The Fairy Tales of Madame D'aulnoy, Newly Done Into English

FAIRY TALES

OF

MADAME D'AULNOY.

ABERDEEN UNIVERSITY PRESS.

THE FAIRY TALES OF MADAME D'AULNOY, NEWLY DONE INTO ENGLISH. WITH AN INTRODUCTION BY ANNE THACKERAY RITCHIE. ILLUSTRATED BY CLINTON PETERS.

LONDON: LAWRENCE AND BULLEN.
MDCCCXCII.

NOTE.

The first twelve and last two stories have been translated by Miss Annie Macdonell ; the others by Miss Lee. The moralising verses at the end of each story have been omitted.

CONTENTS.

b

INTRODUCTION.

I HAVE been asked to write a few lines of preface to the stories which are here once more, after a century or so, presented in a new form to the present generation of children. "To those people of intelligence under the age of fourteen," as a French editor says, "who are prepared to be pleased and convinced," just as their fathers, mothers, grandfathers, great-grandfathers, great-great-grandfathers and grandmothers have been before them. These special stories have fallen out of circulation, since the days when the French ladies and gentlemen all read fairy tales together, and the order of the Terrace was instituted for little Louis XV. The Knights of the Order were to play at games on the Terraces at Versailles with his youthful majesty, and then assemble together (specially on their feast day, the day of St. Bartholomew) and spell out fairy stories for the rest of the afternoon. It was not only children who liked fairy tales in those days; there was a general fashion for them.

People were tired of the long-winded romances of the *Scudéry* times of Louis XIV., they had wearied of the fables and society verses once so popular, and which perhaps required more effort and attention than this later generation was disposed to give, even to its play. Perhaps, too, people were not sorry to turn away from the present, from the disasters in which the reign of Louis XIV. came to a close, and to take to stringing marvels and wonders on to old springs and threads that belonged to a world which they could govern and fashion to their fancy. Besides the little chevaliers of the Terrace, a whole society of well-born ladies seems to have been in the habit of meeting and devoting its leisures to the inditing of marvellous histories. The "Cabinet des Fées" numbers its volumes by decades, and the authors and authoresses of this collection, if they had not much invention of their own, were not afraid of drawing largely from other sources.

Charles Perrault was among the first to recount the popular nursery stories of the time, in his *Histoire de la Mère l'Oye*, published in 1697. Madame d'Aulnoy, who must have been well advanced in years by this time, followed suit, and many other ladies of rank, her friends and contemporaries, seemed to have amused themselves by concocting marvellous and nightmare-like histories. But, as the editor of the French edition of popular tales reminds us, we must not be ungrateful, nor forget that the author of *L'oiseau Bleu* and the *Belle aux Bois* was among them, as was also Madame de Beaumont to whom we owe the charming history of *Beauty and the Beast.*

We are fortunate in possessing portraits of both the chief recounters of fairy lore : that of the Countess D'Aulnoy herself, as well as the engraving of Charles Perrault, deputy-receiver of taxes under Colbert. He in his magnificent wig looks more like a Condé or a Turenne at the head of an invading army than a peaceful knight of the quill, marshalling his figures and his fairy battalions, and prepared to shed his ink for his country ; Madame d'Aulnoy (d'Aulnoi or d'Aunoy, as her name is variously spelt), with her hair beautifully curled, is dressed in draperies disposed in dignified folds, and upheld by a jewelled band which crosses from her shoulder to her waist. Her features are marked and somewhat beakish. French people have a different standard of beauty to ours, and the countess seems to have been considered lovely in her day, witty as well as very agreeable. "She was always ready in conversation," says one of her admirers. "No one knew better how to introduce an anecdote, and her stories were the delight of all." " Pour raconter simplement quelque chose il ne faut pas un grand talent," says Madame d'Aulnoy modestly enough in one of her stories. Her readers will appreciate the pleasant simplicity of her style. Occasionally it rises to eloquence, as in the description of the battle between the Yellow Dwarf and the king who tries to rescue the princess from his spells.*

* Mr. Lang quotes a passage about fairy tales from one of Madame de Sevigné's letters to her daughter. She describes Madame de Coulange's account of the stories that they amused ladies with at Versailles. "They call this *mitonner*, so she ' *mittonnéd* ' us, and spoke to us about a green island where a princess was brought up as bright as the day ! The fairies were her com-

Marie Catherine—Le Jumel—de Berneville, the wife of François de la Motte, Comte d'Aulnoy, was born in the middle of the sixteenth century, and she died in January, 1705, when she was between fifty and sixty years of age. Her father was allied to some of the oldest families in Normandy, and had served for many years in the king's armies. She was the niece of the "celebrated Madame Desloges," we are told, and the mother of Madame de Heere. Madame Desloges lived in the reign of Louis XIII., and by her wit and agreeable conversation attracted many of the most interesting men of the time to her house. Madame d'Aulnoy seems to have inherited this pleasant talent, and we hear much of her conversational powers and agreeable wit. Her mother, who was not sixteen when she was born, sent her away to be brought up by a grandmother. It was not the fashion of the times for parents to bring up their children. For some years the little girl was supposed to be an heiress, and received, so she tells us, much adulation in consequence; but when she was eleven a brother was born, and the relations immediately determined to send little Marie Catherine into a nunnery. The child was in despair, and passionately implored her father to rescue her from this fate. He was not the ruling spirit in the home, says Madame d'Aulnoy in her *Memoirs*, but he did the best he could to help his poor little girl. He advised her to submit quietly, and promised that as soon as she was of an age to be married he would, without telling her mother, find her a suitable husband. These *Memoirs* of Madame d'Aulnoy are to be seen in the British Museum in a "*diverting collection*" of her works, published in English by John Nicholson, at the King's Arms, and Andrew Bell, at the Cross Keys and Bible in Cornhill, in 1707. The *Memoirs* are diverting perhaps, but they are certainly disappointing too, and it is difficult to tell whether they are a real history or the divagations of a fanciful imagination longing for adventure and excitement. The little girl in the convent seems to have read a great many

panions, and the Prince of Pleasure was her lover, and they both came to the king's court one day in a ball of glass. The story lasted a good hour, and I spare you much of it." This letter was written in 1676, and proves, as Mr. Lang tells us, that fairy tales had come to Court some time before Perrault published his *Mother Goose's Tales*. This is Mr. Lang's pretty comment on the arrival of these distinguished visitors at the king's palace: "The stories came in their rustic weeds, they wandered out of the cabins of the charcoal burners, out of the farmers' cottages, and, after many adventures, reached that enchanted castle of Versailles. There the courtiers welcomed them gladly, recognised the truant girls and boys of the fairy world as princes and princesses, and arrayed them in the splendour of Cinderella's sisters."

novels about romantic heroes and "heroesses," as she is made to call
them, and to have tried to pose as a heroess herself a great deal more
than the abbeys approved.   Her mother also disapproved, and was more
than ever set upon making her into a nun : but her father does not forget
his promise.   He comes with her mother to see her one day, and while
her mother sits talking to the abbess in the parlour, her father (so Madame
d'Aulnoy tells us) takes her for a walk in the convent garden, where she is
immediately carried off by three or four masked cavaliers, put into a
carriage and driven rapidly away, while the father goes back to the
convent calling for help.   One of these masked men turns out to be no
less a person than the Comte d'Aulnoy himself, who had planned it all
with M. de Berneville.   They are immediately married, and Madame
d'Aulnoy speaks with cordial dislike of her husband, with whom she
seems to have lived very unhappily from the first, and from whom, whenever anything went wrong, she seems to have run away in disguise.   She
mentions a son casually, and in another book she subsequently mentions
a daughter; and she also tells us that at M. d'Aulnoy's death she married
again, M. de St. Albe.   Her brother having died young, she eventually
succeeded to considerable wealth, but her *Memoirs* scarcely mention any
facts and are chiefly a record of her sentimental emotions.   They come to
an abrupt end with the death of St. Albe.

In the few records—not her own—which remain to us of Madame
d'Aulnoy's life, there should be quite enough emotions to satisfy a
less excitable person, but to none of these events does she make any
allusion.   On one occasion her husband, François de la Motthe, Sieur
d'Aulnoy, having been seized, imprisoned, and falsely accused of high
treason by two Normans, narrowly escaped losing his head.   One of his
accusers was the Marquis de Courboyer (who is curiously enough described
as a " good-natured man ") and the other was Jaques de Crouville, sur-
named Lamière.   Lamière at the last moment, touched by remorse, retracted
the accusation, confessing that he had received a thousand crowns for his
false witness.   The count was discharged on the eve of condemnation, and
the conspirators suffered in his place.   There seem, according to contem-
porary chroniclers, to have been further complications in Madame
d'Aulnoy's life, connected with " the famous and beautiful Madame Angélique Tiquet ".   Madame d'Aulnoy was her friend, and was somewhat compromised during her trial.   Madame Tiquet was decapitated in the Place

de Grève in 1699. The story is a very sad one. Madame Tiquet was born at Metz. She was left an orphan, rich, extraordinarily beautiful, and agreeable. There were many pretenders to her hand; among them was Councillor Tiquet, from Paris. He was greatly in debt, many years older than she was, and his chief object in courting the young heiress was to secure her fortune. He was clever enough to enlist the sympathy of an aunt of Angélique's, who persuaded her to accept him. Madame Tiquet came to live in Paris; she had children, but she felt little affection for her husband. Her fortune, her charm, her rare beauty, attracted a large circle of friends to her house. Among the many amiable and brilliant people who came thither was Madame d'Aulnoy. As time went on the differences between Madame Tiquet and her husband grew more and more bitter. She tried in vain to obtain a separation from him; and, at last, finding her married life intolerable, she urged one of her servants to attempt his life. One evening, when Tiquet was coming home, he was fired at and badly wounded. He had himself carried away from the house, sent for the police, and declared that his wife must have instigated the attack. Friends of Madame Tiquet went to her and urged her to fly; but this she refused to do. She was taken to prison and tried; but, notwithstanding all the sympathy which was shown her, and the extraordinary interest which the trial excited, she was condemned to be beheaded, and her servant to be hung at the same place. The husband delayed and wasted time in petitioning that her confiscated fortune should be returned to him, and then, finally, went to Versailles to ask for a reprieve. It is said that Angélique was so beautiful that the executioner altogether lost his nerve upon the scaffold. It is impossible to know exactly in what way Madame d'Aulnoy was compromised; probably she was among those friends who attempted to plan the poor lady's escape. This seems all the more likely because the countess was a spirited and lively person from all accounts, not easily discouraged or frightened (except indeed by ghosts), and she was evidently fond of adventure, as we see in her records of her journeys through Spain and elsewhere.

Madame la Princesse de Conté seems to have been one of Madame d'Aulnoy's sympathetic readers, for to her are dedicated, with many compliments and salutations, *The Memoirs of the Court of Spain*, which came out at the Hague in 1691. Madame d'Aulnoy may have been about forty years of age when the pretty little brown book, with its old-fashioned type, made its appearance, but it must have been written many years before. It has since been transformed into a handsome annotated volume, with margins, and elaborate and very interesting notes, the work of Madame Carey, who has traced the dates and the facts with admirable patience, and who tells us that Madame d'Aulnoy, although she had excellent opportunities of observing facts, and was in the main accurate, had the singular habit of transcribing entire paragraphs out of the books of other people without any acknowledgment whatever, and also of sometimes adding imaginary adventures when her own struck her as somewhat dull. She is a mysterious person. She gives no hint of the reasons which led her to undertake this long expedition, nor are either of her husbands once mentioned by the widow in the course of the narrative. Madame Carey vouches, however, for the facts which she has been at the trouble of verifying; many of the customs noted still survive in a modified form, others are corroborated by St. Simon and various writers of the time. Madame d'Aulnoy's pictures of the Court of Spain are singularly vivid; her journeys are a curious mixture of reality and fairy tale, but perhaps not more so than many of the books of travel one has lately come across. The impression left by these volumes (which are, I ought to say, anything but suitable for young people) is that of a lively and spirited woman of a past society visiting in Wonderland. Her first start is not at all unlike a chapter out of Alice's well-known adventures. On her arrival at Bayonne, Madame d'Aulnoy is hospitably welcomed by various ladies of the neighbourhood, to whom she has brought introductions. These ladies visit the traveller coming in with cheerful hospitality, carrying for the most part little sucking pigs, tied up with ribbons, under their arms, which little pigs are set down upon the floor to frolic during the rest of the visit. Presently the ladies stand up and execute a dance to amuse the travellers, after which entertainment they all retire with their little pigs, leaving presents behind them of sweetmeats, and stockings, and ornaments, to testify their sympathy. The further adventures of the caravan, as it slowly advances across the mountains from Bayonne into Spain, carrying Madame d'Aulnoy in her litter, with her little girl at her side, fill one with wonder and respect for the courage of the ladies of the seventeenth century, who were not deterred by fatigue and horrible discomfort from such long and wearisome expeditions. Madame d'Aulnoy must have been a very healthy and vigorous woman to survive all the trials she describes—the snows, the floods, the cold, the garlic, and the want of privacy; and also to be able to sit down and write crown octavo letters to her cousin all along the road. Clarissa Harlowe herself would have scarcely equalled her. At Burgos, after a long day's travel, she arrives in time for supper, after which her suite immediately sits down to cards. When she retires for the night, she tells us she is led into a gallery full of beds, about thirty in a row, just as one sees them in hospitals. She remonstrates, saying she wants but four beds—for her daughter, herself, and her two women attendants; but she is told that this is the only available place in the house. " I was hardly in bed," she writes, "when some one knocked gently at the door. My women opened, and were greatly surprised to see the host and hostess come in, followed by a dozen wretches half undressed. I opened my curtain, hearing the noise. The hostess came to my bedside, saying these were honest travellers who were going to occupy the empty beds. 'These people!' cried I; 'you must be out of your mind.' 'I should be out of my mind, indeed,' said the hostess, 'if I left so many beds unoccupied. You, madame, must pay for them, or these gentlemen will remain.' I cannot express to you my fury. I was tempted to send for Don Fernand and my other chevaliers, who would soon have thrown the honest travellers out of the window; but it was not worth a disturbance. I therefore quieted down, and promised to pay twenty sols for each bed (they are hardly dearer at Fontainebleau when the Court is there). The illustrious Spaniards and vagabonds who had had the insolence to come in now retired with a great many curtseys. I couldn't help bursting out laughing the next morning, when I found that these travellers were only neighbours, who were accustomed to renew this performance for the benefit of each fresh arrival." The countess continues her journey in her litter. At last she arrives very early one day in the environs of Madrid, where she is received by a certain Dona Theresa of seventeen, who is married to a man many years older than herself. It was ten o'clock in the morning. Don Augustin was walking in his garden, and presently he invited the countess to visit his wife, who was not yet up. " She wore no cap," says Madame d'Aulnoy; "her hair, parted in the middle, was wrapt in a piece of red silk tied by a ribbon. She had many little pillows to her bed, ornamented with ribbons and trimmed with lace. Her ample night-dress was buttoned by diamonds; her quilt was trimmed with Spanish point, and gold and silk. Her bed was of gilt copper with ornaments of ivory and ebony. As soon as she was up the young lady took a cupful of rouge, put some on her cheeks, on her ears, on her chin, under her nose, and inside her hands, saying that she did not care for it, but that the use was so universal she could not well give it up. One of her women then perfumed her from head to foot with the smoke of some excellent pastilles." When they went to breakfast, the host took the countess by the hand, and led her into a saloon paved with marble, ornamented with pictures, and quite without hangings. "The breakfast was served upon the table for the gentlemen, and a cloth was spread on the carpet, with three covers, for Dona Theresa, my daughter and myself," says the countess. "I was surprised at this; for I am not accustomed to have my dinner on the floor. I said nothing, but never was I more uncomfortable; sometimes I tried leaning on my elbow, sometimes on my hand. My hostess observed nothing, because she thought that the ladies in France always ate as they do in Spain; but at last the gentlemen noticed my uneasiness, and desired absolutely that I should join them at the table. To this I gladly consented, provided that Dona Theresa came too. Her husband called to her to come; but when the poor little lady was installed she was no less embarrassed than I had been on the carpet. She confessed ingenuously that she had never before sat upon a chair; the idea had never occurred to her." It seems that St. Simon describes a great Court ball given by Philip V. where the ladies all sat upon a vast carpet upon the floor. This habit is supposed to have been derived from the Moors.

Madame d'Aulnoy is quick to catch the impression of the moment; she describes pleasantly and graphically the events as they occur. Her peasants, her courtiers, her kings and her queens, her widows, her romantic ladies and gentlemen, her monks, dukes and duchesses, all appear in turn in their quaint costumes, a whole gallery of Velasquez figures. Here is a sketch of a Spanish widow in the year 1679; she comes up in her litter, seeking for a night's lodgings: "Her dress appeared to me very singular, only so beautiful a woman as she was could have kept any charm in it. She wore a coiffe of black stuff, her petticoat to match, and above this a sort of surplice of white linen reaching below the knees, the sleeves were long, fitted to the arm, and falling over the hands; this surplice was not pleated in front, and looked like a sort of pinafore. On her head she wore a piece of muslin covering her throat, and falling to the waist—it might have been the gimp of a religious, but it was of lighter texture. All her hair was hidden away. She wore a great mantle of black silk falling to her feet, and besides this a huge hat tied under her chin. This is the dress of widows and duennas, but I am told that they only wear these hats when they are travelling. If one were to meet a woman thus dressed at night, I am persuaded that without cowardice one might be terrified by the apparition. I must, however, confess that this young lady was of admirable beauty, notwithstanding her ugly mourning. It is never given up in Spain, except in the event of re-marriage; and in all things poor widows are constrained to mourn. The first year of their widowhood they spend in a room hung with black without a single ray of sunshine; they sit cross-legged upon a little mattress. At the end of a year they are allowed grey hangings. They are forbidden pictures, looking-glasses and cabinets, beautiful tables, and all silver ornaments; they dare not wear their jewels or any bright colours. Modest as they may be, they have to live in so retired a fashion that it seems as if their souls were already in the next world. This great constraint is the reason that several very rich ladies, who have beautiful furniture, marry again, in order to have the pleasure of using it."

As a contrast to this, let us take a Spanish gentleman of fashion. A "guapo," which word means, says Madame d'Aulnoy, "a Spaniard, brave, gallant, and even dashing. This young man's hairs were divided in the middle of his head and tied behind with a blue ribbon, four inches wide and two yards long. He had tights of black velvet, buttoned above the knee by five or six buttons, without which it would be impossible to take them off, so closely fitting are they in this country. He had a vest so short that it did not reach the pocket, and a black velvet jacket with long tabs and hanging sleeves. The inner sleeves were of white satin bordered with jet. His shirt was of black silk, greatly puffed. His cloak was of black cloth; and, as he was a 'guapo,' he had twisted his cloak round his arm, because that was more gallant. He also carried a 'broquel' in his hand; that is to say, a sort of very light shield with a point of steel in the middle. In the other hand he carried a spear longer than a pike. He had also a poignard fastened to his belt at the back. His neck-piece, lined with pasteboard, held his head so stiff that he could neither turn his head or bend it." A note of Madame Carey's tells us that this collar, neck-piece, or golille as it was called, had been adopted by King Philip IV., who was so satisfied with this happy idea that he instituted a fête to perpetuate it, and the pious king and his Court went in procession, once a-year, to the chapel on the bridge of the Guardian Angel to render thanks for their stocks. To return to Madame d'Aulnoy, she is not at all of the opinion of Philip IV. She says nothing can be more ridiculous than this stock. It is neither a ruffle, nor a turnover, nor a cravat. A golille resembles nothing at all; is very uncomfortable, and disfiguring. The young man also wore a hat of a prodigious size, lined with black silk, with a great crape all round, like a husband in mourning for his wife. "I am told," says the countess, "that this crape is the most incontestable sign of the finest breeding. His shoes were of fine morocco, like the kid of which we make gloves, very much cut away, and so tight to the feet that they seemed stuck upon them. He wore no heels. As he came in, he made me a Spanish reverence, crossing his legs and curtseying gravely, as women do when they salute. He was very much perfumed; but his visit was not long. He did not forget to tell me that he often went to Madrid, where he exposed his life in every bull-fight." Has one not seen this gentleman hanging up on the walls of the National Gallery? I cannot help quoting one more description from the book of Madame d'Aulnoy's visit to the queen-dowager, when for the first time she had to put on the Court dress of a Spanish lady. "Nothing can be more uncomfortable," says she; "the shoulders are so compressed that they ache again, and it is impossible to raise one's arm. They put me on a stiff petticoat of a fearful size. I knew not what to do with this strange machine; it was impossible to sit down with it. My hair was left floating and tied with narrow ribbon; for this is the indispensable Court head-dress. Finally, I put on the wooden pattens the ladies wore at Court, rather to break my neck with than to walk about in. When we were all dressed, for my cousin and my daughter came too, we were shown into a state-room, where Monsieur le Cardinal came to see us. He remained an hour with us, and then a magnificent breakfast was served; but I could hardly touch anything. There was nothing to choose between the perfumed dishes, or the others flavoured with saffron, onions, pepper, garlic and spices. There was an excellent ham, covered with sugar-plums, of which the sugar was melting in the fat; it was all larded with citron. . . . We hurried away from table, for it was the hour to visit the queen-dowager. After mounting a magnificent staircase, and crossing a great gallery, and many vast and empty apartments, we reached a saloon, of which all the windows were open upon a plain and upon the river. The

carpet, the hangings, the tapestries, were all grey. The queen was standing, leaning against a balcony, and holding in one hand a long chaplet.
We had the honour of kissing her hand, which is small, thin, and white.
She is very pale, of delicate complexion; her face is long and flat; her
eyes are soft; she is of medium size. She was dressed, as are all widows
in Spain, like a nun; not a single hair appearing. I observed that there
were several tucks round her skirt, so as to let it down in case it should be
worn at the bottom. I do not say that this is always done; but it is the
fashion. After some conversation about the king's approaching marriage,
and the portrait of the Princess of Orleans, which had been sent to the
Queen of Spain, a little dwarf as round as a barrel, and not taller than a
water melon, dressed in gold and brocade, with long hair falling to her
feet, entered, and kneeling before the queen, asked her whether she would
be pleased to sup. We offered to retire; but she told us that we might
follow her. She sat down alone, and we all stood around. The ladies-in-
waiting whispered to us they were horribly dull." Poor ladies! they might
well complain. The whole description of the echoing palace—the kneeling, attendants, passing the dishes from hand to hand; the imprisoned
women, queens though they might be, gives one a shiver. The story of
the poor little princess, from the French Court, whose parrot had its neck
wrung because it talked French to its young mistress, is piteous and
ludicrous. But there are sadder things still. Madame d'Aulnoy's
terrible description of the *auto da fé* at Madrid has been already quoted,
and is too painful to be inserted here. Madame d'Aulnoy herself
did not stay to witness it; for, at the very beginning, she was
taken ill, and had to retire. But the king, she says, "dared not
avoid this horrible spectacle, standing with his sword of state upheld
beside him, for it was the cause of religion!" The whole Court,
indeed, was assembled—the king, the queen, the ladies, the ambassadors. The scaffold was adjoining the royal balcony, and the victims implored the royal mercy in vain. No wonder that, in such an age, amid
facts so monstrous and execrable, people turned to imaginary worlds for relief from the devilish superstitions of the time in which they lived. There
is cruelty still among us—injustice, and oppressions, and suffering; but
these things are called openly by their names, and day by day as the truth
grows and spreads from man to man, from generation to generation, the
dark demons still surviving from those mediæval ages dwindle and vanish

in the light of day. Is it the press, that crowing chanticleer, which helps dispel the dark deeds of the night?

Madame d'Aulnoy seems to have left Spain in the spring of 1681, after some two years' residence, for she speaks of her visit to Aranjuez, to take leave of the young queen, now established in Spain, who received her graciously, gave her an enamelled portrait of herself, all set in diamonds, and promised her protection for a young lady, a " demoiselle," very dear to Madame d'Aulnoy, who remained behind in Spain. She carried her own recommendation, so said the queen, graciously, "for she was a French woman ". Can this have been Madame d'Aulnoy's daughter? The *Memoirs of the Court* break off with a promise of further memoirs, and the sad history of the loss of the said enamel, which, however, has never yet been given to the world.

Besides her *Fairy Tales* and her *History of Spain*, Madame d'Aulnoy wrote two or three novels which seem to have been very popular; *Jean de Bourbon* was one, another was called *The Adventures of Hypolite, Comte de Duglas*, of which there are a great many editions, says the editor of *L'Europe Illustre*. "It is a novel," so he goes on, "in which fiction is well supported by historic fact, and where that tender softness of style which characterises the pen of a lady is most seductive!" The editor of the *Biographie Universelle* is not of this opinion; "tous ses personnages parlent le language d'une fade galanterie," he says. There is an anecdote of a young officer, a friend of the writer in *L'Europe Illustre*, who, after reading the *History of the Comte de Duglas*, immediately went off and proposed to a young lady whom he had known for some time, but whom he had not thought of marrying. "You are the cause of my happiness," he exclaimed to his friend, the editor; "for you lent me the book which had so fortunate an influence upon my destiny!" "I congratulated him," says M. Dreux du Radier, "and came to the conclusion that, after all, novels have some use!"

The same writer's somewhat naïve criticism on Madame d'Aulnoy's *Spanish History* is, that there are many interesting facts in it which one does not read anywhere else, but that, unfortunately, one is not able to tell whether or not they are true.

Many of Madame d'Aulnoy's tales have been taken with scarce any variation from the *Pentamerone* of Basile and the *Nights* of Straparola, which latter book, as Dunlop tells us in his history, was printed about the middle of the sixteenth century. He also tells us that Straparola himself had borrowed largely from preceding authors. The ladies and gentlemen who contributed to the many volumes of the "Cabinet des Fées" did not, I imagine, pretend to create their fairies, but rather to conjure up the old ones with new dresses and decorations, just as our pantomimes do every Christmas. Any of us in the nineteenth century, who have thrilled to the stirring and beautiful song of "Ché Faro," as uttered by the sweet voice of Julia Ravogli in "Orfeo," have witnessed a scene reproduced out of one of Madame d'Aulnoy's histories, in which Love, crowned with roses, is sent to assist the wandering prince in his search through Hades for her whom he adores. The prettiest of Madame d'Aulnoy's stories are also the best known, such as *L'oiseau Bleu, The White Cat, Le Prince Lutin,* and a good many others. *Le Nain Jaune, Fortunée, La Biche au Bois,* are also very charmingly told.

Before ending this very imperfect little sketch, I must not omit to say that as time went on the little girl who had travelled in the litter grew up, and also began to write fairy tales. She became Madame de Heere, and is said to have walked in her mother's footsteps.

> " Prose and verse are there,
> Most charming De Heere,
> To prove daughter and mother
> Equal each to the other."

Verses to this effect are quoted as written by the Président de Ventron and addressed to Madame de Heere. He was evidently a lavish admirer of both ladies. To Madame d'Aulnoy he dedicates a quatrain :—

> " Si l'on récompensait tes vers,
> Si l'on payait ton éloquence,
> Qui brille en mille endroits divers,
> Tu pourrais épuiser les trésors de la France ".

The president's enthusiasm must make up for his metre.

ANNE THACKERAY RITCHIE.

GRACIEUSE AND PERCINET.

ONCE upon a time there lived a king and a queen who had but one daughter. For beauty, and gentleness, and quick wit there was no one to be compared with her, and for this reason they called her Gracieuse. She was her mother's only joy. Every morning a beautiful dress was brought to her. Sometimes it would be of gold brocade, sometimes of velvet or satin ; yet all her fine clothes never made her a whit more vain or boastful. She spent every morning with great scholars, who taught her all kinds of learning, and in the afternoon she worked near the queen. For luncheon they brought her basins full of sweetmeats, and more than twenty pots of jam. And so everybody said she was the happiest princess in all the world.

Now at the same court there lived a very rich old maid, whose name was Duchess Grognon, and who was as ugly as she could be. Her hair was as red as fire, and her huge face was all covered with pimples. She had but one bleareye left, and her mouth was so big that it looked as if it were going to gobble everybody up, but then as all her teeth were gone there was nothing to fear in that respect. She had a hump before and behind, and she was lame of both legs. Monsters like her are very jealous of those who are beautiful. She therefore hated Gracieuse with a deadly hatred, and left the court so as not to hear her praises sung, retiring to a castle of her own a little way off. When anyone paid her a visit, and brought her news of all the princess's charms, she would cry out in great wrath: " It is a lie! it is a lie! She is not beautiful! There is more charm in my little finger than in her whole body."

Meanwhile the queen fell ill, and died. Princess Gracieuse was like to die too for grief at having lost so good a mother, and the king was in deep distress for the loss of such a wife. For nearly a whole year he shut himself up in his palace, till at last his doctors, fearing lest he too should fall ill, ordered him to go out and to amuse himself. So one day he went hunting. The heat being very great he entered a great castle, which he saw from the roadside, to rest. Now this was the Duchess Grognon's castle, and as soon as she knew of the king's arrival she came to receive him, and told him that the coolest place in the house was a great arched cellar. It was quite clean, she said, as she begged him to come down there. The king went along with her, and seeing in the cellar two hundred barrels in rows, one above another, he asked whether all these supplies were for herself alone. " Yes, sire," she said, " for myself alone ; but I shall be

delighted to let you taste. Here you find Canary, Saint Laurent, Champagne, Hermitage, Rivesalte, Rossolis, Persicot, Fenouillet. Which do you prefer ? " " Well, to tell the truth," said the king, " I think Champagne is by far the best of all." So Grognon took a little hammer, and went tap-tapping at the barrel, out of which came a thousand pistoles. " What is the meaning of this ? " said Grognon, with a smile. She struck another barrel, tap-tap, and out came a bushel of double Louis-d'ors. " I can't understand this at all," she said, with a still broader smile. On she passed to a third barrel, and went tap-tapping, when out there poured such a stream of pearls and diamonds that the ground was covered with them. "Ah!" she cried, "I am altogether mystified, your majesty. Someone must have stolen my good wine, and put these trifles there instead." "Trifles!" said the king, who was filled with wonder. "By my faith, Madam Grognon, call you these trifles? Why, they are enough to buy ten kingdoms as big as Paris!" "Well," she answered, "I will tell you that all these barrels are full of gold and jewels, and they will be yours if you will marry me." "Ah!" replied the king, who cared for money more than anything else, "I will do so with the greatest pleasure in the world, and to-morrow if you like." "But," she went on, "I have one more condition to make. That is, that I be given authority over your daughter as if I were her mother; that she look to me for everything, and that you leave all control of her to me." "She will be entirely under your authority," said the king. "Here is my hand upon it." Grognon put her hand in his, and together they went out of the treasure-house, the key of which she gave him.

As soon as he returned to his palace, Gracieuse, hearing his steps, ran to meet him, and, kissing him, asked him if he had had good luck at the hunt. "I caught a dove alive," he said. "Ah, sire," said the princess, "give it to me, and I will feed it." "That is not possible," he answered, "for, to speak more plainly, I must tell you I met the Duchess Grognon, and I have promised to marry her." "Oh, heavens!" cried Gracieuse, without thinking what she was saying. "Do you call her a dove? She is more like an owl." "Hold your tongue," said the king, angrily. "I insist on your loving her, and respecting her as if she were your own mother. Go away at once and get dressed, for I wish to go back and see her this very day." The princess was very obedient, and went to her room to get ready. Her nurse saw from her eyes that she was in distress. "What is the matter, dear little one?" she said. "You are crying." "Alas! dear nurse," answered Gracieuse, "who would not cry? The king is going to give me a step-mother, and, worst of all, she is my cruellest enemy—in fact, it is that hideous Grognon. How can I look at her in those beautiful beds that my good mother, the queen, embroidered so exquisitely with her own hands? How can I caress a monster who would like to kill me?" "Dear child," replied the nurse, "your courage should be as great as your birth. Princesses like you must show finer examples than others. And what better can you do than obey your father, and sacrifice yourself to please him? Promise me then that you will not let Grognon see how dismayed you are." The princess found it difficult to make up her mind to this, but the good nurse reasoned with her so wisely that at last she promised to put a good face on the matter, and to be polite to her step-mother. Then she dressed herself in a green robe with a gold ground. Her fair hair fell over her shoulders, floating in the wind, according to the fashion of those days, and on her head was a light crown of roses and jasmines, all the leaves of which were made of emeralds. When she was ready, Venus, the mother of the loves, would have seemed less fair by her side; yet you could read in her face the sadness which she could not altogether overcome.

But let us go back to Grognon. That ugly creature was much taken up with her attire. That she might seem rather less lame she had one shoe made half-a-cubit higher than the other, and to hide her hump she had her bodice stuffed on one shoulder. She stuck in the best made glass eye that could be found, painted her face to make it white, and dyed her red hair black. Then she put on a dress of amaranth satin lined with blue, a yellow petticoat, and violet ribbons. She meant to make her entrance on horseback, for she had heard that the queens of Spain always did so.

While the king was giving his orders, and Gracieuse was waiting the moment when they should set out to meet Grognon, the princess went by herself into the garden, and, entering a little dark wood, she sat down upon the grass. "At last," she said, "I am free to weep as much as I want. There is nobody to hinder me." And with that she began to sigh and weep so much that her eyes looked like two streams of living water. In this condition she felt she could not return to the palace. All at once she saw a page coming towards her, dressed in green satin, with white feathers in his cap, and the comeliest face in the world. Kneeling before her, he said: "Princess, the king awaits you". She was full of admiration for the beauty of this young page whom she did not know, and who she thought must belong to Grognon's suite. "How long," she asked, "have you been amongst the king's pages?" "I am no page of his, madam," he answered. "I am yours, and I wish for no other service." "Mine?" she answered, in astonishment, "but I do not know you." "Ah, princess!" he replied, "I have not dared till now to make myself known to you, but the evil that threatens you from the marriage of the king forces me to speak sooner than I otherwise should have done. I had determined to leave to time and my services the task of declaring my love to you, and . . ." "What! a page!" cried the princess, "a page has the audacity to say he loves me! This is the worst of all!" "Fear not, fair Gracieuse," he said, with respect and tenderness in his looks; "I am Percinet, a prince not unknown for his wealth and his accomplishments, and you may set your mind at rest as to the equality of our stations in life. It is only your birth and your merit which make us unequal. I have loved you long, and I am often near you without your being aware of it. The fairy gift I received at my birth has been of great service in giving me the pleasure of looking upon you. I shall bear you company to-day in this dress, and I hope I may be of use to you." While he was speaking the princess was looking at him with an astonishment she could not master. " It is you then, fair Percinet," she said, " you whom I so longed to see, and of whom such wonderful things are told. What joy to have you for a friend! I no longer fear the wicked Grognon, since you will watch over my safety." They talked still a little while longer, and then Gracieuse returned to the palace, where she found a horse ready harnessed and caparisoned that Percinet had placed in the stable, and which was meant for her it was supposed. She mounted, and, as the horse was very spirited, the page took it by the bridle and led it, turning every moment towards the princess, to have the joy of looking on her face.

When the horse that had been chosen for Grognon appeared near Gracieuse's it looked but a sorry hack, while the saddle-cloth of the princess's beautiful steed was so splendid with jewels that the other looked poor and mean in comparison. The king, who had many things to see after, paid no attention to this, and none of his lords had any eyes but for Gracieuse, whose beauty so dazzled them, and for the page in green, who was handsomer than all the court pages put together.

They met Grognon on the road in an open carriage, uglier and more mis-shapen than any old countrywoman. The king and the princess embraced her, and led forwards her horse. But when she saw the one belonging to Gracieuse, she called out : " Why should that creature have a finer horse than I ? I would rather not be a queen at all, and go back to my own fine castle, than be treated like this." The king at once ordered Gracieuse to dismount and beg Grognon to do her the honour of riding on her horse, and the princess obeyed without a word. Grognon neither looked at her nor thanked her, and she was hoisted up on the pretty horse very much like a bundle of dirty linen. Eight gentlemen held her on, in case she should fall ; and still she was not pleased, but went on mut-tering threats under her breath. They asked her what was the matter. " As I am the mistress," she answered, " I want the page in green to hold the bridle of my horse, as he did when Gracieuse was riding it." So the king ordered the page in green to lead the queen's horse. Percinet cast his eyes towards the princess, and she looked at him without saying a single word. He obeyed, and all the court set out amidst the loud din of drums and trumpets. Grognon was de-lighted ; and for all her flat nose and her crooked mouth, she would not have changed places with Gracieuse.

But, just when they were least thinking of it, the beautiful horse began to rear, and to kick, and to run so fast that no one could stop him. Away he went with Grognon holding on to the saddle and the mane, crying as loud as she could. At last her foot caught in the stirrup, and she fell. The horse dragged her for a long way over the stones, through thorns, and through mud in which she was all but buried. They had all followed after, and they soon came up to her, and found her full of scratches, her head broken in four or five places, and one of her arms fractured. Never was a bride in a more woeful plight. The king was in despair. She was picked up like a glass shivered to atoms; her cap was found lying on one side of the road, her shoes on the other. She was carried to the town, and put to bed, and the best doctors were sent for. But in spite of all her sufferings, she never stopped scolding. "This is one of Gracieuse's tricks," she said. "I am sure she only took that beautiful and vicious horse to make me jealous, and so that I might be killed. If the king does not right my wrongs, I shall go back to my own fine castle, and never look on his face again." The king was told of Grognon's rage. As his ruling passion was avarice, the mere thought of losing the thousand barrels of gold and diamonds made him shudder, and he would have done anything to prevent it. So he ran to the loathsome sufferer, flung himself at her feet, and swore to her that she had only to name a punishment fitting for the offence Gracieuse had committed, and that he would give up the princess to her angry will. She said that was enough, and she would send for Gracieuse. So they went to tell the princess that Grognon was asking for her. The princess became pale and trembled, knowing well enough it was not for caresses she was sought. She looked round on every side for Percinet to come, but not seeing him, she made her way in all sadness to Grognon's chamber. Hardly was she inside when the doors were shut, and four women, like four furies, threw themselves on her by their mistress's orders, pulled off her pretty clothes, and tore her shift from her back. When her shoulders were bare these merciless furies could not endure to look on their dazzling whiteness, and shut their eyes as if they had been looking on snow for a long time. "Lay on, lay on! courage!" cried the pitiless Grognon from her bed. "Flay her till not a little morsel remains of that white skin she thinks so beautiful." In the midst of any other trouble Gracieuse would have wished for the handsome Percinet to come to her aid; but being all but naked, she was too modest to desire him for a witness, and she made up her mind to suffer everything as meekly as a lamb. Each of the four furies held in her hand a bunch of horrible-looking rods, and there were also large brooms out of which they could pluck fresh ones. They beat her mercilessly; and at every stroke Grognon would say: "Harder! harder! you are too gentle with her!" After this nobody would believe but that the princess was flayed from head to foot. Yet, it was not so at all; for the gallant Percinet had put a charm on the eyes of those women, and what they took for rods in their hands were only feathers of every possible colour. As soon as the beating began Gracieuse saw how it was, and was no longer afraid. "Ah, Percinet," she said, under her breath, "how generous of you to come to my aid! What should I have done without you ?" At last the floggers were so exhausted that they could not move their arms any longer, so they bustled her into her clothes, and. put her out of the room, calling her all kind of ugly names. She went back to her own room, and pretending to be very ill, she went to bed, giving orders that no one but her nurse should remain with her. To her she told the whole story, till at last she fell asleep. The nurse went away, and when Gracieuse woke up she saw the page in green in a dark corner of the room, not daring to come near, by reason of the respect he felt towards her. She told him she would never forget, during her whole life long, her obligations to him ; begged him not to leave her to the fury of her enemy, and, in the meantime, to go away, as she had always been told she should not stay alone with boys. He replied that his respect for her must be evident, but that it was only right that he should obey his mistress in every-thing, even at the cost of his own happiness. Thereupon he left her, after advising her to pretend to be very ill in consequence of the cruel treatment she had received.

Grognon was so glad to think of Gracieuse in this condition that she got better twice as soon again as she would have otherwise done, and the wedding was celebrated with great splendour. Now, as the king knew that Grognon liked to be called beautiful better than anything else, he had her portrait painted, and ordered a tournament to be arranged, where six of the best knights of the court should sustain in the face of, and against all comers that Queen Grognon was the fairest princess in the whole world. Many foreign knights came to maintain the contrary. The hideous creature was present throughout the whole proceed-ings, seated on a great balcony covered with gold brocade, and seeing with pleasure how the prowess of her knights was triumphing in her wicked cause. Gracieuse was behind her, and every eye sought hers ; but vain and foolish Grognon thought she was the object of everybody's attention.

There was hardly a knight left who dared dispute the beauty of Grognon, when a young man was seen approaching, carrying a portrait in a diamond box. He would maintain, he said, that Grognon was the most hideous of all women, and that she whose portrait was in his box was the fairest of damsels. At the word he charged the six knights, and threw them to the ground. Six others came up. In the end four-and-twenty had presented themselves, but he was victor over all. Then, opening his box, he told them that for their consolation he would show them his beautiful picture. Everyone recognised it as that of Gracieuse, to whom he made a profound reverence, and then retired without telling his name. But she had no doubt of its being Percinet.

Grognon was well nigh choking with anger. Her throat swelled, and she could not get a word out, but she signed that it was Gracieuse she had to deal with, and when she could find words she raged like a madwoman. "How dare you," she said, "dispute with me the prize of beauty? How dare you cause my knights to be insulted in this fashion? I will have my revenge, or I will die for it!" "Madam," said the princess, "I protest I have no part in what has just happened. If you like, I will attest with my blood that you are the most beautiful lady in the world, and that I am a monster of ugliness." "Oh, you would laugh at me, little one, would you?" answered Grognon, "but my turn will come soon." The king was told of the fury of his wife, and how the princess, half dead with fright, begged him to have pity on her, for if he left her to the tender mercies of the queen, all sorts of evil things would happen to her. Still he was quite unmoved, and only answered: "I gave her to her step-mother. Let her do what she likes with her."

The wicked Grognon waited for night to come with much impatience. As soon as it was dark she had horses harnessed to her carriage. Gracieuse was forced to get into it, and with a strong escort was taken away for a hundred leagues, into a great forest through which no one dared to pass, for it was full of lions, and bears, and tigers, and wolves. When they had reached the middle of the terrible forest they made her get down, and there they left her, in spite of her prayers that they should have mercy. "I do not ask you to spare my life," she cried; "I only ask a speedy death. Kill me and thus save me from all the ills which I must meet with here." She spoke to deaf ears. They would not even answer, and fled from her, leaving this poor unhappy beauty all by herself. For some time she walked on without knowing where she was going, now bruising herself against a tree, now falling, now entangled in the bushes. At length, over-come with grief, she threw herself on the ground, with no strength left to get up. "Percinet," she cried from time to time, "Percinet, where are you? Can you in truth have left me?" At last, just as she had said these words, she suddenly saw the most beautiful and the most astonishing thing in the world. It was an illumination, so magnificent that there was not a tree in the forest from which did not hang several chandeliers filled with candles; while at the other end of an avenue she saw a palace all made of crystal, glistening like the sun. She began to think that Percinet must have something to do with this fresh wonder, and her joy was mingled with fear. "I am alone," she said. "This prince is young, beautiful, and full of affection for me. I owe my life to him. Ah, I must not think of it! Better to die than to love him!" And so saying, she got up, and spite of her fatigue and her weakness, and without a glance at the beautiful castle, she walked in the opposite direction, so troubled and so confused in her mind with all the different thoughts that crowded there that she did not know what she was doing. At that moment she heard a noise behind her.

Fear took hold of her. She thought some wild beast was going to devour her, and looking round in terror, she saw Prince Percinet as beautiful as Love himself. " Are you fleeing from me ? " he said. " Do you fear me when I adore you ? Can you have so poor an idea of me as to think I could be lacking in respect for you ? Come, come away without fear to the Fairy Palace. I shall not enter if you forbid me, but you will find there my mother, the queen, and my sisters, who love you tenderly already from what I have told them of you." Gracieuse, delighted at the mild and gentle manner in which her young lover spoke, could not refuse to mount along with him into a little sleigh, painted and gilded, and drawn with marvellous speed by two stags. In this way he took her to see end-less beautiful spots in the forest. It was daylight everywhere, and they saw

shepherds and shepherdesses gaily dressed, dancing to the sound of flutes and pipes. In other places, by the banks of rivers, there were village lads with their sweethearts feasting and singing merry songs. " I thought this forest was not inhabited," she said; " but I see life and cheerfulness everywhere." " Since you have come, my princess," replied Percinet, " this dark solitude is full of pleasure and gaiety. The loves accompany you, and flowers spring up where'er you tread." Gracieuse dared not answer. She did not wish to take part in this kind of conversation, and she begged the prince to take her to the queen, his mother. So he told the stags to set out for the Fairy Palace. As they were nearing it, beautiful music sounded in their ears, and the queen with two of her daughters, who were all very lovely, embraced her and led her into a great hall, whose walls were of rock crystal. With much astonishment she saw that the story of her own life, up to that very day, was engraved on them, even her drive with the prince in the sleigh, and all in a style so finished, that the works of Phidias and all the sculpture that ancient Greece could boast of were as nothing in comparison. " You have very watchful craftsmen," said Gracieuse to Percinet, " for no sooner do I make a sign or a movement but I see it carved there." " That is because I wish nothing to be lost that relates in any way to you, my princess," he answered. " But alas ! nowhere am I happy or satisfied." She said nothing in reply, but thanked the queen for the way in which she received her. A great feast was served, and Gracieuse ate with a good appetite, so delighted was she to have found Percinet instead of the bears and lions she had feared to meet in the forest. Although she was very tired, he persuaded her to come with him into a saloon all shining with gold and pictures, where an opera was performed. The subject was the Loves of Psyche and Cupid, and it was interspersed with dances and little songs. A young shepherd stepped forward and sang these words :—

> " Why so cruel, lady mine ?
> Dost thou know the love that's thine
> In my true heart burning ?
> Even the tigers fierce and wild,
> 'Neath the power of love grow mild,
> Tame and lamb-like turning.
> Only gentle Gracieuse flees
> When the looks of love she sees,
> All my worship spurning."

She blushed at hearing her name mentioned in this way before the queen and the princesses, and she told Percinet that it grieved her somewhat that everybody should know their secrets. " That reminds one of a maxim," she said, " which I agree with entirely :—

> " ' Discretion adds a grace and charm to wooing ;
> Then tell your love not in the world's ear,
> Lest, as a cruel judge your joys pursuing,
> It makes their harmlessness as crimes appear '."

He asked her pardon for having done anything to displease her. When the opera was finished the queen sent the two princesses to take her to her rooms. Nothing so beautiful as the furniture was ever seen, nor so elegant as the bed and the bed-chamber where she was to sleep. She was waited on by twenty-four maidens dressed as nymphs, the eldest eighteen years old, and each of them a wonder of beauty. When she had gone to bed, exquisite music was played to lull her to sleep, but her astonishment was so great that she could not close her eyes. "All I have seen," she said, "is the work of magic. There is danger in being near a prince so beautiful and so wonderful. I cannot too soon flee away from here." But the thought of escaping was very painful to her. Were she to leave this splendid palace and fall into the hands of cruel Grognon, what different treatment she would experience! Such a step was not to be taken too suddenly. Yet Percinet seemed to her so charming that she did not wish to remain in a palace where he was master.

When she rose they brought her dresses of every colour, trinkets of precious stones of every shape, lace, ribbons, gloves, silk stockings, and all in exquisite taste. Nothing was lacking. Her costume was of chased gold, and never before had she been so finely dressed, never before had she looked so beautiful. Percinet entered her room clad in cloth of gold and green, for green was his colour, because Gracieuse liked it. The comeliest, the handsomest of men beside him would have seemed plain. Gracieuse told him she had not been able to sleep, so much did the memory of her misfortunes torment her, and that she could not but fear what was still to come. "What is there to fear, madam?" he said. "You are sovereign here: you are adored. Would you wish to forsake me for your cruel enemy?" "If I were mistress of my fate," she said, "I should accept your proposal, but I am accountable for my actions to the king, my father, and it is better for me to suffer than to fail in my duty." Percinet said everything he could think of to persuade her to marry him, but she would not consent, and it was almost in spite of herself that he kept her for eight days, during which time he invented all kinds of pleasures to amuse her.

She would often say to the prince: "I should like to know what is passing at Grognon's court, and what kind of explanation she has given of her conduct to me". Percinet said he would send his squire, who was a man of intelligence, to make inquiries. She told him she was sure he did not need anyone to inform him of what was going on, and that he himself could tell her. "Come with me, then," he said, "to the great tower, and you will see for yourself." Thereupon he took her to the top of an enormously high tower, made of rock crystal as the rest of the castle was, and told her to put her foot on his and her little finger in his mouth, and to look towards the town. Then she saw the wicked Grognon with the king, and she heard her crying: "That unfortunate princess has hanged herself in the cellar. I have just seen her. She is horrible to look at, and she must be speedily buried, and you must console yourself for so trifling a loss." But the king began to cry for the death of his daughter. Grognon turned her back on him, and went to her own room. She had a log dressed up with a cap and well wrapped about, and put into a coffin. Then,

by order of the king, there was a grand funeral, where everybody wept and
cursed the step-mother, who, they said, had killed Gracieuse. They all wore
mourning, and the princess on the tower heard the lamentations for her death,
and heard them saying to themselves : " How sad that so young and fair a princess should have perished by the cruelty of this wicked wretch! She ought to
be hacked to pieces and put into a pie ! " And the king, unable to eat or drink,
wept bitterly. Gracieuse, seeing her father in such distress, said : " Ah ! Percinet,
I cannot bear that my father should any longer think I am dead. If you love
me, take me back to him. Whatever he says, I must obey him, however distasteful it may be to me." " My princess," he said, " you will often regret the
Fairy Palace, though I do not dare to think you will regret me. You are
more cruel to me than Grognon is to you." Yet, for all he said, she persisted
in setting off, and took leave of the prince's mother and sisters. He got in with
her into the sleigh, and the stags began to run. As she went out of the palace
gates she heard a great noise, and looking behind her, she saw the whole building
falling in a thousand pieces. " What is this I see ? " she said. " The palace
has vanished ! " " No," answered Percinet; " my palace will be among the
dead. There you will never enter till after you are buried." " You are angry,"
said Gracieuse, trying to soften him. " But, after all, am I not more to be pitied
than you ? "

When they had reached her home, Percinet made the princess, himself, and
the sleigh invisible. Then she went up to the king's room, and flung herself at
his feet. When he saw her he was afraid, and would have fled, for he took her
for a ghost. But she held him, and told him she was not dead, that Grognon
had sent her into the wild-beast forest, where she had climbed to the top of a
tree, and lived on fruits ; and that it was a log that had been buried in her
stead. She begged, for pity's sake, that he would send her to one of his other
castles, where she would no longer be at the mercy of her step-mother's fury.

The king, not sure whether she was telling the truth or not, sent and had
the log dug up, and much astonished was he at Grognon's wickedness. Anyone
else would have had her buried in its place, but he was a poor, weak man, who had
not spirit enough to be really angry. So he petted his daughter a good deal,
and had her to sup with him. When Grognon's minions went and told her that
Gracieuse had come back, and that she was supping with the king, she behaved
like a madwoman, and running to him, she told him that this was not a time
for shilly-shallying; that either he must give up this good-for-nothing girl, or she
herself would this moment depart and never come back any more; and that it was
a mere supposition that it was Princess Gracieuse. This girl that had come was
somewhat like her, but Gracieuse had hanged herself ; she had seen her hanged

with her own eyes, and that to put any faith in the impostures of this creature was to show a lack of consideration for and trust in herself. The king without a word abandoned the poor princess, believing, or pretending to believe, she was not his daughter.

Grognon, delighted, dragged her by the help of her women into a dungeon, where she made her undress. They took away her pretty clothes, and put on a poor rag of coarse linen, and wooden shoes on her feet, and a rough hood on her head. They grudged her even a bundle of straw to lie on, and black bread to eat. In her distress she wept bitterly, longing to be back in the Fairy Palace; but she dared not call Percinet to come to her help, thinking she had used him too ill, and not sure whether he loved her enough to help her again. Meanwhile wicked Grognon had sent for a fairy who was hardly less malicious than herself. " I have here," she said to her, " a wicked little girl whom I have great reason to be angry with. I wish to punish her, and to have always very difficult pieces of work to give her to do, which she will never be able to finish, so that I may beat her as much as I like without her having any reason to complain. Help me to find for her every day a new difficulty." The fairy said she would think about it, and would come back next day. And so she did, bringing with her a skein of thread as big as any four persons, and so fine that it broke if you but breathed on it, and so tangled that it was all in a bunch, without beginning or end. Grognon was delighted, and sending for the fair prisoner, she said: " There, good gossip, get ready your great fists to wind this thread, and remember that if you break the least little bit of it you are lost, for I shall flay you alive with my own hands. Now begin when you like, but I must have it wound before sunset." Then she shut her up in a room under three locks.

No sooner was the princess by herself than she began looking at the huge skein, turning it this way and that, breaking the thread in a thousand places for one knot that she disentangled, till she was so confused that she gave up trying any more to wind it. Throwing it into the middle of the room, she said: " Go, fatal thread! You will be the death of me. Ah, Percinet, Percinet, if my harshness has not too much repelled you, I ask, not your aid, but only that you should come and receive my last farewell." Thereupon she began to cry so bitterly that anyone even less tender than a lover would have been touched. Percinet opened the door as easily as if he kept the key in his pocket. " Here I am, my princess," he said, " ever ready to serve you. I am not capable of forsaking you, though you ill requite my affection." Striking the skein three times with his wand, the broken threads were immediately joined, and with two other strokes the whole was wound with wonderful neatness. He asked her if she wished for anything else from him, and if she would never call for him but when she was in distress.

" Do not reproach me, fair Percinet," she said; " I am unhappy enough already."
" But, my princess, it is in your hands to free yourself from the tyranny of which
you are the victim. Come with me, and let us be happy together. What are
you afraid of ? " " That you do not love me enough," she answered. " I want
your affection for me to be strengthened by time." Percinet, enraged by these
suspicions, took leave of her and went away.

The sun was just about to set, and Grognon was waiting for the hour in a
fever of impatience. At last she came before her time, with the four furies, who
went with her everywhere. She put the three keys into the three locks, and
said, as she opened the door: " I wager the pretty idle hussy has not kept her
fingers going very fast. She will rather have been sleeping to keep her complexion fresh." When she came in Gracieuse gave her the ball of thread, beautifully wound. Grognon could not say anything except that she had soiled it,
that she was a little slut, and for that she gave her two slaps that turned her
pink and white cheeks blue and yellow. Poor Gracieuse bore meekly this
insult which she was not able to protect herself against, and they took her back
to the dungeon, where she was again locked up.

Grognon, deeply disappointed at having failed with the skein of thread, sent
for the fairy, and loaded her with reproaches. " Find something much more difficult," she said, " so that it will be impossible for her to do it." The fairy went away,
and next day she brought a great barrel full of feathers. There were feathers of all
kinds of birds : nightingales, canaries, tarins, goldfinches, linnets, redwings, parrots,
owls, sparrows, doves, ostriches, bustards, peacocks, larks, partridges—I should
never have done if I were to name them all. These feathers were all mixed in such
a way that the birds themselves could not have distinguished them. " Here,"
said the fairy to Grognon, " here is something that will test the skill and try the
patience of your prisoner. Command her to pick out these feathers, and to put
those of the peacocks apart, and those of the nightingales, and to do the same
with all the others, making a heap of each kind. A fairy even would find herself
at a loss with such a task." Grognon was beside herself with joy as she pictured
the despair of the poor princess. She sent for her, threatened her in the same
way as before, and shut her up in the triple-locked room with the barrel, telling
her that the whole work must be done by sunset.

Gracieuse began to handle some of the feathers, but, as it was impossible
for her to distinguish one kind from another, she threw them back again into
the barrel. Again she took some out, and several times she made an attempt,
but seeing that it was an impossible thing she was trying, she said, in a tone of
despair : " Let me die. It is my death they wish for, and it will end my
sorrows. I must not call again on Percinet to help me ; if he cared for me he

would be here already." "And so I am, my princess," cried Percinet, appearing from the depths of the barrel, in which he was hidden. "Here I am to get you out of the difficulty in which you are struggling. Doubt if you can, after so many proofs of my affection, that I love you better than my life." With that, he gave three taps with his wand, and the feathers, coming out by thousands from the barrel, arranged themselves in little heaps all round the room. "What do I not owe you, my lord?" said Gracieuse to him. "Without you I should have given up entirely. Rest assured of my gratitude." The prince tried every means to persuade her to make up her mind to do as he wished, but she asked for time; and however great his sacrifice, he did according to her desire. When Grognon came she was so astonished at what she saw that she did not know what more she could do to torment Gracieuse. All the same she beat her, saying her feathers were badly arranged. Again she sent for the fairy, and flew into a horrible temper with her. The fairy did not know what to answer; for she was stupefied. At last she said she would employ all her skill in making a box which would give the princess a good deal of trouble if she took it into her head to open it. A few days after this she brought a box of a considerable size. "See," she said to Grognon; "tell your slave to carry that somewhere. Tell her she must not open it. She will not, however, be able to resist, and then you will be satisfied." Grognon did exactly as she was told. "Carry this box," she said, "to my great castle, and put it on the table in the cabinet. But I forbid you, on pain of death, to look what is inside." Gracieuse put on her sabots, her coarse linen frock, her woollen hood, and set off. Those who met her by the way said: "That must be some goddess in disguise," for her marvellous beauty could not be hidden. She had not gone far before she felt very tired, and, while she was passing through a little wood skirting a pleasant meadow, she sat down to rest for a little. As she held the box on her knees, she suddenly felt a strong desire to open it. "What could happen to me?" she said. "I shall take nothing out of it, but at least I shall see what is inside." And, thinking no more of the consequences, she opened it. Immediately there came

out such a number of little men and little women, violins, and other musical instruments, little tables, little cooks, little dishes, and last of all the giant of the troop, who was as high as your finger. They leaped about in the meadow, separating into several bands, and began the prettiest ball that ever was seen. While some were dancing, others were cooking, and others eating, the little violins playing beautifully all the time. At first Gracieuse was amused at seeing such an extraordinary thing; but when she was somewhat tired of it, and wanted to put them into the box again, not one of them would go. The little gentlemen and the little ladies ran away, even the very violins; and the cooks, with their saucepans on their heads and their spits on their shoulders, ran off to the woods as soon as she was in the meadow, and into the meadow when she was in the wood. "O reckless curiosity," said Gracieuse, weeping, "you have done my enemy but too good a turn! The only misfortune I could have avoided comes from my own fault. No, I cannot reproach myself enough. Percinet! Percinet!" she cried, "if you still can love a princess who is so thoughtless, come and help me in this the most unlucky adventure that has ever befallen me." She had not to call him thrice before he appeared in his glittering green dress. "Were it not for wicked Grognon," he said, "fair princess, you would never think of me." "Ah, do not so misunderstand my feelings towards you. I am neither insensible to worth, nor ungrateful for kindness. It is true that I try your constancy, but only to crown it when I am convinced of it." Percinet, more pleased than he had ever been before, tapped the box three times with his wand, and immediately the mannikins, the little ladies, the violins, the cooks, the roast meats, everyone of them took their places as if they had never been out of them. Percinet had left his chariot in the wood, and he begged the princess to use it to go to the great castle, and indeed she had much need of this help, so exhausted was she. Making her invisible, he drove her there himself, thus having the pleasure of bearing her company—a pleasure, my chronicle tells me, to which she was not indifferent at the bottom of her heart, though she carefully hid her feelings.

When she reached the fine castle, and asked, in Grognon's name, to have the door of the cabinet opened for her, the governor burst out laughing. "What!" he said, "do you think when you leave your sheep you can enter without more ado into such a beautiful place? Be off! Return where you came from. We don't allow wooden shoes on our fine floors." Gracieuse begged him to write a word stating his refusal, which he did. Then, leaving the great castle, she found kind Percinet waiting outside, who brought her back to the palace. It would be difficult for me to write all the tender and respectful words he said to her by the way, to persuade her to put an end to her unhappiness ; and she told him that if Grognon played her another bad turn she would do as he wished.

When her step-mother saw her come back she threw herself on the fairy, whom she had kept by her, and scratched her, and she would have strangled her if a fairy could be strangled. Gracieuse gave Grognon the governor's note and the box, but she flung both into the fire without even opening them, and, according to her own tale, she would have liked to have thrown Gracieuse in too. But she did not long put off the princess's punishment. She had a great hole made in the garden as deep as a well, and over it a large stone was placed. Then she went to walk in the garden, and said to Gracieuse and all who were with her : " Here is a stone under which I am told there is a treasure. Come now, lift it speedily." Everyone lent a hand, Gracieuse amongst the others, which was just what they wanted. As soon as she was at the edge, Grognon pushed her roughly into the pit, and they let fall the stone that closed it. There was nothing to be hoped for in a case like this. How could Percinet ever find her in the middle of the earth ? She saw the hopelessness of her situation, and repented having waited so long to marry him. " How cruel is fate to me ! " she cried. " Here I am buried alive, and this kind of death is more terrible than any other. You are revenged for my delays, Precinet, but I feared lest you should be as fickle as other men, who change just as soon as they are certain of being loved. In short, I wished to be sure of your heart ; and my natural suspicions have brought me to my present state. Yet," she went on, " could I hope that you would feel my loss, I think death would be easier to bear." She was speaking thus to ease her pain, when suddenly a little door opened, which, in the darkness, she had not seen before. The light streamed through and let her see a garden full of flowers, and fruits, and fountains, grottoes, statues, shrubberies, and arbours. Without a moment's hesitation she entered, and going along a broad walk, wondering to herself what end this adventure would have, she saw the Fairy Castle. She had no difficulty in recognising it, quite apart from the fact that there are not many such made of rock crystal, and that she saw her new adventure engraved on its walls. Percinet appeared with his mother and his sisters. " Do not refuse any longer, fair princess," said the queen to Gracieuse. " It is time my son were made happy, and it is time you were released from the terrible condition in which you live under the tyranny of Grognon." The grateful princess threw herself on her knees, and told her she might do with her as she willed ; that she would obey her in all things ; that she had not forgotten the prophecy of Percinet when she left the Fairy Palace—that this same palace would be among the dead, and that she would not enter it till after she had been buried ; that she looked on his

2

fairy lore with admiration, as she did on his virtue; and that she was willing to marry him. The prince, in his turn, threw himself at her feet, and at that moment the palace resounded with the sound of voices and of instruments.

The wedding feast was of unheard-of splendour. All the fairies from a thousand leagues round came with their magnificent equipages; some in cars drawn by swans, others mounted on dragons, others on clouds, others on fiery globes. Amongst them came the fairy who had helped Grognon to torment Gracieuse, and when she saw the princess never was anyone so surprised. She begged her to forget what was past, and promised she would seek means to repair the wrong she had made her suffer. And in truth she would not stay for the feast; but, mounting again on her car drawn by two terrible serpents, she flew to the king's palace, where she sought out Grognon, and wrung her neck before the guards or her attendants could hinder her.

FAIR GOLDILOCKS.

THERE was once a king's daughter who was so beautiful that nothing in the whole world could be compared with her. And because she was so beautiful they called her Princess Goldilocks; for her hair was finer than gold, wonderfully fair, and it fell in ringlets to her feet. Her only covering for her head was her curly hair and a garland of flowers; her dresses were embroidered with diamonds and pearls; and no one could look on her without loving her.

In a neighbouring country there lived a young king who was not married, and who was very handsome and very rich. When the fame of fair Goldilocks reached him, before he had ever set eyes on her he was already so much in love that he could neither eat nor drink for thinking of her. He determined to send an ambassador to ask her hand in marriage. He had a magnificent coach made for the occasion; and, giving the ambassador more than a hundred horses and lackeys, he charged him well to bring the princess home with him.

When the ambassador had taken leave of the king and had gone away, nothing was spoken of at the court but his mission; and the king, who felt assured of Goldilock's consent, had beautiful dresses made for her, and wonderful fittings for the palace. While the workmen were making preparations anent her coming, the ambassador reached her court and delivered his message. But whether she was not in a good humour that day, or whether the offer was not to her liking, she told the messenger that she thanked the king but that she had no desire to marry.

The ambassador left the princess's court very down-hearted at not being able to bring her home with him. He took back all the gifts the king had sent her; for she had been well brought up, and knew that girls should not accept presents from boys. So she would not take the fine diamonds and all the rest of the things; but, so as not to give offence, she accepted a little packet of English pins.

When the ambassador reached the king's capital, where he was waited for with the greatest impatience, everybody was in deep distress because fair Goldilocks was not with him. The king began to cry like a child, and it was in vain they tried to comfort him. Now at the court was a young lad, who was fair as the day, and indeed in the whole kingdom there was no one so handsome. His charms and his ready wit earned him his name of Avenant. Everybody liked him except those who were jealous that the king showed him favour and made him his daily confidant.

Avenant, hearing them speak of the ambassador's return and of how his embassy had been in vain, said, without thinking very much what he was saying: "If the king had sent me to Princess Goldilocks I am sure she would have come back with me". Then the mischief-makers hastened to the king and said to him: "Your majesty, what do you think Avenant has been saying? —That if you had sent him to the princess he would have brought her back! Who ever heard of such impudence? He thinks he is handsomer than you, and that she would have fallen so much in love with him that she would have followed him anywhere." And now the king flew into such a furious passion that he lost all control of himself. "Ha! ha!" said he. "This spoilt monkey laughs at my misfortune! He thinks he is the better man! Go; shut him up in my great tower, and let him die of hunger."

The king's guards went to fetch Avenant, who by this time had forgotten entirely what he had said, and dragged him to prison with all kinds of violence. The poor boy had only a miserable heap of straw for a bed; and he would have died had it not been for a little stream that flowed along through the bottom of the tower, and of which he drank a little to cool his mouth, which was parched by hunger.

One day, when he was sighing in despair, and was saying, "What does the king blame me for? He has not a more loyal subject than myself, and I have never done him any harm," the king passed hard by the tower. Hearing the voice of him whom he had loved so much, he stopped to listen, in spite of the efforts of those who were with him, who, hating Avenant, said: "Why does your majesty waste your time? Do you not know he is a rascal?" But the king answered: "Let me alone. I want to listen." At the sound of his laments, tears filled the king's eyes, and he opened the door of the tower and called him. Avenant came forward in deep distress, and, throwing himself on his knees and kissing the king's feet, he said: "What have I done that your majesty should treat me so cruelly?" "You laughed at me and at my ambassador," said the king. "You said that if I had sent you to the Princess Goldilocks you would have brought her back." "It is true, your majesty," replied Avenant, "that I should have made her so thoroughly realise your good qualities that I feel sure she would not have refused her consent, and in saying that I said nothing that should have displeased you." The king saw that, after all, Avenant was in the right, and, looking with contempt on those who had slandered his favourite, took him away with him, deeply repenting all he had made him suffer.

After having regaled him with a fine supper, he called him into his private room, and said: "Avenant, I am still in love with fair Goldilocks, but I don't know what to do to gain her consent. I should like to send you to see if you could succeed." Avenant replied that he was ready to obey him in everything, and that he would set out next day. "Ah," said the king, "but I wish to have a fine equipage prepared for you." "That is not needful," he answered. "I want only a good horse and letters from you." The king embraced him, so delighted was he with his eagerness to set out.

It was on a Monday morning he took leave of the king and of his friends to go on his errand, all by himself, quite simply and quietly. He did nothing but think of the means he would use to persuade Goldilocks to marry the king. In his pocket he carried a writing tablet, and when a pretty thought occurred to him for his speech, he got off his horse and sat down under the trees to write, so that it might not go out of his head. One morning he had set out at the first streak of day. While he was crossing a wide plain a very pretty conceit came into his head. So he alighted, and leaned up against the willow trees and poplars on the banks of the little spring that flowed by the side of the meadow. After he had written down his thought he was looking all round, delighted at being in such a beautiful spot, when he saw on the grass a great golden carp, panting, and at the last gasp. While trying to catch the little flies, it had jumped so far out of the water that it had fallen on the grass, and now it lay there like to die. Avenant was sorry for it; and though it was a fast-day, and he might well have taken it for his dinner, instead of doing so he put it back gently into the stream. As soon as Mother Carp touched the cool water she recovered her spirits. She let herself be carried down to the bottom ; and then, coming gaily up to the surface again, she said: "Avenant, I thank you for the kindness you have just shown me. But for you I should have died. You have saved my life, and I shall do as much for you one day." With these few words of good omen she plunged into the water, leaving Avenant in great astonishment at such intelligence and such politeness in a carp.

Another day, when he was going on his way, he saw a crow in great distress. The poor bird was being pursued by a huge eagle. Now, eagles feed greedily on crows, and this one was just on the point of seizing his victim, whom he would have swallowed like a lentil, had not Avenant taken pity on the bird's distress. "There," said he, "see how the strong oppress the weak.

What right has the eagle to eat the crow?" With his bow and arrow, which he always carried with him, he took good aim at the eagle—and then, crack! he shot the arrow into its body and pierced it through and through. It fell dead; and the crow, in great glee, perched itself on a tree, saying: "Avenant, it was most generous of you to come to the aid of a poor crow like me. But I shall not be ungrateful. I'll do as much for you one day."

Avenant, in some surprise at the gratitude of the crow, went on his way. Entering a large wood, while it was yet so early that he could hardly see his way, he heard despairing cries from an owl. "Dear me!" he said, "here is an owl in distress. It must have got caught in some nets." Looking round on every side, at length he saw great nets that the fowlers had spread during the night to catch little birds. "How sad," said he, "that men are only made to torment each other, or to persecute poor animals that do them no harm or injury of any kind!" So saying, he took out his knife and cut the cords. The owl sprang up, but came down again quickly to say: "Avenant, there is no need for many words on my part to make you understand the obligation I am under to you. It speaks for itself. The fowlers would have come and caught me, and without your aid I should have died. I have a grateful heart, and I shall do as much for you one day."

Such were the three adventures of any importance that happened to Avenant on his journey. He was so eager to reach his destination that he did not loiter on his way to the palace of fair Goldilocks. Everything there was wonderful to look at. There were diamonds lying in heaps as if they had been but stones. The dresses, the silver, the sweetmeats—everything was marvellous; and he thought to himself that if she left it all to come with him, his master, the king, would be very lucky. He put on a doublet of brocade, with pink and white feathers in his hat. He dressed and powdered his hair, and washed his face. Round his neck was tied an embroidered scarf, with a little basket attached, and in it a pretty little dog he had bought while passing through Boulogne. Avenant was so handsome, so beautiful to look on, all his movements were so full of grace, that when he presented himself at the palace gate the guards saluted him humbly, and sent in haste to announce to Princess Goldilocks that Avenant, ambassador from the king, her nearest neighbour, requested to see her.

At the name of Avenant the princess said: "That name has a pleasant sound. I feel sure he is handsome, and that everybody likes him." "You say truly, madam," said all the maids-of-honour; "we saw him from the loft when we were arranging your flax, and all the time he was standing under the windows we couldn't do anything but look at him." "Well, that is a fine occupation," replied fair Goldilocks, "to amuse yourselves by gazing at boys! Now then, I want my best embroidered blue satin gown. My fair hair must be curled. Let me have garlands of fresh flowers, and fetch my high-heeled shoes and my fan. And tell them to sweep out my room and my throne; for it is my desire that he shall tell everywhere that I am in truth fair Goldilocks."

And now all her maids made speed to dress her like a queen. They were in such a hurry that they knocked against each other and made but little progres . At last the princess passed into her gallery, with the great mirrors, to see if nothing were lacking in her appearance. Then she ascended her throne, made of gold and ivory and ebony, the scent of which was like balm, and she told her damsels to take instruments and to sing quite softly so that the sound might jar on no one's ears.

Avenant was led to the audience chamber, where he stood so dazzled with admiration that, as he has often said since then, he could hardly speak. Never-

theless he plucked up courage and delivered his speech beautifully, begging the princess that he might not have the disappointment of returning without her. "Gentle Avenant," she said, "all the reasons which you have just given me are excellent, and I assure you I would most willingly do more for you than for another. But you must know that a month ago I was in a boat on the river with all my ladies, when, as they were serving me with luncheon, in taking off my glove, I slipped a ring from my finger, which unluckily fell into the river. It was more precious to me than my kingdom, and I leave you to judge what sorrow its loss caused me. I vowed never to listen to any proposal of marriage till the ambassador who brings it restores my ring. And now think what you have before you, for, were you to speak to me for fifteen days and fifteen nights, you could not persuade me to change my mind."

Avenant was much surprised at this answer. Making her a profound bow, he begged her to accept the little dog, the basket, and the scarf. But she said she wished for no gifts, and charged him to think of what she had just told him.

Returning to his own dwelling, he went supperless to bed, and his little dog, Cabriole, would not eat anything either, and came and lay down beside him. All through the night Avenant never ceased his sighs. "How could I find a ring that fell into a great river a month ago?" he said. "It is nothing but folly to make the attempt. The princess only spoke of it to me to make it impossible for me to obey her." And he sighed in deep distress. Cabriole, listening all the while, said : "My dear master, I beg you not to be down-hearted about your luck. You are too good not to be happy. Let us go as soon as it is day to the river-side." Avenant stretched out his hand to pat him once or twice and returned no other answer. At last, quite overcome with his sorrow, he fell asleep.

When daylight came Cabriole began to cut capers as soon as he awoke. "My master," he said, "get dressed and come out." Avenant had no objection. Getting up, he dressed and went down into the garden, and from the garden he turned his steps unconsciously to the river-side, where he walked along with his hat over his eyes and his arms crossed. All at once he heard a voice calling : "Avenant, Avenant!" Looking all round, and seeing no one, he thought it must have been fancy. He went on walking, and again the voice called : "Avenant, Avenant!" "Who is calling me?" he said. Cabriole, who was very little and who was peering into the water, answered him : "Never again believe what I say if it is not a golden carp I see". Then the big carp appeared and said to him : "You saved my life in the beam-tree meadow, where I should have remained a captive but for you. I promised to do as much for you one day. Well then, dear Avenant, here is fair Goldilock's ring." And Avenant, stooping down, took it out of Mistress Carp's gullet, thanking her over and over again.

Instead of going home he went straight to the palace with little Cabriole, who was very glad he had brought his master to the river-side. The princess was told he wished to see her. "Alas!" she said. "Poor boy! he is coming to bid me farewell. He thinks that what I ask is an impossibility, and he is going home to tell his master so." Avenant, on being announced, presented the ring to her, saying : "Princess, I have fulfilled your command. Will it please you to accept the king, my master, as your husband?" When she saw the ring, the very ring she had lost, she was so astonished, so astonished, that she thought she must be dreaming. "In truth," she said, "dear Avenant, you must be some fairy's favourite, for by yourself it would have been impossible." "Madam," he answered, "I know no fairy, but I had a great wish to obey you." "Then, since you are so willing," she went on, "you must do me another service ; otherwise, I shall never marry. Not far from here there is a prince called Galifron, who has taken it into his head that he wants to marry me. He announced his intention to me with fearful threats that, should I refuse, he would lay waste my kingdom. But could I accept him, think you? He is a giant, taller than a high tower, and thinks no more of eating a man than a monkey would think of eating a chestnut. When he goes to the country he carries little cannons in his pockets, which he uses instead of pistols, and when he speaks very loud those that are near him are struck deaf. I told him I did not wish to marry, and asked to be excused; yet, he has never left off persecuting me, and he kills all my subjects. The first thing to be done, therefore, is for you to fight him and to bring me his head."

Avenant was somewhat stunned by this proposal. He turned it over in his mind for a little while, and then said: "Well, madam, I shall fight against Galifron. I think I shall be beaten, but I shall die like a brave man." The princess was much surprised, and told him all kinds of things to prevent his undertaking the enterprise, but in vain; so he withdrew in order to fetch his armour and all that should be necessary. When he had found all he wanted, he put little Cabriole in his basket, mounted his good horse, and set out for the country of Galifron. He questioned those he met on the way about the prince, and everybody told him he was a real demon, and no one dared go near him. The more he heard this, the more frightened did he become. Cabriole reassured him, saying: "My dear master, while you are fighting, I shall bite his legs. Then he will bend his head to chase me away, and you will kill him." Avenant admired the little dog's spirit, though he knew his help would not avail.

At last he arrived near Galifron's castle. All the roads were covered with the bones and the carcasses of the men he had eaten or torn to pieces. He did not have long to wait for him, for he saw him coming through a wood, his head over-topping the tallest trees, and heard him singing in a terrible voice :—

> " Ho, bring me for lunch
> Fat babies to crunch;
> Not few and not lean,
> Or my appetite keen
> You will not satisfy,
> So hungry am I ! "

Avenant immediately began to sing to the same air :—

> " Here see Avenant stand
> With his spear in his hand,
> In humour defiant
> Though he isn't a giant,
> For there's never a doubt
> But he'll tear your teeth out ".

The rhymes were not very regular, but then he had made the song in a great hurry, and it is a wonder it was not much worse even, so terribly afraid was he. When Galifron heard these words he looked all round and saw Avenant with his

spear in his hand calling him names, one after the other, to make him angry. This was not necessary, for he flew into a terrible passion, and, taking a heavy bar of iron, would have felled Avenant with one stroke had not the crow perched itself on the top of his head, and, making a dart at his eyes, torn them out with its beak. The blood flowed down his face, and like a madman he struck out on all sides. Avenant parried the blows, and with great force he plunged his spear into the giant again and again up to the hilt, wounding him terribly, and causing him to fall from the blood he lost. Then he hacked off Galifron's head, in great spirits at his good fortune, while the raven, who was perched on a tree, spoke thus : " I have not forgotten the service you did me in killing the eagle that pursued me. I promised to pay my debt, and I think I have done so to-day." " It is I who am the debtor, Sir Raven," replied Avenant, " and I remain your servant." Then, putting the horrible head of Galifron on the horse, he rode away.

When he reached the town everybody ran after him, crying : " Here comes brave Avenant, the slayer of the monster ! " so that the princess, who heard the noise quite well, and who trembled lest they should come to tell her of the death of Avenant, did not dare to ask what had happened. But Avenant came in bearing the giant's head, which still struck terror into her, although there was no longer cause for fear. " Madam," he said, " your enemy is dead. I hope you will no longer refuse the king, my master." " Yes, indeed, I will," said fair Goldilocks. " I still refuse him, unless you are able, before I go away, to fetch me some water from the Dark Grotto. Near here there is a deep cavern fully six leagues in circumference. The entrance is barred by two dragons with fire coming out of their eyes and mouths. Once inside you have to go down into a great hole, full of toads and adders and serpents. At the bottom of this hole is a little cave through which there flows the stream of Beauty and of Health. A miracle happens to whoever washes with this water. If you are beautiful, you will always be so ; if you are ugly, you grow fair. If you are young, you never grow any older ; if you are old, you grow young. You can understand, Avenant, that I could not leave my kingdom without taking a supply of this water with me."

" Madam," he answered, " you are already so beautiful that this water is altogether useless to you. But I am an unlucky ambassador, whose death you seek. I go to search for what you desire, well assured that I shall return no more."

Fair Goldilocks did not change her mind, and Avenant set out with his little dog Cabriole for the Dark Grotto to search for the water of Beauty. All who met him on the way said what a pity it was to see so fair a youth going recklessly to his death. " He goes to the grotto by himself, but were he to go a hundred strong he would never succeed. Why does the princess ask such impossible things ? " Avenant went on his way, without saying a word, but he was sad at heart.

When he had climbed to the top of a mountain he sat down to rest for a little, letting his horse graze and Cabriole run after the flies. He knew the Dark Grotto was not far off, and he looked to see if it were not in sight. At last he saw, first a hideous rock black as ink, out of which a thick smoke was coming, and after a moment one of the dragons that shot fire from their mouths and eyes. Its body was yellow and green. It had great claws, and a long tail curled into hundreds of twists. When Cabriole saw all this he was so terrified that he did not know where to hide.

Avenant, quite resigned to death, drew his spear, and went down with a phial which the Princess Goldilocks had given him to fill with the water of Beauty. To his little dog Cabriole he said: " My end is near! I can never get that water which is guarded by the dragons. When I am dead fill this bottle with my blood, and take it to the princess that she may see what her errand has cost me. Then repair to the king, my master, and tell him of my unhappy fate." While he was saying these words he heard a voice calling him: " Avenant, Avenant!" " Who is calling me?" he asked. He saw an owl in the hollow of an old tree, who said to him: " You extricated me from the fowlers' nets in which I was caught, and you saved my life. I promised to do as much for you one day. Now the time has come. Give me your phial. I know all the paths through the Dark Grotto, and I will fetch the water of Beauty for you." Here was good news for Avenant, as you may believe, and he gave him the bottle in haste. The owl entered the grotto without hindrance, and in less than a quarter of an hour he came back carrying the bottle well corked. Avenant, delighted, thanked him with all his heart, and, climbing the hill, again took the way to the town with a glad heart.

Going straight to the palace, he presented the phial to fair Goldilocks, who had nothing more to say. She thanked Avenant, gave all the necessary orders for her departure, and then set out on her journey with him. He seemed to her very charming, and she would sometimes say: " If you had been willing I should have made you king, and need never have left my kingdom ". But he answered: " I would not do such a wrong to my master for all the kingdoms of the earth, though I think you lovelier than the sun ".

At last they reached the capital, where the king, knowing that the Princess Goldilocks was coming, came to meet her with the fairest gifts in the world. Such great rejoicing was there at their wedding that nothing else was spoken of. But fair Goldilocks, who at the bottom of her heart loved Avenant, was never happy but when she saw him, and his praises were ever on her tongue. " I should never have been here had it not been for Avenant," she said to the king. " He had to perform impossible feats for me, and you owe him a great deal. He gave me the water of Beauty, so I shall never grow old, and I shall be beautiful for ever."

Envious people, listening to the queen's words, said to the king: "You are not jealous, but you have good reason to be. The queen is so much in love with Avenant that she can neither eat nor drink. She does nothing but speak of him and of the obligations you are under to him, as if anyone else whom you might have sent would not have done as much." " I believe you are right," said the king. " Let him be cast into the tower, and irons put on his feet and hands." There Avenant saw no one but the gaoler, who used to throw him a bit of black bread through a hole, and give him some water in an earthen dish, but his little dog Cabriole stayed with him to comfort him, and brought him all the news.

When fair Goldilocks heard of Avenant's disgrace she threw herself at the king's feet, and, weeping bitterly, begged him to let Avenant go free. But the more she pleaded the more angry grew the king, thinking that she loved Avenant. He would not relent, so she stopped speaking of the matter, but her heart was very sad.

It occurred to the king that perhaps she did not think him handsome enough, and he had a strong desire to rub his face with the water of Beauty, in order that the queen might love him better that she did at present. This water stood in the bottle on the edge of the mantelshelf in the queen's room. She had put it there so that she might the oftener look at it. But one of the housemaids, when killing a spider with a broom, unfortunately knocked down the bottle, which was broken and all the water spilt. She swept away the traces

quickly, and, at her wits' end what to do, she remembered that she had seen in the king's private room a bottle just like it, full of a clear liquid like the water of Beauty. Without saying a word to anybody, she managed to get hold of it, and placed it on the queen's mantelshelf.

Now the water in the king's room was for causing the death of princes and great lords when they had committed crimes. · Instead of beheading or hanging them, their faces were rubbed with this water, and they fell asleep and woke no more. One evening, therefore, the king took the bottle and rubbed his face well with the contents. Then he fell asleep, and he died. The little dog Cabriole was the first to learn what had happened, and did not fail to go and tell Avenant, who asked him to go to Princess Goldilocks and beg her to take thought of the poor prisoner.

Cabriole slipped quietly through the crowd, for there was great confusion at the court owing to the king's death. " Madam," he said to the queen, " do not forget poor Avenant." She bethought herself of the sufferings he had undergone on her account, and of his great faithfulness. Without saying a word to anyone, she went out and made straight for the tower, where, with her own hands, she took off the irons from Avenant's hands and feet. Then, placing a golden crown on his head and the royal robes on his shoulders, she said : " Come, dear Avenant, I make you a king, and take you for my husband ". Throwing himself at her feet, he poured out his gratitude. Everyone was delighted to own him for their master. Never was there such a wedding feast, and the Princess Goldilocks and fair Avenant lived long together in peace and happiness.

THE BLUE BIRD.

THERE was once upon a time a king who was very rich in lands and money. When his wife died he was inconsolable, and for eight whole days he shut himself up in a little room, and knocked his head against the wall, so desperate was he. They feared lest he should kill himself, and they therefore put mattresses between the tapestry and the wall, so that however hard he might strike his head, he could do himself no harm. All his subjects planned amongst themselves to go and see him, and to say everything they could think of as likely to comfort him in his sorrow. Some of them made up grave and serious speeches; others again went with cheerful, even gay words on their tongues, but none of them made any impression on him. In fact he hardly heard what they said. At last there came before him a woman clad all in black crape, with veil and mantle and long mourning garments, who wept and sobbed so loud and so violently that he was filled with astonishment. She said that, unlike the others, she had come with the object of adding to, rather than of lessening, his grief; for what could be more natural than to sorrow for a good wife? As for her, she had had the best husband in the whole world, and it was her part now to weep for him while she had eyes in her head. Thereupon she redoubled her cries, and the king following her example, began to wail aloud.

He gave her a better reception than he had done to the others, entertaining her with an account of the fine qualities of his dear dead lady, while she waxed eloquent on those of her beloved husband. They talked and talked till they had not a word more to say on the subject of their sorrows. When the cunning widow saw that there was nothing more to be said on the matter, she lifted her veil just a little, and it was some relief to the king in the midst of his distress to look on this poor lady afflicted like himself. Her large blue eyes, fringed with long black eyelashes, she rolled this way and that way, to make the most of their beauty ; and then her cheeks were rosy too. The king looked at her very atten-tively. Gradually he spoke less of his wife ; then he stopped speaking of her altogether. The widow still declared she would always lament her husband, but the king begged her not to sorrow for ever. In the end, to everybody's astonishment, he married her ; and her mourning garments were changed to gowns of green and rose colour. It often happens that you have but to know people's weak points to win their hearts and do with them what you will.

The king had only one daughter by his first marriage, and she was looked on as the eighth wonder of the world. They called her Florine, because she was like Flora, so fresh and young and beautiful was she. She did not care to be dressed very grandly, but liked rather robes of floating taffeta, with jewelled clasps, and garlands of flowers to adorn her lovely hair. When the king married again she was only fifteen years old.

The new queen sent for her own daughter, who had been brought up in the house of her god-mother, Soussio the fairy, though she was none the more graceful or beautiful for that. Soussio had done what she could for her, but without success. Yet she loved her dearly none the less. They called the girl Truitonne,* for her face had as many red spots as a trout. Her black hair was so dirty and greasy that you could not touch it, and oil oozed out from her yellow skin. All the same the queen loved her to distraction, and would speak of nothing but of Truitonne's charms. But as Florine was far more attractive, the queen was in despair. In all kinds of ways she tried to raise quarrels between her and the king, and not a day passed but she and Truitonne did Florine some bad turn. The princess was, however, good-tempered and in-telligent, and endeavoured to take no notice of their bad behaviour.

One day the king said to the queen that Florine and Truitonne were old enough to be married, and that the hand of one of them must be bestowed on the first prince who should come to the court. " I think," said the queen, " that my daughter should be thought of first of all, seeing that she is older than yours ; and as she is far more amiable there can be no hesitation in agree-

* Fr. *truite*, trout.

ing to this." The king did not like disputing, so he said he was quite willing, and the queen might do as she liked.

Some little time after they heard that King Charming was going to pay them a visit. Never was there so splendid and so gallant a prince, and everything in his mind and person answered to his name. When the queen heard of his coming she employed all the embroiderers, and all the dressmakers, and all the craftsmen, to make things for Truitonne. She begged the king to give Florine nothing new; and, by bribing her maids, she had all her dresses, and wreaths, and jewels taken away the very day that Charming arrived, so that when the princess wished to deck herself she could not find so much as a ribbon. Florine was well aware to whom she owed this bad turn. When she sent to buy stuffs the merchants told her the queen had forbidden them to sell her any. So she had nothing to put on but a dirty little frock; and so much ashamed of it was she that she sat down in a corner of the hall when King Charming came in.

The queen received him with much ceremony, and presented her daughter to him, clad in the most splendid apparel, and uglier than usual in her grandeur. When the king turned away his eyes the queen would have liked to persuade herself that it was because Truitonne dazzled him too much, and that he feared the effect of her charms on him; so she always pushed her forward. He asked if there was not another princess called Florine. " Yes," said Truitonne, pointing to her; "she is hiding over there, because she is not very nicely dressed." Florine blushed, and looked at that moment so beautiful, so very, very beautiful, that King Charming was quite dazzled. Rising quickly, he made a deep bow to the princess, saying : " Madam, your incomparable beauty already adorns you too well for you to need any other aid ". " Your majesty," she answered, " I must tell you I am little accustomed to wearing so poor a dress as this, and I should have liked better had you taken no notice of me." " It would have been impossible," cried Charming, "that so lovely a princess should have been anywhere near me and that I should have had eyes for anyone else." "Ah," said the queen, who was much annoyed, " what a waste of time is this ! Believe me, sire, Florine is vain enough already. She doesn't need so many compliments paid to her." King Charming understood at once the motives that made the queen speak in this way, but as he was not in a humour to restrain his feelings he let all his admiration for Florine be seen, and talked to her for three hours on end.

The queen was in despair ; and Truitonne was inconsolable at not being preferred to the princess. They complained loudly to the king, and forced him to consent during King Charming's stay to shut Florine up in a tower, where they would not see each other. So as soon as she had gone back to her room

3

four men with masks carried her off to the top of the tower, and left her there in
the utmost distress.   She knew quite well she was only treated thus to prevent
her from pleasing King Charming, whom she already liked very much and whom
she would willing have accepted as a husband.

As Charming was ignorant of the wrong they had done to the princess, he
was waiting the hour when he would see her again with the greatest impatience.
He spoke of her to those whom the king had ordered to be in attendance on him,
but by the queen's command they told him all the harm they could of her—that
she was vain, and of an uncertain and violent temper, that she was a plague to
her friends and her servants, that she was slovenly, and so avaricious that she
preferred to be dressed like a little shepherdess rather than to buy rich stuffs with
the money the king, her father, gave her.   Charming writhed to hear all this, and
he had much ado to restrain the anger that stirred within him.   " No," he said
to himself, " it is not possible that heaven should have made so evil a soul
to dwell in nature's masterpiece.   I own she was not suitably dressed when · I
saw her, but her evident shame shows she is not used to being in that condition.
What!   So they tell me she could be wicked with that charming look of
modesty and gentleness!   Such a thing could not possibly be : it is easier for
me to believe that the queen slanders her.   She is not a step-mother for nothing,
and Princess Truitonne is such an ugly creature that it would not be strange if
she were jealous of the most perfect being in the world."

While he was thinking over all this, the courtiers who were with him saw
quite well from his manner that he was not pleased at their speaking evil of
Florine.   There was one amongst them sharper than the others, and he, changing his tone and language in order to find out what the prince really felt, began
to pay compliments to the princess.   At this Charming woke up as from a profound sleep, and took part in the conversation, his face showing perfectly the joy
he felt.   Love, how difficult it is to hide thee !   Thou art everywhere visible, on
a lover's lips, in his eyes, in the sound of his voice.   When we love, the signs of
it appear in our every action, in our silence, our conversation, in our joy, in our
sorrow.

The queen, impatient to know if King Charming was really impressed, sent
for those she had taken into her confidence, and she spent the rest of .the night
in questioning them.   All they told her only served to confirm the opinion that
the king was in love with Florine.   But what shall I say of the melancholy condition of that poor princess, as she lay on the floor of the dungeon in that terrible
tower into which the masked men had brought her ?   " It would be easier to
bear," she said, " if they had put me here before I had seen that king, who is so
amiable.   The recollection of him only makes my distress harder to bear, and I

have no doubt that it is to hinder me from seeing him any more that the queen treats me so cruelly. Alas! whatever beauty heaven may have endowed me with will have to be paid for by my happiness!" Then she cried, and cried so bitterly, that her worst enemy would have been sorry for her had she seen her misery.

So the night passed. The queen, who wished to attach King Charming to her by all the marks of attention possible, sent him costumes of a richness and magnificence nowhere else to be found, fashioned after the mode of the country, and also the Order of the Knights of Love, which she had made the king institute on their wedding-day. It was a golden heart enamelled in fire-colour. There were several arrows round it, and one that pierced it through, and the words: *One alone wounds me.* The queen had had the heart for Charming's order cut out of a ruby as big as an ostrich's egg. Each arrow was made of a single diamond as long as your finger, and the chain from which it hung was made of pearls, the smallest of which weighed a pound. In short, since the beginning of the world, a like thing had never been seen. At sight of it the king was so astounded that for some minutes he could not speak. At the same time he was presented with a book, the leaves of which were of vellum, with wonderful miniatures. The cover was of gold, studded with precious stones, and it contained the statutes of the Order of the Knights of Love, written in very tender and very gallant style. They told the king that the princess whom he had seen begged him to be her knight, and that she sent him this present. On hearing this he flattered himself it might be from her whom he loved. "What! the fair Princess Florine!" cried he; "she remembers me in so charming and so generous a fashion." "Your majesty," they said, "you make a mistake in the name. It is from the lovely Truitonne we come." "Then it is Truitonne who begs me to be her knight?" said the king, in a cold and serious manner. "I am sorry not to be able to accept this honour, but a sovereign is not sufficiently his own master to do everything he would like. I know the duties of a knight, and I would like to fulfil them all, but I prefer rather to decline the favours she offers me than to prove myself unworthy of them." So saying, he put back the heart, the chain, and the book in the same basket, and returned all of them to the queen, who, as well as her daughter, was nearly mad with rage at the scornful way in which the stranger king had received so especial a favour.

As soon as he found opportunity he went to the apartment of the king and queen, hoping Florine would be there, and looking about everywhere to see her. Whenever anyone came into the room he turned his head abruptly towards the door, and seemed anxious and disappointed. The wicked queen knew well enough what was passing in his mind, but she did not let him see that she did, and spoke of nothing but pleasure-parties, receiving from him quite foolish answers in return. At last he asked where the Princess Florine was. " Your majesty," said the queen, hotly, " the king, her father, has forbidden her to leave her own apartments till my daughter be married." " And what reason can there be for keeping this fair lady a prisoner ? " " I do not know," said the queen ; " and even if I did I might be excused from telling you." The king was in a fury of passion, and cast black looks at Truitonne as he thought to himself it was on account of that little monster that they robbed him of the pleasure of seeing the princess. Then he left the queen abruptly, for her presence was more than he could bear.

When he was again in his own room he told a young prince who had come with him, and whom he loved dearly, to give any bribe in the world to one of the attendants of the princess, so that he might speak with her a moment. The prince had no difficulty in finding some ladies-in-waiting who were willing to be taken into his confidence, and one of them assured him that every evening Florine would be at a little window overlooking the garden, where she could speak to him, provided he took great precautions to prevent its being known. " For," she added, " the king and the queen are so severe that they would kill me if they discovered that I had favoured Charming's suit." The prince, de-lighted at having thus far succeeded, promised all she wished, and ran to pay his respects to the king, and to tell him the hour appointed. But the faithless waiting-woman did not fail to go and warn the queen of what was going on, and to take her orders accordingly. The queen at once made up her mind to send her daughter to the little window. She gave her instructions what to do, and Truitonne remembered them every one, though she was naturally very stupid.

The night was so dark that it would have been impossible for the king to see the trick that was being played him, even if he had been less confident than he was. So he drew near to the window with such transports of joy as cannot be described, and said to Truitonne all he would have said to Florine, to persuade her to believe what love he felt for her. Truitonne, making the best of the oppor-tunity, told him she was the most unhappy girl in the world to have so cruel a step-mother, and that she would always have to suffer till her step-sister should get married. The king assured her that if she would have him for a husband he would be delighted to share with her his crown and his heart. So saying, he drew the ring from his finger, and putting it on Truitonne's, he told her it was for an everlasting token of his faith, and that she had only to fix the time and they would set off without delay. Truitonne gave what answer she could to all his passionate speeches, but he noticed that there was very little in what she said. This would have grieved him had he not persuaded himself that the fear of being surprised by the queen was a check on her spirits. He only left her on condition that he might come back next night at the same hour, to which she consented with the utmost willingness. The queen was in great hopes after hearing of the success of this interview.

Now the day of their escape being fixed, the king came to take the princess away in a flying chaise, drawn by winged frogs, which one of his friends, a wizard, had made him a present of. The night was very dark. Truitonne crept out of a little door with great mystery, and the king, who was waiting for her, received her in his arms and swore eternal faithfulness to her. But as he had no desire to go flying through the air in this chaise for ever so long without marrying the princess whom he loved, he asked her when she would like their wedding to take place. She told him that she had for god-mother a very cele- brated fairy called Soussio, and that she wished to go and visit her at her castle. Although the king did not know the way, he had nothing to do but tell his big frogs to take them there, for they knew the chart of the whole world, and in no time they landed the king and Truitonne at Soussio's dwelling.

The castle was so brilliantly lighted that there the king would have found out his mistake had not the princess carefully covered herself with her veil. Having asked to see her god-mother she spoke to her in private, telling her how she had entrapped Charming, and begging Soussio to make her peace with him. " But, my daughter," said the fairy, " that is no easy thing. He is much too fond of Florine for that, and I feel certain he will disappoint us." Meanwhile the king awaited them in a hall, whose walls were of diamonds, so clear and transparent that through them he saw Soussio and Truitonne talking together. He thought he must be dreaming. " What," he said, " have I been tricked ? Have the demons brought hither that enemy of our happiness ? Has she come to interfere with my marriage ? My dear Florine is not to be seen. Perhaps her father has followed her ! " All kinds of things suggested themselves to his mind, and he began to be in despair. But it was much worse when they came into the room, and when Soussio said, in a commanding tone : " King Charming, here is Princess Truitonne, to whom you have pledged your word. She is my god-daughter, and I command that you marry her at once." " What, I ? " cried the king. " I marry this little monster ? You must think me of a very docile disposition since you make such a proposal to me. In truth, I have promised her nothing, and if she says anything to the contrary she . . ." " Stop," in- terrupted Soussio, " and never be so bold as to fail in respect for me." " I am quite willing," answered the king, " to give you all the respect that is due to a fairy, provided that you give me back my princess." " And am I not your princess, faithless wretch ? " said Truitonne, showing him the ring. " To whom did you give this ring as a token of fidelity? To whom did you speak at the little window, if not to me?" "What!" he cried; "I have been tricked and deceived! But, no; I shall not be your dupe. Quick there! my frogs, my frogs! I shall depart at once!"

"Ho!" said Soussio, "that is not in your power unless I give leave"; and so saying she touched him, and his feet stuck fast to the floor as if they had been nailed to it. "Though you were to stone me, or to flog me," said the king, "I shall never own another mistress but Florine. On this I am determined, and, knowing that, you can use your power as you like." Soussio tried every means to soften his resolve—gentleness, threats, promises, supplications. Truitonne wept, cried aloud, groaned, flew into tempers, and cooled down again. The king said not a word; and looking at them both with the most scornful air in the world, paid not the faintest attention to all they said to him.

Twenty days and twenty nights passed away in this fashion, during which they never stopped talking, never ate, never slept, never sat down. At last Soussio, tired out, could endure it no longer, and said to the king: "Well, you are indeed stubborn! Why will you not listen to reason? Take your choice: you shall have seven years' penance for having made a promise you have not kept, or you shall marry my god-daughter." The king, who had never uttered a word till now, cried out suddenly: "Do whatever you like with me, only deliver me from this detestable creature!" "I am no more detestable than you," said Truitonne, wrathfully, "you silly little king, coming with your equipage, fit only for the bogs, to my country, to insult and to break faith with me. If you had a particle of honour, would you behave so?" "These reproaches touch me deeply," said the king, in mocking tone. "How foolish not to take so fair a lady for my wife!" "No, no," said Soussio, angrily; "she will never marry you. You have only to fly out of the window if you want to. For seven years you will be changed into a blue bird."

At that moment the king's person changed. His arms were covered with feathers, and turned into wings. His legs and feet became black and shrunken, with hooked claws. His body dwindled in size, and was all covered with long fine feathers, some of them of sky blue; his eyes became round, and shone like two planets; his nose was nothing but an ivory beak; and on his head stood up a white plume in the shape of a crown. He could sing exquisitely and speak too. He uttered a cry of pain to see himself metamorphosed, and flew as fast as ever he could to escape from Soussio's horrible palace.

In the melancholy state into which he had fallen he hopped about from branch to branch, choosing only those trees consecrated to love and sorrow: now on a myrtle, now on a cypress, singing sad songs, in which he lamented the evil fortune that pursued Florine and himself. " Where have her enemies hidden her ? " said he. " What has become of that fair victim ? Does the cruelty of the queen still deprive her of her liberty ? Where can I seek for her ? Am I doomed to spend seven years without her ? Perhaps during that time they will give her in marriage, and I shall lose for ever the hope that sustains my life." All these thoughts so filled Blue Bird with despair that he wished to die.

To return to Truitonne : the fairy Soussio sent her back to the queen, who was most anxious to hear how the wedding had passed off. But when she saw her daughter, and heard from her all that had happened, she flew into a terrible passion, of which the full force fell on poor Florine. " She shall duly repent," said the queen, " of having found favour in Charming's eyes." She went up the tower with Truitonne, whom she had dressed in her grandest clothes. On her head was a diamond crown, and three daughters of the richest barons in the kingdom held the train of her royal mantle. On her thumb was Charming's ring that Florine had noticed the day they had talked together. She was very much surprised to see Truitonne in such gorgeous apparel. " Here comes my daughter, who brings you presents in honour of her wedding," said the queen. " King Charming has married her ; he loves her to distraction, and there never were two happier people." Then they spread out before the princess gold and silver stuffs, jewels, laces, ribbons, in great baskets of gold filigree work. In presenting all these things Truitonne never forgot for a moment to make the king's ring flash ; and Princess Florine, no longer able to hide from herself her misfortune, begged them with cries of despair to take all these miserable presents out of her sight, that she would never again wear anything but black, or rather that she would like now to die. Then she fainted, and the cruel queen, delighted at her success, would not allow anyone to come to Florine's aid. She left her alone in the most deplorable condition, and went and told the king maliciously that his daughter was so excited by her love that nothing could equal the absurd things she did, and that on no account must they allow her to get out of the tower. The king said she might manage the matter as she liked, and he would be satisfied whatever she did.

When the princess recovered from her fainting fit, and began to reflect on the way she was treated, the cruelty of her wicked step-mother towards her, and the hope she was losing for ever of marrying King Charming, her grief became so keen that she cried all night, and in this condition she sat herself down at the window, where she uttered sad and plaintive laments. When day was near she shut the window and wept anew.

The following night she opened the window, and sat heaving deep sighs, sobbing bitterly, and shedding torrents of tears. When day came she retired into her room. But King Charming, or rather the beautiful Blue Bird, flew round and round the palace, thinking his dear princess was inside; and if her laments were sad, his were no less so. He came as near to the windows as he could to peer into the room, but the fear lest Truitonne should see him, and discover who he was, kept him from doing all he wished. " It would cost me my life," said he to himself. " If those wicked princesses find out where I am they will seek to revenge themselves. I must go away if I do not wish to run into the utmost danger." These considerations made him take great precautions, and as a rule he sang only at night-time.

In front of Florine's window was a cypress of a tremendous height, and there the blue bird came and perched. Hardly was he there before he heard the cries of a lady. " How long will my sufferings last?" she said. " Will death not come to my aid? To those who fear him he comes but too soon, but for me, who long for him, he tarrieth cruelly. Ah, cruel queen! what harm have I done you that you should keep me shut up in this horrible prison? Are there not other ways enough in which to torture me? You need only let me look on at the happiness which your wicked daughter enjoys with King Charming." The blue bird had lost not a word of this lament, which filled him with astonishment, and he waited for daylight with the utmost impatience to see the sorrowful lady. But before the dawn she had shut her window and gone out of sight.

The bird, full of curiosity, did not fail to return next night. By the light of the moon that was then in the sky he saw a damsel at the window of the tower, and heard her beginning her lament. " Fortune," she said—" that flatteredst me by setting me in a place of power; that madest me the darling of my father— what have I done that thou shouldst all at once plunge me into the bitterest waters? Should I begin to feel thy changefulness in these my tender years? Return, cruel one; return, if possible, and all I ask of thee is to end my unhappy life." The blue bird listened, and the longer he listened the more persuaded was he that it was his dear princess who was uttering these laments. " Adorable Florine," he said, " the wonder of our days, why do you long that yours should be so soon ended? Your misfortunes are not without a remedy." " Ah! who is it speaks to me with words of comfort?" she cried. " An unhappy king," replied the bird. " He loves you, and will never love anyone else." " A king who loves me?" she said. " Is this some snare my enemy has laid for me? But in the end what would she gain by it? If she seeks to find out what my feelings are, I am ready to make them all known to her." " No, my princess," he answered; " the lover who now speaks to you is not capable of betraying you "; and so saying he flew on to the window-sill. At first Florine was very much afraid of a bird so strange, that spoke as sensibly as a man, though in the gentle notes of a nightingale. But the beauty of its plumage and the words it said reassured her. " Do I in truth see you again, my princess ? " he cried. " Can I taste such perfect happiness and not die for joy ? But, alas ! how ·my joy is troubled by your captivity, and at the shape into which Soussio has changed me for seven years." " And who are you, you charming bird ? " said the princess, caressing him. " You call me by my name," said the king; " and you pretend not to know me ! " " What ! " said the princess ; " the little bird in my hand is King Charming ! " " Alas ! fair Florine, it is but too true," he replied ; " and if anything could console me it is that I have preferred to suffer this rather than give up my love for you." " For me ! " said Florine. " Ah ! do not seek to deceive me. I know, I know that you have married Truitonne. I recognised the ring on her finger as yours. I saw her sparkling with the diamonds you had given her. She came to insult me in my sad captivity, wearing a grand crown and royal mantle that she got from you; and all the while I was laden with chains and irons."

" You saw Truitonne in such a dress ! " interrupted the king. " Her mother and herself have dared to say that these baubles came from me ! Heaven ! is it possible I hear such horrible lies, and that I cannot take my revenge on the spot ? Believe me, they tried to deceive me, and by using your name they managed to make me run away with the hideous Truitonne, but as soon as I discovered my mistake I left her, choosing rather to be Blue Bird for seven long years than break my troth to you."

Florine was in such delight to hear these words from her dear lover that she forgot altogether her sufferings in the prison. What did she not say to him to comfort him for his sad mischance, and to persuade him that she would do no less for him than he had done for her? The day appeared, and the greater number of the officers of the court were already stirring while Blue Bird and the princess were still speaking together. It was terrible to tear themselves apart, and they only did so after promising to see each other in this way every night. The joy they felt at having found each other again was so great that there are no words to describe it. Each of them in turn gave thanks to Love and Fortune, yet Florine was sad on Blue Bird's account. " Who will protect him from the fowlers ? " she said ; " or from the sharp claw of some eagle or famished vulture ? who will devour him none the less greedily that he is a great king. O heaven ! what would become of me if his light and delicate feathers, driven by the wind, were to come to my prison and to announce the danger that I fear ? " For this thought the princess could not close an eye, for when one is in love illusions appear real, and what at another time would be thought impossible seems easy then, so that she spent her day in weeping till the hour came to seat herself at the window.

The lovely bird, hidden in the hollow of a tree, had been all day long think-ing of his dear princess. "How happy I am!" he said, "to have found her again! And how charming she is! And how grateful I am for all her kindness to me!" This tender lover counted every moment of the time of trial during which he could not marry her, and never was the end of anything longed for more passionately. As he wished to pay Florine every attention within his power, he flew to the capital of his kingdom, entered his own room by a broken pane of glass, chose out diamond ear-rings so perfect and so beautiful that nothing in the world could be compared to them. That evening he took them to Florine, and begged her to put them on. "I would do so willingly," she said, "if you saw me during the day, but since I never speak to you but in the night I shall not put them on." The bird promised to choose his time so well that he would come to the tower at any hour she liked. Then she put on the ear-rings, and the night, like the last, was spent in talking.

Next day Blue Bird returned to his kingdom, went to his palace, entered his own room by the broken pane, and carried off the richest bracelets that were ever seen. They were made of a single emerald, cut in facets, with a hole bored through the middle through which to pass the hand and wrist. "Do you think that my love for you needs to be fed by gifts? Ah, how little you know of it!" "No, madam," he answered; "I do not think that the trifles I offer you are needed to safeguard your tenderness for me, but mine would suffer hurt if I neglected any opportunity of showing my attention, and when I am away from you these little trinkets will remind you of me." Florine answered him with many loving words, to which he replied by others none the less so.

The following night the bird, eager to show his love, did not fail to bring to his fair lady a watch just of the right size. It was encased in a pearl, and the excellence of the workmanship excelled even the material it was made of. "What is the use of a watch to me?" she said, by way of a compliment. "When you are away from me the hours seem never-ending. When you are with me they pass like a dream. And thus I can never measure them exactly." "Alas! my princess," cried Blue Bird, "I feel just as you do; indeed I believe I feel this even more keenly than yourself." "After what you suffer by reason of your faithfulness to me," she answered, "I am ready to believe that greater respect and love than you bear me would be impossible."

As soon as daylight appeared the bird flew into the hollow of his tree, where he lived on fruits. Sometimes he would sing beautiful airs, delighting the passers-by, who hearing him and seeing no one, came to the conclusion that it was spirit voices they heard. This opinion became so common that no one dared enter the wood. Endless fabulous adventures were recounted, and in the general terror consisted Blue Bird's safety. Never a day passed but he made some present to Florine, a pearl necklace, or rings with the most brilliant jewels and of the finest workmanship, clusters of diamonds, bodkins, bouquets of precious stones to imitate the colours of flowers, delightful books, medals—in short, an endless number of rare wonders. She never decked herself except in the night-time to please the king, and during the day, having nowhere else to put her fine things, she hid them carefully in her mattress.

Two years passed away like this, and Florine never once uttered a complaint about her imprisonment. And why should she have done so? Every night she had the satisfaction of speaking to her love, and never were such pretty things said as during these conversations. Although she saw no one, and Blue Bird passed the day in the hollow of a tree, they had always a thousand fresh things to say to each other. Their material was inexhaustible, for in their own hearts and minds they found abundant subjects of conversation.

Meanwhile the wicked queen, who kept her in this cruel fashion in prison, was making vain efforts to get Truitonne married. She sent ambassadors to offer her to all the princes whose names she knew, but as soon as they arrived they were sent away without ceremony. "If you had come about Princess Florine, we should have welcomed you gladly," they were told; "but for Truitonne, she may remain a vestal for ever for all anybody cares." Hearing this, Truitonne and her mother were beside themselves with anger against the innocent princess whom they persecuted. "What!" they said, "in spite of her being in prison, this bold hussy comes in our way! How can we ever forgive the evil turns she has done us? She must keep up a secret correspondence with foreign countries. She is a State criminal, and must be dealt with as such. Let us seek her conviction." Their consultation lasted so long that it was nearly midnight when they decided to mount the tower to question the princess. Florine was with Blue Bird at the window, decked in all her jewels, her beautiful hair dressed with a care which is not usual with anyone in distress. Her room and her bed were heaped with flowers, and the Spanish pastilles which she had been burning gave out a delicious scent. Listening at the door, the queen thought she heard a two-part song being sung. Florine had a voice like an angel's, and what she now sang sounded to the queen like a love song. Here are the words of it :—

> " Weary our lot and full of woe,
> And all our days in pain are spent,
> Oh! hard and cruel punishment!
> Because our love we'd not forego!
> Yet may they plot and plague us ever,
> Our constant hearts they cannot sever."

What sighs followed their little concert!

"Ah, my Truitonne, we are betrayed!" cried the queen, suddenly throwing the door open and bursting into the room. At sight of her, Florine was in despair. She closed the little window without delay to give time to Blue Bird to fly off, much more anxious about his safety than her own. But he had not the strength to go. His keen eyes had recognised the danger to which the princess was exposed. He had seen the queen and Truitonne, and he deplored the sad fate that hindered him from protecting his mistress. They approached her like furies ready to devour her. "Your plots against the State are known," cried the queen. "Do not imagine that your rank will save you from the punishment you deserve." "And with whom have I plotted, madam?" answered the princess. "You have been my gaoler for two years, have you not? Have I seen any persons but those you have sent to me?" While she was speaking the queen and her daughter were examining her with the utmost wonder, for her marvellous beauty and her wonderful apparel dazzled them. "And whence, madam, come these jewels that shine brighter than the sun?" said the queen. "Will you have us believe that there are mines of them in this tower?" "I found them here," replied Florine; "that is all I know." The queen looked at her searchingly to see what was passing in Florine's secret heart. "We are not your dupes," she said. "You think you can deceive us: but, princess, we know all you do from morning till night. You have been given all these jewels as a bribe to you to sell your father's kingdom." "Of course I should be the very person to do such a thing," she replied, with a disdainful smile. "An unhappy princess, who has languished in prison for years, can do a great deal in a plot of that kind!" "And for whom then have you decked your hair like a little coquette; for whom does the pastille scent your room; and for whom have you put on such gay apparel, more magnificent than if you had been to appear at the court?" "I have time enough on my hands," said the princess. "It is, therefore, not strange that I spend a few moments on my own adornment. I need hardly reproach myself on account of that, seeing I have to spend so many in weeping for my unhappy lot." "Ha! but we shall see if this innocent damsel has not all the same made a treaty with our enemies." Thereupon she set to searching all round, and coming to the bed, which she had shaken out, she found in it such a quantity of diamonds, pearls, rubies, emeralds, topazes, that she could not think where they had come from. She had determined to hide somewhere papers of such a nature as would ruin the princess. When no one was looking she hid them in the chimney, but by good luck Blue Bird was perched on the top of it, and seeing better than a lynx, and hearing all, he cried: "Take care, Florine; your enemy is seeking to betray you". This voice, so unexpected, frightened the queen to such a degree that she did not dare to do what she had intended. " You see, madam," said the princess, " that the spirits of the air are my friends." " I believe," answered the queen, beside herself with anger, "that you have the demons on your side, but in spite of them your father will know how to right himself." " Heaven grant," cried Florine, " that I may never have worse to fear than my father's wrath! Yours, madam, is more terrible."

The queen left her in great trouble at all she had seen and heard, and took counsel as to what she should do to defeat the princess. They told her that if some fairy or some enchanter had taken her under their protection, it would only irritate them to torment her further, and it would be best to try to discover her secret. The queen approved of this suggestion, and sent a young girl to sleep in her room, who played the part of an innocent, and by her orders told Florine she had come for the purpose of waiting on her. But it was not very likely the princess would fall into such a clumsy trap. Florine looked on her as a spy, and she was more troubled than ever. " What! I can never speak again to the bird that is so dear to me!" she said. " He helped me to bear my sorrows; I comforted him in his: our love was everything to us. What will he do? What shall I do myself?" And thinking on all this, her eyes flowed with tears.

No longer did she dare to sit at the little window, although she heard the bird flying about. She was dying to open it for him, but she feared to run any risk with her dear lover's life. She spent a whole month without showing herself at the window, and Blue Bird was in despair. How he did lament! How was he to live without seeing his princess? Never had he felt more keenly the misfortunes of absence and of his metamorphosis, and he sought remedies in vain for one and the other. He racked his brains and found no comfort.

The princess's spy, who had been watching day and night for a month, was so overcome with fatigue that at last she fell into a deep sleep. Florine noticed this, and opening the little window, she called out :—

> " Bird, with wings of heaven's blue,
> Haste to where I wait for you ".

These are her own words, which it has been thought best to keep unchanged. The bird heard them so distinctly that he came at once to the window. What joy to see each other again! How much they had to tell! Loving words and vows of faithfulness were repeated again and again; and when the princess could not keep from shedding tears her lover was melted with pity, and sought to console her as best he could. At last, the hour of parting having come, they said farewell to each other in the tenderest way, though the gaoler had not yet awakened.

Next day again the spy fell asleep: the princess without delay sat down at the window, saying, as before :—

" Bird, with wings of heaven's blue,
Haste to where I wait for you ".

The bird came at the moment, and the night passed like the other without noise or disturbance, and our lovers were delighted, flattering themselves that the watcher would be so glad to sleep that she would do so every night. And, in fact, the third one passed very happily too. But on the following night the sleeper heard a noise, and lay listening quietly. Then she peered out curiously, and by the light of the moon saw the prettiest bird in the world speaking to the princess, and caressing her with his claws and pecking at her softly. Then she heard some words of their conversation, which astonished her greatly, for the bird spoke like a lover, and Florine answered with affection.

Day dawned: they said farewell; and as they felt a presentiment of coming misfortune, they parted in great sorrow. The princess threw herself on her bed bathed in tears, and the king returned to his hollow tree. Her gaoler ran to the queen, and told her all she had seen and heard. The queen sent for Truitonne and her confidants, and after a long consultation they came to the conclusion that Blue Bird was King Charming. "What an insult!" cried the queen; "what an insult, Truitonne! This insolent princess, who I thought was in such distress, has been enjoying at her ease the pleasant company of that ungrateful wretch. Ah! but I shall have my revenge, and in so deadly a way that it will be heard of!" Truitonne begged her not to lose a moment; and, as she thought the matter concerned her more nearly than the queen, she was beside herself with joy at the thought of all that was going to be done to the hurt of the lover and his mistress.

The queen sent the spy again to the tower, ordering her to show neither suspicion nor curiosity, and to pretend to be in a deeper sleep than usual. She went to bed early, and snored as loud as she could, and the poor princess, deceived, opened the little window and cried :—

> " Bird, with wings of heaven's blue,
> Haste to where I wait for you ".

But all night long she called in vain ; he did not come. For the wicked queen had tied spears and knives and razors and daggers to the cypress, and when he was alighting on it with all speed, these deadly weapons cut his feet. Then he fell on others which cut his wings, till at last, wounded all over, he flew in terrible pain to his tree, leaving a long track of blood. Why were you not there, fair princess, to comfort this royal bird ? But she would have died to see him in such a deplorable condition. He did not care to tend his life in any way, thinking that it must have been Florine who had played him this trick. " Ah, cruel one," he said, in sorrow, " is it thus you reward the purest and the tenderest passion, such as the world can never know again ? If you desired my death, why did you not seek it yourself? Death would have been a precious gift from your hand! I was coming to meet you with such love and confidence. I was suffering for you, suffering without complaint. And now you have sacrificed me to the cruellest of women. She was the enemy of both of us, and you have made your peace with her at my expense. And it is you, Florine, you, who wound me ! You have borrowed Truitonne's hand and aimed it at my bosom ! " And overcome by these sad thoughts, he determined to die.

But his friend the enchanter, who had seen the flying frogs come back with the chariot, but no trace of the king, was so anxious as to what might have happened to him that he went round the world eight times in his search, but in vain. He was just making his ninth round when he entered the wood where the king was. According to the rules which had to be observed, he blew a long blast on the horn, and then called out as loud as he could : " King Charming, King Charming, where are you ? " The king knew the voice for that of his best friend. " Come," he answered ; " come to this tree, and see the unhappy king whom you love drowned in his blood." The enchanter looked all round in surprise without seeing anything. " I am a blue bird," said the king, in a weak and languid tone. Hearing this, the enchanter found him without trouble in his little nest. Any other would have been much more astonished than he was, but there was not a trick of necromancy that was unknown to him. A word or two was enough to stop the blood that was flowing still, and with some herbs that he found in the wood, over which he muttered some magic words, he cured the king as completely as though he had never been wounded. Then he begged him to tell him by what mischance he had been turned into a bird, and also asked him who had wounded him so cruelly. The king satisfied his curiosity, saying that it was Florine who had revealed the sacred mystery of the secret visits he paid to her, and that to make her peace with the queen she had allowed the cypress to be stuck all over with daggers and razors, by which he had been well nigh hacked to pieces. He railed against the faithlessness of the princess, saying he would rather have died than have known the wickedness of her heart. The magician broke out against her and against all women, and advised the king to forget all about her. " Think what a misfortune it would be were you capable of still loving that ungrateful princess. After what she has done you, anything might be expected of her."

But Blue Bird was not of this opinion. He loved Florine still too dearly, and the enchanter, who knew what he was thinking in spite of all the trouble he took to hide it, said to him :—

> " Reason is vain and comfort palls
> In midst of desolation.
> The ear lists only the heart's cries,
> Is closed to consolation.
> Time with his torch will yet ere long
> Light up the darkest spot,
> But till that brighter hour come round
> Comfort availeth not."

And the royal bird agreed. Then he begged his friend to take him home and put him in a cage, where he would be safe from the cat and from murderous weapons. " But," said the enchanter, " will you remain for five years still in a condition so deplorable and so little befitting your duties and your dignity ? For, frankly, you have enemies who declare that you are dead. They wish to take possession of your kingdom, and I fear it may be lost to you before you have regained your former shape." " Could I not go to my palace and carry on the government as I used to do ? " " Ah ! " cried his friend, " that would be diffi-cult. They who would willingly obey a man would hardly own a parrot as master ; and while they would fear you as a king surrounded with splendour and pomp, they would pluck out your feathers when they saw you a little bird." " Ah, how weak men are ! " cried the king ; " a brilliant exterior means after all nothing in the way of merit or virtue, and yet it is well nigh impossible to keep out of the circle of its influence. Ah, well ! " he continued ; " let us be philo-sophers, and despise what may not be ours : our lot will be none the harder." " I do not give up so quickly," said the magician. " I hope to be able to find some means of solving the difficulty."

Florine, poor Florine, in despair at not seeing the king, passed days and nights at the window, with these words ever on her tongue :—

" Bird, with wings of heaven's blue,
Haste to where I wait for you ".

The presence of the spy did not keep her silent, for her distress was such that she became quite reckless. " What has become of you, King Charming ? " she cried. " Have your enemies and mine made you feel the cruel effects of their rage ? Are you a victim to their fury ? Alas, alas ! are you then dead ? Shall I never see you any more ? or, tired of me and my sorrows, have you left me to my unhappy lot ? " And then the tears, the sobs, that would follow her pitiful laments ! How the hours dragged in the absence of a lover so tender, so beloved ! The princess, worn out, ill, thin, and sadly changed, could hardly bear her life any longer, feeling certain that the most terrible fate had overtaken the king.

The queen and Truitonne were joyful ; they were more delighted with their vengeance than they had formerly been annoyed by the offence. And in reality, what offence had been given them ? King Charming had not been willing to marry a little monster whom he had every reason in the world to detest. But now Florine's father grew old, fell ill, and died. The fortunes of the wicked queen and her daughter wore a different face. They were looked on as favourites who had abused their influence, and the people, in rebellion, hastened to the palace, demanding the Princess Florine, owning her as their sovereign. The queen, in a passion, would have liked to have treated the matter with a high hand, and going out on a balcony she threatened the rebels. Then the sedition spread : the doors of her room were forced, the room was pillaged, and the queen was stoned to death. Truitonne fled to her god-mother, the fairy Soussio, for she ran no less a risk than her mother.

The nobles of the kingdom assembled at once, and mounted the tower where the princess was lying very ill, unconscious of the death of her father or the punishment of her enemy. When she heard all the noise she did not doubt but that they were coming to put her to death ; yet she was not afraid, for life was hateful to her since she had lost Blue Bird. But her subjects, throwing themselves at her feet, made known to her the change in her fortunes, news which left her cold and indifferent. Taking her away to the palace, they crowned her.

The infinite care that was taken of her health, and her strong desire to go in search of Blue Bird, helped to cure her, and before long she felt well enough to nominate a council to take charge of the kingdom in her absence. Then choosing out jewels to the value of an immense sum, she set out one night quite alone, without letting anyone know where she was going.

4

The enchanter who was looking after King Charming's affairs, not being powerful enough to undo all that Soussio had done, determined to go and find her, and to propose to her some arrangement by means of which the king would have his natural shape restored to him. Taking the frogs, he flew to the fairy, who at that moment was speaking with Truitonne. There is not very much difference between an enchanter and a fairy. These two had known each other for five or six hundred years, and in that space of time they had had a hundred quarrels and made them up again. She received him very kindly. " Well, and what does my comrade want? " she said. (They all call each other comrades.) " Is there anything I could do for you ? " " Yes, mother," said the magician, " you can do everything I want. I have come on a matter concerning my best friend, a king whom you have ruined." " Ha, ha ! I understand you, comrade," cried Soussio. " He has incurred my wrath, and there is no pardon to be hoped for him unless he will marry my god-daughter. Here she is ; beautiful and charming, as you see. Let him choose."

The enchanter was almost struck dumb at her intense ugliness ; yet he could not make up his mind to go away without making some arrangement with the fairy, for the king had run a thousand risks since he had been in the cage. The nail to which it was hung had got broken, the cage had fallen, and his feathered majesty had suffered much in consequence. Ninet, the cat, was in the room when the accident happened, and scratched his eye with its paw, which all but blinded him. Another time they had forgotten to give him anything to drink, and he was on the way to have the pip when they saved him from it by giving him a few drops of water. A mischievous little monkey, having got loose, caught hold of his feathers through the bars of the cage, and spared him not a whit more than if he had been a jay or a blackbird. The worst of all was that he was on the point of losing his kingdom, and every day the heirs foraged out some fresh stories to prove he was dead. At last the enchanter made an arrangement with Soussio that she would take Truitonne to the palace of King Charming, that she should stay there several months, during which he would make up his mind to marry her; that, in return, Soussio would restore him his own shape, he to be ready to assume the bird's again if he refused to marry.

The fairy gave Truitonne dresses all of gold and silver. Then she mounted her behind herself on a dragon, and they repaired to the land of Charming, who had just arrived with his faithful friend, the enchanter. With three waves of the wand he was again as he had used to be—handsome, amiable, witty, and splendidly attired. But the cutting short of his punishment was dear bought, for the mere thought of marrying Truitonne made him shudder. The enchanter gave him all the best reasons he could think of, but they made but slight impression on the king's mind; and he was less taken up with the govern-ment of his kingdom than with the means of prolonging the time which Soussio had given him before marrying Truitonne.

Meanwhile Queen Florine, disguised in a peasant's dress, her hair all in disorder and hanging over her face, a straw hat on her head, and a canvas bag over her shoulder, set out on her journey, sometimes walking, sometimes riding, sometimes by sea, sometimes by land. She made as much speed as possible, but, not knowing where to turn her steps, she was always in fear lest while she went in one direction her dear king should be in the other. One day she stopped at the side of a stream, where the silver water rushed over little pebbles, and, wishing to bathe her feet, she sat down on the grass, and tying up her fair hair with a ribbon, put her feet in the water, like Diana, bathing on her return from the chase. There passed by a little old woman, quite bent, and leaning on a big stick. Stopping, she said to Florine: "What are you doing there, my pretty maid, so all by yourself?" "My good mother," said the queen, "I do not want for company, for all my sorrows, anxieties, and disappointments abide with me." At these words her eyes filled with tears. "What! so young, and weeping!" said the good woman. "Ah! my daughter, do not distress your-self. Tell me frankly what is the matter, and I hope to be able to comfort you." The queen consented, and told her troubles, the fairy Soussio's part in the business, and, finally, how she was now in search of Blue Bird.

The little old woman drew herself up, shook herself out; her appearance changed all at once, and she became beautiful, young, superbly dressed, and looking at the queen with a gracious smile, she said: "Incomparable Florine, the king you are seeking is no longer a bird. My sister Soussio has restored to him his former shape, and he is now in his own kingdom. Do not despair. You will reach him, and will gain your end. Here are four eggs: you can break them when you are in urgent need of help, and will find in them what will serve you well." And saying these words, she vanished.

Florine felt much consoled by what she had just heard, and putting the eggs in her bag, turned her steps towards the kingdom of King Charming. After walking eight days and eight nights without stopping, she reached the base of a mountain of a prodigious height, all made of ivory, and so steep that you could not set foot on it without falling. Over and over again she tried, but in vain. She slipped, she tired herself out, and in despair at so insurmountable an obstacle, she lay down at the foot of the mountain, with no other desire but to die, when she remembered the eggs which the fairy had given her. Taking one of them, she said: "Let me see if she was not laughing at me, in promising me the help of which I stand in need". As soon as she had cracked it, she found inside little golden grappling irons, which she attached to her feet and hands. As soon as she had them on she climbed the ivory mountain without any difficulty, for the irons stuck into the ground and kept her from slipping. When she was quite at the top, a new difficulty met her—how to get down again —for the whole valley was one sheet of mirror. All round were ranged more than sixty thousand women looking at themselves with the utmost delight, for this mirror was more than two leagues wide and six high ; and there everyone saw herself as she wished to be. The red-haired maiden saw herself with fair ringlets, and brown hair looked black. The old dame saw herself young again, and the young never grew aged there. In short, all one's defects were so well hidden that people came from the four quarters of the globe. It was enough to make one die of laughing to see the grimaces and the affectations of the greater number of those vain creatures. And men were no less attracted by the flattery, for the mirror pleased them too. This one looking at himself would think what beautiful hair he had ; others would seem to themselves to have grown in height, and to have a much finer figure than before, a more soldierly bearing, or a handsomer face. The women whom they laughed at, laughed just as much at them. And this mountain was called by all sorts of different names. No one had ever reached the top, and when Florine was seen up there the ladies broke out into loud cries of despair. "Where is this unlucky girl going? " they said. "Doubtless she is mad enough to walk on our mirror, and at the first step she will break it all." And they set up such a hullabaloo. The queen did not know what to do, for she saw great danger in descending that way. So she broke another egg, out of which came two pigeons and a chariot, which became on the spot big enough for her to get into comfortably. Then the pigeons descended lightly with the queen, without the slightest accident. " My little friends," she said to them, " if you would but take me to the place where King Charming holds his court, it would be a service which would never be for- gotten. The pigeons were willing and docile, and they stopped neither night nor day till they had reached the gate of the town. Florine got down and gave each of them a sweet kiss, a greater reward than a crown would have been.

Oh ! how her heart beat fast as she entered. In order that she might not be recognised she besmeared her face, and then asked the passers-by where she could see the king. Some of them began to laugh. " See the king ! " they said, " little smutty face ? Go away, go away and wash yourself. Your eyes are not good enough to look upon such a monarch." The queen answered nothing but passed on gently, and asked those whom she next met where she should stand to see the king. " He will be coming to the temple to-morrow with Princess Truitonne," they said ; " for at last he has consented to marry her."

Heavens! what news was this! Truitonne, the wicked Truitonne, about to marry the king! Florine thought she would die. She had no strength left to speak or move, and she sat down under a doorway on a heap of stones, her face well hidden by her hair and her straw hat. "Ah! how unhappy I am," she said; "to come here to render the triumph of my rival greater, and to be a witness to her joy. It was because of her then that Blue Bird stopped coming to see me. It was for this little monster that he has been so cruelly faithless to me. While I was plunged in grief and anxiety lest he should be dead, the traitor had changed; and thinking no more of me than if he had never seen me, left me to mourn his too long absence without concerning himself about mine."

When one is very unhappy one's appetite is not usually very good, so the queen sought for a lodging, and went to bed supperless. Rising with the day, she hastened to the temple, and entered only after receiving endless rebuffs from the guards and the soldiers. Then she saw the king's throne and Truitonne's, who was already looked on as queen. What sorrow for a heart so tender and sensitive as Florine's! She went up to her rival's throne, and stood there leaning against a marble pillar. The king was the first to arrive—handsomer, comelier than ever. Truitonne followed, richly clad, but so ugly that she frightened all those who set eyes on her. Looking at the queen, she frowned and said: "Who are you that dares to approach my fair presence, and to stand near my golden throne?" "My name is Mie Souillon," she answered; "I come from a long way off to sell you rarities." Then she rummaged in her sack and drew out the emerald bracelets that King Charming had given her. "Ho, ho!" said Truitonne; "these are pretty bits of glass. Will you have a five sou piece for them?" "Show them to those who know their value, madam," said the queen; "and then we can make our bargain." Truitonne, who loved the king more tenderly than such a monster seemed capable of, was delighted to find opportunities of speaking to him, and approaching his throne, showed him the bracelets, and asked him what he thought of them. At sight of them he called to mind those he had given to Florine, and grew pale, sighed, and remained long without answering a word. At length, fearing lest they should notice evidences of the conflicting thoughts within him, he made an effort, and answered: "These bracelets are worth, I should think, as much as my kingdom. I thought there was but one such pair in the world, yet here are others just like."

Truitonne came back and sat on her throne, where she looked not quite so pretty as an oyster in a shell. Then she asked the queen how much, without overcharging, she would take for these bracelets. "You would never be able to pay me, madam," she said. "I'll rather propose another bargain to you. If you will let me sleep one night in the echo room of the king's palace I shall give you the emeralds." "Very well, little snautty face," said Truitonne, laughing like a madwoman and showing her teeth, which were longer than a wild boar's tusks.

The king never asked where the bracelets came from, not so much from indifference to her who presented them, although she was hardly of a condition to rouse his curiosity, as from an antipathy he could not master that he felt towards Truitonne. Now you must know that while he was Blue Bird he had told the princess that under his apartment there was a little room called the echo room, so ingeniously made that all that was said quite low in it was heard by the king when he lay in his own room; and as Florine wished to reproach him with his unfaithfulness, she could think of no better means.

By order of Truitonne she was brought into this cabinet, and there she began her cries and laments. "The misfortune which I only feared is now but too certain. Cruel Blue Bird!" she said; "you have forgotten me. You love my wicked rival. The bracelets I received from your faithless hand could not recall me to you, so far have I slipped out of your remembrance!" Then sobs interrupted her words, and when she had regained strength enough to speak her cries broke out anew, and went on till daybreak. The valets-de-chambre had heard her all night long groaning and sighing, and told Truitonne, who asked her what noise she had been making. The queen said she was such a sound sleeper that usually she dreamt, and that very often in dreaming she spoke quite loud. As for the king, by a strange fatality he had not heard her, for since ever he had loved Florine he could not sleep, and when he went to bed to rest they gave him opium.

The queen passed a part of the day in a wondering anxiety. "If he heard me," she said, "could he be more cruelly indifferent? If he did not, what shall I do to make him hear me?" She had no more rare curiosities. She had, it is true, beautiful jewels, but it was necessary to find something which would take Truitonne's fancy. She, therefore, had recourse to her eggs. As soon as she broke one out came a little coach of polished steel inlaid with gold. Six green mice were harnessed to it. The driver was a rose-coloured rat, and the postillions, also of the rat family, were of a flax grey. In this coach were four marionettes, livelier and funnier than any of those you would see at St. Germain's or St. Lawrence's Fair. The things they did were extraordinary, especially two little gypsies who could dance a saraband or a jig as well as Leance.

The queen was delighted with this fresh wonder of magic, but she kept it to herself till evening, at which time Truitonne used to go for a walk. Then, stationing herself in one of the avenues, she set the mice off at a gallop with the coach, the rats, and the marionettes. Truitonne was so astonished at this curiosity that she cried out two or three times: " Mie Souillon, Mie Souillon, will you take five halfpence for your coach and mice? " " Ask the learned men and the scholars of this kingdom," said Florine, " the worth of such a curiosity, and I will take whatever the most learned may say is its value." Truitonne, who was always very imperious, said: " Tell me the price of it, and take your dirty face out of my sight ". " To sleep again in the echo chamber," she answered; "that is all I ask." " Well, be off with you, poor wretch," said Truitonne; "you won't be refused that"; and turning towards her ladies-in-waiting, she added: " What a fool she is to get so little profit out of her curiosities ! "

Night came. Florine said the tenderest things she could think of, but all in vain as before, for the king never failed to take his opium. The valets said to each other: "Not a doubt but this peasant girl is mad. What does she talk for all night long?" " All the same," some of them remarked, "neither sense nor tenderness is lacking in what she says." She waited with impatience for the day to see what effect her words had had. "What! is this wretch grown deaf to my voice? Does he no longer hear his beloved Florine? Ah, how weak I am to care for him still, and I deserve the contempt he pours on me!" But it was in vain she reasoned thus; she could not kill the affection she felt for him.

The only thing she could now hope for help from was the one egg left in her bag. She broke it, and out came a pie made of six birds, all larded, cooked, and beautifully dressed. The pie sang in a wonderful fashion, told fortunes, and knew more of medicine than Æsculapius even. The queen, delighted with the wonderful thing, hastened with her talking pie into Truitonne's ante-chamber. While she was waiting for her to come that way, one of the king's valets come up to her, and said: " Mie Souillon, do you know that if the king did not take opium to make him sleep you would certainly drive him wild, for you chatter during the night in such an astonishing fashion?" Florine no longer wondered that he had not heard her, and rummaging in her bag, she said: " I have so little fear of disturbing the king's rest that if you give him no opium to-night, and let me sleep in that same room, all these pearls and all these diamonds will be yours." The valet agreed, and gave her his word on it.

A few minutes after Truitonne came along. Seeing the queen with her pie, pretending as if she were going to eat it, she said : " What are you doing there, Mie Souillon?" " Madam," replied Florine, " I am eating astrologers, musicians, and doctors." At that moment all the birds began to sing more sweetly than sirens, and cried: " Give us a silver penny, and we will tell you your fortune ". A duck appeared to be the leader, and he called out louder than the others : " Quack, quack, quack ! I am a physician; I can cure every ill and every kind of madness except love." Truitonne, more surprised by such wonders than ever she had been in her life, swore: "Bless my heart, but here is a fine pie! I must have it. Come, now, Mie Souillon, what shall I give you for it?" "The usual price," she answered: "let me sleep in the echo room, nothing more." "See," said Truitonne, generously (for she was in a very good temper at having got such a pie), "I'll give you a pistole." And Florine, better pleased than she had yet been, thinking that the king might hear her this time, withdrew, giving thanks to Truitonne.

As soon as night came on she betook herself to the echo room, hoping eagerly that the valet had kept his word, and that instead of giving the king opium, he had given him something to keep him awake. When she knew that everybody else was asleep she began her usual laments. "To what dangers am I exposed in my search for you!" she said. "And all the while you flee me and wish to marry Truitonne. What have I done, cruel man, that you should forget your oaths? Do you remember your metamorphosis, my kindness to you, and our loving conversations?" Then she repeated nearly the whole of them, with a memory which amply proved that nothing was dearer to her than this remembrance.

The king was not sleeping, and he heard Florine's voice so distinctly, and all she said, that he could not understand where the words came from. But his heart, overpowered with sudden tenderness, called back in such a life-like way the memory of his incomparable princess that he felt his separation from her as keenly as he did the moment when the knives had wounded him in the cypress tree. Then on his part he began to speak after the fashion of the queen. "Ah! princess," he said, "you have been too cruel to the lover who adored you. Is it possible you sacrificed me to the enemies of us both?" Florine heard what he said, and did not fail to reply, and to let him know that if he would talk over the matter with Mie Souillon, all the mysteries he had not been able to understand till now would be cleared up. At these words the king, without waiting a moment, called for one of his valets, and asked him if he could not find Mie Souillon and bring her to the palace. The valet said nothing was easier, for she was sleeping in the echo room. The king did not know what to think. How could he believe that so great a queen as Florine should be disguised as Souillon? And how could he believe that Mie Souillon had the queen's voice, and knew her most intimate secrets, unless she were the queen herself? In this uncertainty he rose, dressed quickly, and went by a secret staircase to the echo room. The queen had taken away the key, but the king had one that opened all the doors of the palace. He found her wrapped in a light robe of white taffeta, which she wore under her old clothes. Her beautiful hair hung over her shoulders as she lay on a couch, a lamp some little way off giving only a sombre light. The king entered suddenly, and his love getting the better of his anger, as soon as he recognised her he threw himself at her feet, and bathed her hands in his tears. He thought he must die of joy, of grief, of the thousand different feelings that crowded all at once into his soul.

The queen was no less disturbed. She felt a weight on her heart, and could hardly breathe, but lay looking fixedly at the king without saying a word. When she recovered strength enough to speak, she had none to use for reproaches, and the pleasure of seeing him once more made her forget for some time her grievances against him. At last they came to an understanding : they justified themselves : their tenderness awoke again, and their only trouble was the fairy Soussio.

But just at that moment the enchanter, who loved the king, arrived with a celebrated fairy, the very one who had given the four eggs to Florine. After the first greeting, the enchanter and the fairy declared that they had joined their power together in favour of the king and the queen. Soussio was, therefore, powerless against them, and the wedding need not be delayed.

It is easy to picture the joy of these two young lovers. As soon as daylight came it was known throughout the palace, and everyone was delighted to see Florine. The news reached Truitonne, who ran to the king. What a surprise for her to find her fair rival with him ! When she was just opening her mouth to call Florine names, the enchanter and the fairy appeared and changed her into a sow (*truie*), so that at least a part of her name and her surly temper remained to her. She ran away grunting, grunting, down to the backyard, where the loud laughter she was met with put a climax to her misery.

King Charming and Queen Florine, free from this hateful woman, gave themselves up to planning their wedding feast, and everything was as elegant as it was superb. And it is not difficult to imagine how happy they were after having known so many hardships.

PRINCE ARIEL.

ONCE upon a time there lived a king and a queen who had only one son, of whom they were passionately fond, though he was a very ill-shapen boy. He was as stout as the biggest man and as short as the tiniest dwarf. But the ugliness of his face and the deformity of his body were as nothing compared to his evil disposition. He was a self-willed little wretch, and a nuisance to everybody. From his earliest childhood the king had noticed this, but the queen was foolishly blind to his faults, and helped to. spoil him still more by her excessive indulgence, which let him plainly see the power he had over her. To gain favour with this princess you had but to tell her that her son was handsome and clever. She wished to give him a name that would inspire respect and fear, and after racking her brains for a long time she called him Furibon.

When he was old enough to have a tutor, the king chose for this purpose a prince who had ancient claims on the crown, and who would have maintained them like a man of spirit, if his affairs had been in a better state. But he had long given up all thought of this, and his whole time was occupied with the education of his only son. Never was there a lad gifted with a finer nature, a quicker or keener mind, or a gentler, meeker spirit. Everything he said had a happy turn and a special grace of its own, and in his person he was charming. The king having chosen this great lord to be the guide of Furibon's youth, told his son to be very obedient, but Furibon was a naughty urchin to whom a hundred floggings made no difference. The tutor's son was called Leander, and everybody liked him. The ladies looked on him with much interest, but as he paid no special attention to any of them, they called him the Fair Indifferent. And they laid siege to him to make him change his manner towards them, but for all that he hardly ever left Furibon. Furibon, however, only seemed to them the more hideous now that he appeared side by side with Leander, for he never came near the ladies except to say rude things to them : sometimes to tell them they

hot. After a moment he heard the sound of sighing and sobbing, and looking round everywhere, he saw a man running, then stopping, now crying out, now saying nothing for a while, tearing his hair, beating his body, till Leander had no doubt but that he was some miserable person who had lost his wits. He seemed to be handsome and young. His clothes had once been splendid, but now they were all tattered. The prince, moved with compassion, addressed him : " I see you in so unhappy a condition that I cannot help asking you what is the matter and offering you my services". " Ah! my lord," replied the young man, "there is no remedy for my ills. To-day my dear mistress is going to be sacrificed to a jealous old wretch, who is rich in the world's goods, but who will make her the unhappiest creature in the whole world ! " " She loves you then ? " said Leander. " I may flatter myself she does," he answered. " And where is she ? " said the prince. " In a castle at the farther end of this forest," replied the lover. " Very well, wait for me," said Leander again. " I will bring you good news before very long." And so saying, he put on the little red hat, and wished himself in the castle. He had not reached it before he heard the sound of beautiful music ; and, on entering, the whole palace resounded with the noise of violins and other instruments. He made his way into a great hall thronged with the relatives and friends of the old man and the young damsel. Nothing could have been lovelier than she was, but the pallor of her complexion, the sadness in her face, and the tears that flooded her eyes from time to time, were quite enough to show her suffering.

Leander, who had now turned into the invisible Ariel, remained in a corner to watch some of those who were present. He saw the father and mother of the pretty maiden, who were scolding her for the discontented face she was wearing. When they had returned to their places, Ariel stationed himself behind the mother, and whispered in her ear : " Since you force your daughter to give her hand to this old villain, know for certain that before eight days are over you will be punished by death ". The woman, terrified at hearing a voice and seeing no one, and still more at the threat which had been uttered, screamed aloud and fell down on the floor. Her husband asked what was the matter, and she cried out that she was a dead woman if her daughter's marriage took place, and that for all the riches of the world she would not permit it. The husband laughed at her, and told her she was dreaming ; but Ariel, going up to him, said : " Old sceptic, if you do not believe what your wife says, you will pay for your doubt with your life. Break off your daughter's wedding, and give her up at once to the man she loves." These words produced a wonderful effect. Without more ado they despatched the bridegroom, telling him they would not have broken off the match but for orders from on high. He did not believe what they said, and would have sought to gain his end by trickery, for he was a Norman ; but Ariel shouted so loud in his ear that he was nearly deafened, and to make sure of his departure, he trod so hard on his gouty feet that he nearly squeezed them flat. So they ran to seek for the lover in the wood, who in the meanwhile was in despair. Ariel was waiting for him with the utmost impatience, only less than that of his young mistress. The lover and his bride nearly died of joy. The feast prepared for the old man's wedding served for the happy lovers, and Ariel taking his human shape again, appeared suddenly at the hall door in the guise of a stranger drawn thither by the noise of the feast. As soon as the bridegroom saw him, he ran and threw himself at his feet, calling him every name that his gratitude could suggest to him. Leander spent two days in this castle, and if he had liked he might have ruined them, for they offered him all they possessed ; and he did not quit such good company without regret.

Going on his way, he reached a large city where lived a queen whose great desire was to gather about her court all the handsomest persons in her kingdom. Leander on his arrival had the finest equipage prepared that ever was seen ; for, after all, he had only to shake the rose, and money never failed him. It is easy to imagine that being handsome, young, witty, and, above all, splendid in appearance, the queen and all the princesses received him with every mark of respect and consideration.

This was the most gallant court in the whole world, and not to be in love there was to be laughed at. So wishing to follow the custom, he thought he would play at falling in love, and that when he went away he could leave his love behind him as easily as his suite. And he cast his eyes on one of the queen's maids-of-honour, called Fair Blondine. This lady was very clever, but so cold and so serious that he did not know very well what to do to please her. He arranged wonderful fêtes, and balls, and plays every night. He sent for rarities from all parts of the world, but it seemed to have no effect on her. Still, the more indifferent she was, the more was he determined to gain her favour. What chiefly attracted him was that he believed she had never loved anyone else. But to be certain he thought he should like to try on her the power of the rose. So, as if playfully, he placed it on Blondine's bosom, when suddenly, fresh and blooming as it had been, it withered and faded. That was enough to let Leander know that he had a rival whom she loved. ·He felt this very keenly, and to be convinced of it by his own eyes, he wished himself in Blondine's room in the evening. There he saw a musician come in who had the most villainous face imaginable. This man screeched out three or four couplets he had made for her, the words and the music of which were alike detestable, but she enjoyed them as if they were the finest things she had ever heard in her life. He made faces as if he were possessed, and even these she praised, so mad about him was she; and at last she let this hideous wretch kiss her hand as a reward. Ariel, enraged, threw himself on this impertinent musician; and pushing him roughly against a balcony, flung him into the garden, where he broke his few remaining teeth.

If a thunderbolt had fallen on Blondine she could not have been more surprised. She thought it must be the work of some spirit. Ariel vanished from the room without showing himself, and at once returned to his own quarters, where he wrote to Blondine, heaping on her all the reproaches she deserved. Without awaiting her answer he set off, leaving behind him his equipage, which he presented to his squires and his gentlemen, and rewarding the rest of his people. Then mounting on his trusty Grisdelin, he made up his mind never to fall in love again after what had happened. He set out at full speed. For a long time he was very melancholy, but his good sense and absence from Blondine came to his aid in time. On his arrival in another town he learnt that a great ceremony was to take place that day, on the occasion of the admission of a maiden among the vestal virgins, though she had no wish to be one. The prince was much touched when he heard of this. He felt that the little red hat had only been given him to repair public wrongs and to comfort the distressed. So he hastened to the temple. There the young girl was crowned with flowers, dressed in white, and her long hair falling over her like a mantle. Two of her brothers led her by the hand, and her mother followed her with a great company of men and women. The eldest vestal was waiting for her at the temple door. At that moment Ariel called out: " Stop, stop, wicked brethren, cruel mother, stop! heaven will not consent to this wrong being done. If you go on you will be trampled to death like frogs." They looked round everywhere without finding out where the terrible threats were coming from. The brothers said it must be their sister's lover who was hiding at the bottom of some hole to play the oracle, but Ariel, flying into a rage, took a long stick and beat them soundly. You could see the stick rise and fall about their shoulders like a hammer on an anvil, and the blows at least were real enough. The vestals were seized with terror, and fled, the others following. Ariel remained with the young victim. Taking off his little hat, he asked her in what way he could help her. She told him, with more courage than could have been expected of a girl of her age, that there was a knight whom she cared for very much, but who was poor. Then he shook Fairy Gentille's rose so vigorously that he shot out ten million pounds for her and her lover. The two young people got married, and lived happy ever afterwards.

The last adventure he had was the best of all. Entering a great forest he heard the piteous cries of a young maiden, who he had no doubt was being hurt in some way. Looking all around he saw four men, fully armed, bearing away a damsel who seemed to be about thirteen or fourteen years of age. Advancing as speedily as possible, he cried out : " What has this child done that you should treat her as a slave ? " " And what is that to you, my little lordling ? " said he who seemed to be the leader of the band. " I command you," said Leander, " to let her go at once." " Oh, certainly, certainly ! " they answered, laughing. In great wrath the prince dismounted, and put on the little red hat, for he did not think it would be wise to attack all by himself four men strong enough to be a match for twelve. When he had on his little hat you would have been very clever if you could have seen him. The robbers said : " He is gone. Don't let us mind about him. Seize his horse only." One stopped to guard the young damsel, while the other three ran after Grisdelin, who gave them no end of trouble. " Alas, fair princess ! " said the girl, " how happy I was in your palace ! How can I live without you ? If you knew what has happened to me, you would send your Amazons after poor Abricotine." Leander listened, and without a moment's delay he seized the arm of the robber who kept the girl, and tied it to a tree before he had the time to defend himself, for he did not even know who it was that had bound him. At his cries one of his comrades came running up out of breath and asked him who had tied him to the tree. " I do not know. I have seen no one." " That is only an excuse," said the other. " But I have known for long that you were nothing but a coward, and I shall treat you as you deserve." Thereupon he belaboured him with his stirrup leathers. Ariel was much amused to hear him screaming. Then going up to the second robber he took him by the arm, and fastened him also to a tree, just opposite his comrade, not forgetting to ask him : " Well, my good fellow, and who has dared to attack you ? Are you not a great coward to have permitted it ? " The man answered not a word, but bent his head for shame, unable to imagine how he had been tied to the tree without seeing anyone.

Meanwhile Abricotine took the opportunity of running away, without even knowing where she was going. Leander no longer seeing her, called out to Grisdelin, and the horse, eager to find his master, freed himself by two kicks from the robbers who had caught him, breaking the head of one and three ribs of the other. The first thing to be done now was to rejoin Abricotine, for Ariel thought her very pretty, and he wished to be in the young damsel's company. In a moment he had reached her, and found her so very, very tired that she was leaning up against a tree, hardly able to stand. When she saw Grisdelin coming along so gaily, she cried out : " What good luck ! Here is a pretty horse to carry Abricotine to the Palace of Delights." Ariel heard what she said, but she did not see him. He went up to her ; Grisdelin stopped ; and she sprang on his back.

Ariel clasped her in his arms, and set her gently in front of him. Oh ! how terrified Abricotine was to feel someone there, and yet to see nobody ! She dared not move, and she shut her eyes for fear she should see a spirit, and did not utter a syllable. The prince, who had always his pockets full of the nicest sugar-plums in the world, tried to put some in her mouth, but she shut her teeth and lips quite tight. At last, taking off his little hat, he said : " Why, Abricotine, you are a very timid girl to be so much afraid of me. It was I who saved you out of the robbers' hands." Then she opened her eyes and recognised him. "Ah! my lord," she said, "I owe you everything. It is true I was terrified at being in the company of someone whom I could not see." "I am not invisible," he replied ; " but you have evidently hurt your eyes, and you could not therefore see me." Abricotine believed him, though for all that she was sharp enough as a rule. After talking for some time on things in general, Leander begged her to tell him her age, where her home was, and by what mischance she had fallen into the bandits' hands. " I owe you too much," she said, " not to satisfy your curiosity ; but, my lord, I beg you to give less attention to my story than to the means of getting on our way speedily."

" A fairy, who surpassed every other in fairy lore," began Abricotine, " fell so madly in love with a certain prince that, though she was the first of her race who had been so weak, she married him, in spite of all persuasions to the contrary from the other fairies, who placed before her ceaselessly the wrong she was doing to their kind. They refused to let her live amongst them any longer, and all she could do was to build a great palace on the borders of their kingdom. But the prince whom she had married got tired of her. He was much annoyed because she had the power of seeing all his actions ; and as soon as he showed the least favour to any other lady she made a terrible commotion, and would revenge herself on the prettiest damsel in the world by making her hideously ugly. The prince, feeling very uncomfortable by such an inconvenient amount of affection, set off one fine morning with post horses, and journeyed a long, long way off, to hide himself in a big hole in the depths of a mountain, in order that she might not be able to find him. It was no use. She followed him, and, telling him that a child was about to be born, begged him to return to his palace ; that she would give him money, and horses, and dogs, and arms ; that she would have a riding-school built, and a tennis-court and a mall made for his amusement. All this had no effect on him, for by nature he was very obstinate and fond of lawless pleasures. He said all sorts of rude things to her, and called her an old surly witch. ' It is very lucky for you,' she said, ' that my good temper is greater than your folly, otherwise I would turn you into a cat, and you should pass your life mewling on the spout, or into a filthy toad, dabbling in the mud, or into a pumpkin, or an owl. But the worst I can possibly do is to leave you to your own folly. Stay here, then, in your hole, in your dark cave with the bears. Call the shepherdesses of the neighbourhood round you. In time you will get to know the difference between the low country folks and a fairy like me, who can be as charming as she likes.'

" With this she mounted on her flying car, and sped away as swift as a bird. As soon as she reached her home she transported her palace to an island, drove away her guards and her officers, took women of the Amazonian race and set them round her isle to keep a careful watch so that no men might ever set foot thereon. She called the spot the Isle of Calm Delights, and she used to say that no true pleasures were possible wherein men had any part. She bred up her daughter in this opinion. Never was there such a beautiful maiden. She is the princess I serve," continued Abricotine ; " and, as pleasures reign where she is, no one grows old in her palace. To look at me you would not think it, but I am more than two hundred years old. When my mistress grew up her fairy mother left her her island ; and having given her many lessons in the art of living a happy life, went back to the realm of Faërie once more. And the Princess of Calm Delights governs her state in an admirable fashion. I do not remember in all my life having seen any other men than those robbers who carried me off ; and now you, my lord. Those men told me that they had been sent by a certain ugly, mis-shapen creature called Furibon, who loves my mistress, though he has only seen her portrait. They hung round the island without daring to set foot on it, for our Amazons are too watchful to let anyone land. But I have charge of the princess's birds, and I let a beautiful parrot escape, and fearing I should be scolded, I imprudently left the island to seek for it. So they caught me, and would have taken me away with them had it not been for your help."

" If you really feel grateful," said Leander, " may I not hope, fair Abricotine, that you will let me land on the Isle of Calm Delights, and let me see this wonderful princess who never grows old ? " " Ah ! my lord," she said, " we should be ruined, both you and I, if we did anything of the kind. It should be very easy for you to do without a pleasure which you have never known. You have never been in this palace : imagine to yourself that it does not exist." " It is not so easy as you think," answered the prince, " to wipe out of one's memory the things that take kindly root there ; and I do not agree with you that to banish our sex is a sure means of securing calm delights." " My lord," she replied, " it is not for me to decide. I even confess that if all men were like you I should be glad that the princess should make other laws ; but having only seen five, four of whom were villains, I conclude that the wicked outnumber the good, and that it is therefore best to banish all of them."

While they were speaking, they arrived at the banks of a great river. Abricotine jumped lightly to the ground. " Adieu, my lord," she said to the prince, making him a low bow ; " I wish you so much happiness that the whole earth may be for you an island of delights. Now go away in haste, lest our Amazons see you." " And as for me," he answered, " fair Abricotine, I pray that a tender heart may be given you, so that some memory of me may remain with you." Then he went on his way. In the thickest part of a wood which he saw near the river he unharnessed Grisdelin, so that he might wander about and graze for a little. Putting on the little red hat, he wished himself in the Isle of Calm Delights. His wish was granted at once, and he found himself in a very beautiful and very extraordinary place. The palace was of pure gold, with figures on the roof of crystal and precious stones, representing the signs of the zodiac and all the wonders of nature—the sciences, the arts, the elements, the sea with its fish, the earth with its living things ; Diana at the chase with her nymphs, the noble exercises of the Amazons, the amusements of a country life, shepherdesses with their flocks and their dogs ; rustic labours, agriculture, harvesting, gardens, flowers, bees,—and yet amongst all those different things there was never the image of a man nor a boy, not even a little Cupid ; for the fairy had been too angry with her disloyal husband to show favour to any of his unfaithful sex. " Abricotine has not deceived me," said the prince to himself. " The very idea of men has been banished from this place ; let us see whether they lose much thereby. Entering the palace, at every step he took such wonderful things met his eyes that it was with great difficulty he could withdraw them again. The gold and the diamonds were wonderful, even more for their workmanship than for their intrinsic worth. Everywhere he met maidens of gentle look, innocent and merry, and fair as a sunny morning. Passing through endless vast rooms, he found some full of exquisite china vases, the odour from which, along with the odd colours and designs, delighted him greatly. Some of the rooms had walls of porcelain, so fine that you could see the light through them. Others were of engraved rock crystal, others of amber and coral, lapis lazuli, agate, and cornelian, while the princess's room was all made of great mirrors, for so fair an object could not be too often seen. The throne was made of a single pearl, hollowed out like a shell, in which she sat with perfect ease. It was all hung round with branched candlesticks decked with rubies and diamonds. But this splendour was as nothing by the side of the incomparable beauty of the princess herself. Her childlike air had all the grace of youth with the dignity of a riper age. Nothing could equal the gentleness and the brightness of her eyes. In fact, it was impossible to find fault with her at any point. She was just then smiling graciously to her maids-of-honour, who that day had dressed themselves as nymphs for her amusement. Not seeing Abricotine, she asked where she was. The nymphs replied that they had sought her in vain. . She was nowhere to be found. Ariel was dying to speak to her, and so he imitated the shrill little voice of a parrot (there were several in the room), and said : " Dear princess, Abricotine will come back soon. She was in great danger of being carried off, had not a young prince found her." " You are very pretty, my little parrot," she said, " but I think you are mistaken, and when Abricotine returns she will beat you." " I shall not be beaten," said Ariel, still in the parrot's voice. " She will tell you how much the stranger wished he might come into this palace, to root out from your mind your false ideas against his sex." " Really, my pretty poll," cried the princess, " it is quite a pity that you are not as amusing every day. I would love you dearly." " Ah ! if I need only talk to please you," said Ariel, " I shall not stop talking for a minute." " Well, now," said the princess, " would you not certainly say this parrot was a wizard ? " " He is too much of a lover to be a wizard," he answered.

At that moment Abricotine entered ; and throwing herself at her fair mistress's feet, she told her adventure, and painted the prince's portrait in the brightest and most pleasing colours. " I should have hated all men," she added, " if I had not seen him. Ah ! madam, how charming he is ! In his look and his whole manner there is something noble and spiritual, and as everything he says is most fascinating, I think I have done wisely in not bringing him here." The princess made no answer to this, but went on questioning Abricotine about the prince, as to his name, his country, his birth, where he came from, where he was going to. Afterwards she fell into a deep reverie. Ariel watched everything, and continued to speak in the same voice. " Abricotine is an ungrateful girl, madam," he said. " This poor stranger will die of grief if he does not see you." " Very well, poll, let him die ; and, since you take upon yourself to talk seriously, I forbid you ever to speak to me again of that unknown prince."

Leander was delighted to see that Abricotine's story and the parrot's had made such an impression on the princess, and he looked at her with a pleasure which made him forget his former vows never to fall in love in his life—for there was no comparison between her and the vain Blondine. " Is it possible," he said to himself, " that this masterpiece of nature, this miracle of our days, must stay for ever on an island where no mortal man may dare approach her ! But after all," he went on, " what does it matter that all the rest are banished, since I have the honour of being here, since I see her, hear her, admire her, since I love her better than my life ! "

It was late, and the princess passed into a hall all of marble and porphyry, where fountains were playing, and everthing was pleasant and cool. As soon as she had entered, a symphony began and a sumptuous supper was served.   At the side of the hall there were long aviaries filled with rare birds which Abricotine tended.   Leander had learnt on his travels how to sing like birds ; he used even to invent songs such as no living birds ever sang.   The princess listened, looked in great astonishment, then left the table and came near.   Ariel then gave out a louder, stronger note, and in the voice of a canary he sang these words to an impromptu air :—

> " O ! heavy the tread of the march of life,
> And weary the striving and vain the strife,
> And lonely the way for you and for me
> If Love be not of the company.
> For life is love, and love is life,
> And everything else is useless strife ;
> See, Love is beckoning you and me,
> Haste then and join his company."

The princess, still more astonished, sent for Abricotine, and asked her if she had taught any of the canaries to sing.   She said no, but she thought that canaries were probably as intelligent as parrots.   The princess smiled, and thought all the same that Abricotine had given the birds singing lessons.   Then she sat down to table again to finish her supper.

Leander's journey had been long enough to give him an appetite, and he made his way towards the good things, the very smell of which was grateful to him.   The princess had a blue cat—a very fashionable colour for cats at that period—which she was very fond of, and one of her maidens held it in her arms, saying : " Madam, I assure you Bluet is hungry ".   So they seated him at the table, with a little golden plate and a lace napkin neatly folded.   He wore a golden bell and a pearl collar.   With a voracious appetite he began to eat.   "Oh, ho ! " said Ariel, " a great blue tom-cat, who probably never caught a mouse in his life, and who certainly is not of better birth than I, has the honour of supping with my fair princess !   I would like to know if he loves her as much as I do, and if it is right that I have nothing but the smell of the dishes for my supper, while he munches all the dainty bits ? "   Thereupon he very quietly removed Bluet, sat down himself in the armchair, and took the cat on his lap. No one saw Ariel.   How could they have seen him, for he had his little red hat on ?   The princess put partridge, quail, and pheasant on Bluet's golden plate. The partridge, quail, and pheasant disappeared in a moment, and the whole court said there never was a cat with such an appetite.   The ragouts were excellent, too ; and Ariel taking a fork, and holding it in the cat's paw, tasted them.   Sometimes he took rather much on his fork, and Bluet, who did not understand a joke, mewed, and tried to scratch viciously. Then the princess would say : " Put that tart, or that fricassee, near poor Bluet. Hear how he is crying to have it ! " Leander laughed to himself at such a funny adventure. But now he felt very thirsty, not being used to such long repasts without drinking. So he caught hold of a large melon with the cat's paw, and this satisfied him somewhat, and when supper was nearly over he ran to the sideboard and drank two bottles of delicious nectar.

The princess retired to her room, telling Abricotine to come along with her, and to shut the door. Ariel followed fast after, and made an unseen third to the company. The princess said to her confidant : " Confess, now, that you were exaggerating in drawing the portrait of this unknown prince. It does not seem to me possible for him to be so beautiful as you say." " I assure you, madam," she answered, " that if I have failed in any way it is that I have said too little." The princess sighed, and for a moment she was silent. Then, speaking again, she said : " It was wise of you to have refused to bring him with you ". " But, madam," answered Abricotine, who was in fact a sly little monkey, and who already guessed what was in her mistress's mind, "even if he had come to admire the wonders of this lovely place, what harm could he have done you ? Do you wish to live for ever unknown in a corner of the world, hidden away from the rest of mortals ? What is the use of so much grandeur, pomp, and magnificence if nobody sees it all ? " " Hold your tongue, you little chatterbox," said the princess, " and do not trouble the happy calm which has been mine for two hundred years. Think you, if I had lived an anxious, noisy life, I should have lived so long ? It is only innocent and quiet pleasures that leave no bad effects behind. Have we not heard in the best histories of revolutions in great states, of the unforeseen strokes of fickle fortune, the terrible disturbances caused by love, the griefs of absence and of jealousy ? What is it brings about all these sorrows and troubles ? Nothing but the intercourse of human beings with each other. Now, thanks to the care of my mother, I am free from all these crosses. I know neither bitterness of heart, nor vain desires, nor envy, nor love, nor hate. Ah, let us go on living always in this same calm ! " Abricotine dared not answer. The princess waited some time, and then asked her if she had nothing to say. Abricotine inquired why she had sent her portrait to various courts, where it could only make people miserable, for everyone who saw it would wish to see the original, and, being unable to, they would be in despair. " I confess, in spite of that," replied the princess, " that I would like my portrait to fall into the hands of that stranger, whose name I do not know." " Ah, madam ! " she replied, " is he not already eager enough to see you ? Would you have him more so ? " " Yes," said the princess ; " a certain impulse of vanity, which has been unknown to me till now, breeds this desire in me." Ariel listened to all this without losing a single one of the words: some of them gave him flattering hopes, which were dashed to pieces by others.

It grew late, and the princess went to her room to bed. Ariel would have much liked to have been present when she made her toilette, but though this was possible, the respect he had for her prevented him. It seemed to him that he ought to take no liberties with her but those she might have permitted; and his affection for her was so delicate and so refined that he tormented himself about the smallest things. So he went into a cabinet near the princess's room to have at least the pleasure of hearing her speak. At that moment she was asking Abricotine if she had seen nothing extraordinary during her little journey. "Madam," she said, "I passed through a forest where I saw animals very much like children. They were leaping and dancing about the trees like squirrels. They were very ugly, but wonderfully nimble." "Ah, how I should like to have some of them!" said the princess. "If they were less agile one could catch them." Ariel, who had passed through this forest, knew the animals must be monkeys. Thereupon he wished himself back in their haunts, where he caught a dozen, little and big. Putting them all into a sack, he wished himself at Paris, where he had heard you could have anything you liked for money. So he went to Dautel, a dealer in curiosities, and bought a little golden coach, to which he harnessed six green monkeys, with little trappings of flame-coloured morocco pricked out with gold. Then he hastened to Brioché, a famous marionette showman, where he found two very clever monkeys—one, the more intelligent, called Briscambille, the other Perceforêt. They were very polite and very well-bred. Briscambille he dressed as a king, and put him in the coach; Perceforêt was the coachman, while the rest of the monkeys were pages. Never was seen anything so pretty. He put the carriage and the dressed-up monkeys in the same sack and returned. As the princess had not yet gone to bed she heard the noise of the little coach in her gallery, and her nymphs came to tell her of the arrival of the king of the dwarfs. At that moment the coach with its procession of monkeys entered her room, and the country monkeys did as pretty tricks as even Briscambille and Perceforêt. To tell the truth, it was Ariel who was leading the whole of them. Taking the monkey out of the little golden coach, he made him gracefully present a box covered with diamonds to the princess. She opened it at once, and found inside a letter, in which she read these verses:—

> "Here is pleasure's dwelling-place,
>   Palace bright, 'mid gardens shady;
> Fair the spot and full of grace,
>   Yet not so fair as my fair lady.

" All unseen, I envying see
  Life's cool stream here calmly gliding;
  Bound and struggling restlessly,
  All my passion from her hiding."

It is not difficult to imagine her astonishment. Briscambille made a sign to Perceforêt to come and dance with him, and they excelled all the most celebrated performing monkeys that ever lived. But the princess, uneasy at being unable to guess whence the verses came, sent the dancers away sooner than she would otherwise have done, for they amused her endlessly, and she had laughed at first enough to make her ill. When they were gone she gave herself up entirely to her own thoughts, but she could make nothing of so dark a mystery.

Leander, much pleased by the interest with which his verses had been read, and by the delight of the princess in looking at the monkeys, now thought of taking some rest, of which he stood in much need. But he feared lest he might choose some room occupied by one of the princess's nymphs, and therefore he waited for a time in the great gallery of the palace. When at last he went downstairs, he found an open door, and entering noiselessly, found himself in a room on one of the lower floors—the prettiest, the pleasantest ever seen. The bed was hung with green and gold gauze, draped in festoons, with ropes of pearls and tassels of rubies and emeralds. It was still light enough to enable him to admire all this wonderful splendour. After shutting the door he fell asleep; but the remembrance of his fair princess woke him up several times, and he could not keep from heaving sighs for his great love for her.

He rose so very early that the time dragged till he could see her. Looking about him, he saw a canvas ready prepared, and colours, and he called to mind what his princess had said to Abricotine about her portrait. Now he could paint better than the great masters, and without losing a moment he sat down before a large mirror and painted his own picture; also, in an oval, that of the princess, her face being so present to his imagination that he had no need to see her for this first sketch. Afterwards he touched up the work with her before him, though she was unconscious of his presence; and as it was the desire of pleasing her that gave him the impulse to work, never was a portrait more perfectly finished. He had represented himself as kneeling before her, holding the princess's portrait in one hand and in the other a scroll, on which was written:—

" The likeness graven on my heart is fairer far ".

When she entered the cabinet she was astonished to see there the portrait of a man, and she fixed her eyes on it with the greater wonder inasmuch as she recognised her own as well. The words written on the scroll gave

her abundant matter for curiosity and thought.   At that moment she was alone.
She knew not what to think of such an extraordinary incident; but she persuaded
herself it must be Abricotine who had played her this trick.   The only thing to
do was to find out whether the picture of this knight was painted from her imagination, or if there had been a living model.   Getting up quickly, she ran to
call Abricotine.   Ariel was already in the cabinet with the little red hat, very
curious to hear what
would take place.   The
princess told Abricotine
to cast her eyes on that
picture, and tell her what
she thought.   As soon
as she saw it she cried
out : " Madam, I protest
to you this is the por-
trait of that generous
stranger to whom I owe
my life.   Yes, it is indeed
the same ; there is no
doubt of it.   These are
his features, his figure,
his hair, his whole bear-
ing."   " You pretend to
be surprised," said the
princess, smiling ; " but
it was you that put it
here."   " I, madam ! "
said Abricotine.   " I
swear to you I have
never seen this picture
before in all my life.
Could I be so bold as to
hide anything which
could be of interest to you?   And by what miracle could it have fallen into my
hands ?   I cannot paint.   No man has ever entered this place ; yet—here he is,
and painted along with you."   "I am seized with terror," said the princess.   "Some
demon must have brought it here."   " Madam," said Abricotine, " may it not have
been Love ?   If you think so too, I advise you to have it burned at once."   "What
a pity that would be !" said the princess, sighing.   " It seems to me my boudoir

could have no prettier decoration than this picture." While she said so, she looked at it; but Abricotine persisted in saying she should burn a thing that could only have come there by magic power. "And these words—

"The likeness graven on my heart is fairer far,"—

said the princess: "shall we burn them too?" "We must spare nothing," replied Abricotine, "not even your own portrait." She ran off at once to fetch a light. The princess went and stood near the window, unable to look any longer at a portrait which made such an impression on her heart. But Ariel, unwilling to let them burn it, took advantage of this moment, and ran off with it unseen.

Hardly was he out of the room when she turned round to look again at the magic portrait which pleased her so much. What was her surprise to see it gone! She looked on all sides. When Abricotine came in again the princess asked if it was she who had just taken it away, but Abricotine said "No," and this last adventure really did frighten them.

After hiding the portrait Leander came back. During these days it was a source of much delight to him to hear and see his fair princess. Every day he ate at the table along with the blue cat, whose appetite was none the more satisfied in consequence. Yet Ariel's happiness was far from perfect, since he dared neither speak nor let himself be seen, and without that one has little chance of being loved.

The princess delighted in all beautiful things, and in the present state of her heart she had need of amusement. One day when she was with her nymphs, she told them that she should like very much to know how the ladies of all the different courts in the universe were clad, in order that she might dress according to the finest model. A suggestion was all that Ariel wanted to make him set off on a journey through the whole earth. So, clapping on his little red hat, he wished himself in China, where he bought the finest stuffs and took patterns of the costumes. Then he flew to Siam, where he did the same. He ran through the four quarters of the world in three days, and when he was laden he came back to the Palace of Calm Delights, and hid in a room all that he had brought. When he had in this way collected a number of wonderful curiosities (for money was nothing to him, his rose furnishing a constant supply), he bought five or six dozen dolls, which he had dressed in Paris, for there more than anywhere else in the world fashion has sway. There were costumes of all kinds, and of an untold splendour. All these Ariel arranged in the princess's cabinet.

When she entered she was surprised beyond words. Every doll carried a present, either watches, bracelets, diamond buttons, or necklaces, whilst the princi-

pal one had a case containing a portrait. Opening it, the princess found a miniature of Leander. Her remembrance of the first one made her recognise the
second. She uttered a loud cry, then, looking at Abricotine, she said: " I cannot understand all that has been passing for some time in this palâce. My birds
talk like rational beings. It seems I have only to wish in order to be obeyed. I
twice see the portrait of him who saved you from the bandits. Here are stuffs,
diamonds, embroideries, lace, and wonderful curiosities. Who is then the fairy,
who is the demon, that seeks with such care to please me so?" Leander, hearing
her speak, wrote these words on his tablets, and threw them at the princess's
feet :—

> " Neither sprite am I nor fairy;
> But, though near you still I hover,
> Yet to show my face I'm chary—
> Pity your unhappy lover,
>
> PRINCE ARIEL ".

The tablets were so splendid with gold and jewels that as soon as she saw
them she opened them, and read with the utmost astonishment what Leander
had written. " This invisible creature must be a monster, then," she said,
" since he dares not show himself; but if it were true that he had some attachment for me, he would surely have delicacy enough not to present me with so
attractive a portrait. He cannot love me, else he would not expose my heart to
this trial, or he has such a good opinion of himself that he thinks himself handsomer than he is in reality." " I have heard tell, madam," replied Abricotine,
" that there are spirits made of air and fire; they have no body, and it is only
their mind and their will that act." " I am very glad of it," replied the princess.
" A lover like that could hardly disturb the calm of my life." Leander was delighted to hear her, and to see her so much occupied with his portrait. He called
to mind that in a grotto which she often used to visit was a pedestal on which a
Diana, still unfinished, was one day to be placed. He went and stood there in
a strange dress, crowned with laurels and holding a lyre in his hand, which he
could play better than Apollo. Then he waited patiently for his princess to
come, as she did every day, for it was here she came to dream about her unknown lover. Abricotine's account of her champion, added to the pleasure she
had in looking at Leander's picture, hardly left her a moment of rest. She loved
solitude, and her merry humour had changed so much that her nymphs hardly
recognised her.

When she entered the grotto, she signed to them not to follow her, so they
each went away along separate walks. Meanwhile she threw herself on a grassy
bed, sighing, shedding tears, even speaking, but so low that Ariel could not hear

her. At first he had put on the little red hat, so that she might not see him. When he took it off she gazed on him with the utmost astonishment, imagining that it was a statue, for he tried not to change the attitude he had chosen. It was with a joy mingled with fear that she looked on him. This vision so unexpected filled her with surprise, but in the end the pleasure cast out the fear, and she was just growing used to seeing so lifelike a figure when the prince tuned his lyre and sang these words :—

> " There lurketh here such dangerous art
>   That stones and stones might feel it.
> In vain I vowed to guard my heart,
>   Nor let the fair ones steal it.
> Now, wounded, who will heal it, will heal it ?

> " Is this the Isle of Calm Delights ?
>   Here passion met me on the shore,
> Made me a slave beneath his might ;
>   Yet, spite of freedom heretofore,
> 'Tis here I'd stay for evermore, for evermore."

Although Leander's voice was charming, the princess could not master the terror that seized her. Suddenly she grew pale, and fell in a swoon. Ariel, alarmed, leaped from the pedestal to the ground, and put on his little red hat so that no one might see him. Then taking the princess in his arms, he tended her with the utmost care and eagerness. She opened her beautiful eyes and cast them about on all sides, as if to look for him. She saw no one, but yet she felt someone near her, holding her hands, kissing them, and moistening them with tears. It was long before she dared to speak, her fluttered spirit hovering between fear and hope. She feared the invisible Ariel, but she loved him when he took the figure of the stranger. At last she cried out : "Ariel, brave Ariel, why are you not he whom I desire?" At these words Ariel was on the point of making himself known, but he dared not do it yet. "If I terrify this lady whom I love," he said ; "if she fears me, she will never love me." This thought made him keep silence, and induced him to retire into a corner of the grotto. The princess, thinking she was alone, called for Abricotine, and told her the wonders of

6

the animated statue, whose voice was so heavenly, and that in her swoon Ariel had tended her so well. "What a pity," she said, "that this spirit is deformed and hideous, for could anyone have more gracious and pleasant manners?" "And who told you," said Abricotine, "that he is as you imagine him to be? Did not Psyche think that love was a serpent? Your adventure is something like hers. You are no less beautiful. If it were Cupid that loved you, would you not love him?" "If Cupid and the unknown were the same," said the princess, blushing, "alas! I would indeed love Cupid. But how far I am from such happiness! I am following a chimera, and that fatal portrait of the stranger, added to what you have told me, makes me wish for things so opposed to my mother's precepts that I am sure to be punished." "Ah! madam," said Abricotine, interrupting her, "have you not already trouble enough? Why look forward to the evils that will never come to pass?" It is easy to imagine all the pleasure such a conversation gave to Leander.

Meanwhile little Furibon, still in love with the princess, though he had never seen her, waited impatiently for the return of the four men whom he had sent to the Island of Calm Delights. Only one came back, who gave him an account of what had passed, telling him that it had been defended by Amazons, and that unless he were to lead a great army there he would never enter the island. His father, the king, had just died, and Furibon now found himself sole master. So he gathered together more than four hundred thousand men, and set off at their head. Truly he was a fine general! Briscambille or Perceforêt would have done better than this dwarf, with his war-horse hardly half-an-ell in height. When the Amazons saw this great army they warned the princess, who at once sent Abricotine to the kingdom of the fairies to beg her mother to tell her what she should do to drive little Furibon out of her states. But Abricotine found the fairy very angry. "I know quite well all that my daughter is doing," she said. "Prince Leander is in her palace. He loves her, and she loves him. All my care has not been able to save her from the tyranny of love, and now she is under his fatal sway. Alas! the cruel god is not satisfied with the harm he has done me: he exercises his power on what I love better than my life. Such are the decrees of fate, and I cannot resist them. Return, Abricotine; I do not wish even to hear of the daughter who grieves me in this way."

Abricotine brought back the bad news to the princess, who was on the point of despair. Ariel was near her, invisible, and he saw with extreme sorrow her great grief. He did not dare to speak to her at that moment, but he remembered that Furibon was very avaricious, and that by giving him money he might be induced to go away. So he dressed himself as an Amazon, and wished himself first of all in the forest, that he might secure his horse. He called out : " Gris-delin ! " and Grisdelin came to him, leaping and bounding, for he was very wearied at being so long away from his dear master. But when he saw him dressed as a woman he did not recognise him, and feared some mistake. When Leander arrived at Furibon's camp everybody took him for an Amazon, so hand-some was he. The king was told that a young lady wished to deliver him a message from the Princess of Calm Delights, so, quickly putting on his royal robes, he went and sat on his throne, looking like a big toad playing at being king.

Leander spoke, telling him that the princess, who preferred a quiet, peaceful life to the troubles of war, sent to offer him as much money as he wanted if she might be left in peace ; but that, if he refused her offer, she would take every means to defend herself. Furibon replied that he was willing to show mercy to her, that he accorded her the honour of his protection, and that she had only to send him a hundred thousand billions of pistoles and he would return at once to his own kingdom. Leander said it would take too long to count so many, but that he had only to say how many roomfuls he wished for, and that the princess was generous enough and rich enough not to look to a pistole more or less. Furibon was much astonished that instead of beating him down they proposed to give him even more than he demanded. He thought to himself that he would do well to take all the money he could get ; then he could arrest the Amazon and kill her, so that she might not return to her mistress. So he told Leander he would like thirty very large rooms quite filled with gold pieces, and he would give his word as a king to go back to his own country. Leander was led into the rooms to be filled with gold, and, taking the rose, shook it and shook it till there rained from it torrents of pistoles,* quadruples,+ louis,‡ gold crowns, rose-nobles,§ sovereigns, guineas, sequins. ‖ Nothing could have been prettier than this shower of gold. Furibon was beside himself with joy, and the more gold he saw the more desirous was he of seizing the Amazon and carrying off the princess. As soon as the thirty rooms were full he cried to his guards : " Arrest that cheat !—it is false money she has brought me—arrest her ". All the guards tried to get hold of the Amazon, but at that moment the little red hat was put on, and Ariel disappeared. They thought he had fled outside, and run-ning after him, they left Furibon alone. Then Ariel took him by the hair, and cut off his head as if he had been a chicken, before ever the unfortunate little king could even see the hand that was taking his life.

* Spanish gold coin, about 16s. sterling in value. + Spanish gold coin, generally called doubloon, worth two pistoles. ‡ French gold coin, worth 20s. § Old English gold coin, called so in time of Henry VIII. ‖ An Italian gold coin.

As soon as Ariel had secured the king's head he wished himself in the Palace of Delights. The princess was walking in the grounds, thinking in deep sadness of what her mother had said, and wondering what means she could take to repulse Furibon. It was a very difficult task for her and her little band of Amazons, who could not possibly defend her against four hundred thousand men. All at once she saw a head in the air, no one holding it, which astonished her so much that she did not know what to think. It was much worse when the head was placed at her feet by some unseen hand. Then she heard a voice saying: "Fear no more, dear princess; Furibon will never again do you wrong". Abricotine recognised the voice of Leander, and cried out: "I assure you, madam, that the unseen one who is speaking is the stranger who came to my aid". The princess was astonished and delighted. "Ah!" she said, "if it is true that Ariel and the stranger are the same, I confess I should be very pleased to prove my gratitude to him." Ariel went away, saying: "I want still to work that I may be worthy of her". And he returned to the army of Furibon, the noise of whose death had been spread abroad. As soon as he appeared amongst them in his ordinary dress, everyone came up to him: the captains and the soldiers surrounded him, shouting aloud for joy, proclaiming him their king, and telling him the crown belonged to him. He divided the thirty rooms full of gold generously amongst them, so that the soldiers were made rich for ever. And after some formalities, which assured Leander of the loyalty of the soldiers, he returned to the princess, ordering his army to make their way gradually back to his own kingdom.

The princess had gone to bed when Leander returned to the palace, and the deep respect which he had for her prevented his entering her room. So he went to his own, for he still kept the one below. He was tired enough to be glad of some rest, and this made him forget to shut the door as carefully as he usually did. The princess, who was in a fever of anxiety, got up before the dawn, and in her morning-gown went to her room downstairs. But what was her surprise to find Leander asleep on a bed! She had time enough to look at him without being seen, and to be convinced that it was the person whose portrait was in the diamond case. " It is not possible," she said, "that it is Ariel; for, do spirits sleep? Is that body made of air or fire, as Abricotine said? Does it not fill space?" She touched his hair gently: she heard him breathè, and she could not tear herself away, being half delighted and half alarmed at having found him. Just as she was looking at him with eager eyes, her fairy mother entered with such a terrible noise that Leander awoke with a start. How surprised, how grieved he was to see his princess in the utmost despair! Her mother was dragging her off, loading her with reproaches. Oh, what grief for these young lovers about to be separated for ever! The princess dared not say a word to this terrible fairy, and turned her eyes towards Leander as if to ask for help. He knew well enough that he could not keep her against the wish of so powerful a lady; but he trusted somewhat to his persuasive tongue and the mildness of his manner for appeasing this angry mother. He ran after her, threw himself at her feet, and begged her to take pity on a young king who would never cease to love her daughter, and whose highest happiness would be to make her happy. The princess, encouraged by his example, then clung about her mother's knees, saying that without the king she could not be content, and she owed him much. " You do not know the trouble of love," cried the fairy, "nor the treasons of which lovers are capable. They only fascinate in order to poison us. I have experienced it. Do you wish your fate to be like mine?" "Ah, madam," replied the princess, "is there no exception? Do you not think that the assurances which the king gives you, and which seem so sincere, will shelter me from what you dread?"

But the obstinate fairy let them sigh at her feet. In vain did they moisten her hands with their tears. She took no notice, and she would certainly never have forgiven them had not the lovely Fairy Gentille appeared in the room, shining brighter than the sun. The Graces accompanied her, and she was followed by a troop of loves, of sports, and of pleasures, who sang a thousand pretty songs that had never been heard before, dancing about as merry as children the while. Embracing the old fairy, Gentille said: "My dear sister, I am sure you have not forgotten the services I did you when you wished to return to our kingdom. Had it not been for me you would never have been received. Since then I have asked for nothing in return; but at last the time is come when you can do me a real favour. Forgive this fair princess; give your consent to her marriage with this young king, and I will answer for him that he will never cease to love her. The web of their life will be spun with threads of silk and gold, and their union will give you infinite pleasure, while I shall never forget the kindness you have done me." " I consent to all you ask, dear Gentille," cried the fairy. "Come, my children, come to my arms, and receive the assurance of my love." With that she embraced the princess and her lover. The Fairy Gentille was full of joy, and the whole troop began to sing the wedding hymns; and the soft music having awakened all the nymphs of the palace, they came running in their light gauze robes to learn what was happening. Here was a pleasant surprise for Abricotine! No sooner had she set eyes on Leander than she recognised him; and seeing him holding the princess's hand, she felt sure that they had both been made happy. What confirmed her was that the fairy mother said she would transport the Isle of Calm Delights, with the castle and all the wonders it contained, into Leander's kingdom; that she would dwell with them there, and would heap still greater riches on them. "Whatever your generosity may suggest to you to bestow on me," answered the king, "it is impossible that you can give me anything equal to what I have received to-day." This little compliment pleased the fairy very much, for she belonged to the olden time, when they would compliment each other all day long for some trifle no bigger than a pin-point.

As Gentille had forgotten nothing, she had had, by the power of Brelic-Breloc,* the generals and the captains of Furibon's army brought to the palace of the princess, in order that they might be present at the splendid feast that was about to take place. It was she who took charge of the arrangements; and five or six volumes would not be enough to describe the comedies, the operas, the running at the ring, the music, the gladiator fights, the hunts, and the other splendid amusements of this charming wedding-feast. But, most wonderful of all, each nymph found among the brave soldiers that Gentille had brought to this beautiful spot, a husband as affectionate as if she had known him for ten years. Yet their acquaintance had only lasted four-and-twenty hours; but then the little wand can do even more wonderful things than that.

* Topsy-turvydom.

PRINCESS MAYBLOSSOM.

ONCE upon a time there lived a king and a queen who had had several children born to them. But they all died, and the king and the queen were so sorry, so very sorry, that they could not be comforted. They were very rich, and the one thing they wanted was to have more children. It was five years since the queen's last son had been born, and everybody thought she would not have any more, for she distressed herself so much in thinking of all the little princes who had been so pretty, and who were dead.

At last, however, the queen knew that another child was to be born to her, and all her thoughts, night and day, were of how to preserve the little creature's life, or of the name it would be called by, or its clothes, or of the dolls and the playthings she would give it. A command was sent out, proclaimed by the sound of trumpets, and stuck up in all the public squares, that the best nurses should present themselves before the queen, for she wished to choose one for her infant. So they came from all the four corners of the earth, and there were none but nurses with their babies to be seen. One day then, when the queen was taking the air in a great forest, she sat down, and said to the king : "Sire, call all our nurses together and choose one, for our cows have not milk enough to provide for so many little children". "Very well, my love," said the king. "Come, and let all the nurses be called." So they all came, one after the other, bowing with much respect before the queen. Then they stood up in a row, each with her back against a tree. After they had taken their places, and the king and queen had admired their fresh complexion, their

(87)

beautiful teeth, and their look of health and strength, a little wheelbarrow was seen coming up, pushed along by two ugly little dwarfs, and in it a hideous creature with crooked feet, her knees touching her chin, with a great hump on her back, squinting eyes, and skin as black as ink. In her arms she held a little monkey, which she was nursing, and she was speaking in a jargon they could not understand. She had also come to offer herself as nurse, but the queen drove her away, saying: " Be off, you great ugly thing. You are very ill-bred to come before me with your hideous face, and if you stay another minute I'll have you dragged off." So the sulky creature passed on, muttering aloud, and drawn along by her hideous little dwarfs she went and stuck herself in the hollow of a great tree, from where she could see everything.

The queen thought nothing more about her, and chose an excellent nurse. But as soon as she had named her choice, a horrible serpent, hidden under the grass, stung the nurse's foot, and she fell in a swoon. The queen, much distressed at this accident, cast her eyes on another. Immediately an eagle passed flying by, carrying a tortoise, which he let fall on the poor nurse's head, and broke it in pieces like a glass. The queen, still more distressed, called for a third nurse, who, in her great eagerness to come forward, struck against a bush with great thorns, and put out her eye. " Ah ! " cried the queen. " We are indeed unfortunate to-day. I cannot choose a nurse without bringing some ill-luck upon her. . I must leave the care of them to my doctor." As she was rising to return to the palace she heard a stifled laugh, and turning round, she saw behind her the wicked hunchback, looking like an ape as she sat with her little imp in the wheelbarrow. There she was, laughing at the whole company, and especially at the queen, who was so angry that she wished to go and beat her, feeling sure she was the cause of the evil chance that had happened to the nurses. But the hunchback, with three strokes of her wand, turned the dwarfs into winged griffins, the wheelbarrow into a chariot of fire, and they all flew away together into the air, uttering threats and horrible cries.

" Alas ! my love, we are lost," said the king. " That was the Fairy Carabosse. The wicked creature has hated me ever since I was a little boy on account of a trick I played her, putting sulphur in her broth. Since that time she has been seeking to revenge herself on me." The queen began to cry. " If I had but known her name," she said ; " I would have tried to make friends with her. But now I feel as if I should like to die." When the king saw her so distressed, he said : " Come, my love, let us think what we must do," and he gave her his arm to lean on, for she was still trembling from the fright Carabosse had given her. When the king and the queen were in their room they called their councillors, and shut the doors and windows so that nothing might be heard.

Then they determined to have all the fairies for a thousand miles round present at the birth of the child. So without delay they despatched couriers, and sent letters by them—beautifully written and most polite letters—asking them to be so good as to be present at the birth of the royal infant, and to say nothing about the matter to anybody. For they trembled lest Carabosse should hear of it, and come and spoil everything. And to reward them for their trouble, they were promised a hongreline* of blue velvet, a skirt of amaranth velvet, and slippers of crimson satin, a pair of little gilden scissors, and a case full of fine needles.

As soon as the messengers had set off, the queen began to work along with her maidens and her servants at all the things she had promised the fairies. She knew of a good many who might be expected, but only five came, and they arrived just at the moment when the little princess was born. So they shut themselves up in the queen's room without delay to name their fairy gifts. The first one endowed her with perfect beauty, the second with wonderful cleverness, the third with the power of singing, and the fourth with that of writing both in prose and verse. When the fifth was opening her mouth to speak, a noise was heard in the chimney like a great stone falling from the top of a steeple, and Carabosse, all covered with soot, made her appearance, screeching out: "Here is my gift to the little one, I wish:—

> "That all her youth be overcast
> Till her twentieth year be past".

At these words the queen who was in bed began to cry, and to beg Carabosse to take pity on the little princess. And all the fairies said: "Alas! sister, take away this curse from her! What has she done to you?" But the ugly fairy growled, and made no answer. So the fifth fairy, who had not yet spoken, tried to mend matters by endowing the child with a long life full of happiness after the period of the curse should have passed by. Carabosse only laughed, and began singing all kinds of mocking songs, climbing out of the palace by the same road she had come. All the fairies were in great consternation, but especially the poor queen. She did not forget, however, to give them what she had promised, adding even ribbons, which they are very fond of, and entertaining them hospitably.

The eldest fairy, as she was going away, said that in her opinion the princess, till she was twenty years old, should be kept in some place where she would see no one but the attendants chosen for her, and where she would be closely guarded. Thereupon the king had a tower built, in which there was not

---

* A Hungarian jacket.

a single window, and where you could not see except by candle light. To get in you had to go through a vault which stretched under the ground for a league, and it was through this passage that everything that the nurses and the governesses wanted was brought. Every twenty paces there were great doors, with strong locks, and all along numerous guards were stationed.

The young princess had been called Mayblossom, for she had a complexion of lilies and roses, fresher and brighter than the spring. In everything she did or said she excelled, learning the most difficult sciences as if they were quite easy. And she grew so tall, and so beautiful, that the king and the queen never saw her without shedding tears of joy. Sometimes she would beg them to stay with her, or to take her away with them, for she wearied in the tower, without knowing why. But they always put it off. Her nurse, who had never left her, and who was not lacking in intelligence, told her sometimes what the world was like, and she understood everything at once just as if she had seen it. The king would often say to the queen: " My love, Carabosse will be made a fool of. We are cleverer than she is, and our Mayblossom will be happy in spite of her predictions." And the queen would laugh till the tears came, to think of the annoyance of the wicked fairy. They had had Mayblossom's portrait painted, and had sent pictures of her throughout the whole world, for the time to release her from the tower being at hand, they wished to marry her. At last, only four days were wanting to complete the twenty years, and the court and the town were very joyous at the thought of the approaching liberty of the princess. And their joy was all the greater when they heard that King Merlin wished to have her for his own, and that he was sending his ambassador, Fanfarinet, to ask her hand in marriage.

The nurse, who told the princess everything, brought her this news, telling her that no sight in the world would be so fine as Fanfarinet's entrance. "Ah, how unfortunate I am!" she cried. " I am shut up here in a dark tower, as if I had committed some great crime. I have never seen the sky, nor the sun, nor the stars, whose wonders are so much talked of. I have never seen a horse, nor a monkey, nor a lion, except in a picture. The king and the queen say they are going to release me when I am twenty years old, but they only say that to make me have patience. I know quite well they wish me to die here, though in nothing have I offended them." Thereupon she began to cry, so long and bitterly that her eyes were as big as her fists; and her nurse, and her foster-sister, and the under-nurse, and the woman who sang her to sleep, and the little nursemaid, who all loved her passionately, began to weep too so long and bitterly that nothing was heard but sobs and sighs, till they thought they must choke, so great was their distress. When the princess saw them so ready to grieve with her, she took a knife, and said in a loud voice: "There! I am determined to kill myself on the spot, if you do not find some means of letting me see the grand entrance of Fanfarinet. The king and the queen will never know. Choose, therefore, whether you would rather I should kill myself here, or whether you will do what I ask." At these words the nurse and the others began to cry again still louder, and they all determined to let her see Fanfarinet or die themselves in the attempt. The rest of the night they spent in making plans as to how this could be carried out, but in vain; and Mayblossom, who was in despair, said without ceasing: "Never tell me again that you love me. You would find some means if you did, for I have heard that love and friendship can do anything."

At last they came to the conclusion that a hole would have to be made in the tower, on that side of the town by which Fanfarinet would come. So pushing aside the princess's bed, they all set to work day and night without stopping. By means of scraping, they took away first the plaster and then the little stones, till at last they made a hole through which with much difficulty you might have slipped a fine needle. It was through this opening that Mayblossom saw the light for the first time. She was quite dazzled by it. Looking as she did steadily through the little hole, she saw Fanfarinet appear at the head of his whole troop. He was riding on a white horse which danced to the sound of the trumpets, rearing in a splendid fashion. Six flute-players walked in front, playing the finest opera airs, and six hautboys took up the sound. Then the trumpets and the timbrels struck up. Fanfarinet was dressed in a doublet, embroidered with pearls. His boots were of gold, and scarlet plumes waved on his helmet, and ribbons floated from every part of his dress, while he was so covered with diamonds—for King Merlin had whole rooms full of them—that the sun's splendour was as nothing to his. Mayblossom at this sight was beside herself, and quite exhausted. After considering the matter a little, she swore that she would marry none but the beautiful Fanfarinet, that there was no reason for thinking his master would be as beautiful, and she had no ambition to marry one of high rank; that if she had lived happily in a tower, she could live happily, if need be, in some castle in the country with him, and that she would think bread and water in his company better than chicken and sugar-plums with anybody else. In short, she spoke so much that her women could not think where she had learnt a quarter of what she said. When they pleaded her rank and the wrong she would be doing herself, she bade them be silent, and would not deign to listen to their words.

As soon as Fanfarinet had come into the palace of the king, the queen sent for her daughter. All the streets were carpeted, and the ladies stood at the windows, some with baskets full of flowers in their hands, some with baskets full of pearls, others, what were still better, delicious sweetmeats, to throw at her when she passed by. Her maids were just beginning to dress her when there came to the tower a dwarf, mounted on an elephant. He had been sent by the five good fairies who had given her gifts when she was born. They sent her a crown, a sceptre, a dress of gold brocade, a skirt made of butterflies' wings, worked in the most wonderful way, with a still more marvellous casket, full of jewels of priceless value. Never were such treasures seen. At sight of them the queen was speechless with admiration, but the princess looked at them all indifferently, for she was only thinking of Fanfarinet. They thanked the dwarf, and gave him also a pistole to go and drink their health with, and more than a thousand ells of many coloured ribbons, with which he made himself fine garters, and a breast knot, and a rosette for his hat. Being small, when he had put all the ribbons on, you could no longer see him. The queen said she would go and look for something pretty to send back to the fairies, and the princess, who was very kind-hearted, gave them several German spinning-wheels, with distaffs made of cedar-wood.

When they had arrayed the princess in all the rarest things the dwarf had brought, she seemed to everybody so beautiful that the sun hid itself in spite, and the moon, who is never too shamefaced, dared not appear while she was on the road. She walked on foot through the streets over rich carpets, the assembled people in crowds crying around her: "Ah, how beautiful she is! How beautiful she is!" As she walked in her gorgeous robes between the queen and four or five dozen princesses of the blood—not to speak of more than ten dozen who had come from neighbouring states to be present at the feast—the sky began to darken, and the thunder to rumble, and the rain and the hail to fall in torrents. The queen put her royal mantle over her head, and the ladies their skirts. Mayblossom was just going to do the same when the noise of numberless ravens, and screech-owls, carrion-crows, and other birds of evil omen was heard in the air, their croakings boding nothing good. At the same time an ugly owl, of an enormous size, came swooping down, holding in his beak a scarf of spider's web, embroidered with bats' wings. It let this scarf fall on Mayblossom's shoulders, and great bursts of laughter were heard, a sure enough sign that it was some mischievous trick of Carabosse's planning.

At this terrible sight everybody began to cry, and the queen, more distressed than anyone else, wanted to snatch away the black scarf, which seemed, however, to be nailed to her daughter's shoulders. "Ah!" she said, "this is a trick which our enemy has played us. Nothing can appease her. In vain have I sent her fifty pounds of sweetmeats, as much of our own especial sugar, and two Mayence hams. She has taken no notice of them." While she was lamenting thus, they were all getting wet to the skin. Mayblossom, her head full of the ambassador, was speeding on in perfect silence, thinking to herself that provided she pleased him, she did not care either for Carabosse or for her ill-omened scarf. She was wondering that he did not come to meet her, when all at once she saw him by the king's side. Immediately the trumpets, drums, and violins struck up gaily. The cries of the people redoubled, and in fact there were no bounds to the rejoicing.

Fanfarinet was very ready-witted. Yet when he saw the fair Mayblossom with so much grace and dignity, he was so delighted that instead of speaking he only gaped. You would have said he was drunk, though of a truth he had only taken one cup of chocolate. He was in despair at having forgotten in a moment a speech he had been repeating every day for months, and which he knew well enough to be able to say in his sleep. While he was torturing his memory to call back the words, he kept bowing low before the princess, who, for her part, made half-a-dozen curtsies without knowing what she was doing. At last she spoke, and to relieve him from the trouble in which she saw him, she said : " My Lord Fanfarinet, I feel absolutely certain that every thought of yours is charming, for I know you are full of intelligence. But let us make haste and reach the palace. It is pouring in torrents. The wicked Carabosse wants to drown us, but when we are inside we can laugh at her." He answered her with much gallantry, for the fairy had wisely foreseen the fire that the fair eyes of the princess would light, and it was to temper it she poured out this deluge of water. With these few words he gave her his hand to help her on her way, while low in his ear she whispered : " I feel for you what you would never guess, if I did not tell you myself. It is somewhat difficult for me to do so, but ' evil to him that evil thinks '. Know, therefore, my Lord Ambassador, that I admired you very much when I first saw you on your fine, prancing horse, and I felt full of regret that you should come here on another's errand. There is a remedy to be found for this, if your courage is as great as mine. Instead of marrying you in the name of your master, I shall marry you in your own. I know you are not a prince, but you please me just as much as if you were, and we shall flee away together into some corner of the world. At first it will make some talk. But another girl will do as I have done, or perhaps worse ; and then they will leave us alone and talk of her, and I shall have the pleasure of living with you."

Fanfarinet thought he must be dreaming, for Mayblossom was so magnificent a princess, that unless by some strange caprice of fortune he could have never hoped for this honour she did him. He had not even strength left to answer her. If they had been alone, he would have thrown himself at her feet. As it was, he took the liberty of wringing her hand so vigorously that he hurt her little finger very much. But she never cried out, so infatuated was she. When she entered the palace all kinds of musical instruments began to play, mingled with voices like those of the angels, so exquisite that no one dared to breathe for fear of making too much noise. After the king had kissed his daughter on the forehead and on the two cheeks, he said to her: "My little lambkin (for he gave her all kind of pet names), will you not be glad to marry the son of the great King Merlin? Here is Lord Fanfarinet, who will perform the ceremony for him, and who will take you away into the finest kingdom in the world." "Yes, my father," she said, with a low bow; "I am willing to do anything to please you, provided my good mother gives her consent." "Yes, I give my consent, my darling," said the queen, embracing her. "Come now, let the tables be spread." And this was done in haste. There were a hundred spread in a great gallery, and in the memory of man never was there such feasting. Only Mayblossom and Fanfarinet did not partake, for they only thought of looking at each other, until they became so dreamy that they forgot all that was going on around them. After the feast there was a ball, a ballet, and a play acted, but it was already so late, and everybody had eaten so much, that in spite of all their efforts, the people were sleeping on their feet. The king and the queen, overcome also with sleep, threw themselves on a sofa. The greater part of the dames and cavaliers were snoring, the musicians played out of tune, and the players did not know what they were saying. Only our lovers were wide awake as mice, and looking at each other with soft looks. The princess, seeing that there was nothing to fear, and that the guards lying on their pallets were asleep too, said to Fanfarinet: "Trust me, let us take advantage of so favourable an opportunity, for if I wait for the wedding ceremony the king will give me waiting women and a prince to accompany me to your King Merlin. We had better go now, as quickly as we can."

Getting up, she took the king's dagger, which was studded with diamonds, and the head-dress which the queen had taken off that she might sleep more at her ease. She gave her white hand to Fanfarinet, and as he took it he knelt on the ground and said: "I swear to be for ever faithful and obedient to your highness. Great princess, you do everything for me. What would I not do for you!" They left the palace, the ambassador carrying a dark lantern in his hand, and through very muddy streets they reached the port, where they got into a little boat. There was a poor old boatman in it asleep. They awoke him, and when he saw Mayblossom so beautiful and so gaily dressed, with so many diamonds, and with her spider-web scarf, he took her for the Goddess of Night, and knelt before her. But as there was no time to be lost, she ordered him to set off. It was very venturesome, for neither moon nor stars could be seen, and the air was still full of the storm which Carabosse had caused. It is true there was a carbuncle in the queen's head-dress which shone brighter than fifty lighted torches, and Fanfarinet, indeed, might have done without the dark lantern, the carbuncle having the power of making them invisible. Fanfarinet asked the princess where she would like to go. "Alas!" she said, "I wish to go with you. That is all I care for." "But, madam," he answered; "I dare not take you to King Merlin's court, for there I should be killed like a dog." "Very well," she answered; "let us go to the desert Isle of Squirrels. It is far enough away, so we shall not be followed." Then she ordered the sailor to set off, and though it was only a little boat, he obeyed.

When day was dawning the first thought of the king, the queen, and of everybody, after they had shaken themselves a little and rubbed their eyes, was to complete the princess's marriage ceremony. The queen, in great haste, asked for her grand head-dress to put on her hair. They looked for it everywhere, from cabinets even to saucepans, but it was not to be found. The queen, very anxious, ran up and down stairs, to the cellar, to the attic, everywhere, but it was nowhere to be seen.

The king, for his part, wished to array himself with his magnificent dagger, and in the same way they began to rummage everywhere, opening boxes and caskets, the keys of which had been lost for more than a hundred years. They found all kinds of curious things, dolls that moved their heads and their eyes, golden sheep with their little lambs, lemon peel, pickled walnuts, but none of these made up to the king for his loss. He was so desperate that he tore his beard, and the queen, for company, tore her hair, for

in truth the head-dress and the dagger were worth more than ten towns as large as Madrid.

When the king saw there was no hope of finding either of them, he said to the queen : " My love, take courage, and let us haste to complete the ceremony which already has cost us so dear". When he asked where the princess was, her nurse came forward and said : " Your majesty, I assure you that I have looked for her for more than two hours, and I cannot find her". These words brought the king and queen's grief to a climax, and the queen began to cry like an eagle whose little ones have been taken away, and fell down in a faint. You never saw such a pitiful sight, and they had to throw more than two buckets of Queen-of-Hungary water on her majesty's face before she came to herself. The court ladies and the maids of honour wept, and all the valets cried out : " What ! is the king's daughter really lost ?" The king seeing that the princess was not to be found, said to his chief page: " Go and fetch Fanfarinet, who is sleeping in some corner, that he may come and mourn with us ". So the page went about looking everywhere for Fanfarinet, but he was no more to be found than were Mayblossom, the head-dress, and the dagger. This was another addition to their troubles, and their majesties were in despair.

The king called all his councillors and men-at-arms together, and went with the queen into the great hall, which had already been hung with black. They had put off their gay dresses, and they each wore a long mourning robe, tied round the waist with a cord. When their people saw them in this condition, there was no heart so hard but was ready to break, and the hall resounded with sobs and sighs, while streams of tears flowed over the floor. As the king had had no time to prepare his speech he was three hours before he could say a word. At last he began :—

" Listen now, gentle and simple. I have lost my dear daughter, Mayblossom. I do not know whether she has melted away or whether she has been stolen away from me. The queen's head-dress and my dagger, which are worth their weight in gold, have also disappeared, and what is worse, the ambassador Fanfarinet is no longer to be found. I very much fear that the king, his master, receiving no news, will come and seek for him at our court, and that he will accuse us of cutting him to pieces. I should be more patient if I had any money, but I must own to you that the expenses of the wedding have ruined me. Counsel me, therefore, my dear subjects, as to what I can do to get back my daughter, Fanfarinet, and the property I have lost."

Everyone admired the king's fine speech; he had never spoken so well before. Lord Gambille, the chancellor of the kingdom, then spoke :—

" Your majesty, we regret very much the trouble that has befallen you, and we would have given you our very wives and our little ones, so that you might have less reason to grieve. But evidently all this has been brought about by the Fairy Carabosse. The princess's twenty years had not yet been completed, and since I must speak frankly, I ought to tell you that I noticed she was always looking at Fanfarinet, and he was always looking at her too. So perhaps Love has been playing some of his tricks."

At these words the queen, who was very quick-tempered, interrupted him. " Take care what you are saying, my Lord Gambille. The princess would not be disposed to fall in love with Fanfarinet. I have brought her up too well." Thereupon the nurse, who was listening to everything, came and knelt before the king and queen. " I come to confess to you what has happened," she said. " The princess declared she must see Fanfarinet, or die, so we made a little hole, through which she saw him, and at once she swore she would never marry anyone else." On hearing this everyone was in great distress, for they knew well that Chancellor Gambille was a very keen-sighted man. The queen in great wrath scolded the nurse, the foster-sister, the under-nurse, the woman who had used to sing the princess to sleep, and the little nursemaid, so soundly that they all but died under her reproaches.

Then Admiral Chapeau-Pointu, interrupting the queen, cried out : " Come, let us go after Fanfarinet. There can be no doubt but this rascal has run away with our princess." Everybody clapped their hands at this, saying : " Let us go !" Some embarked by sea, others went by land from kingdom to kingdom, beating drums, and sounding trumpets, and when people gathered round them, they would cry : " Whoever wants to gain a beautiful doll, pots of preserves (dry or liquid), a pair of scissors, a gilded robe, a fine satin cap, has only to tell us where the Princess Mayblossom is who was stolen away by Fanfarinet." But every man answered : " Go elsewhere, we have not seen them ". Those who pursued the princess by sea were more fortunate, for after sailing for a long time they saw one night something shining before them like a great fire. They dared not come near it, not knowing what it might be, but all at once this light seemed to land on the desert Isle of Squirrels.

In truth it was no other than the princess and her lover, and it was the carbuncle they had seen shining. Mayblossom and Fanfarinet disembarked, and after having given a hundred golden crowns to the good man who had brought them, they bade him farewell, making him swear by the eyes in his head to speak of nothing he had seen or heard. The first thing the boatman met was the king's vessels, which he had no sooner recognised than he tried to avoid. But the admiral sent a boat after him, and the good man was so aged and so weak that he had not strength to row fast enough. So coming up with him they brought him before the admiral, who had him searched. They found on him a hundred gold crowns quite new, for they had coined money for the princess's wedding-feast. The admiral questioned him, and so as not to be obliged to answer, he pretended he was deaf and dumb. " Very well," said the admiral, " tie this dumb man to the great mast, and give him a flogging. That is the best cure of all for the dumb." When the old man saw that he meant this, he confessed that a girl, more like an angel than a human creature, and a beautiful knight, had ordered him to take them to the desert Isle of Squirrels. Hearing this the admiral knew it must be the princess, and he sent his fleet to surround the island.

Meanwhile Mayblossom tired out by the sea, having found a green lawn under the shade of thick trees, lay down and fell quietly asleep. But Fanfarinet whose hunger was keener than his love, did not leave her long in peace. " Do you think, madam," he said, waking her up, " that I can remain long here ? I see nothing to eat. Even were you fairer than the dawn, that hardly would suffice, for one must eat. My teeth are very long, and my stomach very empty." " What, Fanfarinet," she answered, " does not the affection I feel for you stand you in stead of everything ? Is your mind not filled with your good fortune ? " " With my misfortunes, rather," he cried. " I would to heaven you were still in your black tower ! " " Sir Knight," she said, graciously, " I beg you, do not be angry. I shall go and search everywhere, and perhaps I may find some fruit." " I wish," he answered, " that you would find a wolf to eat you up ! " The princess, in great distress, ran through the woods, tearing her pretty clothes with the briars, and her white skin with the thorns till she was all full of scratches as if she had been playing with cats. See what it is to fall in love— only trouble comes of it. After having searched everywhere, she came back very sad to Fanfarinet, to tell him she had found nothing, but he turned his back on her, and went away muttering. Next day they searched again, but still all in vain, so that they were three days without eating anything but leaves and some cock-chafers. The princess made no complaint, though she was very delicate. " I would not mind," she said, " if I suffered by myself, and I should not care though I died of hunger, provided you had enough to eat." " It would be all the same to me," he answered, " whether you died or not, provided I had what I want." " Is it possible," she asked, " that my death would make so little difference to you ? Are these the oaths you made me ? " " There is a great difference," he answered, " between a man when he is comfortable, and neither hungry nor thirsty, and an unfortunate wretch like to die on a desert island." " I am in the same danger," she said, " and I make no complaint." " It would ill become you to do so," he replied, harshly. " You wished to leave your father and mother, and go gadding up and down. Well, here we are, in a nice place too! " " But it was for love of you, Fanfarinet," she said, holding out her hand. " I could have done without that," he answered, and then he turned his back on her.

The beautiful princess, overcome with grief, began to cry so bitterly that she would have moved a stone to pity. She sat down near a bush covered with red and white roses. After having looked at them for some time, she said : " How happy you are, young flowers. The zephyrs caress you, the dew moistens you, the sun brings you beauty, the bees love you, the thorns defend you. Everybody admires you. Alas! why should you be happier than I ? " At these thoughts she shed so many tears that the root of the rose tree was quite wet. Then she was much astonished to see that the bush was moving, and the roses opening out, and that the fairest of them all said : " If you had not fallen in love, your lot would be as desirable as mine. Whoever loves is exposed to the utmost dangers. Poor princess, take the honeycomb you will find in the hollow of yonder tree. But do not be so foolish as to give it to Fanfarinet." Off she ran to the tree, not knowing yet whether she was dreaming or whether she was really awake. She found the honey, and as soon as she had done so, she took it to her ungrateful lover. " Here," she said, " is a honeycomb. If I had liked I might have eaten it all by myself, but I would rather share it with you." Without a word of thanks, without even a look, he tore it out of her hands, and ate the whole of it, refusing to give her one little morsel, even adding mockery to his cruelty, saying it was too sweet, that it would spoil her teeth, and a hundred other like taunts.

Mayblossom, still more distressed, sat down below an oak, and spoke to it very much as she had done to the rose tree. The oak, moved with pity, lowered some of its branches and said : " It would be a pity were you to die, May-blossom. Take this pitcher of milk and drink it, and don't give a drop to that ungrateful lover of yours." The princess, very much astonished, looked behind and saw a large pitcher of milk. Her only thought at the moment was of Fanfarinet's thirst after having eaten more than fifteen pounds of honey, and she ran with her pitcher to him. " Drink, my beautiful Fanfarinet," she said, " and don't forget to leave me some, for I am dying of hunger and thirst." But he snatched it roughly from her, drank all the milk up at a single draught, then throwing the pitcher on the stones, broke it in pieces, saying, with a mocking smile : " Those who have eaten nothing are not thirsty ". The princess clasped her hands, and lifting her beautiful eyes to heaven, she said : " I have deserved it. It is a punishment for having so rashly fallen in love with a man whom I did not know, for having run away with him, forgetting my rank, and the misfortune with which Carabosse threatened me." Then she began to cry again, more bitterly than ever she had done in her life, and plunging into the thickest part of the wood, she fell down from sheer weakness at the foot of an elm tree, on which a nightingale was perched and singing beautifully. Shaking his wings he sang these words as if only for Mayblossom's benefit. He had learnt them out of Ovid on purpose :—

> " Love is a traitor, then beware his guile ;
> For all his favours doth he ask a price ;
> Most full of danger when they most entice ;
> Deadliest the poison in his sweetest smile ".

"Who can know that better than I do?" she cried, interrupting her. "Alas! I know only too well the sharpness of his arrows and the hardness of my lot." "Take courage," said the tender nightingale; "and search in this bush. You will find sugar-plums and tarts, but do not be so foolish as to give any to Fanfarinet." The princess had no need of this warning to keep them for herself. She had not yet forgotten the two last tricks he had played her, and besides, she was in great want of food, so she munched the sugar-plums and the tarts all by herself. Greedy Fanfarinet, seeing her eating without him, flew into such a temper that he ran towards her, his eyes flashing with anger, and his sword in his hand to kill her. In a moment she had uncovered the stone on her head-dress, which made her invisible, and going farther off she reproached him with his ingratitude, but in such a way as made him understand well enough that she could not yet bring herself to hate him.

Meanwhile Admiral Chapeau-Pointu had despatched John Caquet, courier-in-ordinary to the council, with his straw boots, to tell the king that the princess and Fanfarinet had landed in the Island of Squirrels, but that, not knowing the country, he feared there might be ambuscades. This news gave great satisfaction to their majesties, and the king sent for a great book, each leaf of which was eight ells in length. It was the masterpiece of a learned fairy, and in it was a description of the whole earth. He found from this book that the Isle of Squirrels was not inhabited. "Go," he said, therefore, to John Caquet, "and command the admiral on my behalf to land at once. He may well be very impatient at the thought of leaving my daughter so long with Fanfarinet, and at all events I am." As soon as John Caquet had reached the fleet, the admiral ordered the drums to beat, and the timbals and the trumpets to sound. Hautboys, flutes, violins, hurdy-gurdies, organs, guitars struck up. What a desperate noise they made! for every instrument of war or peace was heard throughout the whole island. At this noise the princess, in alarm, ran towards her lover to offer him help. He was not brave, and their common terror very quickly reconciled them. "Keep behind me," she said. "I shall walk in front, and uncovering the invisible stone, I shall take my father's dagger and kill a part of our enemies while you kill the others with your sword." So the invisible princess stepped forward amidst the soldiers, and she and Fanfarinet killed them all without being seen. Nothing was heard but cries of "I am dead!" "I am dying!" It was in vain the soldiers drew their swords, they could touch nothing, for the princess and her lover ducked down every time, and the blows passed over their heads. At last the admiral, in great trouble at losing so many men in such an extraordinary way, without knowing who were their assailants, nor how to defend himself, beat a retreat, and returned to his ship to hold a council.

The night being already far advanced, the princess and Fanfarinet took refuge in the thickest part of the wood. She was so tired that she lay down on the grass, and was just falling asleep when she heard a little soft voice whispering in her ear: " Run, Mayblossom, for Fanfarinet is going to kill and eat you ". Quickly opening her eyes, she saw by the light of the carbuncle the wicked Fanfarinet's arm raised ready to plunge his sword into her bosom. For seeing how plump and white she was, and being very hungry, he wished to kill and eat her. She did not hesitate long as to what she should do, but quietly drawing her dagger, which she had kept ever since the battle, she stabbed him so furiously in the eye that he died on the spot. "There, you ungrateful wretch," she cried, "take this last favour from my hands, the one you have best deserved! Be an example to all false lovers in time to come; and may your faithless soul never rest in peace!"

When the first heat of her anger was past, and she thought of her situation, she was nearly as lifeless as he whom she had just killed. "What will become of me?" she cried, weeping. "I am all alone in this island. Wild beasts will come and devour me, or I shall die of hunger." She was almost sorry she had not allowed Fanfarinet to eat her. All of a tremble she sat down, waiting and longing for the light, for she was afraid of ghosts, and especially of goblins. She was leaning against a tree, peering through the darkness, when she saw on one side a grand golden chariot, drawn by six great, tufted hens. The coachman was a cock, and the postillion a fat chicken. In the chariot there was a lady, so very, very beautiful, that she seemed like the sun. Her dress was all embroidered with gold spangles and silver bars. And another chariot she saw, to which six bats were harnessed. The coachman was a raven, and the postillion a black-beetle. And in this chariot was a hideous little monster, dressed in serpent-skin, and on her head for a top knot was a great toad. Never, never was anyone so astonished as the young princess. As she was looking at these wonders, she saw the chariots advance suddenly to meet each other, and the fair lady holding a golden lance, the hideous imp a rusty pike, they began a stern combat, which lasted more than a quarter of an hour.   At last the beautiful lady was victorious, and the ugly one flew away with her bats.   At that moment the beauty stepped down on the ground and addressed Mayblossom.

"Do not fear, dear princess," she said, "that I have come here for any other reason than to do you a service.   The combat I have had with Carabosse was all for love of you.   She wished to have authority to beat you because you came out of the tower four days before the twenty years.   But you saw how I took your part, and that I chased her away.   Enjoy the happiness therefore which I have gained for you."   The grateful princess fell down before her.   "Great Queen of the Fairies," she said, "your generosity delights me.   I do not know how to thank you, but I feel that there is not a drop of the blood which you have just saved which is not at your service."   The fairy kissed her three times, and made her still more beautiful than she had been before—if that were possible.   She ordered the cock to go to the king's ships, and to tell the admiral he might come without fear.   Then she sent the fat chicken to her palace, to fetch the most beautiful dresses in the world for Mayblossom.   The admiral hearing the cock's news, was so delighted that he nearly died of joy.   He hastened to the isle with his men, and even John Caquet seeing how everyone hurried as they landed from the ships, hurried too, like the others, bearing on his shoulder a spit loaded with game.   Hardly had Admiral Chapeau-Pointu gone a league when he saw on the high road the chariot and the hens, and the two ladies in it.   He recognised the princess, and went and flung himself at her feet, but she said that all the honour was due to the generous fairy, who had saved her from the clutches of Carabosse.   So he made her the prettiest speech that was ever spoken on a like occasion.   While he was talking, the fairy interrupted him, crying : "I swear I smell roast beef".   "Yes, madam," answered John Caquet, showing the spit laden with the fine birds.   "If your highness would but taste them ?"   "Very willingly," she said, "but less for my own sake than for the princess's, who is in much need of a good meal."   So they sent off at once to the ships for all that was necessary, and the joy of having found the princess again, added to the good cheer, left nothing to wish for.

The repast being over, and the fat chicken come back, the fairy dressed Mayblossom in a dress of green and gold brocade, sprinkled with rubies and pearls. She tied her fair hair with cords of diamonds and emeralds, and crowned her with flowers, and when she made her get into her chariot, all the stars that saw her passing thought it was the dawn that had not yet disappeared, and they greeted her in passing with : "All hail! Aurora".

After the fairy and the princess had bidden each other a tender farewell Mayblossom said : " And, madam, shall I not tell the queen, my mother, who has done me all this kindness ? " " Fair princess," she answered, " kiss her for me, and tell her I am the fifth fairy who brought you a gift at your birth." When the princess was in the vessel they fired all the guns, and sent off endless rockets. She reached port quite safely, and found the king and queen waiting for her ready to greet her with so much kindness that they gave her no time to ask them to forgive her foolish conduct in the past, though she meant to throw herself at their feet as soon as she had seen them. But the tenderness of her parents prevented her, and they put all the blame on old Carabosse.

Just at that moment the son of the great king arrived, anxious at not having received any news from his ambassador. He had a thousand horses, and thirty lackeys gaily dressed in red with fine gold braid, and he was a hundred times lovelier than the false Fanfarinet. They took care not to tell him the story of the princess's adventures, for that might have made him somewhat suspicious. They told him very gravely that his ambassador being thirsty, and going to draw water to drink, had fallen into the well and got drowned. He had no difficulty in believing this, and the marriage was celebrated amidst joy so great as to blot out entirely the remembrance of past sorrows.

PRINCESS ROSETTE.

ONCE upon a time there lived a king and a queen who had two fine boys. They grew like the day, and were hungry and healthy. The queen never had any children born to her without sending for the fairies to ask what would be their future lot. So at the birth of her next child, a pretty little girl—so pretty that you could not look on her without loving her—the queen entertained in a very hospitable fashion all the fairies who came to see her on the occasion. As they were going away, she said to them: " Do not forget that good custom of yours; and tell me what will happen to Rosette ". (Rosette was the little princess's name.) The fairies said they had left their fortune-books at home, and that they would come back again to see her. " Ah ! " said the queen, " that bodes nothing good. You do not want to distress me by foretelling evil, but let me know all, I beg of you, and hide nothing from me." They excused themselves in all kinds of ways, but this only made the queen more anxious to know what was in their minds. At last, the chief fairy said: " Madam, we fear that Rosette may be a source of great misfortune to her brothers, and that they may die on her account. That is all we can find out about the fate of this pretty little girl, and we are very sorry not to be able to tell you anything more cheerful." They went away, and the queen was so very, very downcast that the king saw it from her face. He asked her what was the matter, and she told him she had gone too near the fire and had burnt all the flax on her distaff. " Is that all ? " said the king. And he went up to the garret and brought her more flax than she could spin in a hundred years.

But still the queen was sad, and he asked her again what was the matter. She told him that when she was standing on the edge of the river, she had let her green satin slipper fall in. " Is that all ? " said the king. And he sent for all the shoemakers in his kingdom, and bought her ten thousand green satin slippers.

But still the queen was sad, and again he asked her what was the matter. She told him that while eating very heartily, she had swallowed the wedding-ring on her finger. The king knew she was not telling the truth, for he had put the ring away carefully; so he said to her: " My dear wife, you are not speaking the truth. Here is your ring, which I put away in my purse." Now she was caught in the very act of telling a lie, and there is nothing in the world uglier. She saw that the king was offended, so she told him what the fairies had predicted about little Rosette, and asked him, if he knew any good remedy, to tell her of it. The king was very down-hearted; so much so, that at last he said to the queen : " I know no other way of saving our two sons but of killing the little girl before she is out of her swaddling clothes ". But the queen cried out that she would rather die herself than consent to such a cruel deed, and that he must think of some other means.

During this time, when they could think of nothing else, the queen learnt that in a large wood near the town there lived an old hermit, who was consulted by persons far and near. " I must go to him also," she said. " The fairies told me the evil, but they forgot to tell me the cure." So early one morning she set out on a pretty little white mule shod with gold, two of her maids accompanying her, each on a beautiful horse. When they came near the wood the queen and her maidens dismounted out of respect, and took their way to the tree where the hermit dwelt. He did not much care for visits from women folks, but when he saw that it was the queen, he said: " Welcome ! What can I do for you ? " Then telling him what the fairies had said of Rosette, she asked his advice ; and he told her she must shut the princess up in a tower, and never let her out. The queen thanked him, made him a handsome present, and came back to tell the king everything.

When the king heard the news he had a great tower built without delay, and there he locked up his daughter. So that she might not be lonely, the king, the queen, and her two brothers went to see her every day. The elder brother was called the big prince, and the younger the little prince. They loved their sister passionately, for she was the prettiest and the most graceful little girl that ever was seen, and a glance from her eye was better to them than a hundred pistoles. When she was fifteen years old, the big prince said to the king : " Father, my sister is old enough now to be married. Shall we not soon dance at her wedding ? " And the little prince said the same thing to the queen ; and their majesties joked with them, but gave them no answer about the marriage. At last the king and queen fell very ill, and died almost on the same day. Everybody mourned very deeply, and put on black clothes, and all the death-bells were rung. Rosette was inconsolable for the death of her good mother. When the funeral of the king and queen was over, the marquises and the dukes of the kingdom led the elder prince to a throne made of gold and diamonds, and seated him on it. He had a beautiful crown on his head, and his garments were of violet velvet, covered with suns and moons. Then all the court shouted thrice: " Long live the king!" And there was nothing heard but sounds of joy.

The king and his brother in the meanwhile said to each other: " Now that we are masters, we must release our sister from the tower, where for long she has been pining ". They had only to cross the garden to reach the tower, which was built in a corner, as high as the builders could make it, for the late king and queen had wished her to stay there always. Rosette, who was embroidering a beautiful gown on a frame in front of her, rose on seeing her brothers, and taking the king's hand she said: " Good-day, your majesty; you are now king, and I ·m your little servant. I beg that you wil release me from the tower, where I a . so very lonely "; and with that she began to cry. The king kissed her, and told her not to cry: for he had come to take her away to a beautiful castle. The prince had his pockets full of sugar-plums, and these he gave to Rosette. " Come along," he said, " let us get out of this hideous tower. The king will soon have you married, so don't distress yourself."

When Rosette saw the beautiful garden full of flowers, and fruit, and fountains, she was so astonished that she could not say a word; for till this day she had seen nothing. She looked all round on every side, walked on for a little way, then stopped to pick fruit from the trees, or flowers from the flower-beds. Her little one-eared dog, Fretillon, as green as a parrot, and an exquisite dancer, ran before her, saying yap, yap, yap, and jumping and capering madly. Fretillon amused the company very much. Suddenly he set off at a run into a little wood. The princess followed him, and great was her astonishment when she saw a huge peacock spreading out its tail; it seemed to her so very, very beautiful that she could not take her eyes off it. The king and the prince coming up wished to know what was amusing her. She pointed to the peacock, and asked what it was. They told her it was a bird which sometimes was eaten. " What!" she said. " Do they dare to kill such a beautiful bird and eat it? I declare that I shall never marry anyone but the King of the Peacocks, and when I am their queen I shall let nobody eat them." The astonishment of the king is not to be told. " But, my sister," he said, " where think you we shall find this King of the Peacocks?" " Wherever you like, your majesty; but I will marry none but him."

After this decision, the two brothers took her to their castle, where the peacock had to be brought, and kept in her room, so fond was she of it. All the court ladies who had not yet seen Rosette hastened to salute her, and to pay their respects to her, some bringing her preserves, some sugar, others dresses trimmed with gold, others beautiful ribbons, dolls, embroidered shoes, pearls, and diamonds. Everywhere they did honour to her ; and she was so well-bred, so polite, kissing their hands, and bowing when anything pretty was given her, that there was not a gentleman or a lady of the court who did not go away satisfied.

While she was in this good company the king and the prince were thinking over what means they would take to find the King of the Peacocks, if there was such a person in the world. They thought it would be necessary to have a por-trait of Princess Rosette painted, so they had this done. It was so like, that only speech was lacking. Then they said to her : " Since you will marry none but the King of the Peacocks, we are going away together to seek him for you through the whole world. If we find him we shall be very glad. Take care of our kingdom till we return."

Rosette thanked them for the trouble they were taking for her, and promised to govern their kingdom well. While they were away, she said, her whole amusement would be in looking at the beautiful peacock, and in making Fretillon dance. They could not help weeping when they said good-bye.

So the two princes set off, asking everyone they met on their way if they did not know the King of the Peacocks. But everyone said : " No, we do not know him ". They passed on and went still further, and such a long, long way did they travel that they reached where no one had ever been before. They came at last to the kingdom of the Mayflies. Never were so many seen before, and they made such a loud buzzing that the king was afraid lest he should become deaf. He asked the one that appeared the most sensible if he knew where he could find the King of the Peacocks. " Sire," said the Mayfly, " his kingdom is thirty thousand leagues from here. You have taken the longest way to reach it." " And how do you know that ? " said the king. " Because," replied the Mayfly, " we know you very well, and every year we spend two or three months in your gardens." Then the king and his brother saluted the Mayfly in the most affectionate manner, and struck up a great friendship with him. They dined together, and went to look with the greatest admiration at all the curiosities of that country, where the tiniest leaf of a tree is worth a pistole. After that they went on their journey again, and as they now knew the way they were not long before they arrived. All the trees they saw laden with peacocks, and the whole place was so full of them that you could hear their cries and chattering two leagues off.

The king said to his brother: " If the King of the Peacocks is himself a pea-cock, how can our sister ever marry him ? We should be mad if we gave our consent. Think what a fine connection she would give us. Why, we should have little peacocks for nephews!" And the prince was no less troubled. "Yes," he said ; " it is indeed a most unfortunate idea that she has taken into her head. I can't think how she has thought of the existence even of a peacock king."

When they reached the great town they saw it was full of men and women, but their clothes were made of peacocks' feathers, and these were everywhere about as if much prized for their beauty. They met the king driving in a pretty little coach of gold and diamonds, drawn by twelve peacocks at full gallop. The king was so very beautiful that the stranger king and the prince were charmed. He had long, flaxen, curly hair, a fair complexion, and a peacock's tail for a crown. When he saw them he thought, since their dress was different from that of the people of the country, they must be foreigners, and to find out he stopped his coach and called them towards him.

The king and the prince came forward. Having made a low bow, they said: " Your majesty, we come from a long distance to show you a beautiful portrait," and they drew from their valise the large picture of Rosette. When the King of the Peacocks had looked well at it, he said : " I cannot believe that there is so beautiful a maiden in the whole world". " She is a hundred times more beautiful than that," said the king. " Ah," said the Peacock King ; " you are laughing at me." " Sire," said the prince, "this is my brother, a king like yourself. That is his title, and I am called the prince. Our sister, whose portrait you see, is the Princess Rosette. We come to ask you if you will marry her. She is beautiful and very good, and we shall give her a bushel of golden crowns." " Ah, but with all my heart!" said the king. " With me she shall lack for nothing. I will love her dearly. But I assure you I demand that she be as beautiful as her portrait, and if she fails in the slightest degree in her re-semblance to it, I shall put you to death." " Very well, we agree," said Rosette's two brothers. " You agree?" said the king. " Then go to prison and stay there till the princess arrives." The princes made no objection, for they were very certain that Rosette was more beautiful than her portrait.

While they were in prison, the king had everything possible done for their comfort, and he went himself to see them very often. In his castle he kept Rosette's portrait, with which he was so infatuated that he never slept day or night. As soon as the king and his brother were in prison, they sent word by post to the princess to pack up quickly, and to come without delay, for at last the Peacock King was waiting for her. But they said nothing about their being prisoners, for fear she should be too anxious. When she received this letter she was so overwhelmed with joy that she was like to die. She told everybody that the Peacock King was found and wanted to marry her. They lit bonfires, and fired cannon, and ate sweetmeats and sugar-plums to their hearts' content, and all those who came to see the princess for three days had bread and jam, and wafers, and hippocras given them. After having dispensed these bounties she left her beautiful dolls to her good friends, and gave her brother's kingdom into the keeping of the wisest old men of the town, charging them to take good care of everything, to spend little, and to save up money against the return of the king. She left her peacock behind in her friends' keeping, only taking with her her nurse and her foster-sister, and her little green dog Fretillon. Then she set out in a boat on the sea, taking with her the bushel of golden crowns, and dresses to last her for ten years even were she to change them twice a-day. She and her companions did nothing but laugh and sing. The nurse asked the boatman : " Are we near, are we anywhere near the kingdom of the peacocks ? " He answered : " No". And again this time she asked : " And now, are we near it, anywhere near it ? " And he answered : " Soon, we shall soon be there". Still another time she said : "Are we near, are we anywhere near it ? " " Yes, yes, we are," he answered. And when he had said that she went to the end of the boat, sat down beside him, and said : " If you wish it, you can be rich for ever". "Very well," he answered. " If you like, you can earn good money." "I have no objections," he said. " Well, then, this night while the princess is asleep you must help me to throw her into the water. After she is drowned I shall dress my daughter up in her fine clothes, and we shall take her to the Peacock King, who will be very glad to marry her. For your reward we shall give you as many diamonds as you like." The boatman was much astonished at the nurse's proposal. He said it was a pity to drown so beautiful a princess, and that he was sorry for her. But she took a bottle of wine and made him drink so much that he was not in a condition to refuse her.

Night having come, the princess went to bed as usual, her little Fretillon snugly rolled up at her feet. Rosette was fast asleep when the wicked nurse, who was very wide awake, went to fetch the boatman. She took him to the princess's room, and then without awaking her, they took her, feather-bed, mattress, sheets, coverlet, and all, her foster-sister helping them in every way, and threw her with all these into the sea. And the princess slept so soundly that she did not awake. But most fortunately her bed was made of phœnixs' feathers, which are very rare, and which have this property, that they never go to the bottom of the water. So that she floated about in her bed, as if she had been in a boat. The water, however gradually wet first her feather-bed and then her mattress, through, and Rosette, beginning to feel the discomfort of this, was turning from one side to the other when Fretillon woke up. His scent was keen, and he smelt the soles and the cod-fish so near that he began to bark loud enough to wake up the other fishes. They began to swim about, the big ones pushing against the princess's bed, which being unattached, turned round and round and round about. Oh, how astonished she was! "Is our boat dancing on the water?" she said. "I am not used to being so uncomfortable as I am to-night." And Fretillon went on barking, barking, in the most desperate fashion. Meanwhile the wicked nurse and the boatman, who were listening from far off, said: "There is that funny little dog and his mistress drinking our healths. Make haste to reach the shore." For they were now opposite the town of the Peacock King.

He had sent to the sea coast a hundred carriages, drawn by all sorts of strange animals—lions, bears, deer, wolves, horses, oxen, asses, eagles, and peacocks, and to the carriage for the Princess Rosette were harnessed six blue monkeys that could jump, and dance on tight ropes, and do all sorts of funny tricks. They had beautiful harness of crimson velvet with golden mountings. Sixty young damsels appeared, chosen by the king to amuse Rosette. They were dressed in all kinds of colours, and lavishly adorned with gold and silver.

The nurse had taken great care to dress her daughter gaily, putting Rosette's diamonds on her head and all over her, and giving her her prettiest gown. But, with all her ornaments, she was uglier than an ape. Her hair was of a greasy black, her eyes squinting, her legs twisted, and she had a great hump in the middle of her back. Besides, she was ill-tempered and sulky, and always grumbling.

When the Peacock King's people saw her come out of the boat, they were so very much surprised that they could not say a word. "What is the matter?" she said. "Are you asleep? Quick, make haste, bring me something to eat! You rascals, I shall have you all hung!" When they heard this they said: "What a hideous creature! And she is as wicked as she is ugly! This is a fine marriage our king is making! Well, we are not astonished! But it was hardly worth while to bring her from the other end of the world." Meanwhile she was carrying things with a high hand, and for no reason at all she was boxing people's ears and hitting them with her fist. As her procession was very long, she went slowly, sitting up proudly like a queen in her carriage. All the pea-cocks perched themselves on the trees to salute her as she passed, meaning to shout "Long live the fair Queen Rosette!" but when they saw her looking so hideous, they called out: "Fie, fie! how ugly she is!" She was mad with rage, and screamed to her guards: "Kill those rascally peacocks that are shouting insults at me". The peacocks flew away fast enough, laughing at her. The wicked boatman, who saw what was going on, said to the nurse under his breath : " Mother, we don't seem to be getting on very well. It is a pity your daughter is not prettier." But she whispered : " Hold your tongue, you fool, else you will spoil everything ".

The king was told by this time that the princess was coming. " Well, now," said he, " did her brothers tell the truth ? Is she more beautiful than her portrait ? " " She will do very well, your majesty," said those to whom he spoke, " if she is as beautiful." " Oh, yes," said the king ; " I shall be satisfied. Let us now go and see her," for he heard by the great noise they were making in the court-yard that she had arrived. The only words he could distinguish out of all they were saying were : " Yes, how ugly she is ! " He thought they must be speaking of some dwarf or of some beast she had perhaps brought with her, for it did not even enter his mind that it could really be herself.

Rosette's portrait, uncovered, was carried at the end of a long pole, and the king walked gravely behind, with all his barons and all his peacocks, and then all the ambassadors from the neighbouring kingdoms. The king was full of impatience to see his dear Rosette. Oh ! when he did see her—he all but died on the spot. He flew into the greatest passion, tore his clothes, and refused to go near her, for she terrified him.

" What ! " he said. " Those two villains I have in my prison have been bold enough to laugh at me, and to propose a monkey like that for my wife ? They shall die ! Go, let them without a moment's delay shut up that insolent woman, her nurse, and the man who brought them here, and cast them into the dungeon of my great tower."

Meanwhile the king and his brother, who were prisoners, and who knew that their sister was about to arrive, had put on their best clothes to meet her. But instead of coming to open the prison and setting them free as they had hoped, the gaoler came with the soldiers and took them down to a cellar which was quite dark and full of hideous beasts, and where they stood in water up to their necks. No one could have been more astonished or distressed than were they. " Alas ! " they said to each other; " this is a sad wedding for us. What can have brought so great a misfortune on us ? " They did not know what in the world to think, except that the king meant to put them to death, and right sorrowful they were.

Three days passed and they had no explanation given them. At the end of that time the Peacock King came to the prison and said the most insulting things to them through a hole. " You have taken the title of king and prince to catch me and to persuade me to marry your sister. But you are rascals, both of you, not worth the water you drink. I shall bring you before the judges, who will settle your case fast enough, and already the rope to hang you with is being made." "King of the Peacocks," answered the other king, angrily, "do not be so hasty in this matter, or you may repent of it. I am as much a king as you. I have a great kingdom. I am rich in suits and crowns, and have broad gold pieces in plenty. Surely you must be joking to talk of hanging us. Have we stolen anything from you?"

When the king heard him speak so boldly he did not know what to think, and he had half a mind to let them go with their sister without putting them to death, but his chief friend, who was a mere flatterer, encouraged him, telling him that if he did not revenge himself everybody would laugh at him, and would take him for a miserable little king not worth a cent. So he swore he would not pardon them, and he ordered them to be tried. The trial did not last long, for to look at the portrait of the Princess Rosette beside the pretender that had come in her place was quite enough. So they were condemned to be beheaded, as liars who had promised the king a beautiful princess, and had given him instead an ugly peasant girl. Then the judge went to the prison with much ceremony to declare the sentence. The prisoners said they had not lied, that their sister was indeed a princess, that she was fairer than the day, and that there was something behind all this that they did not understand, and that if but seven days' grace were given them before being put to death, perchance in that time their innocence would be recognised. It was hard to persuade the King of the Peacocks, who was very angry, to grant them this grace, but at last he consented.

While all these things were passing at the court, we must tell something about poor Princess Rosette. As soon as it was day she was much astonished, and so was Fretillon, at seeing herself in the middle of the sea, with no boat and utterly helpless. Then she began to cry and cry till all the fish were sorry for her. She did not know what to do, nor what would become of her. "Surely," said she, "I have been thrown into the sea by order of the Peacock King. He has repented of marrying me, and to get rid of me without disgrace to himself, he has had me drowned. What a strange man!" she went on. "I should so have loved him, and we should have been the happiest of couples." Thereupon she wept very bitterly, for she could not help loving him. Two days she remained in this condition, floating from one end of the sea to the other, wet to her very bones, chilled to death, and almost benumbed. If it had not been for little Fretillon, who warmed her heart a little, she would have died a hundred times. She was famished with hunger, and seeing oysters, she took as many as she wanted and ate them. Fretillon did not much like them, but he had nothing else to eat. When night came on a great fear took possession of Rosette, and she said to her dog: "Fretillon, keep on barking, for fear the soles eat us up".

He had barked the whole night long, and the princess's bed was not far from the sea-shore. Near them there was a good old man, who lived quite alone in a little hut where nobody ever went. He was very poor, and had no longings for the goods of this world. When he heard Fretillon barking, he was very much astonished, for it was very rarely that dogs passed by there. He thought some travellers must have lost their way, and he went out with the kind intention of putting them on their road again. All at once he saw the princess and Fretillon floating in the sea. The princess at sight of him held out her arms, crying: "Good old man, save me, for I shall perish here. For two days I have been in this condition." When he heard her speaking in this sad voice, he felt great pity for her, and returned to his hut again to fetch a large hook. The water reached to his neck as he went in, and two or three times he thought he should be drowned. At last with tremendous efforts he brought the bed to the shore. Rosette and Fretillon were very glad to be on dry land again, and thanked the good man with much gratitude. Then she took the coverlet in which she was wrapped, and barefooted she entered the hut, where he lit her a little fire of dry straw, and took out of his trunk his late wife's best dress and shoes and stockings, which the princess put on. Clad thus like a peasant, she looked as beautiful as the day, and Fretillon danced round her to amuse her.

The old man saw well enough that Rosette was some great lady, for the covers of her bed were all of gold and silver, and her mattress was of satin. He begged her to tell him her story, promising not to repeat a word if she did not wish him to. She told him everything from one end to the other, weeping very bitterly, for she still believed that it was the King of the Peacocks that had ordered her to be drowned. "How shall we manage, my daughter?" said the old man. "You are such a great princess and used to eating only dainty morsels,

and I have only black bread and radishes. It will be but poor cheer for you. If you will but let me, I shall go and tell the Peacock King that you are here; for of a surety, had he seen you, he would marry you." "Ah, he is a wicked man; he would kill me. But if you have a little basket fasten it round my dog's neck, and he will not have his usual luck if he does not bring us back something to eat." The old man gave the princess a basket, which she tied round Fretillon's neck, saying: "Run off to the place where the best dinner in the whole town is being cooked and bring it back to me". Fretillon ran to the town; and as there was no better pot than the king's, he went into the royal kitchen, found the pot, took very cunningly all that was in it, and returned home. Then Rosette said to him: "Run back again to the larder and take the best of everything there". Fretillon flew back to the larder, carried off white bread, muscatel wine, all kinds of fruits and preserves, and he was so laden that he was quite exhausted.

When the Peacock King wished to dine, there was nothing in his pot nor in his larder. Each one of his servants looked at the other, and the king was in a terrible rage. "Well," said he, "I cannot dine, but this evening let the spit be put on the fire so that I may have good roast meat." The evening being come, the princess said to Fretillon: "Run off to the town, go to the best kitchen, and bring me some good roast meat". Fretillon did as his mistress bade him, and knowing of no better kitchen than the king's, he went in very quietly, while the cooks' backs were turned, and took the whole roast on the spit. It looked delicious, and the very sight of it would have made you hungry. He brought back his basketful to the princess, who sent him back again to the larder to bring all kinds of sweets and sugar-plums. The king, who had no dinner, wished to sup early, but there was nothing for him. He flew into a fearful rage, and went to bed without supper. Next day at dinner and supper the same thing happened, so that the king was three days without eating or drinking; for whenever he sat down to table, it was found that everything had been stolen. His confidant, in great trouble, and fearing the king would die, hid himself in a little corner of the kitchen, and kept his eyes on the boiling pot. How astonished he was to see a little green dog, with but one ear, creep in softly, lift the lid of the pot, and put the meat in its basket. Following it to know where it would go, he saw it run outside the town, and following it still farther, he found himself at the good old man's house. Without delay he went and told the king that it was to a poor peasant's hut that his boil and roast went every evening and morning.

The king was much astonished, and ordered them to go and make inquiries. The confidant, anxious for the king's favour, went himself, taking a guard of archers with him. They found the peasant dining with the princess and eating the king's boiled beef. They were both seized and bound with stout cords, and Fretillon was captured as well. When they had arrived at the palace the king was told. "To-morrow," said he, "is the last of the seven days I gave the wicked men to live. They shall die with those who stole my dinner." Then he strode into the justice chamber. The old man fell on his knees saying he would explain everything. But while he was speaking the king looked on the beautiful princess, and was sorry to see her weep. Then when the good man had declared that she was called Rosette, and that they had thrown her into the sea, in spite of his weakness from his long fast the king gave three leaps for joy, embraced her, and untied the cords with which she was bound, telling her he loved her with all his heart. At once the princes were fetched, but they, thinking it was to take them to their deaths, came out very sad and hanging their heads. The nurse and her daughter were brought too. When they were face to face they all knew each other. Rosette fell on her brothers' necks ; the nurse and her daughter and the boatman fell on their knees, and asked for pardon. The joy was so great that the king and the princess forgave the evil-doers ; and the good old man received a large reward, and stayed for the rest of his life in the palace.

In the end, the Peacock King made every possible amends to the other king and his brother, to show his grief for having treated them so badly ; and the nurse gave Rosette back her fine dresses and her bushel of golden crowns. The wedding-feast lasted for fifteen days. Everyone was full of joy ; even Fretillon had his share, for he ate nothing but partridge wings for the rest of his life.

THE GOLDEN BRANCH.

THERE was once a king whose temper was so austere and morose that all who knew him feared rather than loved him. Very rarely did he show himself; and on the slightest suspicion he would put his subjects to death. And because he was always frowning they called him King Sombre. Now King Sombre had a son who was not in the least like him. There was no other prince in the world so clever, or so gentle, or so generous, or of such various talents. But his legs were crooked; he had a hump higher than his head; his eyes squinted, and his mouth was awry. In short, he was a little monstrosity, and never was so fair a soul the light of so hideous a body. Yet by some strange chance he made himself beloved by all whom he cared to please; and in intelligence he was so much superior to anyone else that no one could hear him talk without being interested. The queen, his mother, wished to call him Torticoli, either because she liked the name, or because, on account of his crookedness, she thought she had hit on the aptest name possible. King Sombre, who thought more of his own greatness than the happiness of his son, cast his eyes on the daughter of a powerful king, one of his neighbours, whose states, if added to his own, would make him formidable throughout the earth. He thought this princess a most fitting match for Prince Torticoli, inasmuch as she would never be able to reproach him for deformity and ugliness, being herself at least as ugly and deformed as he was. She used always to go about in a kind of bowl, for her legs were broken. Her name was Trognon. For all her defects she was the most lovable creature in the world, and it seemed as if heaven had wished to give her compensation for the wrong that nature had done her.

King Sombre asked for and obtained the picture of the Princess Trognon, and placed it in a great hall under a canopy. Then he sent for Prince Torticoli, and commanded him to look on the portrait with favour, since it was Trognon's, and she was to be his wife. Torticoli glanced at it, and then turned away his eyes with a scornful air that displeased his father. "Are you not satisfied?" he asked, in a bitter, angry tone. "No, sire," he answered. "I should never be satisfied to marry a crippled deformity like her." "It is indeed most fitting for you to point out the faults in this princess," said King Sombre, "a hideous little monster like you, whose very look frightens people." "That is the very reason," said the prince, "why I do not wish to wed with just such another monster. It is enough to have to endure the sight of myself. What would it be were there a whole tribe of us?" "You are afraid lest the race of monsters be perpetuated?" said the king, in an angry tone. "Well, your fears are of no avail, for you shall marry her. It is enough that I command. It is your part to obey." Torticoli answered nothing, but with a deep bow he left the hall.

King Sombre was not accustomed to the slightest resistance to his wishes, and his son's put him into a fearful temper. So he shut him up in a tower built expressly for rebel princes. But there had been none there for two hundred years, so everything about it was in very bad repair, and all the rooms and the furniture seemed to be very old. The prince, who was very fond of reading, asked for books, so they let him take some from the library in the tower. At first he thought that this permission was all that was necessary, but when he tried to read them he found they were in a tongue so ancient that he did not understand a word of it. He put them aside, but afterwards he took them up again, trying to make out something of their contents, or at least to amuse himself. King Sombre, feeling sure that Torticoli would get tired of prison, acted as if the prince had given his consent to marry Trognon, and sent ambassadors to the neighbouring king asking for the hand of his daughter, to whom he promised perfect happiness. Trognon's father was delighted to find such a good chance of marrying her, for it was not everybody who would be willing to take on himself the care of the deformed creature. So he accepted King Sombre's proposal, though, to tell the truth, the portrait of Torticoli, which they had brought, did not strike him as very attractive. It also was placed in a magnificent gallery, and Trognon was sent for. As soon as she saw it she lowered her eyes and began to cry. Her father, very angry at the evident dislike she showed, took a mirror, and placing it in front of her, said: "You weep, my daughter? Well, look at yourself, and be convinced after that that you have nothing to weep for." "If I were in any hurry to get married, sire," she answered, "I should perhaps be to blame for my fastidiousness; but I would rather bear my troubles all alone.

I do not wish to share with anyone the misery of looking on my face. Let me remain my whole life long unhappy Princess Trognon. I shall be content—at least I shall make no complaint." No matter how reasonable were her words, the king would not listen to them, and she had to go with the ambassadors who had come for her.

While she is travelling in a litter, like the poor deformed stump she is, let us go back to the tower and see what the prince is doing. None of his keepers dared speak to him, for they had been told to weary him out, to give him bad food, and to exhaust his patience by every kind of cruel treatment. And King Sombre knew how to make people obey him—if not from love, then from fear. But the guards' affection for the prince was very great, and they found means to ease some part of his sufferings. One day when he was walking in a large gallery, thinking sadly of the unhappy lot which had made him so ugly, so unsightly, and which had thrown in his way a princess still more so, he cast his eyes on the windows, which were painted in very bright colours and fine designs. Having a great love for such works of art, he set about examining this one. But he could not understand the subject, for it dealt with things gone by ages since. But one figure particularly struck him—a man so like himself that it might have been his own portrait. This man was in the donjon of the keep searching for something in the wall. There he found a golden screw, with which he opened a cabinet. There were many other things too which struck his imagination, and on nearly all the windows he saw his own portrait. " By what strange chance," he said, " do I play a part in these scenes, seeing I was not born when they took place? And what put it into the painter's head to paint a man like me?" Then he saw on the windows a beautiful lady, with a face so full of intelligence that he could not take his eyes off her. There were, besides, endless different figures, and they were all so full of expression that he really thought that what was only represented by a mixture of colours was actually taking place under his own eyes. He did not leave the gallery till it was no longer light enough to distinguish the pictures. When he went back to his room he took up an old manuscript, the first that came to his hand. The leaves were of vellum, with illuminated borders, and the cover of gold, enamelled with blue and covered with ciphers. He was very much astonished to see in the book the same things that were on the windows of the gallery. He tried to read what was written, but found he could not. All at once he saw on one of the pages a picture of musicians singing, in another games of basset and tric-trac, cards being dealt and dice thrown. Turning over the vellum, there he saw an assembly where they were dancing, all the ladies grandly dressed and wonderfully beautiful. Turning over once more, he smelt the odour of a delicious repast, and there he saw little figures eating, the biggest not a quarter-inch high. One of them, turning towards the prince, said : " To your good health, Torticoli. Try to give us back our queen. If you do so, it will be well with you ; if not, evil will befall you." At these words the prince was seized with terrible fear ; and he trembled so much that at length he let the book fall on one side while he himself fell to the other like a dead man. At the noise of his fall his guards came running. They loved him dearly, and they took every possible means of restoring him to consciousness. When he had recovered enough to speak, they asked him what was the matter. He told them they fed him so insufficiently that he had no strength, and that, having his head full of imaginings, he seemed to see and hear such astonishing things in this book that he had been seized with terror. His guards, in great distress, gave him food in spite of all King Sombre's orders to the contrary. When he had eaten, he took the book, and opening it again in their presence, he found nothing of what he had seen before, which convinced him that he had been mistaken.

Next day he returned to the gallery. Again he saw the paintings on the windows, and the personages in them moved about, walked along paths, hunted stags and hares, fished, built little houses—for all the pictures were very small. And everywhere he saw his own portrait in a dress exactly like his own. The figure was going up to the donjon of the tower to find the golden screw. He thought to himself that as he had eaten well he could no longer suppose that all he saw was a mere vision. " This is too mysterious," he said, " for me to neglect any possible means of knowing more. Perhaps I shall learn something in the donjon." So he went up, and knocking against the wall, one spot seemed to him to give back a hollow sound. Taking a hammer he knocked the plaster down off this part, and found there a golden screw, very finely made. Still ignorant what use to put it to, he saw in a corner of the donjon an old cupboard

of rotten wood. He tried to open it, but he could find no lock. No matter on what side he turned it, it was quite useless. At last he saw a little hole, and having an idea that the screw would be useful here, he put it in. Then pulling energetically he opened the cupboard. But if it was old and ugly outside, it made up for it by its wonderful beauty inside. All the drawers were of cut rock crystal, or amber, or precious stones. When he had drawn out one, he found other smaller ones at the side, above, beneath, and at the back, divided from each other by mother-of-pearl partitions. Pulling out the mother-of-pearl, and then the drawers, he found each one filled with the most beautiful weapons in the world, splendid crowns and wonderful portraits. Prince Torticoli was delighted, and went on pulling out more and more without stopping. At last he found a little key made of a single emerald with which he opened a little door at the back. He was dazzled by a brilliant carbuncle out of which a large box had been made. He drew out the box hastily, but what was his horror to find it full of blood, and a hand lying in it cut off at the wrist and holding a miniature case. At sight of this Torticoli shuddered, his hair stood on end, and his unsteady legs could hardly support him. Sitting down on the ground with the box still in his hand, but with his eyes turned away from so horrible an object, he had a great desire to put it back in the place from where he had taken it. He thought to himself that in all that had taken place up till now there had been something very mysterious. He remembered what the little figure in the book had said to him, that according to his conduct, evil or good would befall him, and he feared the future no less than the present. Reproaching himself after a time for a cowardice unworthy of a great soul, he made a strong effort, and fixing his eyes on the hand, he said : " O unfortunate hand ! Can you not tell me your sad story by some signs? If I am able to serve you, you may rest assured of the generosity of my heart." At these words the hand appeared to be agitated, and moving its fingers, it made signs the sense of which he understood as well as if it had been spoken in articulate words. " You must know," the hand said, " that you can be of the utmost use to him from whom cruel jealousy has separated me. In this portrait you see that beautiful lover for whom I sorrow. Go now at once into the gallery. Watch where the sun's rays strike most keenly. Look there and you will find my treasure." Then the hand stopped moving, and to the various questions the prince asked, it answered nothing. " Where shall I put you ? " he asked. It made some signs which the prince understood to mean that it must be put back in the cupboard. This was done, everything was locked up again, the screw hidden in the same wall he had taken it from, and somewhat more at ease among all these wonders, he went down to the gallery. When he entered, the windows began to rattle and shake in an extraordinary fashion. Looking where the sunbeams were striking, he saw it was on the portrait of a young man, so handsome and with so distinguished an air that it was pleasant to look on him. Raising this picture, he found an ebony panel with gilt mouldings as in the rest of the gallery. He did not know how to take out the panel or even whether he should take it out at all. Looking at the windows, he found that the wainscot could slide up, and raising it at once, he found himself in a vestibule made of porphyry, and decorated with statues. He mounted a wide staircase made of agate, the balustrade of which was of worked gold, and entered a salon made of lapis lazuli. Then walking through endless apartments, where the excellence of the pictures and the richness of the furniture delighted him, he reached at last a little room where all the ornaments were of turquoise. There on a bed of blue gauze and gold he saw a lady who seemed to be asleep. Her beauty was marvellous. Her hair blacker than ebony showed off the whiteness of her skin. She seemed to be restless in her sleep ; her face had a wearied look as if she were ill. The prince fearing to awake her, stepped forward softly. She was speaking, and listening eagerly to what she said, he heard these few words, broken by sighs : " Do you think, traitor, that I can love you, after you have taken my dear Trasimene away from me ? What! before my very eyes you dared to separate that dear hand from that mighty arm ? Is it thus you think to prove to me your respect and your love ? Ah, Trasimene, dear lover, shall I never see you any more ? " The prince noticed that her tears sought a passage between her closed eyelids, moistening her cheeks like the morning dew.

He stayed at the foot of her bed without moving, not knowing whether he ought to awake her or leave her longer in a sleep in which she seemed so unhappy. He had gathered that Trasimene was her lover, and that it was his hand he had found in the donjon. A thousand conflicting thoughts were rushing through his mind, when he heard the sound of sweet music, the mingled song of nightingales and canaries, blending so exquisitely as to surpass the most charming human voices. At that moment an eagle of an extraordinary size came in, flying slowly through the air, and holding in its claws a golden branch laden with rubies in the shape of cherries. It looked fixedly at the sleeping beauty, and seemed to see in her its sun, and spreading out its great wings hovered before her, now rising, now falling again to her feet. After some minutes it turned towards the prince, and coming forward placed in his hand the golden branch with the cherries. Then the singing birds sent out such melody as pierced the vaults of the palace. The prince was so watchful of everything that took place that he felt sure the lady was enchanted, and that the honour of some glorious adventure was reserved for him. Going up to her he knelt down, and touching her with the branch he said : " Fair and charming lady, who sleep by some power unknown

to me, I conjure you to wake up again to life and action ".   The lady, opening
her eyes and seeing the eagle, cried : " Stay, dear lover, stay " ; but the royal

bird uttered a sharp and painful cry, and flew away with his little feathered
songsters.   The lady then turning to Torticoli, said : " It is my heart rather

than my gratitude that now speaks ; I know that I owe you everything, and that you are bringing me back to the light I have not seen for two hundred years. The enchanter who loved me, and who brought so many misfortunes on me, has reserved this great adventure for you. It is in my power to serve you, and I have the greatest desire to do so. Tell me what are your desires and I shall employ the fairy art, which is mine in the highest degree, to make you happy." "Madam," answered the prince, "if your knowledge enables you to divine the feelings of the heart, you must know that in spite of the misfortunes that have been heaped on me, I am less to be pitied than another might be." "That is because you have resources in your mind," said the fairy, "but in any case do not force on me the shame of ingratitude. What do you wish for ? I can do everything, so ask." "I desire," said Torticoli, "that the handsome Trasimene, for whom you sigh, shall be restored to you." "You are too generous," she answered, "to prefer my interests to your own. This great affair will be achieved by someone else —a lady. I will say no more at present. Only be certain that she will not be indifferent to you. But do not any longer refuse me the pleasure of being of use to you. What are your wishes ? " "Madam," said the prince, throwing himself at her feet, "you see my hideous face. I am called Torticoli, in mockery. Make me less ridiculous." "Go, my prince," said the fairy, touching him three times with the golden branch, "go ; you will be so accomplished, so perfect, that never man in times past or time to come will be your equal. Call yourself hence-forth Peerless, for that name will be yours with just right." The prince, in grati-tude, embraced her knees, and by a silence which expressed his joy, left her to guess what was passing in his mind. She made him get up, and when he looked at himself in the mirrors that adorned the room, Peerless no longer recognised Torticoli. He was three feet taller. His hair fell in thick curls on his shoulders. He looked all dignity and grace. His features were regular ; his eyes full of in-telligence. In short, his person was a piece of workmanship worthy of a kind and tender-hearted fairy. "Why may I not reveal to you your destiny, tell you of the obstacles that fortune will place in your way, and teach you how to avoid them ? How delighted I should be to add this service to what I have just done you, but I should be displeasing the higher genius who is guiding you. Go, prince, flee from the tower, and remember that the Fairy Goodheart will always be your friend." At these words she herself, the palace, and the wonders the prince had·seen, disappeared, and he found himself in a thick forest, more than a hundred leagues from the tower, where King Sombre had imprisoned him.

Let us leave him to recover from his natural astonishment while we look on at two other scenes. Let us find out what is going on amongst the guards whom his father had sent to watch him, and what is happening to Princess

Trognon. The poor guards, astonished that the prince did not ask for supper, entered his room, and not finding him, they searched for him everywhere, terribly afraid lest he should have escaped. Their trouble being all in vain, they were in despair, for they feared that King Sombre who was so cruel would put them to death. After having discussed all the possible ways of appeasing his anger, they came to the conclusion that one of them should go to bed and hide his face, while they would say that the prince was very ill. Shortly afterwards they would pretend he was dead, and they would bury a log and this would get them out of the difficulty. The plan seemed to them perfect, and at once they set about carrying it out. The shortest of the guards had a great hump fastened on to him and went to bed. Then they told the king that his son was very ill, but he thought they only said so to work on his feelings, and he refused to relax any of his severity. This was just what the terrified guards wanted, and the more they pretended to urge him the more indifference did King Sombre show.

As for Princess Trognon, she arrived in a little vehicle no higher than your arm, and which was carried in a litter. King Sombre went to meet her. When he saw how deformed she was, and how she sat in a bowl, her skin covered with scales like a codfish, her eyebrows that met each other, her large, flat nose, her mouth stretching round to her ears, he could not help saying : " In truth, Princess Trognon, it is very fitting that you should despise my Torticoli! I confess he is very ugly, but, to tell the truth, he is not so ugly as you." " Your majesty," she answered, " I am not vain enough to take offence at any disagreeable things you may say to me. Perhaps you do so as a sure means of persuading me to love your charming Torticoli : but I declare to you that in spite of my miserable bowl and my many faults, I do not wish to marry him, and I prefer to be Princess Trognon rather than Queen Torticoli." King Sombre was very angry at this answer. " I assure you," he said, " that I will have no contradiction. The king, your father, should be your master, and he has placed you in my hands." " There are things," she answered, " in which we have the power of choice. It has been against my will that I have been brought here, I give you warning, and I shall look upon you as my worst enemy if you force me to consent." The king, still more angry, left her. She was given an apartment in the palace, where she was waited on by ladies who received orders to convince her that her best part was to marry the prince.

Meanwhile the guards, who feared lest they should be discovered and that the king should come to know that his son had escaped, hastened to tell him he was dead. Hearing this, he was overcome by a grief of which they had not thought him capable. He cried, he shrieked, and venging himself on Trognon for his loss, he sent her to the tower in the place of his dear, lost son. The poor princess's grief was as great as her astonishment when she found herself a prisoner. She was full of spirit, and she spoke her mind respecting so cruel a proceeding, hoping they would repeat her words to the king; but no one dared to speak to him on the subject. She thought, too, she could write to her father about the bad treatment she received, and then he would come and deliver her; but her attempts in this direction were useless, for they intercepted her letters and gave them to King Sombre. So long as she lived in hopes that her letters would bring her help, she was in less distress, and every day she walked in the gallery to look at the pictures on the windows. Nothing surprised her more than the number of different things which were there represented, and to see pictures of herself in her bowl. "Since I have been in this country," she said, "the painters have taken a strange pleasure in painting me. Are there not enough ridiculous faces without mine? Or do they wish by placing mine near that young charming shepherdess to enhance her beauty still more by contrasting her with me?" Then she looked at the portrait of a shepherd who was beautiful beyond description. "How much is anyone to be pitied," she said, "whom nature has treated as badly as she has done me! And how happy it must make one to be beautiful!" As she said this the tears stood in her eyes, and catching a glimpse of herself in a mirror, she turned away abruptly. Suddenly to her astonishment she saw behind her a little old woman with a hood on her head, who was even uglier than herself, while the bowl in which she dragged herself along was worn out and full of holes. "Princess," said the old woman, "the choice is given you between virtue and beauty. I have been listening to your touching laments. If you desire beauty, you will be coquettish, vain, and very gay. If you choose to remain as you are, you will be good, respected, and very humble-minded." Trognon looked at the old woman who spoke to her, and asked her if beauty was incompatible with goodness. "No," said the good woman to her, "but so far as you are concerned, it is decreed that you can only have one of them." "Well," said Trognon, in a firm voice, "I prefer my ugliness to beauty." "What! you prefer to frighten those who look at you?" asked the old woman. "Yes, madam," said the princess. "I would rather have every misfortune in the world than fail in virtue." "I have brought my yellow and white muff on purpose," said the fairy. "If you blow on the yellow side, you will be like that beautiful shepherdess whom you thought so charming, and be loved by a shepherd whose portrait you have looked at more than once. If you blow on the white side, you will be strengthened in the path of virtue on which you now set out so courageously." "Ah! madam," answered the princess, "do not refuse me this favour. It will console me for all the contempt I have had poured on me." So the little old woman gave her the muff of virtue and beauty. And Trognon made no mistake, but blowing on the white side, thanked the fairy, who vanished immediately.

Trognon was delighted at the good choice she had made; and however much she might envy the incomparable beauty of the shepherdess on the painted windows, she consoled herself by thinking that beauty passes like a dream, that virtue is an everlasting and unchangeable treasure which endures longer than life. She still had hopes that the king, her father, would head a great army, and come and take her away from the tower. She waited the moment of his coming with the utmost impatience, and was dying to mount to the turret to see him arrive with the help she looked for. But how could she climb so high? She crawled about in her room more slowly than a tortoise, and when at any time she wanted to mount anywhere, her women had to carry her. However, she hit on a very original plan. Knowing the clock was in the turret, she took the weights off and put herself in their place. When they wound up the clock, she was hoisted to the top. Once there, she looked hastily through the window over the country, but seeing nothing coming, she drew back to rest a little. While she was leaning up against the wall that Torticoli, or, as we should say, Prince Peerless, had broken down and built up again rather badly, the plaster fell and so did the golden screw, rattling on the floor near Trognon. Seeing it, she picked it up and examined it to find out if it were any use to her. Now, as she was very clever, she saw quickly enough that it was meant to open the cupboard which had no lock. She succeeded in doing this, and was no less delighted than the prince had been on finding all the rare and beautiful things it contained. There were four thousand drawers, all filled with jewels, antique and modern. At last she found the little golden door, the carbuncle box, and the hand swimming in blood. Shuddering, she would have cast it away from her, but it was not in her power to let it go, for a secret attraction prevented her. "Alas!" she said in distress, "I would rather die than remain longer with this hand." But in a moment she heard a sweet, pleasant voice that said to her: "Take courage, princess; your happiness depends on this adventure". "Ah, what can I do?" she asked, trembling. "You must take this hand into your own room," said the voice, "hide it under your pillow, and when you see an eagle, give it to him without a moment's delay." However frightened the princess was, the voice had something so persuasive about it that she did not hesitate to obey; and so she put back the treasures and curiosities as she had found them without taking a single one. Her guards, who feared that she too had escaped, searched for her, and were very much astonished to find her in a place where she could not, they said, have reached except by enchantment. She was three days without seeing anything of importance. She dared not open the beautiful carbuncle box, for the bleeding hand terrified her too much. At last one night hearing a noise against the window, she drew aside her curtain, and saw by the light of the moon an eagle flying about. She rose as quickly as she could, and dragging herself along the floor, she opened the window. The eagle entered, flapping its wings noisily, as if to express delight. Without a moment's hesitation she gave him the hand, which he seized with his claws, and was gone. In his place was a young man, the handsomest and the comeliest that ever was seen. His brow was wreathed with a diadem, his dress was covered with jewels, and in his hand he held a portrait. It was he who spoke first. "Princess," he said to Trognon, "for two hundred years a wicked enchanter has imprisoned me here. We both of us loved the wonderful Fairy Goodheart (for that is the name of my queen). She favoured me, and he was jealous. His art was greater than mine, and he determined to use it for my ruin. So he told me in a masterful manner that he forbade me to see her any more. Such a command was not in accord either with my love or with my rank, so I defied him ; and the fair lady I adore was so offended with the enchanter's conduct, that in her turn she forbade him ever to come near her again. Then the cruel wretch determined to punish us both. One day when I was with her, in great delight because of a portrait she had given me, and that I was looking at, but thinking it not a thousandth part so beautiful as the original, he appeared, and with a blow from his sabre cut my hand from my arm. Fairy Goodheart felt the pain more keenly than myself, and fell fainting on her bed. All at once I saw I was covered with feathers, and I was changed into an eagle. Every day I was allowed to see the queen, but I could not come near her, nor awake her. I only had the consolation of hearing her uttering constant sighs, and speaking of her dear Trasimene. I also knew that at the end of two hundred years a prince would call back Goodheart to the light of day, and that a princess by restoring me my hand would give me back my former shape. A fairy, who is interested in your fame, has arranged it in this way. It was she who so carefully locked up my hand in the cupboard in the donjon, she who has given me the power to-day of expressing to you my gratitude. Say, princess, what would give you most pleasure, and it shall be yours at the moment." "Great king," answered Trognon, after some moments of silence, "if I do not reply at once, it is not because I am in doubt as to my desires, but I confess to you that I am little used to such astonishing adventures, and I think it must be a dream rather than a reality." "No, madam," answered Trasimene, "it is no dream. You will see the results of it as soon as you tell me the gifts you wish for." "If I asked all those I stand in need of to make me perfect," she said, "however powerful you may be, it would be difficult to satisfy me. But I really care only for the most essential. Therefore make my soul as beautiful as my body is ugly and deformed." "Ah, princess," cried King Trasimene, "you delight me by a choice so good and worthy. Therefore your body will become as beautiful as your soul and mind." He touched the princess with the portrait of the fairy. She heard her bones go crack, crack. They stretched out, they fitted into their right places. She stood up, tall, beautiful, straight, her skin whiter than milk, her features regular, her bearing at once dignified and modest, her face refined and pleasant. "What wonder is this!" she cried. "Is this I? Is it possible?" "Yes, madam," replied Trasimene, "it is you. The wise choice you made of goodness has brought about the happy change you now experience. What a pleasure for me, after what I owe you, to be destined to help towards it! But now cast away for ever the name of Trognon, and take that of Radiant instead, for you are worthy of it, from your brilliancy and your charms." At that moment he disappeared, and the princess, without knowing by what means she had come, found herself at the edge of a little river, in a shady place, the pleasantest that could anywhere be found.

She had not yet seen herself, but now the water of this stream was so clear, that looking in it, she saw with the greatest surprise, that she was the same shepherdess whom she had admired so much in the windows of the gallery. In truth, like her, she had a white dress trimmed with fine lace, the prettiest ever a shepherdess wore; her girdle was of little roses and jasmine, her hair adorned with flowers. Close to her hand she found a crook, painted and gilded, while a flock of sheep were feeding along the bank. The sheep dog hearing her voice seemed to know her and came up and fawned on her. What could she think of all these fresh wonders! She had been born, and till now she had lived, the ugliest creature imaginable, but then she was a princess. Now she was fairer than the morning star, but she was only a shepherdess; and the loss of her rank she could not but feel somewhat. Worn out by these different thoughts at last she fell asleep. She had been awake all night, as I have already said, and the journey she had taken, although she had not known it, was a hundred leagues long. So she was rather tired. Her sheep and her dog gathered at her side, seemed to be keeping watch over her, and giving her the care she owed to them. The sun could not scorch her though it shone ever so brightly, for the leafy trees protected her, and the delicate, fresh grass on which she had lain down, seemed as if it were proud of so fair a load.

> Here the violets thickest bloom
>   Peeping from their hiding places,
>   See them lift their little faces,
> Breathing out their sweet perfume.

The birds sang together in sweet harmony, and the zephyrs held their breath for fear they should awake her. A shepherd tired out by the heat of the sun, having espied the spot from far off, made for it as quickly as possible, but seeing young Radiant he was so astonished that had it not been for a tree to lean against, he would have fallen on the ground. In truth he recognised her as the same maiden whose beauty he had admired in the gallery windows and in the vellum book: for the reader of course has guessed that the shepherd was Prince Peerless. Some unknown attraction had kept him in this country, and he had been admired by all who had seen him, and among the shepherds he was no less distinguished by his skill in everything, his handsome face, his quick wit, than he had formerly been by his birth. He gazed on Radiant with an eagerness and delight he had never felt till now. He knelt before her, examined all the different points that made of her such a perfect whole, and his heart was the first to pay that tribute which no one since has been able to refuse. While he stayed dreaming near her, Radiant woke up, and seeing Peerless by her side in gay shepherd's dress, she looked at him, and recalled him, for she had seen his portrait in the tower. " Fair shepherdess," he said, " what happy fate has led you here? You come, doubtless, to receive our incense and our vows. Ah, already I feel that I shall be the first to pay my homage." " No, shepherd," she said, " I have no wish to claim honours that are not due to me. I wish to remain a simple shepherdess, for I love my flock and my dog. Solitude has charms for me. I seek for nothing else." " What! young shepherdess, in coming to this spot, you mean to hide yourself from those who dwelt here? Is it possible," he went on, " that you are so evilly disposed towards us? At least, except me, since I am first to offer my services." " No," replied Radiant, " I do not wish to see you oftener than the others, though already I have an unaccountable feeling of respect for you. But tell me of some good shepherdess with whom I can find a home, for being unknown here, and of an age when I cannot dwell alone, I shall be very glad to have her protection." Peerless was delighted with this commission, and took her to a neat little cabin, charming in its simplicity. There dwelt a little old woman, who very rarely went out, because she could hardly walk. " See, good mother," said Peerless, leading Radiant forward, " here I bring you an incomparable damsel, whose very presence will make you young again." The old woman embraced her, and said in a pleasant voice that she was welcome, that she was sorry to lodge her so poorly, but that at least she would lodge her very well in her heart. " I did not think," said Radiant, " I should find here so kind a welcome and such courtesy. I assure you, good mother, I am delighted to be with you. Do not refuse," she added, turning to the shepherd, " to tell me your name, so that I may know to whom I am obliged for this service." " My name

9

is Peerless," answered the prince, "but at present I do not wish to be called anything but your slave." "And as for me," said the little, old woman, "I wish to
know the name of the shepherdess whose host I am." The princess said she was
called Radiant, and the old woman seemed charmed with so lovely a name, while
Peerless said a hundred pretty things on the subject.

The old shepherdess, fearing lest Radiant should be hungry, brought her a
shining earthen vessel, some sweet milk, some brown bread, fresh eggs, newly-
churned butter, and cream cheese. Peerless ran to his hut, and brought strawberries, nuts, cherries, and other fruits, all garnished with flowers ; and to have
the chance of staying longer with Radiant he asked her permission to eat with
her. Alas ! it would have been difficult to refuse him. She had great pleasure
in his company, and however cold she pretended to be she knew quite well that
her presence was not a matter of indifference to Peerless.

When he had left her she sat thinking of him for a long time, while his
mind was full of her. He saw her every day when he led his flocks into the same
pasture where hers were feeding, and where he sang love songs to her. He played
the flute and the pipes for her to dance to, which she did with such grace and
accuracy as filled him with admiration. Now each of them was thinking a great
deal of the series of astonishing adventures which had happened to them, and
they both began to be uneasy. Peerless never left her alone if he could help it.

> Wherever Radiant went he followed fast,
> And while beseeching looks on her he cast,
> All the delights and charms of love he told.
> Such burning passion could not leave her cold.
> But fearing danger, though she knew not why,
> She fled whene'er the shepherd she did spy.
> 'Tis hard to flee when pleasure is in staying—
> Peerless had watched at times her eyes betraying
> Far other thoughts than hate. But now in vain
> He seeks to win some tender look again.

She avoided him with the utmost care, and reproached herself endlessly for her
affection for him. "What !" she said, "I am so unhappy as to be in love,
and that with a miserable shepherd ! What a sad fate is mine ! I preferred
goodness to beauty, yet it seems heaven in rewarding me for this choice, has
made me beautiful, but only for my misfortune. Without these vain attractions,
this shepherd that I hide from would never have set himself to please me, and I
should not have the shame of blushing for my feelings towards him." Her tears
left her always filled with sad thoughts, and she was the more troubled at seeing
the misery of her dear shepherd.

He too was overcome with melancholy. He wished to declare to Radiant the greatness of his birth, in the hopes that she would be perhaps influenced by vanity, and would listen to him more willingly. But after all he thought she might not believe him, and if she asked for some proof, he had no means of giving her such. "How cruel is my lot!" he cried. "Although before I was hideous to look at, at all events I was my father's heir, and a great kingdom makes up for many faults. Now it would be useless to present myself either to him or to his subjects, for none of them would recognise me, and all the kind Fairy Goodheart has done for me in taking away my name and my ugliness, ends in making me a shepherd, and placing me under the spell of an unkind shepherdess who cannot endure me. O cruel star," he said with a sigh, "shine on me with more favour, or give me back my deformity and with it my former carelessness!"

Such were the sad laments of the lover and his mistress, each ignorant of the truth about the other. But one day when Radiant had been doing her best to keep out of Peerless's way, he on the contrary had made up his mind to speak to her, and to have a pretext which should not offend her. So he took a little lamb, decked it with ribbons and flowers, put a collar of coloured straw on it, worked so beautifully that it was a little master-piece. . He himself had a mantle of rose-coloured taffeta, trimmed with English lace. Thus with his crook decked with ribbons and his scrip slung over his shoulder, all the Aladdins in the world would have made but a poor show beside him.

He found Radiant sitting on the bank of a stream, which flowed slowly through the thickest part of the wood. Her sheep were scattered here and there, for the melancholy of the shepherdess prevented her caring for them. Peerless greeted her timidly, giving her the little lamb, and looking at her tenderly. "What have I done, fair shepherdess," he said, "to be so marked out for your hatred? You blame your eyes if they so much as look at me, and you seek to flee me. Is my love for you such a crime? Can you ever hope to be loved with more. purity or faithfulness? Have not my words and my actions shown my respect and the warmth of my feeling? But doubtless you love some one else. Your heart already belongs to another." But she answered him :—

> "Shepherd, list, an you would know
> Why henceforth I flee you,
> My poor heart is troubled so,
> When my eyes do see you.
>
> "If, perchance, I loved you less
> Hardly would I hide me,

> But since all my looks confess,
>   I fear what may betide me.
>
> " Duty I would bid begone
>   While you near me hover ;
>   Slowly drag the footsteps on
>   When one flees a lover.
>
> " Fare you well, and, for my peace,
>   Fare you well for ever !
>   Leaving you, my life may cease,
>   Yet—here our ways must sever. "

And so saying, Radiant moved away.   The prince, full of love and despair,
would have followed her, but his· grief became so great that he fell unconscious
at the foot of a tree.   Ah, severe and too-timid virtue, why do you fear a man
who has loved you from his tenderest years ?   He is incapable of doing you
wrong, and his affection is altogether innocent.   But the princess distrusted
herself as much as him.   She could not but own the merits of this charming
shepherd, and she knew well how necessary it is to avoid what we are tempted
to love too much.

No harder task could have been hers at that moment, tearing herself away
from the person she loved more tenderly and more dearly than any one she had
ever seen.   She could not help turning her head sometimes just to look if he
were following, and she saw him fall down as if dead.   She loved him, yet she
would not give herself the consolation of going to his aid.   When she was on
the plain she lifted her eyes piteously, and clasping her hands, cried : " O virtue !
O glory !   O high estate !   See how I sacrifice my happiness to you !   O
fate !   O Trasimene !   I give up my fatal beauty.   Give me back my former
ugliness, or give me back, without the need to blush for it, the lover whom I
leave behind."   Then she stopped, hesitating whether to flee or to return.   Her
heart called to her to go back to the wood where she had left Peerless ; but her
virtue was stronger than her tenderness, and she took the generous determination not to see him.

Since she had been living in these parts, she had heard tell of an enchanter
who dwelt with his sister in a castle he had built on the borders of the island.
Their fairy lore was the talk of every one, and every day new wonders came to
light.   She felt that it must be a magic power at least that should blot out of
her heart the picture of the charming shepherd, and without saying a word to
her kind hostess who had received her and treated her as a daughter,
she set off, her mind so full of her troubles that she never thought of the danger

there might be in so young and beautiful a maiden travelling all by herself. She stopped neither night nor day, neither ate nor drank, in such haste was she to reach the castle and be cured of her love. But passing through a wood she heard some one singing, and it seemed as if she heard her name uttered in the voice of one of her companions. Stopping to listen she heard these words:—

> "The comeliest shepherd of the plain was Peerless,
> And all his heart on Radiant fast was set,
> Proud of his love, and confident, and fearless,
> He poured his passion out whene'er they met.
> But his young mistress of his love made light,
> Though when her lover wandered from her sight,
> She'd sigh and sigh until he came again;
> And ne'er such sigh for him was heaved in vain.
> Upon the grass together they would sit,
> And what was taught him by his love and wit
> He'd sing and pipe the summer morning long,
> And stop to hear from her sweet mouth his song."

"Ah! but this is too bad," she said, shedding tears. "Ah, treacherous shepherd, you have boasted of the harmless favour I have granted you! You dared to think my weak heart would be more ready to listen to your love than my own duty. You have spoken your wicked desires aloud, and yours is the fault that my name is sung in the woods and the plains." And at that moment she felt so very angry that she thought she could have looked upon him with indifference, and perhaps even with hatred. "It is useless," she said, "for me to go farther to seek a remedy for my ill. I have nothing to fear from a shepherd whom I know to be so undeserving. I shall return to the hamlet with that shepherdess I have been listening to." She called her as loud as she could, but there came no answer, yet nevertheless from time to time she heard some one singing near her. She became uneasy and afraid. The truth was, this wood belonged to the enchanter, and no one could pass through it without meeting with some sort of adventure. Radiant, more uncertain than ever, hastened on her way out of the wood. "Has the shepherd whom I feared become of so little consequence to me now that I should permit myself to see him again? Is it not rather that my heart, in league with him, is seeking to deceive me? Oh! let me flee, let me flee away; it is the best thing an unhappy princess like me can do." So she went on her way to the enchanter's castle; and once there she entered without hindrance. She crossed several great courts, where the grass and the bramble-bushes grew so high, that you would have thought no one had walked there for a hundred years, and when she pushed them aside her hands were full of scratches. She went into a hall, where the daylight only came through a little hole, and which was hung with bats' wings. Twelve cats, suspended from the ceiling, served as a chandelier, and made mewling enough to drive any one distracted. On a long table there were twelve big mice fastened down by their tails, with a piece of lard lying before each of them, which they could not reach. The mice were in terror of the cats, and were dying of hunger within sight of good pieces of lard. The princess was thinking of the suffering of these animals when she saw the enchanter come in in a long black robe. On his head for a cap he wore a crocodile, and never was so terrible a head-

dress seen. The old man wore spectacles, and held a whip in his hand made of twenty long serpents, all alive. Oh, how frightened the princess was! How she longed at that moment for her shepherd, her sheep, and her dog! Her only thought was of flight, and without a word to this terrible man, she ran to the door. But the door was all covered with spiders' webs. She took one away, and found another. She took that away, and found a third. When she took the third away a new one appeared in front of still another. In fact, these tiresome spider-web curtains were altogether numberless. The poor princess came to an end of her strength, and her arms were not strong enough to support the webs. She wished to sit down on the ground to rest for a little, but there she felt long thorns going into her. Jumping up again, she tried once more to get out, but ever another web appeared when she had torn the first away. The wicked old man looked on at her all the while, laughing as if he would choke. At last he called to her, saying: "You may spend the rest of your life trying, but you will never succeed. You seem to be young, and you are the prettiest of all pretty things. If you like, I will marry you. I will give you these twelve cats you see hanging from the ceiling to do what you like with, and those twelve mice on the table will be yours too. The cats are princes, and the mice princesses. The minxes, at different times, have had the honour to be loved by me, for I have always been amiable and gallant, but none of them would marry me. The princes were my rivals, and happier than I. I was seized with jealousy. I found the means of enticing them here, both princes and princesses, and as they were caught they were turned into cats or mice. The fun of it is that they hate each other just as much as they used to love each other, and what more perfect vengeance could I find ? " " Ah, sire," said Radiant, " turn me into a mouse. I deserve it just as much as these poor princesses." " What ! " said the magician, " you will not love me, then, you little Bo-peep ? " " I have made up my mind to love no one," she answered. " Oh, you little silly ! " said he. " I shall give you such nice things to eat. I shall tell you stories, and give you the prettiest clothes in the world. You will always drive in a coach, or be carried in a litter, and you will be called madam." " I have made up my mind to love no one," replied the princess once more. . " Take care what you are saying," cried the enchanter angrily. " You will long repent of this." " No matter," said Radiant, " I have made up my mind to love no one." " Oh, very well, cold-hearted creature," said he, touching her ; " since you will not love anybody, you shall be turned into a special kind of animal. Henceforth you shall be neither flesh nor fish. You shall have neither blood nor bones. Because you are still in your fresh youth, you shall be green ; you shall be light and nimble ; you shall live in the meadows as you lived before, and your name shall be Grasshopper." At that instant Princess Radiant was turned into the prettiest grasshopper in the world, and, regaining her liberty she made off at once for the garden.

As soon as she was free to utter her laments, she cried in distress : " Ah ! my bowl ; my dear bowl, what has become of you ? This then is what your promises end in, Trasimene ! Was it this sad fate you kept for me two hundred years long ? A beauty as little lasting as the flowers of spring, and in the end a covering of green crape, a queer little body, neither flesh nor fish, and with neither blood nor bones ! I am indeed unhappy ! Alas ! a crown would have hidden all my defects. I would have found a husband worthy of me, and if I had remained a shepherdess, dear Peerless's one desire would have been to win my heart. He is but too well revenged for my cruel contempt. Here I am, a grasshopper, fated to sing day and night, when my heart full of bitterness would rather bid me weep." So spoke the grasshopper hidden amongst the delicate grass on the edge of the stream.

But what was Prince Peerless doing away from his beloved shepherdess ?

The cruel manner in which she had left him pained him so much that he had not the strength to follow her. Before he could have reached her, he had fainted, and he remained for a long time quite unconscious at the foot of the tree where Radiant had seen him fall, till at length the coolness of the ground, or some unknown power, brought him back to life. He did not dare to go to her cottage that day. Turning over in his mind some of the last verses she had said to him—

> " If perchance I loved you less
> Hardly would I hide me "—

he began to be more hopeful, and felt sure that with time and care he would breed in her a little gratitude. But what were his thoughts when, going to the old shepherdess's hut where Radiant lodged, he learnt that she had not been there since the day before? He was like to die for anxiety, and took his leave full of troubled thoughts. As he sat grieving by the river-side, he felt over and over again the impulse to throw himself in, and to end his troubles with his life. At last, taking a small dagger, he carved these verses on the bark of a beamtree :—

> " Clear stream that wanders through the valleys fair,
> Green meadow lands that once my pleasure were,
>   But now my misery,
> She whom I loved, and whom you sure have taken
> As model for your charms, has now forsaken
>   Both you and me.
> Henceforth my business in this world is sorrow—
> From dawn to dusk, again from eve to morrow,
>   What but to weep ?
> Young tree, upon whose tender bark I write
> The story of my love and of her flight
>   In letters deep,
> Forgive the pain. Your wounds are records weak
> Of what is branded on my spirit meek
>   In marks of fire.
> Her name is rather your adorning ; while I—
> Now she is gone, to lay me down and die
>   Is my desire. "

He could write no more, for at that moment he was accosted by a little old woman who wore a ruff round her neck, a farthingale, a fillet about her white hair, and a velvet hood. There was something venerable about her antique air. " My son," she said, " the words you utter are very bitter. I beg of you to tell me what is the cause of your sorrow." " Alas ! good mother," said Peerless,

" I deplore the absence of a lovely shepherdess who has fled from me. I have resolved to seek for her throughout the whole earth, till so be I have found her." "Go in yonder direction, my child," she said, pointing to the road leading to the castle where poor Radiant had been turned into a grasshopper. "I have a feeling that you will not have to search for her long." Peerless thanked her, and begged that the God of Love would look kindly on her.

The prince met with no other adventure on his way to stop him, but on reaching the wood near the castle of the magician and his sister, he thought he saw the shepherdess. He hastened to follow her, but she still went on. "Radiant," he cried, "Radiant, whom I adore, stay a little, deign to hear me!" The phantom sped on faster, and in this pursuit the day went by. When night came on, he saw lights sparkling in the castle, and he thought to himself the shepherdess was perhaps inside. So he ran, and entered without hindrance. Going upstairs, he found in a magnificent hall an old fairy, tall and horribly thin. Her eyes were like two lamps whose light had been put out, and you could see through her cheeks. Her arms were like lathes, her fingers like spindles; a black, leathery skin covered her skeleton form. Yet, all the same, she had put rouge and patches on her cheeks, and wore green and pink ribbons, a mantle of silver brocade, a crown of diamonds on her head, and jewels all over.

"At last, my prince," she said, "you reach the spot where I have been waiting for you long. Think no more of your little shepherdess. A love so unfitting your rank should make you blush. I am the Queen of the Meteors. I wish you well, and I can be of endless service to you if you will love me." "Love you, madam!" cried the prince, looking at her indignantly. "Love you, madam! Am I master of my heart? No, I could never consent to such unfaithfulness, and I feel even that were I to change the object of my love, you would not take her place. Choose amongst your meteors some influence that pleases you. Love the air, or the winds, but leave mortals in peace."

The fairy was enraged. Waving her hand twice, she filled the gallery with horrible monsters, against whom the young prince had to defend himself with his skill and courage. Some of them had several heads and several arms; others had the face of a centaur or a siren; some were lions with men's faces, some were sphinxes, and flying dragons. Peerless had nothing but his crook and a small spear which he had armed himself with at the beginning of his journey. From time to time the tall fairy would make the fray to cease, and ask him if he loved her. And always he said he had vowed to be a faithful lover, and he could not change. Tired out with his persistence, she made Radiant appear. "Well," she said, "you see your mistress at the foot of this gallery. Think what you are doing. If you refuse to marry me she will be torn to pieces by tigers before your eyes." "Ah! madam," cried the prince, throwing himself at her feet, "I would willingly die to save my mistress. Spare her life by taking mine." "It is not a question of your death, traitor," replied the fairy, "it is a question of your heart and your hand." While they were speaking the prince heard the voice of his shepherdess as if she were mourning. "Will you let me be devoured?" she said. "If you love me make up your mind to do what the queen commands you." The poor prince hesitated. "Ah, Goodheart," he cried, "have you then forsaken me, after so many promises? Come, come and help us." Hardly had he uttered the words when he heard a voice saying these words distinctly :—

     "Let fate take its course; only be faithful, and seek the Golden Branch".

The tall fairy who had thought she had won the day by means of so many different illusions, was in despair at finding such a powerful obstacle across her path as the protection of Goodheart. "Get out of my sight, you miserable stubborn prince!" she cried. "Since your heart is so enflamed, be a cricket, friend of the heat and of the fire." And at that moment the handsome, the splendid Prince Peerless became a little black cricket, who would have burnt himself alive in the first fireplace or the first oven, if he had not called to mind the friendly voice that had bidden him hope. "I must seek the Golden Branch," he said, "and then perhaps I shall regain my own shape. Ah, if I could but find my shepherdess, what would be lacking for perfect happiness?"

The cricket made haste out of the fatal palace, and without knowing where he should go. He recommended himself to the care of the beautiful Fairy Goodheart. Then he took his departure without baggage and without noise, for a cricket fears neither robbers nor misadventures by the way. At his first resting-place, which was in the hollow of a tree, he found a grasshopper in a melancholy condition and unable to sing. The cricket, having no idea that this was a reasoning intelligent being said: "And whither is Gammer Grasshopper bound for?" "And you, Gaffer Cricket, whither away?" This answer very much astonished the love-sick cricket. "What," he cried, "you can speak?" "What? well, I like that!" she cried. "Do you think a grasshopper should be less privileged than a cricket?" "I can speak perfectly well," said the cricket, "because I am a man." "According to that," answered the grasshopper, "I should be able to speak better than you, because I am a woman." "Is then your lot like mine?" said the cricket. "Yes, it must be the same," answered the grasshopper. "But now tell me where you are going." "I should be delighted," the cricket went on, "if we could bear each other company for a long while. I heard a voice which came from I know not where, which said :—

     ' Let fate take its course, and seek the Golden Branch '.

It seemed to me it could only be meant for me. So without delay I set off, though I know not whither I am bound."

This conversation was interrupted by two mice running as fast as ever they could. Seeing a hole at the foot of the tree, they flew in there head foremost, and all but choked the cricket and the grasshopper, who took refuge as they could in a little corner. " Ah, madam," said the biggest mouse, " I have a pain in my side with having run so fast. How does your highness?" "I wrenched off my tail," said the youngest. " Otherwise I should still be fastened to the old wizard's table. Did you see how he ran after us ? How lucky we are to have got away from his wretched palace !" " I am just a little afraid of the cats and the rat-trap, princess," said the big mouse, " and I fervently wish I may soon reach the Golden Branch." " You know the way then ? " said the mouse princess. " Do I know it ? I should think I do, madam, as well as the way to my own house," answered the other. "This branch is wonderful. You want only one of its leaves to be rich for ever. It supplies you with money. It breaks the charms of magic. It gives beauty, and preserves youth. So before daybreak let us set out on the road." " We shall have the honour of your company, this good cricket here and myself, if you are agreeable, ladies," said the grasshopper, "for we also are like you, pilgrims to the Golden Branch." The two parties exchanged compliments with each other. The mice, be it understood, were princesses whom this wicked enchanter had attached to the table ; and as for the cricket and the grasshopper, their courtesy most clearly showed their rank.

All of them woke early next morning, and set off together very silently, for they feared lest any hunters on the watch, hearing them speak, might take them and put them into cages. At last they arrived at the Golden Branch. It was in the middle of a wonderful garden, the walks of which were strewn with little Eastern pearls, rounder than peas, instead of sand. The roses were of pink diamonds, and the leaves of emeralds, the pomegranate flowers of garnets, the marigolds of topazes, the jonquils of yellow brilliants, the blue-bottles of turquoises, the tulips of amethysts, opals, and diamonds. In fact, endless were the number and the variety of these beautiful flowers, and they shone brighter than the sun.

Here it was then, as I have already said, the Golden Branch, the same that Prince Peerless received from the eagle, and with which he touched Fairy Goodheart when she was enchanted. It had grown as high as the tallest trees, and was loaded with rubies, which hung from it like cherries. As soon as the cricket, the grasshopper, and the two mice came near it, they took their own natural shapes again. What joy for them ! And what delight did not the prince feel at the sight of his fair shepherdess ! He threw himself at her feet, and was in the midst of telling her how happy this pleasant and so little expected surprise made him when Queen Goodheart and King Trasimene appeared in such splendour as was in keeping with the magnificence of the garden. Four Cupids armed from top to toe, bows by their sides, quivers on their shoulders, supported with their arrows a little pavilion of gold and blue brocade, beneath which two beautiful crowns were seen. "Come, dear lovers," cried the queen, stretching out her arms; "come and receive from our hands the crowns which your virtue, your birth and your faithfulness deserve. Your pains are going to be turned into pleasures. Princess Radiant," she said, "this is the prince who was destined for you by your father and his. He did not die in the tower. Take him for your husband, and leave to me the care of your peace and happiness." The princess in great delight threw herself on Goodheart's neck, and seeing her tearful face the fairy understood that it was excess of joy that took from her the power of speech. Peerless threw himself on his knees before the generous fairy. He kissed her hands respectfully, and poured out his thanks in great confusion. Trasimene caressed him tenderly, and Goodheart told them, in a few words, how she had scarcely ever left them, that it was she who had proposed to Radiant to blow into the yellow and white muff, that she had taken the form of an old peasant, so that the princess might lodge with her, and that it was again she who had told the prince in which direction he should follow his shepherdess. "In truth," she went on, "you have had troubles which I would have saved you if I had been able to. But, after all, the pleasures of love are worth their price." A soft symphony was heard murmuring around them, and the Loves made haste to crown the young lovers. The marriage took place, and while this ceremony was going on, the two princesses, who had just lost their mouse shape, conjured the fairy to use her power to deliver from the wizard's castle the unfortunate mice and cats who were languishing there. "This is too memorable a day," said she, "to refuse you anything." With that she struck the Golden Branch three times, and all who had been imprisoned in the castle made their appearance in their own natural shape, and found their mistresses again. The generous fairy, wishing that every one should have a share in the rejoicing, gave them the cupboard in the donjon to share between them. This present was worth more than ten kingdoms in those days. Their pleasure and their gratitude can easily be imagined. Goodheart and Trasimene finished the great work with a generosity which surpassed all they had ever done before, declaring that the palace and the garden of the Golden Branch would in future belong to King Peerless and Queen Radiant. A hundred kings paid tribute to them, and they had a hundred dependent kingdoms.

THE BEE AND THE ORANGE TREE.

ONCE upon a time there lived a king and a queen who lacked but one thing to make them happy, and that was to have children. The queen was already old, and had given up all hope of having any, when she gave birth to the prettiest little girl that ever was seen. Great was the joy in the royal household. Every one began to seek for the princess a name which should express their love for her. At last she was called Aimée, and the queen had these words, *Aimée, daughter of the King of Happy Isle*, engraved on a turquoise heart, which she hung round the princess's neck, thinking it would bring her luck, as turquoises are supposed to do. But the rule did not hold good, for one day when they had taken her on the sea to give the nurse a holiday in the most beautiful summer weather, suddenly a terrific tempest arose, so that it was impossible to land; and as the vessel was a small one only for use near the shore, it was soon shattered to pieces. The nurse and all the sailors perished. The little princess, asleep in her cradle, floated on the water, and at last she was cast up on the shore of a beautiful country, where, however, very few people dwelt since the ogre Ravagio and his wife Tourmentine had gone to live there—for they ate up everybody. Ogres are terrible people. When once they have tasted raw human flesh they will hardly eat anything else, and Tourmentine always knew how to make somebody come their way, for she was half a fairy.

She smelt the poor little princess a mile off, and ran to the shore to find her before Ravagio should have reached her. One was as greedy as the other, and never were such hideous creatures seen, each with one squint eye in the middle of their foreheads, their mouths as big as ovens, their large flat noses, their long asses' ears, their hair all standing on end, and their humps in front and behind. Yet when the ogress saw Aimée in her beautiful cradle, swaddled in golden brocade, and playing with her little hands, her cheeks like roses white and red, her tiny cherry mouth, laughing and half open as if smiling to the hideous monster who was coming to devour her, moved by a feeling of pity which she had never felt before, Tourmentine determined to nurse her and not to eat her yet at all events. She took her in her arms, tying the cradle on her back, and in this fashion she returned to her cavern. "See, Ravagio," she said to her husband, "here is raw flesh, fine and plump and fat, but, by my head, I declare you shall not put your teeth in it. It is a pretty little girl, and I am going to nurse her. We shall marry her to our young ogre, and their little ogres will one day be curiosities to see. They will amuse us in our old age." "Very well," said Ravagio. "You are very clever even for your size. Let me see this child; she seems wonderfully pretty." "Well, do not eat it," said Tourmentine, giving him the little one into his great paws. "No, no," said he, "I would rather die of hunger." And thereupon Ravagio, Tourmentine and the little ogre began caressing Aimée in such a human fashion that it was a wonder to see them.

But the poor child, who only saw these hideous creatures round her, and not a sign of her nurse; began to screw up her little face and then to cry as loud as ever she could, till Ravagio's cavern rang again. Tourmentine, fearing lest this should annoy him, took her and carried her into the woods, the little ogres following after. There were six of them, each one uglier than the other. As I have already told you, the ogress was a kind of fairy, her power being contained in an ivory wand, which she held in her hand when she wished for anything. So now she took the wand and said : "In the name of the royal Fairy Trusio, I command the most beautiful hind of our forests to come here this very minute. Let it be meek and gentle, and let it leave its fawn and come and suckle this little darling that fortune has sent me." At that moment a hind appeared, to the great delight of the little ogres. Coming near, it gave the princess of its milk, after which Tourmentine took her back to the cave, the hind running after with leaps and bounds, the little one looking and caressing it. When she cried in her cradle there was the hind always ready to feed her, and there the little ogres to rock her to sleep.

It was in this way the king's daughter was brought up, while night and day her parents wept for her, and while her father, thinking her at the bottom of the sea, was making up his mind to choose another heir. When the king spoke of this matter to the queen she told him to do what seemed right, for her dear Amy was dead, and she could hope for no more children. He had waited long enough, she said, and after the fifteen years that had passed since she had lost her, it would be out of the question to expect ever to see her again. The king, there-fore, determined to ask his brother to chose from among his sons the one most worthy of reigning, and to send him the prince at once. The ambassadors being given their letters of state and all the necessary instructions, set out on their way. They had a long distance to go, but their good ships and a favourable wind brought them speedily to the king's brother, who ruled over a great kingdom. He received them very well, and when they asked him to let them take one of his sons home with them to be their master's heir, he wept for joy. He told them that since his brother had left the choice to him, he would send his second son, the one he would have chosen to succeed himself, whose character so well befitted his high birth that every desirable quality was found in him in perfection.

Prince Aimé (for so was he called) was sent for, and though the ambassa-dors had been led to expect great things of him, when they saw him they were astonished. He was eighteen years old, and Love, the tender god himself, was less fair to look upon. But his was a beauty which in no way took away from the noble martial bearing which wins respect and affection. He was made aware of his royal uncle's strong desire to have him at his court, and his father's inten-tion to send him off forthwith. So his equipage being got ready, he said fare-well, went on board, and set out on the open sea.

Leave him there awhile, and may good fortune be his guide! Let us go back to Ravagio and see what our young princess has been doing. She grew in beauty every year, and of her it may be truly said that the charms of the Graces and the goddesses together were not as hers. And when she was in that deep cavern with Ravagio, Tourmentine, and the little ogres, it seemed as if the sun and the stars and the skies had come down to visit it. The cruelty she saw amongst these monsters only served to make her the more gentle, and since she had become aware of their terrible appetite for human flesh, her whole mind was given to saving any poor creature that might fall into their hands. Indeed, in this way, for their sakes she often ran the risk of drawing down all the ogres' rage upon herself. And this would have happened one day or another if the young ogre had not loved her as the apple of his eye. What will a strong affec-tion not bring about? For this little monster had grown quite gentle from looking on the fair princess and loving her.

But, alas, what was her sorrow when she thought that she must marry this hideous lover! Though she knew nothing of her birth, she felt sure from the richness of her swaddling clothes, the golden chain and the turquoise, that she came of a good stock, and the feelings of her heart told her this still more plainly. She did not know how to read or write, nor was she learned in languages. She spoke the ogres' jargon, and lived in absolute ignorance of everything; yet, nevertheless, her principles were as good and her manners and temper as sweet as if she had lived all her life in the most refined court in the whole world.

She had made herself a dress out of a tiger-skin, leaving her arms half bare. She carried a quiver and arrows on her shoulder, and a bow at her girdle. Her fair hair was tied with a bit of sea-weed, and floated at will in the wind over her throat and down her back. Her sandals were of sea-rushes too. Thus attired, she haunted the woods like a second Diana, and she would never have known her own beauty if the crystal streams had not served her as natural mirrors, in which she gazed, yet grew no vainer, nor more disposed to look on her own face with favour. The sun had done with her complexion as it does with wax—whitened it; nor could the air of the sea make it tawny. Her only food was the fruits of

her hunt or her fishing, and such expeditions were a pretext many a time for leaving the terrible cavern and the sight of more hideous things than could anywhere else be found. "Ah, heaven!" she said, shedding tears, "what have I done that this cruel ogre should be my fate? Why didst thou not rather let me perish in the sea? Why didst thou save a life which must pass so miserably? Wilt thou have no pity on my sorrow?" So would she entreat the gods, praying to them for help.

When the weather was very stormy, and she thought the sea might have cast some poor creatures on the shore, thither she went to care for them tenderly, and to prevent their coming in the way of the ogres' cave. One night it happened that a tremendous storm was raging. As soon as it was light she rose and ran to the sea-shore. There she saw a man holding on to a plank and struggling to gain the shore in spite of the force of the waves that ever drove him back. The princess, wishing to help him, pointed out by signs the easiest landing-place, but he neither saw nor heard her. Sometimes he was so near that there seemed only a step between him and the land, when a wall of water covered him, and he disappeared from sight. At length he was driven on the sand, and there he lay motionless. Aimée drew near, and in spite of his pale face, which seemed to betoken death, she used every means she knew of to bring him back to life. She used always to carry with her certain herbs, the scent of which was so powerful that it roused people from the longest swoons, and these she pressed now into his hands, and rubbed his lips and his temples with them. When he opened his eyes he was so astonished at the beauty and at the dress of the princess, that he hardly knew whether it was a dream or real. It was he who spoke first. She answered, but they did not understand each other in the least, and looked one at the other attentively, half in astonishment, half in pleasure. The only men the princess had ever seen were poor fishers whom the ogres had caught, and whom she had saved as I have already said. What could she think then when she saw the comeliest and most magnificent man in the whole world? For of course it was Prince Aimé, her cousin, whose fleet, shattered by a furious tempest, had struck upon the rocks. Driven about helplessly by the winds, all the crew had perished, or had reached some unknown shore. The young prince was struck with astonishment that in such savage garments and in a country which seemed a wilderness, so beautiful a damsel could be found, and his recent impressions of the princes and ladies he had seen only served the more to persuade him that this lady he saw before him had not her equal anywhere. In their mutual astonishment they still went on talking without understanding each other's words, their eyes and their gestures being the interpreters of their thoughts. The princess after a few moments suddenly called to mind the danger which this stranger was exposed to. She became so very sad and disheartened that her feelings showed themselves on her face. The prince fearing she was ill, hastened to help her, and would have taken hold of her hands, but she repulsed him, making signs as well as she could for him to go away. Then she set off running before him, and coming back signed to him to do the same thing. So he ran away and returned. But when he had come back she got angry, and taking her arrows aimed them at his heart as if to show him he would be killed. He thought she meant to take his life, and kneeling on the ground he awaited the stroke. When she saw this she was at her wit's end what to do and how to express her meaning. Looking at him tenderly, she said: "Ah, must you then be the victim of the terrible ogres? Must

I with these eyes that now have the joy of looking on you, see you torn to pieces and pitilessly devoured?" She wept, and the prince in sad confusion understood not a word of what she was saying. However, one thing she made him understand, that she did not wish him to follow her. Taking him by the hand she led him into a very deep cave with an opening looking towards the sea. She used often to go and lament her misfortunes there, and would sleep there when the sun was too scorching for her to return to the ogres' cave, and as she was very deft and skilful with her hands, she had hung it round with a tissue of butterfly wings of different colours, and on interlaced reeds forming a kind of couch she had spread a covering of sea-weed. She had put branches of flowers in great deep shells which served as vases and which she filled with water to keep the bouquets fresh. There were all kinds of other pretty things that she had made, some with fish and shells, others with sea-weed and reeds, and about all these trifles, in spite of their simplicity, there was something so graceful that it was easy to see from them the good taste and the skill of the princess. The prince was so astonished at all this elegance that he thought this cave must be her home. He was delighted to be with her, and though he was not fortunate enough to make her understand the admiration she filled him with, he already felt that he should prefer to see her and to live near her to all the crowns to which his birth and the desires of his family called him. She made him sit down, and then to show that she wished him to stay there till she had brought him something to eat, she undid the rush that fastened a part of her hair, and tied one end of it to the prince's arm and the other to the little bed. Then she left him. He was dying to follow her, but he was afraid of displeasing her, and he gave himself up to the thoughts which the presence of the princess had driven away. "Where am I?" he said. "Into what country has fortune led me? My ships are lost, my men are drowned. Everything fails me. Instead of the crown which was offered to me, I find a miserable cave where I am forced to seek shelter. What will become of me here? What sort of people shall I find here? To judge by the damsel who came to my aid, they are gods, but the fear she had lest I should follow her, that hard and barbarous language which sounds so harshly in her beautiful mouth, lead me to dread some adventure still more terrible than what has already happened!" Then he went over very carefully in his mind all the incomparable points of beauty in the young barbarian. His heart took fire. He longed impatiently for her return, and her absence seemed the greatest evil of all. Yet she came back with all the speed possible. The prince had not been out of her mind a single instant, and love was such a new experience to her that she did not fear it, but thanked heaven for having saved the prince from the perils of the sea, and begged that he might be preserved from the dangers with which the ogres threatened him. She was so laden and she had walked so quickly that when she got back she felt somewhat faint under the great tiger-skin that served her for mantle. She sat down, and the prince was at her feet in great distress at her suffering, for in truth he felt worse than she did. After a little she recovered, and showed him all the little dishes she had brought him, amongst which were four parrots and six squirrels cooked in the sun, strawberries, cherries, raspberries and other fruits. The plates were of cedar and calambac * wood, the knife was of stone, the napkins of large leaves of trees, very soft and pliable. She had brought two shells, one containing clear water and the other to drink out of.

The prince showed his gratitude by every sign of head and hands he could think of, and she, with a gentle smile, let him see that all he did was pleasing to her. But the hour for parting having come, she made him clearly understand that she was going away. Both began to sigh, and both to weep tenderly, yet each to hide their tears from the other. The princess got up and made for the entrance, but the prince uttered a loud cry and threw himself at her feet, begging her to remain. She knew well enough what he meant, but she put him aside, assuming a severe manner, and let him see that he must early learn the habit of obedience to her. In truth, he passed a terrible night. And the princess no less so, for when she reached the cavern and found herself in the midst of the ogres and their little ones, and looked at the hideous young ogre, the monster who was to be her husband, and thought of the charms of the stranger whom she had just left, she was on the point of throwing herself head foremost into the sea. Besides, she was in terror lest Ravagio or Tourmentine should smell human flesh, and should go straight to the cave and devour Prince Aimé. All these terrors kept her awake the whole night. At dawn she rose and took the road to the shore. She ran, she flew, laden with parrots, monkeys, a bustard, fruits, milk, and all the best things she could find. The prince had not undressed. He had undergone so much fatigue on the sea, and he had slept so little during the night that towards day he fell into a light slumber. "What!" she said, waking him, "I have been thinking of you since ever I left you. I have not even shut my eyes; but you can sleep!" The prince looked at her, and listened without understanding. Then he said, kissing her hands : "What joy, dear child; what joy to see you again! It seems an age since you left the cave." He spoke to her for long without remembering that she could not know what he was saying. When he remembered he sighed deeply and was silent. Then she spoke, saying she was terribly anxious lest Ravagio and Tourmentine should

---

* A fragrant wood, called also agal or eagle wood.

discover him ; that she dared not hope that he might remain safely in this cave, and that if he went away she would die, but that she would see him go rather than see him devoured, and so she begged him to make his escape. Here her eyes filled with tears, and she clasped her hands before her in a piteous fashion. He could not understand what she meant, and in desperation he threw himself at her feet. At last she pointed out the road to him so many times that he understood some part of her signs, and he made it clear, in his turn, that he would die rather than leave her. So keenly did she feel this proof of the prince's friendship that to show him how sensible of it she was, she took off the gold chain and turquoise heart which the queen, her mother, had fastened round her neck, and put it on the prince's arm with the utmost grace. Though overpowered by this favour he could not help seeing the inscription engraved on the turquoise. Looking carefully at this he read—

Aimée, daughter of the King of Happy Isle.

Never was any one so astonished. He knew that the name of the little princess that had been lost was Aimée. He did not doubt but that this heart had been hers, but he was not yet sure if this beautiful savage were the princess, or if the sea had cast up the jewel on the sand. He looked at Aimée with keen glances, and the more he looked at her the more he seemed to see a certain family likeness in her manner and in certain features, but it was more especially the feelings of tenderness within his soul that assured him that this barbarian was indeed his cousin. She looked on with astonishment at all he did, while he raised his eyes to heaven as if to give thanks, gazing at her and weeping, taking her hands and kissing them fervently ; then thanking her for all the gifts she had brought him, and giving them back to her again as if to make her understand that a lock of her hair would be more precious to him. And this he asked of her, but it was not easy for him to obtain the boon.

Four days passed away in this manner. Every morning the princess brought him what he needed in the way of food. She stayed with him as long as possible, and the hours went by very quickly, though the pleasure of conversing with each other was debarred them. One evening, when she was late of returning home, and feared she would be scolded by the terrible Tourmentine, she was much surprised to receive a most friendly welcome, and to find a table laden with fruits. When she asked permission to take some, Ravagio told her they were there specially for her ; that the young ogre had gone to gather them ; that at last the time had come to make him happy, and that in three days he wished to marry her. This was indeed news for her. Could anything be more terrible for this lovely princess? She all but died of fright and grief, but hiding her pain, she answered that she would willingly obey if only they would give her a little more time. Ravagio became angry, and cried out: "There is nothing to prevent my eating you!" The poor princess fell senseless with fright into the clutches of Tourmentine and the young ogre, who loved her so well that he entreated Ravagio, so that his anger was softened. Aimée did not sleep a wink that night. She waited for the day impatiently, and as soon as it appeared she ran to the cave. When she saw the prince she wept aloud piteously, shedding floods of tears. As for him, he could hardly move. His affection for fair Aimée had made more progress in four days than is usually the case in the same number of years. He was dying to ask her what was the matter, and though she knew this quite well she could not explain her meaning. At last she took down her long hair, and put a crown of flowers on her head. Taking Aimé's hand in her own, she made it clear to him by signs that she would soon be doing the same thing to another than himself, till at last he understood the unhappy fate that awaited him, and that she was going to be married. He thought he must die at her feet. He knew neither the roads nor the means of escape, nor did she. They wept, they looked at each other, and made signs to each other that they would rather die together than be apart. She remained with him till evening, but night came on sooner than they expected. Full of thought, she paid little attention to the paths she was treading, and took a little-used road through a wood, and there a great thorn pierced her foot through and through. Happily she was not very far from the cavern, but she found it difficult to reach it with her bleeding foot. Ravagio, Tourmentine, and the little ogres came to her aid. It hurt her very much when the thorn was taken out, but they pounded herbs and applied them to the wound. She went to bed in the greatest possible anxiety about her dear prince. "Alas!" she said, "I shall not be able to walk to-morrow. What will he think when he does not see me? I let him know that my marriage was arranged, and he will think I have had to give in to it. Who will bring him food? Whatever he does he must die, for if he comes in search of me he is lost, and if I send a little ogre to him Ravagio will hear of it." She burst into tears, and sobbed. She wished to rise early, but it was impossible for her to walk; her wound was too bad. And Tourmentine, who saw her go out, stopped her, and said that if she went another step she would eat her up.

Meanwhile the prince, who saw the hour pass by when she was in the habit of coming, began to be uneasy and full of fear. And as the time went on he grew still more afraid. Any punishment in the world would have been easier to bear than the anxieties to which his love made him a victim. He forced himself to wait in patience, but the more he waited the less was his hope. At last, ready to die if need be, he set out resolved to seek his dear princess. He walked on without knowing where he was going, and followed a beaten path he found at the entrance of the wood. After having walked for an hour he heard a noise, and seeing the cavern, from whence a thick smoke was rising, he thought he might learn some news of her there. Scarcely had he set his foot inside when he saw Ravagio, who, taking hold of him with violence, was just going to devour him when the cries he uttered in his struggles reached the ears of his dear princess. At that voice she felt as if nothing could stop her, and coming out of her own hole she rushed into the one where Ravagio was holding the poor prince. She was all pale and trembling, as if she had been going to be the victim. Throwing herself before the ogre, she begged him to keep this human flesh for the day of her wedding with the young ogre, promising that she herself would eat of it. Hearing this, Ravagio was so pleased to think that the princess was falling in with his habits that he let the prince go, and shut him up in the hole where the little ogres slept. Aimée asked leave to feed him well, so that he might be fat and do honour to the feast, and the ogre gave her leave. So she brought the prince the best she could find of everything. When he saw her come in, the joy he felt comforted him in his wretchedness, but when she showed the wound on her foot his grief broke out anew. They wept for long together. The prince could not eat, and his dear mistress cut little morsels with her delicate hands and gave them to him with such grace that it was impossible to refuse them. She bade the little ogres bring fresh moss, which she covered over with birds' feathers, and then she signed to the prince that his bed was there. Tourmentine calling her, she could say no other farewell but by giving him her hand, which he kissed with such tenderness as cannot be described, while she let her eyes express all her thoughts.

Ravagio, Tourmentine, and the princess slept in one of the recesses of the cavern, while the young ogre and the five little ogres slept in the other. Now in Ogreland it is the custom every night for the ogre, the ogress, and the little ones to put on their heads fine golden crowns in which they sleep. This is their only kind of splendour; but they would rather be hanged or strangled than fail to do it. When they had all fallen asleep, the princess, whose thoughts were with her dear lover, began to reflect that in spite of the promises of Ravagio and Tourmentine not to eat him, if they were hungry during the night, as they nearly always were when there was human flesh about, all hope for him was gone; and her anxiety on his account became so violent that she all but died of terror. After thinking the matter over for some time she got up, put on her tiger-skin in haste, and groping her way noiselessly along, she reached the cavern where the little ogres were sleeping. Taking the crown from the first one that came in her way, she placed it on the prince's head, who was wide awake, but who did not dare to seem so, not knowing who was performing this ceremony. Then the princess went back to her own little bed.

Hardly had she got into it, when Ravagio, thinking what a fine meal the prince would make, and growing hungrier every minute at the thought, got up and went to the hole where the little ogres slept. As he did not see clearly, for fear of taking the wrong one, he felt with his hand, and seizing the one that had no crown, munched him up like a chicken. The poor princess, hearing the noise which Ravagio made in munching the bones of the unfortunate little ogre, fainted and nearly died of fear lest it should be her lover; while as for the prince, who was still nearer, he felt all the terrors of his situation.

Day brought a great relief to the princess. She ran to see the prince, and let him understand by signs her fears and her impatience to see him out of reach of the murderous teeth of these monsters. She spoke kindly to him, and he would have poured out kind words to her had not the ogress, coming to see her children, noticed the blood with which the cavern was full, and found out that the little baby ogre was missing. The shrieks she uttered were terrible, and Ravagio realised the harm he had done—but too late to remedy it. He whispered in her ear that being hungry he had chosen the wrong victim, thinking he was eating human flesh. Tourmentine pretended to be consoled, for Ravagio was cruel, and if she had not taken his excuses in good part, she would perhaps have been eaten up herself.

But, alas! what terrible anxiety did the princess suffer. Never for a moment did she give up searching for some means of saving the prince. And as for him, what were his thoughts with respect to the terrible home of this charming maiden? He could not make up his mind to go away while she was here, for death would have seemed sweeter than such a separation. And this he made her understand, when by repeated signs she begged him to flee and to take steps to save himself. They mingled their tears, and taking each other by the hand, each in their own tongue swore faithfulness and everlasting love one to the other. She could not help showing him the clothes she had worn when Tourmentine found her, and the cradle in which she had lain, and the prince recognised on them the arms and the device of the King of Happy Isle. This sight delighted him, and his joy was so evident that the princess guessed that the cradle had told him something of importance. She was dying to hear what it might be, but however hard he tried, how could he make her understand whose daughter she was, and the kinship between them? All she understood was that she had reason to be very happy. The hour for retiring came, and they went to bed as they had done the night before. The princess, a prey to the same fears, rose quietly, went to the cavern where the prince was, gently took the crown from one of the little ogres, and put it on her lover's head. He dared not detain her, however much he wished to, for the respect he felt for her and his fear of displeasing her restrained him. The princess had never had a happier thought than putting the crown on Aimé's head. Without this precaution all would have been lost, for the cruel Tourmentine, starting out of her sleep and remembering the prince she had thought as beautiful as the day and so very appetising, began to be much afraid that Ravagio would go and eat him all by himself. So she thought the best plan was to be beforehand with him. She slipped away, without a word, to the little ogres' hole, where she passed over quietly those that had crowns on—among whom was the prince—and in three mouthfuls the little uncrowned ogre was gobbled up. Aimé and his princess heard everything, trembling with fear; but Tourmentine having made this expedition now wished for nothing but sleep, and they were safe for the rest of the night. " Heaven help us!" said the princess. " Inspire us with what we should do in such a terrible extremity." And the prince prayed no less fervently. At times he thought of attacking these two monsters and fighting with them. But how could he hope to win in the struggle ? They were tall as giants, and their skin was pistol proof, so that very sensibly he came to the conclusion that only ingenuity could bring them out of this terrible place.

As soon as it was day and Tourmentine had found the bones of her little ogre, she set up a frightful howling, and Ravagio was no less distressed. A hundred times they were on the point of throwing themselves on the prince and princess and killing them mercilessly. They were both hidden in a little dark corner, but the cannibals knew only too well where they were, and of all the dangers they had met with this one seemed the most imminent. Aimée set a-thinking and racking her brains, and all at once she bethought herself of the ivory wand which Tourmentine used, and which did wonders, though the ogress herself did not know how. " If, in spite of her ignorance," said the princess, "most astonishing things come to pass, why should there not be as much power in my words ? " Full of this idea she ran to the cavern where Tourmentine slept and searched for the wand, which was hidden at the bottom of a hole. When she had it in her hands she cried: " In the name of the royal Fairy Trusio, I desire to speak the tongue that is spoken by him whom I love ". And she would have wished for other things, but Ravagio came in at the moment. So the princess was silent, and putting the wand in its place, came back very quietly to the prince. " Dear stranger," she said, " your sorrows give me more pain than my own." At these words the prince was all astonishment and confusion. " Adorable princess," he said, " I understand you. You speak my language, and surely I may hope that you also understand that my suffering is less for myself than for you, and that you are dearer to me than my life, dearer than light or than all that is loveliest in nature." "My words are simpler," answered the princess, "but they are none the less sincere. I feel as if I would give all that I have in my sea-cave, my sheep, my lambs, in short, everything I possess, only for the pleasure of looking on you." The prince thanked her a thousand times for her goodness to him, and begged her to tell him who had taught her in such a short time all the terms and all the refinements of a language which had till now been unknown to her. So she told him of the power of the enchanted wand, while he in his turn made known to her her birth and their kinship. The princess was overpowered with joy, and as naturally she had great mental gifts, everything she said was so subtle and so well expressed that the prince felt his affection for her growing more and more.

They had no time to arrange their plans. The first thing to be thought of was to flee from those angry monsters, and to seek as soon as possible a shelter where they might be free to love each other, which they vowed to do for ever, and to wed as soon as they could. The princess told her lover that as soon as she saw Ravagio and Tourmentine asleep she would go and fetch their great camel, and that they would mount on it and ride away wherever heaven should please to lead them. The prince was so glad that he could hardly contain his delight, and though there was reason enough for terror, still the hopeful prospect before them made their present ills easier to bear.

The night so longed for came at last. The princess took some flour, and with her white hands she kneaded a cake into which she put a bean. Then holding the ivory wand in her hand, she said : "Bean, little bean, in the name of the royal Fairy Trusio, I command you to speak when it may be necessary, until you are cooked". She put this cake under the hot cinders, and went to the prince who was waiting for her impatiently in the little ogres' wretched hole. "Come away," said she, "the camel is tied in the wood." "May love and good fortune be our guides!" answered the young prince in a low voice. "Come, come, my Aimée; come seek a happy, peaceful home." She had not forgotten to take with her the ivory wand when in the moonlight they set out. Finding the camel, they took the road without knowing where they were going.

Meanwhile Tourmentine, who could not forget her sorrow, turned over and over in her bed without being able to sleep. She stretched out her arm to feel whether the princess was already in her little bed, and not finding her, she cried, in a voice like thunder: "Where are you then, child?" "Here I am, near the fire," answered the bean. "Will you go to bed?" said Tourmentine. "Very soon," replied the bean. "Go to sleep, go to sleep." Tourmentine was afraid to awake her Ravagio, and was silent; but after two hours again she groped in Aimée's little bed, crying: "What, you little jade, you will not go to bed?" "I am warming myself as fast as I can," answered the bean. "I wish you were roasting in the middle of the fire for your trouble," said the ogress. "So I am," said the bean; "I couldn't be more so." And so they went on talking, the bean keeping up the conversation very cleverly till, towards daybreak, Tourmentine again calling the princess, the bean, now thoroughly cooked, did not answer. This silence made the ogress uneasy, so she got up in a great state, looked, called, and searched all round in much alarm. Princess, prince, and little wand, all gone! Then she cried aloud, so that the woods and the valleys rang again: "Awake, my dear one, awake, my brave Ravagio, your Tourmentine has been deceived, and our two human prisoners have taken their flight". Ravagio opened his eye, leaped into the middle of the cavern like a lion, roaring, bellowing, howling, and foaming at the mouth. "Come!" said he, "come, my seven-league boots! bring hither my seven-league boots, till I pursue the runaways! I'll have their blood before they have gone far." And he put on the boots, which enabled one of his legs to take a seven-league step. Alas! how could the fugitives go fast enough to escape such a pursuer?

You will be astonished to hear that, having the ivory wand, they did not go faster than he, but the fair princess was new to the fairy art. She did not know how much she could do with such a wand, and it was only in great difficulties that light dawned on her. The pleasure of being together, and able to speak to each other, and the hope that they might be allowed to escape, quieted their fears as they went on their way. It was the princess who first saw the terrible Ravagio. "Prince," she cried, "we are lost. See this hideous monster coming on us like a thunderbolt!" "What can we do?" said the prince. "What will become of us? Ah, if I were but alone I should not regret my life, but yours, dear mistress, is in danger!" "I am in despair. If the wand does not come to our aid," said Aimée, weeping, "we must make up our minds to die. In the name of the royal Fairy Trusio, I desire that our camel become a pond, the prince a boat, and myself an old boatwoman to guide it." And at the moment the pond, the boat, and the boatwoman took shape. When Ravagio reached the water's edge, he cried out: "Holloa there! Ho! old Mother Everlasting! Haven't you seen a camel, a young man, and a maiden pass by?" The old woman, standing in the middle of the pond, put her spectacles on, and looking at Ravagio, signed to him that she had seen them, and that they had gone into the meadow. The ogre believing her, took the road to the left. The princess then wishing to appear in her own shape again, touched herself with the wand three times, and struck the boat and the pond with it. She was young and beautiful again in a moment, and so was the prince. Mounting the camel, they turned to the right in order not to meet their enemy.

While they were going on their way in all haste, in hopes of finding some one of whom they might ask the road to Happy Isle, they lived on the wild fruits and drank of the water of the streams, and slept under trees in terror all the while lest the wild beasts should come and devour them. But the princess had her bow and arrows, with which she would have tried to defend herself, and the danger did not frighten them so much as to prevent them from realising the happiness of having escaped from the cavern and of being together. Since they had been able to speak the same language, they said the prettiest things in the world to each other, for love is wont to sharpen intelligence, and indeed they had no need of this help, for nature had given them both much grace of mind and a lively wit. The prince told the princess how very impatient he was to reach his father's home or hers without delay, since she had promised that, provided their parents gave their consent, she would marry him. What perhaps will not be easily believed is that, till that happy day should come, they lived alone together in the woods behaving towards each other so respectfully and so sensibly, though he was in a position to do what he liked, that never was so much affection and goodness found together.

After Ravagio had scoured the mountains, forests, and plains, he returned to his cavern, where Tourmentine and the little ogres waited for him impatiently. He came home laden with five or six persons who had unhappily fallen into his clutches. "Well," cried Tourmentine, "have you found them and eaten them, the runaways, the thieves, the carrion? Haven't you kept a scrap for me?" "I think they must have flown," answered Ravagio. "I have hunted on every side like a wolf, and have not seen them—only an old woman in a boat on a pond, who gave me news of them." "And what did she say to you?" said the impatient Tourmentine. "That they had gone to the left," said Ravagio. "By my head," said she, "but you have been made a fool of. I feel sure that it was to their very selves you talked. Go back again, and if you catch them have no mercy." So Ravagio greased his seven-league boots, and set off again like a madman. Our young lovers were just coming out of the wood, where they had passed the night; when they saw him they were both afraid. "My Aimée," said the prince, "here is our enemy. I feel I could fight him. Are you brave enough to escape by yourself?" "No," she cried. "I shall not leave you. Cruel one, do you doubt my affection? But let us not lose a moment. Perhaps the wand may be of help to us. In the name of the royal Fairy Trusio," she cried, "I desire that the prince be changed into a portrait, the camel into a pillar, and myself into a dwarf." The change took place, and the dwarf began to blow a horn. Ravagio, who was coming on with great strides, said : " Tell me, you unnatural imp, have you seen a pretty boy, a little maid, and a camel pass by ? " " Now will I tell you," said the dwarf. " It is known to me that you are in quest of a gentle youth, a fair lady, and the animal on which they ride. I saw them yesterday at this hour ambling along in joy and contentment. The gentle knight received the praise and guerdon of the jousts and tournaments which were being held in honour of Merlusine, whose living picture here you see. Many fine gentlemen and brave knights broke lances there on hauberk, helmet, or buckler. The conflict was rude, and the reward a very beautiful golden clasp, adorned with pearls and diamonds. As I was taking my departure the unknown lady said to me : ' Dwarf, my friend, without more words I ask a boon of you for the sake of your dearest friend '. ' If it be in my power it will not be denied, and I will grant it,' said I. ' In case, then,' she said, ' that you should see the great and wonderful giant with the eye in the middle of his forehead, beg him very courteously to go on his way in peace and leave us to do the same.' Then she pricked her palfrey, and they went away." " In which direction ? " said Ravagio. " Towards that green meadow on the edge of the wood," said the dwarf. " If you are not telling the truth," said the ogre, " be assured, you hideous imp, that I shall eat you up and your pillar and your picture of Merlusine and all." " There is no villainy or falsehood in me," said the dwarf; " my mouth is no lying one, and no living man has ever been deceived by me. But make haste if you would kill them before the sun sets." The ogre went away. The dwarf assumed her own shape, and, touching the pillar and the portrait, they too took their own forms again.

What joy for the lover and his mistress ! " Nay," said the prince, " but I have never before felt such keen alarm, dear Aimée. As my affection for you every moment grows stronger, so do my anxieties increase when you are in danger." " And as for me," she replied, " I don't think I was in the least afraid, for Ravagio does not eat pictures ; I alone was exposed to his fury, and I would give my life to save yours."

Ravagio ran, but all in vain, for he found neither lover nor mistress. Tired out like a dog he returned to the cavern. " What, you come back without our prisoners ? " cried Tourmentine, tearing her bristling hair. " Do not come near me or I shall strangle you." " I have met nobody," said he, " but a dwarf with a pillar and a picture." " By my head," she replied, " it was they. What a fool I am to leave my revenge to you, as if I were not big enough to look after it myself ! Well, well, I am off. I shall put the boots on this time, and I shall go with no less speed than you." So she put on the seven-league boots, and went away. How could the prince and princess go fast enough to escape these monsters with their accursed seven-league boots ? They saw Tourmentine coming, clad in a wonderful serpent's skin of motley colours. Over her shoulder she carried a bar of iron, enormously heavy, and looking round carefully on every side as she did, she must have seen the prince and princess if at that moment they had not been in the depths of a wood. "The case is hopeless," said Aimée, weeping. "Here is that cruel Tourmentine, whose very look freezes my blood. She is cleverer than Ravagio. If either of us speaks to her she will recognise us, and without more ado will eat us up. Our end is coming, I assure you." "O God of Love," cried the prince, "do not abandon us! Hast thou beneath thy rule any hearts more tender, any affections purer than ours ? Ah, my dear Aimée," he went on, taking her hands and kissing them fervently, "is it fated you should die in so cruel a way ? " " No," she answered. " No; I feel within me a courage and a resolution which give me hope. Come, little wand, do your duty. In the name of the royal Fairy Trusio, I desire the camel to be a box, my dear prince a beautiful orange tree, while I, turned into a bee, fly round him." According to her custom, she gave each of them three taps, and the change took place soon enough for Tourmentine, who came up just then, not to see it happening.

The hideous fury was quite out of breath, and sat down under the orange tree, where Princess Bee took pleasure in stinging her all over; and though the ogress's skin was tough enough, the bee pierced it, and made her cry out. As Tourmentine lay rolling and struggling on the grass, she looked like some bull or young lion attacked by flies, for this bee was as bad as a hundred such; and Prince Orange-tree was in deadly fright lest the princess should allow herself to be caught and killed. At last Tourmentine went away all bleeding, and the princess was just about to take her own shape again, when unhappily some travellers passing through the wood, and seeing the ivory wand which was very pretty to look at, picked it up and carried it off. Nothing more unfortunate could have happened. The prince and princess had not lost the power of speech, but that was very poor comfort in their present condition. The prince, overcome with grief, uttered his laments aloud, which added greatly to the sorrow of his dear Aimée. Sometimes he would say :—

> "Long had I waited, and when hope at last ·
>   Was mine, and joy had come in sight,
> All my clear sky was sudden overcast,
>   All my fair season with a deadly blight.
> O God of Love! whose power is greater still
>   Than Fortune's cruel intent to bereave me,
> Watch o'er my mistress's heart, and form her will
>   That she may ever love, and never leave me."

"Ah, how unhappy I am!" he went on. "Here I am pent up under this bark. Here I am an orange tree. I cannot move, and what will become of me if you leave me, dear little bee? But," he added, "why should you leave me? You will find on my flowers delicious dew, and a liquor sweeter than honey, on which you can feed. My leaves will serve you for a bed of rest, where you will have nothing to fear from the malice of spiders." As soon as the orange tree ended his lament, the bee answered him :—

> "My love is fixed. No wavering to and fro
> Thou hast to fear.
> My heart thou madest thine : it resteth so,
> Thy weariness to cheer."

And then she added: "Do not be afraid that I shall ever leave you. Neither lilies, nor jasmines, nor roses, nor any of the flowers in the most beautiful gardens could tempt me to such faithlessness. You will see me flying round you ceaselessly, and you will know that the orange tree is no less dear to the bee than the prince was to Princess Aimée." And then she shut herself into one of the largest flowers as into a palace, and true affection, which finds resources everywhere, did not fail in its comfort here.

The wood where the orange tree grew was the favourite walk of a princess who lived in a magnificent palace. She was young and beautiful and clever, and her name was Linda. She had no wish to marry, for she feared that any one whom she might take for a husband would not always love her. And as she was very rich she had a splendid castle built, where she received only ladies and old men, who were more learned than gallant. And no other knights might approach her. The heat of the day having kept her in her room rather longer than she would have liked, she went out in the evening with her ladies to walk in the woods. The scent of the orange blossom astonished her, for she had never seen the tree before, and was delighted to find it. No one knew by what chance it had come there, and it was quickly surrounded by all this great company. Linda would not let them pick a single flower, and they took it into her garden, where the faithful bee followed. Linda, delighted with its delicious scent, sat down under it, and just as she was picking some flowers before going into the palace, the watchful bee came out buzzing from under the leaves where she had placed herself as sentinel and stung the princess with such a force that she all but fainted. There was no more question of plucking the flowers from the orange tree, and Linda went home very ill.

When the prince was free to speak to Aimée, he said : "What spite have you, dear bee, against young Linda? You have stung her cruelly." "How can you ask me such a question?" she answered. "Have you not delicacy enough to see that you should feel affection for none but me, that the whole of you belongs to me, and that I am defending my property when I defend your flowers?" "But," said he, "you see them falling, and it does not trouble you. Would it not be the same if the princess decked herself with them, put them in her hair, or wore them in her bosom?" "No," said the bee, in a somewhat vexed tone, "it is not at all the same thing. I know, you ungrateful creature, that you care more for her than for me. There is of course a great difference between a lady, refined and richly clad, of high rank, and an unfortunate princess whom you have seen dressed in tiger-skin, in the midst of monsters that have only taught her harsh and savage manners, and whose beauty is not dazzling enough to strike you." Here she wept as much as a bee is capable of weeping, and some of the flowers of the tender orange tree were wet with her tears. Aimé was so sorry to have wounded his princess that all his leaves grew yellow, several of his branches withered, and he was like to die. "What have I done then," he cried, "beautiful bee? What have I done to draw down your wrath on me? Ah, you doubtless wish to leave me. You are already tired of being attached to an unfortunate creature like myself." They spent the night reproaching one another, but at dawn, a gentle zephyr that had been listening to them, induced them to make up their quarrel, and it could not have done them a better turn.

Meanwhile Linda, who was dying to have a bunch of orange blossom, rose very early in the morning, and went to her garden to pluck some. But as soon as she put out her hand, she felt herself stung so violently by the jealous bee that her courage failed her. She returned to her own room in a very bad temper. "I do not understand," she said, "what kind of tree this is that we have found, but as soon as I wish to pluck the tiniest bud from it, the flies that guard it attack me with their stings." One of her maidens, a quick-witted, merry girl, said to her, laughing: "I am of opinion, madam, that you should arm yourself like an amazon, and like Jason when he went to capture the Golden Fleece, go boldly, and take the finest flowers of this pretty tree". Linda liked this idea, and at once gave orders for a helmet covered with feathers, a light cuirass, and gauntlets to be made for her, and at the sound of trumpets, timbrels, fifes, and hautboys, she entered her garden, followed by all her ladies, armed like herself. They called this sport the War of the Flies and the Amazons. Linda drew her sword with much grace, and then striking the finest branch of the orange tree, she cried: "Come out then, terrible bees, come on. I defy you! Are you valiant enough to defend what you love?" But what did Linda and those who were with her think when they heard a piteous "Alas!" followed by a deep sigh, proceeding from the trunk of the tree, and saw blood flowing from the branch that had been cut? What a wonder was this! Taking the bleeding

branch, she in vain placed the parts together to join them, and she was seized with terror and horrible anxiety. The poor little bee, in despair at the sad adventure of her dear orange tree, was on the point of rushing to seek her death by the same fatal sword, to avenge her dear prince, but she bethought herself it would be better to live for him, and thinking what remedy he stood in need of, she asked his consent to let her fly to Araby to bring him balm. And after he had at last consented, and they had said a tender and touching adieu to each other, she set out for that part of the world, with only her instinct to guide her. But in truth it was Love brought her there, and as he goes faster than the swiftest flies, by his aid she made a speedy journey, and brought back wonderful balm on her wings and at the end of her little feet, with which she cured the prince. It is true that the cure was due less to the excellence of the balm than to his pleasure in seeing the Princess Bee take so much care of his hurt. Every day she applied balm to it, and it had need, for the branch that had been cut was one of his fingers, and indeed had he suffered a little more of the treatment Linda had given him, neither arms nor legs would have remained. Oh! how keenly did the bee feel the sufferings of the orange tree, and how she reproached herself with being the cause of them, by her over-eagerness in defending its flowers.

Linda, in terror at what she had seen, neither slept nor ate. At last she determined to send for the fairies, to try to get some enlightenment on a matter that seemed to her so extraordinary. So she sent off ambassadors, and loaded them with presents, to request the fairies to come to her court. Among the first to come to Linda's palace was Queen Trusio. There never was any one so learned in the fairy art. She examined the branch and the orange tree, smelt the flowers, and distinguished a human odour that surprised her. Not a charm was there but she tried, and all the most powerful ones too, so that all at once, the orange tree disappearing, they saw the prince, the handsomest, the comeliest alive. At this sight Linda was struck motionless with admiration, and by some still keener feeling. She was already becoming more than indifferent to him, when the young prince, all whose thoughts were of his dear bee, threw himself at Trusio's feet. "Great queen!" he said, "I owe you everything. You give me back life itself in restoring me my own shape, but if you wish me to be your debtor for all my peace and joy, which is more even than the light you call me back to, give me my princess." And as he said these words he took up in his hands the little bee, on which he always kept his eyes. "I shall do as you wish," replied kind Trusio. And she began her ceremonies again, and Princess Aimée appeared, so charming that not a lady was there but was envious of her. Linda was secretly hesitating whether to feel joy or disappointment at so extraordinary an occurrence, and more especially at the change of the bee into human shape. But at last reason got the better of an affection which as yet was only in the bud, and she caressed Aimée over and over again, while Trusio begged her to tell her story. Aimée was too good-natured to delay satisfying them on this point, and the grace and the air of distinction with which she talked interested all who were present. When she told Trusio what wonders she had done in her name, and by her wand, a cry of joy arose in the hall, and each one begged the fairy to complete her great work.

Trusio on her side felt extreme pleasure at all she heard, and folded the princess closely in her arms. "Since I have been so useful to you without knowing it, you may think, dear Aimée, how glad I am to do you a service now that I do know you. I am a friend of your father, the king, and your mother, the queen. Let us be off at once then in my flying car to Happy Isle, where both of you will receive the welcome you deserve." Linda begged them to remain for a day with her, during which she presented them with rich gifts, and Princess Aimée cast off her tiger-skin and put on garments of exquisite beauty. Imagine now the joy of those tender lovers. Yes, if you can. But to do so you would have had to undergo the same mishaps, to have been among the ogres, and been changed into all sorts of different shapes. At last they set off. Trusio drove them through the air to Happy Isle, where they were received by the king and the queen as became those whose presence could least be expected and yet was most longed for. Aimée's beauty and goodness, together with her bright wit, made her the admiration of her age, and her dear mother loved her to distraction. The fine qualities of Prince Aimé charmed no less than his handsome face. When their marriage took place it was celebrated with great splendour. The Graces came in their festive attire. The Loves were there without even having been asked, and by special order of theirs the eldest son of the prince and princess was called Faithful Love. Since then he has had many different names given him, and among them all it is very difficult to distinguish him as Prince Faithful Love, the fruit of this charming, happy marriage. Happy they who really do meet with him !

THE GOOD LITTLE MOUSE.

ONCE upon a time there lived a king and a queen who loved each other so very, very much that they were all in all to each other. The one always knew what was in the other's mind and heart. Every day they hunted hares and stags in the forest, or fished for soles and carps in the river, or went to balls and danced the bourée* or the pavan,† or to grand banquets where they ate roast meats and sugar-plums, or to the play and the opera. They laughed and sang and invented all kinds of games to amuse themselves. In short, never were any two people so happy. And their subjects followed their example, and each man was merrier than his fellow. For all these reasons this kingdom was called the Land of Joy.

Now King Joyous had a neighbour who lived in quite a different way. He was the sworn enemy of every kind of pleasure, and only took delight in fighting and quarrelling. There was always a scowl on his face; his beard was long, and his eyes were hollow. He was skinny and shrunken, and always clad in black; and his greasy, dirty hair stood on end. His amusement was to see the passers-by knocked down and killed. Criminals he hung with his own hands, and to torture them gave him the keenest joy. Whenever he heard of a good mother who loved her little girl or boy, he sent for her, and before her eyes he broke their arms or wrung their necks. This kingdom was called the Land of Tears.

The fame of King Joyous' happiness came to the ears of the wicked king, who was very envious, and who made up his mind to levy a great army and go and fight his neighbour, and press him hard, till he should be dead or seriously

---

* National dance of Auvergne, in quick time.
† A slow dance in which the cavaliers and ladies wore long mantles or trains. These spreading out like peacocks' tails gave the name to the dance. L. pavo.

wounded. From all parts he gathered recruits. He collected arms, and ordered cannons to be made. Then everybody was terrified, and said: "Whomsoever this wicked king attacks he will give no quarter to".

When all his preparations were made he marched towards King Joyful's country, who, hearing the evil tidings, immediately set about defending himself. The queen nearly died of fright. " Sire," she said, weeping, " we must flee. Get all the money you can, and we shall go away to the other end of the world." But the king answered: " Madam, I have too much courage for that. I would rather die than be a coward." So, gathering his men round him, he bade the queen a tender farewell ; and, mounting his beautiful steed, rode away.

When he was lost to her sight she began to weep sadly, and clasping her hands, she said : " Alas ! for the child that is to be born to me ! If the king is killed in the wars, I shall be a widow and a prisoner, and the wicked king will harm me in every possible way." So for this thought she could neither eat nor sleep. The king used to write to her every day, but one morning when she was looking over the battlements she saw a courier riding at full speed. " Ho, courier !" she called. " What news ? " " The king is dead," he cried, " the battle is lost; and the wicked king will be here in a moment." The poor queen fell down in a swoon. They bore her away and laid her on her bed, while all her women stood round, here one weeping for her father, there another for her son. It was the saddest of all sights.

And now, all at once, they heard shrieks of murder and pillage ! It was the wicked king come with all his miserable people, and they were killing without distinction all who came in their way. He entered the palace armed to the teeth, and went to the queen's chamber. When she saw him come in, she was so terrified that she hid herself in her bed, and put the coverlet over her head. Twice or thrice he called her, but she answered not a word. Then he got angry, and in a great rage he said : " I verily believe you are laughing at me. Do you know that your life is in my hands at this moment ? " And, finding where she was, he snatched her cap off her head, so that her lovely hair fell down over her shoulders, and twisting it three times round in his hand, strung her up on his back by it like a sack of wheat. So he carried her off on his great black horse. She begged for mercy, but he only laughed, and said : " Cry then, and make your moan. It only amuses me, and makes me laugh."

He took her away to his own country, vowing all the time he would hang her. But his people told him it would be a pity, for a child would soon be born to her. When he knew that, it occurred to him that if the child were a daughter he might wed her with his son, and, to know which it would be, he sent for a fairy who dwelt on the borders of his kingdom. When she had come, he treated her more hospitably than was his custom ; and then took her up into a tower, at the top of which the poor queen had a little scantily-furnished room. Her bed was a mattress not worth a penny, laid on the floor, and there she wept day and night. When the fairy saw her she was deeply touched, and making her a curtsey, whispered while she embraced her: " Take courage, madam ; your sorrows will not last for ever. I hope to be of service to you." The queen, somewhat consoled by these words, kissed her, and begged her to take pity on a poor princess, who once had enjoyed a great fortune, and had seen it all vanish away. They were speaking together when the wicked king interrupted them with : " Come along now, don't make such a fuss ; I brought you here to tell me whether this slave is to bear a boy or a girl ". The fairy answered : " A girl, and she will be the most beautiful and the most accomplished princess that ever was seen ". She then wished the child endless gifts and honours. " If she is not beautiful and accomplished," said the wicked king, " I will hang her to her mother's neck, and I will hang her mother on a tree, and no one shall hinder me." And so saying he went out along with the fairy, without casting a glance at the good queen, who was weeping bitterly. " For, alas ! " she said to herself, " what can I do ? If I have a pretty little girl, he will give her to his monkey of a son, and if she is ugly he will hang both of us. What an unhappy lot is mine ! Could I not hide her somewhere, so that he might never see her ? "

The time of the little princess's birth was drawing near, and the anxieties of the queen grew worse every day. She had no one to share her grief with, or to console her. The gaoler who guarded her only gave her three peas cooked in water the whole day long, with a little morsel of black bread. She became thinner than a herring, till she was nothing but skin and bone. One evening while she was spinning for the wicked king, who was a great miser and made her work day and night, she saw a very pretty little mouse come in through a hole. " Alas, little one," she said, " what are you seeking here ? I have only three peas for my food all the day long, so, if you don't like fasting, run away." The little mouse ran here and there, dancing and cutting capers like a little monkey, and the queen was so amused that she gave it the only pea she had left for her supper. " Here, little one," she said, " eat this ; I have no more, but I give it you with a good will." As soon as she had done this, she saw on the table an excellent partridge, exquisitely cooked, and two pots of jam. " In truth," she said, " the good one does is never lost." She ate a little, but her appetite had gone through long fasting. She threw some sweets to the mouse, and it munched them up, and then began to jump about in a livelier way than it had done before supper. Next morning early the gaoler brought the queen's three peas, having put them in a large dish just to mock her. The little mouse came softly and ate them all up, and the bread too. When the queen wished to dine, she found nothing left, and she was very angry with the mouse. "It is a naughty little beast," she said, "and if it goes on doing this I shall die of hunger." When she went to cover up the large dish, which was empty, she found in it all kinds of good things to eat. But while she was eating, the thought came to her that in two or three days perhaps the wicked king would put her child to death, and she rose from the table to weep. Then, lifting her eyes to heaven, she said: "Are there no means of escape?" As she said this she saw the little mouse playing with long pieces of straw. Picking them up, she began to work. "If I have straw enough," she said, "I shall make a covered basket to put my little girl in, and I will give her through the window to the first charitable person who will take care of her." She set to work, therefore, with a good heart. She had plenty of straw, for the mouse was always dragging some into the room, and jumping about all the while. At meal-times the queen gave it her three peas, and found in exchange all sorts of dishes. This astonished her very much, and she never stopped wondering who could be sending her such excellent things.

The queen was looking through the window one day, to see how long the cord should be which she must fasten to the basket to let it down, when, below, she saw a little old woman leaning on a staff, who said to her: "I know your trouble, madam, and if you like I will help you ". "Alas! dear friend," said the queen, "you will do me a great service if you come every evening to the foot of the tower. I shall let down my poor child to you. You will feed it, and I shall try to pay you well, if I am ever rich." "I am not fond of money," the old woman answered, "but I like good things to eat. There is nothing I care so much for as a fine plump mouse. If you find any in your garret, kill them, and throw them down to me. I shall not be ungrateful, and your baby will thrive well." When the queen heard this she began to cry, and did not say a word in reply, and the old woman, after waiting for some time, asked her why she was weeping. "Because," she said, "only one mouse comes to my room, and it is so pretty and so sweet that I cannot make up my mind to kill it." "What!" said the old woman, angrily, "you care more for a silly little mouse that gnaws at everything than the child that is to be born to you! Very well, madam, you are not to be pitied. Remain, if you wish, in such good company. I shall find plenty of mice without you; I haven't the least doubt about that." And she went away scolding and muttering.

Although the queen found a nice meal prepared for her, and the mouse came and danced before her, she never once lifted her eyes from the ground where she had fixed them, and the tears ran down her cheeks. That night a princess was born, a miracle of beauty; and, instead of crying as other children do, she smiled to her dear mother, holding out her little hands as if she understood everything. The queen caressed and kissed her with great tenderness, thinking sadly: "Poor darling! Dear child, if you fall into the hands of the wicked king it is all over with you." So she put her in the basket, with a label fastened to her swaddling clothes, on which was written :—

This unhappy little girl is called Joliette;

and when she had left her for a moment without looking at her she opened the basket again, and found her much prettier still. Then she kissed her and wept yet more bitterly, not knowing what she should do.

But now the little mouse comes, and gets into the basket with Joliette. "Ah, little creature," said the queen, "it has cost me much to save your life. Perhaps I may lose my dear Joliette. Anyone else would have killed you and given you over to the old glutton, but I could not consent." "Do not repent of what you have done, madam," began the mouse; "I am not so unworthy of your friendship as you may think." The queen was half dead with fright at hearing the mouse talk, but her terror grew much worse when she saw its little snout taking the form of a face, its paws becoming hands and feet, and its whole body growing suddenly larger. At last the queen, who hardly dared to look any more, recognised in the mouse the fairy who had come with the wicked king, and who had treated her so tenderly.

"I wished to test your heart," said the fairy; "I know now it is good, and that you are capable of friendship. We fairies, though we possess immense treasures and riches, seek love as the only consolation in life, and we find it rarely." "Is it possible, fair lady," said the queen, embracing her, "that, being so rich and powerful as you are, you have difficulty in finding friends?" "Yes," she answered, "for we are only loved because it is to people's advantage to show us affection, and we do not care for that. But when you loved me in the shape of a little mouse you had no selfish motive. Then I wished to put you to a still harder test, and so I took the form of an old woman. It was I who talked to you at the foot of the tower, and you then, as always, were true to me." So saying she embraced the queen, kissed the little princess's red lips three times, and said : "My gifts to you, my daughter, are, that you be your mother's comfort, that you be richer than your father, and that you live for a hundred years, ever beautiful, never ill, never wrinkled, never old ". The queen in great delight thanked her, and begged her to take Joliette away and care for her, adding that she gave her the child for a daughter.

The fairy accepted the gift and thanked the queen. Putting the little one into the basket she let it down. But she stopped for an instant to change herself into a little mouse again, and when she went down herself afterwards by the cord the child was not to be found. She mounted again in a great fright. "All is lost," she said to the queen ; "my enemy, Cancaline, has carried off the princess. You must know that there is a cruel fairy who hates me, and unhappily, being older than I, she has more power. I do not know how to get Joliette out of her wicked clutches."

When the queen heard such sad news she thought she must die of grief. She wept very bitterly, and begged her good friend to do what she could to find the little one again, at whatever cost.

But meanwhile the gaoler came to the queen's room, and, finding that the child had been born, he went to tell the king, who hastened to demand the princess. But she told him that a fairy, whose name she did not know, had come and taken her away by force. Now the wicked king stamped his foot and bit his nails till he had none left. "I told you I should hang you," he said, "and I am going to keep my promise at once." At the word he dragged the poor queen into a wood, climbed up a tree, and was just going to hang her when the fairy made her invisible, and, giving him a great shove, made him fall from the top of the tree, breaking four of his teeth. While they were trying to mend them, the fairy bore the queen away in a flying car to a beautiful castle, where she took great care of her. If only she had had the Princess Joliette with her she would have been quite happy, but it was impossible to discover where Cancaline had hidden her, though the little mouse did her very best.

Time went on, and softened the queen's great sorrow. Fifteen years had already gone by, when a rumour was spread abroad that the wicked king's son was going to marry his turkey-herd, though the little creature was unwilling.

It was very surprising that a turkey-herd should refuse to be queen ; nevertheless the wedding garments were got ready, and to see such a beautiful wedding people came from a hundred leagues round. The little mouse went too, wishing to see the turkey-herd at her leisure. Going into the poultry-house she found her dressed in coarse linen, bare-footed, and with a dirty cloth on her head. There were gold and silver garments, and diamonds, and pearls, and ribbons and laces lying on the ground; the turkeys were trampling on them, making them filthy, and spoiling them. The little herd was sitting on a large stone, while the wicked king's son, who was deformed, blind, and lame, was saying rudely: "If you will not give me your heart, I shall kill you". But she answered, proudly: "I shall not marry you; you are too ugly. And you are like your cruel father. Leave me alone with my little turkeys—I like them better than all your finery." The little mouse looked at her with admiration, for she was as beautiful as the sun. As soon as the wicked king's son went away, the fairy took the form of an old shepherdess, and said: "Good-day, little one; what fine fat turkeys you have got here!" The young turkey-herd looked at this old woman with eyes full of gentleness, and said: "They want me to leave them for a miserable crown—what do you say about it?" "My little girl," said the fairy, "a crown is a very fine thing; you neither know the value nor the weight of it." "Oh, yes, I do," the herd replied, promptly, "and for that reason I will never wear it. But I do not know who I am, nor who my father is, nor my mother. I have neither parents nor friends." "You have beauty and goodness, my child," said the wise fairy, "and these are better than ten kingdoms. Tell me, I beg you, who brought you here, since you have neither father, mother, relations, nor friends?" "It was a fairy called Cancaline who was the cause of my coming here. She used to beat me, and would knock me down without any cause or reason. So one day I ran away, and, not knowing where to go, I stopped in a wood. The wicked king's son came to walk there, and he asked me if I should like to go and be a servant in his yard. I was quite willing, so I had the turkeys given to my charge. He used to come constantly to see them, and he saw me too. Alas, without any desire on my side, he has fallen so very much in love with me that he will not leave me alone."

The fairy, hearing this, began to think the turkey-herd must be Princess Joliette; so she said to her: "Tell me your name, my daughter". "My name is Joliette, at your service." Then the fairy no longer doubted but that it was she, and, throwing her arms round her neck, she was like to have eaten her up with caresses. Thereupon she said to her: "Joliette, I have known you for a long time; I am glad you are so good, and so well-bred; but I would wish you to be cleaner, for you are like a little scullion. Here, take these pretty clothes and put them on."

Joliette, who was very obedient, at once cast away the dirty clothes; and, shaking her head a little, her hair, which was fair as sunlight and fine as golden threads, covered her from head to foot, falling in curls to the ground. Then taking in her delicate hands some water from a stream that ran near the poultry-house, she washed her face, which became as fair as an Eastern pearl. It seemed as if roses were blowing on her cheeks and lips, and her sweet mouth breathed the scent of thyme from the woods and the gardens. Her figure was straighter than a reed. In winter you might have taken her skin for snow, in summer for lilies.

When she was adorned with the diamonds and the beautiful clothes, the fairy thought her a miracle of beauty, and said to her: "Who do you think you are, dear Joliette, for you look a very fine lady now?" "In truth," she answered, "I think I am the daughter of some great king." "Would you be very pleased if this were so?" said the fairy. "Yes, good mother," replied Joliette, with a curtsey. "Very well," said the fairy, "be easy in your mind then; I shall tell you more to-morrow."

In haste she repaired to her beautiful castle, where the queen was busy spinning silk. The little mouse called to her: "Your majesty, will you give me your distaff and your spindle for the best news you could ever hear?" "Alas!" said the queen, "since the death of King Joyous, and the loss of my Joliette, I wouldn't give a pin for all the news of the world." "Now, now! don't go on so," said the fairy, "the princess is in the best of health; I have just seen her; and she is so beautiful, so very beautiful, that she can be a queen if she likes." And she told her the story from one end to the other, the queen weeping for joy to know that her daughter was so beautiful; and for sadness to think that she kept turkeys. "When we were great sovereigns in our kingdom," she said, "and lived in such magnificence, my poor husband and myself, we never could have believed that our child would one day keep turkeys." "It is that cruel Cancaline," said the fairy, "who, knowing how I love you, just to spite me, has reduced her to that condition; but she will come out of it, or I shall burn my books." "I do not wish her to marry the wicked king's son," said the queen. "Therefore, let us set out to-morrow to fetch her, and bring her here."

Now it happened that the wicked king's son, being very angry against Joliette, went and sat under a tree, and wept and howled aloud. His father, hearing him, went to the window and called out to him: "What are you crying for? What a fool you are!" "Because your turkey-herd will not love me," he answered. "What! she will not love you?" said the wicked king. "I insist on her loving you, or else she dies!" He called for his men-at-arms, and said to them: "Go and fetch her, for I shall punish her so that she will be sorry for her obstinacy". They went to the poultry-yard, and found Joliette in a beautiful dress of white satin, embroidered with gold and red diamonds, and more than a thousand yards of ribbon. Never, never, in the wide world was seen such a lovely damsel. They hardly dared speak to her, thinking she must be a princess. "I beg of you, tell me whom you are looking for here," she asked. "Madam," they answered, "we are looking for a miserable little girl called Joliette." "Alas!" she said, "I am Joliette. What do you want of me?" They took hold of her in haste, bound her feet and her hands with thick cords for fear she might run away, and in this fashion they took her to the wicked king, who was with his son. When he saw that she was so lovely, he could not help being somewhat touched, and there is no doubt he would have taken pity on her, had he not been the wickedest and the cruellest man in the world. "Ah ha! you little good-for-nothing, you little toad, so you will not love my son? He is a hundred times handsomer than you, and one of his looks is worth more than the whole of your person. Come here, love him at once, or I will have you flayed." The princess, shaking like a little pigeon, knelt before him, saying: "Sire, I beg of you not to flay me. That would hurt me too much. Leave me one or two days to think what I ought to do, and then you may do what you will with me." His son, who was desperate, wished her to be flayed, but they decided between them to shut her up in a tower, where she would not even see the sun.

Just then the good fairy came in the flying car with the queen. When they learnt all the news, the queen began to weep bitterly, saying she was ever unfortunate, and that she would rather her daughter were dead than that she should marry the wicked king's son. But the fairy said: "Take heart, I am going to tire them out so that you will be fully satisfied and revenged".

When the wicked king was going to bed the fairy turned herself into a little mouse, and hid under his pillow. As soon as he tried to fall asleep, she bit his ear. Very angry, he turned on his other side, and then she bit his other ear. "Murder!" he cried, and called for his attendants. When they came they found his two ears bitten and bleeding so freely that they could not stop the blood. While they were looking everywhere for the mouse, she did the same thing to the wicked king's son, who called his valets and showed them his ears all bitten, and had plasters put on them. The little mouse went back to the wicked king's room, who was now somewhat drowsy. She bit his nose and began to gnaw it. He put his hands up, but she bit and scratched them. He cried out: "Have mercy, I am lost!" Then she went into his mouth and nibbled at his tongue, his lips, his cheeks. His servants came and saw him in a fearful condition, hardly able to speak, so wounded was his tongue. He signed to them that a mouse had done it, and they looked in the mattress, the bolster, in every little corner. But it was not there, having gone to treat the son still worse, eating up his good eye, and he had but one. Rising like a madman with his sword in his hand, he rushed, blind as he was, to his father's room, who also had taken his sword, and who was storming and swearing that he would kill everybody if they did not catch the mouse. When he saw his son so desperate he burst out into abuse of him, and the son, who was in a burning rage, not recognising his father's voice, threw himself on him. The wicked king in wrath gave him a great blow with his sword, and received one in return. Both fell in a great pool of blood. All their subjects, who hated them mortally, and who only served them out of fear, no longer having cause to be afraid of them, fastened cords to their feet and dragged them to the river, saying they were very happy to be rid of them.

And now the wicked king was dead and his son too. The good fairy, who knew this, fetched the queen, and they went together to the black tower where Joliette was imprisoned under forty locks. At three raps of the fairy's hazel wand the great door opened, and so did the others. They found the poor princess very sad and very silent. The queen threw herself on her neck. "My dearest one," she said, "I am your mother, Queen Joyous," and she told her the story of her life. When Joliette heard such good news she nearly died of joy, and throwing herself at the queen's feet, she embraced her knees, bathed her hands with her tears, and kissed her a thousand times. She caressed the fairy tenderly, who had brought for her baskets full of priceless jewels, gold, diamonds, bracelets, pearls, and the portrait of King Joyous surrounded with precious stones, all of which she placed before her. But the fairy said: "This is not a time for play. We must carry out a great revolution in the state. Let us come and speak to the people in the great hall of the castle."

She went first with a grave and serious face, the train of her dress sweeping more than ten ells behind her. The queen's dress of blue velvet, embroidered with gold, had a longer train still, for they had taken their finest clothes with them. Then they had crowns on their heads which shone like suns. Princess Joliette followed them, beautiful and modest, a perfect wonder to see. They bowed to all they met on the way, to the poor as well as the great, and all the people followed them, very eager to know who these fair ladies might be. When the hall was quite full, the good fairy said to the subjects of the wicked king that she wished to give them for a queen the daughter of King Joyous, whom they saw before them, that they would live happy under her rule, that if they would accept her she promised to seek a husband for her as perfect as herself, who would be always merry, and who would chase away sadness from every heart. At these words they all cried: "Yes, yes; we will! Too long have we been sad and miserable." And at that moment a hundred kinds of instruments struck up on all sides. Every one took his neighbour's hand and they danced in rings, singing round the queen and her daughter and the good fairy : "Yes, yes ; we will ".

Such was their welcome, and never was joy like theirs. Tables were spread, and they feasted and drank, and then went to bed to sleep soundly. When the young princess woke, the fairy presented to her the handsomest prince that ever saw the light. She had been to fetch him in the flying car from the other end of the world. He was as lovely as Joliette, and as soon as she saw him she loved him. As for him, he was charmed with the princess, and the queen was beside herself with joy. A feast and the most splendid garments were got ready, and the wedding was celebrated with endless merrymaking.

THE RAM.

I N those happy days when the fairies were alive, there reigned a king who had
three daughters. They were beautiful and young, and they were good;
but the youngest was the most lovable and the most beloved, and her name was
Merveilleuse. Her father the king, gave her more dresses and ribbons in a
month than he did the others in a year. But she had such a kind little heart
that she shared everything with her sisters, so that they were the best of friends.

Now the king had evil-minded neighbours who, tired of peace, waged such
a terrible war against him that he feared he should be overthrown unless he took
means to defend himself. So he gathered together a large army and took the
field with it. The three princesses remained with their governor in a castle
where every day good news of the king reached them, sometimes that he had
taken a city, and sometimes that he had gained a battle. At last his success
was such that he conquered his enemies, and drove them out of his states.
Then he returned with speed to his castle to see his little Merveilleuse again,
whom he loved so much. The three princesses had three satin dresses made
for them—one green, one blue, and the third white. Their jewels matched their
dresses; the green one had emeralds, the blue turquoises, the white diamonds.
Thus adorned, they came into the king's presence singing verses they had composed on his victories :—

> " Home from full many a hard-fought field,
> Where the proud foe was forced to yield,
> Receive our greetings, father, king.

And when the bells their loudest ring,
And everywhere the feasts are spread,
Hear in our shouts, our songs, our glee,
Echoes of our strong loyalty."

When he saw them so beautiful and so gay he embraced them tenderly, but he gave Merveilleuse more caresses than the others. A splendid feast was prepared, and the king and his three daughters sat down to it; and as it was his habit to draw meanings out of everything, he said to the eldest: " Now, tell me, why did you choose a green dress ? " " Your majesty," she said, " having heard of your great deeds, I thought that green would show my joy and my hope that you would return." " That is very prettily said," said the king. " And you, my daughter," he went on, " why did you choose a blue dress ? " " Your majesty," said the princess, " as a sign that I should pray without ceasing for you to the gods, and because in looking on you I seem to see the sky and the most beautiful stars." " Why," said the king, " you speak like an oracle." " And you, Merveilleuse, what reason had you for dressing in white ? " " Sire," she answered, " because it becomes me better than any other colour." " What ! " said the king, very much annoyed, " was that your only thought, you vain little monkey ? " " I thought of pleasing you," said the princess ; " and, it seems to me, that was my only duty." The king, who loved her, thought her answer made up for everything, and said he liked her wit, and that it was even clever not to have stated her meaning all at once. " Now," said he, " I have had a good supper. I don't want to go to bed so soon, so tell me the dreams you dreamt the night before I came back."

The eldest said she had dreamt that he was going to bring her a dress, the gold and the jewels on which shone brighter than the sun. The second said she had dreamt that he was bringing her a dress and a golden distaff to spin her linen with. The youngest said she had dreamt that on her second sister's wedding day he held a golden ewer in his hands, and that he said to her : " Come, Merveilleuse, come here till I give you water to wash with ".

The king, very angry at this dream, frowned and made the ugliest face possible, so that every one knew he was annoyed. Going to his room he went quickly to bed, but he could not get his daughter's dream out of his head. " This insolent little wretch," said he, " would like me to become her servant. I am not surprised she chose the white satin gown without thinking of me. She considers I am not worthy of her consideration, but I shall take steps to prevent her wicked design before she can carry it into effect."

He rose in a passion of rage, and though it was not yet day, he sent for the captain of the guards and said to him : " You heard Merveilleuse's dream : it means strange things against me, and I desire you to take her at once into the forest and kill her. When you have done this, you shall bring me her heart and her tongue, for I will not have you deceive me, and if you fail to carry out these orders I shall put you to death." The captain of the guards was very much astonished to hear so cruel an order. Yet he did not wish to contradict the king for fear of angering him still more, and of making him give the commission to some one else. So he told him he would take the princess away, and that he would kill her and bring him her heart and her tongue.

He went at once to her room, but had some difficulty in entering, for it was still very early. He told Merveilleuse that the king was asking for her, and she got up at once. A little Moorish girl called Patypata carried the train of her dress, and her monkey and the dog that always followed her ran after her. The monkey was called Grabugeon, and the dog Tintin. The captain of the guard made Merveilleuse come downstairs, telling her the king was in the garden taking the air. Thither she went, the captain pretending to look for him, and not finding him, he said: "The king has gone into the forest". So opening a little gate he led her into the forest. The daylight was beginning to appear, and when the princess looked at her conductor she saw he had tears in his eyes, and that he was so melancholy he could not speak. "What is the matter with you?" she said, with an air of charming sweetness. "You seem very sad." "Ah, madam, who would not be," he said, "at the most terrible order that ever was given? The king wishes me to kill you here, and to bring your heart and your tongue back to him. If I fail to do so, he will put me to death." The poor princess terrified, turned pale and began to cry silently, looking like a little lamb being led to the slaughter. Fixing her sweet eyes on the captain of the guards, and looking at him without any anger, she asked: "Shall you have the courage to kill me, seeing I never did you any harm, and never said anything but good of you to the king? If I had deserved my father's anger I would endure the consequence without a murmur, but alas! I have shown him so much respect and affection that he cannot with justice complain of me." "Do not fear, fair princess," said the captain of the guards, "that I am capable of lending my hand to so cruel a deed. I would rather resign myself to the death with which I am threatened. But even if I were to stab myself you would not be any the more secure, and some means must be found whereby I may return to the king and make him believe that you are dead."

"How can we do so?" said Merveilleuse, "for he wants you to bring back my tongue and my heart, and without these he will not believe you." Patypata, who had heard all, but whom neither the princess nor the captain of the guards had even noticed, so full of sadness were they, now stepped forward bravely, and

12

flung herself at Merveilleuse's feet. "Madam," she said, "I come to offer you my life. You must kill me. I shall be only too glad to die for so kind a mistress." "Far be such a thing from me, my dear Patypata," said the princess, kissing her; "after so tender a proof of your love, your life is no less precious to me than my own." Grabugeon then came forward and said: "You are right, princess, to love so faithful a servant as Patypata. She can be more useful to you than me. I offer you my tongue and my heart with joy, desiring as I do to make my name remembered in Monkeyland." "Ah, my darling Grabugeon," replied Merveilleuse, "I cannot endure the thought of taking your life." "It would be insupportable to me," cried Tintin, "good dog as I am, that another than myself should give his life for my mistress. I should die for you if any one ought to." Thereupon arose a great dispute between Patypata, Grabugeon, and Tintin, and they set a-quarrelling about the matter; but at last Grabugeon, more agile than the others, climbed to the top of a tree, and flinging itself down head foremost was killed at once. However sorry the princess was, she agreed, since the monkey was dead, that the captain of the guards should take out its tongue. But it was found to be so small (for the monkey was no bigger than your fists) that with great sorrow they came to the conclusion that the king would not be deceived by it.

"Alas! my dear little monkey, now you are dead," said the princess, "and yet your death has not saved me." "That honour is reserved for me," interrupted the little Moor. And so saying, she took the knife they had used for Grabugeon and plunged it into her throat. The captain of the guards would have cut out her tongue, but it was so black that he dared not hope to deceive the king by means of it. "Am I not very unhappy?" said the princess, weeping. "I lose all I love, and my fortune does not improve." "If you had been willing," said Tintin, "to accept my proposal, you would have had only me to regret, and I should have had the happiness to be the only one regretted."

Merveilleuse kissed her little dog, crying so bitterly that she was quite exhausted. Then she walked hastily away. When she looked back she no longer saw her conductor, and stood there with her little Moor, her monkey, and her dog all dead. She could not go away without burying them in a hole that she found by chance at the foot of a tree, on which she afterwards wrote these words:—

> "Here three faithful mortals lie:
> To save my life they chose to die".

At last she thought of her own safety, and as there was none for her in this forest, so near her father's castle that the first passer-by could see and recognise her, or where the lions and wolves could eat her up like a chicken, she began to walk as fast as she could. But the forest was so wide, and the sun so burning that she was nearly dead from heat, terror, and fatigue. On all sides she looked but she saw no end to the forest. Everything frightened her, and she was in constant terror lest the king should run after her to kill her. The sad cry she uttered it is impossible to describe.

As she walked along following no certain path the bushes tore her pretty dress and wounded her white skin. At last she heard a sheep bleating. "Doubtless," she said, "there are shepherds here with their flocks. They will be able to guide me to some hamlet, where I may hide under the disguise of a peasant. Alas!" she went on, "it is not always kings and princes that are happiest. Who in all this kingdom would believe that I am a fugitive; or that my father, without cause or reason, seeks my death, which to avoid I am forced to disguise myself?"

Thus reflecting she went towards the place from which the bleating came, but what was her surprise on reaching a wide stretch of ground surrounded by trees, to see a great ram, whiter than snow, with golden horns, round his neck a garland of flowers, strings of pearls of an extraordinary size twisted about his legs, and wearing chains of diamonds. The creature was lying on orange flowers, while a pavilion of gold cloth suspended in the air prevented the sun from hurting him. A hundred sheep gaily decked were standing round, not nibbling the grass, but having coffee, sherbet, ices, lemonade, strawberries, cream, and sweetmeats. Some were playing at basset, others at lansquenet. Several had golden collars enriched with beautiful designs, some had their ears pierced or were decked out in ribbons and flowers. Merveilleuse was so astonished that she stood almost motionless. She was looking for the shepherd of so extraordinary a flock when the beautiful ram came forward by bounds and leaps. " Come, divine princess," he said, " do not fear animals so gentle, so peaceful as we are." " Here is a wonder! Talking sheep!" "Ah, madam," he answered, "your monkey and your little dog spoke very prettily; was that less astonishing?" " A fairy," answered Merveilleuse, " had given them the gift of speech, therefore the wonder had grown less astonishing to me." " Perhaps something of the same sort happened to us," answered the ram, smiling in his sheepish style. " But, princess, what brought you here?" "My misfortunes, Sir Ram," she said. " I am the most unhappy maiden in the world, and am in search of a hiding-place against the anger of my father." " Come, madam," answered the sheep, "come with me. I offer you one that no one else will know of, and you will be sole mistress of it." " I cannot follow you," said Merveilleuse. " I am so tired that I am like to die."

The ram with the golden horns ordered them to bring a coach, and in a moment six goats were seen coming harnessed to a pumpkin of such an enormous size that two persons could sit inside it very comfortably. The pumpkin was dry, and it was lined with soft cushions of down and velvet, and the princess stepped in feeling great admiration for so novel a carriage. The master ram got in with her, and the goats ran as hard as they could to a cave, the entrance to which was barred by a large stone. This the gilded ram touched with his foot, and it fell aside at once. Then he told the princess to enter without fear. She thought the cavern looked terrible, and if she had been less alarmed nothing would have forced her to go in. But in such a state of terror was she that she would have even thrown herself into a well.

She did not hesitate, therefore, to follow the ram, who, walking before her, made her go down and down so far till she thought she must at least be going to the Antipodes, and she feared at times lest he should be taking her to the kingdom of the dead. At last she suddenly discovered a vast plain variegated with a thousand different flowers, the scent of which was sweeter than any she had ever felt. A great river of orange-flower water flowed all round, while streams of Spanish wine, of rossolis, of hippocras, and a thousand other sorts of liqueurs formed cascades and charming little streams. This plain was covered with strange trees. There were whole avenues of such, where partridges, better larded and better cooked than you find them at La Guerbois's, hung from the branches. There were other walks where the trees were laden with quails, young rabbits, turkeys, chickens, pheasants, and ortolans. In certain places where the air seemed darker, it rained lobsters and soups, ragouts of sweetbreads, white puddings, sausages, tarts, pasties, preserves (dry and liquid), sovereigns, crowns, pearls, and diamonds. The strangeness, but, above all, the usefulness, of this shower would have attracted a goodly company if the big ram had been of a rather more sociable temper, but all the chronicles that tell of him assure us that he was graver in his manner than a Roman senator.

As it was the finest season of the year when Merveilleuse arrived in this beautiful spot, she saw no other palace than a great forest of orange trees, jasmine, honeysuckles, and little musk roses, the branches of which, intertwined one with the other, formed cabinets, halls, and rooms all furnished with gold and silver gauze, with great mirrors, hanging lamps, and beautiful pictures.

The master ram told the princess she was now queen of these parts, that for several years he had abundant reason for sorrow and tears, but that he only needed her to make him forget his grief. "The way you treat me, dear ram," she answered, "has something very generous about it, and all I see here seems so extraordinary that I do not know what to think." Hardly had she ended these

words when she saw before her a troop of nymphs of admirable beauty, who presented her with fruit in amber baskets; but when she wished to come near them,
their bodies seemed gradually to vanish. She stretched out her hands to touch
them, but feeling nothing, she knew they were but shadows. "Ah, what is
this?" she cried; "with whom am I here?" She began to cry, and King Ram
(for so he was called), who had left her for some moments, coming back to her
and seeing her in tears, was in despair and like to die at her feet.

"What is the matter, fair princess?" he said. "Has any one here failed
in the respect which is due to you?" "No," she answered. "I have nothing
to complain of, I only confess to you that I am not used to living with ghosts
and with talking sheep. Everything here terrifies me, and however much
obliged I may be to you for having brought me, I should be still more so if you
would take me back again to the world." "Do not be afraid," replied the ram;
"only be so good as to listen to me calmly, and you shall learn my sad story:—

"I was born to a throne. The long line of kings I had for ancestors
had assured me the possession of the finest kingdom in the universe. My
subjects loved me. I was feared and envied by my neighbours, and respected,
not without cause. It has been said that never was a king so worthy of esteem.
I was not ill-looking personally. I was very fond of hunting, and one day,
having ridden far for the pleasure of pursuing a deer, and having in this way
outstripped my companions somewhat, I saw it all of a sudden plunge into a
pond. I spurred on my horse, as imprudently as rashly, but on going forward
a little, I felt instead of the coolness of the water, an extraordinary heat. The
pond dried up, and through an opening out of which came terrible flames, I fell
to the bottom of a precipice which was all on fire.

"I thought I was lost, when I heard a voice saying: 'Less fire than this,
ungrateful man, would never warm your heart!' 'What! who is it complains
of my coldness?' I called. 'An unhappy lady,' answered the voice, 'who
loves you without hope." At that moment the fire went out, and I saw a fairy
whom I had known from my earliest years, whose age and ugliness had always
disgusted me. She was leaning on a young slave who was exquisitely beautiful,
wearing golden chains that showed clearly enough her condition. "What
wonder is this?' I said to Ragotte, for such was the name of the fairy. 'Is
it happening by your orders?' 'And by whose orders should it be done then?'
she answered. 'Did you not know before my feelings towards you? Must I
undergo the shame of expressing them? Have my eyes that were at one time
so sure of their aim lost all their power? Think how I humble myself in confessing my weakness to you, for though you may be a great king you are less
than an ant before a fairy like me.'

" ' I am whatever you like to call me,' I said, in an impatient manner and voice. ' But, after all, what do you want with me ? Is it my crown, my towns, or my treasures ? " ' Ah, you wretch !' she replied, disdainfully; ' my scullions, if I liked, could be more powerful than you. I ask your heart. My eyes have begged for it thousands and thousands of times; you did not hear them, or rather, you did not wish to hear them. If you had been engaged to another,' she continued, ' I should have let you go on with your courtship without interference, but I have been too eager in informing myself of your doings not to have discovered the indifference that reigns in your heart. Well, now, love me,' she added, screwing up her mouth to make it prettier, and rolling. her eyes. ' I shall be your little Ragotte. I shall add twenty kingdoms to the one you possess, a hundred towers full of gold, five hundred full of silver—in short, whatever you wish.'

" ' Madam Ragotte,' I answered, ' it is not in the bottom of a hole where I thought I was to be roasted that I should wish to make a declaration to a lady of your merit. I beg you by all the charms which make you adorable to set me free, and then we shall plan together what I can do to please you.' ' Ah ! you traitor !' she cried, ' if you loved me you would not seek the road back to your kingdom. In a grotto, in a fox's den, in the woods, in the deserts, you would be content. Do not think I am so easily deceived. You are planning how to escape, but I warn you, you must stay here, and the first thing you have to do is to keep my sheep. They are very intelligent, and speak at least as well as you.'

"And so saying she went forward to the plain where we now are, and showed me her flock. I paid no attention, for that beautiful slave who was with her seemed to my eyes a wonder. My looks betrayed me, and the cruel Ragotte seeing this, threw herself upon her, and plunged a bodkin with such force into her eye that the adorable creature fell lifeless on the spot. At this fatal sight I darted on Ragotte, and with my spear in my hand I would have sacrificed her to the memory of so dear a spirit, if by her power she had not rendered me motion-less. My efforts being in vain, I fell to the ground, and I was seeking every possible means of killing myself to deliver me from the misery with which I was overpowered when, with a mocking smile, she said to me : ' I wish you to recognise my power. Now you are a lion ; you will become a ram.' Then she touched me with her wand, and I saw myself metamorphosed into my present shape. I did not lose the use of speech, nor the capability of misery, because of my unhappy condition. ' You shall be five years a sheep,' she said, ' and absolute master in this beautiful spot ; while far from you, and out of sight of your hand-some face, I shall think of nothing but the hate I bear you.'

" She disappeared, and if anything could have consoled me for my misfortunes it would have been her absence. The talking sheep here owned me for their king. They told me they were unhappy creatures who in one way or another had given offence to the revengeful fairy, and that she had turned them into a flock, though the punishment of some would not last so long as others. And in fact," he added, " from time to time they regain their former shape and leave the flock. As to the others, they are rivals or enemies of Ragotte whom she has killed, and who will remain lifeless for a century or less, and who afterwards will return into the world. The young slave whom I have told you about is one of these. I have seen her several times, and always with pleasure, though she would not speak to me, and when I wanted to go near her I was grieved to find that she was but a shadow. But having noticed that one of my sheep was constantly by the side of this little phantom, I divined he was her lover, and that Ragotte, jealous of his love, had taken him away from her. For this reason I kept apart from the shadowy slave, and for three years I have felt no longing for anything but for my liberty. That is what takes me sometimes into the forest. There I saw you, fair princess," he continued, " sometimes in a chariot, which you drove with more skill than the sun when he drives his, sometimes at the chase, on a horse that seemed untameable by any other than you, or again when running lightly with the princesses of your court you gained the prize like another Atalanta. Ah ! princess, if every time when my heart was making its secret vows to you, I had dared to speak to you, what should I not have said ? But how would you have received the declaration of a miserable ram like me ? "

Merveilleuse was so troubled by all she had heard up to that moment that she hardly knew what to answer. She expressed herself, however, in so pleasant a way as to leave him some hope, and told him she now feared the shadows less since they would live again one day. " Alas ! " she continued, " if my poor Patypata, my dear Grabugeon, and pretty Tintin, who died to save me, could have had such a fate, I should no longer be lonely here."

In spite of King Ram's misfortunes, he had none the less great privileges. " Go," said he to his chief equerry, a fine-looking sheep, " go and fetch the little Moor, the monkey, and the dog ; their shades will entertain our princess." The next moment Merveilleuse saw them, and though they did not come near enough for her to touch them, their presence was an infinite comfort to her.

King Ram had much intelligence and great delicacy, and could converse in the most charming way. He loved Merveilleuse so passionately that she came also to look on him with favour and afterwards to love him. And who could help loving a pretty sheep, so gentle, so affectionate, especially when he is known to be a king, and that his metamorphosis will not last for ever? So the princess's days passed quietly away, waiting for a happier time to come. The ram, ever attentive, had no other thought but of her, and arranged banquets and concerts and hunts for her, his flocks helping him, and even the shadows taking part.

One evening when his couriers returned, for he sent regularly for news, and received always the freshest, they told him Merveilleuse's eldest sister was about to be married to a great prince, and that nothing so magnificent as the preparations for the wedding had ever been seen. " Ah! " cried the young princess, " how unfortunate I am not to see so many fine things. Here I am underground with shadows and sheep, while my sister appears apparelled like a queen. Every one will come to pay respects to her. I alone shall have no part in her joy." "Why do you complain, madam? " said the king of the sheep to her. " Have I said you might not go to the wedding? Set off as soon as you please, but promise me to return. If you will not, you will see me die at your feet, for the affection I feel for you is too strong for me to lose you and yet live."

Merveilleuse, much touched, promised the ram that nothing in the world would hinder her return. He gave her an equipage befitting her birth, and she dressed herself superbly, forgetting nothing that could add to her beauty. She drove away in a mother-of-pearl coach drawn by six dun-coloured hippogriffs, just come from the Antipodes, and accompanied by a large number of officers richly clad and very handsome, who had been sent for from a distance to form the guard of honour.

She arrived at her father's palace just when the marriage ceremony was taking place. As soon as she entered, every one who saw her was struck by the brilliancy of her beauty and her jewels. Nothing was heard round her but acclamations and praises. The king looked at her with an attention and a pleasure which made her fear lest she should be recognised, but he was so firmly convinced of her death that he had not the least suspicion who she was. But the fear of being stopped prevented her from staying till the end of the ceremony. She left abruptly, leaving a little coral box, ornamented with emeralds, on which was written in diamonds *Jewels for the Bride*. They opened it at once, and what was there not inside? The king, who had hoped to meet her again and who was most eager to make her acquaintance, was in despair at not seeing her, and he gave an absolute order that if ever she came back, all the doors should be shut after her, and she should be detained.

Though Merveilleuse's absence had been a short one, it had seemed more than a century to the ram. He waited for her by the side of a stream in the thickest part of the forest, where he had spread out vast treasures as an offering to her in gratitude for her home-coming. As soon as he saw her, he ran to meet her, leaping and bounding like a real ram, caressing her tenderly over and over again, lying down at her feet, kissing her hands, telling her all his anxieties and his impatience, his passion lending him an eloquence which charmed the princess.

After some time the king was arranging the marriage of his second daughter. Merveilleuse learnt this, and begged the ram to let her go, as she had done before and see a fête in which she was so much interested. At this proposal he felt a pang which he could not subdue, a secret warning of evil to come. But as misfortunes cannot always be avoided, and as his love for the princess was more to him than his own comfort, he had not the heart to refuse her. "You wish to leave me, madam," he said. "Well, for this the consequence of my misfortune, my unhappy fate is more to blame than are you. I consent to what you ask, and I shall never make a greater sacrifice."

She assured him she would not stay longer than she had done before ; that any delay that kept her from him would be a pain to her, and she begged him not to be anxious. Travelling in the same fashion as on her former visit, she arrived just as the ceremony was beginning, and in spite of the close attention being paid to it, a cry of joy and admiration arose at her entrance, which drew the eyes of all the princes on her. They could not help looking at her, and seeing her rare beauty, they were ready to believe [that she was more than mortal.

The king was delighted at seeing her again, and never took his eyes off her except when he was giving the order to shut all the doors to detain her. When the ceremony was all but over the princess got up in haste, wishing to steal away amidst the crowd, and she was very much astonished and distressed at finding the doors closed. The king greeted her with such great respect and humility as re-assured her, begging her not to deprive them so soon of the pleasure of seeing her and of entertaining her at the great feast which he was giving to the princes and

princesses. Leading her into a magnificent room where all the court was assembled, he himself brought a golden basin and a ewer full of water to wash her beautiful hands. At that she could contain herself no longer, but fell at his feet and embraced his knees, saying: " Now has my dream come to pass. You have brought me water to wash with on my sister's wedding day, and no harm has happened to you in consequence."

The king recognised her with less difficulty, inasmuch as more than once she had reminded him of Merveilleuse. " Ah, my dear daughter," he said, embracing her and weeping. " Can you forget my cruelty? I desired your death because I thought your dream meant the loss of my crown. And so it does," he added. " Here are your two sisters married; they each have one, and mine will be for you." So saying he rose and placed it on the princess's head, and cried: " Long live Queen Merveilleuse!" All the court shouted too, and the young queen's two sisters came and fell on her neck, caressing her over and over again. Merveilleuse did not know what she was doing for gladness. She cried and laughed at the same time, embracing some one here, speaking to another there, and thanking the king. Amidst all this she did not forget the captain of the guards, to whom she owed so much. She asked after him eagerly, but they told her he was dead, a loss she felt most keenly.

When she sat at table, the king begged her to tell him all that had happened since the day when he had given the cruel orders concerning her, and without a moment's hesitation she began her tale, with perfect grace, everybody lending an eager attention.

But while in the company of the king and her sisters she was forgetting how the time passed. Her lover, the ram, saw the hour of her return go by, and he became so anxious that he could not restrain himself. " She does not wish to come back any more," he cried; " my unfortunate ram's face does not please her. Ah, too unhappy lover that I am! What will become of me without Merveilleuse? Ragotte, you cruel fairy, what a revenge you have taken for my coldness towards you!"

A long time he mourned thus, and seeing night coming on, and no sign of the princess, he ran to the town. When he reached the king's palace, he asked for Merveilleuse, but as every one already knew her story, and did not wish her to return with the ram, they sternly refused to let him see her. The cries and laments he uttered would have moved any but the guards at the palace gate. At last, overcome by his sorrow, he threw himself on the ground and died.

The king and Merveilleuse in the meanwhile were not aware of the sad tragedy that had just taken place. He proposed to his daughter to ride in a coach, so that all the town might see her by the light of the thousand torches in the windows and in the great squares. But what a sight did she see on her way out of the palace—her dear ram stretched on the pavement, all the life gone out of him! Throwing herself out of the coach, she ran to him, weeping and groaning, for she knew her delay had caused the death of the royal ram. In her despair, she was like to die herself.

This was taken as a striking example, therefore, that people of the highest rank are subject, like others, to fortune's blows, and that often the worst luck comes to them just when they think all their wishes are about to be fulfilled.

FINETTE CENDRON.

THERE was once upon a time a king and a queen who managed their affairs very badly. They were driven out of their kingdom, and had to sell first their crowns, then their clothes, their linen, their laces, their furniture, bit by bit, in order that they might have bread to eat. The pawnbrokers were tired of buying, for every day something new was sold. When at last they were stripped of nearly everything they possessed, the king said to his wife: "Here we are exiled from our kingdom, with nothing left us to live on. We must therefore earn our own and our poor children's bread. Think, then, what we shall do, for till now I have only followed kingcraft, which is very easy." The queen, who was very clever, asked eight days to think about the matter. At the end of that time, she said: "There is no reason why we should be miserable, your majesty. All you have to do is to make nets to catch birds in the woods and fish in the sea. While the lines are wearing out I shall make others for you. As for our three daughters, they are lazy minxes, and no mistake, who think they are still great ladies, and play at being such. They must be sent away, so far away that they will never come back; for it would be impossible for us to give them the fine clothes they would desire."

The king began to weep when he saw he must part from his children, for he was a kind father; but the queen was mistress. He agreed, therefore, to all her proposals, and said: "To-morrow morning rise early, and take your three daughters wherever you think suitable". While they were planning this, Princess Finette, the youngest girl, was listening through the keyhole. When she had found out the intention of her father and mother, she ran off as fast as ever she could to a large grotto, a long way from home, where the Fairy Merluche, her god-mother lived.

Finette took with her two pounds of fresh butter, some eggs, milk, and some flour to make a nice cake for her god-mother, so that she might get a good welcome from her. Very merrily did she set out on her journey, but the farther she went the more tired she grew. The soles of her shoes were quite worn through, and her pretty little feet were so torn that it was pitiful to see them. At last she had to give up, and sitting down on the grass, she began to cry.

A beautiful Spanish jennet passed by, saddled and bridled, with more diamonds on its saddle-cloth than would buy three whole towns. On seeing the princess, it began feeding quietly by her side, and bending its knee, it seemed to bow before her. "Pretty one," she said, taking hold of the bridle, "will you carry me to my god-mother, the fairy? I shall be so grateful if you will, for I am so tired that I am like to die. And if you help me now, I will give you nice oats, and hay, and fresh straw to lie on." The horse bent down almost to the ground before her, and little Finette jumped on its back, whereupon it set off running as lightly as a bird. At the entrance of the grotto, it stopped as if it had known the way, as indeed it did; for it was Merluche, knowing that her god-daughter was coming to see her, who had sent this beautiful horse.

When she was inside, she made three low bows to her god-mother, and taking the hem of her dress, she kissed it, saying : " Good-day, god-mother, how are you? Here is some butter, some milk, some flour, and some eggs, which I have brought to make a nice cake for you, just as we do at home." " Welcome, Finette," said the fairy; " come till I give you a kiss." So saying, she kissed her twice, which made Finette very happy, for Madam Merluche was not a common fairy. "Now, god-daughter," said she, "I want you to be my little maid. Take down my hair and comb it." The princess undid it, and combed it, in the cleverest possible way. " I know quite well," said Merluche, "why you came here. You overheard the king and the queen, who want to lead you away and lose you, and you wish that no such evil thing may happen to you. Well, you have only to take this ball of thread. It will never break. Fasten one end to the door of your house, and keep it in your hand. When the queen has left you, it will be easy to return by following the thread."

The princess thanked her god-mother, who filled a bag for her with beautiful dresses all of gold and silver, and after kissing her, mounted her again on the beautiful horse, and in two or three minutes she was landed at the door of their majesties' hut. "My little friend," said Finette to the horse, "you are very pretty, and very good, and you run faster than the sun. I thank you for your trouble, and now go back to where you came from." She entered the house very quietly, and hiding her bag under her pillow, went to her bed as if nothing had happened.

As soon as day dawned, the king awoke his wife, saying: "Come, madam, come, get ready for the journey". She got up immediately, put on her thick shoes, a short skirt, a white camisole, and took a stick in her hand. Then she called her eldest daughter, whose name was Fleur d'Amour; her second, Belle-de-Nuit; and her third, Fine-Oreille, or Finette, as she was usually called. "I learnt in a dream last night," said the queen, "that we must go and see my sister. She will entertain us well, and we can eat and laugh as much as ever we like." Fleur d'Amour, who was miserable at living in this lonely place, said to her mother: "Very well, madam, let us go wherever you please. Provided that I get away from here, it doesn't matter to me." The two others said the same. So after bidding good-bye to the king, all the four set off. They went such a very long way that Fine-Oreille began to be much afraid she would not have thread enough, for they had gone nearly a thousand leagues. She used always to walk behind her sisters, passing the thread deftly through the bushes. When the queen thought that her daughters would not be able to find their way back, she went into a large wood, and said: "My little lambs, go to sleep now. I shall be the shepherdess who watches round her flock, for fear the wolf should eat them." So lying down on the grass they fell asleep, and the queen left them there, thinking she should never see them again. Finette had shut her eyes, but was not asleep. "If I were a wicked girl," she said, "I should go away at once, leaving my sisters here to die, for they beat me and scratch me till the blood comes. But in spite of all their cruelty, I will not leave them." So she awoke them, and told them the whole story. They began to cry, and begged her to take them along with her, and said they would give her lovely dolls, and their little silver dolls' house, and their other toys, and their sugar-plums. "I know well enough that you will do nothing of the kind," said Finette, "but all the same, I will be a kind sister to you." And getting up, she followed her thread, and the princesses did so too, so that they got home almost as soon as the queen.

Stopping at the door, they heard the king saying: "My heart is very sore at seeing you coming back by yourself". "Well, but we didn't know what to do with our daughters," said the queen. "Yet, if you had brought my Finette back," replied the king, " I should not mind about the others, for they care for nobody." Tap, tap, came their knock. "Who is there?" said the king. " Your three daughters," they answered, " Fleur d'Amour, Belle-de-Nuit, and Fine-Oreille." The queen was all of a tremble. " Do not open the door," she said ; " it must be their ghosts, for they themselves could not have come back." And the king, who was just as great a coward as his wife, said : " You are deceiving me ; you are not my daughters." But Fine-Oreille, who was quick-witted, said to him : " Father, I am going to bend down. Look at me through the cat's hole, and if I am not Finette, I'll let you beat me." The king looked as she had told him, and as soon as he recognised her, he opened the door to them. The queen pretended that she was very glad to see them, and told them she had forgotten something, and that she came to fetch it, but assuredly she would have found them again. And they made as if they believed her, and went up to their sleeping-place in a pretty little garret for the night.

" Well, sisters," said Finette, " you promised me a doll; give it me then." " And how can you expect it, you little monkey?" said they. " It is all on account of you that the king does not love us." Thereupon they took their distaffs and beat her without mercy. When they had chastised her well, she went to bed, but with so many scars and swellings that she could not sleep. So she heard the queen saying to the king: " I shall take them in another direction, still further off, and I am sure they will never return ". When Finette heard this plan, she got up very quietly, meaning to pay another visit to her god-mother. Going into the poultry-house, she took two chickens and a fine cock, and wrung their necks, then two little rabbits that the queen was feeding up with cabbage against the next time they should be having a feast ; and putting them all in a basket, she set off. But she had not gone a league, groping all the way, and in terror of her life, when the Spanish jennet galloped up to her, snorting and neighing. She thought it was all up with her, and that soldiers were coming to capture her, but when she saw the pretty horse all by itself, she mounted, delighted to go on her way in this comfortable fashion ; and very soon she was at her god-mother's house.

After the usual greetings, she gave her the chickens, the cock, and the rabbits. Then she begged Merluche to help her by good counsel, making known to her how the queen had sworn to take them away to the end of the world. Merluche told her god-daughter not to be miserable, and giving her a sack full of ashes, she said : " You will carry the bag in front of you, and shake it as you go. You will walk on the ashes, and when you want to return, you need only look for your footprints. But do not bring your sisters back. They are too wicked, and if you bring them, I will never see you any more." Finette took leave of her, taking with her by Merluche's orders some thirty or forty millions of diamonds in a little box which she put in her pocket. The horse was quite ready, and carried her off as before.

When day broke the queen called the princesses, and when they came she said to them: "The king is not very well. Last night I dreamt that I must go and gather flowers and herbs in a certain country where they are very good. They will make him young again, therefore let us set out at once." Fleur d'Amour and Belle-de-Nuit, who could not believe their mother was anxious to get rid of them, were very sorry to hear this. However they had to set off; and they went so far that never was such a long journey made before. Finette, who did not say a word all the while, kept behind the others, shaking the ashes very cleverly, not letting the wind or the rain spoil any of them.

The queen, fully persuaded they could never find the way again, noticed one evening that her three daughters were fast asleep, so she took 'advantage of this to leave them and return home. When daylight came, and Finette knew that her mother was no longer with them, she awoke her sisters. "We are alone," she said; "the queen has gone away." Fleur d'Amour and Belle-de-Nuit began to cry, to tear their hair, and to beat their faces with their fists. "Alas!" they exclaimed; "what shall we do?" Finette was the kindest girl in the whole world, and again she took pity on her sisters. "Think what risk I am running," she said; "for when my god-mother gave me the means of returning, she forbade me to tell you the way, and said if I disobeyed her she would never see me again." Belle-de-Nuit threw herself on Finette's neck, and so did Fleur d'Amour, caressing her so tenderly that before long they all three returned together to the king and the queen.

Their majesties were very much astonished at seeing the princesses again, and spoke of it all night long. And the youngest girl, who was not called Fine-Oreille * for nothing, heard them making up a fresh plot for the queen on the morrow to take them again into the wilds. She ran and awoke her sisters. "Alas!" she said to them, "we are lost. The queen is determined to take us to some desert and leave us there. It is your fault that my god-mother is angry, and that I dare not go and find her as I always did before." They were very much troubled, and one said to the other: "What shall we do, my sister, what shall we do?" At last Belle-de-Nuit said to the others: "There is no need to distress ourselves. Old Merluche hasn't the whole stock of cleverness in the world. We need only take peas with us and sow them along the road, and by the traces of their growth we can come back." Fleur d'Amour thought this a

---

* Sharp Ear.

capital plan, so they took a large quantity of peas, and filled their pockets. But Fine-Oreille, instead of carrying peas, took the bag with the pretty clothes, and the little box of diamonds, and as soon as the queen called them to be off, they were quite ready.

"I dreamt last night," she said to them, "that in a country which I need not name there are three handsome princes waiting to marry you. I am going to take you there to see if my dream is true." The queen walked on in front, and her daughters after her, sowing their peas, and quite easy in their minds, having no doubt but that they would return home again. This time the queen travelled farther than she had ever done before; but one dark night she left them, and came back to the king. Very tired was she when she reached home, but very glad not to have the cares of such a large household on her shoulders.

The three princesses, after sleeping till eleven o'clock in the morning, woke up. It was Finette that first perceived the queen's absence, and though she expected it, she could not help crying, having, so far as getting back was concerned, more confidence in her god-mother's help than in her sisters' cleverness. In a great fright, she told them the queen had gone, and that they must follow her as soon as possible. "Hold your tongue, you little monkey," said Fleur d'Amour; "we'll be able to find the road whenever we like. We don't want you to interfere unless your opinion is asked." Finette did not dare to answer, but when they tried to find the way, not a mark or a footpath could be found. The pigeons, of which there are a great number in that country, had eaten up the peas, and so the princesses began to cry and howl. After being two days without food, Fleur d'Amour said to Belle-de-Nuit: "Sister, have you nothing to eat?" "No," she answered. She asked Finette the same thing. "No more have I," she replied, "but I have just found an acorn." "Ah! give it to me," said one. "Give it to me," said the other; and each of them wanted to have it. "One acorn would hardly satisfy three of us," said Finette; "let us plant it; another will grow out of it for our use." They agreed, though there seemed little likelihood that a tree would grow in a country where there were none, and where only cabbages and lettuces were to be seen. The princesses ate of these, and if they had been very delicate, they would have died a hundred times. Nearly every night they lay down under the stars, and every morning and every evening went in turns to water the acorn, saying: "Grow, grow, pretty acorn!" And it began to grow visibly. When it had grown to some height, Fleur d'Amour wished to climb up on it, but it was not strong enough to bear her, and feeling it bend under her weight, she got down. The same thing happened to Belle-de-Nuit. Finette, lighter than the others, stopped longer, and they asked her: "Do you see nothing, sister?" "No, I see nothing," she answered. "That is because the oak is not high enough," said Fleur d'Amour; so they went on watering it, and saying: "Grow, grow, pretty acorn!" Finette never failed to climb up twice a day, and one morning when she was there, Belle-de-Nuit said to Fleur d'Amour: "I have found a bag our sister has hidden. What can be in it?" Fleur d'Amour said Finette had told her it was old lace she was mending. "Well, I think there are sugar-plums in it," said Belle-de-Nuit. She was greedy, and wanted to see what was in it. She did find the laces of the king and the queen, but they served to hide Finette's beautiful clothes and the box of diamonds. "Well, was there ever such a wicked little creature?" she cried. "Let us take them all and put stones in their place." This they did without delay. When Finette came back, she did not notice what her sisters had done, for she did not think of ornaments in a desert. Her one thought was of the oak, which was growing to be the finest ever seen.

One time when she had climbed up and her sisters as usual asked her if she saw nothing, "I see," she cried, "a large house, so beautiful—so very, very beautiful, that I cannot describe it to you. The walls are of emeralds and rubies, the roof of diamonds, and it is all covered with golden bells; the weathercocks turn and turn with the wind." "That is not true," they said; "it is not so beautiful as you say." "Believe me, it is," replied Finette; "I don't tell lies. Come and see for yourselves, for my eyes are quite dazzled." Fleur d'Amour climbed up into the tree, and when she saw the castle, she could speak of nothing else. Belle-de-Nuit, who was very curious, would not be behind-hand, and climbing up, she was just as delighted as her sisters. "Certainly," they said, "we must go to that palace; perhaps we shall find handsome princes there who will only be too happy to marry us." All the evening long they spoke of nothing but their plan. Then they lay down on the grass, and when Finette seemed to be asleep, Fleur d'Amour said to Belle-de-Nuit: "Do you know what we must do, sister? Get up and let us dress ourselves in the rich dresses Finette has brought." "You are right," said Belle-de-Nuit; so they got up, curled their hair, powdered their faces, stuck on beauty spots, and dressed themselves in gold and silver gowns, all covered with diamonds. Never was seen such a magnificent sight.

Finette, not knowing that her wicked sisters had robbed her, took her bag with the intention of dressing, and she was in great distress at only finding pebbles. At the same time she saw her sisters decked out like suns. She wept, and reproached them with their breach of faith to her, but they only laughed and mocked at her. "Would you really dare," she said, "to take me to the castle without any pretty dresses or ornaments at all?" "We have not too many for ourselves," replied Fleur d'Amour, "and we'll beat you if you talk any more about it." "But," Finette went on, "these dresses are mine. My god-mother gave me them. You have no part in them." "If you speak another word," they said, "we shall kill you, and bury you, and nobody will know anything about it." And poor Finette, afraid to anger them, followed them quietly, walking some steps behind, just as if she were their servant.

The nearer they came to the house, the more wonderful it seemed. "Hi!" said Fleur d'Amour and Belle-de-Nuit, "what a good time we are going to have! What good cheer we shall partake of as we sit at the king's table. But as for Finette, she will wash the dishes in the kitchen, for she is just like a scullion, and if any one asks who she is, let us take care not to call her our sister, but rather the little village herd." Finette, who was full of intelligence, and very pretty, was in great distress at such ill-treatment. When they went up to the gate of the castle they knocked, and at once a hideous old woman came to open the door to them. She had only one eye, in the middle of her forehead, but it was bigger than five or six ordinary eyes; her nose was flat, her complexion dark, and her mouth was so horrible that it made every one afraid to look at it; she was fifteen feet high, and thirty feet in girth. "Oh, you miserable girls," she said, "what brings you here? Do you not know that this is the ogre's castle, and that all of you together would hardly be enough for his breakfast? But I am better than my husband. Come in, I shall not eat you up all at once. You may have the comfort of living two or three days more." When they heard the ogress speaking in this fashion, they ran away, thinking they could escape, but one of her strides was as good as fifty of theirs, and running after them, she caught them by their hair or by the skin of their necks. Bundling them under her arm, she threw all three of them into the cellar, which was full of toads and adders, and where you walked on the bones of those that had already been eaten.

As she wanted to crunch up Finette on the spot she ran to fetch vinegar and salt to eat her as a salad, but hearing the ogre coming, and thinking the princesses' skin white and delicate, she made up her mind to eat them all by herself. So she hastily put them into a large tub where they could only see out through a hole.

The ogre was six times as tall as his wife. When he spoke the house shook : when he coughed you would have thought it was claps of thunder. He had only one eye, a large, ugly one, his hair stood all on end, and he leant on a log which he used for a stick. In his hand he held a covered basket out of which he drew fifteen little children that he had stolen on the road, and whom he swallowed as if they had been fifteen fresh eggs. When the three princesses saw him, they shook with terror under the tub, and dared no longer cry aloud for fear he should hear them. But low to themselves they said : " He'll eat us all alive ; how can we escape ? " The ogre said to his wife : " I smell fresh meat, give me some ". " Indeed," said the ogress, " you always think you smell fresh meat. It is four sheep that passed by." " Oh, I make no mistake," said the ogre. " I smell fresh meat for certain. I am going to look everywhere for it." " Look for it, then," she said, " but you won't find any." " If I find it," answered the ogre, " and if you are hiding it, I shall cut off your head to make me a ball." In terror at this threat she said to him : " Don't be angry, my little ogre, I am going to tell you the truth. To-day there came here three young maidens whom I kept, but it would be a pity to eat them, for they know how to do everything. As I am now old I need rest ; our beautiful house, as you see, is in very bad order ; our bread is not baked properly ; our soup no longer tastes good to you, and I don't look so beautiful in your eyes since I have been killing myself with work. They will, therefore, be my servants, so I beg of you not to eat them just now. If you wish to at some future time you can do as you like."

The ogre found it very hard to promise not to eat them up at once. " Let me have my own way," he said ; " I shall only eat two of them." " No, you shall not eat any of them." " Very well ; I shall only eat the little one." But she answered : " No, you shall not eat one of them ". At last, after quarrelling for a long time, he promised not to eat them ; while the ogress thought to herself: "When he goes to the hunt I shall eat them and tell him they have run away".

The ogre came out of the cellar and ordered them to be brought before him. The poor girls were nearly dead with fright ; but the ogress reassured them. When he saw them he asked them what they could do, and they told him they could sweep and sew and spin perfectly ; that their stews were so delicious that you would like to eat the plate even on which they were served ; and as for their bread, cakes, and pies—why, people came for them from a thousand miles round. The ogre was greedy, and so he said : " Now, then, set these fine cooks to work at once ". " But," said he, turning to Finette, " when you have lit the fire, how can you tell if the oven be hot enough ? " " My lord," she answered, " I throw butter in, and then I taste it with my tongue." " Very well," he said, " light the fire then." The oven was as big as a stable, for the ogre and ogress ate more bread than two armies. The princess made an enormous fire, which blazed like a furnace ; and the ogre, who was standing by, ate a hundred lambs and a hundred sucking pigs while waiting for the new bread. Fleur d'Amour and Belle-de-Nuit kneaded the dough. " Well," said the great ogre, " is the oven hot ? " " My lord," replied Finette, " you will see presently." And so saying she threw a thousand pounds of butter into the oven. " I should try it with my tongue," she said, " but I am too little." " I am big enough," said the ogre, and bending down he went so far into the oven that he could not draw back again, so that he was burned to the bones. When the ogress came to the oven she was mightily astonished to find a mountain of cinders instead of her husband.

Fleur d'Amour and Belle-de-Nuit, who saw that she was in great distress, comforted her as they could, but they feared lest her grief should be consoled only too soon, and that regaining her appetite she would put them in a salad, as she had meant to do before. So they said to her: " Take courage, madam ; you will find some king or some marquis who will be happy to marry you ". At that she smiled a little, showing her teeth, which were longer than your finger. When they saw she was in a good humour, Finette said : " If you would but leave off wearing those horrible bear-skins, and dress a little more fashionably ! We could arrange your hair beautifully, and you would be like a star." " Come then," she said, " let us see what you can do ; but be sure that if I find any ladies more beautiful than myself I shall hack you into little bits." Thereupon the three princesses took off her cap, and began to comb and curl her hair, entertaining her all the while with their chatter. Then Finette took a hatchet, and with a great blow from behind, severed her head from her body.

Never was there such joy. They climbed up to the roof of the house to amuse themselves by ringing the golden bells; they ran through all the rooms, which were of pearls and diamonds, and furnished so richly that they nearly died of joy. They laughed, they sang. Nothing was lacking. They had wheat, and sweetmeat, fruits, and dolls, as many as they liked. Fleur d'Amour and Belle-de-Nuit slept in beds hung with brocade and velvet, and they said to each other: " Here we are richer than was our father in his kingdom, but we want husbands. No one will come here, for this house is certainly looked on as a death-trap, and nobody knows of the death of the ogre and his wife. We must go to the nearest town to show ourselves off in our fine clothes, and it will not be long before we find honest merchants who will be glad enough to wed with princesses." As soon as they were dressed they told Finette that they were going for a walk, and that she must stop at home to look after the house and the washing, so that when they came back everything might be neat and clean; that if it were not they would beat her soundly. Poor Finette, stricken with grief, stopped alone in the house, sweeping, cleaning, washing, without a moment's rest, and always crying. " How unhappy I am," she said " to have disobeyed my god-mother ! All kinds of evils happen to me. My sisters have stolen my beautiful clothes to dress themselves in. Without me the ogre and his wife would still be alive and well ; and of what benefit is it to me that I killed them ? It would have been as good to have been eaten by them as to live as I live now." When she had said this she was almost choked with her tears. Then her sisters came back, loaded with Portuguese oranges, preserves, and sugar, saying to her: " Oh, what a fine ball we have been to ! And what a crowd was there ! The king's son was dancing ; we had a great many attentions paid us. But come now, pull off our shoes, and wash us. That's all you are good for." Finette did as she was told, and if by any chance a word of complaint escaped her, they threw themselves on her, beating her till she was senseless.

Next day they went again, and returned to tell of all the wonders they had seen. One evening, when Finette was sitting near the fire on a little heap of cinders, for want of anything else to do, she peered into the crevices of the chimney, and as she looked she found a little key, so old, and so rusty, that it gave her a great deal of trouble to clean it. When it was polished, she found it was gold, and she thought that a golden key must be for opening some beautiful little chest. So she began to run through the whole house, trying the key in all the locks, till at last she found it fit a casket of perfect workmanship. Opening this, she found in it dresses, diamonds, lace, linen, and very costly ribbons. She said nothing about her good fortune to her sisters, but waited impatiently till they should go out next day, and as soon as they had gone out of her sight, she dressed herself in such a way that she was more beautiful than the sun or the moon.

Thus decked out, she went to the same ball where her sisters were dancing, and though she wore no mask, she was so changed for the better that they did not recognise her. As soon as she made her appearance in the assembly a murmur of voices arose, some expressing their admiration, some their jealousy. She was asked to dance, and she excelled all the ladies in that as she did in beauty. The mistress of the house coming up to her and making her a deep bow, begged to know what she was called, so that she might ever keep in remembrance the name of so distinguished a lady. With much courtesy she answered that she was called Cendron. Not a lover was there but forgot his mistress for Cendron : not a poet but made verses to her. Never did a name make such a sensation in such a short time, and the echoes brought nothing back but Cendron's praises. No one had eyes enough to look on her, or voice enough to sing her praises.

Fleur d'Amour and Belle-de-Nuit, who at first had made a great noise wherever they appeared, now seeing the reception given to the new-comer, were bursting with rage. But Finette kept clear of all their spite with the most perfect grace possible. To look at her you would have said she was born to rule, and Fleur d'Amour and Belle-de-Nuit who never saw their sister but with soot on her face and grimier-looking than a little dog, had so forgotten all about her beauty that they did not recognise her at all, and paid court to Cendron like the others. As soon as the ball was nearly over she set off quickly, reached home, undressed in haste, and put on her rags again. When her sisters came back they said : " Ah ! Finette, we have just been seeing a young princess who is quite charming. She is not an ugly ape like you. She is white as snow, and redder than roses. Her teeth are of pearl and her lips of coral. Her dress must weigh more than a thousand pounds, for it is all of gold and diamonds. Ah, how beautiful ! how lovely she is ! " And Finette would answer between her teeth : " I was like that, I was like that ". " What are you muttering ? " they said. And Finette answered still lower : " I was like that ". This little enter-tainment lasted for a long time. Hardly a day passed but Finette put on new clothes, for it was a fairy casket, and the more you took from it, the more there was in it, and the clothes that came out of it were so fashionable that ladies took her for their model.

One evening when Finette had danced more than usual, and had stopped rather late, in her desire to make up for lost time and to get home before her sisters, she walked as fast as ever she could, and let fall one of her slippers, which was of red velvet embroidered with pearls. She did all she could to find it again on the road, but the night was so dark that her trouble was in vain, and she had to go in with only one foot shod.

Next day, Prince Chéri, the eldest son of the king, on his way to the chase, found Finette's slipper. He ordered them to pick it up, looked at it, turned it this way and that, kissed it, cherished it, and bore it away with him. From that day he would not eat. He grew thin and changed, was as yellow as a quince, melancholy, and spiritless. The king and queen, who loved him to distraction, sent in all directions for fine game and preserves for him. But to him these seemed less than nothing, and he only looked at them all, and would not answer the queen when she spoke to him. They sent to fetch doctors from all parts, even from Paris and Montpellier.* When they arrived they were shown the prince, and having watched him three days and three nights without once leaving him, they came to the conclusion that he was in love, and that he would die if a remedy were not provided.

The queen, who loved him tenderly, wept oceans of tears because she could not find out whom he loved and so arrange for his marriage. She brought the most beautiful ladies to his room, but he would not even look at them. At last she said to him one day : " My dear son, you will kill us with grief, for you are in love, and you hide your feelings from us. Tell us whom it is you long for, and she shall be yours even were she but a simple shepherdess." The prince, assured by the queen's promises, drew the slipper out from below his pillow, and showed it to her. " Madam," he said, " this is the cause of my illness. I found this dear little pretty slipper when I was going to the chase, and I shall never marry any but the lady whom it fits." " Very well, my son," said the queen, " do not grieve, we will send in search of her." And she went to tell the news to the king, who was very much astonished. Without delay he ordered that an announcement should be made with drums and trumpets that all the girls and all the women should come and try on the slipper, and that whosoever it should fit should wed with the prince. When all the ladies had heard the announcement they washed their feet with all sorts of waters, pastes, and pomades. There were some who peeled their feet, so that the skin should be more beautiful, others pared them, or fasted, to make them smaller. In crowds they set out to try on the slipper, but not one would it fit, and the more unavailing attempts were made the greater was the prince's distress.

Fleur d'Amour and Belle-de-Nuit one day dressed themselves so fine that they were a wonder to see. " Where are you going ? " said Finette. " We are going to the great city," they answered, " where the king and the queen dwell,

---

* A famous French School of Medicine.

to try on the slipper which the king's son found; for if it fits one of us, the prince will marry her and she shall be a queen." "And might I go too?" said Finette. "You, in truth!" said they. "You are a silly little goose. Be off and water the cabbages, you good-for-nothing."

Finette at once thought of putting on her finest clothes to go and try her luck with the others, for she had some idea that she would have a good chance. But what troubled her was that she did not know the way, for the ball they had danced at was not in the great town. She dressed in all her splendour, in a gown of blue satin covered with stars of diamonds, a sun made of them on her head, a full moon on her back, and all shining so brilliantly that you could not look at her without flinching. When she opened the door to go out she was very much astonished to find the beautiful Spanish jennet that had carried her to her god-mother. She caressed him, saying: "Welcome, little one; for you I am obliged to my god-mother, Merluche". Then it bent down, and she rode on it like a nymph. It was all covered with golden bells and ribbons, and its saddle cloth and bridle were priceless. As for Finette, she was far more beautiful than the fair Helen.

The jennet trotted lightly along to the music of the bells, cling, cling, cling. Fleur d'Amour and Belle-de-Nuit hearing the sound, turned and saw her coming. But what was their surprise at that moment, when they recognised that it was Finette Cendron! They themselves were all draggled, and their fine clothes covered with mud. "Sister," said Fleur d'Amour to Belle-de-Nuit, "I declare to you that that is Finette Cendron." The other said the same; and Finette passing close by at the moment, they were bespattered by her horse's hoofs, and their faces splashed with mud. And Finette laughed as she said: "Your highnesses, Cinderella despises you as much as you deserve"; then riding past them like an arrow she was gone. Belle-de-Nuit and Fleur d'Amour looked at each other. "Are we dreaming?" they said. "Who could have given Finette her fine clothes and the horse? What an astonishing thing! She is in luck. She will put the slipper on, and our journey will be in vain."

While they were mourning over their disappointment, Finette reached the palace, and as soon as she came in sight, every one thought she was a queen. The soldiers presented arms, the drums began to beat, the trumpets sounded, and all the doors were flung open. Those who had seen her at the ball ran in front of her, calling out: "Room, make room for the fair Cendron, the wonder of the world!" With such pomp, she entered the dying prince's room, who, casting his eyes on her, was enchanted, and full of desire that her foot might be small enough to fit the slipper. Without delay, she put it on, and showed the other one which she had brought on purpose. "Long live Princess Chéri!"

they burst out. " Long live the princess who will be our queen ! " The prince rose from his bed, and came forward to kiss her hands, and she thought him handsome and full of wit as he poured his compliments upon her. The king and queen, who had been told the news, hastened to the spot, and the queen taking Finette in her arms, called her her daughter, her darling, her little queen. She gave her beautiful gifts, and the generous king added more. The cannons were fired, there was music of violins, and of pipes, and all kinds of instruments, and nothing was heard but the sounds of dancing and merriment.

The king, the queen, and the prince begged Cendron to give her consent to the marriage. " No," she said, " I must first of all tell you my story," which she did very shortly. When they heard that she was born a princess, they were still more delighted, and almost besides themselves with joy. But when she told them the names of the king and queen, her father and mother, they knew that it was they themselves who had conquered their kingdom, and told her so. Then she swore she would not consent to the marriage till they gave back her father's estates. This they promised, for having more than a hundred kingdoms, one more or less was of very little consequence.

In the meanwhile Belle-de-Nuit and Fleur d'Amour arrived, and the first news they heard was that Cendron had put on the slipper. They did not know what to say or to do, and would have liked to have gone back without seeing her, but when she heard they were come, she ordered them to appear before her, and instead of scowling at them, and of punishing them as they deserved, she rose and came forward to embrace them tenderly. Then presenting them to the queen, she said : " Madam, these are my sisters, who are very amiable ; I beg that you will love them." So astounded were they at Finette's goodness, that they could not utter a word. She promised them that they should return to their own kingdom, which the prince wished to restore to their family. At these words they threw themselves on their knees before her weeping for joy.

Never was there such a wedding-feast. Finette wrote to her god-mother, and put her letter along with magnificent gifts on the beautiful jennet. In the letter she begged her to find the king and queen, to tell them of her good fortune, and to say they might return to their kingdom when they liked. Merluche, the fairy, carried out these instructions perfectly, and Finette's father and mother went back to their own estates, and her sisters became queens like herself.

FORTUNÉE.

ONCE upon a time there was a poor labourer who, knowing he was about to die, wished to leave nothing behind him that his son and daughter could quarrel about after his death, for he loved them tenderly. " Your mother brought me for a dowry," he said, "two stools and a straw mattress. These, with my hen, would have been my only belongings, had not a pot of pinks and a silver ring been given me by a great lady who lived for some time in my poor cottage. When she went away, she said to me : 'My good man, here is a present for you. Be careful to water the pinks, and to keep the ring in a safe place. I may also tell you that your daughter will be wonderfully beautiful. Call her Fortunée ; and give her the ring and the pinks to comfort her for being so poor.' So, dear Fortunée," the good man went on, "you shall have both these, and the rest of my belongings I leave to your brother."

The labourer's two children appeared to be satisfied. Their father died, and they wept, and afterwards they shared his belongings without any dispute. Fortunée thought her brother loved her, but once when she was about to sit down on one of the stools, he said to her in an angry tone: " You keep your pinks and your ring, but don't meddle with my stool. I like order in my house." Fortunée, who was very gentle, began to cry quietly, and remained standing, while Bedou (that was the brother's name) sat there as fine as if he had been a learned doctor. Supper time came on ; Bedou had a beautiful, fresh egg which his only hen had laid, and he threw the shell towards his sister, saying : " See, I have nothing else to give you ; if that isn't enough, go and hunt for frogs ; there are plenty in the marsh near by ". Fortunée answered nothing, but lifting her eyes to heaven she wept again ; then she went to her own room. She

(203)

found it filled with a delicious scent, which she knew, of course, must be from her pinks. She went up to them, saying, in a sad voice: "Pretty pinks, with all your different colours so fair to see, how you comfort my sad heart by your sweet scent. Never fear that I shall let you want for water, or with cruel hand wrench you from your stalks. I shall take care of you, for you are all I have in the world." Then she looked to see if they wanted watering. They were very dry, so she took the pitcher and ran out in the moonlight to the stream some little way off. As she had walked very fast, she sat down on the bank to rest, but hardly had she done so before she saw a lady, whose majestic air beseemed the large number of attendants who accompanied her. Six maids-of-honour held up the train of her robe, while she leaned on two others. Her guards marched before her, richly clad in amaranth velvet embroidered with pearls. They carried an armchair spread with cloth of gold, on which she presently sat down, and a portable canopy was quickly set up over her head. At the same time there were others spreading a table all covered with golden vessels and crystal vases. An excellent supper was served on the banks of the stream, and the soft murmur of the water seemed to blend with the different voices that were singing these words :—

> " Soft and low the summer air
> Gently stirs the woodlands there ;
> Bright flowers glittering on the sod
> Mark where Flora's feet have trod ;
> 'Neath the cool shades hear the choirs
> Of birds that sing their soft desires ;
> Would you catch the soft notes too ?
> Lovers plenty wait for you."

Fortunée hid in a little corner, not daring to move, so surprised was she with all that was happening. After a moment the queen said to one of her squires: " It seems to me that I see a shepherdness near that bush. Bring her here." So Fortunée came forward ; and though she was naturally very timid, she did not fail to make a deep bow to the queen, and she did it with so much grace that those who saw her were much astonished. Taking the hem of the queen's robe in her hand she kissed it, and then stood before her with her eyes cast down, the pink blush on her cheek showing up the whiteness of her complexion. Altogether you could not fail to see in her manners that air of mild simplicity that is so charming in young people. " What are you doing here ? " the queen asked her. " Are you not afraid of robbers ? " "Alas ! madam," said Fortunée, " I have only a cotton frock; so what good would it do them to rob a poor shepherdess like me ? " " You are not rich then ? " replied the queen, smiling.

" I am so poor," said Fortunée, " that my whole inheritance from my father is a pot of pinks and a silver ring." " But you have a heart," added the queen. " If some one wished to take it from you, would you give it away ? " " I do not know what it means to give away my heart, madam," she replied. " I have always heard that without one's heart one cannot live ; that when it is wounded one must die, and in spite of my poverty I am not sorry to live." " You will always be right, my pretty girl, to defend your heart. But tell me," the queen went on, " did you have a good supper this evening ? " " No, madam," said Fortunée, " my brother ate up everything." The queen ordered them to lay a place for her, and setting her down at the table, she gave her all the best things on it. The young shepherdess was so struck with admiration, and so touched with the queen's kindness, that she could hardly eat a morsel. " I would like very much to know," said the queen, " what you were doing so late at the stream." " Madam," she answered, "there is my pitcher ; I was fetching water to water my pinks." So saying she bent down to take hold of the pitcher which was near her ; but when she showed it to the queen she was much astonished to find it turned into a golden one, all covered with diamonds and filled with deliciously-scented water. She dared not take it away with her, fearing it was not her own. " I give it to you, Fortunée," said the queen. " Go and water the flowers which you take such good care of, and do not forget that the Queen of the Woods means to be a friend to you." At these words the shepherdess threw herself at her feet. " After giving you my very humble thanks, madam," she said, " for the honour you do me, I make so bold as to ask you to wait here a moment. I am going to fetch you the half of what belongs to me, my pot of pinks. It can never be in better hands than yours." " Very well, Fortunée," said the queen, gently stroking her cheeks. " I will remain here till you return." Fortunée took her golden pitcher, and ran to her little room ; but while she had been away her brother Bedou had gone in, taken away her pot of pinks, and put a big cabbage in its place. When Fortunée saw this miserable cabbage she was in despair, and hesitated whether she should go back to the stream or not. At last she made up her mind to do so, and kneeling down before the queen she said : " Madam, Bedou has stolen my pot of pinks ; I have only my ring left, and I beg you to take it as a proof of my gratitude ". " If I take your ring, pretty shepherdess," said the queen, " you will be ruined." " Ah ! madam," she answered, with a pretty air of grace, " if I have your favour I cannot be ruined." The queen took Fortunée's ring and put it on her finger. Then she got into her chariot of coral, decked with emeralds, which was drawn by six white horses, more splendid than the equipage of the sun. Fortunée followed her with her eyes as long as she could, till the turns in the forest roads hid her from her sight. Then she went back to Bedou, her mind full of this adventure.

The first thing she did on entering her room was to throw the cabbage out of the window. But she was much astonished to hear a voice crying: "Ah! you have killed me!" She could not understand what these cries could mean, for cabbages are not in the habit of talking. As soon as it was day, Fortunée, anxious about her pot of pinks, went outside to look for it, and the first thing she found was the miserable cabbage. Giving it a kick, she said: "What are you doing here? Do you think you do as well in my room as my pinks?" "If I had not been put there," replied the cabbage, "I should never have thought of intruding." Fortunée trembled, for she was very much afraid. But the cabbage spoke once more. "If you will only put me back amongst my kind, I will tell you in two words that your pinks are in Bedou's bed." Fortunée, in despair, did not know how to get possession of them, but she was kind enough first to plant the cabbage, and then taking up her brother's favourite hen, she said: "Naughty creature! I shall make you pay for all the trouble that Bedou gives me". "Ah! shepherdess," said the hen, "let me live, and as I am of a very talkative humour, I shall tell you the most interesting things. Do not think that you are the daughter of the labourer in whose house you have grown up? No, fair Fortunée, he was not your father. But the queen who gave you life had already had six daughters, and—as if she could have borne a son if she had wished—her husband and her father-in-law told her they would stab her if she did not give them an heir. The poor queen, in great distress, was about to have another child. They shut her up in a castle, surrounded her with guards, or rather executioners, who were ordered to kill her if she bore another daughter. The princess, terrified at the danger that threatened her, neither ate nor slept. But she had a sister who was a fairy, and she wrote to tell her of her fears. The fairy, too, was to bear a child, whom she knew would be a son. When he was born, therefore, she packed her son comfortably in a basket, which she gave in charge to the winds, telling them to carry the little prince into the queen's room, and exchange him for the daughter whom she would bear. This plan was, however, of no use, for the queen, not receiving news from her sister the fairy, took advantage of the good nature of one of her guards, who pitied her and let her escape by a cord ladder. As soon as you were born, the poor queen, seeking a hiding-place, came to this hut half dead with fatigue and pain. I was an industrious woman," said the hen, "and a good nurse, so she gave you in charge to me, telling me all her sorrows, with which she was so overcome that she died before she had time to tell us what should be done with you. As I have been very fond of talking all my life, I could not keep from telling this adventure. So one day there came here a beautiful lady, to whom I related everything I knew about it. She touched me immediately with her wand, and I was turned into a hen, and never could speak any more. My grief was terrible, and my husband, who was from home when the change occurred, never knew the truth. When he came back he looked for me everywhere, till at last he thought I was drowned, or that the beasts of the forest had devoured me. The same lady who had done me such a wrong passed by here a second time ; she ordered him to call you Fortunée, and made him a present of a pot of pinks and a silver ring. But while she was in the hut, there came five-and-twenty of your royal father's guards, who were seeking you with evil intentions. She muttered some words, and they were all turned into green cabbages, one of which it was you threw out of the window last night. I had never heard him speak till now. I myself could not speak either, and I know not how my voice has come back to me."

The princess was very much astonished at the wonders which the hen told her of. She felt stirred with pity for her, and said : " I am deeply sorry, my poor nurse, that you were turned into a hen. I should very much like to give you back your former shape if I could. But despair of nothing. It seems to me that all the things you have just told me about cannot always remain as they are now. Meanwhile I am going to look for my pinks, for I love them better than anything else."

Bedou had gone to the wood, never imagining that Fortunée would think of rummaging in his bed. She was delighted that he was from home, and was hoping she would find no difficulty, when all at once she saw a great quantity of enormous rats ready for fight. They were drawn up in battalions, with the bed in question behind them, and the stools by their sides. Some large mice formed a reserve force, bent on fighting like Amazons. Fortunée was much surprised, and dared not go nearer, for the rats were attacking her, biting her, and making the blood flow. " What ! " she cried, " my pinks, my dear pinks, will you remain in such bad company ? " All at once the thought struck her that perhaps the perfumed water which she kept in the golden pitcher might have some special virtue, so she ran to fetch it, and threw some drops of it on the host of rats and mice. In a moment the rabble scampered off, each one to his hole, while the princess bore away her beautiful pinks in haste. They were nearly dead, so much in want of water were they, and she poured on them all she had in her golden pitcher. She was smelling them with great delight when she heard a very sweet voice which came from amongst the leaves and which said : " Wonderful Fortunée ! behold the happy day so longed for, when I may declare my feelings to you ; for the power of your beauty is such, that even flowers are conscious of it". The princess trembling and astonished at having heard a cabbage and a hen talk, and now a pot of pinks, and at having seen an army of rats, turned pale and fainted.

At that moment Bedou arrived. His work and the heat of the sun had so excited him, that when he saw that Fortunée had come to seek for her pinks, and had found them, he dragged her to the door and put her out. Hardly had her cheeks touched the cool earth before she opened her beautiful eyes, and saw standing by her the Queen of the Woods, ever charming and dignified. "You have a wicked brother," she said to Fortunée, "I saw how cruelly he threw you out here. Do you wish to be revenged on him?" "No, madam," she said, "I do not know what anger is, and his evil nature cannot change mine." "But," said the queen, "I have a strong conviction that this coarse labourer is not your brother; what do you think?" "All the facts that I am aware of go to prove that he is, madam," replied the shepherdess, modestly, "and I must believe them." "What!" said the queen, "have you not heard that you were born a princess?" "I have just heard it," she answered; "yet dare I venture to boast of a thing of which I have no proof?" "Ah, dear child," said the queen, "how I like to see you in this humour! I know now that the obscure bringing up you have had has not stifled the noble blood in your veins. Yes, you are a princess, and it has not been in my power to save you from the misfortunes which you have experienced up till now."

Here she was interrupted by the arrival of a young man, who was fairer than the day. He was dressed in a long doublet of green and gold silk, fastened with large buttons of emeralds and rubies and diamonds. On his head was a crown of pinks, and his hair hung down over his shoulders. As soon as he saw the queen, he bent one knee to the ground and greeted her respectfully. "Ah! dear Pink," she said, "the unhappy term of your enchantment has come to an end by the help of fair Fortunée. What joy to see you!" And she clasped him close in her arms, and then turning towards the shepherdess she said: "Fair princess, I know all that the hen has told you; but what you do not know is, that the zephyrs, whom I had ordered to exchange my son for you, carried him to a flower-bed while they were searching for your mother, who was my sister. Meanwhile a fairy who knew the most secret things, and with whom I had long been on bad terms, so cleverly seized the opportunity she had been on the watch for ever since the birth of my son, that she changed him on the spot into a pot of pinks, and for all my skill I could not prevent this misfortune. Stung with grief, I used all my art to find a remedy, and I could think of nothing better than to bring Prince Pink to the place where you were being brought up, guessing that when you would have watered the flowers with the delicious water which I had in the golden vase, he would speak, he would love you, and that after that nothing would disturb your peace. I had even in my possession the silver ring which it was necessary for me to receive from your hand, as a sign that the hour was at hand when the charm should lose its force, in spite of the rats and the mice that our enemy sent out to hinder you from touching the pinks. So, dear Fortunée, if my son marries you with this ring, your happiness will never end. Look now if the prince seems to you handsome enough to take him for a husband." " Madam," she replied, blushing, " you heap favours on me. I know that you are my aunt, that by your skill the guards sent to kill me were turned into cabbages, and my nurse into a hen. In proposing to marry me to Prince Pink, you do me more honour than I deserve. But, may I tell you why I hesitate ? I do not know what his feelings are for me, and I begin to feel for the first time in my life that I would not be satisfied if he did not love me." " Have no doubts on that point, fair princess," said Pink ; " for long you have impressed me as you wish to impress me now, and if I had been able to speak, what should I not have told you every day as to how my affection was growing, burning within me ? But I am an unfortunate prince to whom you are quite indifferent." Then he repeated these verses to her :—

" Ah ! kinder was my lot before,
　When I, a flower, was all your care,
When on my blossoms you set store,
　And happier were that I was fair ;
For your dear eyes I bloomed anew,
　For you I gathered perfume sweet ;
And when I looked in vain for you
　While far off tarriéd your feet,
My faded petals told a tale
　Of a poor heart that down would sink,
And a poor life that 'gan to fail.
　Then water cool you'd bid me drink,
And kisses sweet would be my food,
　And I was whole and bloomed again,
My soul aglow with gratitude ;
　To prove my passion I was fain ;
Oh ! how I longed some fairy power
　Would break the charm that bound so fast
My being in a fragile flower !
　My prayers are answered now at last.
I see you, love you, and can speak
　My love, and all my soul's desire—
Only, alas ! in vain I seek

14

What once was mine. Your looks retire,
Your words their former feeling lack.
Gods ! did I of my lot complain ?
My human shape I give you back
Ah, let me be a flower again ! "

The princess seemed very pleased with Pink's gallantry, and praised highly the verses he had made on the spot, and though she was not used to hearing verses, she spoke of them like a person of good taste. The queen, who was impatient at seeing her still dressed as a shepherdess, touched her with her wand, and wished for her the richest dresses that ever were seen. At the word her white cotton frock changed into silver brocade embroidered with carbuncles. From her hair, which was piled high on her head, a long veil of gauze and gold fell down. Her black hair sparkled with diamonds, and her complexion, which had been of dazzling whiteness, became like blooming roses, till the prince could hardly bear to look on its brilliancy. "Ah ! Fortunée, how beautiful and charming you are ! " cried he, with a sigh. "Will you not comfort me in my distress ? " "Nay, my son," said the queen, "your cousin will not resist our prayers."

While she was speaking, Bedou passed by on his way to work, and seeing Fortunée like a goddess, he thought he must be dreaming. She called him in a kindly voice, and begged the queen to have pity on him. "What! after having ill-treated you so ? " she said. "Ah, madam," replied the princess, " I am incapable of revenge." The queen kissed her, praising her generous feeling. "To please you," she added, " I am going to make the ungrateful Bedou rich." Thereupon his hut became a palace, beautifully furnished and full of money. But his stools did not change, neither did his bed, to remind him of his former state. And the Queen of the Woods sharpened his wits, softened his manners, and changed his face. Then Bedou felt capable of gratitude, and poured out his thanks to the queen and the princess.

Afterwards by a touch of her wand, the cabbages became men, and the hen a woman. Only Prince Pink was dissatisfied, and sighed as he stood by his princess, begging her to look more kindly upon him. At last she consented. She had never seen a handsome prince before, and the handsomest was as nothing to this one. The Queen of the Woods, delighted by so happy a marriage, took every pains to make all the arrangements as sumptuous as possible. The merrymaking went on for several years, and the happiness of this loving couple lasted their whole life long.

BABIOLE.

THERE was once a queen who had nothing left to wish for but to have children. She could talk of nothing else, and would constantly say that the Fairy Fanferluche, who had been present at her birth, and who bore a grudge against the queen, her mother, had flown into a rage, and had wished her nothing but ill-luck.

One day, as she sat alone grieving by the fireside, she saw a little old woman, no bigger than your hand, come down the chimney, riding on three reeds. On her head was a branch of hawthorn; her gown was of flies' wings, and two nutshells served for shoes. She rode through the air, sweeping three times round the room, and then stopped in front of the queen. "For a long time," she said, "you have been grumbling at me, saying I am to blame for your misfortunes, and that I am responsible for all that happens to you. You think, madam, that it is my fault you have no children. I come to announce to you the birth of an infanta, but I warn you she will cost you many a tear." "Ah! noble Fanferluche," exclaimed the queen, "do not deny me your pity and your aid; I undertake to do everything in my power for you if you will promise that the princess shall be a comfort to me and not a grief." "Fate is stronger than I," replied the fairy. "All that I can do to prove my affection for you is to give you this hawthorn. Fasten it to your daughter's head as soon as she is born ; it will protect her from many perils." And, giving her the haw-thorn, she vanished like a flash of lightning.

The queen remained sad and pondering. "What ! " she said, "do I really desire a daughter who is to cost me many sighs and tears ? Should I not be happier without her ? " When the king, whom she dearly loved, was with her her troubles seemed more bearable. Her child would soon be born, and in pre-paration for the event she gave her attendants strict charge to fasten the haw-thorn on the princess's head directly she should come into the world. She kept the branch in a golden box covered with diamonds, and valued it above all her possessions.

At length the queen gave birth to the loveliest creature that ever was seen. Without delay the hawthorn was fastened on her head, and at the same instant, wonderful to relate ! she turned into a little monkey, and jumped and ran and capered about the room—a perfect monkey and no mistake ! At this metamor-phosis all the ladies uttered horrible cries, and the queen, more alarmed than any one, thought she should die of despair. She ordered the flowers to be taken off the creature's head. With the greatest difficulty the monkey was caught ; but it was in vain that the fatal flowers were removed. She was already a monkey, a confirmed monkey. She could not suck nor do anything else like a child, and cared only about nuts and chestnuts.

"Wicked Fanferluche !" exclaimed the queen, sorrowfully, "what have I done that you should treat me so cruelly ? What is to become of me ? What a disgrace for me, that all my subjects should think I have brought a monster into the world ! and how horrified the king will be at seeing such a child ! " With tears she entreated her ladies to advise her what to do in this serious case. " Madam," said the oldest, "you must persuade the king that the princess is dead, and we must shut up this monkey in a box and cast it to the bottom of the sea ; it would be a terrible thing to keep an animal of this sort any longer."

The queen had some scruple in making up her mind ; but when she was told that the king was coming into her room, she became so confused and dis-tressed that without further consideration she bid the lady-in-waiting do what she liked with the monkey.

It was carried into another apartment and shut up in a box. One of the queen's servants was ordered to throw it into the sea ; and he at once set off with it. Now was the princess in the greatest danger ; for the man, seeing that the box was beautiful, was very unwilling to throw it away. Sitting down by the sea-shore, he took the monkey out of the box, and, not knowing it was his sovereign, resolved to kill her. But while he held it in his hand a loud noise startled him and made him turn his head. He saw an open chariot drawn by six unicorns, glittering with gold and precious stones, and in front marched several trumpeters. A queen in royal robes and with a crown on her head was seated on cushions of cloth of gold, and held her four-year-old son on her knee.

The servant recognised the queen, for she was his mistress's sister and had come to rejoice with her. But as soon as she learned that the little princess was dead, she set out in great sadness to return to her own kingdom. She was startled from a deep reverie by her son crying out: "I want the monkey! I will have it"; and, on looking, the queen saw the prettiest monkey that ever was. The servant looked about for means of escape, but they would not let him go. The queen gave him a large sum of money; and, finding the monkey a gentle little plaything, called her Babiole, who thus, in spite of the cruelty of fate, fell into the hands of her aunt.

When she reached her own realms the little prince begged her to give him Babiole for a playmate. He wished her to be dressed like a princess; so every day new frocks were made for her. She was taught to walk only on her feet; and a prettier and nicer-looking monkey could nowhere be found. Her face was black as a jay's, and she wore a little white hood with bright red tufts at the ears. Her hands were no bigger than butterflies' wings, and the expression of her bright eyes was so intelligent that no one could be astonished at her accomplishments. When the prince, who was very fond of her, caressed her, as he was always doing, she took great care not to bite him; and when he cried she cried too.

She had been living four years with the queen when, one day, she began to stutter like a child trying to speak. Every one was astonished, and still more so when she began to talk in a sweet and clear voice, and so distinctly that not a word was lost. Here was a marvel! Babiole talking! Babiole making herself understood by words! The queen sent for the monkey to amuse her; and, to the great disappointment of the prince, she was taken to the queen's apartment. It cost him some tears; and, to console him, dogs, cats, birds, and squirrels were given him, and even a pony, called Criquetin, who danced the saraband;* but all that did not make up for a word from Babiole. As for her, she was less at her ease with the queen than with the prince. She had to reply like a sybil to a hundred witty and learned questions that she did not always understand. Directly an ambassador or a foreigner arrived she had to appear in a gown of velvet or brocade with stiff bodice and ruff. If the court was in mourning she wore a long mantle and crape, a costume that tired her very much. She was no longer permitted to eat what was to her taste: the doctor gave the

---

* A slow dance in triple time.

orders, and these did not at all please her; for she was as self-willed as only a monkey born a princess could be.

The queen gave her masters who cultivated her bright wit. She excelled in playing on the harpsichord; and a wonderful instrument had been made for her out of an oyster-shell. Painters from the four quarters of the globe, and especially from Italy, came to paint her. Her fame flew from one end of the earth to the other, for never before had a talking monkey been heard of.

The prince, as beautiful as Cupid, and as full of grace and wit, was a prodigy no less extraordinary. He came to see Babiole, and sometimes played with her; and now and then their talk would turn from merry jests to serious subjects, and to moralising. Babiole had a heart; and it had not been metamorphosed like the rest of her little person; and she became so exceedingly fond of the prince that her affection began to be harmful to her. The unhappy Babiole did not know what to do. She passed her nights on the top of a window shutter, or in the chimney corner, and would not enter her clean, soft, downy, and padded basket. Her governess (for she had one) heard her often sigh, and sometimes she would utter her laments aloud. Her melancholy grew with her intelligence; and she never saw herself in a mirror without trying in her vexation to break it. For, as it used to be said, once an ape, always an ape, so Babiole could not get rid of the evil disposition natural to her race.

The prince had grown up. He liked hunting, dancing, the drama, feats of arms, and books, and rarely now gave the monkey a thought. With her it was quite otherwise. She loved him better at twelve than she had at six; but when she reproached him for his neglect he thought he made the amplest amends that could to be expected of him when he gave her a rosy apple or some candied chestnuts.

At last the fame of Babiole began to make a great sensation in Monkeyland, and Magot, the king of the monkeys, was greatly desirous of marrying her. For that purpose he sent a magnificent embassy to ask her hand from the queen. It was not difficult to explain his intentions to his chief ministers, but it would have been infinitely hard to express them to others without the aid of parrots and the birds commonly called magpies. They chattered a great deal; and the jays, who accompanied the procession, felt in honour bound to make as much noise as their companions.

A big ape, called Mirlifiche, was chief of the embassy. He had a coach made of pasteboard, on which were painted the loves of the King Magot with Monette, a monkey renowned throughout Monkeyland, who had died a cruel death by the claws of a wild cat that had taken her playfulness seriously. The delights that Magot and Monette had enjoyed during their married life, and the profound sorrow with which the king had wept for her after her death, were there depicted. Six white rabbits, of first-rate breed, drew the coach, called by distinction the state carriage. Behind came a chariot, in which were the monkeys destined to wait on Babiole. You should have seen how they were dressed! It really seemed as if they were going to a wedding. The rest of the procession was composed of little spaniels, young greyhounds, Spanish cats, Muscovy rats, a few hedgehogs, sly weasels, and greedy foxes. Some drove the chariots, others carried the baggage. Mirlifiche, graver than a Roman dictator, wiser than a Cato, rode a young hare, that ambled better than an English gelding.

The queen knew nothing of this magnificent embassy until it arrived at her palace. Hearing shouts of laughter from the people and the guards she put her head out of the window, and beheld the most extraordinary cavalcade she had ever seen in her life. Immediately Mirlifiche, followed by a considerable number of monkeys, approached the chariot of the ladies of his troop, and, giving his paw to the big one, called Gigona, he helped her to get down. Then letting loose the little parrot, who was to act as his interpreter, he waited while the beautiful bird was presented to the queen and begged an audience.

The parrot, mounting gently in the air, went to the window from which the queen was looking out, and said in the prettiest tone of voice imaginable: " Madam, his grace Count Mirlifiche, ambassador of the celebrated Magot, king of Monkeyland, begs an audience of your majesty, to discuss a very important question ". " Pretty parrot," said the queen, caressing him, " first you must eat some roast meat and have something to drink. After that, you may go and tell Count Mirlifiche that he is heartily welcome to my realm, and so are all who accompany him. If he is not too much fatigued by his journey, he can presently enter the audience chamber, where I, on my throne, will await him with the whole court."

At these words the parrot kissed his claw twice, saluted the guard, sang a little tune to give vent to his joy, and taking to his wings again and perching on Mirlifiche's shoulder, whispered in his ear the favourable answer he had just received. Mirlifiche was fully sensible of the honour, and told the magpie Magot, who had been appointed as sub-interpreter, to ask one of the queen's officers to be good enough to give him a room in which to rest for a few moments. Accordingly, a saloon paved with coloured and gilded marble, one of the handsomest in the palace, was opened, and he entered with a part of his suite. But since monkeys are naturally very inquisitive, they smelt out a certain corner in which many pots of preserves had been stored. Immediately the gluttons set on it. One seized a crystal cup full of apricots, another a bottle of syrup; some took patties, others marzipan. The winged creatures who accompanied them were vexed at the sight of a repast where there was neither hemp nor millet seed; and a jay, by profession a great talker, flew into the audience chamber, and, respectfully approaching the queen, said: "Madam, I am too much your majesty's obedient servant to be a willing party to the havoc that is being made in your delicious preserves. Count Mirlifiche has already eaten three pots himself; he was gobbling up the fourth without the slightest respect for your royal majesty, when, deeply grieved, I came to warn you." "Many thanks, little jay, for your friendly thought," said the queen, smiling, "but you need not be so zealous for my pots of preserves; I relinquish them for the sake of Babiole, whom I love with all my heart." The jay, somewhat ashamed of the attack he had just made, withdrew without a word.

A few moments later the ambassador entered, accompanied by his suite. He was not dressed quite in the fashion, for since the famous Fagotin, who made such a brilliant figure in the world, had returned home, a good model had been lacking. He wore a sugar-loaf hat with a bunch of green feathers, a shoulder-belt of blue paper covered with gold spangles, deep frills to his breeches, and carried a cane. The parrot, who passed for something of a poet, having composed a very solemn harangue, advanced to the foot of the throne on which the queen was seated. Addressing Babiole, he spoke thus:—

> " Learn the power of your eyes' bright fire
> By the love that they in King Magot inspire!
> These monkeys, birds, cats—all this splendid array
> Are here, at his word, and his passion display.

Monette, the queen, beloved of her race—
Except you, none had ever so comely a face—
By a wild cat's claws she was mangled and torn,
And Magot, the king, was left all forlorn.
The king to her memory faithfulness swore,
And to love her for ever and evermore;
But you, from his heart, by your sweet perfection,
Have chased of his first love all recollection.
In you now, madam, he finds all his delight;
And, could you but measure his passion's height,
No doubt but your heart, framed in pity's fashion
To cure his love, would share his passion.
For once on a time he was hearty and gay,
But now he is weak and thin alway
As if pain bore him company every hour—
Ah! madam, indeed he feels love's power!
The olives and nuts that he found so good
Are now to his palate but tasteless food;
He dies!—'tis you alone that can save—
You alone can keep him on this side the grave.
On all the delights that your coming await
In our happy land, can I not dilate.
There figs and grapes will fail you never,
And the finest fruits are in season ever."

The parrot had no sooner finished his speech than the queen looked at Babiole, who was covered with confusion. Before replying, the queen, wishing to find out her feelings, asked the parrot to explain to the ambassador that, as far as she was concerned, she favoured his master's suit. The audience finished, she withdrew, and Babiole followed her into her closet. " My little one," she said, " I shall be very sorry to part with you, but it is not possible to refuse Magot, who asks your hand in marriage, for I have not yet forgotten that his father sent two hundred thousand monkeys into the field to carry on a great war against mine. They ate so many of our subjects that we were obliged to make an ignominious peace." " You mean, madam," answered Babiole, impatiently, " that, to avoid his wrath, you are resolved to sacrifice me to this wretched monster, but I at least implore your majesty to grant me a few days in which to make up my mind." " That is but fair," said the queen; " nevertheless, if you will take my advice, decide quickly. Consider the honours in store for you, the magnificence of the embassy, and the number of ladies-in-waiting sent to you. I am sure that Magot never did for Monette what he has done for you." " I do not know what he did for Monette," replied little Babiole, disdainfully, " but I do know that I care very little for these marks of affection for me." Then she rose, and, gracefully curtseying, sought the prince to tell him her troubles. As soon as he saw her, he cried out: " Well, my Babiole, when are we to dance at your wedding?" " I do not know, sir," she said, sadly; " but I am so wretched that I have no longer the strength to keep my secret from you; and, although it ill becomes my modesty, I must confess to you that you are the only one I wish for a husband." " Husband!" said the prince, bursting out laughing, " husband, little one! Well, that is delightful! but all the same, I trust, you will excuse me if I do not accept your proposal, for, to tell the truth, in our persons, our appearance, and our manners, we are not exactly a match." " I agree with you," she said, " especially since our hearts are not alike. For a long while I have seen that you are ungrateful, and I am extremely foolish to love a prince who so little deserves it." " But, Babiole," said he, " think of the trouble I should be in to see you perched on the top of a sycamore, holding on to a branch by the end of your tail. Come now, let this be a joke, and for your honour and mine marry the monkey king, and, in token of our firm friendship, send me your first little Magot." " It is fortunate for you, sir, that my nature is not entirely that of a monkey. Any other than myself would have already torn out your eyes, bitten off your nose, and wrenched off your ears; but I leave you to the reflections your unworthy conduct will one day cause you." She could say no more. Her governess came to fetch her, the ambassador Mirlifiche having entered her apartment with magnificent presents.

There was a costume made of a spider's web, embroidered with tiny glow-worms, an egg-shell case for combs. A white-heart cherry served for a pin-cushion, and all the linen was trimmed with paper lace. In a basket there were several carefully-chosen shells, some to serve for ear-rings, others for bodkins, all of them shining like diamonds; and, what was even better, a dozen boxes full of sweetmeats, and a little glass chest with a hazel-nut and an olive inside. But the key of this was lost, and Babiole troubled little about it.

The ambassador gave her to understand, in the chattering language of Monkeyland, that his sovereign was more touched by her charms than he had ever been by those of any other monkey; that he intended to build her a palace at the top of a fir tree; that he sent these gifts and the fine preserves as a mark of his attachment; and that indeed the king, his master, could prove his affection in no better way. " But," he added, " the strongest testimony to his love, and that which you ought to feel most deeply, is, madam, the trouble he has been at to have his picture painted, so that you may anticipate the pleasure of seeing him." He then displayed the portrait of the King of the Monkeys, seated on a huge log, eating an apple.

Babiole turned away her head that she might not look longer on so ugly a face, and after some little display of temper gave Mirlifiche to understand that she thanked his master for his esteem, but that, as yet, she had not made up her mind whether she intended to marry at all.

Meanwhile, the queen determined not to draw down on herself the anger of the monkeys, and, believing there would be little difficulty in sending Babiole wherever she wished her to go, had everything prepared for her departure. At this news, despair took possession of Babiole. The prince's disdain on one hand, the queen's indifference on the other, and more than all that, the prospect of such a husband, made her resolve to run away. It was not a very difficult matter, for, since she could speak, she was no longer tied up, and came and went as she liked, and would enter her room as often by the window as by the door.

She set out as quickly as possible, jumping from tree to tree, from branch to branch, until she came to the bank of a river. The violence of her despair blinded her to the danger she was running into in attempting to cross by swimming. Without the least consideration she threw herself in, and immediately went to the bottom. But there she did not lose consciousness; she saw a magnificent grotto, adorned with shells. She hastened in, and was received by a venerable old man, whose white beard reached to his waist. He was lying on a bed of reeds and irises, with a crown of poppies and wild lilies on his head, and propped up against a rock, from whence flowed several springs that fed the river.

"Well! what brings you here, my little Babiole?" said he, reaching her his hand. "Sir," she replied, "I am an unfortunate monkey; I am running away from a hideous ape, to whom they wish to marry me." "I know more about you than you think," added the wise old man. "It is true you detest Magot, but it is equally true that you love a young prince who cares nothing for you." "Ah! sir," cried Babiole, sighing, "do not let us speak of him. The recollection of him only makes my sorrows harder to bear." "He will not be always insensible to love," continued the King of the Fish; "I know he is reserved for the most beautiful princess in the world." "Unhappy wretch that I am!" continued Babiole; "then he will never be mine!" The old man smiled, and said: "Do not grieve, my good Babiole. Time is a wonderful master. Only take care not to lose the little glass chest Magot sent you, and that you have, perchance, now in your pocket. I can tell you no more. Here is a tortoise that travels at a good rate. Seat yourself on her; she will take you where you have to go." "After what I owe you," said Babiole, "I cannot help wishing to know your name." "I am called," he said, "Biroquoi, father of Biroquie, a river, as you see, of considerable size and fame."

Babiole mounted her tortoise with the greatest confidence. For a long time they floated over the water, and at length, by what seemed a very round-about way, the tortoise gained the bank. It would be difficult to imagine anything prettier than the side saddle and the rest of the trappings. There were even little horse-pistols, for which two crab-shells served as cases.

Babiole was journeying on with the utmost confidence in wise Biroquoi's promises when she suddenly heard a great noise. Alas! alas! it was the ambassador Mirlifiche, with all his attendants, returning to Monkeyland, sad and sorrowful at Babiole's flight. A monkey belonging to the troop had, during the halt for dinner, climbed a nut tree, in order to throw down nuts to feed the little ones; but no sooner had he reached the top of the tree than, looking round on every side, he saw Babiole on the poor tortoise, who was

slowly making her way across the open country. At sight of her he began to shout so loudly that the assembled monkeys asked him, in their language, what was the matter. He told them, and immediately the magpies and jays were let loose, and they flew to where she was. On their report, the ambassador, the monkeys, and the rest of the company ran and stopped her.

Here was a misfortune for Babiole! Nothing more unlucky or disagreeable could possibly have happened. She was forced to get into the state carriage, which was immediately surrounded by the most vigilant monkeys, by a few foxes, and a cock who, perched on the top, kept guard day and night. A monkey led the tortoise along as a rare animal, and so the cavalcade continued its journey, to the great sorrow of Babiole, whose sole companion was Madam Gigona, a cross-grained and disagreeable monkey.

At the end of three days, which passed without adventure, the guides having lost their way, they reached a large and magnificent city, whose name they did not know; but, seeing a beautiful garden with the gate standing open, they stopped there, and plundered it, as if it had been a conquered country. One crunched nuts, another gobbled cherries, a third despoiled a plum tree. Indeed, there was not the smallest monkey but joined in the pillage, and laid in a store.

You must know that this city was the capital of the kingdom where Babiole was born; her mother lived there, and since she had had the misfortune to see her daughter changed into a monkey by means of a hawthorn branch, had never allowed a monkey, a baboon, or an ape to remain in the kingdom, nor, indeed, anything that could recall to her mind the deplorable and fatal circumstance. A monkey was looked upon as a disturber of the public peace. Think, then, what was the astonishment of the people to see a pasteboard coach, a chariot of painted straw, and all the rest of the most extraordinary cavalcade that was ever seen since tales were tales, and fairies fairies!

The news spread quickly to the palace. The queen was paralysed; she thought the whole race of monkeys meant to make an attack on her government. She immediately summoned her council, who, by her orders, found the whole troop guilty of high treason, and, not wishing to lose the opportunity of making such an example of them as should be remembered in the future, she sent her officers into the garden with orders to seize them all. Big nets were cast over the trees, and the capture was soon effected.

In spite of the respect due to the rank of an ambassador, this high office was most contemptuously treated in the person of Mirlifiche, who was pitilessly cast into the depths of a cellar under a big empty cask, where he and his companions were imprisoned, with the lady monkeys, both matrons and damsels, who accompanied Babiole.

As for Babiole, she felt a secret joy at this fresh disturbance. When misfortunes reach a certain point nothing further is dreaded, and death itself seems desirable. Such was her condition, for her heart was full of the prince who disdained her, and her mind occupied with the horrible thought of King Magot, whose wife she was on the point of becoming.

Besides, we must not forget to mention that she was so prettily dressed, and her manners were so distinguished, that those who had seized her, stopped to look at her as something quite marvellous, and when she spoke to them they were still more surprised, for they had already heard of the wonderful Babiole. The queen who had found her, and who did not know of her niece's metamorphosis, had often written to her sister that she possessed an extraordinary monkey, and begged her to come and see it, but the unhappy queen would pass over that sentence without reading it.

At length the warders, carried away by admiration, brought Babiole into a big gallery and made her a little throne. She sat on it more like a sovereign than a captive monkey, and the queen, happening to pass by, was so vastly taken with her pretty face and the charming compliments she paid her, that, in spite of herself, the nature within her made appeal for the infanta. She took her in her arms; and, as for the little creature, feelings she had never known before stirred within her. She threw herself on the queen's neck and spoke such loving and engaging words that all who heard her were delighted. "No, madam," she exclaimed, "it is not the fear of approaching death, with which I am told you threaten the unfortunate race of monkeys, that terrifies me and makes me try to please you and soften your heart. The cutting short of my life is by no means the greatest misfortune that can happen to me, and I have in me feelings so far above my condition that I should regret any step whatsoever that might be taken to preserve my life. It is you yourself I love. Your crown is of far less consequence to me than your goodness."

I ask you, what reply could be made when Babiole spoke such winning words? The queen said not a word, but opened her two eyes wide, seemed to consider, and felt her heart strangely stirred.

She carried the monkey into her closet, and when they were alone she said to her: "Tell me your adventures without a moment's delay, for I feel that of all the animals who inhabit the menageries, and whom I keep in my palace, you will be the one I shall love most. I assure you that for your sake I will pardon the monkeys who accompany you." "Ah! madam," she exclaimed, "I ask nothing for them. By ill-luck I was born a monkey, and that same ill-luck gave me intelligence that will cause me suffering till I die. For what must I feel when I see myself in my mirror: little, ugly, and sooty, my hands covered with hair, with a tail, and with teeth ever ready to bite; while, at the same time, I do not lack intelligence, and have taste, refinement, and quick feelings?" "Do you know what it is to love?" said the queen. Babiole sighed, but did not answer. "Oh!" continued the queen, "you must tell me if you love a monkey, a rabbit, or a squirrel; for, if you are not already too deeply pledged, I have a dwarf who will just suit you." At that proposal Babiole looked so disdainful that the queen burst out laughing. "Don't be angry," she said, "and tell me how it is that you can speak."

"All that I know of my adventures," replied Babiole, "is that your sister had scarcely left you after the birth and death of your daughter, when going along the sea-shore she saw one of your servants on the point of drowning me. At her command I was taken from him. By a miracle, that equally astonished everybody, speech and reason were given to me. Masters, who taught me several languages and to play musical instruments, were provided for me. At length, madam, I became aware of my misfortune, and— but," she exclaimed, seeing the queen's face pale and covered with a cold perspiration, "what is the matter, madam? I observe an extraordinary change in your appearance." "I am dying!" said the queen, in a weak, almost inaudible voice, "I am dying; my beloved and only too unhappy daughter! have I at last found you again!" At these words she swooned. Babiole, terrified, ran and called for aid. The queen's ladies hurried to give her water, to unlace her and put her to bed. Babiole crept in with her, and she was so small that no one noticed her.

When the queen had recovered from the long swoon into which the princess's words had thrown her, she desired to be left alone with the ladies who knew the fatal secret of her daughter's birth. She told them what had happened, and they were so dismayed that they did not know what advice to give.

But the queen commanded them to tell her what they considered it expedient to do in this lamentable case. Some said the monkey must be strangled, others that she should be shut up in a den; others, even, that she should be again thrown into the sea. The queen wept and sobbed. "She has so much intelligence," said she; "what a pity to see her reduced to this miserable condition by an enchanted bouquet! But, after all," continued she, "she is my daughter; it is I who brought on her the wicked Fanferluche's anger. Is it right that she should suffer on account of that fairy's hatred for me?" "Yes, madam," exclaimed her old lady-in-waiting, "your reputation must be saved. What would the world think if you declared that a little monkey was your daughter? It's not in nature to have such children when one is as beautiful as you." The queen lost patience at hearing her talk thus. But the old lady and the others were equally persistent that the little monster must be got rid of; and, finally, she determined to shut Babiole up in a castle, where she would be well fed and kindly treated, for the rest of her life.

When Babiole heard that the queen intended to put her in prison, she slipped quietly out by the side of the bed, and, throwing herself from the window on to a tree in the garden, escaped to the big forest, and left everybody in confusion at her loss.

She spent the night in the hollow of an oak, where she had leisure to reflect on the cruelty of her fate. What caused her most distress was to be forced to leave the queen; but she preferred voluntary exile and the preservation of her liberty to the loss of it for ever.

As soon as it was light she continued her journey, without knowing where she wished to go, thinking and thinking a thousand times over of the strangeness of this most extraordinary adventure. "What a difference," she exclaimed, "between what I am and what I was meant to be!" Tears flowed freely from poor Babiole's little eyes.

Directly day appeared she set out, fearing the queen would send after her, or that one of the monkeys escaped from the cellar would take her, against her will, to King Magot. She went on by slow degrees without following road or path until she reached a great desert, where there was neither house, nor tree, nor fruit, nor grass, nor spring. She entered it without thinking; and, only when she began to feel hungry, recognised too late that travelling in such a country was exceedingly imprudent.

Two days and two nights went by without her being able to catch even a grub or a fly. The fear of death seized on her, and she was so weak that she was on the point of swooning. She sank down on the ground; and, remembering the olive and the hazel nut in the little glass box, she thought they might make her a slight repast. Delighted at this ray of hope, she took a stone, broke the box to pieces, and crunched the olive.

But she had scarcely put her teeth in it when a great quantity of scented oil came pouring out upon her paws, which immediately turned into the most beautiful hands in the world. Her surprise was extreme: she took the oil and rubbed herself all over. Oh! wondrous! she immediately became so beautiful that there was nothing in the world like her. She felt that she had big eyes, a small mouth and a well-shaped nose. She was dying for a mirror; and at length managed to improvise one out of the biggest piece of the glass box. And when she saw herself, what joy! What a delightful surprise! Her clothes grew in size like herself; her head was well dressed; her hair fell in thousands of curls; her complexion was fresh as the flowers in spring. The first moments of surprise over, hunger made itself more acutely felt, and her distress vastly increased. "What!" she said, "so young and so beautiful, a born princess, and I must perish in this barren place! Oh! wretched fate that led me here! How strangely is my destiny shaped! Have you made so delightful and unexpected a change in me only to make my troubles greater? And you, venerable river Biroquie, who so generously saved my life, will you leave me to perish in this frightful solitude?"

In vain did the infanta implore help—the whole world was deaf to her voice. Hunger tormented her to such a degree that she took the hazel nut and cracked it; but, in throwing away the shell, she was greatly surprised to see come out of it architects, painters, masons, upholsterers, sculptors, and ever so many other sorts of workmen. Some made designs for a palace, others built it; others, again, furnished it. Some decorated the rooms, and some cultivated the gardens; everything shone with gold and azure. A magnificent banquet was served; sixty princesses, more beautifully dressed than queens, accompanied by squires and followed by pages, came to her with charming compliments, and invited her to the feast that awaited her. Babiole at once, without waiting to be entreated, advanced quickly, with the air of a queen, into the hall, where she ate ravenously of the food.

Scarcely had she left the table when her treasurers brought her fifteen thousand chests, big as hogsheads, filled with gold and diamonds. They asked her if she was agreeable that they should pay the workmen who had built her palace. She replied that was only right, on condition that they would also build a city, marry, and remain with her. They all consented; and, although the city was five times bigger than Rome, it was finished in three quarters of an hour. Surely these were wonders enough to come out of a little hazel nut!

The princess was considering in her mind whether she should send an imposing embassy to her mother, and some reproachful messages to her cousin, the young prince. While the necessary measures were being taken she amused herself with looking on at the tilting, where she always awarded the prize, with cards, the play, hunting and fishing, for a river had been brought into her domain. The fame of her beauty spread over the whole world : kings from the four corners of the earth came to her court with giants taller than mountains, and pigmies smaller than rats.

It happened that on a certain day a great tournament was being held. Several knights entered the lists. They got angry with each other, came to blows, and were wounded. The princess, in great wrath, came down from the balcony to see who were the guilty men : but when they were disarmed, what was her distress to see the prince, her cousin! If he was not dead, he was very nearly so, and she thought she must herself die of surprise and grief. She had him carried into the finest apartment of the palace, where nothing necessary for his cure was wanting—physicians from Chodrai, surgeons, salves, broths, and syrups. The infanta herself made the bandages and prepared the lint. Her eyes moistened them with tears, and such tears must have been balm to the sick man. For, indeed, he was ill in more ways than one; not to reckon a half-dozen sword thrusts, and as many cuts from a lance which pierced him right through, he had been for some time at the court *incognito*, and had fallen a victim to the power of Babiole's charms to an extent past recovery. It is then easy to imagine something of what he now felt, when

15

he could read in the kindly princess's face that she was in the utmost trouble because of the condition to which he was reduced.

I shall not stop to record all the things his heart prompted him to say in thanking her for the kindness she showed him. Those who heard him were surprised that a man so ill could show so much affection and gratitude. The infanta, who blushed more than once, begged him to be silent; but the emotion and the ardour of his words excited him to such an extent that she saw him suddenly seized by a frightful agony. Until then she had remained perfectly calm, but now she entirely lost her self-control, tore her hair, uttered loud cries, and made everybody think that her heart was easily given away, since, in this short time, she had become so fond of a stranger. For in Babiola (as she had called her kingdom) it was not known that the prince was her cousin, and that she had loved him since her childhood.

It was while travelling that he had stopped at her court, and, as he knew no one to present him to the infanta, he thought nothing would serve him better than to perform before her five or six heroic feats: for instance, to cut off the legs and arms of the knights of the tournament. But he did not find them amiable enough to permit this. There was only in consequence a wild confusion; the strongest overcame the weakest, and, as I have already said, the weakest was the prince.

Babiole, in despair, ran along the high road without carriage or guards. Entering a wood, she fell swooning at the foot of a tree, where the Fairy Fanferluche, who never slept, and only sought opportunities of doing evil, came and carried her off in a cloud which was blacker than ink, and travelled faster than the wind. For some time the princess remained unconscious, but at length she came to herself. Never did surprise equal hers at finding herself so far from the earth, and so near the heavens. The floor of the cloud was not solid, so that in running here and there she seemed to be walking on feathers, and when it partly opened she had much ado to keep from falling off. There was no one to whom she could complain, for the wicked Fanferluche had made herself invisible. She had time to think of her beloved prince, and of the condition in which she had left him, and her soul was filled with the saddest thoughts. "How!" she exclaimed, "can I survive him whom I love, or how can dread of a speedy death find a place in my heart! Ah! if the sun would scorch me it would be doing me a good turn, or if I could drown myself in the rainbow, how happy I should be! But, alas! the whole zodiac is deaf to my cries: the archer has no arrows, the bull no horns, the lion no teeth. Perhaps the earth will be kinder, and on the sharp point of a rock I may meet my death. Oh, prince! my beloved cousin, if you were only here to see me take the most tragic leap a despairing lover can imagine." With these words she ran to the edge of the cloud, and threw herself off like an arrow shot from a tight strung bow.

All who saw her thought the moon was falling; and as the moon was then on the wane, many of its worshippers, who were some time without seeing it again, went into deep mourning, and persuaded themselves that the sun had played it this wicked trick out of jealousy.

However desirous the infanta might be of dying, she did not succeed. She fell into the glass bottle in which the fairies generally exposed their ratafia to the sun. But what a bottle! No tower in the universe was so big! Fortunately it was empty, or she would have been drowned like a fly.

The six giants who guarded it immediately recognised the infanta. They were the same who dwelt in her court, and they loved her. The malicious Fanferluche, who did nothing by chance, had transported them there each on his winged dragon, and when the giants slept the dragons guarded the bottle. While Babiole was there, there were many days when she regretted the loss of her monkey's skin. She lived like the chameleons on air and dew.

The infanta's prison was known to none. The prince was ignorant of its existence. He was not dead, and continually asked for Babiole. He saw by the melancholy of all those who attended him that there was some cause of general grief at the court. His native good-breeding prevented him from seeking to discover it. But when he was convalescent he begged so hard for news of the princess that they had not the courage to conceal her loss from him. Those who had seen her enter the wood declared she had been devoured by lions, and others believed she had killed herself out of despair; others again maintained that she had gone out of her mind, and was wandering over the world.

Since the last suggestion was the least terrible, and somewhat revived the prince's hopes, he decided it was so, and set out on Criquetin, whom I mentioned before—although I did not remark that he was the eldest son of Bucephalus, and one of the best horses of that age. Riding with a loose rein, letting his horse go at hazard, he called the infanta's name aloud, but the echoes alone replied.

At length he reached the bank of a broad river. Criquetin was thirsty, and went into the water to drink; and the prince, according to his custom, began to shout with all his might: " Babiole, beautiful Babiole, where are you ? "

He heard a voice whose sweetness seemed to delight the wave; it said to him : " Approach, and you shall know where she is ". At those words the prince, as brave as he was loving, gave two pricks of the spur to Criquetin, swam out and found a gulf where the water rushed down more rapidly. He sank to the bottom, fully persuaded that he was going to be drowned.

He arrived safely at the abode of the good Biroquoi, who was celebrating his daughter's marriage with one of the richest and most important rivers of the land. All the fishy deities were in the grotto; tritons and mermaids made pleasant music, and the river Biroquie, lightly clad, danced olivettes * with the Seine, the Thames, the Euphrates, and the Ganges, who had certainly come a long way to enjoy each other's society. Criquetin, who was a well-bred horse, stopped respectfully at the entrance of the grotto, and the prince, whose manners

were even better than those of his horse, making a low bow, asked if a mortal like himself was permitted to appear among so fine a company.

Biroquoi took up the word, and replied in an affable manner that they would be honoured and pleased were he to do so. "I have been expecting you, sir, for some days," he continued. "I am devoted to your interests, and those of the infanta are dear to me. You must rescue her from the fatal place where the vindictive Fanferluche has imprisoned her. She is shut up in a bottle."

---

* Olivette, a kind of dance in use among the Provençals after the gathering in of the olives.

"What do you tell me!" exclaimed the prince, "the infanta in a bottle?" "Yes," said the wise old man, "she suffers greatly; but I warn you, sir, that unless you follow my advice it is not easy to overcome the giants and dragons who guard her. You must leave your good horse here, and mount a winged dolphin I have been training for you for a long time past." He ordered the dolphin, saddled and bridled, to be brought, and it pranced and curvetted so finely that Criquetin was jealous.

Biroquoi and his companions made haste to arm the prince. They put on him a shining cuirass made of the scales of golden carps; his helmet was a big snail-shell, shaded by a large cod's tail, raised up to form an aigrette; a naiad girded him with an eel belt, from which hung a formidable sword made of a long fish bone. Afterwards he was given a great tortoise-shell for a shield; and so equipped there was never a little gudgeon that would not have taken him for the god of the soles, for, to speak the truth, this young prince had a certain air seldom found among mortals.

The hope of soon finding the charming princess he loved, inspired him with a gladness he had been unable to feel since her disappearance, and the faithful chronicler of this tale remarks that he ate with a good appetite at Biroquoi's board, and thanked the company in no common words. He bade his Criquetin farewell, and mounted the flying fish, which immediately set out.

At the end of the day the prince found himself so high up that, in order to rest a little, he entered the kingdom of the moon. The strange and rare things he discovered there would have delighted him had he been less anxious to get his infanta out of the bottle in which she had been living for several months.

Day had scarcely dawned when he saw her surrounded by the giants and dragons that the fairy, by the power of her wand, had set over her. So little did the fairy dream that any one could be strong enough to deliver her, that she relied on the vigilance of her terrible guards to keep her in suffering.

The beautiful princess was pitifully looking at the heavens, and addressing her sad laments to them, when she saw the flying dolphin and knight who came to rescue her. She would not have believed the adventure possible had she not known, from her own experience, that to certain people the most extraordinary things are always happening. "Is this knight," she said, "transported into the air by the malice of the fairies? Alas! how I pity him if a bottle or a decanter is to serve him for a prison, like me!"

While she was reflecting thus, the giants, who saw the prince above their heads, thought it was a kite, and cried one to the other: "Catch it; catch the cord, it will amuse us"; but when they stooped to pick it up, he cut and thrust at them, and hacked them to pieces like a pack of cards you cut in half and scatter to the winds. At the noise of this great combat the infanta turned her head and recognised her young prince. What joy to be certain he still lived! but what terror to see him in so evident danger in the midst of those terrible giants and dragons who were throwing themselves on him! She cried aloud in terror, and the thought of the danger he was in nearly killed her.

However, the magic fish bone with which Biroquoi had armed the prince's hand did not strike in vain, and the nimble dolphin, who raised himself, and came down just at the right moment, was also a wonderful help; so that in a very short time the ground was covered with the monsters.

The impatient prince, seeing his infanta through the glass, would have dashed it in pieces had he not feared wounding her. So he descended instead by the neck of the bottle. When he was at the bottom he threw himself at Babiole's feet and respectfully kissed her hand. "Sir," said she, "it is right, if I am to deserve your esteem, that I should tell you the reasons that induced me to take so tender an interest in your preservation. You must know that we are near relations; that I am the daughter of the queen, your aunt, and the very same Babiole you found in the shape of a monkey by the sea-shore, and who afterwards was weak enough to show towards you an affection you disdained." "Ah, madam!" exclaimed the prince. "Can I believe so extraordinary a tale? You were a monkey! You loved me! I knew it; and my heart was capable of refusing the greatest happiness in the world!" "I should now," replied the infanta, smiling, "have a very poor opinion of your taste if you could then have felt any affection for me. But, sir, let us depart; I am tired of being a prisoner, and I fear my enemy. Let us go to the queen, my mother, and tell her these extraordinary things, that must surely be of great interest to her." "Come, let us go, madam," said the anxious prince, mounting his winged dolphin, and taking her in his arms; "let us restore to her, in your person, the most charming princess in the world."

The dolphin rose up gently, and shaped his course towards the capital, where the queen was passing her sad life. Babiole's flight had left her not a moment of peace. She could not help thinking of her and recalling the pretty things she had said to her; and, monkey as she was, the queen would have given half her kingdom to see Babiole again.

When the prince arrived he disguised himself as an old man and asked for a private audience. "Madam," he said, "since my earliest youth I have studied the art of necromancy. You must know, therefore, that I am not ignorant of the hatred Fanferluche has for you, and the terrible results it has caused. But dry your tears, madam; Babiole, whom you remember so ugly, is now the most beautiful princess in the world. You will soon have her with you if you will forgive the queen, your sister, for the cruel war she has waged against you, and conclude the peace by the marriage of your infanta with your nephew, the prince." "I cannot delude myself that what you tell me is true," replied the queen, weeping; "good old man, you wish to alleviate my distress; I have lost my daughter, I have no longer a husband; my sister claims my kingdom, her son is as unjust as she is, they persecute me; I will never make an alliance with them." "Fate decrees otherwise," he continued; "I am chosen to inform you of it." "Well, and where would be the good, if I did consent to this marriage? The wicked Fanferluche has too much power and malice; she would never be reconciled to it." "Do not disturb yourself about that, madam," replied the old man; "only promise me that you will offer no opposition to the desired marriage." "I promise everything," exclaimed the queen, "if only I may see my beloved daughter once more."

The prince left her, and ran to the spot where the infanta was waiting for him. She was surprised at his disguise, and he was obliged to tell her that for some time the interests of the two queens had been greatly opposed, and that there had been much ill-feeling between them, but that he had just gained his aunt's consent to what he wished. The princess was enchanted. She repaired to the palace, and all who looked on her saw in her so perfect a likeness to her mother that they eagerly followed to find out who she was.

As soon as the queen saw her, her heart was so mightily stirred that no other testimony was needed to the truth of the story. The princess threw herself at the feet of the queen, who clasped her in her arms. At first they were silent, wiping away each other's tears with a thousand tender kisses; and then they said everything that such an occasion could suggest. Then the queen, casting her eyes on her nephew, welcomed him very kindly, and repeated to him what she had promised the magician. She would have gone on speaking, but, hearing a noise in the courtyard of the palace, she put her head out of the window, and had the pleasant surprise of seeing that the queen, her sister, had arrived. The prince and the infanta, who were also looking out, recognised in her suite the venerable Biroquoi; and even the good Criquetin was there too. Each party shouted for joy at the sight of the other; and they hastened to meet once again with a delight that cannot be described. The far-famed marriage of the prince and the infanta was immediately concluded in defiance of the Fairy Fanferluche, whose cunning and malice were thus equally confounded.

THE YELLOW DWARF.

THERE was once a queen who had lost all her children except one daughter, who was all the world to her. But, being a widow, and loving the young princess as the dearest thing on earth, she was so fearful of losing her that she never corrected her faults. Thus the maiden, whose beauty was extraordinary and divine rather than mortal, and who was destined to wear a crown one day, became so headstrong and so vain of her budding charms that she looked down on everybody.

Her mother, by her caresses and indulgence, encouraged her in the belief that there was nobody worthy of her. She was nearly always dressed as Pallas or Diana, attended by the greatest ladies of the court attired as nymphs. And, to put the finishing stroke to her vanity, the queen called her Toutebelle: and having had her picture painted by the most skilled artists, sent it to several kings with whom she kept up a close friendship. When they gazed on the picture, not one of them was proof against the irresistible power of her charms. Some fell ill, others went out of their mind, and the more fortunate who reached her side in good health, no sooner set eyes on her than they became her slaves.

Never was there such gallantry and courtesy at any court. Twenty kings vied with each other to please her; and, after spending three and four hundred millions on a single fête, they thought themselves only too well recompensed if they obtained from her a word, such as "How pretty!" Their adoration delighted the queen. Not a day passed but there came to her court seven or eight thousand sonnets, and as many elegies, madrigals, and songs, sent by all the poets of the universe. Toutebelle was the one and only subject of the prose and verse of the authors of the time. Yet these poems served for nothing but lighting bonfires, and they sparkled and burned better than any kind of fuel.

The princess was fifteen years old, but no one dared aspire to the honour of becoming her husband; and yet there was no one who did not desire to be the happy man. But how were they to touch a heart like hers? They would have thought little of being hanged five or six times a-day just to please her, but she would have regarded it as a mere trifle. Her lovers murmured loudly against her cruelty, and the queen, who wished her to marry, did not know how to persuade her to make up her mind. "Will you not," she used sometimes to say, "lay aside a little of the intolerable pride that causes you to look with contempt on all the kings who come to our court? I want you to marry one of them. You have no desire to please me." "I am so happy," replied Toutebelle. "Allow me, madam, to remain as I am, calm and indifferent. If I once lost my peace of mind you would be sorry." "Yes," replied the queen; "I should be sorry if you loved some one beneath you; but consider those who ask you, and learn that nowhere are others to be found like them."

That was true; but the princess's idea of her own merits was such that she thought herself worth something better still; and by degrees her obstinacy in remaining single began deeply to grieve her mother, who repented, but too late, of having been so indulgent.

Uncertain what she ought to do, she determined to go all by herself to see a celebrated fairy called the Fairy of the Desert. But it was no easy matter to get at her, for she was guarded by lions. The queen would have found it impossible had she not long since learnt that you had to throw them a cake made of millet seed, sugar candy, and crocodiles' eggs. She kneaded the cake herself, and put it in a little basket which she carried on her arm. Unaccustomed to so much walking, she became tired, and lay down at the foot of a tree to take some rest. Before she was aware of it she had fallen asleep, and on awaking found that the cake was no longer in the basket; and, to complete her misfortune, she heard the lions approaching. They had scented her, and were making a great noise.

"Alas!" she cried, sorrowfully, "what will become of me? I shall be eaten up." She wept, and, having no strength to run away, remained by the tree where she had slept. At the same time she heard a sound like "Chet!

Chet! Hem! Hem!" Raising her eyes, she looked all round her, and saw on the tree a little man no bigger than your arm, eating oranges. "Oh! queen," he said to her, "I know you well, and I know the fright you are in lest the lions should eat you up; and you have every reason to be afraid, for they have eaten many others. To add to your misfortune, you have no cake." "I must make up my mind to die," said the queen, sighing. "Alas, I should be less distressed if my dear daughter were married!" "What? You have a daughter!" cried the yellow dwarf, who was so called from the colour of his complexion and the orange tree in which he lived. "Truly, I rejoice, for I have been seeking a wife over sea and land.' Come now, if you promise to give her to me I will undertake to protect you from lions, tigers, and bears." The queen looked at him, and was scarcely less afraid of his hideous little face than of the lions. She seemed to be pondering, and she answered not a word. "What! you hesitate, madam?" he cried. "Then you do not care much for your life?" At the same moment the queen saw the lions on the top of a hill running towards her.

They had each two heads, eight feet, four rows of teeth, and their skin was as hard as shell, and as red as morocco leather. At that sight the poor queen, more fearful than a dove at the sight of a kite, exclaimed with all her might: "Sir Dwarf! Toutebelle is yours". "Oh!" he said, with a contemptuous air, "Toutebelle is too beautiful; I don't want her; keep her." "Ah, sir," continued the distressed queen, "do not refuse her. She is the most charming princess in the world." "Well," he replied, "I will take her out of charity: but remember the gift you make me." The orange tree immediately opened; the queen rushed headlong inside. It closed again, and the lions caught nothing.

The queen was so upset that she did not notice a door which had been contrived in this tree. At last she saw it, and opened it. It looked on a field of nettles and thistles, and was surrounded by a muddy ditch, while a little further off was a low thatched hut, out of which came the yellow dwarf with a sprightly air. He wore wooden shoes and a yellow frieze jacket. He had no hair on his head, big ears, and looked a perfect little villain.

"I am delighted, mother-in-law," he said to the queen, "for you to see the little castle in which your Toutebelle will live with me. With the nettles and thistles she can feed an ass to ride on. Under this rustic roof she will be protected from stress of weather. She will drink of this water and feed on the fat frogs that live in it; and then she will have me beside her day and night, handsome, lively, and gallant as you see me; for I should be sorry if her shadow were a closer companion to her than I."

The unhappy queen, suddenly realising the miserable existence the dwarf promised her beloved daughter, and unable to endure so terrible a thought, fell prostrate on the floor, unconscious and without strength enough to utter a single word. While in this condition, she was put to bed with the greatest care, and in the finest night-cap, trimmed with the prettiest ribbon knots she had ever worn in her life. The queen, when she awoke, remembered what had happened, but she thought it must have been a delusion, for, finding herself in her palace in the midst of her ladies with her daughter by her side, there seemed no evidence of her having been in the desert, of her having encountered such great danger, nor of the dwarf having saved her on the hard condition of obtaining Toutebelle's hand in marriage. And yet this night-cap of valuable lace and the knot of ribbons were quite as surprising as the dream she thought she had dreamt. These things preyed on her mind to such an extent that she could scarcely speak, eat, or sleep for the extraordinary melancholy that took possession of her.

The princess, who loved her with all her heart, was exceedingly uneasy, and entreated her over and over again to tell her what was the matter. But the queen would put her off by telling her sometimes that it was caused by her bad health, sometimes that one of her neighbours was threatening her with a great war. Toutebelle saw that these replies were plausible enough, but that there was something more behind which the queen was trying to hide from her. Unable to endure her anxiety any longer, she determined to seek the celebrated Fairy of the Desert, whose wisdom was known far and wide. She was also desirous of asking her advice as to whether she should remain single or marry; for everybody was strongly urging her to choose a husband. She took care to knead with her own hands the cake which was to appease the fury of the lions; and, pretending to go to bed early in the evening, she went out by a little secret stair-case, her face covered with a long white veil that reached to her feet; and thus, alone, she took her way towards the grotto where the wise fairy lived.

But reaching the fateful orange tree, of which I have already spoken, she saw that it was full of fruit and flowers, and was seized with a longing to pluck some. Placing her basket on the ground, she gathered and ate a few oranges. But when she wished to pick up her basket and her cake it was no longer there. As she stood there uneasy and unhappy at her loss, she suddenly saw in front of her the hideous little dwarf I mentioned before. "What is the matter with you, my fine maiden? Why do you weep?" said he. "Alas! who would not weep?" she replied. "I've lost my basket and my cake, and I can never reach the Fairy of the Desert safely without them." "Well, and what do you want with her, pretty maid?" said the ugly little man. "I am her relative, her friend, and, to say the least, as clever as she is." "The queen, my mother," replied the princess, " has for some time been so terribly melancholy that I fear for her life. I cannot help thinking that I am perhaps the cause, for she wants me to marry. I confess to you that as yet I have found no one worthy of me. All these reasons make me desirous of speaking with the fairy." " Don't take the trouble, princess," said the dwarf; " I am better able than she to explain these matters to you. The queen is in trouble because she has promised you in marriage." " The queen has promised me! " she said, interrupting him. " Ah, doubtless you are mistaken; she would have told me, and I have too much interest in the matter for her to have pledged me without my consent." " Beautiful princess," said the dwarf, suddenly falling on his knees, " I flatter myself that this choice will not be displeasing to you when I tell you that it is I who am destined to such happiness." " My mother wishes you to be her son-in-law! " exclaimed Toutebelle, falling back a step or two; " was ever any one so mad as you? " " I care very little for the honour," said the dwarf, testily. " Here come the lions. In three bites they will avenge me for your unjust contempt."

At the same moment the princess heard them coming with loud roars. " What is to become of me? " she exclaimed. " Am I thus to end my fair days? " The wicked dwarf looked at her, and smiled contemptuously. " You will at least have the satisfaction of dying unmarried," said he, " and of not allying your shining merit with a miserable dwarf like myself." " Do not be angry, I beg of you," said the princess, clasping her beautiful hands; " I would rather marry all the dwarfs in the world than perish in this frightful way." " Look at me well, princess, before pledging your word," he replied, " for I have no desire to entrap you." " I have looked at you enough and to spare. The lions are on me; my terror grows. Save me! save me! or I shall die of fear." Indeed, scarcely had she uttered these words before she swooned; and, without knowing how, she found herself in her own bed in the most beautiful nightgown trimmed with the prettiest ribbons, and a little ring made of a single red hair which clung so closely that it would have been easier to have torn off her skin than to have removed the ring from her finger.

When the princess saw these things and remembered what had happened in the night, she fell into a melancholy that surprised and alarmed the whole court. The queen was the most distressed of all, and asked her hundreds and hundreds of times what was the matter. But she persisted in concealing her adventure. At length the estates of the realm, impatient to see their princess married, after holding a council, came to the queen begging her to choose a husband. She said that was exactly what she wished to do, but that her daughter showed so much repugnance that she advised them to go and talk to her themselves. They did so without delay. Since her adventure with the yellow dwarf Toutebelle's pride had been greatly humbled, and she could conceive no better way of getting out of the difficulty than by marrying some great king, with whom the ugly little man would be in no position to dispute so glorious a prize. Thus she replied more favourably than could have been expected: that, although she should have considered herself happy in remaining single all her life, she consented to marry the King of the Gold Mines. He was a powerful, handsome prince, who had loved her with the utmost passion for some years, and who, so far, had had no reason to flatter himself that his love was returned.

When he learned the delightful news his supreme joy can be easily imagined, and also the rage of all his rivals at losing for ever the hope that fed their passion. But Toutebelle could not marry twenty kings; it had given her trouble enough to choose one, for her vanity did not fail her, and she was entirely persuaded that no one in the world could be compared with her.

Everything necessary for the greatest fête imaginable was prepared. The King of the Gold Mines sent such enormous sums that the whole sea was covered with the ships that brought them. He sent to the most elegant and brilliant courts, and especially to that of France, to procure the most valuable things to adorn the princess, although her beauty was so perfect that she had little need of ornaments to set it off. The King of the Gold Mines, seeing himself on the point of becoming happy, never left the side of the charming princess.

It was to her interest to know him well, and, studying him with care, she discovered in him so much merit and intelligence, such lively and delicate feelings—in short, so beautiful a soul in so perfect a body—that she began to feel for him something of what he felt for her. These were happy times for both, when, in the loveliest gardens in the world, they were free to speak to each other all their passion. Those delights were often accompanied by music. The king, always gallant and loving, made poems and songs for the princess. Here is one which pleased her very much :—

> "These woods and meadows don their gayest dress,
> Shine out their best to greet your loveliness;
> And west winds blow and fairest flowers up-spring,
> While loving birds their sweetest roundels sing.
> All nature hastes, in humour gay,
> Homage to love's own queen to pay."

They were at the height of their joy. The king's rivals, disconsolate at his good fortune, returned to their homes overwhelmed with the keenest sorrow, unable to be present at Toutebelle's wedding. They bade her farewell in so touching a manner that she could not but pity them. "Ah, madam," said the King of the Gold Mines, "of what are you robbing me? You grant your pity to lovers who are only too well paid for their distresses by a single one of your glances." "I should be sorry," replied Toutebelle, "if you had not observed the compassion I show these princes, who are losing me for ever; it is a proof of your delicacy which I prize. But, sir, their condition is so different from yours. You have so much reason to be pleased with me, and they have so little, that you should not carry your jealousy further." The King of the Gold Mines, ashamed at the kindly way in which the princess took a thing that might have annoyed her, threw himself at her feet, and, kissing her hands, asked her pardon a thousand times.

At last the long-expected and much-desired day arrived: when everything was ready for Toutebelle's wedding, musical instruments and trumpets announced the great fête through the city. The streets were laid with red cloth, strewn with flowers, and the people rushed in crowds to the great courtyard of the palace. The queen was so excited that she had scarcely been to bed at all; and she rose before the dawn to give the necessary instructions and to choose the precious stones with which the princess was to be decked. She was covered with diamonds to her very shoes, which were made of them. Her gown of silver brocade was trimmed with a dozen sunbeams, of countless price indeed; but there! what could have been more brilliant?—only the beauty of the princess herself. A magnificent crown adorned her head; her hair hung down to her feet; and her dignified bearing marked her out from all the ladies attending her. The King of the Gold Mines was no less perfectly appointed and magnificent. His joy appeared in his countenance and in all his actions. No one went to greet him without returning loaded with gifts; for round his banqueting hall he had had placed a thousand casks filled with gold, and big velvet bags embroidered with pearls filled with gold pieces. Each one held a hundred thousand. They were given indiscriminately to all who came for them; so that this little ceremony, which was not the least useful and pleasant part of the wedding, attracted many persons who would scarcely have appreciated the other entertainments.

As the queen and the princess were on their way to join the king they saw two big turkey cocks, dragging a very ill-made box, enter the long gallery where they were. Behind them came a tall old woman, whose advanced age and decrepitude were not less surprising than her exceeding ugliness. She leaned on a crutch, and wore a black silk ruff, a red velvet hood, and a ragged farthingale. She went three times round with the turkey cocks without saying a word; then, stopping in the middle of the gallery and brandishing her crutch in a threatening manner: "Ho! ho! queen!—Ho! ho! princess!" she shouted. "You think you can break with impunity the promise you gave my friend, the yellow dwarf! I am the Fairy of the Desert. Without him, without his orange tree, do you not know my big lions would have eaten you up? Such insults are not endured in Fairyland. Consider quickly what you intend to do; for I swear by the cap on my head that you shall marry him or I will burn my crutch."

"Ah! princess," said the queen, in tears, "what do I hear? What have you promised?" "Ah! mother," replied Toutebelle, sorrowfully, "what did you promise yourself?" The King of the Gold Mines, angry at what was going on and because the wicked old woman had come in the way of his happiness, approached her, sword in hand, pointing it at her throat. "Wretched woman," he said, "depart from this place for ever, or your life shall pay for your wickedness."

He had scarcely spoken these words when the lid of the box jumped right up to the ceiling with a fearful noise, and out came the yellow dwarf, mounted on a big Spanish cat. He placed himself between the Fairy of the Desert and the King of the Gold Mines. "Rash youth," he said, "do not seek to injure this most distinguished fairy. It is with me that you have to reckon. I am your rival; I am your enemy. The faithless princess who intends to marry you has given me her promise, and accepted mine. Look if she has not a ring made of one of my hairs. Try to take it from her, and even by that slight test you will see that your power is less than mine." "Wretched monster," said the king, "you are actually bold enough to call yourself the adorer of this divine princess, and to lay claim to so splendid a possession? Consider, you are an ugly little imp, whose hideous face hurts one's eyes. I should have already taken your life had you been worthy of so glorious a death." The yellow dwarf, mortally offended, struck his spurs into the cat, which set up a horrible mewing, and, jumping first to one side and then to the other, frightened every one except the brave king. He was grappling with the dwarf when the creature drew a large cutlass with which he was armed, and, challenging the king to a combat, with a strange noise rushed down into the courtyard of the palace.

With hasty strides the wrathful king followed him. Hardly were they face to face, and the whole court on the balconies, than the sun growing suddenly red as if stained with blood, darkness came on so that they could scarcely distinguish each other. Thunder and lightning seemed bent on the destruction of the world; and the two turkey cocks looked by the side of the wicked dwarf like two giants, taller than the mountains, casting forth fire from their mouths and eyes in such quantities that you might have taken them for a fiery furnace. All these things would not have terrified the brave heart of the young monarch. The boldness of his look and actions reassured all who were anxious for his preservation, and even, perhaps, somewhat troubled the yellow dwarf. But his courage was not equal to seeing the condition to which his beloved princess was reduced. The Fairy of the Desert, like Tisiphone, her head covered with long snakes, was mounted on a winged griffin and armed with a spear, with which she struck the princess such cruel blows that she fell into the queen's arms bathed in blood. The tender mother, more hurt by the blow than her daughter, uttered the most piteous cries and laments. At this the king lost his courage and his presence of mind, and, giving up the combat, ran to help the princess, and to die with her. But the yellow dwarf did not give him time to reach her. With his Spanish cat he sprang on to the balcony where she was, tore her from the hands of the queen and of all her ladies, and, jumping on to the roof of the palace, disappeared with his prey.

The king, stupefied and motionless, was regarding with the uttermost despair so extraordinary an event, and one in which he had the misfortune to be quite powerless, when, to add to his ill-luck, he felt a veil come over his eyes, which deprived him of all sense of sight; while some one with remarkable strength carried him away into the vast region of air. What a tale of misfortunes! Love, cruel love! is it thus you treat those who own you for their conqueror?

The wicked Fairy of the Desert, who had come to help the yellow dwarf to carry off the princess, had scarcely looked at the King of the Gold Mines when, her savage heart feeling the worth of the young prince, she wished to make him her prey. So she carried him to the depths of a horrible cave and loaded him with chains which she had fastened to a rock, hoping that the fear of a speedy death would make him forget Toutebelle, and induce him to do whatever she wished. As soon as they arrived she restored his sight without giving him his liberty, and, borrowing from the fairies' art the grace and charm nature had denied her, she appeared before him as a lovely nymph whom chance had led to that spot.

"Whom do I see here?" she cried. "What! it is you, charming prince? What ill fortune has come upon you and keeps you in so sorry an abode?" The king, deceived by these false appearances, replied: "Alas, lovely nymph, I have no idea what the fiendish fury who brought me here wants of me. Although she deprived me of the use of my eyes when she carried me off and has not appeared since, I did not fail to recognise, by the sound of her voice, that she was the Fairy of the Desert." "Ah, sir," cried the pretended nymph, "if you are in the power of that woman you will not get free until she has married you. She has played this trick on more than one hero, and she is the least manageable person in the world with regard to her infatuations." While she was pretending to sympathise with the king's distress, he looked at the nymph's feet, and saw that they resembled those of a griffin. The fairy, in her various metamorphoses, might always be recognised by these; for she was unable to change that part of her griffin nature.

The king took no notice, and went on speaking in a confidential tone: "I have no aversion," he said, "for the Fairy of the Desert, but I cannot brook that she should protect the yellow dwarf from me and keep me chained like a criminal. What have I done to her? I loved a charming princess; but, if she restores me my liberty, I feel that gratitude would oblige me to love only her." "Are you speaking sincerely?" asked the deluded nymph. "Do not doubt it," replied the king; "the art of feigning is unknown to me, and I confess that the idea of a fairy flatters my vanity more than a mere princess; but, even were I dying of love for her, I should always show her nothing but hatred until I was set free."

The Fairy of the Desert, deceived by these words, resolved to carry the king away to a place as delightful as the present solitude was horrible. Forcing him to get into her chariot, to which she had yoked swans instead of the bats that usually drew her, she flew from one end of the earth to the other.

But what were the prince's feelings when, traversing the vast region of air, he saw his beloved princess in a castle of steel, whose walls, struck by the sun's rays, formed glowing mirrors that burned all who attempted to approach them! She was in a grove, lying by the side of a stream. One of her hands supported her head, while with the other she seemed to be wiping away her tears. As she lifted her eyes to heaven, as if to ask its aid, she saw the king pass with the Fairy of the Desert, who, employing the fairy art in which she was skilled to appear beautiful in the eyes of the young monarch, seemed, in fact, in those of the princess the most wondrously fair lady in the world. "What!" she exclaimed, "am I not wretched enough in this inaccessible castle to which the horrible yellow dwarf has brought me? To add to my misfortunes, must I be persecuted by the demon of jealousy? By so strange an adventure must I learn the faithlessness of the King of the Gold Mines? He thought in losing sight of me that he was freed from all the oaths he made me. But who is this formidable rival, whose fatal beauty surpasses mine?"

While she was speaking thus the amorous king felt sick at heart at flying with such speed from the beloved object of his vows. If he had had less knowledge of the fairy's power he would have tried everything to get away from her, either by killing her, or by any other means his love and courage might have suggested. But what could he do against so powerful a personage? Only time and cunning could free him from her clutches.

The fairy had seen Toutebelle, and sought to discover in the king's eyes the effect of the sight on his heart. "I am better able than any one," he said, "to tell you what you desire to know. The unexpected meeting with an unfortunate princess, to whom I was attached before I knew you, has somewhat moved me, but you rank so far above her in my heart that rather than be faithless to you I would die." "Ah, prince," she said, "may I flatter myself that I have inspired in you such a strong affection?" "Time will convince you, madam," he said; "but, if you wish to prove to me that I have found favour with you, do not refuse me your assistance for Toutebelle." "Think what you are asking," said the fairy, frowning and looking askance at him. "You wish me to use my skill against the yellow dwarf, who is my best friend, and take out of his hands a haughty princess, whom I cannot but regard as my rival?" The king sighed, and answered never a word. What could he have replied to this keen-sighted person?

They reached a vast meadow brilliant with a thousand different flowers. A deep river surrounded it, and many a rivulet flowed gently under the thick-spreading trees, in whose shade it was always cool. In the distance rose a magnificent palace, the walls of which were of transparent emerald. Immediately the swans that drew the fairy alighted under a portico with a pavement of diamonds and a roof of rubies. Then appeared on all sides a thousand beautiful ladies, who received her with great shouts of joy, singing these words :—

> "When love would fain subdue a heart
> Resistance but augments the smart:
> The warrior, most famed in fight,
> Must soonest yield to Cupid's might".

The Fairy of the Desert was charmed to hear them sing the story of her love. She led the king into the most magnificent chamber ever seen within the memory of fairy; and, that he should not think himself absolutely a prisoner, left him there a few minutes. He felt pretty certain that she was not far off, and that, hidden in some place, she was watching what he did. So he went up to a large mirror, and, addressing it, said : "Faithful counsellor, show me what I can do to make myself agreeable to the charming Fairy of the Desert, for the desire to please her is never out of my mind". Then he combed and powdered his hair, put on a patch, and, seeing on a table a coat more splendid than his own, hastily put it on. The fairy entered, so carried away by her joy, that she was unable to restrain it. "I see," she said, "the care you take to please me; without any effort you have discovered the secret; judge then, sir, if, when you wish it, it will be difficult."

The king, who had his reasons for saying pretty things to the old fairy,

was not sparing of them, and, little by little, gained permission to walk along
the sea-shore. By her art she had made the sea so terrible and stormy that
there were no pilots bold enough to sail it. Thus she had nothing to fear from
the indulgence she showed her prisoner; and he found some consolation for his
troubles in being able to dream in solitude, without the interruptions of his
wicked gaoler.

After walking for some time on the sand, he bent down and wrote these
lines with a stick he carried in his hand :—

> " Here am I free
> To ease my grief with pouring out my tears,
> For that my loved one never more appears.
> O wind-toss'd sea !
> That scal'st heaven's height,
> Searchest hell's night,
> Driving poor mortals from this churlish shore !—
> The winds torment thee with an endless strife,
> Yet my heart struggleth more.
> O cruel fate, that bore Toutebelle away,
> O heaven, that said my loved one might not stay,
> Wilt thou not take my life ?
> Fair goddess of the wave,
> If that thou ever yet hast felt love's power,
> Come from thy deepest cave,
> And help the lover in his darkest hour ! "

While he was writing he heard a voice, which, in spite of himself, attracted
his whole attention, and, seeing that the waves began to swell, he looked all
around, and saw a woman of extraordinary beauty. Her only covering was her
long hair, which, gently stirred by zephyrs, floated on the water. She held
a mirror in one hand and a comb in the other. Her body ended in a long
fish's tail with fins. The king was very much surprised at so strange an
encounter. As soon as she was within speaking distance, she said to him : " I
know the sad plight to which you are reduced by the loss of your princess, and
by the strange passion the Fairy of the Desert has for you. If you like, I will
take you away from this fatal place, where, it may be, you will languish for more
than thirty years." The king did not know what reply to make to the proposal :
not from any lack of desire for his liberty, but because he feared the Fairy of the
Desert had only borrowed this shape to deceive him. As he hesitated the mermaid, who divined his thoughts, said : " Do not think I am setting a trap for
you ; I am too sincere to wish to serve your enemies. The doings of the Fairy
of the Desert and of the yellow dwarf have incensed me against them. I see

your beautiful princess every day. Her beauty and merit alike make me pity her. I again repeat that, if you have confidence in me, I will save you." "I trust you so entirely," cried the king, "that I will do everything you command; but, since you have seen my princess, give me news of her." "We should lose too much time talking," said she. "Come with me; I will take you to the castle of steel, and leave on this shore a figure so nearly resembling you that the fairy will be deceived:"

She then cut some sea rushes, made a big bundle of them, and, breathing on them three times, said: "Sea rushes, my friends, I command you to remain stretched out on the sand, without moving, until the Fairy of the Desert comes to carry you off". The sea rushes had all the appearance of being covered with

skin, and were so like the King of the Gold Mines that nothing more wonderful was ever seen. They were dressed in a coat like his, and were pale and feeble to look like the drowned king. Then the good mermaid made the king seat himself on her big fish tail, and both, equally pleased, sailed out to sea.

"I will now tell you," said she, "that when the wicked yellow dwarf carried off Toutebelle, notwithstanding the wound the Fairy of the Desert had inflicted on her, he put her behind him on his terrible Spanish cat. She lost so much blood and was so disturbed by the adventure that her strength failed, and she remained in a swoon the whole way. But the yellow dwarf would not stop to restore her to consciousness until he was safely arrived in his terrible castle of steel. There he was received by the most beautiful ladies in the world, whom he had stolen away. Each vied with the other in her eagerness to serve the princess. She was placed in a bed made of cloth of gold, embroidered with pearls bigger than nuts." "Ah," exclaimed the King of the Gold Mines, interrupting the mermaid. "He has married her. I am faint; I shall die." "No, sir," said she, "make yourself easy; Toutebelle's firmness preserved her from the violence of the horrid dwarf." "Go on, I beg of you," said the king. "What more have I to tell you?" replied the mermaid. "She was in the wood when you passed. She saw you with the Fairy of the Desert, who was so disguised that she seemed her superior in beauty. Her despair cannot be imagined; she thinks you love the fairy." "She thinks I love her! Oh, ye gods!" cried the king, "into how fatal an error has she fallen! and how shall I undeceive her?" "Consult your heart," replied the mermaid, with a charming smile. "When a man is so passionately in love he has no need of advice." By this time they had reached the castle of steel. The side looking seawards was the only part that the yellow dwarf had not fortified with the formidable walls that burned up everybody.

"I know," said the mermaid to the king, "that Toutebelle is by the side of the same stream where you saw her when you passed; but, since you will have foes to vanquish before reaching her, here is a sword with which, provided you do not let it fall, you can undertake anything and brave the greatest dangers. Farewell; I shall betake myself to the shade of the rock you see there. If you have need of me to help you further with your beloved princess, I shall not fail you; for the queen is my best friend, and it was to serve her that I came to your aid." So saying, she gave the king a sword made of a single diamond, brighter than the sun's rays. He well understood its use; and, unable to find words strong enough to express his gratitude, he begged her to supply those that would describe what a grateful heart is capable of feeling for such good service.

We must now tell something of what has been happening to the Fairy of the Desert. Since her charming lover did not return, she hastened in search of him, betaking herself to the shore with a hundred damsels of her suite, all bearing magnificent presents for him. Some carried large baskets filled with diamonds, others golden vases wonderfully wrought, several containing ambergris, coral, and pearls. Others bore on their heads bales of stuffs of inconceivable richness; others, again, fruits, flowers and even birds. But what were the feelings of the fairy, who was following this fine and numerous company, when she saw the sea rushes so like the King of the Gold Mines that no difference could be discovered? At the sight, struck with astonishment and the keenest sorrow, she uttered a terrible cry, which pierced the heavens and made the mountains tremble and re-echo even to the depths of hell. The faces of the furies, Megara, Alecto, and Tisiphone themselves, could not have been more terrible to look on than hers. Throwing herself on the king's body, she wept, she howled, she tore in pieces fifty of the most beautiful damsels who had accompanied her, sacrificing them to the spirit of her dead lover. Afterwards she summoned eleven of her sisters, fairies like herself, begging them to aid her in building a magnificent mausoleum for the young hero. There was not one who was not deceived by the sea rushes. This may seem surprising, for the fairies knew everything; but the clever mermaid knew even more than they did.

While they were providing the porphyry, the jasper, the agate, and the marble, the statues, the inscriptions, the gold, and the bronze to immortalise the memory of the king whom they thought dead, he was thanking the good mermaid and imploring her to grant him her protection. She promised with the best grace in the world, and vanished from his sight. Nothing remained but to advance towards the castle of steel.

So, guided by his love, he walked with great strides, looking about eagerly for his adored princess. But he was not long without occupation. Four terrible sphinxes surrounded him, and, sticking their sharp claws into him, would have torn him in pieces, had not the diamond sword been as useful as the mermaid had foretold. It scarcely glittered in the eyes of the monsters before they fell helpless at his feet. Giving each a mortal wound, he advanced further and saw six dragons covered with scales harder to pierce than iron. However alarming the encounter was he did not lose heart, and, making use of his formidable sword, cut each one of them in half. He hoped he had now overcome the greatest difficulties; but there still remained an embarrassing one. He met four-and-twenty nymphs, beautiful and charming, holding long wreaths of flowers, and by their means barring his passage. "Where do you wish to go, sir?" said they. "We are the guardians of this place; if we let you pass endless disasters will happen to you and to us. We entreat you not to persist. Would you stain your victorious hand with the blood of four-and-twenty innocent damsels who have never done you any harm?" At this sight the king remained dumbfounded and undecided, not knowing what to do. He, who professed to respect the fair sex and to be their knight to the death, must, on this occasion, destroy them. But a voice that he heard suddenly gave him strength. "Strike! strike! spare no one," said the voice, "or you will lose the princess for ever!"

Then, without answering the nymphs, he rushed into their midst, broke their wreaths, attacked them without quarter, and scattered them in a moment. It was one of the last obstacles he was to find, and he at length entered the little wood where he had seen Toutebelle: she was beside the stream, pale and languishing. He approached her trembling, and would have thrown himself at her feet, but she drew back as quickly as if he had been the yellow dwarf. "Do not condemn me unheard, madam," he said; "I am neither faithless nor guilty; I am unfortunate enough to have displeased you without intending it." "Ah! cruel one!" she exclaimed, "I saw you ride through the air with a woman of extraordinary beauty. Did you set out on that journey against your will?" "Yes, princess," he replied, "it was against my will. The wicked Fairy of the Desert, not satisfied with chaining me to a rock, carried me off in a chariot to one of the ends of the earth, where, if it had not been for the unexpected aid of a good mermaid who brought me here, I should be languishing now. I come, princess, to snatch you from the hand that keeps you captive. Do not refuse the help of the most faithful of all lovers." He threw himself at her feet, but in laying hold of her gown unfortunately dropped his famous sword. The yellow dwarf, who was hidden under a lettuce, no sooner saw it out of the king's hands than, knowing its power, he threw himself upon it and seized it.

The princess uttered a heartrending cry on seeing the dwarf; but her lamentations only served to exasperate the little monster. Uttering two words in his own jargon, two giants appeared, who loaded the king with chains and irons. "Now," said the dwarf to the princess, "I am master of my rival's destiny; but I will grant him his life and permission to leave this place, if you will agree to marry me without delay." "Ah! Let me rather die a thousand deaths!" said the love-stricken king. "Alas!" cried the princess. "What more terrible than that you should die?" "And what more frightful," replied the king, "than that you should become the victim of this monster?" "Let us then die together," continued she. "Let me, my princess, have the consolation of dying for you." "Nay, rather do I consent," she said to the dwarf, "to your wishes." "In my sight!" replied the king; "in my sight, you would take him for your husband, cruel princess? Life would be hateful to me." "No," said the yellow dwarf. "The betrothal will not take place in your presence; I dread too much a favoured rival."

At these words, in spite of the tears and cries of Toutebelle, he stabbed the king to the heart and stretched him at his feet. The princess, who could not live after her lover's death, fell on his body, and it was not long before her soul joined his. Thus perished the unhappy prince and princess; and the mermaid could give them no help, for all the power of her magic lay in the diamond sword.

The wicked dwarf was better pleased to see the princess dead than in the arms of another; and the Fairy of the Desert, having heard what had happened, destroyed the mausoleum she had built, conceiving for the memory of the King of the Gold Mines as great a hatred as she had felt affection for his person before. The only favour the good mermaid, in despair at the ill-fortune, could obtain from Destiny was to change the lovers into palm trees. The two perfect bodies became two beautiful trees, bearing ever a faithful love one to the other, embracing each other with their intertwined branches, and in this tender union immortalising their loves.

GREEN SERPENT.

ONCE upon a time there was a great queen who gave birth to twin daughters. She invited twelve fairies who lived in the neighbourhood to come and see them, and bestow gifts on them according to the custom of the time. And a very convenient custom it was! for the fairies' power very often remedied what Nature had done ill, although occasionally it spoiled what Nature had done very well.

When the fairies were all in the banqueting hall, a magnificent repast was served. Just as they were sitting down to table, Magotine entered. She was the sister of Carabosse, and was equally wicked. The queen trembled at the sight, fearing some disaster, for she had not invited her to the feast; but carefully concealing her anxiety, she went to find for Magotine a green velvet armchair embroidered with sapphires. As Magotine was the oldest of the fairies, they all moved to make room for her, and each whispered the other: "Let us hasten to bestow our gifts on the little princess, in order to anticipate Magotine".

On the offer of the armchair, Magotine said rudely that she did not want it; she was tall enough to eat standing. But she made a great mistake, for, as the table was rather high, she could not even see it, so small was she! This vexed her so greatly that her ill-temper increased. "Madam," said the queen, "I beg you to sit down to table." "If you had wanted me," said the fairy, "you would have invited me with the rest; you only ask handsome people with fine figures and magnificently attired like my sisters to your court; as for me,

(249)

I'm too old and ugly. But, all the same, my power is as great as theirs, and without boasting at all, even greater." The fairies urged her so much to sit down to table that she at last consented. A golden basket was placed on it, containing a dozen packets of precious stones; the first-comers helped themselves, and there were thus none left for Magotine, who began to mutter below her breath. The queen went to her closet, and brought her a casket of perfumed Spanish leather, covered with rubies and filled with diamonds; she entreated Magotine to accept it, but the fairy shook her head, saying: " Keep your jewels, I have enough and to spare. I only came to see if you had remembered me, and you had entirely forgotten my existence." So saying, she struck her wand on the table, and all the good things upon it immediately turned into fricasseed serpents. The fairies, in great alarm, threw down their serviettes, and left the banqueting hall.

While they were discussing the evil trick Magotine had just played them, the cruel little fairy approached the cradle where the princesses lay wrapped in the prettiest cloth of gold swaddling clothes imaginable. " My gift to you," she said quickly to one, " is that you shall be the ugliest creature in the world." She was on the point of laying a like curse on the other when the fairies ran up in great agitation and prevented her. Wicked Magotine broke a window-pane, and passing through it like a flash of lightning, disappeared from view.

No matter what gifts the good fairies bestowed on the princess, the queen was less sensible of their kindness than of the pain of finding herself mother of the ugliest creature in the world. She took her in her arms, and was grieved to see her grow uglier from one minute to the next. She tried in vain to keep from crying in the presence of the fairies, but she could not control herself, and they showed her all the pity imaginable. " What shall we do," they consulted, " to console the queen ? " They held a great council, and afterwards told her not to grieve so deeply, since, at an appointed time, her daughter would be very happy. " But," interrupted the queen, " will she become beautiful ? " " We cannot," they replied, " explain ourselves more fully : let it suffice you that your daughter will be happy." She thanked them, and did not fail to load them with presents, for, although the fairies are very rich, they always like to receive gifts. The custom has since passed to all the peoples of the earth, and time has not destroyed it.

The queen called her elder daughter Laidronette, and the younger Bellotte. The names suited them admirably; for Laidronette became so ugly, that in spite of her great intelligence, it was impossible to look at her; her sister grew very beautiful and was most charming. When Laidronette was twelve years old, she threw herself at the feet of the king and queen, and begged their permission to shut herself up in the castle of solitude, in order to hide her ugliness, and not grieve them any longer. They loved her, her ugliness notwithstanding, and it cost them something to consent, but there was Bellotte, and that sufficed to console them.

Laidronette asked the queen to send with her only her nurse and a few officers. "You needn't fear that any one will run away with me, and for myself, I confess, fashioned as I am, I should like to avoid even the light of day." The king and queen granted her request, and she was conveyed to the castle of her choice. It had been built many centuries before. The sea came right up to the windows, and did duty for an ornamental canal. A vast forest near at hand furnished pleasant walks, and meadows shut in the view. The princess played musical instruments, and sang divinely. She spent two years in that pleasant solitude, and wrote several books of reflections, but the desire of seeing her parents again made her get into her coach and go to the court. She arrived exactly on Bellotte's wedding day. Everybody was filled with joy, but at the sight of Laidronette they all looked annoyed. Neither the king nor queen embraced or caressed her, and for all welcome they told her she had grown much uglier, and advised her not to appear at the ball; if however she wished to see it, some place might be arranged whence she could view it. She replied that she had not come to dance, nor to listen to the music, but she had been so long in the lonely castle that she could not help leaving it to pay her duty to the king and queen. She knew, to her keen regret, that they could not endure her, and she intended returning to her solitude, where the trees, flowers and springs did not reproach her for her ugliness every time she went near them. The king and queen, observing her sorrow, told her she could remain with them two or three days. But having a heart, Laidronette replied that if she spent that time in such pleasant company, it would pain her too much to leave them. They were too anxious for her to go to seek to prevent her, and coldly told her she was right.

Princess Bellotte gave her for a wedding gift an old riband she had worn all the winter on her muff, and the king she was marrying presented her with some purple silk for a petticoat. Had she consulted her own feelings, she would have thrown the riband and silk in the faces of the generous donors who treated her so ill; but she had too much spirit, wisdom and intelligence to show her annoyance, and set out with her faithful nurse on her return to the castle. So full of sorrow was her heart that during the whole journey she did not open her lips.

Walking one day in the thickest part of the forest, she saw under a tree a big green serpent. Raising his head, he said : " Laidronette, you are not alone in misfortune. Look at my horrible form, and learn that I was born even more beautiful than you." The princess, greatly alarmed, heard only half of what he said, and for several days, fearing such another encounter, dared not stir out. At length, weary of always being alone in her room, she one evening quitted it, and went to walk by the sea-shore. She was pacing slowly along, thinking over her sad fate, when she saw a little gilded boat, painted with a thousand different devices, come towards her. The sail was of brocade of gold, the mast of cedar-wood, and the oars of calambac. Chance alone seemed its steersman, and as it stopped close to the shore, the princess, curious to see its beauties, stepped in. She found it adorned with crimson velvet with a gold ground, the nails being made of diamonds. But all of a sudden the boat left the shore, and the princess, alarmed at her danger, took the oars to try and return, but all her efforts were of no avail. The wind raised the waves up mountains high, she lost sight of land, and seeing nothing but sea and sky, abandoned herself to her fate, sure that the worst was about to happen, and that she owed this bad turn to Magotine. "I must perish," she cried; "but what secret impulse makes me fear death? Alas! so far, I have known none of the pleasures that could make me hate it. My ugliness alarms even my nearest relatives; my sister is a great queen, while I am banished to the depths of a desert, where all the society I have found is a talking serpent. Would not death be preferable to a wearisome existence like this?"

These reflections dried the princess's tears. She looked boldly to see from what quarter death would come, and seemed to be inviting it not to delay, when she saw a serpent on the waves approaching the boat. He said: "If you are willing to receive help from a poor green serpent like me, I can save your life". "Death strikes less terror to my heart than you do," exclaimed the princess; "and if you want to do me a favour, never show yourself in my sight." Green Serpent made a long hissing sound, which he meant for a sigh, and answering never a word, plunged into the sea. "What a horrid monster!" said the princess to herself; "he has green wings, a many-coloured body, ivory jaws, fiery eyes, and long, bristling hair. Ah! I would rather die than owe my life to him. But," she went on, "what makes him follow me so persistently? and how comes it that he speaks like a reasoning being?" She was considering thus when a voice replying to her thought said: "Learn, Laidronette, that Green Serpent is not to be despised; and were it not too cruel a thing to say, I could assure you that he is less ugly in his degree than you are in yours. But so far from wishing to anger you, if you would only consent, I should like to mitigate your sorrow."

The voice vastly surprised the princess, and what it said was so little credible, that she had not strength enough to keep back her tears. But suddenly reflecting : "What ! " she cried ; " reproached with my ugliness as I am, I will not lament my death. What is the use of being the most beautiful woman in the world ? I must die all the same. It ought rather to console me and prevent me regretting my life."

While she moralised, the boat drifting at the mercy of the waves struck a rock, and scarcely two pieces of the wood held together. The poor princess found her philosophy of no avail in so pressing a danger ; she discovered a few pieces of wood, and imagining she was clinging to them she felt herself lifted up, and reached in safety the foot of a big rock. Alas ! what were her sensations on finding she was tightly embracing Green Serpent ! Seeing her great alarm he moved a little aside, and cried out : " If you knew me better you would fear me less, but it is my cruel fate to terrify everybody ". He immediately threw himself into the water, and Laidronette was left alone on the great rock.

Casting her eyes around, she saw nothing to lessen her despair. Night was coming on ; she had nothing to eat, and knew not where to find shelter. " I thought," she said, sadly, "to end my days in the sea. Doubtless the last scene of all is to be here ; some sea monster will devour me, or I shall perish of hunger." She seated herself on the top of the rock. As long as the light lasted she looked out over the sea, and when night was over all the earth she took off her silk petticoat, covered her head and face with it, and anxiously awaited what might happen.

At length she fell asleep ; and it seemed to her that she heard a sound as of various musical instruments. She felt convinced she was dreaming, but after a moment she heard these lines sung, lines which seemed composed for her :—

> " Here within this palace gay
> May you suffer Cupid's dart !
> Here shall gladness be our part,
> Sorrows all he'll drive away.
> Here within this palace gay
> May you suffer Cupid's dart ! "

The attention with which she listened to these words completely roused her. " What happiness and what ill-fortune are in store for me ? " she said. " In my condition, can happy days be possible for me ? " In terror, she opened her eyes, fearing to see herself surrounded by monsters. But imagine her astonishment, when, instead of the horrible and barren rock, she found herself in a chamber all panelled with gold. The bed on which she was reclining was in keeping with the splendour of the most beautiful palace in the world ; she asked herself question after question, unable to believe she was actually awake. At last she got up and opened a glass door that led on to a spacious balcony, whence she descried all the beauty that Nature, seconded by art, could produce : gardens full of flowers, fountains, statues and rare trees ; forests in the distance ; palaces whose walls were adorned with precious stones and roofs of pearl, and so marvellously were they wrought that each was a masterpiece. The sea, calm and peaceful, was covered with numerous ships of all sorts, and the sails, streamers, and pennants tossing in the wind, produced the most charming possible effect.

"Oh, ye gods ! ye just gods ! " she exclaimed, "what.do I see ?   Where am I ?   What a remarkable change !   What has become of the terrible rock that seemed to threaten the heavens with its cloud-capped points ?   Was it I who nearly perished yesterday, and was saved by the aid of a serpent ? "   In her distress she broke out into laments, now walking to and fro, now stopping still. At length she heard a noise in the room.   Turning back into it, she saw coming towards her a hundred pagodas, adorned and built in a hundred different ways. The biggest were about an arm's length in height, and the smallest not more than four fingers ; some beautiful, graceful, and pleasant looking ; others hideous, and of a terrible ugliness.   They were of diamonds, emeralds, rubies, pearls, crystal, amber, coral, porcelain, gold, silver, brass, bronze, iron, wood, clay ; some without arms, others without feet, with mouths reaching from ear to ear, squint eyes, flat noses.   In short, there is not greater unlikeness between the creatures who inhabit the world than there was between those pagodas.

Those who presented themselves before the princess were the deputies of the kingdom.   After making her a speech containing many wise reflections they told her, to amuse her, that they had for some time been travelling about the world, but that in order to obtain their sovereign's consent they swore in setting out never to speak ; and so scrupulous had they been that they would not move either head, feet, or hands.   The greater number, however, could not help doing so, while they were thus travelling about the world.   When they returned, they delighted their king by the recital of all the most secret affairs of the different courts in which they had been received.   "It is, madam," added the deputies, " a pleasure we will sometimes give you, for we are commanded to omit nothing in our power to amuse you.   Instead of bringing you presents, we shall divert you with our songs and dances."   They immediately began to sing these words, dancing a round dance with tambourines and castanets :—

" Joy is more delightful
That follows after pain ;
Joy is more delightful
After ills despiteful :
Young lovers, do not break your chain,
Let fortune you disdain,
Yet happiness you'll gain ".

When they had finished, the deputy who was spokesman said to the princess : " Here, madam, are a hundred pagodinas who are appointed to the honour of attending you : everything you most desire will be accomplished, provided you remain with us ". The pagodinas then appeared. They carried baskets in proportion to their size, filled with a hundred different things, so pretty, so useful, so well made, and so rich that Laidronette could not leave off admiring, praising and loudly expressing her wonder at the marvels she saw. The most distinguished of the pagodinas, a little diamond figure, suggested that as the heat was increasing, she should enter the bathing grotto. The princess walked in the direction pointed out, between two rows of body-guards of most laughable size and appearance. She found two basins of crystal ornamented with gold, and filled with choicely perfumed water, a canopy of cloth of gold was arranged over them. She asked why there were two basins, and was told that one was for her, and the other for the King of the Pagodas. " But," she cried, " where is he ? " " Madam," was the reply, " he is just now at the wars ; you will see him on his return." The princess asked if he was married ; she was told no, that he was so charming that so far he had not found any one worthy of him. She did not carry her curiosity further, she undressed and went into the bath. Immediately the pagodas and pagodinas began to sing and to play on musical instruments. Some had lutes made of a walnut-shell, others violas made of an almond-shell, for it was necessary to suit the instruments to their size. But everything was so exact and harmonised so well that nothing could be more delightful than these concerts.

When the princess came out of the bath, a magnificent dressing-gown was presented to her. Pagodas, playing the flute and the hautboy, walked before her ; pagodinas followed her, singing songs in her honour. Thus she entered a room where her toilette was prepared. Immediately pagodinas who did duty as ladies of the bed-chamber and ladies' maids came and went, dressed her hair, attired her, praised her, applauded her. There was no longer any thought of ugliness, of purple silk petticoat, or of worn-out riband.

The princess was veritably astonished. " What," she said, " can procure me this extraordinary delight ? I was on the point of perishing. I was awaiting death and could hope for nothing else, when suddenly I find myself in the most beautiful and magnificent place in the world, where my presence too seems to give so much pleasure!" She possessed so much intelligence and goodness of heart, and her manners were so pleasing, that all the little creatures were charmed with her.

Every day on rising new clothes, new laces, new jewels were brought her. It was certainly a great pity she was so ugly, but in consequence of the great care taken in dressing her, she who had never been able to endure the sight of herself, began to find herself less hideous. The pagodas constantly told her the most secret and curious things that went on in the world. They told her of treaties of peace and leagues of war; of the treachery and quarrels of lovers, and the unfaithfulness of mistresses, of despairs, reconciliations, and disappointed heirs, of frustrated marriages and old widows who married again most unseasonably, of treasures discovered, of bankruptcies and fortunes made in a moment, of fallen favourites and besieged cities, of jealous husbands and flirting women, of thankless children and ruined towns. Indeed what did they not tell the princess to amuse and divert her? Some of the pagodas were most surprisingly swollen and puffed out. On asking the reason they told her: "As we are not allowed when on our travels to laugh or to speak, and as we continually see very laughable things and the greatest absurdities, the effort not to laugh causes us to swell in this way. It is in fact a dropsy caused by suppressed laughter, of which we are cured when we return here." The princess admired the good humour of the pagoda race, for people might indeed become inflated by constantly suppressing laughter at all the absurd things they must infallibly see.

Every evening one of the finest plays of Corneille or Molière was represented. Balls were of frequent occurrence. So that no possible effect might be lost, the tiniest figures danced on the tight-rope that they might be better seen, and the repasts served to the princess would have done for the banquets of some solemn festival. Books, serious, amusing, and historical, were brought to her; indeed the days passed like minutes. As a matter of fact, however, the pagodas, highly intelligent as they were, were of a ridiculous minuteness. It often happened when going a walk that she put thirty of them into her pocket to amuse her, and it was the pleasantest thing in the world to hear them chattering in their little voices, shriller than those of marionettes.

Once when the princess was unable to sleep, she said: "What will become of me? Shall I always remain here? My life passes more pleasantly than I could have dared to hope, yet my heart lacks something, and I cannot tell what it is. I begin to feel that a series of the same pleasures, varied by no events, is very insipid." "Ah! princess," replied a voice, "is it not your own fault? If you would love, you would at once be conscious that it is quite possible to be happy for a very long time in a palace or even in a lonely desert with one we love." " What pagoda is speaking to me?" she said. " What pernicious advice he gives me, opposed to all the peace of my life." " It is no pagoda," came the reply, " that warns you of what must be sooner or later. It is the un-happy monarch of this kingdom who adores you, and only dares confess it in the greatest fear and trembling." " A king adores me!" said the princess. " Has he eyes, or is he blind? Has he seen that I am the ugliest creature in the world?" " I have seen you, madam," replied the invisible king, " and to me you are not what you represent yourself to be, and whether on account of your person, your merits, or your misfortunes, I can only repeat that I adore you, and that my timid and respectful love compels me to hide myself." " I am deeply grateful to you," rejoined the princess. " Alas! what should I do if I loved any one?" " You would make one happy who cannot live without you," he said, " and without your permission he would never dare to appear." " No," said the princess, " I do not wish to see anything that might attract me." Nothing further was said, but for the rest of the night she was greatly taken up with the circumstance.

Notwithstanding her resolution to say nothing about it, she could not help asking the pagodas if their king had returned. They replied: " No". That answer, which agreed ill with what she had heard, somewhat disturbed her, and she went on to ask if their king was young and good-looking. They told her he was young, handsome, and everything that was charming; she asked if they often heard from him, and they replied: " Every day". " But does he know," she added, " that I am in his palace?" " Yes" was the rejoinder, " he knows every-thing about you, and so great is his interest in you that couriers are sent from hour to hour to take him news of you." She was silent, and began to reflect much more deeply than had been her custom.

When she was alone the voice spoke to her. At one time she was afraid of it; at another it gave her pleasure, for it invariably said the most gallant things. " Notwithstanding my firm resolve never to love," said the princess, " and the good reason I have to keep out of my heart an emotion that can only cause me misery, I confess I should like to know a king whose taste is so eccentric as yours, for if you really do love me, you are probably the only person in the world who could care for a woman as ugly as I am." " Think whatever you like of my taste, beloved princess," replied the voice, " I find justification enough in your merit; indeed it is not for that reason I am compelled to hide myself. The cause is so sad that if you knew it, you could not withhold your pity." The princess then urged the voice to explain, but it spoke no more, and

17

only long-drawn sighs were heard. She was greatly disturbed by all this; although her lover was invisible and unknown he was most attentive, and she was beginning to wish for more suitable society than that afforded by the pagodas. She was, in fact, getting very weary, and could only find pleasure in the voice of her invisible lover.

On one of the darkest nights in the year, awaking out of her sleep, she perceived some one close to her bed; she thought it was the pagodina of pearls, who, being much more intelligent than the others, sometimes came to talk with her. The princess stretched forth her arms to take hold of her; her hand was at once seized, pressed and kissed; she felt tears fall on it, and she was so startled that she could not speak. She had no doubt that it was the invisible king. "What do you want of me?" she said, with a sigh. "Can I love you without knowing you, or seeing you?" "Ah! madam," was the reply, "what are the conditions of pleasing you? It is impossible for me to show myself. The wicked Magotine, who played you such an evil trick, has condemned me to a penance of seven years; five have already gone, but two still remain, and if you were willing to take me for your husband, you could sweeten their bitterness. You think me very bold, and that what I ask of you is absolutely impossible; but if you knew the ardour of my passion, or the greatness of my misfortunes, you would not refuse the favour I beg of you."

As I have already said, Laidronette was becoming very weary; she found that, as far as intelligence went, he was all that could be desired, and under the specious name of a generous pity the invisible king won her heart and love. She replied that she required a few days in which to make up her mind. It was indeed a great thing to have brought matters so far, to a delay of a few days, for he had not dared to indulge hope. The fêtes and concerts were redoubled, and only wedding hymns were sung before her, and presents, which surpassed anything she had ever seen, were continually brought her. The tender voice, ever assiduous, made love to her as soon as it was night, and the princess retired early, in order to have more time to converse with it.

At length she consented to marry the invisible king, and promised not to look upon him until his penance was at an end. "Therein lies everything for you and me," he said. "If you give way to indiscreet curiosity, I should have to begin my penance all over again, and you would share the hardship with me: but if you can refrain from following the bad advice that will be given you, you will find that I shall be exactly to your taste, and you will at the same time recover the marvellous beauty taken from you by the wicked Magotine." The princess, enchanted with that new hope, swore a thousand times to her husband to do nothing contrary to his wishes. The marriage was concluded without noise or splendour; but the heart and soul were not the less content.

As all the pagodas sought eagerly to amuse their new queen, one of them brought her the story of Psyche that a fashionable author had just written out in beautiful language; she found in it many things that bore upon her own adventure. She was seized with so violent a desire to receive her father and mother, her sister and brother-in-law, at the palace, that nothing the king could say could drive the fancy from her mind. "The book you are reading," he added, "will teach you what were Psyche's misfortunes. I beg of you take heed and avoid them." She promised even more than he asked, and a vessel of pagodas carrying presents and letters from Queen Laidronette to her mother was despatched. She implored her to pay her a visit in her kingdom, and for that occasion only the pagodas had permission to speak elsewhere than in their own country.

The loss of the princess had evoked a feeling of tenderness in her near relatives. They thought she was dead, and thus her letters were the more eagerly welcomed at the court. The queen, who was dying to see her daughter again, did not delay a moment in setting out with her daughter and son-in-law. The pagodas, who alone knew the road to their kingdom, acted as guides to the royal party, and when Laidronette saw her parents she thought she should die of joy. She read the story of Psyche over and over again as a safeguard against her replies to all the things her family said to her. She had enough to do, and got into confusion a hundred times a-day. Sometimes the king was with the army. Sometimes he was ill and so bad-tempered that he did not wish to see any one. Now he was on a pilgrimage, then he was hunting or fishing. It seemed she was fated to say nothing that carried any weight, and that cruel Magotine had bereft her of her good sense. Her mother and sister talked over the matter together, and came to the conclusion that Laidronette was deceiving them, and perhaps deceiving herself. With ill-judged zeal they determined to speak to her. They accomplished the task with so much skill that a thousand fears and doubts crept into Laidronette's mind. For a long time she had not permitted all they could say to have the least effect on her; but she now confessed that, so far, she had never seen her husband. His conversation, however, was so full of charm that to be happy it was only necessary to hear him. She told them further that his penance was to last two years more, and at the end of that period not only would she see him, but she would become as beautiful as the day-star. "Ah! wretched girl," exclaimed the queen, "how clear is the snare laid for you! Is it possible you can be simple enough to believe such tales? Your husband is a monster; it cannot be otherwise, for all

the pagodas over whom he rules are the most grotesque creatures possible."
" I rather believe," replied Laidronette, " that he is the God of Love himself."
" What a mistaken notion ! " exclaimed Queen Bellotte; " Psyche was told she
had a monster for a husband, and found him to be Cupid himself. You persist
in believing your husband is Love and assuredly you will discover him to be a
monster. Any way set your mind at ease, enlighten yourself on so simple a
matter." The queen was of the same opinion, and her son-in-law even more
strongly so.

The poor princess was so confused and disturbed that, after sending away
her family with presents that more than made up for the purple silk and the
muff riband, she determined, happen what might, to see her husband. Ah!
fatal curiosity. A thousand terrible examples cannot cure us, and dearly indeed
did the unfortunate princess pay for her indiscretion. She would have been
very sorry not to follow the example of her predecessor, Psyche, so she concealed a lamp and with its aid looked upon the invisible king, so dear to her
heart. But how terrible were her shrieks, when, instead of Love, gentle, fair,
young, and altogether charming, she saw hideous Green Serpent with his long
bristling hair. He awoke, transported with rage and despair: " Oh! cruel
one ! " he cried, " is this the reward of my great love ? " The princess heard
no more, she swooned with fear, and Serpent was already far away.

Hearing the noise caused by this tragedy, some of the pagodas rushed in.
They put the princess to bed, and assisted to restore her. When she came to
herself, her condition may be more easily imagined than described. How she
reproached herself for the evil she had brought upon her husband ! She loved
him tenderly, but abhorred his form, and would have given half her life never to
have seen him.

The entrance of several pagodas with terrified countenances interrupted her
sad reflections. They informed her that a number of ships full of marionettes,
with Magotine at their head, had entered the harbour unopposed. The marionettes
and pagodas are eternal enemies, and are rivals in a thousand things. The
marionettes have even the privilege of speaking wherever they like, a thing the
pagodas are denied. Magotine was their queen. Her hatred for poor Green
Serpent and unfortunate Laidronette led her to assemble troops, and determine
to attack them just when their sorrows should be at their height.

It was not difficult to succeed in her designs : for the queen was in such
grief, that although urged to give the necessary orders she refused, assuring
them that she knew nothing about war. By her command, however, the
pagodas that had been found in besieged cities, and in the closets of great
generals, were assembled. She ordered them to provide for everything, and

then shut herself up in her closet, regarding all the events of life with the utmost indifference.

Magotine's general was the celebrated Punchinello, who knew his business well, and who had a large reserve force, consisting of wasps, cockchafers, and butterflies, who were able to do wonders against a few frogs and light-armed lizards. They had been for a long time in the pay of the pagodas, who were more formidable in name than in valour.

Sometimes Magotine amused herself by watching the fight. Pagodas and pagodinas surpassed themselves, but with a stroke of the wand the fairies destroyed all the superb edifices, and the delightful gardens, woods, meadows, and fountains were buried in the ruins. Queen Laidronette was compelled to become a slave to the most malicious fairy that ever lived. Four or five hundred marionettes brought her to Magotine. "Madam," said Punchinello, "I venture to present to you the Queen of the Pagodas." "I have known her for a long while," said Magotine; "she was the cause of an affront I received the day of her birth, and I shall never forget it." "Alas! madam," said the queen, "I thought you were sufficiently avenged; the gift of ugliness you bestowed on me would have more than satisfied a less vindictive person than yourself." "How she talks," said the fairy, "just like a newly fledged doctor; your first work shall be to teach my ants philosophy; prepare to give them a lecture every day." "How am I to manage it, madam?" said the miserable queen; "I do not know philosophy, and if I did, are your ants capable of understanding it?" "Listen to the logician!" shouted Magotine. "Well, queen, you shall not teach them philosophy, but in spite of yourself, you shall afford the world an example of patience it shall be difficult to imitate."

Then she had iron shoes brought in; they were so tight that Laidronette could not get her feet into them, but she had to put them on all the same; and the poor queen wept and endured the pain. "Here," said Magotine, "is a distaff filled with cobweb; in two hours you must spin it as fine as your hair." "I do not know how to spin," said the queen; "but although it seems impossible, I will endeavour to obey you." She was immediately taken to the depths of a dark grotto, and after leaving her some brown bread and a pitcher of water, the entrance was closed up by a big stone.

When she tried to spin the horrid cobweb, the heavy spindle fell to the ground hundreds and hundreds of times. She had patience enough to pick it up as often, and to begin the task over and over again; but it was always in vain. "Now," she said, "I perfectly recognise the measure of my misfortune; I am in the power of the implacable Magotine, and she, not satisfied with depriving me of my beauty, wishes to take my life." She began to weep, going over in her mind the happiness she had enjoyed in the Kingdom of Pagody, and throwing her distaff to the ground : " Let Magotine come when she pleases," she said, " I cannot do what is impossible ". She heard a voice that said : " Ah ! queen, your indiscreet curiosity is the cause of all your tears : but I cannot witness the suffering of her I love. I have a friend of whom I have never spoken, the Fairy Protectress ; I trust she will be of great use to you." Three knocks were then heard, and although no one appeared, the cobweb was spun and wound off. At the end of the two hours, Magotine, hoping for a cause of quarrel, ordered the stone to be removed from the entrance, and she went into the grotto, attended by a numerous cortège of marionettes. " Let us see," said she, " the work of a lazy girl who can neither sew nor spin." " Madam," said the queen, " I certainly did not know, but I found it necessary to learn." When Magotine saw the strange circumstance she took the ball of cobweb thread, saying : " You are indeed skilful, and it would be a vast pity not to make use of you. Make nets with this thread, strong enough for catching salmon." " I beg your pardon," replied she, " but it's scarcely strong enough for flies." " You are very fond of arguing, my fine friend," said Magotine, " but it is not of the least use." She left the grotto, ordered the big stone to be replaced at the entrance, and assured the queen that if the nets were not finished in two hours she was lost.

" Ah ! Fairy Protectress," said the queen, " if it is true that my misfortunes can in any way touch you, do not refuse your aid." In the same moment the nets were finished. Laidronette was intensely surprised, and thanked in her heart the kind fairy who did so much for her ; she thought with pleasure that she doubtless owed such a friend to her husband's love. " Alas ! Green Serpent," she said, " you are very generous to continue loving me after the evil I have done you." No reply was forthcoming, for Magotine entered, and was greatly astonished to find the nets so industriously wrought, since it was not work for ordinary hands. " Do you dare to tell me," she said, " that you have woven these nets yourself ? " " I have no friend at your court, madam," said the queen, " and even if I had, I am so closely imprisoned that it would be difficult for any one to speak to me without your permission." " As you are so clever and skilful, I shall find you very useful in my kingdom."

She at once commanded the fleet to be prepared ; all the marionettes were ready to depart. She had the queen fastened in big iron chains, fearing she might through some impulse of despair throw herself into the sea. The unhappy princess was one night deploring her sad fate, when by the light of the moon she perceived Green Serpent quietly approaching the vessel. " I always fear to alarm you," he said ; " although I have no reason to treat you with con-

sideration, you are infinitely dear to me." " Can you forgive my indiscreet
curiosity ? " she asked, " and may I tell you without displeasing you ?

> " My Serpent ! O love ! art thou come to me
> To stay my heart's weary longing for thee ?
> Dear, tender spouse ! do I see thee again ?
> Ah ! cruel, alas ! was solitude's pain !
>   Sorrowful in misery,
>   Weeping I have yearned for thee."

Serpent replied in these lines :—

> " Hearts apart needs must smart,
>   Weeping duly, loving truly—
> When gods vent their wrath in this world of woe,
> Wreaking their vengeance with pitiless blow.
>   Torture no worse can they ever devise
>   Than his, who alone in solitude sighs."

Magotine was not one of those fairies who are sometimes caught napping ;
the desire of doing evil kept her always wide awake. Thus she did not fail to
hear the conversation of King Serpent and his wife. She interposed like a fury.
" Ah, ah ! " she said, " you meddle with rhyming and make your laments in the
tones of Apollo. Indeed, I am very glad. Proserpina, who is my best friend,
has asked me to provide her with some poet on hire. It's not that she lacks them,
but she wants more of them. Go then, Green Serpent, finish your penance in her
gloomy kingdom, and present my compliments to the charming Proserpina."
The unfortunate serpent immediately departed with long-drawn hisses. He left
the queen in the deepest grief; she thought nothing further could possibly happen
to her. In her misery she exclaimed : " By what crime have we displeased
you, cruel Magotine ? I had scarcely entered the world when your infernal
curse deprived me of my beauty and made me hideous. How can you possibly
assert that before my reason was developed and I knew myself, I could be guilty
of any misdeed ? I am sure that the unhappy king you have just sent to Hades
is equally innocent; but put an end to it all and let me die now at once; it is
the only favour I ask of you." " If I granted your request you would be too
happy," replied Magotine ; " you must first fetch water from the inexhaustible
spring."

Directly the ships reached the country of the marionettes, cruel Magotine
tied a millstone round the queen's neck and ordered her to climb to the top of a
mountain far beyond the clouds. Once there she was to gather four-leaved
clover, fill her basket with it, and then come down to the depths of the valley

and, in a pitcher full of holes, fetch enough of the water of discretion to fill the fairy's big glass. The queen replied that it was not possible to obey; the mill-stone was ten times heavier than she was, the broken pitcher could never hold the water, and she could not therefore make up her mind to undertake a thing so impossible. "If you fail," said Magotine, "be very sure Green Serpent shall suffer." That threat so greatly alarmed the queen that without considering her complete inability to do what was required of her, she attempted to walk on; but alas! it would have been quite useless had not the Fairy Protectress, whom she summoned, come to her aid. "This," she said, "is the just reward of your fatal curiosity; you have only yourself to thank for the state into which Magotine has brought you." But she conveyed Laidronette to the mountain, filled her basket with the four-leaved clover in spite of the dreadful monsters who guarded it and made supernatural efforts to defend it, for by a stroke of the wand the Fairy Protectress made them gentler than lambs.

She did not wait for the thanks of the grateful queen to finish giving her all the aid that lay in her power. She presented her with a little chariot drawn by two white canaries who spoke and sang to perfection. She told her to go down the mountain and to throw her iron shoes at two giants armed with clubs who guarded the spring, and they would fall without offering the least resistance. She was then to give the pitcher to the little canaries who would easily be able to fill it with the water of discretion. Directly they brought it she was to rub her face with it and she would at once become the most beautiful creature in the world. The fairy advised Laidronette not to remain at the spring, or to climb to the top of the mountain again, but to stop in a pleasant little wood she would find on her road, and stay there for three years. Magotine would think she was all the while engaged in fetching the water in her pitcher, or that one of the numerous dangers of the journey had caused her death.

The queen embraced the Fairy Protectress, and thanked her a hundred times for all her kindness. "But," she added, "neither the happy issue of my journey nor the beauty you promise me can give any joy so long as Green Serpent remains a serpent. "That will only be until you have lived for three years in the wood," said the fairy, "and have delivered the water and the clover to Magotine."

The queen promised the Fairy Protectress to do everything that she told her. "But, madam," she added, "am I to be three years without hearing anything of Green Serpent?" "You deserve to be without news of him all your life," said the fairy, "for could there be anything more cruel than to compel him, as you have, to begin his penance all over again?" The queen replied nothing; her tears and her silence sufficiently testified to her sorrow. She got into the little chariot. The canaries conducted her to the bottom of the valley where the giants guarded the spring of discretion. She promptly took off her iron shoes and threw them at their heads; the giants at once fell lifeless to the ground. The canaries took the pitcher and mended it with such remarkable skill that it did not seem it could ever have been broken. The name of the water made Laidronette desirous of drinking it. " It will make me," she said, " more prudent and discreet than in the past. Alas! if I had had those qualities, I should be still in the Kingdom of Pagody!" After she had drunk a long draught, she bathed her face and became so exceedingly beautiful that you would have taken her rather for a goddess than a mortal.

The Fairy Protectress then appeared and said: " You have just done a thing that pleases me vastly; you knew this water had the power of beautifying both your mind and body; I wanted to see which of the two would have the preference. You gave it to your mind and I praise you for it; on account of that action your penance will be shortened by four years." " Do not lessen my troubles," replied the queen, " I deserve them all; but comfort Green Serpent, who merits none." " I will do my best," said the fairy, embracing her; " and now since you are so beautiful, I should like you to discontinue the name Laidronette that no longer suits you, and call yourself Queen Discreet." With these words she disappeared, leaving her a little pair of shoes, so pretty and so beautifully embroidered that she hardly liked to put them on.

When she had re-entered her chariot, holding her pitcher full of water, the canaries took her straight to the wood. There never was a pleasanter place; myrtles and orange trees united their branches to form long sheltered alleys and arbours which the sun could not penetrate. A thousand gently-flowing streams and springs helped to adorn the beauteous spot. But the strangest thing was that all the animals there could speak, and gave the canaries the warmest welcome imaginable. " We thought," they said, " that you had deserted us." " The time of our penance is not yet ended," rejoined the canaries, " but the Fairy Protectress bade us bring this queen here; take heed to amuse her as much as possible." At the same moment she was surrounded by animals of all sorts, who paid her great compliments. " You shall be our queen," they said, " and receive from us every attention and consideration." " Where am I?" she cried; " by what supernatural power are you able to speak to me?" One of the canaries, who had remained near her, whispered: " You must know, madam, that certain fairies being on their travels were vexed to see men and women fallen into grievous faults; they thought at first that warning them to change their evil ways would be enough, but that was of no avail, and becoming suddenly very angry indeed, they put them into penance. Those who talked too much they changed into parrots, jays, and hens; lovers and their mistresses into pigeons, canaries, and little dogs ; people who were too fond of good eating into pigs ; angry persons into lions. In fact, the number of those they put in penance is so great that this wood is populated by them, and you will find here persons of all ranks and dispositions."

"From what you have just told me, my dear little canary," said the queen, "I feel sure I am right in thinking that you are here only for having loved too well." "Yes, madam," replied the canary, "that is so. I am the son of a Spanish nobleman, and in our country love holds such despotic sway over all hearts that it is not possible to escape it. An ambassador from England arrived at the court ; he had a daughter of great beauty, but of an intolerably haughty and cold disposition. Nevertheless, I became attached to her and loved her distractedly ; sometimes she seemed sensible of my attentions, while at others she repulsed me so cruelly that I lost patience. One day when she had driven me to despair, a venerable old dame confronted me and blamed me for my weakness ; all she could say only served to make me more obstinate, and, perceiving it, she grew angry. 'I condemn you,' she said, 'to become a canary for three years, and your mistress a wasp.' I was at once conscious of the most extraordinary change imaginable ; my distress notwithstanding, I could not refrain from flying into the ambassador's garden, to discover the fate of his daughter. But I had scarcely entered it, before I saw a big wasp buzzing four times as loud as any other. I hovered round her with the eagerness of a lover whom nothing could keep away. Several times she tried to sting me. 'If, beautiful wasp,' I said, 'you desire my death, you need not use your sting. Only command me to die, and I will cheerfully obey you.' She vouchsafed no reply, and settled on the flowers, who doubtless suffered for her ill-temper.

"Overwhelmed by her disdain and my own condition, I flew away, following no particular route. I at length reached Paris, one of the most beautiful cities in the world; I was tired, and threw myself on a clump of trees in a walled enclosure, and quite unconscious how it came about, found myself at the door of a cage painted green and ornamented with gold. The furniture and the apartment were of surprising magnificence ; a young lady caressed me and spoke to me with a charming gentleness. I did not live long in her room without learning her heart's secret ; she was visited by an enraged bully, who, not satisfied with loading her with unjust reproaches, beat her unmercifully, leaving her almost dead in the hands of her attendants. I was in no small degree distressed at witnessing such unworthy treatment, and I was the more displeased to perceive that the more he beat her, the stronger became the charming woman's affection for him.

"I wished night and day that the fairies who turned me into a canary would reduce their ill-assorted love to order. My desire was granted. Just as the lover was beginning his ordinary beating, the fairies suddenly appeared in the room. They loaded him with reproaches, and condemned him to become a wolf; they turned the long-suffering woman into an ewe, and sent them to the wood. As for myself, I easily found means to fly away ; I wanted to see the different courts of Europe. I went to Italy, and by chance fell into the hands of a man, who often having business in town, and wishing his wife, of whom he was very jealous, never to see any one, shut her up from morning to night; he, therefore, destined me for the honour of amusing the beautiful captive, but she had other matters to occupy her. A certain neighbour, who had long loved her, was in the habit of coming at evening time down the chimney, sliding from the top to the bottom, and arriving blacker than any demon. The keys, which were in the possession of the jealous husband, only served to make him feel the more secure. I was ever dreading some miserable catastrophe, when the fairies entered by the key-hole, and not a little surprised the loving pair. 'Go into penance,' said they, touching their wands; 'let the chimney-sweep become a squirrel and the cunning woman a monkey; the husband, who is so careful to keep the keys of his house, shall become a watch-dog for ten years!'

"I should have too many things to relate to you, madam," added the canary, "were I to recount my various adventures. From time to time I was obliged to repair to the wood, and scarcely ever came without finding new animals, for the fairies continued to travel, and people to vex them with their manifold faults, but during the time you dwell here, you can amuse yourself with the adventures of its inhabitants." Many of them immediately offered to tell her theirs whenever she liked; she thanked them most politely, but desiring rather to reflect than to talk, she sought a solitary spot where she could be alone. As soon as she found one, there arose in it a little palace, and the finest repast imaginable was served her; it was only of fruits, but of very rare fruits, brought by the birds, and as long as she stayed in the wood she wanted for nothing.

Sometimes there were fêtes delightful by their oddity : lions danced with lambs, bears told soft tales to doves, and serpents grew gentle for the sake of linnets. A butterfly carried on an intrigue with a panther; in fact, nothing was classified according to its species, and it was not a question of being tiger or sheep, but only of the persons the fairies punished for their faults.

They all loved and adored Queen Discreet; they made her judge in their disputes, and she had absolute power in the little republic. If she had not continually reproached herself for the misfortunes of Green Serpent, she might have endured her own with some sort of patience. But when she thought of his sad condition, she could never forgive herself her indiscreet curiosity. The time for leaving the wood having arrived, she informed her little guides, the faithful canaries, who assured her of a happy return. To avoid farewells and regrets that would have cost her some tears, she slipped away during the night; the affection and respect shown her by these reasoning animals had greatly touched her.

She forgot neither the pitcher full of the water of discretion, nor the basket of clover, nor the iron shoes, and when Magotine believed her dead, she suddenly appeared before her, the millstone round her neck, the iron shoes on her feet, and the pitcher in her hand. The fairy uttered a loud cry, and asked her whence she came. "Madam," she said, "I spent three years in fetching water in the broken pitcher, and at the end of that time discovered a way to make it stay in." Magotine burst out laughing, to think of the fatigue the poor queen must have suffered; but looking at her more attentively: "Why, how is this?" she exclaimed; "Laidronette has become quite charming! How have you come by this beauty?" The queen told her she had washed in the water of discretion, and so the miracle had come to pass. At this information, Magotine, in despair, threw her pitcher to the ground. "Oh! power that braves me," she cried, "I can avenge myself. Make ready your iron shoes," she said to the queen, "you must go on my behalf to Proserpina and ask of her the elixir of long life; I always dread falling ill, and even dying. If I had the antidote, I should have no longer cause to fear; take heed therefore not to uncork the bottle or to taste the liquor, for you would thus diminish my share."

This command took the queen completely aback. "How am I to get to Hades?" she asked; "can those who go there return? Alas! madam, will you never grow tired of persecuting me? Under what star was I born? My sister is far happier than I am; no longer can I believe that the constellations are the same for all." She began to weep, and Magotine, in triumph to see her shed tears, burst out laughing. "Go, go," she said; "do not delay a moment a journey that is to prove so advantageous to me." She then put some stale nuts and brown bread into a wallet, and the queen set out, resolved to end her troubles by breaking her head against the first rock she came across.

She walked on some time, unheeding the way she was going, taking first one side and then another, thinking how extraordinary a command it was to send her thus to Hades. When she was tired, she lay down at the foot of a tree and began to dream of poor Green Serpent, thinking no more of her journey. But, suddenly, she saw Fairy Protectress, who said: "Do you know, beautiful queen, that to rescue your husband from the gloomy abode where, by Magotine's orders, he dwells, you must go to Proserpina?" "If it was possible I would go even much farther," she replied, "but I do not know how to reach that abode of darkness." "Here," said the fairy, "is a green branch; strike it on the ground, and speak these verses distinctly." The queen embraced her generous friend, and then said :—

> "Love! thine aid I fain would borrow,
>   Who canst the lord of thunder quell,
> Mitigate my soul's sad sorrow,
>   Ope then for me the path to hell.
>
> "You have caused your flame to shine
>   'Neath the world, where dead men dwell.
> Pluto sighed for Proserpine,
>   Ope then for me the path to hell.
>
> "Shall I never see again
>   My faithful loved one by my side ?
> More than mortal is my pain,
>   And death's solace is denied."

She had hardly finished her prayer, when a young child, beautiful beyond belief, came forth from the depths of a cloud of azure and gold, and sank down at her feet. A crown of flowers encircled his head. By his bow and arrows, the queen recognised that he was Love, and approaching her, he said :—

> " No more shall you grieve,
>   For the heavens I leave
> To wipe the tear-drops away from your eyes.
>   Everything for your sake
>   Will I undertake ;
> Once more shall you see the loved one you prize.
>   Green Serpent again
>   Sweet life shall regain,
> And with punishment dire his foe we'll chastise."

The queen, astonished at the brilliance that surrounded Love and enchanted with his promises, cried :—

> " To hell will I go, and that hideous place
>   Shall seem to possess a beauteous grace
> If there once more my love I see,
>   Without whom life hath no charm for me ".

Love, who rarely speaks in prose, after striking the earth three times with his bow, sang these words most beautifully :—

> " Earth that knowst Love, grant thou my prayer ;
>   Ope wide thy gates, admit us there,
> Where saddened shores bound darkened lands,
>   And Pluto great the realm commands ".

The earth, obedient, opened wide, and by a dark descent, where there was every need of a guide as brilliant as Love, the queen reached Hades. She dreaded meeting her husband in the form of a serpent; but Love, who sometimes busies himself in doing kindnesses to those who are unfortunate, had foreseen everything, and had already commanded Green Serpent to become what he was before his penance. However great was Magotine's power, she could do nothing against Love. So the first thing the queen found was her husband, and she had never seen him under so handsome a form; he, likewise, had never seen her so beautiful as she had become: however a presentiment, and perhaps Love, who was with them, helped them to divine who they were. The queen at once said to him with exquisite tenderness :—

> " The cruel Fate that binds thee here
>   Controls me also with her law ;
>   My only wish to feel thee near,
>   Thus satisfied for evermore.

> " Gladly beat our hearts united,
>   Fearlessly in Hades' shades ;
>   Joyous love by love requited ;
>   For ever vanquished, terror fades."

The king, transported by the most ardent passion, replied with all that could testify to his enthusiasm and joy ; but Love, who likes not to lose time, invited them to approach Proserpina. The queen paid her respects on behalf of the fairy, and begged for the elixir of long life. It was, in fine, the watchword of these good people, and she at once gave her a very badly-corked phial, so that the queen could, if she wished, gratify her curiosity with the greatest ease. Love, who is no novice, set her on her guard against a curiosity that would again prove fatal, and quickly leaving those gloomy regions, the king and queen returned to the light. Love did not desert them—he conducted them to Magotine, and lest she should see him hid himself in their hearts ; his presence, however, inspired the fairy with such kindly feelings that, although she was ignorant of the cause, she received her former victims most cordially, and by a supernatural effort of generosity restored to them the Kingdom of Pagody. There they at once returned and enjoyed in the future as much good fortune as in the past they had suffered disaster and trouble.

PRINCESS CARPILLON.

THERE was once an old king who consoled himself for a long widowhood by marrying a beautiful princess he dearly loved. He had a son by his first wife, hunchbacked and squint-eyed, who was extremely annoyed at his father's second marriage. "The position of an only son," he reasoned, "made me feared and loved; but if the young queen has children, my father, who can do as he likes with his kingdom, will not take into account that I am the eldest, and will disinherit me in their favour." He was ambitious, full of malice and dissimulation. But he did not allow his annoyance to be seen, and secretly consulted a fairy said to be the cleverest in the world.

Directly she saw him she divined his name, rank and errand. "Prince Hunchback," she said, for so he was named, "you are too late: the queen will have a son, and I will do nothing to prevent it; but if the boy dies or anything happens to him, I will take care that she does not have another." This promise comforted Hunchback a little. He implored the fairy not to forget, and determined to play his little brother some evil trick as soon as he should be born.

Accordingly after a short time a son was born to the queen, the handsomest child imaginable. It was noticed as an extraordinary thing that the figure of an arrow was imprinted on his arm. The queen loved her child so dearly that she wished to nurse him herself; at which Prince Hunchback was extremely annoyed, because a mother's vigilance is far greater than that of a nurse, and it is easier to deceive a nurse than a mother.

Hunchback, however, only sought to attain his end, and feigned a love for the queen and all affection for the little prince; at which the king was delighted. "I should never have believed," he said, "that my son possessed such a good disposition, and if it continues I'll leave him a part of my kingdom." Such promises did not satisfy Hunchback, who wanted all or nothing. One evening he gave the queen some preserves which contained opium. She fell asleep, and the prince, who had hidden behind the tapestry, quietly took the little prince away, and put in his place a big cat well wrapped up so that the nurses might not discover the theft. The cat cried and the nurses rocked the cradle, but at last he made such strange sounds that they thought he was hungry. They awoke the queen, and she, still half asleep, thinking to hold her beloved babe, took him in her arms to feed him. But the wicked cat bit her. She uttered a loud cry, and looking down what must she have felt to see a cat's head instead of that of her son? Her grief was so great that she thought she should die at once. The noise, made by the queen's waiting-women, aroused the whole palace. The king seized his dressing-gown, and rushed to her apartments. The first thing he saw was the cat in the same cloth of gold wrappings that his son ordinarily wore. The cat had been thrown on the floor where he lay, uttering the strangest cries. The king, greatly alarmed, asked what it all meant, and was told that no one knew, but the little prince was nowhere to be found. They had searched for him high and low, and the queen was badly wounded. The king entered her room, and found her in indescribable distress, and not wishing to increase hers by his own, forced himself to try and console her.

Meanwhile Hunchback had given his brother to a man who was his confidant and partisan. "Take him to a distant forest," he said, "and leave him naked in the spot most exposed to wild beasts, that they may eat him, and he may never be heard of more. I would take him myself, so much I fear you will not do my commission properly, but I am bound to appear before the king. Go, then, and be sure that when I am king, I shall not prove ungrateful." With his own hands he put the child into a covered basket. As he had been accustomed to caress him, the infant already knew him, and smiled, but hard-hearted Hunchback was no more moved than a rock. He then went to the queen's room, half-dressed on account of his haste, as he explained. He rubbed his eyes like a man not yet awake, and when he learned the bad news of his step-mother's wound, and saw the cat, he uttered such sorrowful cries that he took as much consoling as if he had been really distressed. He seized the cat, and, with a ferocity natural to him, twisted its neck, saying he did so on account of the wound it had inflicted on the queen.

No one suspected him, although he was wicked enough; but he concealed his crime under pretended tears. The king and queen were therefore pleased with their infamous son, and commissioned him to send to all the fairies to try and find out what could have become of the child. Anxious to put an end to these inquiries, he brought them many different and mysterious answers, all tending to the same thing: that the prince was not dead, but, for reasons that could not be given, he had been carried off for a short time, and would be restored to them quite unharmed. It was, therefore, useless to search for him. Hunchback thought this would set their minds at rest, and what he hoped took place. The king and queen flattered themselves they would one day see their son again, but the wound became so inflamed that the queen died of it, and the king, overwhelmed with grief, did not stir out of his palace for a whole year: he was always hoping for news of his son, but none came.

The man who carried the child off walked on without stopping the whole night. At dawn he opened the basket, and the pretty child smiled up at him, as had been his wont when the queen took him in her arms. "Oh, poor little prince," he said, "what a wretched fate is yours! Alas! you will serve for food, like a young lamb, to some hungry lion. Why did Hunchback choose me to assist in bringing about your death?" He closed the basket again, in order to hide the pitiable sight, but the child, who had had nothing to eat all night, began to cry with all his strength. The man plucked some figs and put them in the child's mouth. The sweet-tasting fruit quieted him a little, and the man carried him the whole day until the next night, when he came to a vast and gloomy forest. He did not much like entering it, fearing to be eaten up himself; but the next day he ventured in, still carrying the basket.

The forest was so large, that look in what direction he pleased, he could not see the end of it; but in a spot concealed by the trees he espied a rock towering up into many points. "Doubtless," he said, "there lies the den of the most cruel beasts, and since I cannot save the child, I must leave him there." As he drew near the rock an enormous eagle came forth, flying round as if he had left there something very precious; in fact, she kept her little ones there in the depths of a sort of grotto. "You will be the prey of the king of the birds, poor child," said the man. Then he unwrapped the child, and placed him among the three eaglets. The nest was large, and sheltered from the inclemency of the weather. It was no easy matter to put the prince into it, because the side on which it could be approached was very steep, and inclining to a frightful precipice. He went away sighing, and saw the eagle returning with all possible swiftness to her nest. "Ah! it's all over," he said, "the child must die." He set off quickly, not wishing to hear his last cries, and, returning to Hunchback, told him that his brother was no more.

The cruel prince embraced his faithful servant, and gave him a diamond ring, assuring him that when he was king he would appoint him captain of his guards. When the eagle returned to her nest she must have been somewhat surprised at the sight of the new inmate, but whether she was surprised or not, she exercised the laws of hospitality better than most people. She went close to her nursling, stretched out her wings and warmed him, and in fact gave him all her attention. A particular instinct caused her to seek fruits for him; she pecked them, and poured the juice into the prince's little red mouth, and fed him as carefully as if she had been his mother.

When the eaglets were a little older, the eagle took them by turns, on her wings or in her talons, and accustomed them to look at the sun without blinking. Sometimes the eaglets left their mother and flew round her for a while, but the little prince could do nothing of the sort, and when she took him up into the air he ran great risk of falling and killing himself. But fortune favoured him. She procured him this extraordinary nurse, and prevented him from falling.

Four years passed. As soon as the eaglets were old enough, they left their mother, and returned no more to the nest. The prince, who was unable to go far, remained on the rock. The eagle, prudent and timid on his account, and fearful lest the child should fall down the precipice, carried him to the other side, and put him in a safe place, that wild beasts could not reach.

Cupid was scarcely so beautiful as the young prince. The heat of the sun could not spoil the lilies and roses of his complexion. His features were so regular that the most famous painters could imagine nothing more beautiful. His hair was already long enough to cover his shoulders, and his whole appearance so noble, that a more majestic and beautiful child had never been seen. The eagle loved him with the most extraordinary affection. She brought him only fruit for food, understanding the difference between him and her eaglets, to whom she brought raw flesh. She was the despair of all the shepherds of the neighbourhood, mercilessly carrying off their lambs. Nothing was talked about but the eagle's depredations. At length, weary of nourishing her at the expense of their flocks, they resolved to seek out her eyrie. They divided into parties, followed her with their eyes, traversed the mountains and valleys, and for a long time could not find her. But one day some of them saw her settle down on the big rock. The most determined among them risked the perils of the ascent. She was at that time carefully nourishing two little eaglets; but much as she loved them, her affection for the prince was even greater, because she had known him longer. When the shepherd discovered her nest, she was not there, and it was easy to destroy it, and take everything it contained. But what was their surprise when they found the prince? It was so extraordinary a thing that their meagre intelligence could scarcely take it in.

The eaglets cried when they were carried off with the child, and the eagle heard them. She hastened to swoop down on the robbers, and they would have felt the full effect of her anger had not one of the shepherds killed her with an arrow. The young prince, greatly distressed, uttered pitiful cries, and wept bitterly to see his nurse fall. The shepherds then walked away in the direction of their village. The next day a barbarous ceremony I will now describe was to take place.

For a long time that country had served as a retreat for the ogres. The people, reduced to despair by such dangerous neighbours, sought a means of driving them away, but without success. The terrible ogres, enraged at the hatred shown them, redoubled their cruelties, and devoured, without exception, everything that came in their way.

One day when the shepherds were assembled for the purpose of deliberating on a course of action in regard to the ogres, a man of gigantic stature appeared in their midst. Half his body was that of a stag covered with blue fur. He had goat's feet, a club on his shoulder, and a shield in his hand. He said: "Shepherds, I am the Blue Centaur. If you will give me a child every three years, I promise, with the aid of a hundred of my brothers, to make fierce war on the ogres, and drive them away."

The shepherds found it very difficult to pledge themselves to so cruel a thing, but the oldest among them said: "Is it any better, my friends, for the ogres to eat our fathers, children, and wives every day? We shall lose one to save many. Do not let us refuse the centaur's offer." Thus they consented and promised with many oaths to keep their word to the centaur, and give him a child as he asked.

He went away and soon returned with his brothers, who were as gigantic as himself. The ogres were as brave as they were cruel. Many battles were fought, in which the centaurs were victorious, and at last the ogres were forced to flee. The Blue Centaur then demanded his reward, and everybody said he was quite justified in doing so, but when it came to the point of delivering up the child, no family was found willing to part with theirs. Mothers hid their children even in the bosom of the earth. The centaur, however, would stand no nonsense, and after waiting eight and forty hours told the shepherds they would have to give him as many children as he remained days among them. The delay cost them six little boys and six little girls. This settled the matter, and every three years a solemn festival was held, at which the poor, innocent child was delivered up to the centaur.

It happened that the tribute was to be paid on the very day after the finding of the prince in the eagle's nest, and although a child had already been provided, it may easily be believed that the shepherds gladly substituted the prince. The uncertainty about his birth, for they were so simple they sometimes thought the eagle was his mother, and his marvellous beauty decided them to give him to the centaur, who was so fastidious that he would only eat pretty children. The mother of the child that was to have been the centaur's victim suddenly passed from the horrors of death to the sweetness of life. They made her deck out the prince in the garments prepared for her son. She combed his long hair, and placed a wreath of small red and white wild roses on his head; she dressed him in a long robe of fine white linen, with a girdle of flowers. And thus attired, he was told to walk at the head of the children who accompanied him. But how can I describe the look of majesty and nobility that already shone in his eyes? He who had never seen anything but eagles, and who was still so young in years, was neither awkward nor unpolished. He acted as if he thought the shepherds were there only to give him pleasure. "What a pity," they whispered to each other, "that this child should be eaten up. Can we not save him?" Many of them wept, and it was quite impossible to remain unmoved.

It was the centaur's custom to appear on the top of a rock, club in one hand and shield in the other, and there in an awful voice to shout to the shepherds: "Leave me my prey and withdraw". Directly he saw the child who was being led to him, he became extremely joyful, and shouting so loudly that the mountains trembled, he said: "This is the best breakfast I've ever had. I can eat that little boy without pepper and salt." The shepherds and shepherdesses, looking at the poor child, whispered: "The eagle spared him, but this monster will kill him". The oldest shepherd took him in his arms, kissed him many times, and said: "My child, my darling child, I know you not at all, and yet am conscious of knowing you only too well. Must I take part in your funeral? What does fortune mean by protecting you from the eagle's sharp talons and crooked beak, and then delivering you to-day to the ravenous appetite of this horrible monster?"

While the shepherd was moistening the prince's rosy cheeks with his tears, the boy played with his grey locks and smiled at him in childish fashion. The greater the pity he inspired, the more slowly the old shepherd advanced. "Hurry yourself," cried the famished centaur; "if you force me to come down and approach you, I shall eat a hundred." He rose up impatiently and was swinging his club when there appeared in the air a big globe of fire, surrounded by an azure cloud. Everybody looked attentively at the extraordinary sight. Gradually the globe and cloud came down and opened. From it issued a diamond chariot in which sat the most beautiful woman imaginable. On her head was a golden helmet adorned with white feathers. The visor was up and her eyes shone like the sun. Her rich cuirass, and the fiery lance in her hand, proclaimed her an amazon.

" Shepherds, how is this ? " she exclaimed. " Are you inhuman enough to give such a child to the cruel centaur ? It is time to release you from your promise. Justice and reason are opposed to such barbarous customs. Do not fear the return of the ogres. I, the fairy amazon, will prevent it. From this moment I take you under my protection." " Madam," cried the shepherds and shepherdesses, stretching out their hands to her, "this is the greatest piece of good fortune we could have." They could say no more, for the enraged centaur challenged her to combat. He was savage and obstinate, but the fiery lance burned him wherever it touched him, and his horrible shrieks ended only with his life. He fell entirely burnt, and such a noise did his fall make, that it was as if a mountain had been overturned. The terrified shepherds hid themselves, some in a neighbouring forest, others in the depths of hollow rocks whence you could see everything without being seen.

There the shepherd, holding the little prince in his arms, had taken refuge, much more anxious about the fate of the beautiful child than about anything that concerned himself and his family, although such a matter surely deserved consideration. After the centaur's death, the amazon took a trumpet and played on it such melodious notes that the sick who heard it rose up whole, and all were conscious of a secret joy for which they were unable to account.

At the sweet sounds of the trumpet, shepherds and shepherdesses assembled. The fairy amazon, to reassure them, drew nearer, gradually lowering her chariot till it was within three feet of the ground. It rolled along on a cloud so transparent that it seemed made of crystal. The old shepherd, who was called the Sublime, appeared, holding the little prince. " Draw near, Sublime," said the fairy, " there is nothing to fear. I desire that in the future peace should reign here, and that you may enjoy the rest you came to seek. But give me the child whose adventures have already been so remarkable." The old man, with a low obeisance, put the child into her arms. She caressed him a thousand times, kissed him, seated him on her knees, and spoke to him, although she knew he understood no language and could not speak. He uttered cries of joy and sorrow, gave forth sighs and made inarticulate sounds, for he had never heard any one speak.

He was, however, dazzled by the amazon's shining armour, and stood up on her knees in order to touch her helmet. The fairy smiled at him and told him as if he could understand her : " When you are old enough to bear arms, my son, you shall certainly have them ". After again tenderly caressing him she gave him back to Sublime. " Good old man," she said, " you are not unknown to me ; do not disdain to take care of this child. Teach him to despise the vanities of the world, and to rise superior to the blows of fortune. He may

be born to a brilliant lot, but I believe it is better to be good than powerful.
Man's happiness should not only consist in outward greatness; to be happy you
must be virtuous, and to be virtuous you must know yourself. You must be
able to restrain your desires, to be as contented in mediocrity as in opulence.
You must gain the esteem of men of merit, despise no one, and be ever ready to
sacrifice without regret the good things of this unhappy life. But what am I
thinking of, venerable shepherd? I am telling you things you know much better
than I do, but in truth I repeat them less for you than for the other shepherds
who are listening to me. Farewell to you all; summon me when you need me.
The same lance and hand that have just killed the centaur will be always at your
service."

The confusion and delight of Sublime and all his comrades was so great
that they could not reply to the fairy's kind words. In their embarrassment and
joy they humbly prostrated themselves before her, and while they were thus
occupied the fiery globe, gently rising to the middle region of the air, vanished
with the amazon and her chariot.

The timid shepherds dared not at first approach the centaur. Dead as he
was they still feared him, but at length they took courage and determined to
erect an enormous funeral pile and reduce him to ashes, lest his brethren, hearing
what had happened, should come to avenge his death. This advice being found
good, they lost no time in ridding themselves of the odious corpse.

Sublime carried the little prince to his hut. His wife was ill, and his two
daughters had been unable to leave her to go to the ceremony. "Here, shepherdess," he said, "is a child beloved by the gods, and protected by a fairy
amazon; for the future you must look upon him as your own son, and make
him very happy." The shepherdess was charmed with the gift, and took the
prince on her bed. "At least," she said, "if I cannot give him the lofty teaching
he will receive from you, I can bring him up carefully and love him as my own
son." "That is exactly what I ask of you," said the old man, and gave him
into her charge. When his two daughters looked at him they were enchanted
with his incomparable beauty, and with the gracefulness of his little person.
They at once began to teach him their language, and never was there so quick
and bright an intellect. He understood the most difficult things with an ease
that astonished the shepherd, and he was soon advanced enough to take lessons
only from the old man, who was eminently suited to give him valuable teaching,
for he had been king of a fine and flourishing land. An usurper, his neighbour
and enemy, had secretly carried on successful intrigues and won over to his side
some discontented spirits who furnished him with means to surprise the king and
his family: he shut them up in a fortress and there left them to perish miserably.

So remarkable a change did not destroy the virtue of the king and queen, and they endured with courage all the outrages put upon them by the tyrant. Soon after their misfortune the queen gave birth to a daughter. She already had two charming little girls, who when they were old enough shared in their parents' distress. At the end of three years the king gained over one of his gaolers. The man agreed to bring a little boat so that they might cross the lake in whose midst the fortress was situated. He provided them with files for removing the iron bars from the windows, and ropes by which they could descend. They chose a very dark night. The plans were carried out successfully and noiselessly. The gaoler helped them down the walls, which were terribly high; the king descending first, then his two daughters, then the queen. Last of all came the little princess in a big basket. But, alas! it had been carelessly fastened to the rope, and they heard it fall to the bottom of the lake. If the queen had not swooned with grief, her cries and laments would have roused the whole garrison. The king, terribly distressed at the accident, made as thorough a search as the darkness of the night allowed. He found the basket, but the princess was no longer in it, and he then began to row in order to save himself and the rest of the family. On the shore of the lake were horses provided by the gaoler to take the king wherever he desired to go.

During their imprisonment the king and queen had had plenty of time for moralising, and they had discovered that the greatest luxuries of life are of little account when rightly valued. That, added to the new misfortune that had befallen them in the loss of the little princess, determined them not to go to the kings, their neighbours and allies, where most likely they would only be in the way, but to settle in a very fertile and delightful plain. Then the king, exchanging his sceptre for a crook, bought a big flock of sheep and became a shepherd. They built a little rustic cottage, bounded on one side by the mountains and on the other by a brook full of fish. They were happier there than they had been on the throne. No one envied their poverty. They feared neither traitors nor flatterers. The days passed peacefully, and the king often said: "Ah! if men could be cured of ambition, how happy would they be! I have been a king and am now a shepherd, and I prefer my hut to my palace."

It was under this wise philosopher that the young prince studied. He did not know his master's rank, and the master was equally ignorant of his pupil's high birth, but he recognised his noble qualities and aspirations, and could not believe he was any common child. He noticed with pleasure how he always put himself at the head of his comrades with an air of superiority that procured him their respect. He was always forming little armies, building forts and attacking them. He went hunting, and, in spite of all the shepherd king might say, ran the greatest risks. All this convinced him that the boy was born to rule. But while he is growing up, let us return to his father's court.

Prince Hunchback, seeing that his father was already very old, took scarcely any further heed of him. He grew impatient at waiting so long for the succession, and to console himself demanded an army for the purpose of conquering a neighbouring kingdom whose fickle people had made overtures to him. The king was willing, provided that before his departure he would witness a deed he desired all the nobles of the country to sign, to the effect that if ever his younger son returned—it would be easy to make sure it was he by the arrow on his arm—he should be sole heir to the crown. Hunchback was not only present at the ceremony, but himself signed the deed, although his father had thought it too cruel a thing to ask of him. But as he felt perfectly certain of his brother's death, he risked nothing, and thought great value would be attached to so amiable an act. The king summoned the estates of the realm, harangued them and distressed all who heard him by his tears in speaking of the loss of his son. He made the nobles sign the deed, and commanded that it should be deposited in the royal treasury, and, lest it should be forgotten, ordered several authentic copies to be made.

Prince Hunchback then bade his father farewell, and put himself at the head of a fine army to attempt the conquest of the kingdom to which he was invited. After many battles, he killed his enemy with his own hand, took the capital city, established garrisons and governors everywhere, and returned to his father. He presented him with a young princess named Carpillon, whom he had brought back as a captive.

She was so exceedingly beautiful that nothing nature had so far formed, or that the imagination could conceive, could be compared to her. The king was enchanted with her at first sight, and Hunchback, who had known her some time, was so deeply in love with her that he had not a moment's peace ; but as much as he loved her, she hated him. He invariably spoke to her as a master to his slave, and she so much disliked his cruel ways that she did her best to avoid him.

The king gave her apartments in the palace, and women to attend on her, for the misfortunes of so young and beautiful a princess touched him. When Hunchback told him he wished to marry her, the king replied : " I consent on condition she has no objection ; but it seems to me that your society always makes her melancholy ". " That is because she loves me," said Hunchback, " and dares not let it be seen. The forced constraint embarrasses her. When she is my wife, you will see her happy." " I should like to think so," said the king ; " but are you not making a little too sure ? " His father's doubts deeply offended Hunchback. " You, madam," he said to the princess, " are the cause of the king's severity to me, a most unusual thing ; perhaps he is in love with you ; tell me the truth and choose the one you like best ; as long as I see you queen I shall be content." He spoke thus in the hope of discovering her senti- ments, for he had no intention of changing his own. Young Carpillon, who did not as yet know that most lovers are cunning and sly, fell into the snare. " I confess, sir," she said, " that if I was my own mistress, I would have nothing to do with either of you, but if my evil fortune compels me to the sad necessity of making a choice, I prefer the king." " And why ? " replied Hunchback, forcing himself to keep calm. " Because," she added, " he is gentler than you. He is king now, and will not perhaps live very long." " Ha ! ha ! you little wretch," cried Hunchback, " you prefer my father, so that you may shortly be queen- dowager ; but let me tell you it will never be, since he does not give you a thought. It is I who am so kind, and very ill-placed kindness it is too, for your ingratitude is intolerable ; but if you were ten times more ungrateful, you should still be my wife."

Princess Carpillon learned a little too late that it is sometimes dangerous to say out all you think, and to remedy the mischief remarked : " I should be glad to know your sentiments, and am glad you love me enough to overlook my unkindness. Already I esteem you, sir. Try to make yourself loved." The prince fell headlong into the snare, palpable as it was ; but when a man is in love he is usually very stupid, and inclined to tell himself all manner of flattering tales. Carpillon's words made him gentler than a lamb. He smiled and squeezed her hands so tightly that he almost hurt her.

Directly he left her she went to the king's apartments, and throwing herself at his feet, said : " Protect me from the greatest of all misfortunes. Prince Hunchback wants to marry me, and I confess to you, I hate him. Do not be as unkind as he is. My rank, my youth, my family's misfortunes deserve the pity of a great king like yourself." " Fair princess," he said, " I am not surprised that my son loves you. It is a thing common to all who see you ; but I will never forgive him if he fails in respect to you." " But, sir," she went on, " he regards me as his prisoner, and treats me as a slave." " It was with my army he conquered your father," said the king ; " if you are a captive you are mine, and I restore you your liberty, happy in that my advanced age and white hairs protect me from becoming your slave." The grateful princess thanked the king a thousand times, and, followed by her attendants, withdrew.

When Hunchback learned what had happened he felt it keenly, and when the king forbade him to think any more of the princess his rage increased. After such signal service, he feared she could not help wishing well to the king.

" I shall have to labour all my life, and perhaps in vain," he said ; " I am not fond of wasting my time." " I am sorry," replied the king, " because I love you ; but it cannot be otherwise." " We shall see," said Hunchback insolently, going out of the room ; " you dare to carry off my prisoner! I would rather die." " The woman you call your prisoner was mine," added the king angrily, " now she is free ; I intend she shall be mistress of her fate, and shall not be dependent on your caprice."

Had not Hunchback withdrawn, the argument might have been carried too far. He now conceived the idea of making himself master of the kingdom and the princess. While he had been in command of the troops he had won their favour, and the seditious spirits among them willingly supported his evil design. The king was informed that his son was plotting to dethrone him, and, as he was the stronger, the king's only course was one of gentleness. He sent for Hunchback and said: " Is it true that you are ungrateful enough to desire to take my throne from me and set yourself on it ? You see I am on the brink of the grave ; do not hasten my end. Has not my wife's death and the loss of my son been trouble enough ? It is true that I am opposed to your designs on the Princess Carpillon ; but in that I consider you as much as her. For is it possible to be happy with a woman who does not love you ? But, if you are willing to run such a risk, I consent to everything; give me time to speak to her and decide her in favour of the marriage."

Hunchback wanted the princess more than the kingdom ; for he possessed the one he had just conquered, and told the king he was less desirous of reigning than was believed ; had he not himself signed the deed disinheriting him in case of his brother's return? and he declared he would continue to respect it provided he might marry Carpillon. The king embraced him, and went in search of Carpillon, who was greatly alarmed at the turn affairs had taken. Her governess was never far from her. She made her come into her closet, and, weeping bitterly, said : " Is it possible that after all the promises given me by the king, he can be cruel enough to sacrifice me to Hunchback ? Indeed, my dear friend, if I must marry him, my wedding-day will be the last of my life, for it is not so much his deformity that repels me as his evil heart." " Alas! princess," replied the governess, " you are not doubtless aware that the inclinations of daughters of great kings are scarcely ever consulted. If they marry a kind-hearted and handsome prince, they may thank chance for it, but no one thinks of anything but the interests of the state." Carpillon was on the point of replying when she was informed that the king was awaiting her in her apartments. She raised her eyes to heaven as if to ask its aid.

There was no necessity for the king to explain his determination. She knew exactly, so admirable was her penetration; the beauty of her mind was even greater than that of her person. "Ah! sire," she exclaimed, "what do you tell me?" "Fair princess," he said, "do not regard your marriage with my son as a misfortune. I implore you to consent with a good grace. The violence he does your feelings sufficiently testifies to the ardour of his own. If he did not love you so passionately, he could find more than one princess who would be enchanted to share with him the kingdom he already possesses, and the one he hopes for on my death. But he desires only you; neither your disdain nor contempt has wearied him, and you may rest assured that he will do everything in his power to please you." "I thought I had found a protector in you," she replied; "but I am mistaken. You forsake me, but the just gods will not desert me." "If you knew all my efforts to prevent the marriage," rejoined the king, "you would be convinced of my affection. Alas! Heaven gave me a son I dearly loved; his mother nourished him herself, but one night he was taken out of his cradle, and a cat, that bit the queen so severely she died of the wound, was put in his place. If the beautiful infant had not been snatched from me, he would now be the comfort of my old age; my subjects would respect him, and I should have offered you my kingdom with him. Hunchback, who is now master of the situation, might be thankful if he was suffered to remain at the court. The misfortune of losing my son extends even to you, princess." "It is I alone," she replied, "who am the cause of what has happened; look upon me as guilty, and punish me rather than marry me." "At that time, fair princess, you were in no position to do either good or ill to anybody. I do not accuse you of my misfortunes, but if you do not wish to add to them, receive my son kindly, for he is the strongest here, and can work you terrible mischief." Her tears formed her only reply, and as Hunchback was impatient to know the result of the interview, the king found him in his room, and told him the Princess Carpillon agreed to the marriage, and that he would give the necessary orders for the solemn ceremony. The prince was overcome with joy, and immediately sought out the best lapidaries, merchants, and embroiderers. He bought the most beautiful things imaginable for his mistress, and sent her big gold baskets full of a thousand curiosities. She received them with some appearance of pleasure. Then he visited her in person and said: "Were you not very foolish, Madam Carpillon, to refuse the honour I wished to do you? for, not counting my amiability, I am considered very intelligent; and I shall give you so many gowns, diamonds, and all sorts of beautiful things that no queen in all the world will be able to rival you."

The princess replied-coldly that the misfortune of her family made it less suitable for her to deck herself out than for others, and she begged him not to make her such handsome presents. "You would be right," he said, "not to adorn yourself if I did not wish it, but you ought to try and please me. Everything will be ready for our wedding in four days. Amuse yourself, princess, and give what orders you like, for you are already absolute mistress here."

After his departure, she shut herself up with her governess, and told her that if she did not assist her to escape she should kill herself on her wedding-day. The governess pointed out the impossibility of escape, and the cowardice of committing suicide to avoid the ills of life; and, moreover, tried to persuade her that her virtue would contribute to her tranquillity, and that without loving Hunchback passionately, she would esteem him enough to be happy with him.

Carpillon did not give in; she said that so far she had reckoned on her assistance, but that she knew what to do. If everybody deserted her she should not abandon herself, and to great evils it was necessary to apply strong remedies. She opened the window, and now and again leaned out in perfect silence. The governess, fearing she meant to throw herself out, knelt down, and looking tenderly at her, said: "Madam, what do you want of me? I will obey you even at the risk of my life." The princess embraced her, and asked her to purchase a shepherdess's costume and a cow, and she would escape when she could. She declared that all attempt to dissuade her from her purpose was useless; it would only be wasting time, and she had none too much. To aid her in getting away unnoticed, a doll must be dressed and put into her bed, and it must be given out that she was ill.

"You see, madam," said the poor governess, "to what danger I expose myself. Prince Hunchback will be sure to think I was a party to your plan, and to find out where you are, will put me to the torture, and then have me burned alive: after that, say I do not love you!"

The princess was much distressed. "I should like you to escape," she said, "two days after me; till then it will be easy to deceive everybody." They plotted so cleverly that the very same night Carpillon had the dress and the cow.

All the goddesses from High Olympus, those who found the shepherd Paris, and a hundred dozen besides, would not have looked so lovely in rustic costume. Carpillon set off alone by the light of the moon, sometimes leading her cow by a cord, sometimes making it carry her; she went at hazard in the greatest trepidation. If the least little breeze stirred in the bushes, if a bird flew out of its nest, or a hare came forth from its hiding-place, she imagined thieves or wolves were coming to kill her.

She walked on all night, and would have walked on all day, had not the cow stopped to feed in a meadow. The princess, fatigued by her heavy wooden clogs, and the weight of her grey frieze gown, lay down on the grass beside a brook, and took off her yellow linen cap, in order to fasten up her fair hair which, escaping on all sides, fell in curls to her feet. She looked about to make sure that no one could see her until she had put it right again; but notwithstanding her precaution, she was surprised by a lady fully armed, except the head, whence she had removed a golden helmet covered with diamonds. "Shepherdess," she said, "I am tired; will you give me some milk from your cow?" "With pleasure, madam," replied Carpillon, "if I had something to put it in." "Here

is a cup," replied the amazon—for it was she—handing her a very beautiful one of porcelain. But the princess had not the least idea how to milk a cow. "What," said the lady "has your cow no milk, or do you not know how to milk it?" The princess began to weep, ashamed of appearing so awkward in the presence of this extraordinary person. "I confess, madam," she said, "I have not been long a shepherdess. My duty is to lead the cow to pasture, my mother does the rest." "You have a mother then?" continued the lady, "and what does she do?" "She is a farmer's wife." "Near here?" added the lady. "Yes," replied the princess. "I feel a liking for her; I am glad she has such a beautiful daughter, and should like to see her; take me to her." Carpillon knew not what to reply; she was not accustomed to telling falsehoods,

and did not know she was speaking to a fairy. In those days fairies were not so common as they have since become. She lowered her eyes, her face grew crimson, and she said: "When once I am out in the fields, I dare not return till evening. I entreat you, madam, do not force me to vex my mother, who, if I disobey her, will very likely ill-treat me."

"Oh! princess, princess," said the fairy, smiling, "you cannot keep up a falsehood or play the part you've undertaken without my help. Here's a bunch of gillyflowers; be sure that as long as you hold it Hunchback, from whom you are escaping, will never recognise you. When you reach the great forest, ask the shepherds you will find tending their flocks there to show you where Sublime lives. Go to him and tell him you come from the fairy amazon, who begs him to let you live with his wife and daughter. Farewell, beautiful Carpillon; I have been your friend for a long time." "Alas! madam," exclaimed the princess, "since you know me and love me, will you leave me? I need your help so greatly." "The bunch of gillyflowers will never fail you," she replied; "my time is precious; you must fulfil your destiny."

So saying, she vanished from Carpillon's sight, who was frightened almost to death. Recovering a little, she continued her way, having no idea where the big forest was. But she said to herself: "The clever fairy, who appears and disappears, who recognises me in peasants' dress without ever having seen me, will guide me where I ought to go". She grasped the bunch of flowers tightly, whether she walked or rested, but she made scarcely any progress, for although she was brave enough, she was little accustomed to such hard walking: as soon as she came to stones, she fell down and her feet bled. She was obliged to lie down on the ground under some trees; she feared everything, and often felt very anxious about her governess.

And she did not think of that poor woman without reason; her zeal and fidelity have few examples. She arrayed a big doll in the princess's night-cap, made of fine linen, and adorned with knots of ribbon. She moved about the room very softly for fear, she said, of disturbing her, and scolded when anybody made a noise. The king was informed of the princess's illness; he was not surprised, and ascribed the cause to her displeasure and to the constraint she was putting on herself. But when Prince Hunchback learned the bad news, his grief was inconceivable; he wished to see her, and the governess had much ado to prevent him. "At least," he said, "let my physician see her." "Ah! sir," she exclaimed, "only that is wanting to bring about her death; she hates doctors and medicines. But do not alarm yourself; only a few days' rest is needed. It is a nervous attack she will sleep off." She thus prevented him worrying her mistress, and always kept the doll in her bed. But one evening just as she was preparing to flee, because she felt sure the prince would make fresh attempts to enter, she heard him at the door raging like a madman, and without waiting for her to open it, he forced it in.

The cause of his fury was that some of the princess's women had discovered the deceit, and fearing punishment, had at once informed Hunchback. The violence of his anger cannot be described; he hastened to the king, thinking he had a hand in the matter, but the surprise depicted in his face clearly showed his ignorance. Directly he saw the poor governess, he made a rush at her, and taking her by the hair, said: " Restore Carpillon to me, or I'll tear out your heart ". Her tears formed her only reply, and kneeling, she vainly implored him to listen to her. He immediately dragged her himself down to a deep dungeon, and would have stabbed her had not the king, who was as good as his son was wicked, forced him to let her live in that horrible prison.

The amorous and angry prince gave orders for the princess to be sought over sea and land; he himself rushed about everywhere like a madman. One day, when dreadful weather—thunder, lightning, and hail—frightened her, Carpillon took shelter with her cow under a big rock. It happened that Prince Hunchback, who, with all his attendants, were wet through, took refuge in the same spot. When she perceived him so close to her, she was much more frightened of him than of the thunder. She held the bunch of gillyflowers with both hands, fearing one would not be enough, and remembering the fairy, said: " Do not forsake me, charming amazon ". Hunchback looked at her. " What do you fear, you decrepit old dame ? " he said. " If the thunder killed you, what would it matter ? Are you not on the brink of the grave ? " The young princess was no less astonished than delighted to hear herself called old; she had her doubts that the bunch of flowers worked the miracle, and not to enter into conversation, she pretended to be deaf. Hunchback, perceiving she could not hear, said to his confidant, who was ever at his side: " If I was feeling a little more cheerful, I would take this old woman to the top of the rock and throw her off just for the pleasure of seeing her break her neck; nothing could be more delightful ". " But, sir," replied the villain, " if it would give you any pleasure, I am quite willing to take her there whether she is agreeable or not, and you shall see her body bound from point to point of the rock like a ball, and the blood flow even to where you stand." " No," said the prince, " I haven't time; I must continue my search for the ungrateful creature who is the cause of all the miseries of my life."

So saying, he put spurs to his horse, and went off at full gallop. The princess's joy may easily be imagined, for certainly the conversation was of an alarming nature. She did not forget to thank the fairy amazon, whose power she had just proved, and continuing her journey, reached the place where the little cottages of the shepherds of that country were situated. They were very pretty; each had its garden and spring. The vale of Tempé and the banks of Lignon were not more delightful. For the most part the shepherdesses were beautiful, and the shepherds omitted no means of pleasing them; the trees were carved with a thousand names and love-ditties. When they saw her, they left their flocks and followed her respectfully, charmed with her beauty and dignified bearing. The meanness of her clothes, however, surprised them, for, although they led a simple, rustic life, they prided themselves on being very richly dressed.

The princess inquired which was the dwelling of the shepherd Sublime, and they eagerly led her there. She found him seated in a dale with his wife and daughters; a rivulet gently murmured at his feet; he was weaving rushes into a basket for holding fruit, and his two daughters were fishing.

When Carpillon approached them, she was conscious of a feeling of respect and affection that greatly surprised her, and when they saw her, they were so moved that they changed colour. " I am," she said, humbly greeting them, " a poor shepherdess, and by the recommendation of the fairy amazon whom you know, I offer you my services; I hope that, out of consideration for her, you will receive me kindly among you." " My daughter," said the king, rising and saluting her in his turn, " the fairy is perfectly right in thinking we hold her in great honour; you are most welcome, and with no other recommendation than your own charms, our house would be open to you." " Approach, fair girl," said the queen, holding out her hand, " come, let me embrace you; I feel very kindly towards you, and you must look upon me as your mother, and my daughters as your sisters." " Alas! my good mother," said the princess, " I do not deserve that honour; it would be enough to be your shepherdess and tend your sheep." " My daughter," replied the king, " we are all equal here; your credentials remove any distinction between you and our children; come, sit by us, and let your cow feed with our sheep." She still made difficulties, obstinately declaring she had come only to assist in the household work. It would have been very awkward for her had they taken her at her word; but, in truth, to look at her was enough to know that she was born rather to command than obey, and it may be also taken for granted that a fairy of Amazon's importance would not have lent her protection to any ordinary being.

The king and queen were conscious of an inexplicable astonishment and admiration. They asked her if she had come far; she said, yes: if she had father and mother; she answered, no: and, as far as was consistent with politeness, she replied to all their questions in monosyllables. " And what is your name, my child ? " said the queen. " I am called Carpillon," she said. " It's a strange name," rejoined the king, " and unless given for some particular reason, is very uncommon." She answered nothing, and took one of the queen's spindles to wind off the thread. When they saw her hands, it was as if she had drawn two moulded snow-balls from the folds of her sleeves, so dazzlingly white were they. The king and queen exchanged a glance of intelligence, and said: " Your gown is very hot, Carpillon, for this time of year, and your clothes very hard for a child like you; you must dress yourself in our fashion." " Mother," she replied, "we dress like this in my country, but if you desire it, I will dress myself differently." They were glad of her obedience, and greatly admired the modest expression of her beautiful eyes and countenance.

Supper time having arrived, they rose and all entered the house together. The princesses had caught some fish, and there were fresh eggs, milk, and fruit. " I am surprised," said the king, " that my son is not yet returned ; his love of the chase leads him further than I like, and I am always dreading some accident." " So am I," said the queen ; " if you prepare it, we will wait so that he may sup with us." " No," said the king, "that is precisely what I do not wish ; on the contrary, I beg you, when he comes in, not to speak to him, and to treat him very coldly." " You know his good heart," added the queen ; " he will be so grieved that he will be ill." " I cannot help it," said the king, " he must be corrected."

They sat down to the table. When the meal was nearly at an end, the young prince entered ; he carried a roe on his shoulders, his hair was damp with perspiration, and his face was covered with dust. He leaned on a lance he usually carried, his bow was fastened to one side and his quiver of arrows to the other. Even in this condition there was something so noble in his face and bearing that no one could look at him without attention and respect. " Mother," he said, addressing the queen, " the desire of bringing you this roe led me far and wide over the hills and plains to-day." " My son," said the king, gravely, " you seek rather to give us anxiety than pleasure ; you know what I have already said to you about your passion for the chase, but you take no pains to correct it." The prince grew red, and felt the more annoyed to see a stranger there. He replied that another time he would return earlier, or, if his father desired it, would not go hunting at all. " That is enough," said the queen, who loved him dearly. " My son, I thank you for your gift ; come, sit by me, and eat, for I'm sure you must be hungry." He was somewhat disconcerted by the serious manner in which the king had spoken to him, and scarcely dared lift his eyes, for if he was rash in danger, he was docile and very diffident with those to whom he owed respect.

However he recovered himself, sat down by the queen and looked at Carpillon, who had scarcely waited as long to look at him. As soon as their eyes met, their hearts were so agitated that neither of them knew to what to ascribe their confusion. The princess blushed and lowered her eyes, but the prince continued to gaze at her ; she slowly raised her eyes to his, and held them there a long while ; their surprise was mutual, and it seemed to them that nothing in the world could equal what they saw. " Is it possible," said the princess to herself, " that among all the people I saw at court, none came up to this young

19

shepherd ? " In his turn he thought : " How comes it that this enchanting girl is a simple shepherdess ? Oh ! that I were a king to set her on a throne and make her mistress of my realms ! How happy I should be then ! "

Dreaming thus, he forgot to eat. The queen, thinking this cold reception was the cause, took every care to console him ; she brought him, with her own hand, exquisite fruits on which she set a high value. He begged Carpillon to taste them, and she, without thinking who offered them, said sadly : " I do not care for them ". He left them coldly on the table. The queen did not notice it, but the elder of the two princesses, who did not dislike him, and would doubtless have dearly loved him, had it not been for his difference in rank, observed it with some sort of ill-humour.

After supper, the king and queen withdrew ; the princesses did all the household work, one milked the cows, tke other looked after the cheese. Carpillon was eager to help, but she was not accustomed to such things. She did nothing that was of the least use, so that the two princesses called her, laughingly, the fair blunderer ; but the prince, already in love, helped her. He went to the spring with her, carried the pitchers, drew the water, and returned heavily laden, for he would not let her carry anything. " But what do you mean, shepherd ? " she said, " am I to play the lady here ? I who have worked all my life, have I come to this plain to rest ? " " You will do whatever you like, charming shepherdess," he replied ; " but do not deny me the pleasure of offering you my slight help on these occasions." They returned together and reached the house more quickly than he wished, for although he scarcely dared speak to her, it gave him the greatest delight to be with her.

They both spent a restless night ; their inexperience prevented them from guessing the cause, but the prince awaited with impatience the hour of seeing the princess again, and she already dreaded meeting him. The new trouble that the sight of him awakened in her diverted her somewhat from her other overwhelming sorrows. She thought so often of him that she thought less of Prince Hunchback. " Why, oh ! capricious fortune," she said, " do you bestow grace, good looks and charm on a young shepherd who has merely to tend sheep, and malice, ugliness and deformity on a great prince destined to rule a kingdom ? "

Since her metamorphosis into a shepherdess, Carpillon had not troubled to look at herself, but now a certain desire of pleasing sent her in search of a mirror. She found one belonging to the princesses, and when she saw her head-dress and gown she was much confused. " What a figure !" she exclaimed ; " what do I look like ? I cannot any longer be buried in this thick stuff." She took some water and washed her face and hands. They became whiter than lilies. She then found the queen, and kneeling, presented her with a splendid diamond ring (for she had brought her jewellery with her). " My good mother," she said, "some time ago I found this ring ; I do not know its value, but I think it must be worth some money. I beg you to take it as a proof of gratitude for your kindness to me, and buy me gowns and linen so that I may be like the shepherdesses of this land."

The queen was surprised to see such a beautiful ring in the young girl's possession. " I will keep it for you," she said, " but I will not take it from you. Besides, you will this morning receive all you need." She had in fact procured from a small town hard by the prettiest peasant's dress imaginable. The head-dress, the shoes, everything was perfect ; attired thus, she looked more beautiful than the dawn. The prince on his part had not been neglectful ; he had put a wreath of flowers round his hat, and adorned the belt to which his scrip was fastened and his sheep-hook with them. He brought a bouquet for Carpillon and presented it to her with all a lover's timidity, and intelligent as she was she received it in an embarrassed manner. When they were together she scarcely spoke a word, and was always dreaming, and he, on his part, did much the same. On his hunting expeditions, instead of following the roes and bucks, if he found a spot suitable for communing with himself about Carpillon, he remained in that solitary place, composing verses, singing couplets to his shepherdess, speaking to the rocks, woods and birds. He had quite lost the cheerful disposition that made all the shepherds eagerly seek his society.

But since it is difficult to love much and not to fear what we love, he dreaded offending his shepherdess by declaring his feelings towards her; he dared not speak, and although she saw that he preferred her to all the others, and this preference was enough to assure her of his feelings, yet she was sometimes troubled by his silence and sometimes glad of it. "If he does love me," she said, "how am I to receive such a declaration? If I am angry, it may cause his death; if I treat him kindly, I should die myself of shame and grief. I, born a princess, to listen to a shepherd! Oh! unworthy weakness, I shall never consent. I must not change my heart with my costume, and already I have only too many things to reproach myself with since I have been here."

The prince had a beautiful voice, and even had he sung less well, the princess, already prepossessed in his favour, would doubtless have taken the same pleasure in listening to him. She often made him sing little songs, and they were so tender and pathetic that she could not choose but listen. He continually recited to her the verses he had composed, and she well knew that she herself was their subject. These are they :—

> " If there could be
> A divinity
> With beauty fair as thine
> Who should offer beside
> The whole world wide
> To make me feel her charms divine,
> I'd find it a pleasure
> To despise all her treasure
> And offer my vows at thy shrine ".

Although she pretended to pay no more heed to that one than to the others, she could not help giving it a preference that delighted the prince, and made him a little bolder. He went on purpose to a spot shaded by willows and hornbeams; he knew that Carpillon led her lambs there every day: with a bodkin he wrote on the bark of a tree :—

> " In vain within this spot secluded
> Peace and pleasure I espy;
> Me long since has rest deluded,
> And for very love I sigh ".

Just as he had finished, the princess arrived; he pretended to feel confused, and after a short silence: "You see," said he, "an unhappy shepherd who grieves for foolish things, evils of which he should complain only to you ". She made no reply, and lowering her eyes, gave him all the time he could want for declaring his feelings.

While he was speaking, she turned over in her mind what she ought to reply to a man by no means indifferent to her, a fact that led her willingly to excuse him. "He is ignorant of my birth," she mused, "his boldness is excusable, he loves me, and does not imagine that I am above him; when he learns my rank—but do not the high gods desire the hearts of mortals? Are they angry because they are loved?" "Shepherd," she said, when he stopped speaking, "I pity you, and that is all I can do for you, for I do not desire to love—my misfortunes are already too many; alas! then, what would be my fate if I added to them the troubles of some love promise?" "Rather say, shepherdess," he exclaimed, "that if you are miserable, nothing could better console you. I should share all your troubles, and my one desire will be to please you; you could give over to me the care of your flock." "Heaven be praised!" she said, "if that were my only care!" "Can you have others?" he said, eagerly; "you, so young, so fair, without ambition, knowing nothing of the empty vanities of the court? But doubtless you love some one here; a rival makes you so cruel to me." So saying, he changed colour, and became sad, for the thought tortured him cruelly. "I must tell you," she replied, "that you have a rival I hate and abhor; you would never have seen me had I not been forced to fly from his eager pursuit of me." "May be, shepherdess," he said, "you will fly from me in the same way; for if you hate him because he loves you, in your eyes I must be the most hated of men." "Whether I do not believe him," she replied, "or whether I regard you more favourably, I do not think I should take so much trouble to run away from you as from him." The shepherd was overcome with joy at those kind words, and from that moment took the greatest trouble to please the princess.

Every morning he searched for the most beautiful flowers for his garlands; he decked her crook with ribbons of all the colours of the rainbow. He would not allow her to expose herself to the heat of the sun. When she came with the flock along the river side, or into the wood, he bent the branches, fastened them carefully together, and thus made shady arbours where the turf formed natural seats; all the trees bore her name; he carved verses on them that spoke only of Carpillon's beauty, he sang of her alone; the young princess witnessed all these tokens of the shepherd's passion, sometimes with love, sometimes with anxiety. She loved him without acknowledging it, and did not dare to examine herself for fear of discovering too tender sentiments; but does not the possession of such a fear prove what it is we fear?

The young shepherd's love for the shepherdess could not be kept secret; everybody perceived it and approved; who could blame him in a place where all things loved? To see them was to feel sure they were born for each other they were both perfect; surely the gods had entrusted one of their masterpieces to their land, and every effort must be made to keep them there. Carpillon was conscious of a secret joy when she saw how everybody liked a shepherd she found so charming; but when she thought of the difference of rank she was troubled, and determined, in order to leave the heart free, never to make her sentiments known.

The king and queen, who loved her exceedingly, were not sorry to see this dawning passion; they looked upon the prince as their son, and the perfection of the princess charmed them no less. Did not the amazon send them? they said, and did not she fight the centaur for the child? Undoubtedly the wise fairy destines them for each other: we must await her commands.

In this condition things remained; the prince was always lamenting Carpillon's indifference, for she carefully concealed her feelings. One day, however, during the chase, he was unable to escape from an infuriated bear that, springing suddenly out of the depths of a rock, threw itself upon him, and would have destroyed him had not his skill equalled his courage. After struggling for a long time at the top of a mountain, they rolled in a tight embrace to the bottom. Carpillon and her companions happened to be in that place; they could not, of course, see what was happening above them, and great was their horror when a man and bear rolled down. The princess recognised her shepherd at once, and uttered cries of grief and horror. The shepherdesses ran away, but Carpillon remained a spectator of the fight, and, love increasing her strength, was even bold enough to thrust her sheep-hook in the terrible beast's mouth, and enabled her to be of some use to her lover. When he saw her, the fear that she must share his danger increased his courage to such a degree that he thought no more of his own life, but only how he could best save that of the shepherdess. He succeeded in killing the bear at her very feet, but fell down himself half dead from the effects of two wounds he had received. Oh! what feelings were hers when she saw him bleed, and that the blood stained his clothes! She could not speak, the tears streamed down her face, she bowed her head on her knees, and suddenly breaking the silence, said: "Shepherd, if you die I shall die with you; in vain have I hidden my most sacred feelings; learn them now, and know that my life is bound up with yours." "What greater happiness could I have, fair shepherdess!" he exclaimed; "whatever happens to me, I am happy."

The shepherdesses who had run away returned with some shepherds whom they had informed of what they had seen. They came to the assistance of the prince and princess, for she was as ill as he. While they were cutting branches to make a sort of litter, the fairy amazon suddenly appeared in their midst. "Do not be uneasy," she said; "let me touch the young shepherd." She took his hand, and putting her golden helmet on his head, " I forbid you to be ill, dear shepherd," she said. He immediately rose, and the helmet, of which the visor was up, showed a martial expression on his countenance, and bright shining eyes that well corresponded with the hopes the fairy had conceived of him. He was astonished at the way in which she had cured him, and at the majesty of her bearing. Overcome with admiration, joy, and gratitude, he threw himself at her feet, and said: " Great queen, a single word, a single look from you has cured me; but, alas! I have a wound in my heart, I do not desire to cure; deign to ease it and improve my fortune that I may share it with this beautiful shepherdess." The princess blushed at those words, for she knew the fairy amazon recognised her, and she feared she would be displeased with her for encouraging a lover so far beneath her. She dared not look at her, and her sighs struck pity to the fairy's heart. " Carpillon," she said, " this shepherd is not unworthy of your esteem ; and you, shepherd, who desire a change in your condition, rest assured that shortly a very great one will take place." She vanished in her usual fashion directly she had spoken these words. They were led in triumph to the village by the shepherds and shepherdesses who had come to their aid. They placed the lovers in their midst and crowned them with flowers in sign of the victory they had gained over the terrible bear. They took it with them and sang these words about Carpillon's affection for the prince :—

" In these forests everything
Works a charm ;
Each day joy to us shall bring
Free from harm.
A shepherd, famed for beauty rare,
In these groves
Hath captivated e'en the fair
Daughter of Loves."

Thus they reached Sublime's house and told him what had happened, of the courage with which the shepherd had defended himself against the bear, of the generosity with which the shepherdess had assisted him, and of what the fairy amazon had done for them. The king, delighted with the tale, hastened to impart it to the queen. " Undoubtedly," he said, " the boy and girl are no common beings ; their great perfection and beauty, and the care the fairy amazon takes of them, points to something extraordinary." The queen, suddenly remembering the diamond ring Carpillon had given her, said : " I always forgot to show you a ring the young shepherdess delivered to my keeping with an air of dignity very uncommon, begging me to accept it and provide her with clothes such as were worn in this country." " Is the stone beautiful ?" said the king.

" I only looked at it for a moment," said the queen, " but here it is." She gave him the ring, and no sooner did he see it than he exclaimed : " O God ! what do I see ? Do you not recognise a present I received from you ? " So saying, he pressed a spring of which he knew the secret ; the diamond flew back, and the queen saw a portrait of herself she had had painted for the king, and had tied round her little girl's neck for a plaything when she was an infant in the tower. " Ah, sire," she said, " what strange chance is this ? It renews my grief; but let us speak to the shepherdess ; we must know more."

She called her and said : " My daughter, I have waited for your confession until now, and I should have been much pleased had you made it of your own accord. But since you persist in hiding from us who you are, it is only fair to tell you that we know ; the ring you gave me has solved the enigma." " Alas ! mother," replied the princess, kneeling beside her, " it is from no want of confidence that I concealed my rank ; I thought you would be distressed to see a princess in my condition. My father was king of the Peaceful Isles ; his reign was disturbed by an usurper who imprisoned him and his queen in a tower. After three years of captivity, with the help of a gaoler, they escaped. Under cover of the night, they let me down in a basket, but the rope gave way. I fell into the lake, and, without knowing how it happened that I was not drowned, some fishermen found me in the nets they had cast for catching carp, and by my size and weight took me for one of the big carp for which the lake was famous. When they saw me they were disappointed, and thought of throwing me back into the lake as food for the fish ; but, in the end, they decided to keep me and take me to the tyrant ; he knew at once, through my family's escape, that I was a little unfortunate helpless princess. His wife, who was childless, pitied me, kept me with her, and brought me up under the name of Carpillon. Possibly one wanted to make me forget my family, but my heart always told me who I was, and it is indeed a great misfortune to have feelings not in keeping with one's fate. However, a prince called Hunchback wrested from my father's usurper the kingdom he was so peacefully enjoying.

" The change of government made my fate still worse. Hunchback carried me off as one of the most splendid ornaments of his conquest, and resolved to marry me quite against my inclination. In such an extremity I determined to run away, dressed as a shepherdess, and leading a cow. Prince Hunchback searched for me everywhere, and would doubtless have recognised me had not the fairy amazon kindly given me a bunch of gillyflowers as a protection from my enemies. She was equally kind, my dear mother, in sending me to you," continued the princess, " and if I did not tell you of my rank, it was from no want of confidence, but only to spare you pain. I do not, however, complain," she went on; "ever since the day you received me among you I have known peace, and I confess a country life is so sweet and innocent that it is no great hardship to give up that of the court."

As she spoke with much vehemence, she did not observe that the queen was weeping and that the king's eyes were moist; directly she finished they eagerly clasped her in their arms, keeping her there some time in silence. She was equally affected, and following their example, began to weep, and it is impossible to describe the pleasant and sorrowful thoughts of these three illustrious and unfortunate beings. At length the queen, with an effort, said: "Is it possible, dear child of my heart, that after grieving so greatly for your loss, the gods restore you to your mother to console her in her misfortune? Yes, my daughter, you behold her who bore you and who nourished you in your earliest infancy, and here is he who is the author of your being. O light of our eyes! O princess! whom heaven in its wrath took from us, with what joy we celebrate your happy return!" "And I, illustrious mother, dearest queen, in what words and by what actions can I express the respect and love I feel for you both? You protected and sheltered me in my misfortunes at a time when I had no hope of ever seeing you again." They redoubled their caresses, and several hours passed. Carpillon then withdrew; her parents forbade her to mention what had happened, fearing the curiosity of the shepherds; for the most part they were very dense, yet they might desire to penetrate a mystery that in no way concerned them.

The princess kept the secret from all to whom she was indifferent, but she could not keep silence to her young shepherd; how can we be silent when we love? She continually reproached herself for concealing her origin, and thought: "Under how great an obligation he would be to me if he knew that born in the purple I stooped to him, but love makes little distinction between the sceptre and the sheep-hook! Can the greatly vaunted chimerical grandeur of a court satisfy our souls? No, only virtue can do that; it places us above thrones and forces us from them. The shepherd who loves me is virtuous, intelligent and amiable; what could a prince be more?"

As she was indulging in these thoughts, she saw him at her feet; he had followed her to the river side, and giving her a garland of the most beautiful and varied flowers, said: "Where have you been, fair shepherdess? I have been seeking you for some hours, and await you impatiently." "Shepherd," she replied, "I have been occupied in a strange affair, and I should be much to blame if I did not tell you of it, but remember that this mark of confidence exacts eternal silence on your part. I am a princess, my father was a king, and I have just found him in the person of Sublime."

This news disturbed the prince to such a degree that he had not strength enough to interrupt her while she related her story with all the kindness imaginable. Indeed he had some cause for fear, because the good shepherd who had brought him up might, since he was a king, refuse him his daughter, and she herself, reflecting on the difference between a great princess and a poor shepherd, might withdraw the favour she had shown him. "Ah, madam," he said, sadly, "I am lost, I must die: you are of royal birth and have found your family, while I am an unfortunate creature who knows neither country nor fatherland: an eagle served me for a mother and her nest for a cradle. If, hitherto, you have deigned to regard me with favour, in the future you will turn from me." The princess considered a moment, and without replying took a pin that fastened her beautiful hair and wrote on the back of a tree :—

> " Love you a heart that loves you dearly ? "

The prince then carved these words :—

> " Passion most ardent my heart inflames ".

And the princess put beneath :—

> " Enjoy then of loving the happiness great,
> And know that thy love is returned ".

The prince, overcome with joy, threw himself at her feet. " You flatter my distressed heart, adored princess," he said, "and by your new kindness you preserve my life; remember what you've just written in my favour.". " I cannot forget it," she replied, graciously; "you may depend on my heart. I care more for your interests than for my own." Their conversation would undoubtedly have been prolonged had there been more time, but it was necessary to lead the flocks home, and they hastened to return.

Meanwhile the king and queen conferred as to their course of action in respect of Carpillon and the young shepherd. As long as she had remained unknown, they had regarded the dawning passion rising in their young hearts with approval; the perfect beauty they possessed, their intelligence, and the grace of all their actions made them desire their union. But when they learned that Carpillon was their daughter, while the shepherd was probably some outcast exposed to the wild beasts in order to save the necessity of rearing him, they took quite a different view of the matter. They resolved to tell Carpillon she must no longer permit him to cherish hope, and must seriously tell him she did not intend to settle in that land.

The queen soon summoned her, and spoke to her very kindly. But of what avail are words in such terrible distress? The young princess tried in vain to console herself; her face now brilliantly red, now deathly pale, her eyes dim with sorrow, clearly testified to her condition. Ah! how she repented of her confession! But she assured her mother, with submission, that she would obey her; she had scarcely strength enough to throw herself on her bed, where she lay weeping and moaning.

At length she got up, for she had to lead her flock to pasture; but instead. of going towards the river, she went far into the wood, and lying on the moss, she bowed her head and fell a-dreaming. The prince, who could not rest away from her, went in search of her, and suddenly presented himself before her. At sight of him she uttered a loud cry as if surprised, and hastily rising, went off without looking at him. He, astounded at this strange conduct, followed her, and stopping her, said: "Why, shepherdess, while condemning me to death, do you wish to escape the pleasure of seeing me die before your eyes? You have indeed changed towards your shepherd; you have already forgotten your promise of yesterday." "Alas!" she said, looking at him sadly, "of what crime do you accuse me? I am unhappy: I am obeying orders I cannot avoid; pity me, and keep away from the places I frequent; indeed, it must be so." "I am to shun you, divine princess!" he said, folding his arms with a melancholy air, "and you are yourself capable of pronouncing so cruel and little-deserved a command? What do you suppose will be the effect on me? Can I crush the flattering hope you permitted me to indulge, and continue to live?" Carpillon, as despairing as her lover, fell down lifeless and voiceless; at that sight he was agitated by a thousand different thoughts: his mistress's condition assured him that she had no part in the cruel command, and that in some degree alleviated his distress.

He did not lose a moment in coming to her assistance: a stream that trickled under the grass furnished water to throw in her face, and the doves hidden behind a bush whispered he might steal a kiss. However that might be, she soon opened her eyes, and pushing away her lover, said: "Fly, leave me; if my mother came, would she not have every right to be angry?" "Must I leave you to be eaten by bears and wild boars?" he said, "or during a long swoon in these deserted wilds, to be stung by some asp or snake?" "Everything must be risked," she said, "except the queen's displeasure."

While they were holding a conversation so full of affection and regard, their guardian, the fairy, suddenly appeared in the king's room. She was armed as usual, and the precious stones with which her helmet and cuirass were adorned were scarcely as bright as her eyes. Addressing the queen, she said: "You are scarcely grateful, madam, for the recovery of your daughter, who, without my aid, would have been drowned, since you are about to cause the death of the shepherd I entrusted to your care. Think no more of the difference between him and Carpillon; it is time to unite them. Make all ready for the wedding; I desire it, and you shall never repent it."

With these words, without awaiting their reply, she left them. She disappeared from view, leaving behind her a long track of light like a sunbeam.

The king and queen were much surprised and felt glad the fairy's orders were so positive. "There can be no doubt," said the king, "that this unknown shepherd's rank is equal to Carpillon's. His protectress is too noble to desire the union of two persons unsuited to each other. It is she, as you perceive, who saved our daughter from drowning in the lake. How have we deserved her protection ? " ." I have often heard," replied the queen, " that there exist good and bad fairies, who, according to their disposition, have affection or hatred for families ; evidently the fairy amazon is favourable to us." They were talking thus when the princess returned, looking sad and ill. The prince, who had only dared to follow her at a distance, arrived shortly after, so melancholy that a mere glance at him showed what was passing in his mind. During the meal the poor lovers, who were usually the gayest of all, spoke never a word and hardly dared to raise their eyes.

As soon as they left the table, the king went into his little garden, and asked the shepherd to accompany him. At this command he grew pale, and trembled in all his limbs, and Carpillon, thinking her father was going to send him away, was equally frightened. Sublime entered a summer-house and sat down. Looking at the prince, he said : "My son, you know the love with which I have brought you up. I have considered you a gift of the gods to support and console my old age, and, to prove my affection, I have chosen you to be the husband of my daughter, Carpillon. You have sometimes heard me deplore her loss. Heaven has restored her to me, and desires that she should be yours, and I, too, wish it with all my heart ; are you the only one who is not willing ? " " Oh ! my father," exclaimed the prince, kneeling, " dare I believe what I hear ? Am I really so fortunate in that your choice has fallen on me, or do you wish to know my sentiments towards this beautiful princess ? " " No, my son," said the king, "you have no need to hover between hope and fear ; I mean to conclude the marriage in a few days." " You overwhelm me with kindness," replied the prince, kneeling, " and if I express my gratitude awkwardly, the excess of my joy is the cause." Sublime made him get up, and assured him again and again of his regard, and although he did not reveal to him his high rank, he gave him to understand that his birth was far above the condition to which fortune had reduced him.

But Carpillon's anxiety was so great that she could not rest until she had followed her father and her lover into the garden. Hidden behind some trees, she observed them from a distance. When she saw the shepherd at the king's feet, she thought he was asking not to be sent away, and not wishing to know more, she ran into the depths of the forest, speeding along like a fawn pursued by dogs and huntsmen; she feared nothing, neither the ferocity of wild beasts, nor the thorns that caught her on either side. Echo repeated her sad laments, and she seemed to be seeking death when the shepherd, impatient to tell her the good news, hastened after her. "Where are you, my shepherdess, my beloved Carpillon?" he shouted; "if you hear me, do not flee. We are to be happy."

As he uttered these words, he spied her at the bottom of a dell surrounded by huntsmen who were attempting to put her up behind a little deformed hunchback mounted on a horse. At this sight and at the sound of his mistress's cries for help, he advanced swifter than an arrow shot from the bow, and with no other weapon than his sling, gave the man who was carrying off his shepherdess so unerring and terrible a blow, that he fell from his horse with a dreadful wound in his head.

Carpillon fell also; the prince was beside her directly, trying to defend her against her ravishers. But his resistance was of no avail; they seized him and would have cut his throat on the spot if Prince Hunchback, for it was he, had not signed to his people to spare him, for he said: "I wish him to die of many different tortures". They contented themselves with binding him in thick ropes, and as the same bonds served for the princess, they were able to talk together.

A litter was made for the wicked Hunchback: directly it was ready they set off before any of the shepherds had discovered the accident that had befallen the young lovers. Sublime knew nothing of what had happened. His anxiety may easily be imagined when night came on and they did not return. The queen was equally alarmed, and several days were spent in searching and weeping for them, but without avail.

Prince Hunchback had not forgotten Princess Carpillon, but time had cooled his ardour; when he was not amusing himself in committing a few murders and cutting the throats of all who displeased him he went hunting, and was often seven or eight days without returning home. It was on one of these occasions that he saw the·princess. Her grief was so great and she took so little heed of what might befall her that she had not her bunch of gillyflowers with her, so that as soon as he saw her he recognised her.

"Oh! of all misfortunes this is the greatest," said the shepherd, softly, "we had, alas, just reached the happy moment of being united for ever." He told her what had passed between Sublime and himself. Carpillon's regret may be easily understood. "I am then to cost you your life," she said, bursting into tears; "I am myself leading you to torture, you for whom I would give my life. I am the cause of your misfortunes, and by my own carelessness have fallen again into the barbarous hands of my most cruel persecutor."

They conversed thus until they reached the town in which the good old king, wicked Hunchback's father, lived; he was informed that his son was being brought back in a litter, because a young shepherd in defending his shepherdess had dangerously wounded him with a blow of the stone from his sling. The king, distressed even to tears that his only son should be in such a condition, ordered the shepherd to be thrown into a dungeon. Hunchback gave secret commands that Carpillon should receive the same treatment: he had fully made up his mind either to marry her or to torture her to death. The two lovers were only separated by a door that was so ill-made that when the sun was at its height they had the sad consolation of seeing each other through the chinks; during the rest of the day and night they could only converse.

What tender and passionate things they said! Everything the heart could feel and the mind conceive they expressed in words so pathetic that they wept bitterly, and may be, if we repeated them, they would draw tears from our readers.

Hunchback's confidants visited the princess every day and threatened a speedy death if she did not purchase her life by consenting with a good grace to their marriage. She received the proposals with a firmness and disdain that made them despair of success. As soon as she could speak to the prince, she said: " Do not fear, my shepherd, that dread of the most cruel tortures will make me unfaithful; although it has not been granted us to live together, we can at least die together ". " Do you intend to console me, fair princess ? " he replied. " Alas ! would I not rather see you in the arms of the monster than in the power of the executioner ? " She did not agree with these sentiments, accused him of weakness, and assured him that she would show him how to die courageously.

Hunchback's wound being a little better and his love irritated by the princess's obstinate refusals, in his rage he determined to put her to death with the shepherd who had ill-treated him. He appointed the day for this mournful tragedy, and begged the king, with all the senators and nobles of the kingdom, to grace it with his presence. Hunchback was there in an open litter to feast his eyes on the horrid spectacle. As I said before, the king did not know that Carpillon was a prisoner. When he saw her led to the torture in company with the poor governess whom Hunchback condemned with her, and the young shepherd more beautiful than the day, he ordered them to be brought to the terrace where he sat surrounded by all the court.

Without waiting for the princess to speak and complain of her unworthy treatment, he hastened to cut the ropes that bound her, and, looking at the shepherd, was moved with kindness and pity. " Rash young man," he said, forcing himself to speak harshly, " who inspired you with boldness enough to attack a great prince and to bring him to the point of death ? " At the sight of the venerable old man dressed in the royal robes, the shepherd was conscious of an impulse of respect and confidence he had never felt before. " Great king," he said, with admirable courage, " the danger of this beautiful princess was the cause of my rashness. I did not know your son, and how was I to recognise him in an action so violent and so unworthy of his rank ? "

He emphasised his words with gesture and accent ; his arm was bare and the arrow on it too plainly visible for the king not to see it. " Oh ye gods ! " he exclaimed, " am I mistaken, or do I see in you my beloved long-lost son ? " " No, great king," said the fairy amazon from the upper air, where she appeared mounted on a magnificent white horse, " no, you are not mistaken, this is your son ; I protected him while he was in the eagle's nest whither his cruel brother had ordered him to be taken ; he must console you for the loss of the other." So saying, she swooped down on guilty Hunchback, and striking her fiery lance to his heart, made short work of him, and he was burned as if by lightning.

She then approached the terrace and presented the prince with arms. " I promised them to you," she said ; " they will make you invulnerable and the greatest warrior in the world." At the same moment the warlike sounds of a thousand trumpets and instruments of war were heard, but the noise soon gave way to a sweet symphony that sang melodiously the praises of the prince and princess. Fairy amazon dismounted, approached the king, and begged him to give at once the orders necessary for the wedding : she sent a little fairy, who appeared directly she was summoned, to fetch the shepherd king, the queen and their daughter, and ordered her to return speedily. No sooner had she departed than she came back with those illustrious and unfortunate persons. What happiness after their prolonged troubles ! The palace resounded with cries of joy never before equalled.

Fairy amazon gave orders everywhere ; one of her words did more than a thousand people. The wedding was solemnised with a magnificence previously unknown. King Sublime returned to his realms, and Carpillon had the great happiness of taking with her her beloved husband. The old king, enchanted with a son so worthy of his affection, grew young again—at least his old age was so full of joy that he lived a great while longer.

THE BENEVOLENT FROG.

THERE was once a king who for a long time had been engaged in a war with his neighbours. After many battles, the enemy laid siege to his capital. The queen was at that time in delicate health, and, fearing for her safety, the king begged her to retire to a castle he had had fortified. With prayers and tears the queen tried to persuade him to let her stay with him and share his fate, but in vain, and he put her into the chariot prepared for her departure, amid loud expressions of grief. The king ordered his guards to accompany her, and told her he would try and get away unnoticed, and come and pay her a visit. He indulged her with the hope merely to soothe her, for the castle was a very long way off, and surrounded by a thick forest; only those well acquainted with the road could possibly reach it.

The queen departed much distressed at leaving her husband exposed to the dangers of war. She travelled by short stages lest the fatigue of so long a journey should cause illness; at length, very miserable and wretched, she reached the castle. When she had somewhat recovered, she explored the surrounding country, and found it most unpleasing. Wherever she looked she saw vast desert tracts, whose ugliness caused her much grief. She gazed at them sadly, and sometimes said: "What a contrast this place is to that in which I have lived all my life! If I stay here much longer I shall die. I've no one to speak to in this solitary spot; how can I relieve my anxiety? What have I done to the king that he should banish me? He certainly wishes to make me feel the bitterness of his absence when he sends me to so unpleasant a place."

Thus she complained, and although he wrote to her every day, and gave her very favourable news of the siege, she became more and more miserable, and at length resolved to return to the king. But the officers who accompanied her

(304)

had orders not to take her back until the king should send a special messenger. For that reason she kept her determination to herself, and ordered a small chariot to be built to hold one person only, saying she should sometimes like to accompany the hunt. She drove it herself, and followed the hounds so closely that she went along quicker than the huntsmen themselves. By this means she had absolute command of the chariot, and could get away whenever she liked. The only difficulty was her ignorance of the forest roads, but she indulged the hope that the gods would be good to her, and guide her aright. After performing sacrifice to them, she commanded a great hunt to be held; everybody was to take part in it, she in her chariot as usual, and each was to take a different route, in order to leave no possibility of retreat to the wild beasts. The young queen, full of the joy of soon seeing her husband, had dressed herself very prettily; her broad-brimmed hat was adorned with feathers of many colours, her jacket was trimmed with precious stones, and this, added to her beauty, which was quite out of the common, made her seem a second Diana.

When her people were entirely absorbed in the pleasures of the chase, she gave rein to her horses, whipped them up, and shouted to them; off they went at full gallop, and then running away at the top of their speed, the chariot flew along faster than the wind, and the eye could scarcely follow it. Too late the queen repented of her rash action. "Whatever was I thinking of?" she said; "as if I could manage these spirited, untractable horses all by myself; alas! what will become of me? If the king, who loves me so dearly and sent me away from him in order to assure my safety, knew of my danger, what would he do? This is how I repay his loving care of me, and the child of whom I am to be the mother will be with myself the victim of my imprudence." The air resounded with her sorrowful wailing; she implored aid of the gods, of the fairies, but both had forsaken her. The chariot was upset, she had not strength to jump out quickly enough, and her foot was caught between the wheel and the axle-tree; nothing short of a miracle could save her.

She remained wholly unconscious, stretched on the ground at the foot of a tree; her face was covered with blood. When she came to herself, she saw near her a woman of gigantic stature, clothed in the skin of a lion. Her arms and legs were bare, her hair tied up with the dried skin of a snake, whose head hung over her shoulders; a thorn club in her hand served for a stick to lean on, and a quiver full of arrows was fastened at her side. The sight of such an extraordinary creature convinced the queen she must be dead, for it never occurred to her that after so terrible an accident she could still be living, and speaking, she said: "I am not surprised that it should be so difficult to resolve to die, since what is to be seen in the other world is so frightful." The giantess heard her, and could not help laughing at the queen for thinking herself dead. "Take courage," she said, "you are still in the land of the living, but your fate is none the less sad. I am the Fairy Lioness, and I dwell close here; you must come and live with me."

The queen looked at her sadly and said: "Madam Lioness, be good enough to take me back to my castle, and then demand of the king any ransom you please. He loves me so dearly that he would not refuse even half his kingdom." "No," she replied, "I am rich enough, but for some time now I have been growing weary of my loneliness; and you are intelligent and will perhaps amuse me." She then assumed the shape of a lioness, and taking the queen on her back, carried her to the depths of her grotto, and cured her wounds by rubbing her with a cordial.

Picture the surprise and grief of the queen, when she found herself in that horrible place! It was reached by ten thousand steps that led to the centre of the earth; the only light came from some big lamps that were reflected in a quicksilver lake, full of monsters who would have terrified a less timid queen; owls, screech-owls, ravens, and other birds of evil omen abounded; in the distance was a mountain whence flowed a sluggish stream composed of all the tears shed by unhappy lovers; the sad Loves had gathered them into a reservoir. The trees were bare of leaves and fruit, the ground was covered with marigolds, briers and nettles. The food was suitable to the climate of such a detestable country: a few dried roots, horse-chestnuts and bedeguars was all it could offer to appease the hunger of the unfortunate creatures who fell into Lioness's hands.

Directly the queen was sufficiently recovered to be able to work, the fairy told her that, as she would have to live with her all her life, she had better build herself a little house. The princess could not refrain from weeping: " Alas !" she exclaimed, " what have I done to you, that you would keep me here ? If my death, which is, I feel sure, not far off, would give you any pleasure, kill me at once. It is the only kindness I dare hope for from you; do not condemn me to live a long and miserable life away from my husband." Lioness mocked at her grief, and advised her to dry her tears and try and please her; indeed if she did not do so, she would be the unhappiest woman in the world. " Is there no way of touching your heart ? " replied the queen. " I am extremely fond," she said, " of fly pasties, and should be very glad if you could catch enough to make me a pie of large size and excellent quality." " But," said the queen, " there are none here, and if there were, I could not see to catch them by this dim light, and even if I got possession of them, I don't know how to make pastry, so that I cannot possibly execute your orders." " That does not matter," said hard-hearted Lioness, " I shall give you what commands I please."

The queen did not reply. She thought that, in spite of the fairy's cruelty, she had only one life to lose, and, in her condition, what was there to regret ? Instead of looking for flies, she sat down under a yew and began her sad com-plainings, " What grief will be yours, my beloved husband," she said, " when you come to seek me and find me gone ! You will think I am dead or untrue ; I would rather you should weep for my death than for the loss of my affection. Perhaps the broken chariot and the ornaments I had put on to make myself pleasing in your eyes will be found in the forest. You will then be certain of my death, and will very likely bestow on another the affection you had for me. But since I am not to return to the world, I shall never know it."

She would have continued in this strain for ever so long, if she had not heard above her head the miserable croaking of a raven. She looked up, and by the faint glimmer that lighted the shore saw a big raven holding a frog with the intention of devouring it. " Although nothing here is likely to have pity on me," she said, " I will attempt to rescue the poor frog, for she is as unfortunate in her degree as I am in mine." Using the first stick that came to hand, she forced the raven to relax its hold. The frog fell down, was stunned for a moment or two, and, on recovering her froggish wits, said : " You are the only kind-hearted person I have met since curiosity brought me to this place." " By what miracle are you able to speak, little frog ? " replied the queen, " and who are the people you have met here ? as yet I have seen no one." " All the monsters who dwell in the lake," was the reply, " were once in the world ; some on the throne, some the trusted counsellors of their sovereigns, others were the mis-tresses of kings and cost the state much blood : these last have become leeches.

Fate sends them here for a time, but they return no better than when they came."
"So many wicked people together," said the queen, "are not likely to improve each other; but, with regard to yourself, my talkative frog, what are you doing here?" "Curiosity led me here," she replied: "I am a demi-fairy; my power is limited in some directions, and very far-reaching in others; if Lioness found me in her kingdom, she would surely kill me."

"But," said the queen, "if you are a fairy or a demi-fairy, how comes it that a raven was going to devour you?" "That I can explain in two words," replied the frog; "my power resides in a little hood of roses. When it is on my head I fear nothing, but unfortunately I left it in the marsh, and so the wretched raven came swooping down upon me; I confess, madam, that failing your aid, I should now be dead. Since I owe my life to you, if I can do anything to lessen your sufferings, command me as you please." "Alas! my dear frog," said the queen, "the wicked fairy whose prisoner I am has commanded me to make her a fly pasty. Now, there are no flies here, and if there were I could not see to catch them by this dim light, and thus I am in great danger of dying from her beatings." "Leave it to me," said the frog; "in a very short time I will provide you with the flies." She then rubbed herself all over with sugar, and more than six thousand frogs of her acquaintance did the same. They went to a place that abounded in flies, for the wicked fairy kept a store of them for the express purpose of tormenting certain unfortunate persons. As soon as the flies smelt the sugar, they stuck to it, and the helpful frogs returned with great speed to the queen. Never had there been such a large take of flies, or a more excellent pasty than that the queen made for Lioness. She was extremely surprised to receive it, failing to understand how the queen had been able to catch the flies.

Since she was exposed to the inclemency of the poisonous atmosphere, the queen determined to commence building her hut, and cut down cypress trees for the purpose. The frog generously offered her services, and putting herself at the head of those of her friends who had assisted to procure the flies, they helped the queen to erect the prettiest little building imaginable. But she was scarcely installed in it when the monsters of the lake, envying her rest and comfort, tormented her with the most horrible uproar ever heard. Dreadfully frightened, she got up and fled, exactly what the monsters desired. A dragon, formerly the tyrant of one of the finest kingdoms of the universe, took possession of it.

The poor queen attempted to complain, but the monsters jeered and hooted at her, and Fairy Lioness told her that if in the future she deafened her with her lamentations, she would give her a sound thrashing. She was obliged to be silent, and had recourse to the frog, who had proved herself so kind. They wept in company, for when the frog wore her hood of roses she laughed and cried like a human being. "I am so fond of you," she said, "that I will rebuild your house and drive all the monsters of the lake to despair." She prepared the wood, and the rustic palace was so quickly finished that the queen retired to it for the night.

The frog, anxious to do all she could for the queen's comfort, made her a bed of wild thyme. When the wicked fairy discovered that the queen did not lie on the bare ground, she sent for her and asked: "What men or gods are protecting you? The land here, watered by a rain of burning sulphur, never produces so much as a sprig of sage, and I hear that notwithstanding sweet-smelling plants grow under your feet!" "I do not know the reason, madam," said the queen; "if I attribute it to anything, it is perhaps to the child shortly to be born to me, who is, I trust, to be less unfortunate than I am."

"I am most desirous," said the fairy, "of having a bouquet of rare flowers; try to procure them for me. If you are unsuccessful blows will be your reward; I give them very often, and with sure effect." The queen began to weep; such threats were scarcely reassuring, and the impossibility of finding the flowers threw her into despair.

She returned to her dwelling; her friend the frog came to see her. "How sad you seem," she said. "Alas! my dear friend, who would not be sad?" said the queen. "The fairy wants a bouquet of beautiful flowers; where am I to find them? You see those that grow here, but if I do not satisfy her it is all over with me." "Sweet princess," said the frog, graciously, "I must try to pull you out of the difficulty: there is a bat living here, the only one with whom I am acquainted. She's a good creature, and moves about faster than I do; I'll give her my hood of roses, and with its assistance she'll find you the flowers." The queen made a low curtesy, for to embrace the frog was an impossibility.

She gave her orders to the bat, who returned a few hours later, hiding the most lovely flowers under her wings. The queen took them directly to the wicked fairy, who was more surprised than ever, unable to understand by what miracle the queen had procured them.

The princess was always thinking of ways of escape. She told the frog of her desire, and she said: "Madam, let me consult my little hood, and we will act according to its advice". She took it, placing it on some straw, burned in front of it a few sprigs of juniper, some capers, and two green peas; she croaked five times, and the ceremony over, put on her hood of roses again and began to speak like an oracle.

"Fate, ruler of all things," she said, "forbids you to leave this place; you will here become the mother of a princess more beautiful than Venus herself; do not trouble yourself about anything, time alone will relieve you."

The queen looked down, a few tears fell from her eyes; but she decided to trust her friend. "At least," she said, "do not forsake me, and since my child is to be born here, be with me at the time." The kind-hearted frog promised, and comforted the queen as best one could.

But it is time to return to the king. While his enemies kept him besieged in his capital, he was not able to send messengers continually to the queen: but after some sallies against the enemy he compelled them to raise the siege. He was far less joyful about this great event than that he could now without fear seek the queen. He had not heard of the accident, none of his officers had dared to inform him of it. They had found the broken chariot, the runaway horses, and the amazon ornaments she had put on when she set out to find the king, and never doubted her death for a moment. They supposed she had been devoured by wild beasts, and therefore thought it best to assure the king that she had died suddenly. He thought he should die of grief at such sad news. Dishevelled hair, the shedding of many tears, pitiable cries, sobs, sighs, and other of the usual accompaniments of bereavement were not wanting to the occasion.

After spending several days without seeing or desiring to see any one, he returned to the capital and entered on a long mourning, felt more deeply at heart than could be testified by any outward trappings. The neighbouring kings sent ambassadors with messages of condolence, and after the ceremonies consequent on such misfortunes, he granted his subjects a period of peace, exempted them from service in war, and obtained for them excellent opportunities of profitable commerce.

The queen was unaware of those events. In course of time she became the mother of a little princess, as beautiful as the frog had predicted; they called her Moufette, and with great difficulty the queen obtained Lioness's permission to rear her; she was so cruel and savage that she would have much preferred to eat her.

Moufette, the marvel of her time, had reached the age of six, and the queen, looking at her with an air of mingled love and affection, said continually: "Ah! if only the king could see you, my sweetest, how delighted he would be and how he would love you! but perhaps at this very moment he is beginning to forget me; he imagines us buried for ever in the horrors of death, and most likely the place in his heart that once was mine is now occupied by another."

These melancholy reflections were accompanied with many tears. Frog, who loved her faithfully, seeing her weep, said one day: "If you like, madam,

I will go and find your husband; the journey is long and my rate of progress slow, but sooner or later I should doubtless reach him ". The proposal was accepted with joy; the queen clasped her hands and made Moufette clasp hers also in sign of the obligation she was under to Madam Frog for undertaking such a task. The queen assured her the king would not be ungrateful. " But," she continued, " what is the use of telling him I am living in this miserable place? He cannot possibly deliver me." " Madam," rejoined the frog, " you must leave that to the gods; let us do all that depends on us."

They said their farewells. The queen wrote to the king with her own blood on a piece of linen, for she had neither ink nor paper. She advised him to trust implicitly in the kind-hearted frog, who would tell him all about her adventures.

The frog took a year and four days to ascend the ten thousand steps that led from the dark plain where the queen lived to the world, and she took another year to make her preparations, for she was too proud to appear at a great court like an obscure little frog from the marshes. She had a litter made large enough to hold two eggs comfortably; it was of tortoise-shell lined with lizard skin. Fifty of the little green grasshoppers that skip about the meadows were her ladies-in-waiting; each was mounted on a snail, with a side-saddle, the leg over the saddle-bow in the most approved fashion. Several water-rats dressed as pages walked in front of the snails whom she constituted her body-guard. There never was a prettier sight; her hood of roses ever fresh and full of bloom suited her admirably. She was in her way something of a coquette, and had put on rouge and patches; it was said that she painted like most of the ladies of that country; but on examination, it was discovered that only her enemies said such things.

She was seven years on the journey; during that time the queen suffered more grief and trouble than can possibly be described, and without Moufette to console her, would never have lived through it. Every time the marvellous little creature opened her mouth or said a word, her mother was enchanted; indeed it was only the Fairy Lioness who did not yield to her charms. When the queen had lived six years in that horrible place, the fairy decided, on condition that all she killed should be hers, to take her hunting.

How delighted the queen was to see the sun once again! So unaccustomed to the light had she become, that she was almost blinded. Moufette was so clever, that although she was only five or six years old, her shots never missed the mark, and by this means the mother and daughter somewhat lessened the fairy's cruelty.

Frog pursued her way by day and night over mountains and valleys, till at last she found herself near the capital city where tne king dwelt. She was surprised to see nothing but dancing and feasting everywhere; the people laughed and sang, and the nearer she approached the town, the greater was the joy and jubilation.   The procession from the marshes surprised everybody; they all followed it, and by the time they entered the town, the crowd became so large that she had much difficulty in reaching the palace.   There everything was in great splendour.   The king, nine years a widower, had at last yielded to his subjects' entreaties, and was on the point of marrying a princess less beautiful, it is true, than his wife, but very charming all the same.

The good frog got out of the litter and entered the king's palace, followed by the whole cortège.   There was no need to ask an audience; the monarch, the fiancée, and all the princes were too anxious to learn the reason of her coming to make any difficulty.   " Sire," she said, " I do not know if the news I bring will give you joy or pain; the marriage you are about to celebrate convinces me that you are untrue to the queen."   " Her memory is always dear to me," said the king, with tears he was unable to keep back; " but you must know, charming frog, that kings cannot always do as they like; for nine years my subjects have been urging me to marry again; I owe them heirs, and my choice has fallen on this young and charming princess."   " I advise you not to marry her," said the frog; " polygamy is a capital crime, and the queen is not dead.   Here is a letter she entrusted to me, written with her blood : you have a little daughter called Moufette, who is more beautiful than the heavens themselves."

The king took the piece of rag on which the queen had scrawled her few words, kissed it, moistened it with his tears, held it up for the whole assembly to see, saying that he recognised the queen's handwriting, and asked the frog a thousand questions, to which she replied with vivacity and intelligence.   The future bride, and the ambassadors bidden to the wedding, pulled long faces.   The most distinguished of them said : " Sire, how, on the mere word of a toad, can you break so solemn an engagement?   This scum of the marsh is insolent enough to come and tell lies at your court, and you actually give heed to what she says."   " Let me inform you, your excellency," replied the frog, " that I am no scum of the marsh, and, since I must display my power, come, fays and fairies, appear."   The frogs, rats, snails, lizards, with herself at their head, were seen no longer under the form of those ugly little animals, but as persons of tall and majestic stature, with faces pleasant to look on, and eyes brighter than stars ; each wore a crown of precious stones on his head, and on his shoulders a royal cloak of velvet lined with ermine, and a long train borne by dwarfs. At the same time trumpets, small drums, big drums and hautboys pierced the clouds with their melodies and warlike sounds; the frogs and fairies began to dance a ballet, and they were so light that the least spring from the ground sent them up to the ceiling of the room. The king and the future queen had scarcely recovered from their surprise when they suddenly saw the dancers change into flowers, jasmine, jonquils, violets, pinks, and tuberoses, but they went on dancing all the same just as if they had legs and feet. It was a living flower-bed, and its graceful motion was as pleasing to the eye as to the smell.

The next instant the flowers disappeared, and were replaced by fountains; they rose rapidly, and fell into the ornamental water that flowed at the foot of the castle walls; it was covered with gilded and painted boats, and they were so pretty that the princess invited her ambassadors to go with her for a sail. They were quite willing, thinking all this a fête that would end in a happy marriage.

But directly they had embarked, the boat, the river, and the fountains disappeared, and the frogs became frogs again. The king asked where the princess was. The frog replied: " Sire, you ought to have no other wife than the queen ; if I were not so great a friend of hers I should not trouble myself about your affairs, but she is a woman of such lofty character, and your daughter Moufette is so charming, that you should not lose a moment in going to their assistance." " I confess, Madam Frog," said the king, " if I did not believe my wife dead there is nothing in the world I would not do to see her again." " After all the marvels I've shown you," she replied, " it seems to me you ought to be fully convinced of the truth of what I tell you. Leave your kingdom in the hands of a trusty counsellor, and do not defer setting out. Here is a ring that will enable you to find the queen and to speak to the Fairy Lioness, although she is the most terrible creature in the world."

The king no longer gave a thought to the princess he had been on the point of marrying, and as his passion for her diminished, his former love for the queen acquired new strength.

After making the frog very handsome presents, he set out alone. " Do not despair," she said at parting: " you will have to overcome great difficulties, but I do not doubt you will succeed in your purpose." The king, somewhat consoled, gave himself up to the guidance of the ring.

As Moufette grew older, her beauty became so perfect that all the monsters of the quicksilver lake fell in love with her; dragons of horrible appearance fawned at her feet. Although they had been there from her birth, she could never get accustomed to the sight of them, and hid her face on her mother's breast, saying: " Shall we stay here long ? Will our misfortunes never end ? " The queen indulged her in comforting hopes, but at heart she despaired; the absence of the frog, her silence, and the long period since any news had been heard of the king distressed her greatly.

The Fairy Lioness gradually made it a rule to take them hunting. She was dainty, and liked the game they killed for her, and as a reward gave them the head or the feet, but it was something to permit them to see daylight once more. The fairy took the form of a lioness, carried the queen and her daughter on her back, and thus they traversed the forests.

The king, led by the ring, stopping once to rest in a forest, saw them go by swift as an arrow from the bow: they did not see him, and when he tried to follow them, they vanished from his sight.

The queen's troubles had not impaired her beauty, and she seemed to him more lovely than ever. His passion was re-kindled, and never doubting that the young princess with her was Moufette, he resolved to die a thousand deaths rather than give up the attempt to recover them.

The good little ring led him to the gloomy region where the queen had lived for so many years, and he was not a little surprised to descend so far into the interior of the earth; however, what he saw there still more astonished him. The Fairy Lioness, who knew all things, had learned the day and hour of his arrival; she would have given much if her presiding genius had ordered things differently. But she determined to offer all resistance in her power.

In the middle of the quicksilver lake she built a palace of crystal that floated on the wave. In it she imprisoned the queen and her daughter, and then harangued the monsters who were in love with Moufette. "You will lose this beautiful princess," she said, "if you do not assist me in defending her against a knight who is coming to carry her off." The monsters promised to do all in their power; they surrounded the palace; the least heavy took up position on the roof and walls, others at the gates, and the rest in the lake.

The king, advised by his faithful ring, went first to the fairy's grotto; she awaited him in the shape of a lioness. Directly she saw him, she threw herself upon him; he drew his sword with a valour she had not expected, and as she stretched out her paw to strike him to the earth, he cut it at the joint, that is, exactly at the elbow. She uttered a loud cry and fell down; he approached her, placed his foot on her breast, and swore he would kill her, and although she was invulnerable, she felt a little afraid. "What do you want of me?" she said, "what do you demand?" "I want to punish you," he replied, boldly, "for carrying off my wife, and unless you restore her, I shall strangle you without delay." "Look at the lake," she said, "and see if she is in my power." The king looked in the direction pointed out, and saw the queen and his daughter in the crystal castle, that without rudder or oar floated on the quicksilver lake like a ship.

He thought he should die of joy and grief; he called them as loudly as he could, and they heard him. But how to get at them ? While he was seeking a way, Fairy Lioness vanished.

He ran along the shores of the lake, and as soon as the palace came near enough for him to reach it, it started off again with terrible swiftness, and his hopes were ever disappointed in the same way. The queen, who feared he would end by growing weary, shouted to him not to lose courage, that the Fairy Lioness wanted to tire him out, but that true love could not be repulsed by the greatest difficulties. She and Moufette stretched forth their hands to him in supplication. At that sight the king was filled with new courage ; he raised his voice and swore by Styx and by Acheron to pass the rest of his life in that gloomy place rather than leave it without them.

Great perseverance was necessary : he spent his time as disagreeably as possible ; the ground covered with thorny briars served him for a bed ; for food he had only wild fruits, more bitter than gall, and had also to sustain frequent combats with the monsters of the lake. A husband who endures such miseries in order to recover his wife certainly belongs to the fairy age, and his actions help to fix the date of my story.

Three years passed, and the king had not gained the least advantage. He was almost disheartened, and determined a hundred times to throw himself into the lake ; he would have done so if he had been able to see that such an act would be of the slightest use to the queen and princess. He was as usual wandering from one side of the lake to the other, when a hideous dragon called him, and said : " If you will swear by your crown and sceptre, by your royal cloak, by your wife and daughter, to give me a certain toothsome morsel I am most desirous of eating, whenever I think good to demand it, I will take you on my wings, and in spite of all the monsters of the lake who guard the crystal castle, I will rescue the queen and Princess Moufette."

" Ah ! my dearest dragon," exclaimed the king, " I swear to you and all your kin that you shall eat your fill, and I shall ever remain your humble servant." " Do not pledge yourself unless you mean to keep your word," replied the dragon, " for if you break your promise, misfortunes so terrible that you would remember them for the rest of your life will arise." The king renewed his protestations ; he was dying with impatience to set his beloved queen free ; he mounted the dragon as if it had been the finest horse possible. The monsters opposed their advance, they fought, and nothing was heard but the sharp hissing of serpents, nothing was seen but fire, sulphur and saltpetre falling everywhere pell-mell. At length the king reached the castle, and there they renewed their efforts. Bats, ravens, owls, defended the entrance, but the dragon, with his claws, teeth, and tail, cut to pieces the boldest of them. The queen, on her part, seeing the great fight, shattered the walls with a kick, and out of the fragments made weapons to help her husband. They were at last victorious, the long-parted husband and wife fell into each other's arms, and the miracle ended with a clap of thunder that dried up the lake.

The useful dragon vanished with the rest, and not knowing how he had come there, the king found himself with his wife and Moufette in his capital city, seated in a magnificent apartment at a well-loaded table. Never was there astonishment or joy like theirs. All the people came to see their queen and the young princess, who, to add to the wonder of it all, was so beautifully dressed that the brilliance of her jewels was almost too dazzling.

It is easy to imagine that every sort of amusement went on at the court; the masquerades, running at the ring, and tournaments attracted the greatest princes in the world, and they were all struck by Moufette's beauty. Among those who seemed the handsomest and the most skilful, Prince Moufy had certainly the advantage; all he did was warmly applauded, he was vastly admired, and not least by Moufette, who had hitherto only associated with the serpents and dragons of the lake. Every day he tried new ways of pleasing her, for he loved her passionately; he offered himself as a suitor, and informed the king and queen that his principality was of a beauty and extent that deserved special attention.

The king told him that Moufette was free to make her own choice of a husband; he did not intend to force her inclination in any way, and was only anxious to please her and make her happy. The prince was delighted; in their various meetings he had learned that he was not indifferent to her. When at length they came to an explanation, she told him that if he was not her husband no other man should be. Moufy, overcome with joy, threw himself at her feet, and implored her in the most affectionate terms to remember the promise she had given him.

He then informed the king and queen of the progress he had made with Moufette, and entreated them not to delay his happiness any longer. They gladly consented. Prince Moufy possessed such noble qualities that he seemed the only man worthy of possessing Moufette. The king was quite willing for their betrothal to take place before the prince returned to Moufy, where he was obliged to go in order to make arrangements for the marriage; but rather than go away without the certainty of being made happy on his return, he would never have departed at all. Princess Moufette could not bid him farewell without many tears; she was troubled by some indescribable presentiment. The queen, seeing the prince overwhelmed with grief, gave him her daughter's portrait, begging him for the love he bore them not to spend a long time in arranging a very magnificent entry, but to return very soon. He said: "Madam, I have never had greater pleasure in obeying you than on this occasion; my heart is too deeply engaged for me to neglect anything that conduces to my happiness".

He travelled post, and Princess Moufette occupied herself in his absence with the musical instruments she had been learning for some months, and on which she played remarkably well. One day when she was in the queen's room the king entered all in tears, and taking his daughter in his arms exclaimed: "O my child! O unhappy father! unfortunate king!" He could say no more for sighing; the queen and princess, much terrified, asked him what was the matter, and he told them that there had just arrived a giant of immeasurable height, who gave himself out to be the ambassador of the dragon of the lake; he, in accordance with the promise exacted from the king when he helped him to fight and conquer the monsters, demanded the Princess Moufette to make her into a pie for his dinner. The king was pledged by the most solemn oaths to give him whatever he wanted, and in those days no one ever broke his word.

When the queen heard the sad news she uttered heartrending cries, and clasped her daughter tightly in her arms. "He shall take my life," she said, "before he shall deliver my daughter to that monster; let him take our kingdom and all our possessions. Unnatural father! can you be guilty of such cruelty? What! my child made into a pie! I cannot endure the thought: send the barbarous ambassador to me; perhaps he will be moved by my distress."

The king did not reply; he spoke to the giant, and brought him to the queen, who, throwing herself at his feet, with her daughter besought him to have pity on them, to persuade the dragon to take all they possessed and spare Moufette's life. But he told them the matter had nothing to do with him, and that the dragon was extremely obstinate and extremely greedy; when he saw his way to enjoying some toothsome delicacy not all the gods themselves could prevent him. He advised them as a friend, since it was quite possible that even greater misfortunes might happen, to consent with a good grace. At these words the queen fainted, and her daughter, had she not been obliged to come to her mother's assistance, would have done the same.

The sad news was scarcely spread through the palace before the whole town knew it. Then, as all the people adored Moufette, nothing was heard but the sound of weeping and wailing. The king could not make up his mind to give her to the giant, and the giant, who had already been waiting several days, began to get tired and to utter terrible threats. Meanwhile the king and queen said: "What worse can happen to us? If the dragon came and devoured us we could not be more distressed; if he makes our Moufette into a pie we are lost." Then the giant informed them that he had received letters from his master, who agreed to spare the princess's life if she would marry a nephew of his; this nephew was exceedingly handsome, and there was no reason why she should not be very happy with him.

The proposal somewhat lessened their grief; the queen spoke to the princess, but she infinitely preferred death to such a marriage. "I could not," she said, "save my life by being untrue. You promised me to Prince Moufy; I will never be another's. Let me die; my death will ensure the peace of your lives." The king came in and spoke to his daughter as his affection for her prompted. She was firm, however, and in the end he resolved to take her to the top of a mountain whence the dragon was to fetch her.

Everything was prepared for the great sacrifice; those of Iphigenia and Psyche were not so mournful; only black garments, pale and terrified countenances, were to be seen. Four hundred maidens of the highest rank, clad in long white robes, and crowned with cypress, accompanied her; she was carried in an open litter of black velvet so that all the people might look on that masterpiece of the gods. Her hair, tied with crape, hung down over her shoulders, and the crown on her head was of jasmine and marigolds. The grief of her parents who followed, sunk in the most profound melancholy, seemed to be the only thing that touched her. The giant, fully armed, walked by the side of the litter, and looking greedily at her, seemed desirous of eating her himself. The air resounded with sighs and sobs, the road was flooded with tears.

"Ah, frog, frog, you have indeed forsaken me!" said the queen; "alas! why did you give me your help in the gloomy plain, since you refuse it me now? It would have been better to have died then; in that case I should not see all my hopes disappointed now! I should not see my beloved Moufette on the point of being devoured!"

While she was lamenting thus, they slowly advanced, and at length reached the summit of the fatal mountain. The cries and lamentations increased with such strength that never was there a more distressing scene; the giant bade everybody say their last farewells and withdraw. All obeyed, for in those days men were very ignorant and never tried to find remedies for their misfortunes.

The king and queen with all the court ascended another mountain whence they would be able to witness what happened to the princess. They had not to wait long before they perceived in the air a dragon half-a-league long; although his wings were large, his body was so heavy that he could scarcely fly; it was covered with thick blue scales and long burning stings; his tail formed fifty and a half twists and turns; each of his claws was as big as a windmill, and his open mouth exposed to view three rows of teeth as long as those of an elephant.

But while he gradually came nearer, the faithful frog, mounted on a sparrow-hawk, flew swiftly to Prince Moufy. She wore her hood of roses, and although he was shut up in his closet, entered without a key and said : " What are you doing here, unfortunate lover ? You are dreaming of Moufette's charms, who at this moment is exposed to the most terrible misfortunes. Here is a rose leaf ; by breathing on it I turn it into a very rare horse." Immediately a green horse appeared with twelve feet and three heads ; one emitted fire, another bomb-shells, and the third cannon-balls. She gave him a sword, eighteen ells long and lighter than a feather ; she clothed him in a single diamond which he put on like a coat, and although it was harder than a rock, it was so pliable that it was not at all uncomfortable. " Go," she said, " rush, fly to the defence of the woman you love ; this green horse will take you to her, and when you have rescued her tell her the share I have had in the matter."

" Generous fairy," exclaimed the prince, " I cannot now show you my gratitude, but I declare myself for ever your faithful slave." He mounted the three-headed horse, which immediately began to gallop with its twelve feet ; its speed was greater than that of three of the best horses, so that in a very short time the prince reached the mountain-top, where he saw his princess alone, and the horrible dragon slowly approaching her. The green horse began to send forth fire, bomb-shells, and cannon-balls, a proceeding that in no slight degree surprised the monster ; he received twenty balls in his breast ; his scales were consequently somewhat injured, and the bombs put out one eye. He became furious, and made as if to throw himself on the prince ; but the eighteen-ell sword was so excellent that he wielded it with ease, sometimes plunging it up to the hilt into the monster's side, or using it like a whip. Without the diamond coat, which was impenetrable, the prince must have felt the effect of the creature's claws.

Moufette recognised him from a distance, because the diamond that covered him was very clear and bright ; she was seized with the most mortal terror. But the king and queen began to feel some rays of hope, for it was such an extraordinary thing for a horse with three heads and a dozen feet, emitting fire and flame, and a prince in a diamond casing, armed with a formidable sword, to come just at the right moment and fight so valiantly. The king hoisted his hat on his cane, and the queen tied her handkerchief to the end of a stick, to make signs to the prince and encourage him. The whole suite did the same. The prince had, however, no need of encouragement ; his passion and his mistress's danger were enough to stimulate him.

What efforts did he not make ? The ground was covered with stings, claws, horns, wings, and dragon scales ; the monster's blood flowed from a thousand wounds; it was blue, and that of the horse was green, a fact that made the ground of a strange colour. The prince fell five times, but he always got up again, and leisurely mounted his horse, and then there were cannonades and Greek fires such as had never been seen before. At length the dragon's strength gave way; he fell, and the prince struck him a blow in the belly that made a ghastly wound. But what will hardly be believed, and is yet as true as the rest of the tale, is that out of the wound came the handsomest and most charming prince ever seen. His coat was of blue velvet on a gold ground, embroidered with pearls, and on his head he wore a Grecian helmet trimmed with white feathers. He ran with open arms to embrace Prince Moufy. "What do I not owe you, my generous deliverer!" he said. "You have set me free from the most horrible prison in which a monarch was ever shut up. I was put there by the Fairy Lioness, and have languished there sixteen years, and her power was so great that against my will she would have forced me to devour the beautiful princess; lead me to her, that I may explain my misfortune."

Prince Moufy, surprised and delighted at so extraordinary an adventure, was equally polite, and hastened to join Moufette, who was thanking the gods a thousand times for such unhoped-for happiness. The king and queen and the court were already with her; everybody spoke at once, nobody listened, and they all wept for joy as much as they had before shed tears for grief. At length, so that nothing might be wanting to their joy, the good frog appeared in the air, mounted on a sparrow-hawk with golden bells on its feet. When their tinkle-tinkle was heard, all raised their eyes and saw the hood of roses shining like the sun, and the frog as lovely as the dawn. The queen approached her, and took hold of one of her little paws. The wise frog at once became a great queen with a charming face. "I come," she said, "to do honour to Princess Moufette, who preferred to risk her life rather than be untrue to her lover; such an act is rare in our day, but it will be even rarer in the ages to come." She then put myrtle wreaths on the lovers' heads, and striking three blows with her wand, the dragon's bones formed themselves into a triumphal arch to commemorate the great event that had just taken place.

They all wended their way to the town, singing wedding songs as joyfully as they had before chanted funeral hymns. The marriage was solemnised the next day, and the joy amid which it was celebrated may be easily imagined.

THE HIND IN THE WOOD.

ONCE upon a time there was a king and queen who were perfectly happy. They loved each other dearly, and were adored by their subjects ; but every one regretted there should be no heir. The queen felt sure that if she had a child the king would love her even more, and never omitted each spring to drink the water for which the district was famous. People came in crowds, and large numbers of foreigners from all quarters of the globe were to be seen there. The springs were situated in a wood, and were surrounded by marble and porphyry, for every one took pleasure in adorning them. One day, when the queen was sitting by the springs, she asked her attendants to leave her alone. She then began her usual complaints : " How unhappy I am," she said, " to have no children ! The poorest women have plenty of them, while I have for five years been imploring the gods to grant my desire, but without success ; am I to die without knowing the delight of being a mother ? "

She noticed that while she was speaking the water of the spring became agitated; a big lobster appeared and said: "Great queen, you shall have your desire. Not far from here is a magnificent palace, built by the fairies, but it is very difficult to find, because it is surrounded by clouds too thick for mortal eye to pierce; however, I am your very humble servant, and if you will entrust yourself to a poor lobster, I will take you there."

The queen listened without interrupting. She was surprised at the novelty of a talking lobster, and accepted the offer, remarking that it could not, however, walk backwards like the fish. The lobster smiled, and immediately assumed the form of a handsome old woman. "Well, madam," she said, "I promise not to walk backwards; look upon me as one of your friends, for I only wish your happiness."

She came out of the water perfectly dry; her gown was white, lined with crimson, and her grey hair was tied up with green ribbons. A more elegant old lady was never seen; she saluted the queen, who embraced her, and without further delay the old lady led the queen down a path she had never seen before; for although she had been in the wood thousands and thousands of times, she had never walked down that particular path. How should she have done so? It was the fairies' road to the spring, and was usually shut in by briers and thorns. But when the queen and her guide appeared, the briers brought forth roses, the jasmine and the orange trees twined their branches to form an arcade of leaves and flowers, the ground was covered with violets, and a thousand different birds sang enchantingly in the trees.

Before the queen had recovered from her astonishment, her eyes were dazzled by the brilliance of a palace built entirely of diamonds; the walls, roof, ceilings, floors, staircases, balconies, even the terraces were all of diamonds. She could not help giving a loud cry of admiration, and asked her companion if what she saw was a phantom or a reality. "Nothing could be more real, madam," she replied. The palace gates opened, and six fairies came forth, but what fairies! they were the most beautiful and magnificent ever seen. They curtesied low to the queen, and each presented her with a flower of precious stones to form a bouquet; there was a rose, a tulip, an anemone, a columbine, a pink, and a pomegranate. "Madam," they said, "we cannot give you a greater mark of our respect than allowing you to visit us here, and we are very glad to announce that you will become the mother of a beautiful princess. You are to name her Desirée, for it cannot be denied you have long desired her; do not fail to summon us as soon as she is born, for we want to endow her with all sorts of good qualities. To bring us to you, you have merely to take the bouquet we have given you and name each flower aloud, thinking of us all the while."

The queen, overjoyed, threw her arms round their necks, and embraced them for more than half-an-hour. They then invited her to enter the palace, of which it is impossible to give any adequate description. The architect of the sun was responsible for the design, and he had really reproduced that luminary in miniature. The brilliance was almost too much for the queen, and she had to keep shutting her eyes. They took her into the garden; she had never seen such fine fruit; the apricots were bigger than a man's head; it was impossible to eat a cherry without cutting it into four, and the flavour was so delicate that after eating it the queen never wished to take any other sort. There was an orchard of artificial trees which were alive and growing just like the others.

To describe the queen's great joy is impossible, or how much she talked of the little Princess Desirée, and how often she thanked the kind creature who had told her such a pleasant piece of news, but I can assure you that no expressions of affection and gratitude were forgotten. The fairy of the spring, as she well deserved, had her full share, and the queen remained in the palace till evening. She loved music, and heard singing as of heavenly angels; she was loaded with presents, and thanking her hostess, the queen departed with the fairy of the spring.

All the household had been greatly distressed at her absence, and had searched for her very anxiously; they could not imagine what had become of her. They feared some bold stranger had carried her off, for she was both young and beautiful. Thus they all rejoiced exceedingly at her return, and since the hopes just communicated to her had put her into a very good humour, everybody was charmed with her agreeable and brilliant conversation.

The fairy of the spring left her near her home; compliments and embraces were renewed at parting, and as the queen remained eight days longer at the springs, she did not fail to pay other visits to the fairies' palace in company with the delightful old lady, who always appeared first as a lobster and then assumed her natural form.

According to promise, a princess was born to the queen, and was called Desirée. The queen took the bouquet, named the flowers one after the other, and immediately the fairies arrived. Each had a chariot of a different sort; one was of ebony drawn by white pigeons, another of ivory drawn by ravens, another of cedar and calambour. These were their carriages in time of peace, for when they were angry they used flying dragons, snakes emitting flame from eyes and mouth, lions, leopards, panthers who carried them from one end of the globe to the other in less time than it takes to say good-morning. But on this occasion they were in excellent humour.

They entered the queen's room gaily and majestically, accompanied by dwarfs bearing presents. After embracing the queen and kissing the little princess, they displayed the layette : it was of such fine and good quality of linen that it would wear a hundred years ; the fairies wove it in their leisure time. The lace surpassed the linen in beauty ; the design executed with the needle or bobbin showed pictures of the history of the world. Then they showed the swaddling clothes and bed coverings that had been expressly embroidered with designs forming a thousand different children's games ; since embroiderers had existed, nothing so marvellous had been produced. But when the cradle appeared, the queen uttered an exclamation of delight, for it excelled all the rest of the things. It was made of a very rare wood costing a hundred thousand crowns a-pound. It was supported by four little Cupids, each a masterpiece, for such was the victory of art over material that although they were made of diamonds and rubies, it was impossible to praise them too highly. Moreover, the fairies had endowed them with life, and when the child cried they rocked her and put her to sleep, a convenience the nurses greatly appreciated.

The fairies took the little princess, dressed her with their own hands, and gave her more than a hundred kisses, for she was already so beautiful that to see her was to love her. They observed that the babe was hungry, and striking the ground with their wands, a nurse appeared perfectly suited to the infant. It now only remained for them to bestow gifts on her ; the fairies hastened to do so : one gave her virtue, another intelligence, a third miraculous beauty, the fourth good fortune, the fifth health and long life, and the last guaranteed her success in all she undertook.

The queen, delighted beyond measure, was thanking the fairies a thousand times for the favours they had bestowed on the little princess, when a lobster, so big that it could hardly get through the doorway, entered the room : " Ungrateful queen," she exclaimed, " you have forgotten me. Do you not remember the fairy of the spring and my kindness in taking you to my sisters ? You summoned them and forgot me. A presentiment of your conduct made me assume the form of a lobster the first time I spoke to you, to mark that your affection would go back instead of forward."

The queen, inconsolable for her mistake, interrupted her and asked to be forgiven. She said she thought she had named her flower with the rest, that it was therefore the bouquet of precious flowers that had deceived her, she was altogether incapable of forgetting the obligations she owed her. The queen entreated her not to withdraw her friendship, and particularly not to remove her favour from the princess. The fairies, fearing she should bestow misery and evil fortune on the princess, joined with the queen in the attempt to lessen her anger. " My dear sister," they said, " we entreat your highness not to be angry

with a queen who never intended to displease you : throw off your lobster disguise and let us see you in all your beauty."

I have already mentioned that the fairy of the spring was something of a
coquette, and her sisters' praises somewhat mollified her. " Well," she said,
" I will not bring on Desirée all the evil I had intended, for I certainly meant to
do her harm, and nothing should have prevented me, but I warn you, that if she
sees daylight before her fifteenth birthday, she will repent it and perhaps lose
her life." Neither the queen's tears nor the fairies' entreaties could change the
sentence. She withdrew, walking backwards, for she would not lay aside her
lobster disguise.

Directly she had gone, the sad queen asked the fairies to advise her how
she could best save her daughter from the threatened evils. They held a
council, and after much discussion, decided it would be best to build a palace
without doors or windows, to make a subterranean passage leading into it, and
let the princess live there until the fatal age at which misfortune threatened was
past.

The building was begun and ended by three strokes of the wand. It was
of white marble, green on the outside, the ceilings and floors were of diamonds
and emeralds that formed flowers, birds, and many pretty things. The hangings and carpets were of coloured velvet, embroidered by the fairies themselves,
and, as they were learned in history, they delighted in depicting interesting and
remarkable events, the future as well as the past, and the heroic deeds of the
greatest king in the world * filled many tapestries.

> Mark you now his piercing eye !
>   Like the ancient God of Thrace ;
> See how proudly he rides by,
>   Full of courage, full of grace.
>
> And he rules by wisdom's lore ;
>   For, O France ! how peacefully
> Dost thou rest from shore to shore ;
>   Other nations envy thee.
>
> To depict his varied charms
>   All the greatest painters vie :
> Dauntless he 'mid war's alarms ;
>   Matchless he in clemency.

The wise fairies invented this means of teaching the young princess the
different events in the lives of heroes and great men.

* Louis XIV.

Wax candles furnished light, and there were so many of them that the day-light was scarcely missed. Tutors came to her, and her intelligence, vivacity, and skill were so great that she nearly always divined what they had to teach her, and the professors were continually surprised by the remarkable things she said at an age when other children scarcely knew their nurse's name; but the fairies' gifts did not include ignorance and stupidity.

Her beauty equalled her intelligence; even those least likely to be attracted by it were enchanted, and the queen would never have left off looking at her had not duty called her to the king's side. The good fairies visited the princess occasionally; they brought her precious gifts, elegant, pretty, well-made gowns fit for the wedding of the most charming princess. But of all the fairies Tulip loved her best, and anxiously warned the queen not to let her see daylight before she was fifteen. "Our sister of the spring is revengeful," she said; "whatever care we take of this child, she will harm her if she can, so, madam, it is impos-sible to be too vigilant." The queen promised to be on her guard, but as the time when her beloved daughter might safely leave the castle drew near, she had her portrait painted and taken to all the great courts of the world. The princes no sooner looked at it than they admired it, and one of them was so struck by it that he refused to part with it. He put it in his closet, shut him-self up with it and talked to it in the most passionate manner as if it had been alive and could understand.

The king, seeing his son so seldom, inquired what he was doing with him-self, and what made him so much less gay and cheerful than formerly. Some of the courtiers, eager to tell, for such is very often their character, informed him that it was greatly to be feared the prince would go out of his mind because he spent whole days shut up alone in his closet, and yet talked just as if there was some one there.

This information made the king anxious. "Is it possible," he said, "that my son should lose his reason? He was always so intelligent; you know how he has always been admired. Although he seems sad, he looks perfectly sen-sible. I must talk to him, and try to discover what is wrong with him."

Accordingly the king sent for him, ordered the courtiers to withdraw, and after a few questions, to which the prince paid scant attention and answered very wide of the mark, asked him what had caused the change in his appearance and humour. The prince, seizing the moment as favourable, threw himself at his father's feet. "You are determined," he said, "to marry me to the Black Princess. You find advantages in that match which I cannot promise you with the Princess Desirée, but, sire, I perceive charms in the one I do not recognise in the other." "And when have you seen these ladies?" asked the king.

" Their portraits have been brought to me," replied Prince Warrior—he was so named because he had won three great battles—"and I confess my passion for Princess Desirée is so great that if you do not retract the promise given to the Black Princess I shall die, happy in leaving a world where all hope of possessing the woman I love is at an end."

" It is, I suppose, with her portrait," said the king, " that you are pleased to hold conversations that make you a laughing-stock to the whole court. They think you mad, and if you knew all I have suffered on your account you would be ashamed of such weakness." " I cannot blame myself for my passion," said the prince; "when you see the portrait of this beautiful girl, you will understand my feelings." " Go and fetch it at once," said the king impatiently, and looking so annoyed that if the prince had not felt certain of the magical power of Desirée's beauty he would have been greatly distressed. He brought the picture to the king, and he was almost as much enchanted with it as his son. " Well, my dear Warrior," he said, " I consent to what you wish. The presence of such a lovely princess at my court will renew my youth. I will despatch ambassadors to the Black Princess without delay, to announce to her that I must break my word. Even at the risk of a war, I will do as I say."

The prince knelt and respectfully kissed his father's hand. He was so joyful that the courtiers hardly recognised him. He urged the king to send ambassadors not only to the Black Princess but also to Desirée, and for the latter embassy wished him to choose a very wealthy and capable man, because on such an occasion it would be well to make an imposing appearance and possess powers of persuasion. The king fixed on Becafigue, a very eloquent young noble, with a rent-roll of a hundred millions. He loved Prince Warrior passionately, and to please him ordered the most magnificent equipage and most gorgeous liveries that could be procured. He made the greatest possible haste, for the prince's love increased daily, and he incessantly implored him to set out. " My life," he said, confidentially, " is ebbing away. I grow distracted when I think how likely it is that the princess's father has pledged his word to another, and may not be willing to break his promise for me, and I shall thus lose her for ever." In order to gain time, Becafigue reassured him, for he was anxious that the expense he was at should do him honour. He had eighty coaches shining with gold and diamonds; the most highly finished miniatures did not come up to those with which they were adorned. There were fifty coaches besides, twenty-four thousand pages on horseback, with the rest of the cortège to match.

At the farewell audience the prince embraced his ambassador affectionately : " Remember, my dear Becafigue," he said, " that my life depends on the negotiation of this marriage; leave nothing undone to gain my adorable princess ".

He entrusted to him a thousand presents as remarkable for the gallantry of their design as for their splendour. Amorous devices were engraved on diamond seals, watches were set in carbuncles adorned with Desirée's monogram, and heart-shaped ruby bracelets, and indeed everything most likely to please her, abounded.

The ambassador also took with him the prince's portrait, painted by so skilful an artist that it spoke and made pretty speeches. It did not reply to everything said to it, but very nearly. Becafigue promised the prince to leave no means untried to procure him what he wanted, and added that, as he was taking with him plenty of money, should the king refuse to give him the princess, he would bribe one of her women and carry her off. "Ah!" exclaimed the prince, "I cannot agree to that; she would be offended at so disrespectful a proceeding." Becafigue made no reply, and set out on his mission.

Rumour of his coming and his errand preceded him. The king and queen were delighted; they held his master in high esteem, and had heard of the prince's great deeds, yet they were more pleased with his personal merits, and felt certain that if they sought through the wide world for a husband for their daughter they could not find one more worthy of her. A palace was prepared for Becafigue's reception, and the court was ordered to appear in its very greatest magnificence.

The king and queen had made up their minds that the ambassador should see Desirée, but Fairy Tulip came to the queen and said: "Be sure, madam, not to take Becafigue to our child"—for thus she spoke of the princess—"it would be dangerous for her to see him just yet, and do not send her to the king until after her fifteenth birthday. I am certain, if she goes before, some misfortune will occur." The queen embraced the good Tulip and promised to follow her advice, and they then paid the princess a visit.

The ambassador arrived. The passing of the procession took twenty-three hours, for there were six thousand mules with bells and shoes of gold, and trappings of gold-embroidered velvet and brocade. The streets were crowded, everybody turned out to see the sight, and so glad were they of his coming that the king and queen went in person to meet him. Since they can so easily be imagined, it is useless to repeat here the speech Becafigue made, and the compliments that passed on both sides. but he was extremely surprised when his request to see the Princess Desirée was refused. "It is not from caprice, Sir Becafigue," said the king, "that we deny what you have every right to demand; you must hear our daughter's strange story.

"At the time of her birth a fairy conceived a great hatred for her, and threatened her with a terrible misfortune if she say daylight before the age of fifteen : she dwells, therefore, in an underground palace. We had decided to take you to visit her, but Fairy Tulip advised us not to do so." " Then, sir, am I to return without her?" said Becafigue. " You are willing, you declare, to give her in marriage to my master's son who awaits her with the utmost impatience, and yet you allow yourself to be influenced by such trifles as fairies' predictions! Here is Prince Warrior's portrait, which I was asked to give her; it is so excellent a likeness that when I look at it I seem to see him in person." He exhibited it, and the portrait, only instructed how to speak to the princess, said : " Lovely Desirée, you cannot imagine with what ardour I await you ; come soon to our court to adorn it with your matchless beauty ". The king and queen were so astonished that they asked Becafigue to give it to them to take to the princess ; he was delighted to do so, and entrusted it to their care.

The queen had not informed her daughter of what was going on, and had forbidden her attendants to tell her of the ambassador's arrival. But they had not obeyed her, and the princess knew that a marriage was in contemplation for her ; she was, however, so prudent that she did not let her mother think she suspected anything. When the prince's portrait, which made her affectionate and gallant speeches, was shown her, she was extremely surprised, for she had never seen anything to equal it ; the prince's good looks, intelligent expression, and regular features astonished her as much as what it said. " How would you like," said the queen, smiling, " to have a husband like this prince?" " Madam," she replied, " it is not for me to choose ; I shall be satisfied with anyone you destine for me." " But," continued the queen, " would you not think it fortunate if my choice fell on him?" Desirée lowered her eyes, blushed, and made no reply. The queen took her in her arms and kissed her many times : she could not help shedding tears at the thought of so soon losing her daughter, for in three months she would be fifteen ; but, concealing her grief, she told her all about the illustrious Becafigue's embassy, and gave her the exquisite presents he had brought for her. She admired them, and praised them in most tasteful terms ; but, from time to time, her glance wandered to the prince's portrait with a pleasure hitherto unknown to her.

The ambassador, seeing it was useless to hope they would give him the princess, had to rest content with their solemn promises, and returned to inform his master of the result of his negotiations. When the prince learned that it would be three months before he could have his beloved Desirée, his laments distressed the whole court. He neither slept nor ate, he became melancholy and dreamy, and his brilliant complexion took the colour of marigolds. He spent whole days lying on a couch in his closet, gazing at the princess's portrait, and writing it letters as if it had been able to read them. His strength gradually declined, he fell dangerously ill, and neither physician nor doctor was needed to discover the cause.

The king was in despair; never had a father loved his son more tenderly. He now saw himself on the verge of losing him, and his grief may be better imagined than described. There was no means of curing him; all he wanted was Desirée, and without her he must die. The sorrowing father, therefore, resolved as a last chance to go in person to the king and queen and implore them in pity for the prince's condition not to delay a marriage that, if they waited till the princess's fifteenth birthday, would never take place at all.

It was, of course, a most unusual proceeding, but it would have been still more extraordinary if he had allowed so well-loved a son to die. There was, however, one insurmountable difficulty, the king's advanced age only permitted him to travel in a litter, a mode of progression far too slow for his son's impatience, so that he again sent the trusty Becafigue travelling post, and bearing pathetic letters to induce the king and queen to accede to his wishes.

During this time Desirée found quite as much pleasure in looking at the prince's portrait as he did at hers. At every possible opportunity she visited the place where it was kept, and in spite of all her efforts to hide her sentiments, they were easily discovered. Gilliflower and Long-Thorn, her ladies-in-waiting, saw that her mind was disturbed. Gilliflower loved her passionately and faithfully; Long-Thorn was secretly jealous of her. Her mother had been the princess's governess, and was now her lady-in-waiting, and would have continued to love her well, but she adored her daughter, and seeing her hatred of the princess, ceased to care for her well-being.

When his mission was known, the ambassador despatched to the court of the Black Princess was scarcely well received; the Ethiopian was a very vindictive person, and considered it cavalier treatment first to make her promises, and then to send and say he would have nothing more to do with her. She had seen a portrait of the prince and had fallen passionately in love with it, and when Ethiopians become Cupid's victims they are more extravagant in their passion than others. She asked the ambassador: "Does not your master consider me rich and beautiful enough? Look round my realms; you can scarcely find any of greater extent. Come into my treasury and you will see more gold than is contained in the mines of Peru. Look at my jet black complexion, my flat nose and thick lips; is anything wanting that makes a woman handsome?" "Madam," replied the ambassador, who feared a beating worse than that administered to the Turks, "as much as a subject dares, I blame my master's conduct, and if heaven had placed me on a throne, I know with whom I should hope to share it." "That speech will save your life," she said; "I had determined to begin my revenge with you, but since you are not the instigator of the prince's actions, it would be an injustice. Go, tell him that, since I could never love a dishonourable man, I am glad to be released from my promise." The ambassador, who desired nothing so much as permission to depart, no sooner obtained it than he availed himself of it.

But the Ethiopian was too deeply offended with Prince Warrior to forgive him. She got into an ivory chariot drawn by six ostriches that went at the rate of ten leagues an hour. She hastened to the palace of the fairy of the spring, who was her god-mother and best friend; she told her what had happened, and begged her to help her to be revenged. The fairy sympathised with the princess, and consulted the book of all knowledge. She discovered that Prince Warrior had renounced the Black Princess for Princess Desirée, that he loved her distractedly, and had fallen sick with his longing to see her. That news rekindled the fairy's anger; it had been almost extinguished, and as she had not seen Desirée since the time of her birth, it is most likely that had it not been for the Black Princess she would never have done her any harm. "What!" she exclaimed, "this wretched Desirée is always doing something to annoy me. No, my dearest princess, I will not allow you to suffer such an affront; I will enlist the heavens and elements in your behalf. Go home and rely on your god-mother." The Black Princess thanked her, and made her presents of flowers and fruit, which she received with much condescension.

Meanwhile the ambassador Becafigue had travelled with all possible speed to the capital of Desirée's father. He threw himself at the feet of the king and queen, and told them in the most pathetic words how the prince would die without Desirée, and that as she would be fifteen in three months, it was impossible any misfortune could happen to her in so short a time; moreover, he took the liberty to warn them that such a firm belief in fairies was scarcely in keeping with their high position. In fact, in the end his hearers were convinced by his eloquence. They wept in concert over the prince's sad condition, and told Becafigue it would be some days before they could give him a reply. He rejoined he could only allow them a few hours; his master was dying, and thought the delay was caused by the princess's hatred of him. The royal pair then promised to let him know their decision in the evening.

The queen hastened to her daughter's palace, and told her all that had happened. Desirée was so overcome with grief that she fainted, a circumstance that clearly showed her feelings in regard to the prince. "Do not distress yourself, my dear daughter," said the queen; "his cure lies in your hands; I am only anxious on account of the threats of the fairy of the spring at your birth." "I think, madam," she replied, "that by taking certain precautions we can outwit the wicked fairy. For instance, cannot I travel in a close carriage so that I need not see the daylight? It could be opened at night to admit food, and thus I should reach Prince Warrior without accident."

The idea commended itself to the queen, and when the king was made acquainted with it he also approved. Becafigue was summoned, and received a promise that the princess should set out very soon, and that he might at once return to his master with the good news. In order not to delay her departure, they informed him they should not wait to provide the equipage and trousseau suited to her rank. The ambassador, overjoyed, threw himself at their feet, thanked them, and set off, without, however, having seen the princess.

Had Desirée been less prepossessed in the prince's favour, she would have felt the separation from her parents very keenly, but there are sentiments that stifle all the rest. A coach was constructed for her, with the outside of green velvet, ornamented with gold plaques, and lined inside with silver brocade, embroidered in pink; there were no windows, it was very large, and closed as tightly as a box. The keys were given to the charge of one of the first lords of the kingdom.

Flutt'ring about her, the Graces were seen,
Joy and gay laughter and pleasure serene.
Cupids adoring her played round her feet,
Eager to follow her presence so sweet.
Calm and majestic her dignified grace,
Heavenly tenderness shone from her face.
Swayed were all hearts by her attributes rare,
Perfect in truth was this pure maiden fair;
Many her virtues not spoken of here.
Equal in charms, she was Adelaide's peer
When here once she came with Hymen as guide,
Bearer of peace to the whole country side.

As a numerous suite would have been embarrassing, she was accompanied by only a few officers. After giving her most beautiful jewels, and some handsome gowns, after farewells that almost suffocated the king, queen, and court, in their efforts to keep from weeping, she was shut up in the dark coach with the ladies-in-waiting, Long-Thorn and Gilliflower.

It has perhaps been forgotten that Long-Thorn did not love the princess, while she had been deeply smitten with Prince Warrior's speaking portrait. In fact, so severely had Cupid's dart wounded her, that when they were on the point of setting out she told her mother that if the princess's marriage took place she should die; if, therefore, she wished to save her life, she must find a means of breaking off the match. In order to pacify her, the lady-in-waiting promised she would try to make her happy.

When the queen sent her beloved child away, she recommended her beyond everything to this bad woman's care. "What a precious trust I am confiding to you!" she said; "it is dearer to me than my life. Take good care of my daughter's health, and above all guard her carefully against seeing daylight, for then all would be lost. You know the misfortune with which she is threatened, and Prince Warrior's ambassador has promised me that until she is fifteen she shall be placed in a castle where she shall see no other light than that of wax candles." The queen heaped presents on the woman in order to make more sure of her. She promised to watch over the princess, and directly on their arrival to write the queen everything that had happened.

The king and queen, trusting her fully, felt no further anxiety, and were thus a little consoled for their daughter's departure. But Long-Thorn, learning from the officers who opened the carriage every evening to give them food that they were getting near the town where they were expected, urged her mother to carry out her plan without delay, for if the king or prince came to meet them it would be too late. About mid-day, when the heat of the sun is greatest, she suddenly cut the imperial of the coach with a big knife she had had made for the purpose, and then for the first time Princess Desirée saw daylight. She had scarcely looked at it when, sighing deeply, she jumped out of the coach in the form of a white hind, and ran to the neighbouring forest where she concealed herself in a gloomy spot to lament in solitude the beautiful form she had just lost.

The fairy of the spring, who was the cause of this unlucky adventure, finding that the princess's companions knew their duty, and that some were following her into the wood, while others set off to the town to inform Prince Warrior of the accident, called up a dreadful storm. The thunder and lightning were so terrific that they frightened the most courageous, and thus by means of her vast knowledge the fairy succeeded in carrying the faithful servants far away from the place where their presence was troublesome.

Only Long-Thorn, her mother, and Gilliflower remained. The last ran after her mistress, making the woods and rocks resound with her cries and lamentations. The other two, delighted to be left alone, did not lose a moment in carrying out their plans. Long-Thorn put on Desirée's handsomest gown; the royal cloak made for the wedding was of unparalleled magnificence, and every diamond in the crown was two or three times as big as your fist; the sceptre was of a single ruby, the globe she held in the other hand was a pearl bigger than your head; it was very precious and exceedingly heavy, for to convince the people that she was the princess, Long-Thorn considered it wise to omit none of the royal attributes.

Thus attired, Long-Thorn, accompanied by her mother as train-bearer, went towards the town. The false princess walked in a most dignified manner, thinking the king and prince would come to meet her, and, in fact, they had scarcely gone any distance when they perceived a troop of cavalry. In its midst were two litters shining with gold and precious stones, borne by mules and decorated with large bunches of green feathers, the princess's favourite colour. The king who was in one and the prince in the other did not know what to think of the ladies who were approaching them. The most eager of the horsemen galloped up to them and, from the splendour of their costume, judged them to be persons of distinction. They dismounted and addressed them respectfully : "Will you be good enough," said Long-Thorn, "to tell me who are in those litters ? " "Ladies," they replied, "the king and his son, who come to meet Princess Desirée." "Go, if you please," she said, "and tell them I am she. A fairy, jealous of my happiness, dispersed my attendants by means of a terrible storm, but my lady-in-waiting here has charge of my jewels and of letters from my father."

The cavaliers kissed the hem of her robe and speedily announced to the king that the princess was approaching. "What ! " he exclaimed, "she comes on foot and in broad daylight ! " They then informed him of what she had told them. The prince, burning with impatience, summoned them, and without asking them any questions, said : "Come now, confess, is she not a miracle of beauty, a prodigy, a most perfect princess ? " To the prince's great surprise, they made no answer. "There is so much to praise," he continued, "that I suppose you prefer to be silent." "Sir," said the boldest of them, "you will see her yourself directly ; apparently the fatigue of the journey has affected her appearance." The prince was greatly astonished, and had he not been too weak would have jumped out of the litter in order to satisfy without delay his impatience and curiosity. The king, however, got out of his, and advancing with all his court, came up with the pretended princess ; but, directly he saw her, he uttered a loud cry, and falling back a few paces : "What do I see ? " he said, "what perfidy ! " "Sire," said the lady-in-waiting, boldly coming forward, "here is Princess Desirée, with letters from the king and queen. I also deliver over to you the casket of jewels entrusted to my care at our setting out."

The king preserved a gloomy silence, and the prince leaning on Becafigue approached Long-Thorn. O ye gods ! How did he feel when he saw the girl ? Her extraordinary appearance almost produced terror in the spectator. She was so tall that the princess's gown scarcely came below her knees, she was frightfully thin, her nose was like a parrot's beak, and was of a bright red colour; her teeth were black and uneven, and indeed she was as ugly as Desirée was beautiful.

The prince, whose mind had been entirely filled with his beautiful princess, was almost paralysed with horror at the sight of this girl: he had not the strength to utter a word. He looked at her in astonishment, and turning to the king, said: "I am betrayed; this person is not in the least like the lovely picture that won my heart; I have been deceived, and my life will be the cost." "What do you mean, sir?" said Long-Thorn. "How have you been deceived? I promise you you will make no mistake if you marry me." Her impertinence and arrogance knew no bounds, yet the lady-in-waiting almost surpassed her. "My dear princess," she said, "what sort of a country can this be? Is this the way to receive a lady of rank? What inconsistency! What conduct! Your father must obtain satisfaction." "That will be rather for us," said the king. "We were promised a beautiful princess and instead are sent a skeleton, a mummy, frightful to behold! I am no longer surprised this treasure should have been shut up for fifteen years. Your king wanted to make a dupe of some one, and, since he has chosen us, we will be revenged."

"What outrageous behaviour!" exclaimed the pretended princess. "How foolish I was to trust the promises of such people! See how wrong it is to let a painter flatter you a little! But does it not happen every day? If princes refused their brides for that reason, not many of them would marry."

The king and his son were too angry to reply: they got into their litters again, and without any ceremony one of the horsemen put the princess up behind him, and the lady-in-waiting was treated in the same way. By the king's orders, they were taken to the town and shut up in the castle of the three gables.

Prince Warrior was so overcome by the blow that for a time he was unable to find words in which to express his grief. When at length he found himself able to give vent to it, he had much to say about the hardness of his fate. He was still in love, and the object of his passion was a portrait. His hopes were gone, his delightful imaginings about Desirée had all been castles in the air; death was preferable to marriage with the woman whom he believed to be Desirée. In the depths of his misery, he felt he could no longer endure life at court, and determined, as soon as his health allowed it, to leave the palace secretly and spend the rest of his life in some solitary place.

He did not speak of his plan to any one except Becafigue; he felt convinced he would follow him everywhere, and often talked over with him the shabby trick that had been played on him. As soon as he began to feel better he departed, leaving a letter for the king promising to return when his grief had become less keen. He begged him meanwhile to think of their common vengeance and not to set the ugly princess free.

The king's grief on reading his son's letter may be easily imagined. Indeed, the separation from so beloved a child almost cost the father his life. While everybody was occupied in comforting him, the prince and Becafigue were journeying far away, and at the end of three days found themselves in a big forest. The thickly growing trees made it so dark, the fresh grass and the murmuring brooks made it so pleasant, that the prince, tired out with the long journey, for he was not yet entirely recovered from his illness, dismounted; he threw himself sadly on the ground, his hand supporting his head, and he was so weak that he could scarcely speak. "Sir," said Becafigue, "while you are resting I will go and find some fruit, and have a look round this place." The prince replied only by a sign of assent.

It is so long since we left the hind in the wood that I must now speak of the matchless princess. She wept like a hind in despair when she saw her form mirrored in the brook. "What do I see?" she said. "I have to-day undergone the strangest change the fairies' power could devise for an innocent princess. How long will this change last? Where can I hide to be out of the reach of lions, bears, and wolves? How can I live on grass?" She asked herself a thousand such questions, and suffered the most cruel agony possible. The only consoling circumstance was that she was as beautiful a hind as she had been a princess.

Being exceedingly hungry, Desirée nibbled grass with a good appetite, and was vastly astonished to find such a thing possible. She lay down on the moss, and spent the night in the greatest terror. She heard the cries of wild beasts near her, and often forgetting she was a hind, attempted to climb a tree. The dawn reassured her a little; she admired its beauty, and the sun seemed to her something so wonderful that she could not leave off looking at it: all she had heard of it fell far short of the reality. It was her only consolation in that desolate spot, where she remained for several days quite alone.

Fairy Tulip, who had always loved the princess, although much distressed at her misfortune, was extremely vexed with her mother and herself for paying so little attention to her advice; she had told them over and over again that if the princess left the subterranean castle before she was fifteen, mischief would follow. However, she could not leave her to the anger of the fairy of the spring, and it was she who led Gilliflower to the forest in order that her faithful friend might be a comfort to the princess in her misfortune.

The beautiful hind was quietly feeding beside the brook, when Gilliflower, overcome with fatigue, lay down to rest and sadly began to wonder in which direction she ought to go to find her mistress. The hind saw her, jumped the brook, which was both wide and deep, and threw herself on Gilliflower and tenderly caressed her. She was greatly surprised, uncertain if the animals of that district had a particular affection for men, a circumstance that made them almost human, or if she knew her, for it was passing strange that a hind should be accomplished enough to do the honours of the forest so perfectly.

She looked at her attentively, and saw with extreme astonishment tears fall from her eyes; she then felt sure it could be no other than her princess. She kissed her feet with as much respect and affection as if they had been her hands. She spoke; the hind understood her but could not reply; the tears and sighs of both were redoubled. Gilliflower promised her mistress not to abandon her; the hind made signs with her head and eyes that she was glad and felt comforted in her trouble.

They remained together nearly the whole day. The hind, fearing lest her faithful Gilliflower would be hungry, led her to a place in the forest where she had observed wild fruit growing; she ate a great quantity, for she was famished. The meal ended, she became very anxious about where they could sleep; for she could not make up her mind to remain in the forest exposed to all the dangers of the night. "Are you not afraid, beautiful hind," she said, "to spend the night here?" The hind raised her eyes to heaven and sighed. "But," continued Gilliflower, "you have already traversed a part of this solitude; are there no houses, no woodcutters, charcoal burners, or hermits?" By a shake of the head the hind showed that she had seen no one. "O ye gods!" exclaimed Gilliflower, "I shall never see the morrow, even if I am lucky enough to escape tigers and bears. I am certain I should die of terror. But you must not think, my dear princess, that I should regret life on my own account; it is entirely on yours. Alas! could anything be more miserable than to leave you in this place, destitute of all comfort?" The little hind began to weep, and sobbed almost like a human being.

Fairy Tulip, who loved her tenderly, was touched by her tears; notwithstanding her disobedience, she had always watched over her, and now suddenly appearing before her, said: "I am too sorry for you to scold you". The hind and Gilliflower interrupted her, the former by licking her hands and caressing her, the latter imploring her to take pity on the princess and restore her to her natural form. "That is not in my power," said Tulip. "She who has worked this mischief is too influential, but I can shorten the time of penance, and make it less disagreeable by permitting the princess to leave her hind form directly night takes the place of day; she must assume it again, how-

22

ever, each day at dawn, and roam the plains and forests like the rest of the species."

It was certainly something to cease being a hind at night, and the princess testified her joy by leaps and bounds that greatly delighted Tulip. " Go down that narrow path," she said, " you will find there a hut not so bad for so rustic a situation." With these words she vanished. They obeyed her, took the route indicated, and came upon an old woman seated on her door-step weaving a wicker basket. Gilliflower made a curtesy, and said : " Will you give me and my hind shelter ? I want a small room." " Yes, my fair daughter," she replied, " I will gladly give you a retreat here. Come in, you and your hind." She led them into a very pretty room, panelled with cherry-wood ; it contained two little white beds with fine linen sheets, and it was all so simple and clean that the princess has said since that nothing could have been more to her liking.

As soon as night was over all the earth, Desirée ceased to be a hind ; she kissed her beloved Gilliflower, thanked her for following her fortunes, and promised when her penance was over to do all in her power to render her happy. The old woman knocked gently at the door, and without going in, gave Gilliflower excellent fruit of which the princess ate with much appetite. They then went to bed. When daylight appeared, Desirée became a hind again and began to scratch at the door. Gilliflower opened it and, although it was not for long, they showed a sincere regret at parting ; the hind darted into the thickest part of the wood, and began to roam about as usual.

I have already mentioned that Prince Warrior had stopped in the forest, and that Becafigue had gone in quest of food. It was late when he reached the old woman's cottage. He addressed her politely, and asked her for the things he needed for his master. She at once filled a basket for him. " If you spend the night here," she said, " without shelter of some kind, I fear an accident may happen to you. The accommodation I can offer you is very poor, but it will at least put you out of the reach of lions." He thanked her, and told her he was with a friend to whom he would point out the wisdom of accepting her kind offer. The prince was prevailed on to come to the good woman's house. She was waiting at the door, and very quietly led them to a room similar to that of the princess and only divided from it by a partition wall.

The prince, as usual, passed a disturbed night ; as soon as the first rays of the sun shone in at his window, he rose and took his way into the forest in the hope of diverting his misery, telling Becafigue he preferred to be alone.

For some time he walked on without any fixed purpose, and at last reached a mossy spot sheltered by trees, out of which darted a hind. He could not help following her ; the chase had been his ruling passion, but since another passion had possessed his heart, he had not indulged in it to any great extent. All the same he now followed the poor hind, and from time to time let fly arrows that, although they did not wound her, nearly caused her to die of fear. Her friend Tulip protected her, and it certainly needed a fairy's helping hand to prevent the serious effects of such well-aimed shafts. The hind was excessively fatigued ; she was altogether unaccustomed to so much exercise. At length she turned down a path, and happily the hunter lost sight of her ; finding himself extremely tired, he desisted from following her.

After a day spent in that manner, the hind joyfully welcomed the hour for retiring, and turned her steps towards the house where Gilliflower was impatiently awaiting her. Directly she reached her room, she threw herself on her bed out of breath and worn out. Gilliflower, eager to know what had happened, caressed her. At the appointed hour the princess resumed her natural shape, and throwing her arms round her favourite's neck, said : "Alas ! I thought I had nothing to fear but the fairy of the spring and the wild inhabitants of this forest, but I was chased to-day by a young huntsman whom I hardly looked at, so anxious was I to get away. The arrows he aimed at me threatened inevitable death ; indeed, I cannot tell by what good fortune I escaped." "You must not go out again, my princess," replied Gilliflower ; "you must spend the time of your penance in this room. I will go to the nearest town and purchase books to divert our minds ; we will read the newest fairy tales, and ourselves compose songs and poems." "My dear girl," said the princess, "the delightful thought of Prince Warrior is enough to occupy my mind pleasantly, but the same power that forces me to be a hind during the day makes me against my will act as they do ; thus I run, jump, eat grass, and at those times the confinement of a room would be intolerable to me." She was so fatigued that as soon as she had satisfied her hunger, she closed her beautiful eyes till dawn appeared. Then the usual change took place, and she returned to the forest.

The prince likewise rejoined his friend in the evening. "I spent my time," he said, "in hunting the most beautiful hind I have ever seen ; she escaped me a hundred times with the most wonderful skill. I aimed so surely that I cannot conceive how I missed her ; as soon as it is light I must go and look for her, and I shall not fail to find her." In fact, the prince was anxious to erase from his mind the face of a woman whom he now thought did not exist, and was, therefore, not sorry to occupy himself with the chase. He went early to the same spot where he had first seen the hind. But she, fearing a repetition of yesterday's disagreeable adventure, took good care not to go there. The prince searched everywhere, and walked about for a long time. It was very hot, and he was much delighted to find apples whose rosy colour was greatly to his taste; he gathered some and ate them, and was soon sleeping soundly, lying on the fresh grass under trees that seemed the trysting-place of a thousand melodious birds.

While he slept the timid hind, eager to discover a place of shelter, came to the very spot where he was. If she had seen him sooner, she would have fled, but as she was so near him, she could not help looking at him. His deep slumber gave her courage, and she had leisure to examine his features. But imagine her state of mind when she recognised him! His charming image had become so deeply impressed on her memory that she could not have forgotten it in so short a time. O Cupid, Cupid, what is your purpose? Is the hind to die by the hands of her lover? Yes, indeed, she is exposed to that danger; there is no possibility of safety. She lay down some paces from him, and her joy at the sight of him was so great that she could not take her eyes off him for a moment. She sighed and moaned, and becoming bolder, she went nearer, touched him, and he woke up.

He was much surprised to recognise the hind that had given him so much trouble, and that he had sought so long in vain; he could not at all understand her familiarity. She did not wait until he tried to seize her, but ran away at the top of her speed, and he followed as quickly as he could. Now and again they stopped to take breath, for both the beautiful hind and the prince were still tired from yesterday's chase; but it must be confessed that what most retarded the hind's flight was parting from him who had inflicted on her a more serious wound with his charms than with his arrows. He noticed that she often turned her head towards him as if to ask him if he intended to kill her, and whenever he was on the point of coming up with her, she made fresh attempts to escape. "Ah! if only you could understand me, little hind," he exclaimed, "you would not fly from me; I love you, and want to make a pet of you, you are so charming; I will take the greatest care of you." But the sound of his words was lost in the air, and they did not reach her.

After going all round the forest, the hind, too fatigued to continue running, slackened her pace, and the prince, feeling more joyful than he had believed possible, came up with her. He saw that all her strength was spent, and she lay, a little half-dead creature, expecting her life to be taken by her conqueror; but, on the contrary, he began to caress her. "Beautiful hind," he said, "there is nothing to fear; I want to take you away with me, and keep you with me always." He cut down some branches skilfully, bent them, covered them with moss, and scattered roses over them that grew on the bushes hard by; taking the hind in his arms, he supported her head against his neck, and laid her gently on the improvised couch. He sat near her, and from time to time gathered fine grass which she ate out of his hand.

Although the prince knew she could not understand him, he went on talking to her. Notwithstanding the pleasure she felt in his society, as night came on she began to grow anxious. "What would happen," she said to herself, "if he saw me suddenly change my form? He would be startled, and would avoid me, or if not, there would be everything to fear alone with him in this forest." She thought continually of some way of escape, when luckily he himself provided the means. Thinking she must be thirsty, the prince went in search of a brook to which he might take her. While he was gone she stole off and reached the cottage where Gilliflower was awaiting her. She threw herself on her bed, night came, the change took place, and she related the day's adventure.

"Would you believe it?" she said, "my Prince Warrior is in this forest; he is the hunter who has been chasing me for two days, and at last he caught me and caressed me again and again. His portrait falls far short of the original, he is a hundred times handsomer than the painting. Even the disorder and fatigue consequent on hard hunting took off nothing from his good looks, but rather added indescribable attractions. Am I not unfortunate to be obliged to avoid him, the prince destined for me by my nearest relatives, who loves me, and whom I love in return? Why should a wicked fairy conceive a dislike to me on the day of my birth, and make all my life miserable?" She began to weep; Gilliflower tried to console her with the hope that her troubles would soon be turned into pleasures.

When the prince had found a stream, he returned to his beloved hind; but she was no longer where he had left her. In vain he searched for her, and felt as much annoyed with her as if she had been a reasoning being. "I am always," he said, "it seems, to have to complain of that deceitful and faithless sex!" Very melancholy he returned to the old woman's house, and in relating his adventure with the hind to his friend, accused her of ingratitude. Becafigue could not help smiling at the prince's anger, and advised him to punish the hind the next time he met her. "That is my only reason for remaining here," replied the prince; "afterwards we will pursue our journey further."

Day returned, and with it the princess resumed the form of a white hind. She was undecided how to act; whether to go to the prince's usual haunts, or to take a different route and so avoid him. She chose the latter course, and went far away; but the prince, equally cunning, did the same, thinking she would try that trick, and found her in the thickest part of the forest. She had just begun to think herself safe when she saw him. Over the bushes she sprang and leaped, and, as if she dreaded worse treatment on account of the trick she had played him, she was swifter than the wind. But as she was crossing a path, he took such sure aim that he shot her leg with his arrow. She felt a violent pain, and her strength deserting her, she fell down.

Cruel and barbarous Love, what were you thinking of? You permit a matchless girl to be wounded by her tender lover! But the sad accident was inevitable, for the fairy of the spring destined it to be the turning-point of the adventure. The prince was much distressed to see that the hind was bleeding. He applied herbs to the wound to relieve the pain, and again improvised a couch with branches. He held the hind's head against his knees. " You have only yourself to blame, fickle creature," he said, " for your suffering. Why did you forsake me yesterday? You will not have the chance to-day, for I intend to take you with me." The hind made no reply; indeed what could she have said?

She was in the wrong, and was unable to speak; it is certainly of rare occurrence that those who are in the wrong keep silence. The prince caressed her again and again. " How sorry I am to have wounded you," he said; " you will hate me for it, and I want you to love me." It would seem that some hidden genius inspired him what to say to the hind. At length it was time to return to his old hostess; he burdened himself with his prey, and it gave him no little trouble; he led it, carried it, and sometimes dragged it.

The hind had not the least desire to go with him. " What will happen," she said, " when night comes and I am alone with the prince? I would sooner die." She made herself as heavy as possible, and he began to perspire with the exertion; it was not far to the cottage, but he saw that without help he would be unable to get there. He decided to fetch his faithful Becafigue, but before he left his prey, fearing she would escape, he tied her with many ribbons to the trunk of a tree.

Alas! who would have dreamed that the most beautiful princess in the world would one day be treated thus by the prince who loved her! She tried in vain to break the ribbons, but her efforts only drew the knots tighter. She was almost on the point of strangling herself with a slip-knot he had tied most unskilfully when Gilliflower, tired of being shut up in her room, went out to get some air, and came to the place where the poor hind was struggling. Her consternation at her mistress's condition may easily be imagined. The ribbons were knotted in so many different places that she was not very quick at undoing them, so that just as she was ready to take the hind away the prince and Becafigue arrived on the scene.

"Although my respect for you, madam, is very great," said the prince, "allow me to protest against the theft you are committing. I wounded the hind, she is mine, I love her, and entreat you to leave her to me." "Sir," replied Gilliflower, politely, for she was both nice-looking and well-bred, "the hind was mine first. I would rather lose my life than my hind; if you wish to make sure she knows me, let me set her free. Come, my little white darling, embrace me." The hind threw herself on the girl's neck. "Kiss my right cheek"; the order was obeyed; "touch my heart"; she laid her foot on it; "sigh," and she sighed. The prince could no longer doubt the truth of Gilliflower's words. "I give her up to you," he said, politely, "but I confess I am very sorry to do so." She at once departed with her hind.

They did not know that the prince lived in their house; he followed them, and was surprised to see them enter the good old woman's cottage. He reached it soon after, and, impelled by curiosity, asked the woman who the young lady was; she replied that she did not know, she had received her and the hind, she paid well and lived in the completest isolation. Becafigue asked where her room was situated and heard it was next to his, separated only by the partition wall.

When they gained their apartment, Becafigue told the prince he was the most mistaken of men if the girl with the hind had not lived with Princess Desirée, and he felt sure he had seen her at the palace when he had acted as ambassador there. "Why do you revive my recollection of that fatal undertaking? By what chance could she be here?" "That I cannot tell, sir," added Becafigue, "but I should like another look at her, and as nothing but a wooden framework divides us I am going to make a hole." "What useless curiosity," said the prince sadly, for Becafigue's words had brought back all his sorrows. He opened the window that looked on to the forest and fell a-dreaming.

Meanwhile, by Becafigue's exertions, a hole was made through which he saw the lovely princess dressed in a gown of silver brocade, embroidered with gold and emeralds and worked with flowers in red silk. Her hair fell in long curls over her beautiful shoulders, her complexion was brilliant and her eyes were shining. Gilliflower was on her knees binding up the arm which still bled copiously. They both seemed much troubled by the wound. "Let me die," said the princess; "death is preferable to the wretched life I am leading, to be a hind all day, to see the man whom I was destined to marry, without being able to speak to him, and tell him my wretched story! Alas! if you knew how pathetic were the things he said to me, what a sweet-sounding voice he has, what noble and attractive manners, you would pity me even more than you do, for my inability to explain matters to him."

Becafigue's astonishment at all he saw and heard may be easily imagined. He ran to the prince, tore him from the window with more joy than can be expressed. "Sir," he said, "come to the wall without delay, you will see the original of the portrait that enchanted you." The prince no sooner looked than he recognised his princess; if he had not feared he must be the victim of some strange sorcery, he would have been beside himself with joy, but how could he reconcile such a surprising encounter with Long-Thorn and her mother who were shut up in the castle of the three gables, and who designated themselves respectively Desirée and her lady-in-waiting?

His inclination was, of course, to think it all right; we are ever ready to persuade ourselves of what we wish, and on such an occasion the one thing to do was to seek an explanation. He, therefore, without delay, knocked gently at the door of the princess's room. Gilliflower, thinking it was the good old woman, and needing her help to bind up the princess's wound, hastened to open it, and was vastly surprised to see the prince, who immediately entered, and threw himself at Desirée's feet. His great joy prevented him making any coherent speech, so that, notwithstanding my efforts to learn what he said in those first moments, I have found no one able to tell me. The princess's answers were equally confused, but Love, that so often serves as interpreter to the dumb, made a third at the interview and convinced the lovers that never before were such charming things said. And certainly it was all very tender and pathetic; tears, sighs, vows, and smiles played a part. Thus the night passed and day began to break; Desirée had not given a thought to its approach, and she never again became a hind. She noticed the circumstance, and nothing could equal her joy. The prince was too dear to her not to be allowed to share her gladness. She told him her story with a charm and natural eloquence excelling that of the cleverest men and women.

"My lovely princess," he exclaimed, "was it you I wounded in the form of a white hind? How can I atone for so great a crime? Will it be enough if I die of grief before your eyes?" He was so distressed that his grief was depicted in his face. This troubled Desirée more than her wound; she assured him it was very slight, and that she rather took pleasure in a misfortune that had been productive of so much good.

Her manner of saying this was so kind that he could not but believe her protestations. To explain everything on his side, he told her of the fraud of Long-Thorn and her mother, adding that he must hasten to inform his father of his good fortune in finding Desirée, because he intended to wage war with her father in revenge for the affront he thought had been put upon him. Desirée begged him to send letters by Becafigue. He was about to obey her when a loud sound of trumpets, clarions, big drums and little drums was heard in the forest. It seemed as if a large concourse of people was passing close to the little house. The prince looked out of the window, recognised several officers and his own flags and standards: he ordered them to halt till he could join them.

The army was delighted; the men thought the prince meant to lead them against Desirée's father. The king, in spite of his great age, was commanding them in person. He was in a litter of gold-embroidered velvet, followed by an open chariot in which were Long-Thorn and her mother. Prince Warrior, perceiving the litter, hastened up to it, and the king embraced him very tenderly. "Where do you come from, my dear son?" he exclaimed; "how could you grieve me by going away?" "Sire," replied the prince, "deign to hear my story." The king got out of the litter, and withdrawing to a retired spot, his son told him of the fortunate meeting and of Long-Thorn's villainy.

The king was delighted, clasped his hands and raised his eyes to heaven in token of gratitude. Princess Desirée looked more beautiful than all the stars together. She mounted a magnificent horse that curvetted finely; her head was adorned with feathers of many colours, and the biggest diamonds imaginable were to be seen on her gown. She wore the costume of a huntress. Gilliflower, who accompanied her, was equally resplendent. This was the result of Tulip's protection; she had looked after everything carefully and successfully. The pretty wooden house had been built on purpose for the princess, and in the guise of an old woman Tulip had entertained her for several days.

When the prince had recognised his troops, and had gone to meet his father, Tulip entered Desirée's room, cured the wound in her arm by breathing on it, and gave her the rich garments in which she appeared before the king. He said all that was kind and suited to the occasion, and entreated her not to delay becoming his subjects' queen, for he went on: " I am determined to give up my kingdom to Prince Warrior in order to make him more worthy of you ". Desirée replied with all the politeness to be expected from a highly bred lady, and then looking at the two prisoners in the chariot who had covered their faces with their hands, generously demanded their pardon, and that they might be allowed the use of the chariot to take them wherever they wished to go. The king consented, all the while admiring her kind heart and praising her highly.

The army was ordered to return, and the prince mounted his horse to accompany his lovely princess. They were received in the capital with great shouts of joy. The preparations made for the wedding were of a very solemn character on account of the presence of the six kind fairies who loved the princess. They gave her the richest presents imaginable; among others, the magnificent palace where the queen had visited them suddenly appeared in the air, borne by fifty thousand Cupids. They placed it in a beautiful plain by the river side. After a gift like that, no other seemed of any importance.

Faithful Becafigue asked his master to speak to Gilliflower, and when he wedded the princess, to marry him to her. The prince was quite agreeable, and the girl was very glad to find so advantageous a match in a foreign land. Fairy Tulip, who was more generous than her sisters, gave her four gold mines in the Indies, so that her husband might not be able to say he was richer than she. The marriage festivities lasted for several months, some new entertainment was forthcoming every day, and the whole world has sung the White Hind's adventures.

THE WHITE CAT.

ONCE upon a time there was a king who had three brave and handsome sons. He feared they might be seized with the desire of reigning before his death. Certain rumours were abroad that they were trying to gain adherents to assist them in depriving him of his kingdom. The king was old, but as vigorous in mind as ever, and had no desire to yield them a position he filled so worthily. He thought, therefore, the best way of living in peace was to divert them by promises he could always escape fulfilling.

He summoned them to his closet, and after speaking kindly, added: "You will agree with me, my dear children, that my advanced age does not permit me to attend to state affairs so closely as formerly; I fear my subjects may suffer, and wish therefore to give one of you my crown, but it is only fair that in return for such a gift you should seek ways of making my intention of retiring into the country pleasing to me. It seems to me that a clever, pretty, and faithful little dog would be a pleasant companion for me; so without choosing my eldest son rather than my youngest, I declare that whichever of the three brings me the most beautiful dog shall be my heir." The princes were surprised at their father's desire for a little dog, but the two youngest thought they could turn it to their advantage, and gladly accepted the commission; the eldest was too timid and too respectful to press his rights. They took leave of the king; he gave them money and jewels, adding that in a year, without fail, they must return, and on the same day, and at the same hour bring him their little dogs.

Before their departure they repaired to a castle about a league from the town; there they brought their most intimate friends, and gave a great feast, at which the three brothers swore eternal friendship, that they would conduct the matter in hand without jealousy and annoyance, and that the successful one should share his fortune with the others. At length they set out, deciding that on their return they would meet at the same castle, and go together to the king; they would take no attendants with them, and changed their names in order not to be recognised.

Each took a different route. The two eldest had many adventures, but I shall only relate those of the youngest. He was handsome, and of a gay and merry disposition; he had a well-shaped head, great stature, regular features, beautiful teeth, and was very skilful in all exercises befitting a prince. He sang pleasantly, and played charmingly on the lute and theorbo. He could also paint; in short, he was extremely accomplished, and his valour reached almost to rashness.

A day scarcely passed that he did not buy dogs—big, little, greyhounds, bull-dogs, boar-hounds, harriers, spaniels, poodles, lap-dogs; as soon as he had a very fine one, he found one still finer, and therefore let the first go and kept the other; for it would have been impossible to take about with him, quite alone, thirty or forty thousand dogs, and he did not wish to have gentlemen-in-waiting, valets or pages in his suite. He was walking on without knowing where he was going, when night, accompanied by thunder and rain, overtook him in a forest where he could no longer see the paths.

He took the first road that offered, and after he had walked for a long time, saw a light, and felt sure there was a house near in which he could take shelter till the next day. Guided by the light, he came to the gates of a castle, the most magnificent imaginable. The gate was of gold covered with carbuncles, whose bright and pure brilliancy lighted up all the surroundings. That was the light the prince had seen from afar; the walls were of transparent porcelain painted in many colours, illustrating the history of the fairies from the creation of the world; the famous adventures of Peau d'Ane, of Finette, of Orange Tree, of Gracieuse, of the Sleeping Beauty in the Wood, of Green Serpent, and a hundred others were not omitted. He was delighted to recognise Prince Lutin, who was a sort of Scotch uncle. The rain and the bad weather prevented him remaining longer in a place where he was getting wet through, and besides, in those places where the light of the carbuncles did not reach, he could not see at all.

He returned to the gold door; he saw a stag's foot fastened to a diamond chain; he admired its magnificence, and the security in which the inhabitants of the castle must live; for he said: "What is there to keep thieves from cutting the chain and tearing out the carbuncles? they would be rich for ever."

He pulled the stag's foot and heard a bell ring, and from its sound judged it to be of gold or silver; in an instant the door was opened, he saw a dozen hands in the air, each holding a torch. He was so astonished that he hesitated to enter, when he felt other hands pushing him from behind somewhat violently. He walked on very uneasily and at great risk; he put his hand on his sword hilt. On entering a vestibule incrusted with porphyry and lapis lazuli, he heard two enchanting voices singing these words:—

" Within the bounds of this bright place
Is nought to fear and nought to flee,
Save the enchantment of a face,
If you would live still fancy-free ".

He could not imagine that if harm was intended to him later, so kind an invitation should be given now, and feeling himself pushed towards a big coral door that opened as soon as he approached it, he entered a saloon of mother-of-pearl, and then several rooms variously decorated, but so rich in paintings and precious stones that he was as if enchanted. Thousands and thousands of lights, hanging from the roof of the room, lighted some of the other apartments, which contained just the same lustres, girandoles and shelves full of wax

candles; indeed, such was the magnificence that it is difficult to believe it possible.

After passing through sixty rooms, the hands that were guiding him stopped; he saw a big and commodious armchair approach the fire-place quite alone. At the same moment the fire was lighted, and the hands, which seemed to him very beautiful, white, small, plump and well-proportioned, undressed him, for, as I already said, he was wet, and they feared he might take cold. He was presented, without seeing any one, with a shirt beautiful enough for a wedding-day, with a dressing-gown of some material frosted with gold, embroidered with small emeralds to form monograms. The bodiless hands pushed to a table where everything necessary for the toilet was set out. Nothing could be more magnificent. They combed his hair with a lightness and skill that were delightful. Then they dressed him, but not in his own clothes; they brought him others much richer. He silently wondered at all that was taking place, and sometimes could not quite control a certain impulse of fear.

When he was powdered, curled, perfumed, adorned and made more beautiful than Adonis, the hands led him into a hall resplendent with gildings and furniture. Looking round you saw the histories of the most famous cats; Rodillardus hung up by the feet at the Council of Rats, Puss in Boots, Marquis of Carabbas, the cat who wrote, the cat who became a woman, the sorcerers who became cats, their nocturnal revels and all their ceremonies; nothing could be more curious than these pictures.

The table was laid for two, with gold knife, fork and spoon for each; the sideboard was magnificent with a number of rock crystal vases and a thousand precious stones. The prince did not know for whom the two covers were intended; he perceived cats taking their places in a little orchestra built on purpose; one held a book in which was written the most extraordinary music imaginable, another a roll of paper with which he beat time, and the rest had small guitars. Suddenly each began to mew in a different key, and to strike the strings of their guitars with their sharp claws; it was the strangest music ever heard. The prince would have thought himself in hell, if the palace had not been too wonderful to give probability to such a thought, but he stuffed up his ears and laughed heartily at the different postures and grimaces of the novel musicians.

He was thinking over his various adventures since his entrance into the castle, when he saw a little figure no bigger than your arm enter the hall. The little creature was shrouded in a long, black crape veil. Two cats conducted her; they were in mourning, with cloaks and swords at their sides; a numerous procession of cats followed; some carried rat-traps full of rats and others mice in cages.

The prince was more astonished than ever; he did not know what to think. The little black figure approached him, and raising her veil, he saw the most beautiful white cat that ever was or ever will be. She looked very young and sad; she began to mew so softly and prettily that it went straight to the heart. She said to the prince: " King's son, you are welcome; my cat-like majesty is glad to see you." " Madam Cat," said the prince, " it is very kind of you to receive me so cordially, but you do not appear an ordinary animal; your gift of speech and your magnificent castle are strong proofs to the contrary." " King's son," replied White Cat, " I beg you to leave off making me compliments; I am very simple in speech and manner, but I have a kind heart. Come," she continued, " let supper be served and the musicians cease, because the prince does not understand what they say." " Are they singing anything, madam ? " he replied. " Certainly," she went on, " we have excellent poets here, and if you stay with us a little while you will be convinced of it." " It is only necessary to hear you to believe it," said the prince, politely; " you seem to be a most rare cat."

Supper was brought, the bodiless hands waited at table. First two dishes were put on the tables, one of young pigeons and the other of fat mice. The sight of the one prevented the prince from eating the other, imagining that the same cook had prepared them both. But the little cat, guessing by his expression what was passing in his mind, assured him that his kitchen was separate, and that he might eat what was given him without fear of its being rats or mice.

There was no need to repeat it; the prince felt quite sure the beautiful little cat would not deceive him. He was surprised to see that on her paw she wore a miniature. He asked her to show it him, thinking it would be Master Minagrobis. He was astonished to see a young man so handsome that it was scarcely creditable nature could have formed one like him and who resembled him so closely that it would not have been possible to paint his portrait better. She sighed, and becoming more melancholy, remained perfectly silent. The prince saw there was something extraordinary beneath; however, fearing to displease or annoy the cat, he dared not ask. He told her all the news he could think of, and found her well informed about the various interests of princes, and other things that happened in the world.

After supper White Cat invited her guest to enter a hall containing a stage on which twelve cats and twelve monkeys danced a ballet. The former were dressed as Moors and the latter as Chinese. Their leaps and capers may easily be imagined, and now and again they exchanged blows with their paws. Thus the evening ended. White Cat bade her guest good-night; the hands which had been his guides all along took charge of him again, and led him to an apartment just opposite the one he had seen. It was less magnificent than elegant. It was carpeted with butterflies' wings, whose varied colours formed a thousand different flowers. There were also very rare birds' feathers, never seen perhaps except in this place. The beds were of gauze, fastened by a thousand knots of ribbons. There were large mirrors reaching from the ceiling to the floor, and the chased gold frames represented a thousand little Cupids.

The prince went to bed in silence, for he could not carry on a conversation with the hands; he did not sleep well and was awakened by a confused noise. The hands took him out of bed, and dressed him in hunting costume. He looked out into the courtyard, and saw more than five hundred cats, some of whom led hounds in the leash, others sounded the horn; it was a great fête. White Cat was going hunting and wished the prince to join her. The helpful hands gave him a wooden horse, which galloped at full speed, and stepped grandly. He made some difficulty about mounting, saying that he was far from being a knight-errant like Don Quixote; but his resistance was of no avail, and he was put on the wooden horse. It had housings and saddle of gold and diamond embroidery. White Cat was mounted on the handsomest and finest monkey ever seen. She did not wear her long veil, but a dragoon hat, which lent her such a determined expression that all the mice of the neighbourhood were in terror. Never was there a pleasanter hunt; the cats ran quicker than the rabbits and the hares, so that when they caught them White Cat had the quarry made in front of her, and a thousand skilful and delightful tricks were done. The birds, too, were scarcely safe, for the cats climbed the trees, and the wonderful monkey carried White Cat even into the eagles' nests, so that she might dispose of the eaglets according to her pleasure.

The hunt ended, she blew a horn about a finger's length, but with so loud and clear a sound that it could easily be heard ten leagues off. When she had blown it two or three times, she was surrounded by all the cats of the country: some were in the air driving chariots, others in boats came by water; never had so many been seen before. They were all dressed differently. White Cat returned to the castle with the pompous procession, and begged the prince to come too. He was most willing, although it seemed to him that so many cats savoured somewhat of uproar and sorcery, and the cat who could speak astonished him more than all the rest.

As soon as she reached home she put on her long black veil; she supped with the prince. He was hungry and ate with a good appetite; liqueurs were served him which he drank with great pleasure, and immediately forgot the little dog he was to take the king. He only thought of mewing with the White Cat, that is, to keep her pleasant and faithful company; the days passed in pleasant fêtes, fishing, hunting, ballets, feasts, and many other ways in which he amused himself capitally; sometimes the White Cat composed verses and songs of so passionate a character that it seemed she must have a tender heart, and that she could not speak as she did without loving; but her secretary, an elderly cat, wrote so badly that although her works have been preserved, it is impossible to read them.

The prince had forgotten even his country. The hands of which I spoke continued to serve him. He sometimes regretted he was not a cat, in order that he might spend his life in that pleasant company. "Alas!" he said to White Cat, "how grieved I shall be to leave you, I love you so dearly! Either become a woman or make me a cat." She was much amused at his wish, and made mysterious answers of which he understood nothing.

A year passes so quickly when you have neither cares nor troubles, and are in good health. White Cat knew when he ought to return, and as he had quite forgotten it, she reminded him. "Do you know," she said, "that you have only three days in which to find the little dog your father wants, and your brothers have found beauties?" The prince then remembered, and astonished at his carelessness, exclaimed: "By what secret charm have I forgotten the thing more important to me than anything in the world? Unless I procure a dog wonderful enough to win me a kingdom, and a horse speedy enough to travel so long a distance in time, it is all up with my fame and fortune." He began to feel very anxious and distressed.

White Cat to comfort him said: "King's son, do not vex yourself, I am your friend. You can stay here another day, and although it is five hundred leagues from here to your country, the wooden horse will take you there in less than twelve hours." "I thank you, beautiful cat," said the prince; "but it is not enough to return to my father: I must take him a little dog." "Stay," said White Cat, "here is an acorn which contains one more beautiful than the dog-star." "Oh!" said the prince, "Madam Cat, you are laughing at me." "Put the acorn to your ear," she continued, "you will hear it bark." He obeyed, and heard the little dog say bow-wow; the prince was overjoyed, because a dog that

could get into an acorn must be very tiny.   He was so anxious to see it that he
wanted to open it, but White Cat told him it might be cold on the journey, and it
would therefore be better to wait till he was with his father.   He thanked her a
thousand times, and bade her a tender farewell.   " I assure you," he added,
" time has passed so quickly with you that I somewhat regret leaving you, and
although you are queen here, and the cats who form your court are more intelligent and more gallant than ours, I cannot help inviting you to come with me."
The cat's only reply to this was a deep sigh.

They parted ; the prince was the first to arrive at the castle where the
meeting with his brothers had been arranged to take place.   They joined him
very soon, and were surprised to see a wooden horse in the courtyard that leaped
better than all those in the riding schools.

The prince came to meet them.   They embraced each other affectionately,
and related their adventures ; but our prince did not tell his brothers his real adventures, and showed them a wretched dog which served as turnspit, saying he
considered it so pretty that it was the one he destined for the king.   No matter
how they loved one another, the two eldest were secretly glad of the youngest's
foolish choice ; being at dinner, one trod on the other's foot as if to say there
was nothing to fear on that score.

The next day they went on together in the same coach.   The king's two
eldest sons brought little dogs in baskets, so beautiful and delicate that one
scarcely dared to touch them ; the youngest brought the miserable turnspit,
which was so dirty that no one could bear it.   When they reached the palace,
they were greeted and welcomed by all ; they entered the king's rooms.   He did
not know in whose favour to decide, for the dogs brought by his two eldest sons
were almost equally beautiful, and they were already disputing the succession,
when the youngest brought them into harmony by drawing out of his pocket the
acorn White Cat had given him.   He quickly opened it, and they saw a little
dog lying on cotton wool.   He passed through a ring without touching it.   The
prince put him on the ground, and he began to dance with castanets as lightly
as the most famous Spanish girl.   He was of a thousand different colours, his
silky hair and ears dragged on the ground.   The king was greatly puzzled, for
it was impossible to find anything to say against the beauty of the little dog.

But he had not the least desire to give away his crown.   The tiniest gem
of it was dearer to him that all the dogs in the world.   He told his children he
was pleased with their labours, and they had succeeded so well in the first thing
he had asked of them that he wished to prove their skill further before fulfilling
his promise ; so that he gave them a year to look by sea and land for a piece of
linen so fine that it would pass through the eye of a needle used for making

Venice point-lace. They were all vastly distressed to be obliged to go on a new quest. The two princes, whose dogs were not so beautiful as that of the youngest, agreed. Each departed his own way without so much affection as the former time, because the turnspit had greatly cooled their love.

Our prince mounted his wooden horse again, and without caring to find other help than that he might hope from White Cat's friendliness, he speedily departed, and returned to the castle where he had been so kindly entertained. He found all the doors open, the windows, roofs, towers and walls were lighted by a hundred thousand lamps that produced a marvellous effect. The hands that had waited on him so well came to meet him, took the bridle of the wooden horse and led it to the stable, while the prince entered White Cat's room.

She was lying in a little basket on a very nice white satin mattress. Her toilette was neglected and she looked out of spirits; but when she saw the prince, she leaped and jumped to show him her joy. "Whatever reason I had," she said, "to hope that you would return, king's son, I dared not expect too much, and I am usually so unfortunate in the things I wish that this event surprises me." The grateful prince caressed her; he related the success of his journey, which she knew probably better than he, and that the king wanted a piece of linen fine enough to go through a needle's eye; that in truth he thought the thing impossible, but he intended to rely on her friendship and help. White Cat, looking serious, said she would think over the matter; fortunately, there were cats in the castle who spun excellently; she would see that what he wanted was prepared, thus he would have no need to go further afield in search of what he could more easily procure in her palace than in any other place in the world.

The hands appeared, carrying torches, and the prince and White Cat following them, entered a magnificent gallery that extended along the bank of a river, where a splendid display of fireworks took place. Four cats, who had been duly tried with all the usual formalities, were to be burned. They were accused of eating the roast meat provided for White Cat's supper, her cheese, her milk, and of having plotted against her person with Martafax and L'Hermite, famous rats of the country, and held as such by La Fontaine, a truthful writer; but all the same it was known that there was a good deal of treachery in the matter, and that most of the witnesses were bribed. However it might have been, the prince obtained their pardon. The fireworks did no one any harm, and there never were more beautiful rockets.

A very excellent supper was afterwards served, which pleased the prince more than the fireworks, for he was very hungry, and his wooden horse travelled at the greatest speed possible. The days that followed were spent in the same way as those that preceded, with a thousand different fêtes devised by White

Cat's ingenuity to amuse the prince. He is perhaps the first man who entertained himself so well in the company of cats.

It is true that White Cat had a charming, flexible and versatile mind. She
was more learned than cats usually are. The prince was sometimes astonished.
" No," he said, " what I see so surprising in you is not a natural thing; if you
love me, charming puss, tell me by what miracle you think 'and speak so
correctly that you would be received into the most famous academies of learned
men ? "   " Cease to ask questions, king's son," she said, " I am not allowed to
reply; you can carry your conjectures as far as you please, I shall not oppose
them; be contented that I never show my claws to you, and take a tender
interest in all that concerns you."

The second year passed as quickly as the first; everything the prince wished
for was immediately brought him by the hands; whether it was books, jewels,
pictures, antique medals, he had only to say I want such and such a jewel that
is in the cabinet of the Mogul or of the King of Persia, such a statue from
Corinth or Greece, and he immediately saw before him what he desired, without
knowing who brought it or whence it came. That was not without its charms,
and it is sometimes a pleasant diversion to become possessed of the most
beautiful treasures of the earth.

White Cat, who never ceased to watch over the prince's interests, warned
him that the time of his departure was drawing near, that he need not be anxious
about the linen he wanted, since she had had made for him a most wonderful
piece; she added that she wished this time to give him an equipage worthy of
his rank, and without awaiting his reply, she made him look out into the courtyard. He saw an open barouche enamelled with flame-coloured gold, with a
thousand elegant devices that pleased the intelligence as well as the eye.
Twelve snow-white horses yoked together in fours drew it, harnessed in flame-
coloured velvet embroidered with diamonds, and decorated with gold plates.
The inside of the barouche was equally magnificent, and a hundred coaches,
with eight horses, filled with nobles of fine appearance, superbly dressed, accompanied the barouche. It was also attended by a thousand body-guards, whose
coats were so thickly embroidered that you could not see the material; and what
was strangest, White Cat's portrait appeared everywhere: in the decoration of the
barouche, on the coats of the guards, or fastened with a ribbon, like an order,
round the necks of those who formed the procession.

" Go," she said to the prince, " appear at your father's court in so sumptuous a manner that your magnificence may impress him with awe, so that he
will not refuse you the crown you deserve. Here is a walnut; do not crack it
until you are before him; it contains the piece of linen you asked of me."

" Good White Cat," he said, " I confess I am so deeply sensible of your kindness that if you would consent, I would rather spend my life with you than amid all the glory I have reason to expect elsewhere." " King's son," she replied, " I am convinced of your good heart, a very rare commodity among princes ; they want to be loved by all without loving anything or any one themselves, but you are the exception that proves the rule. I shall not forget the affection you show for a little white cat, who is good for nothing but to catch mice." The prince kissed her paw and departed.

It would be difficult to understand the speed at which he travelled, if we did not know already that the wooden horse had taken less than two days to do the five hundred leagues to the castle, so that the same power that animated that horse worked in the others, and they were only twenty-four hours on the road. They halted nowhere until they reached the king's palace, where the two eldest brothers had already repaired, so that not seeing the youngest they applauded his forgetfulness and whispered : " This is very fortunate ; he is either dead or sick, he will not be our rival in this important business ". They exhibited their pieces of linen, which were indeed so fine that they went through the eye of a big needle, but could not get through that of a small one, and the king, glad of the pretext, showed them the particular needle he meant, and which the magistrates by his orders brought from the treasury of the town, where it had been carefully preserved.

There was much grumbling over this. The princes' friends, and particularly those of the oldest—for his piece of linen was the best—said that it was open chicanery, in which there was great cunning and evasion. The king's supporters upheld that he was not compelled to keep to the proposed conditions. At length, to make them all agree, a delightful sound of trumpets, drums, and hautboys was heard ; it was the arrival of the prince and his fine equipment. The king and his two sons were all vastly astonished at its magnificence.

After greeting his father very respectfully and embracing his brothers, he took the walnut out of a box ornamented with rubies, and cracked it, thinking to find in it the famous piece of linen, but instead there was a hazel nut; he cracked that, and was surprised to see a cherry stone. They looked at each other; the king smiled and laughed at his son for being credulous enough to believe a walnut could contain a piece of linen; but why should he not have believed it, since he had already found a little dog contained in an acorn? He cracked the cherry stone, which contained its kernel; then a loud murmur arose in the room, and nothing could be heard but that the youngest prince had been duped. He made no reply to the courtiers' jests; he opened the kernel and found a grain of wheat, and in the grain of wheat a millet seed. In truth, he began to get distrustful, and murmured between his teeth: "Why, cat, White Cat, you have made game of me". He felt at that moment a cat's claw on his hand, which scratched him so severely that he bled. He did not know if this was to encourage him or to make him lose heart. However, he opened the millet seed, and the people were no little astonished when he drew from it a piece of linen four hundred ells long, so wonderful that all the birds, beasts, and fishes were painted on it, with trees, fruits, and plants of the earth, the rocks, the curiosities and shells of the sea, the sun, moon, stars and planets of the heavens; further, there were the portraits of the kings and other sovereigns that had reigned in the world, those of their wives, mistresses, children and subjects, not omitting the least important of them. Each in his condition assumed the character that suited him best, and wore the costume of his country. When the king saw the piece of linen, he became as pale as the prince was red from his prolonged efforts to find it. The needle was brought, the piece of linen passed backwards and forwards through the eye six times. The king and the two eldest princes preserved a dismal silence, although the beauty and rarity of the linen compelled them to say that nothing in the world could be compared to it.

The king uttered a deep sigh, and turning to his children, said: "Nothing consoles me more in my old age than your deference to my wishes. I therefore desire to put you to a further proof. Go and travel for a year, and at the end of that time he who brings back the most beautiful girl shall marry her and be crowned king on his wedding-day. It is absolutely necessary that my successor should marry. I swear, I promise that I will not again put off the reward."

Our prince strongly felt the injustice. The little dog and the piece of linen deserved ten kingdoms rather than one, but he was too well-bred to oppose his father's will, and without delay got into the barouche again. The whole procession accompanied him, and he returned to his beloved White Cat. She knew the day and hour of his arrival. The road was strewed with flowers, a thousand perfume burners smoked on all sides, and especially in the castle. She was seated on a Persian carpet, under a canopy of cloth of gold, in a gallery whence she could see |him coming. He was received by the hands that had always waited on him. All the cats climbed up to the gutters in order to welcome him with a terrible mewing.

"Well, king's son," she said, "you have again returned without a crown?" "Madam," he replied, "your kindness has certainly given me the best chance of gaining it, but I am convinced that the king would have more trouble in giving it away than I should have pleasure in possessing it." "No matter," she said, "you must neglect nothing that can make you deserve it. I will help you this time, and since you must take a beautiful girl to your father's court, I will find you one who will cause you to win the prize. Now let us amuse ourselves; I have ordered a naval combat between my cats and the terrible rats of the country. My cats will doubtless be uncomfortable, for they fear the water, but otherwise they would have had too great an advantage, and things ought before all to be fair." The prince admired Madam Puss's prudence; he praised her highly, and accompanied her to a terrace that looked on the sea.

The cats' ships consisted of big pieces of cork, on which they floated comfortably enough. The rats had joined together several egg-shells to form their vessels. The combat was obstinately kept up; the rats threw themselves into the water, and swam far better than the cats, so that twenty times they were conquerors and conquered, but Minagrobis, admiral of the cats' fleet, reduced the rats to the extremity of despair. He greedily ate up the leader of their fleet, an old experienced rat, who had been thrice round the world in good vessels, where he was neither captain nor sailor, but only a parasite.

White Cat did not wish those poor wretches to be entirely destroyed. She knew how to rule her people, and thought that if there should be no more rats or mice in the land, her subjects would live in an idleness very harmful to them. The prince spent that year like the others in hunting, fishing, and games, for White Cat played chess extremely well. Now and again he could not help asking her fresh questions as to the miracle by which she was able to speak. He asked her if she was a fairy, or if she had become a cat by some change of shape. But she always said only what she wanted to say, and replied only what she wished; and she did this by so many phrases that meant nothing at all, that he clearly saw she did not wish to share her secret with him.

Nothing passes more swiftly than days spent without trouble or care, and if the cat had not been wise enough to remember the time for returning to the court, it is certain that the prince would have entirely forgotten it. She told him the evening before that it only rested with him to take to his father one of the most beautiful princesses the world had ever seen; that the time for destroying the fatal work of the fairies had at length arrived, and to do that it was necessary for him to cut off her head and tail, and throw them at once into the fire. " I," he exclaimed, "White Cat, my love, am I to be cruel enough to kill you? Ah, you doubtless want to prove my heart, but be sure it will never be wanting in the affection and gratitude it owes you." "No, king's son," she continued, "I do not suspect you of ingratitude, I know your merit; it is neither you nor I who rule our fate in this matter. Do what I wish; we shall both begin to be happy, and you will know on the faith of a rich and honourable cat that I am indeed your friend."

The tears came into the prince's eyes at the mere thought of cutting off his cat's pretty little head. He said everything loving and tender he could think of to dissuade her, but she obstinately replied that she wished to die by his hand, and that it was the only way of preventing his brothers from obtaining the crown; in fact, she urged him so ardently that trembling he drew his sword, and with a shaking hand cut off the head and tail of his good friend, the cat. Immediately the most charming change imaginable took place. White Cat's body grew tall, and suddenly turned into a girl, whose beauty cannot be described; never was there any so perfect. Her eyes enchanted all hearts, and her sweetness captivated them. Her stature was majestic, and her bearing noble and modest; her mind was versatile, her manners attractive; indeed, she was superior to everything that was most amiable.

The prince was so surprised, and so agreeably surprised at the sight, that he thought he must be enchanted. He could not speak, he could only look at her, and his tongue was so tied that he could not express his astonishment; but it was a very different thing when he saw an extraordinary number of lords and ladies enter the room, who, with their cats' skins thrown over their shoulders, bowed low to their queen, and testified their joy at seeing her again in her natural state. She received them with marks of kindness that were enough to prove the character of her disposition. And after holding her court for a few moments, she gave orders that she should be left alone with the prince, and spoke to him thus :—

" Do not imagine, sir, that I have always been a cat. My father ruled over six kingdoms. He loved my mother dearly, and allowed her to do exactly as she liked. Her ruling passion was travel, so that shortly before I was born she set out to visit a certain mountain, of which she had heard the most wonderful accounts. On the way she was told that near the place where she then was, was an ancient fairy castle of very great beauty, so at least report said, for, as no one had ever entered it, it could not be proved a fact; but it was well known that the fairies' garden contained the best and most delicately-flavoured fruits ever eaten.

" The queen was seized with a violent desire to taste them, and turned her steps in the direction of the castle. She reached the gate of the magnificent building that shone with gold and azure on all sides. But she knocked in vain ; none appeared, it seemed that everybody was dead. The difficulties only served to increase her desire, and she sent for ladders so that they might get over the garden wall. They would have succeeded if the walls had not visibly increased in height although no one worked at them ; they tied the ladders together, but they gave way under the weight of the climbers, who were either crippled for life or killed outright.

" The queen was in despair. She saw big trees loaded with fruits that seemed delicious ; she felt she must taste them or die ; she ordered sumptuous tents to be pitched before the castle, and she and all her court remained there six weeks. She neither ate nor slept ; she did nothing but sigh and talk of the fruit in the inaccessible garden. At length she fell dangerously ill, and no one could cure her, for the inexorable fairies had not as much as appeared since she had established herself near the castle. All her officers were greatly distressed. Only weeping and sighs were heard while the dying queen asked her attendants for fruits, but would only have what was denied her.

" One night, when she was somewhat drowsy, she saw when she woke a little ugly decrepit old woman seated in an armchair by her bedside. She was surprised her attendants should have allowed any one she did not know to come so near her. The old dame said : ' We consider your majesty very importunate in wishing so obstinately to eat of our fruits, but since your life is in danger my sisters and I have agreed to give you as many as you can carry away, and as many as you like while you remain here, provided you make us a present '. ' Ah ! my dear mother,' exclaimed the queen, ' speak ; I will give you my realms, my heart, my soul, provided I may have the fruit ; no price is too great for it ! ' ' We desire your majesty,' she said, ' to give us the daughter shortly to be born to you ; at her birth we shall come and fetch her away and bring her up among us. We shall endow her with all the virtues, with beauty and knowledge ; in

short, she will be our child ; we shall make her happy, but remember you will
see her no more until she is married.   If you like the proposal I will cure
you at once and take you to our orchards ; although it is night, you will be able
to see clearly enough to choose what you please.   If you do not like what I have
said—well, good-evening, madam, I shall go home to bed.'   ' Although the conditions you impose on me are very hard, I accept them rather than die, for it is
certain I have not a day to live.   Cure me, wise fairy,' she continued, ' and do
not let me be a moment longer without enjoying the privilege you have just
granted me.'

"The fairy touched her with a small gold wand, saying : ' May your majesty be freed from the sufferings that keep you in this bed !'   It seemed to her
immediately as though she had put off a very heavy and uncomfortable gown,
which had oppressed her.   In some places, seemingly where her malady had
been most acute, the burden still weighed upon her.   She called her ladies-in-
waiting, and told them with cheerful looks that she felt extremely well, was
going to get up, and that the gates of the fairy palace, so fast bolted and
barricaded, would be open for her to eat and carry away as much of the fruit as
she pleased.

" The ladies thought the queen was delirious, and dreaming of the fruits she
longed for ; instead therefore of answering her, they began to cry and awoke the
physicians to come and see in what a condition she was.   The delay exasperated
the queen : she asked for her clothes and was refused ; she got angry and became very flushed.   They thought it was the effect of the fever.   However, the
physicians felt her pulse, went through the usual formalities and could not deny
that she was in perfect health.   Her ladies, seeing the fault their zeal had made
them commit, tried to mend it by dressing her quickly.   They asked her pardon
and were forgiven : she hastened to follow the old fairy, who had been waiting
for her all the time.

" She entered the palace, where nothing was wanting to make it the most
beautiful place in the world.   This you will easily believe, sir," said Queen
White Cat, " when I tell you it is the very castle in which we are ; two other
fairies, a little younger than my mother's guide, received them at the door and
welcomed them kindly.   She begged them to take her at once into the garden,
and show her the trees on which she would find the best fruit.   ' They are all
equally good,' they told her, ' and if you were not so anxious to pluck them yourself, we have merely to bid them come !'   ' I entreat you, ladies,' said the queen,
' give me the pleasure of seeing so extraordinary a thing.'   The oldest put her
fingers to her mouth, and whistled three times ; then she shouted : ' Apricots,
peaches, nectarines, cherries, plums, pears, white heart cherries, melons, grapes,

apples, oranges, lemons, currants, strawberries, raspberries, come at my bidding!' 'But,' said the queen, 'those you summon, ripen at different seasons.' 'It is not so in our orchard,' they said. 'We have all the fruits the earth produces always ripe, always good; they never go bad!'

"Directly they all came, rolling, creeping along, pell-mell, without getting bruised or harmed; so that the queen, eager to satisfy her longing, took the first that offered, and rather devoured than ate them.

"When she was somewhat satisfied, she asked the fairies to let her go to the trees that she might have the pleasure of choosing the fruit with her eye, before plucking it. 'We willingly consent,' said the three fairies, 'but remember your promise. You can no longer go back from it.' 'I am sure,' she replied, 'it is very pleasant here, and if I did not love my husband so dearly, I should ask you to let me live here too; so that you need have no fear I shall retract.' The fairies, extremely pleased, opened all their gardens and enclosures; the queen stayed with them three days and three nights without wishing to go, so delicious was the fruit. She gathered some to take with her, and as it never spoiled she loaded four thousand mules with it. The fairies added to the fruit gold baskets of exquisite workmanship to put it in, and several curiosities of great value. They promised to give me the education of a princess, to make me perfect, choose a husband for me, and to inform my mother of the day of the wedding, to which they hoped she would come.

"The king was delighted at the queen's return; the whole court rejoiced with him. There were balls, masquerades, running at the ring, and banquets, where the queen's fruits were served as a delicious feast. The king ate them in preference to everything else that was offered him. He did not know the treaty she had made with the fairies, and he often asked her the name of the land from which she had brought such good things. She told him they were to be found on an almost inaccessible mountain; at another time, that they came from the valleys, then from a garden, or a big forest. So many contradictions surprised the king. He questioned those who had accompanied her, but as she had forbidden them to tell the adventure to any one, they dared not speak of it. As the time of my birth drew nearer, the queen, anxious about her promise to the fairies, fell into a terrible melancholy; she sighed every moment and changed colour rapidly. The king grew very uneasy, and urged the queen to tell him what distressed her. With great difficulty she told him what had passed between her and the fairies, and how she had promised her daughter to them. 'What!' exclaimed the king, 'we are to have no children; you know how I long for them, and for the sake of eating two or three apples you were capable of promising your daughter. You cannot have any affection for me.' He overwhelmed her with a thousand reproaches, which nearly caused my mother to die of grief; but he was not content with that: he shut her up in a tower and surrounded it with guards to prevent her having communication with anybody but the servants who waited on her, and changed those who had been with her at the fairy castle.

"The bad feeling between the king and queen threw the court into great consternation. Everybody put off his rich clothes in order to don those suitable to the general grief. The king, on his part, seemed inexorable; he never saw his wife, and directly I was born, had me brought to his palace to be fed and cared for, while the queen remained a most unhappy prisoner. The fairies knew everything that was going on; they became angry, they wanted to gain possession of me; they looked upon me as their property, and that it was a theft from them to keep me. Before seeking a revenge in proportion to their anger, they sent an embassy to the king, asking him to set the queen at liberty, and take her into favour again, and to give me to their ambassadors in order to be brought up by them. The ambassadors were so small, and so deformed—they were ugly dwarfs—that they had not the gift of persuading the king to do what they wished. He refused roughly, and if they had not speedily departed worse might have befallen them.

"When the fairies learned my father's course of action, they became very indignant; and after inflicting the most desolating evils on his six kingdoms, they let loose a terrible dragon which poisoned all the places he passed through, devoured men and children, and killed the trees and plants by breathing on them.

"The king was in the depths of despair; he consulted all the wise men in the kingdom about what he ought to do to secure his subjects from these overwhelming misfortunes. They advised him to seek through all the world for the cleverest physicians, and the most excellent remedies, and to promise life to all the condemned criminals who would fight the dragon. The king, pleased with the counsel, followed it, but without result, for the mortality continued, and every one who went against the dragon was devoured; then he had recourse to a fairy who had protected him from his earliest youth. She was very old, and scarcely ever left her bed; he went to her and reproached her for permitting fate to persecute him thus, and for not coming to his assistance. 'What do you want me to do?' she said; 'you have annoyed my sisters; they are as powerful as I am, and we seldom act against each other. Appease them by giving them your daughter; the little princess belongs to them You have closely imprisoned the queen; what has she done that you should treat so amiable a woman so badly? Fulfil the promise she gave, and I undertake that good shall come of it.'

"My father loved me dearly, but seeing no other way of saving his kingdoms, and delivering himself from the fatal dragon, he told his friend that he would trust her, and give me to the fairies since she declared I should be cherished, and treated as became a princess of my rank; that he would set the queen free, and that she had only to tell him who was to carry me to the fairy castle. ' You must carry her in her cradle,' said his fairy friend, ' to the mountain of flowers; you can even remain near and see what will happen.' The king told her that in a week he would go with the queen; meanwhile she might inform her sisters of his decision, that they might make what preparations they thought proper.

" When he returned to the palace, he released the queen with as much affection and ceremony as he had made her prisoner in anger and rage. She was so dejected and changed that he would hardly have recognised her if his heart had not assured him that it was the same woman he had so deeply loved. He entreated her with tears in his eyes to forget the troubles he had caused her, assuring her that they would be the last she would experience from him. She replied that she had brought them on herself by her imprudence in promising her daughter to the fairies, and if anything could excuse her, it was her present condition. The king then told her he intended to deliver me to their keeping. It was now the queen who objected; it seemed to be fated that I was always to be a subject for discord between my father and mother. She wept and groaned without obtaining her desire, for the king was too well aware of the fatal consequences, and our subjects continued to die as if they had been guilty of the faults of our family. At length she consented, and everything was prepared for the ceremony.

" I was put into a mother-of-pearl cradle ornamented with everything pretty that art could imagine. It was hung with wreaths and festoons of flowers made of precious stones, and the different colours catching the sun's rays became so dazzling that you could not look at them. The magnificence of my clothing surpassed that of the cradle. All the fastenings of my robes were composed of big pearls, and twenty-four princesses of the blood carried me on a sort of light litter; their ornaments were not ordinary, and they were only allowed to wear white, as befitted my innocence. The whole court accompanied me, each in his rank.

" While they were ascending the mountain, the sound of a melodious symphony was heard coming nearer, and at length the fairies, thirty in number, appeared. They had asked their good friend to accompany them; each was seated in a pearly shell bigger than that in which Venus rose from the sea; and the shells were drawn by walruses that moved uneasily on dry land. The fairies were more magnificently escorted than great queens, but they were exceed-

ingly old and ugly. They carried an olive branch to signify to the king that his submission found favour with them, and they covered me with such extraordinary caresses that it seemed they intended to live only to make me happy.

" The dragon who had avenged them on my father followed them fastened in diamond chains. They took me in their arms, kissed me, endowed me with many precious qualities, and then began the fairy dance. It was very merry, and it is incredible how those old ladies leaped and sprang ; and the dragon, who had eaten so many people, approached crawling. The three fairies, to whom my mother had promised me, seated themselves on him and placed my cradle in their midst, and striking the dragon with a wand, he unfolded his big, scaly wings, finer than crape, and of a thousand different colours ; thus they repaired to the castle. My mother, seeing me in the air at the mercy of the furious dragon, could not help uttering loud cries. The king consoled her with the assurance given him by his good friend that no harm should come to me, and that I should be as well taken care of as if I had remained in the palace. She became calmer, although it was very sad to lose me for so long, and to be her-self the cause of such a misfortune, for if she had not desired to eat the fruit in the garden, I should have remained in my father's kingdoms and should not have suffered all the misfortunes I have still to relate to you.

" Learn then, king's son, that my guardians had purposely built a tower in which were a thousand beautiful apartments for all the seasons of the year, magnificent furniture, interesting books, but no door, and you had to get in by the windows, which were extremely high up. On the tower was a beautiful garden adorned with flowers, fountains and arbours which procured shade even in the hottest season. Here the fairies brought me up with a care that surpassed everything they had promised the queen. My clothes were always in the fashion, and so splendid that if any one had seen me they would have thought it was my wedding-day. They taught me everything that belonged to my age and rank. I did not give them much trouble, for there was scarcely anything I did not un-derstand with the greatest ease ; they liked my gentleness, and as I had never seen any one except them I might have lived contented with them for the rest of my life.

" They always visited me, mounted on the furious dragon I have already mentioned ; they never spoke of the king or queen ; they called me their daughter, and I thought I was. No one lived with me in the tower except a parrot and a little dog they had given me for my amusement, for the animals were endowed with reason, and spoke perfectly.

" One of the sides of the castle was built on a deep road, so full of ruts and trees that it was almost impassable, so that since I had lived in the tower I had

never seen any one there. But one day when I was at the window chatting
with the parrot and dog I heard a noise. I looked all round and saw a young
knight who had stopped to listen to our conversation ; I had never seen any one
like him, except in pictures. I was not sorry that an unexpected meeting should
afford me such an opportunity, and having no idea of the danger that is attached
to the satisfaction of contemplating a pleasant thing, I came forward to look at
him, and the longer I looked, the more pleasure I felt. He made me a low bow,
and fixed his eyes on me, and seemed greatly troubled to know how he might
speak to me ; for my window was very high, and he feared to be overheard,
well knowing that I was in the fairy castle.

"Night suddenly came on, or to speak more correctly, it came without our
perceiving it. He sounded his horn two or three times very prettily and then
departed ; it was so dark that I could not see which way he went. I was in a
dream and no longer took the same pleasure as before in chatting with my parrot
and dog. They told me the prettiest things imaginable, for fairy animals are
intelligent, but I was pre-occupied and knew not how to dissemble. Parrot
noticed it ; he was cunning and did not betray what was passing in his mind.

"I did not fail to rise with the dawn. I ran to my window and was agreeably surprised to see the young knight at the foot of the town. He was magnificently dressed. I flattered myself that it was somewhat on my account, and I
was not mistaken. He talked to me through a kind of speaking trumpet, and by
its aid told me that, having been hitherto insensible to all the beauties
he had seen, he was suddenly so impressed with me, that unless he saw
me every day of his life he should die. I was charmed with the compliment, and much distressed at not daring to reply to it, for it would
have been necessary to shout with all my might, and so risk being better
heard by the fairies than by him. I threw him some flowers I had in my
hands ; he received them as a marked favour, kissed them several times and
thanked me. He then asked me if I should like him to come every day at the
same time to my windows, and, if so, I was to throw him something. I took a
turquoise ring from my finger and hastily threw it him, signing him to go away
quickly because I heard the Fairy Violent mounting her dragon to bring me my
breakfast.

"The first words she said on entering the room were : ' I smell the voice of
a man here ; search for him, dragon '. Imagine my feelings. I was paralysed
with fear lest he should go out by the other window and follow the knight in
whom I was already greatly interested. ' My dear mamma ' (for it was thus the
old fairy liked me to call her), ' you are joking when you say you smell a man's
voice ; has a voice any smell ? and even if it has, who is the mortal daring

enough to ascend this tower?' 'What you say is true, my daughter,' she replied; 'I am delighted you argue so nicely, and I suppose it must be the hatred I have for men which sometimes makes me think they are not far from me.' She gave me my breakfast and my distaff. 'When you have finished eating, spin,' she said, 'for you are very idle and my sisters will be angry.' I had been so taken up with my unknown knight that I had found it impossible to spin.

"As soon as she was gone, I saucily threw the distaff on the ground, and ascended the terrace to see farther over the country. I had an excellent spy-glass; nothing impeded my view; I looked on all sides, and discovered my knight on the top of a mountain. He was resting under a rich pavilion of some gold material, and was surrounded by a large court. I supposed he must be the son of some king who was a neighbour of the fairies' palace. As I feared if he returned to the tower he would be discovered by the terrible dragon, I told my parrot to fly to the mountain, seek out the man who had spoken to me, and beg him on my part not to return, because I dreaded my guardians' vigilance, and that they might do him some mischief.

"Parrot acquitted himself of the mission like a parrot of intelligence. It surprised everybody to see him come swiftly and perch on the prince's shoulder and whisper in his ear. The prince felt both pleasure and pain at the message; my anxiety for his welfare flattered him, but the difficulty of seeing and speaking to me overwhelmed him, without, however, turning him from his purpose of pleasing me. He asked Parrot a hundred questions, and Parrot in his turn asked him a hundred, for he was curious by nature. The king entrusted him with a ring for me instead of my turquoise; it was formed of the same stones, but was much more beautiful than mine; it was cut in the shape of a heart, and orna-mented with diamonds. 'It is only right,' he added, 'that I should treat you as an ambassador; here is my portrait, only show it to your charming mistress.' He fastened the portrait under his wing and brought the ring in his beak.

"I awaited my little messenger's return with an impatience I had never before felt. He told me my knight was a great king; that he had received him most kindly, and that I might rest assured he only wished to live for me; that in spite of the danger he ran in coming to my tower, he was determined to risk everything rather than give up the pleasure of seeing me. That news worried me greatly, and I began to weep. Parrot and Bow-wow consoled me as well as they could, for they loved me dearly; then Parrot gave me the prince's ring and showed me the portrait. I confess I was extremely glad to be able to examine closely the man I had only seen in the distance. He seemed even more charm-ing than I had imagined; a thousand thoughts, some pleasant, others sad, came

24

into my mind, and gave me an extraordinary look of anxiety. The fairies perceived it, and said to each other that doubtless I was feeling bored, and they must, therefore, think about finding me a husband of fairy race. They spoke of several, and fixed on the little King Migonnet, whose kingdom was five hundred thousand leagues from their palace, but that was of no consequence. Parrot overheard this fine advice, and told me of it. 'Ah!' he said, 'I pity you, my dear mistress, if you become Migonnet's queen; his appearance is enough to frighten any one. I regret to say it, but truly the king who loves you would not have him for a footman.' 'Have you seen him, Parrot?' I asked. 'I should think so,' continued he; 'I have been on a branch with him.' 'What! on a branch?' I replied. 'Yes,' he said; 'he has the claws of an eagle.'

" Such a tale distressed me strangely. I looked at the charming portrait of the king; I thought he could only have given it to Parrot so that I might have an opportunity of seeing him, and when I compared him with Migonnet I could hope for nothing more in life, and determined to die rather than marry him.

" I did not sleep the whole night through. Parrot and Bow-wow talked to me. I slept a little towards morning; and as my dog had a keen scent he smelt that the king was at the bottom of the tower. He woke Parrot. ' I bet,' he said, ' the king is down below.' Parrot replied : ' Be quiet, chatterbox ; because your eyes are always open and your ear on the alert, you object to others resting '. ' But let us bet,' said Bow-wow again ; ' I know he is there.' Parrot replied : ' And I know very well he is not ; did I not carry a message from my mistress forbidding him to come?' ' Truly, you're imposing nicely on me with your prohibitions,' exclaimed the dog. ' A passionate man only consults his heart ' ; and thereupon he began to pull his wings about so roughly that Parrot grew angry. Their cries awoke me ; they told me the cause of the dispute ; I ran, or rather flew, to the window. I saw the king, who stretched out his arms, and told me, by means of his trumpet, that he could not live without me, and implored me to find means to get out of the tower, or for him to enter it ; he called all the gods and the elements to witness that he would marry me and make me one of the greatest queens in the world.

" I told Parrot to go and tell him that what he hoped seemed to me almost impossible ; but that relying on the promise he had made me and on his oaths, I would attempt to do what he wished. But I implored him not to come every day, because he might be seen, and the fairies would give no quarter.

" He went away greatly rejoiced at the hope I held out ; but when I thought over what I had just promised, I was in the greatest possible embarrassment. How to get out of a tower that had no doors, the only assistance being Parrot and Bow-wow ! to be so young, inexperienced, and timid ! I therefore determined not to attempt a thing in which I could never succeed, and sent Parrot to tell the king so. He almost killed himself then and there; but at length he ordered him to persuade me either to come and see him die, or to console him. 'Sire,' exclaimed the feathered ambassador, 'my mistress has the will but lacks the power.'

"When he related to me all that had taken place I was more distressed than ever. Fairy Violent came and found my eyes red and swollen; she declared I had been crying, and that if I did not tell her the reason she would burn me, for her threats were always terrible. I replied, trembling, that I was tired of spinning, and that I wanted some small nets to catch the little birds that pecked the fruit in my garden. 'What you desire,' she said, 'need cost you no more tears. I will bring you as much twine as you like'; and in fact I had it the same evening; but she advised me to think less of working than of making myself beautiful, because King Migonnet was expected shortly. I shuddered at the terrible news and said nothing.

"When she was gone, I began to make two or three pieces of netting; but what I really worked at was a rope ladder, and, although I had never seen one, it was very well made. The fairy did not provide me with as much twine as I wanted, and continually said: 'But, my daughter, your work is like Penelope's, it never advances, and you are never tired of asking me for more material'. 'Oh! my dear mamma,' I said, 'it is all very well to talk, but don't you see that I am not very skilful, and burn it all? Are you afraid I shall ruin you in twine?' My look of simplicity rejoiced her, although she was of a very disagreeable and cruel disposition.

"I sent Parrot to tell the king to come one evening under the windows of the tower, that he would find a ladder there, and would know the rest when he arrived. I made it fast; determined to fly with him; but when he saw it he did not wait for me to come down but eagerly ascended it, and rushed into my room just as I was preparing for my flight.

"I was so delighted to see him that I forgot the danger we were in. He repeated his oaths, and implored me not to delay making him my husband. Parrot and Bow-wow were witnesses of our marriage; never was a wedding between people of such high rank concluded with less splendour and fuss, and never was any couple happier than we were.

"Day had scarcely dawned when the king left me: I told him the fairies' terrible plan of marrying me to the little Migonnet; I described his appearance, and he was as horrified as I was. After his departure the hours seemed to me as long as years. I ran to the window, I followed him with my eyes in spite of the darkness, but what was my astonishment to see in the air a fiery chariot drawn by winged salamanders who travelled at such speed that the eye could scarcely follow them. The chariot was accompanied by several guards mounted on ostriches. I had not leisure enough to examine the creature which thus tra-versed the air; but I imagined it must be a fairy or a sorcerer.

"Soon after Fairy Violent entered my room. 'I bring you good news,' she said; 'your lover has been here for some hours; prepare to receive him; here are clothes and jewels.' 'Who told you,' I exclaimed, 'that I wanted to be married? it is not at all my desire; send King Migonnet away. I shall not put on a pin more, whether he thinks me beautiful or ugly; I am not for him.' 'Oh! indeed,' said the fairy, 'what a little rebel! what a little idiot! I do not permit such conduct, and I will make you . . .' 'What will you do to me?' I asked, quite red with the names she had called me. 'Could any one be worse treated than I was, in a tower with a parrot and a dog, seeing every day the hideous and terrible dragon?' 'Oh! you ungrateful little thing,' said the fairy, 'did you deserve so much care and trouble? I have often told my sisters we should have a poor reward.' She sought them and told them our dispute; they were all greatly surprised.

"Parrot and Bow-wow remonstrated with me, and said if I persisted in rebelling, they foresaw that bitter misfortunes would happen to me. I was so proud of possessing the heart of a great king that I despised the fairies, and the advice of my poor little companions. I did not dress myself, and did my hair all crooked so that Migonnet might find me unpleasing. Our interview took place on the terrace. He came there in his fiery chariot. Never since there were dwarfs had one so small been seen. He walked on his eagle's feet and on his knees all at the same time, because he had no bones in his legs, and he supported himself on diamond crutches. His royal cloak was only half-an-ell long, and a third of it dragged along the ground. His head was as big as a bushel measure, and his nose so big that he carried a dozen birds on it, in whose chirping he delighted. His beard was so tremendous that canaries made their nests in it, and his ear projected an arm's length beyond his head, but it was scarcely noticed because of a high, pointed crown he wore to make himself appear taller. The flame of his chariot roasted the fruits, and dried up the flowers and fountains of my garden. He came to me, arms open to embrace me; I held myself so upright that his chief squire had to lift him up, but directly he was near me I fled into my room, shut the door and windows, so that Migonnet went back to the fairies very angry with me.

"They asked him to forgive my rudeness, and to appease him—for he was to be feared—they determined to bring him into my room at night while I was asleep, to tie my hands and feet, and put me with him into his burning chariot, so

that he might take me away with him. The matter once decided, they scarcely scolded me for my rudeness; they only said I must think how to make up for it. Parrot and Bow-wow were surprised at this gentleness. 'Do you know, my mistress,' said the dog, 'I do not augur well from it; the fairies are strange creatures, and very violent.' I laughed at these fears, and awaited my beloved husband most impatiently; he was too anxious to see me to be late. I let down the rope ladder, fully resolved to return with him; he ascended with light step, and spoke to me so tenderly that I dare not recall to memory what he said.

"While we were talking with as much security as if we had been in his palace, suddenly the windows of the room were darkened. The fairies entered on their horrible dragon, Migonnet followed in his fiery chariot, with all his guards and their ostriches. The king, without fear, laid hold of his sword, and only thought of protecting me from the most horrible calamity, for, shall I tell you, sir? the savage creatures set their dragon on him, and it devoured him before my very eyes.

" In despair at his misfortune and mine, I threw myself into the horrid monster's mouth, wishing him to swallow me as he had just swallowed all I loved best in the world. He was very willing, but not so the fairies, who were more cruel than he was. 'We must reserve her,' they said, 'for longer torment; a speedy death is too good for that unworthy girl.' They touched me and I at once became a white cat. They brought me to this magnificent palace, which belonged to my father. They changed all the lords and ladies into cats; of some they allowed only the hands to be seen, and reduced me to the deplorable condition in which you found me, informing me of my rank, of the death of my father and mother, and that I could only be delivered from my cat-form by a prince who should exactly resemble the husband they had torn from me. You, sir, possess that likeness," she continued, "the same features, same expression, the same tone of voice. I was struck by it directly I saw you. I was informed of all that had happened and will happen; my troubles are at an end." "And mine, beautiful queen," said the prince, throwing himself at her feet, "will they be of long duration?" "I already love you more than my life, sir," said the queen. "We must go to your father and see what he thinks of me, and if he will consent to what you desire."

She went out, the prince took her hand, and she stepped into a chariot more magnificent than those he had hitherto seen. The rest of the equipment equalled it in such a degree that all the horses' shoes were of emerald with diamond nails. Probably that is the only time such a thing was seen. I do not relate the pleasant conversation of the queen and the prince; it was unique in its charm and intelligence, and the young prince was as perfect as she was ; so that their thoughts were most beautiful.

.. When they were near the castle where the prince was to meet his two eldest brothers, the queen went inside a little crystal rock whose points were all adorned with rubies and gold. It had curtains all round, so that you could not see it, and it was carried by handsome young men magnificently attired. The prince remained in the chariot, and perceived his brothers walking with very beautiful princesses. When they recognised him they drew near to receive him, and asked him if he had brought a mistress with him. He said he had been unfortunate enough during all his travels only to meet very ugly women, and the most beautiful thing he had brought was a little white cat. They began to laugh at his simplicity. " A cat !" they said ; "are you afraid that our palace will be eaten up by mice." The prince replied that he was certainly not wise to make his father such a present, and each then took his way to the town.

The elder princes and their princesses got into barouches of gold and azure, the horses wore feathers and aigrettes on their heads, and nothing could have been more brilliant than the cavalcade. Our young prince followed, and then the crystal rock that everybody looked at with admiration.

The courtiers hastened to tell the king that the three princes had arrived. " Do they bring beautiful women with them ? " asked the king. " It is impossible that they should be surpassed," was their reply. He seemed vexed at the answer. The two princes eagerly entered with their wonderful princesses. The king welcomed them kindly, and did not know to which to award the prize. He looked at the youngest, and said : " This time you come alone ? " " Your majesty will see in that rock a little white cat," replied the prince, " which mews so prettily and is so gentle that she will charm you." The king smiled, and himself opened the rock, but, as he approached it, the queen by a spring shattered it to pieces, and appeared like the sun which has been for some time hidden by a cloud ; her fair hair was flowing over her shoulders, and fell in long curls to her feet ; her head was encircled with flowers ; her gown was of a light white gauze, lined with pink silk ; she rose and made the king a low curtesy, who, in the excess of his admiration, could not help exclaiming : " This is the matchless woman who deserves my crown ".

" Sire," she said, " I am not come to take from you a throne you fill so worthily. I possess, by inheritance, six kingdoms : allow me to offer you one, and give the same to each of your sons. As a reward, I only ask for your affection, and this young prince for my husband. We shall have quite enough with three kingdoms." The king and the court uttered cries of joy and astonishment. The marriage was celebrated at once, and also the marriage of the two

princes, so that the court spent many months in amusements and delights.
Then each went to rule his own kingdom.   The beautiful White Cat was
immortalised as much by her goodness and generosity as by her rare merit and
beauty.

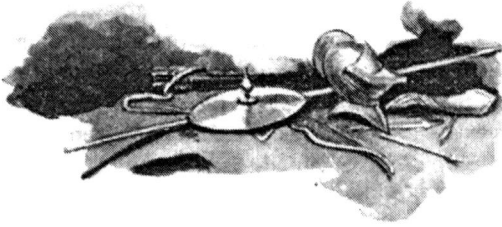

BELLE-BELLE.

ONCE upon a time there was a king who was very powerful, and at the same time very gentle, and greatly loved by his people, but his neighbour the Emperor Matapa was even more powerful than he. They had carried on great wars with each other; in the last the emperor won an important battle, and having killed or made prisoner the greater part of the king's captains and soldiers, laid siege to his capital city, took it, and made himself master of all the treasure it contained. The king had scarcely time to save himself and his sister the queen-dowager, a young widow possessing wit and beauty, but of a haughty, passionate and unsympathetic disposition.

The emperor transferred the king's jewels and furniture to his own palace ; he brought away with him a great number of soldiers, young girls, horses, and many things that he might find useful or that might please him. When he had laid waste the larger part of the conquered kingdom, he returned to his own, where he was joyfully welcomed by the empress and his daughter.

But the conquered king did not patiently submit to the indignity that had been put upon him. He assembled a few troops, out of which he formed a small army, and to increase it, published a decree, enacting that the gentlemen of the kingdom should serve in person, or send one of their children ; they were to be well provided with arms and horses, and must be willing to support all his undertakings.

Near the frontier lived an old nobleman eighty years of age, of great wisdom and intelligence, but fortune had treated him so ill that after possessing great wealth he was reduced to comparative poverty; he would have endured it patiently had it not been for his three beautiful daughters. They were too sensible to grumble at their misfortunes, and if by chance they spoke of them to their father, it was rather to console him than to add to his troubles.

They were living a quiet, unambitious life under their rustic roof when the king's edict reached the ears of the old man; he called his daughters, and looking sadly at them, said: "What are we to do? The king commands every person of rank in his kingdom to serve against the emperor, or failing obedience, he condemns them to pay a heavy fine. I cannot pay the tax; thus I am in a terrible case; it means death or ruin." His three daughters were as distressed as he was, but they entreated their father to take courage, because they felt sure they would be able to discover some remedy for his trouble.

In fact, the next morning the eldest sought her father, who was walking sadly in his orchard. "Sir," she said, "I come to beg you to let me join the army; I am of tall stature, and fairly strong; I will accoutre myself like a man, and can pass for your son; if I do not perform heroic deeds, I shall at least save you the journey or the tax." The count kissed her tenderly, and at first opposed such an extraordinary plan; but with great firmness, she pointed out that she saw no other remedy, and at last he consented.

It was then merely a question of providing her with a costume suitable to the part she was to play. Her father gave her arms, and the best horse of the four that served for the labour of the farm; the farewells and regrets were tender on all sides. After travelling for several days, she passed alongside a meadow, bordered by quick-set hedges. She saw a shepherdess in great trouble, trying to get one of her sheep out of a ditch into which it had fallen. "What are you doing, my good shepherdess?" she said. "Alas!" replied the shepherdess, "I'm trying to save my sheep which is drowning, and I'm so weak that I have not strength enough to pull it out." "I pity you," she said, and without offering to help her, went off. The shepherdess at once cried out: "Farewell, beautiful girl!" Our heroine's surprise cannot be expressed. "How," said she, "can she possibly recognise me? The old shepherdess scarcely saw me for a moment, and she knows I am disguised; what am I to do? I shall be recognised by every one, and if the king finds me out, how ashamed and angry I shall be! He will think my father a coward, who tries to avoid danger." Upon reflection, she thought it best to return home.

The earl and his daughters were speaking of her, and counting the days since her departure, when she entered; she told them of her adventure, and her father said he had foreseen it. If she had taken his advice she would never have started, for it is impossible not to recognise a girl in disguise. This threw the whole family into fresh embarrassment; they did not know what to do, when the second girl in her turn sought the count. "My sister," she said, "had never ridden on horseback, and it is not surprising that she should have been recognised; if you let me go instead, I promise you will have no reason to regret it."

Nothing the old man could say in opposition to her plan was of the least avail. He therefore consented to her departure; she wore a different costume, took other arms, and rode another horse. Thus equipped, she embraced her father and sisters over and over again, resolved on serving the king well; but passing by the same meadow where her sister had seen the shepherdess, she also saw the sheep at the bottom of a ditch, and the shepherdess occupied in pulling it out. "Unfortunate shepherdess that I am!" she exclaimed, "half of my flock has perished in this manner; if some one would help me I could save this poor animal; but every one avoids me." "What! shepherdess," said the girl, "you take so little care of your sheep that you let them fall into the water!" and without offering further consolation she put spurs to her horse.

The old woman shouted with all her might: "Farewell, lovely girl!" These few words distressed our amazon in no slight degree. "How unlucky!" she said, "I, too, am recognised; I am no more fortunate than my sister, and it would be ridiculous for me to join the army with so feminine an appearance that everybody would recognise me." She at once returned to her father's house, very sad at the ill-success of her journey.

He welcomed her kindly, and praised her prudence in returning; but that did not prevent their troubles beginning again with as much force as ever; already they had cost them the material of two useless costumes and many smaller things. The good old man grieved in secret because he did not wish his daughters to witness his sorrow.

At last the youngest entreated him most urgently to grant her the same favour as he granted her sisters. "Perhaps," she said, "it is presumptuous on my part to hope for better success than they; but still I should like to try my luck. I am taller than they; you know I hunt every day, and the exercise has given me some talent for war, and my great desire to lessen your troubles endows me with extraordinary courage." The count loved her much more than her two sisters; she looked after him so well that he regarded her as his one consolation; she read interesting stories to amuse him, and watched over him when he was ill, and all the game she killed was only for him, so that he used even stronger arguments to dissuade her from her plan than those he had used with regard to her sisters. "Will you leave me, my dear daughter?" he said. "Your absence would cause my death; even if fortune favoured you, and you returned covered with laurels, I should not have the pleasure of seeing your triumph, for my advanced age, and the lack of your sweet presence, will end my days." "No, my father," said Belle-Belle, as they called her, "do not think I shall be long away; the war must come to an end: if I saw any other means of satisfying the king's commands I should be glad enough; for let me confess to you, if my going away causes you trouble, it gives me even more." He at last let her have her way. She made herself a very simple costume; those of her sisters had cost so much, and the count was so poor, that she was obliged to take a wretched horse because her sisters had lamed the others; she was not, however, at all discouraged. She embraced her father, received his blessing, and after mingling her tears with those of her father and sisters, departed.

Passing through the meadow of which I have already spoken, she found the old shepherdess, who was still trying to pull a sheep out of the ditch. "What are you doing, shepherdess?" said Belle-Belle, stopping. "I am doing nothing, sir," replied the shepherdess; "since daybreak I've been busy about this sheep. My labours are of no avail, and I'm so tired that I can scarcely breathe; every day some new misfortune happens to me, and no one comes to my assistance."

"Truly, I pity you," said Belle-Belle, "and to prove my compassion I will help you." She dismounted, and her horse was so docile that she did not tie him up to prevent his running away; then, jumping over the hedge, she set to work so bravely that she soon rescued the sheep. "Do not weep, my good mother," she said to the shepherdess; "here is your sheep, and considering the length of time he has been in the water, he seems pretty cheerful."

"You have done a kindness to one who will not be ungrateful. I recognise you, lovely Belle-Belle. I know where you are going and all your plans. Your sisters passed by this meadow. I recognised them too, and knew what was in their minds. But they seemed so hard-hearted, and their behaviour to me was so ungracious, that I took measures to prevent them continuing their journey. You have acted very differently, and you will profit by it, Belle-Belle, for I am a fairy, and am glad to heap benefits on those who are deserving. Your horse is horribly skinny; I will give you another." She touched the ground with her crook, and Belle-Belle immediately heard the sound of neighing behind a bush. She looked, and perceived the most beautiful horse imaginable. He began to run and leap in the meadow. Belle-Belle, who loved horses, was delighted to see one so perfect in every way. The fairy called the beautiful steed, and touching it with her crook, said: "Faithful Comrade, be better caparisoned than the Emperor Matapa's best horse". Immediately Comrade had a saddle cloth of green velvet embroidered with diamonds and rubies, a saddle to match, and a bridle of pearls, with gold bosses and bit; indeed, nothing more magnificent could possibly be found.

"What you see," said the fairy, "is the least that is to be admired in this horse. He has many talents that I must point out to you. Firstly, he only eats once a-week, and there is no need to groom him; he knows the past, the present, and the future; moreover, he has been long in my service. I have educated him as if for myself. When you want information on any matter, or if you have need of advice, you must ask him, and he will give you such wise counsel that sovereigns would be most fortunate if they had advisers like him; you must, therefore, consider him your friend rather than your horse. Then your costume is not to my liking. I will give you one which will suit you better." She struck the ground with her crook, and out came a big trunk covered with Levant morocco, and studded with diamonds: Belle-Belle's initials were on the lid. The fairy sought in the grass for a gold key made in England, and opened the box with it. It was lined with embroidered Spanish leather. Inside were twelve coats, twelve cravats, twelve swords, twelve ostrich plumes; everything by the dozen. The coats were so heavy with embroidery and diamonds that Belle-Belle could scarcely lift them. "Choose the one you like best," said the fairy; "and as for the others, they will follow you wherever you go. You have only to stamp your foot on the ground, and say: 'Leather trunk, come to me full of coats; leather trunk, come to me full of linen and lace; leather trunk, come to me full of jewels and money'. You will at once see it, whether you are in the open country or in your room. You must also choose a name, for Belle-Belle is not suited to the part you are to play; it seems to me you might call yourself Fortuné. But it is only right that you should make my acquaintance, and I will therefore assume my ordinary shape." Her old skin fell off, and she looked so marvellous that Belle-Belle was dazzled; her gown was of blue velvet, lined with ermine, her hair bound with pearls, and she wore a magnificent crown on her head.

Overcome with admiration, Belle-Belle threw herself at her feet with every mark of respect and gratitude. The fairy raised her, and tenderly embraced her, advising her to choose a costume of green and gold brocade. Belle-Belle obeyed, and mounting her horse, proceeded on her way, so impressed with all the extraordinary things that had just taken place that she could think of nothing else.

She asked herself by what unexpected good fortune she had gained the protection of so powerful a fairy, "For really," she said, "I was not needed to pull her sheep out of the ditch; one stroke of her wand could bring a whole flock from the Antipodes if it had betaken itself there. It was, however, a fortunate thing that I was able to help her, since the trifle I did for her has caused her to do so much for me; she knew my heart, and my disposition pleased her. Ah! if my father could only see me now, magnificent and rich, how glad he would be! but I can at least share the gifts she has bestowed on me with my family."

Thus reflecting, she reached a beautiful, well-populated city; all eyes were turned on her. The people followed and surrounded her, saying: " Have you ever seen a knight so handsome, so well mounted, and so richly clad ? How gracefully he manages his splendid horse ! "

She was treated most courteously. When she was about to enter the inn, the governor, who had been in the streets and had admired her in passing, sent a gentleman to invite her to the castle. Fortuné (for so we must call her in future) replied that not having the honour of the governor's acquaintance, he could not take such a liberty, but that he would visit him later, and begged him to lend him one of his servants to carry something of importance to his father. The governor sent him a very trustworthy man, and Fortuné made him promise to return in the evening when his despatches would be ready.

He shut himself up in his room, and stamping with his foot, said: " Leather trunk, come to me full of diamonds and gold coins ". The trunk at once appeared, but there was no key, and where was he to look for it ? It was a pity to break open a gold lock enamelled in different colours ; and, moreover, what was there not to be feared from a locksmith's indiscretion ? Directly he mentioned the treasures, the knight would be robbed and perhaps killed.

He searched everywhere for the gold key, but in vain. " What misery," he exclaimed ; " I cannot avail myself of the fairy's kindness, nor let my father share her gifts." He thought the best plan would be to consult his horse ; he went down to the stable and whispered : " I entreat you, my Comrade, tell me where the key of the leather trunk is to be found ". " In my ear," he replied. Looking in his horse's ear, Fortuné perceived a green ribbon ; he pulled it out, and there was the much-desired key. He opened the leather trunk, which contained more diamonds and gold coins than could be put into a big cask. The knight filled three small boxes, one for his father and one for each of his sisters. He gave them to the messenger, and begged him to travel night and day without stopping until he reached the count's dwelling.

The messenger made all speed, and when he told the good old man that he came from his son, and brought him a very heavy box, the father wondered what could be inside, for Belle-Belle had departed with so little money that it did not seem possible she could have bought anything, or even paid a messenger's expenses. He opened the letter first, and when he read what his beloved daughter had written, he thought he should die for joy. The sight of the jewels and gold proved the truth of her words ; it was, however, very strange that on opening their boxes, Belle-Belle's sisters found only pieces of glass and counter- feit coins, the fairy being unwilling that they should share in her gifts. They thought their sister intended to make fun of them, and were inexpressibly annoyed. Seeing their anger, the count gave them the greater part of his jewels, but as soon as they touched them, they were changed like the others; then they recognised that some unknown power was working in a hostile fashion against them, and they begged their father to keep what remained for himself.

Fortuné did not await his messenger's return; his journey was too important, for he must obey the king's commands. He went to the governor's house, and the whole town assembled there to see him; his person and bearing were so charming that no one could help admiring and liking him. All he said was delightful to listen to, and the crowd round him was so great that he could not imagine to what to attribute so extraordinary a thing, for living always in the country he had seen very few people.

He continued his way on his excellent horse, who conversed most pleasantly on the news of the day, or on the most remarkable events in ancient and modern history. "My dear master," he said, "I am enchanted to be yours, you are frank and honourable; I am disgusted with certain people among whom I lived a long while, and who made me hate life, so unbearable was their society. One of the men professed affection for me, and when he spoke in my presence placed me above Pegasus and Bucephalus, but when my back was turned he treated me like the sorriest hack; he even praised my faults in order that I might contract greater ones. It is true that one day, tired of his caresses, which, properly speaking, were treachery, I kicked him so violently that I broke nearly all his teeth, and I never see him now without saying with great sincerity: "It is not fair that a mouth which opens so often to hurt those who do you no harm should be as pretty as that of others". "Ho, ho!" exclaimed the knight, "you are very -mischievous; did you not fear that in his anger the man would run his sword through your body?" "It would not have been of the least consequence, sir," rejoined Comrade, "since, as soon as he had formed such an intention, I should have known of it."

Speaking thus, they reached a vast forest. Comrade said to the knight: "Master, there is a man here who would be of great use to us; he is a wood-cutter and is endowed". "What do you mean by that?" interrupted Fortuné. "Being endowed means that he has received one or more gifts from the fairies," added the horse; "you must get him to go with us." By this time they had reached the place where the woodcutter was at work. In a gentle, insinuating manner, the young knight asked him several questions about the forest, whether there were any wild beasts in it, and if hunting was allowed. The woodcutter gave very intelligent replies. Fortuné inquired where all the men were who had helped him to fell so many trees. The man said he had cut them all down by himself, that it had been the work of only a few hours, and that he must fell many more to make himself anything of a load. "What! do you intend to carry all that wood away to-day?" said the knight. "Oh, sir," replied Strong-Back (for that was his name), "I am not a man of ordinary strength." "Do you make a good living?" asked Fortuné. "I earn very little," replied the woodcutter. "We are poor folk in this place; each man does his work himself, and does not expect his neighbour to do it for him." "Since you inhabit so poor a country," added the knight, "and it is in your power to go elsewhere, come with me; you shall want for nothing, and if at any time you wish to return, I will pay the expenses of the journey." The woodcutter thought he could not do better, so he left his quarters and accompanied his new master.

When he had passed through the forest and had reached the open, he saw a man tying up his legs with ribbons, and leaving so little space between them that it appeared impossible for him to walk. Comrade stopped and said to his master: "Sir, there is another of these fairy-gifted men; you will want him and must take him with you". Fortuné went up to him, and with his native grace asked him why he tied up his legs. "I am preparing for the hunt," he answered. "What!" said the knight; "do you mean to say you can run faster bound like that?" "No, sir," he rejoined, "I am aware that my speed will be less, but that is what I want, for when my legs are free there is not a stag, roe, or hare that I do not outstrip; thus they escape, and I never enjoy the delight of catching them." "You seem to be a remarkable man," said Fortuné; "what is your name?" "I am called Fleet-Foot," said the hunter, "and I am known in this country." "If you would like to travel," said the knight, "I should be very glad if you would come with me. You shall not have much trouble, and I will treat you very well." Fleet-Foot, who was only moderately happy, willingly accepted the proposal. So Fortuné, accompanied by his new servant, proceeded on his journey.

The next day, he came upon a man on the edge of a marsh, who was putting a bandage over his eyes; the horse said to his master: "Sir, I advise you to take that man into your service". Fortuné asked him why he put a bandage over his eyes. "Because," was the answer, "I see too clearly. I see the game stirring more than four leagues off, so that every shot kills more than I want; I am, therefore, obliged to put a bandage over my eyes, and, although then I only see dimly, I destroy the partridges and other small game in the country in less than two hours."

"You are very skilful," rejoined Fortuné. "I am called Good-Shot," said the man, "and I would not relinquish the occupation for anything in the world." "I am, however, most desirous of suggesting that you should travel with me," said the knight; "you can exercise your talent just the same." Good-Shot made some difficulties, and was more troublesome to win over than the others, for such men are generally fond of liberty : however, he gave in at last, and the knight left the marsh.

Some days later, passing by a meadow, he observed in it a man lying on his side. Comrade said to his master: "That man is also fairy-gifted; I foresee that he will be very useful to you". Fortuné entered the meadow, and asked him what he was doing. " I want a particular kind of herb," he said, " and I am listening to those about to sprout to see if the one I require is among them." " What ! " said the knight, " is your hearing so keen that sounds beneath the earth reach you, and you can discover what is going to come forth!" "For that reason," said the listener, " I am called Quick-Ear." "Well! Quick-Ear," continued Fortuné, " are you inclined to accompany me ? I will pay you well." The man, delighted at so pleasant a prospect, did not hesitate to take his place with the rest.

Going on his way, the knight saw a man near the high road whose inflated cheeks produced a most absurd effect ; he was standing erect, and looking towards a high mountain two leagues off, on which were fifty or sixty windmills. The horse said to his master: " He is one of the fairy-gifted, be careful not to lose the opportunity of taking him with you ". Fortuné, who, as soon as he appeared or spoke, was able to prevail on them all, approached the man, and asked him what he was doing. " I am blowing a little, sir," he said, " to make the mills grind." " It seems to me you are very far off," replied the knight. " On the contrary," rejoined the blower, " I find I am too near ; and, if I did not keep back half my breath, I should have already overturned the mills, and, perhaps, the mountains on which they stand : in this way, I unwillingly cause many evils, and I tell you, sir, that I have been very badly treated by my mistress. When I went to sigh in the woods, my sighs uprooted the trees and made terrible havoc, so that I was called in that country Impetuous." " If any one here objects to your presence," said Fortuné, " and you like to come with me, here are people who will keep you company ; they also have extraordinary talents." " I have so natural a curiosity for everything that is out of the common," replied Impetuous, " that I accept your proposal."

Fortuné, well contented, travelled on. When he had crossed some fairly open country, he saw a large pond, fed by several springs ; on the bank was a man who looked at him with attention. " Sir," said Comrade to his master, " here is a man who is lacking to your company ; if you can induce him to go with you, it would be no bad thing." The knight approached him, saying : " Will you tell me what you are doing ?" " Sir," replied the man, " you will see, as soon as the pond is full, I shall drink it at one draught ; for I am still thirsty, although I have emptied it twice." In fact, he bent down, and when he got up, there was not enough water for the very tiniest fish. Fortuné was not less surprised than all his company. "What!" he said, "are you always so thirsty?" "No," said the water-drinker, "I only drink like this when I've eaten something too salt, or when it is a matter of some wager. I am known by the name of Drinker." "Come with me, Drinker," said the knight, "I will give you wine to drink, and that is better than water." The man was greatly pleased at the promise, and at once began to march with the rest.

The knight was already in sight of the place of meeting, where all the king's subjects were to assemble, when he espied a man eating so greedily that although there might have been more than sixty thousand Genoese rolls by him, he seemed determined not to leave a single crumb. Comrade said to his master: "Sir, only that man is now wanting; I pray you persuade him to come with you". The knight approached him, and smiling, said: "Are you determined to eat all that bread for your breakfast?" "Yes," he replied; "my only regret is that there is so little, but the bakers are such idle fellows, they don't care in the least whether you are hungry or not." "If you need so much every day," added Fortuné, "you would cause a famine in any country." "O sir," rejoined Glutton (for so he was named), "I should be very sorry to have such an appetite always; neither my property nor that of my neighbours would be sufficient. It is true that from time to time I like to regale myself in this way." "Friend Glutton," said Fortuné, "come with me, and I promise you good cheer; you shall not repent choosing me for your master."

Comrade, who was not lacking in intelligence and foresight, warned the knight that it would be well to forbid his men to boast of their unusual gifts. Without delay, he called them and said: "Listen, Strong-Back, Fleet-Foot, Good-Shot, Quick-Ear, Impetuous, Drinker, and Glutton. I advise you, if you wish to please me, to keep your talents secret, and I promise to care so much for your happiness that you will be content." Each swore to obey his orders. Soon after, the knight, more charming by reason of his beauty and dignified bearing than by his magnificent costume, entered the capital, riding his excellent horse, and accompanied by his gifted servants. He did not delay to have liveries of gold and silver made for them; he gave them horses, lodging in the best inn, and awaited the day fixed for the review; but the whole town talked of nothing but of him, and the king hearing of his reputation, was most eager to see him.

The troops assembled in a large plain, and thither came the king, the queen-dowager, and all the court; in spite of the misfortunes the state had suffered, the court was still very magnificent. Fortuné was dazzled by so much luxury. But if that attracted his attention, his matchless beauty did not less attract the illustrious company; everybody asked who the handsome and good-looking young knight was, and the king, passing by the place where he was standing, made him a sign to approach.

Fortuné immediately dismounted, and made the king a low bow; he could not help blushing at the attention with which he looked at him; and the colour added brilliance to his complexion. " I should be very glad," said the king, " to know who you are, and what you are called." " Sire," he replied, "my name is Fortuné, though, so far, there is no reason why I should be so called; for my father, who is count of the frontier, although born to a property that befitted his rank, is now very poor." " Fortuné," replied the king, "your god-mother has not served your interests badly in bringing you here; I feel a great liking for you, and I remember your father rendered great services to mine. I will requite them in your person." "That is only fair," said the queen-dowager, who had not yet spoken; " and as I am your elder, my brother, and know in greater detail than you all that the count of the frontier did during many years for the good of the realm, I beg you to leave to me the charge of rewarding this young knight."

Fortuné, delighted to receive so kind a welcome, could not thank the king and queen enough; he did not, however, enlarge on his feeling of gratitude, thinking it more respectful to be silent than to talk too much. The little he did say was so suitable and to the point that all applauded him; then he mounted his horse again, and mixed with the nobles who accompanied the king; but every moment the queen summoned him to ask a thousand questions, and turning to Florida, her dearest friend, whispered: " What do you think of this knight? Could there be a nobler air or more regular features? I confess I've never seen anything more charming." Florida found it easy to agree with the queen, and she added high praise, for the knight seemed not less charming to her than to her mistress.

Fortuné could not help from time to time looking at the king; he was the handsomest prince imaginable, and his manners were most prepossessing. Belle-Belle, who in assuming her disguise had not renounced her sex, felt a real affection for him.

After the review, the king told him he feared the war would be bloody, and resolved, therefore, to attach him to his person. The queen-dowager, who was present, exclaimed that she had had the same thought, that he must not be exposed to the dangers of a long campaign, that the office of high-steward at her palace was vacant, and that she would give it to him. " No," said the king, " I wish to make him my chief equerry." They disputed about the pleasure of advancing Fortuné; and the queen, fearing to make known the secret passion already taking possession of her heart, yielded the knight to the king.

Every day he summoned the leather trunk, and took from it a new costume. He was certainly more magnificent than any prince at the court, so that the queen sometimes asked him how his father was able to go to such expense. At other times she teased him: "Confess the truth," she said; "you have a mistress, and it is she who sends all the beautiful things we see." Fortuné blushed, and respectfully answered the queen's questions.

He acquitted himself admirably of his office. His heart, sensible of the king's merit, was more attracted to him than under the circumstances was exactly desirable. "What a fate is mine!" he said. "I love a great king without the hope that he loves me, or that he should take any heed of what I suffer." The king, on his side, overwhelmed him with kindness, and only considered well done the things accomplished by the handsome knight. The queen, deceived by his disguise, thought of the means of contracting a secret marriage with him; the difference in their rank was the only circumstance that troubled her.

She was not the only one who was attracted by Fortuné; the most beautiful ladies of the court felt his influence in spite of themselves. He was overwhelmed with love-letters, assignations, gifts, and gallantries, to which he responded with such great indifference that they all suspected he had a mistress in his own country. It was not that he did not desire to appear to advantage at the fêtes; he carried off the prizes at the tournaments; he killed more game in the hunt than all the others; he danced at the ball with more grace and skill than any of the courtiers; indeed it was a delight to see and hear him.

The queen wished to spare herself the shame of declaring her passion. She charged Florida to give him to understand that he ought not to regard with indifference the favour of a young and beautiful queen. The commission greatly embarrassed Florida; she could not escape the fate of the greater part of those who had seen the knight, and she found him so charming that she was unable to put her mistress's interests above her own; so that every time the queen gave her an opportunity of talking to him, instead of speaking of the beauty and the noble qualities of the princess, she only spoke of her bad temper, of what her women suffered in consequence, of the injustice she did them, and of the bad use she made of the power she had usurped in the kingdom; then comparing her sentiments: "I was not born a queen," she said, "but, truly, I ought to be one. I am generous enough to be kind to every one. Ah! if I were of that august rank," she continued, "handsome Fortuné should be happy! he should love me from gratitude, if not from inclination."

Dismayed by this speech, the young knight knew not what to reply, and carefully avoided being alone with her. The queen, in her impatience, continually asked Florida how she was influencing Fortuné ? " He thinks so little of himself," she said, " and is so bashful that he will not believe what I tell him of your favour, or he pretends not to believe it, because some other passion occupies his heart. " " I agree with you," said the queen, alarmed ; " but would he not sacrifice everything to his ambition ? " " And," replied Florida, " would you owe his heart to your crown ? When a woman is young, beautiful, and of rare merit, like yourself, is it necessary to rely on the glamour of a diadem ? " " To subjugate a rebel heart," exclaimed the queen, " a woman has recourse to everything." Thus Florida knew there was no longer any possibility of curing her mistress of her infatuation.

The queen was always hoping for some good result from her confidant's care on her behalf ; but the small progress Florida made with Fortuné obliged the queen to seek the means of conversing with him herself. She knew that he walked every morning in a little wood situated just under the windows of her apartments. She rose with the dawn, and looking in the direction in which he would come, saw him strolling carelessly along with a melancholy air. She called Florida. " You have spoken the truth," she said ; " doubtless Fortuné is in love with some one in this court, or in his own country, see how sad he looks." " I have observed it also in his conversation," replied Florida, " and you would do well to forget him, madam." " It's too late," said the queen, with a deep sigh ! " But since he has gone into the arbour let us join him ; I wish you only to accompany me." The girl did not dare to prevent the queen, but she would have greatly liked to do so, because she feared in the end she would make Fortuné love her, and, besides, a rival of such high rank is always dangerous. When the queen had advanced a little way into the wood, she heard the knight singing. He had a very nice voice, and had set these words to a new tune then in vogue :—

> " How difficult it is,
> With tenderness to love, to live in tranquil peace !
> Enchanting happiness !
> The more I know thy bliss, the more I fear 'twill cease.
> Incessantly the care
> Of unknown future Fate oppresses me with fear,
> When of my earnest prayer,
> My heart's most fervent wish, accomplishment is near."

In this song, Fortuné expressed his feelings towards the king, and described the kindness that prince had shown him, his own dread of being recognised and forced to leave a court where he was better off than in any other place in the world. The queen, while listening, felt extremely troubled. "What can I do?" she whispered to Florida; "the ungrateful fellow despises the honour of pleasing me, he esteems himself happy, seems satisfied with his conquest, and sacrifices me to another." "His is an age," replied Florida, "when reason does not reign paramount, and if I dared offer your majesty advice, it would be to forget a foolish youth who is incapable of taking advantage of his good fortune." This was scarcely what the queen wished her confidant to say; she gave her a furious glance, and advancing hastily, suddenly entered the arbour where the knight was resting. She feigned surprise at finding him there, and was annoyed that he should see her in deshabille although she had omitted nothing that could lend it elegance and magnificence.

When he saw her the knight would have withdrawn out of respect, but she begged him to remain and accompany her in her walk. "I was awakened this morning," she said, "by the birds' delightful singing; the pure air and cool weather invited me to listen to them at closer quarters. How happy they are! Alas! they know only pleasure, sorrow does not trouble their life." "It seems to me, madam," replied Fortuné, "that they are not entirely free from care and anxiety; they have always to fear the fatal shots or the deceitful nets of the hunter; it is not only birds of prey that make war on these innocents. When a severe winter freezes the ground and covers it with snow, they die for want of a little hemp or millet seed; and every year they must find a new mistress." "Then, sir knight," said the queen, smiling, "you think that a trouble. Why, there are men who delight in doing so a dozen times a-year. You seem surprised," she continued; "your heart then is made of different stuff, if you have not yet changed." "I have no means, madam, of knowing of what I am capable," said the knight, "for I have never loved; but I am bold enough to believe that if I did love any one, it would be for all my life." "You have never loved," exclaimed the queen, looking at him so fixedly that the poor knight kept changing colour; "you have never loved! Fortuné, how can you say that to a queen who reads in your eyes and on your countenance the passion that occupies your heart, and who has just heard the words you have set to the new tune now in vogue?" "It is true, madam, that I composed those verses," he said, "but I had no special reason for writing them. Every day my friends ask me to write drinking songs, although I drink nothing but water; others again ask for love ditties, and thus though neither a lover nor a drinker, I sing of Cupid and Bacchus."

The queen's emotion was so great that she could hardly keep calm. His words rekindled the hope Florida had tried to take from her. "If I could think you sincere," she said, "I should be much surprised that you have not found any one in this court charming enough to win your affection." "Madam," replied Fortuné, " I am so fully occupied in discharging the duties of my office, that I have no time for sighing." " Then you really love no one?" added she, passionately. " No, madam," he said, " I am not gallant enough. I am a sort of misanthrope who loves his liberty, and would not part with it for anything in the world." The queen sat down, and looking at him affectionately, rejoined: " There are chains so beautiful and glorious that one must be happy to wear them ; if fortune destines such for you, I advise you to renounce your liberty ". Speaking thus, her eyes only too clearly revealed her meaning, and the knight's strong suspicions were confirmed. Fearing the conversation might go too far, he took out his watch, and pushing the hand on a little, said : " I ask your majesty to permit me to go to the palace ; it is the hour of the king's rising, and he commanded me to be there ". " Go, heartless creature," she said, sighing deeply ; " you are quite right to be attentive to my brother, but it would not be wrong if you dedicated some of your duty to me."

The queen followed him with her eyes, then lowered them, and reflecting on what had passed, blushed with shame and anger. What added to her vexation was that Florida witnessed it, and she observed a look of triumph in her face that seemed to say she would have done better to have taken her advice than to have spoken to Fortuné. She considered for some time, and taking her tablets wrote these lines which she had set to music by the Lulli of her court :—

> " Thou seest ! thou seest ! at last
>   The torments I disdain ;
> My conqueror ! unmoved
>   Thou witnessest my pain.

> " Before him has my heart
>   Its cruel wound displayed,
> With all that should be hid
>   Nor ever be betrayed.

> " And hast thou marked his scorn,
>   Contempt and cruelty ?
> Ah ! could I but hate him,
>   I know that he hates me.

> " But fruitless are such hopes,
>   And vain is my desire,
> For nought but love for him
>   Can he in me inspire."

Florida played her part with the queen very well ; she did her best to console her, gave her some return of hope, of which she stood greatly in need.

" Fortuné feels so far beneath you, madam," she said, " that maybe he did not understand what you meant; it seems to me a very great deal that he has assured you he loves no other." It is so human to hope that the queen took heart again. She did not see that Florida in her malice, and convinced that the knight cared nothing for the queen, wanted to make her speak more explicitly to him, so that he, might anger her the more with the indifference of his response.

He, on his side, felt greatly embarrassed. His situation was most uncomfortable, and, if it had not been that his affection for the king kept him there in spite of himself, he would have quitted the court without any hesitation. He was careful only to see the queen at the hours of her receptions and in the king's suite; she, perceiving this change of conduct, gave him many opportunities of making love to her, of which he did not avail himself. One day when she went into her garden she saw him walking in a grove that led to the little wood. She called to him, and he fearing to displease her by pretending not to hear, respectfully approached her.

" Do you remember, sir knight," she said, " the conversation we had in the arbour some time ago ? " " Madam," he replied, " I could not possibly forget such an honour." " Doubtless the questions I asked you," she added, " gave you pain, for since that day you have carefully avoided giving me the opportunity of putting others to you." " As chance alone procured me that favour," he said, " it seems to me I should have been bold to seek others." " Say rather, ungrateful youth," she continued, growing red, " that you have avoided my presence; you know my sentiments only too well." Fortuné cast down his eyes with a confused and modest air, and as he hesitated to reply, the queen said: " You are much disconcerted; go, do not attempt to answer me, I understand you only too well ". She would, perhaps, have said more, but she perceived the king coming to walk in the garden.

She went to meet him, and observing his melancholy expression, implored him to tell her what was the matter. " You must know," said the king, " that for a month past I have been informed that a dragon of enormous size has been ravaging all the country side. I thought it would be possible to kill him, and gave the necessary orders, but all attempts have failed; he devours my subjects, their flocks, and everything that comes in his way; he poisons the rivers and springs, or drinks them up, and dries up the grass and plants on which he lies." While the king was speaking, the irritated queen turned over in her mind a sure means of revenging herself on the knight.

" I was aware," she replied, " of the bad news. Fortuné, whom you saw with me, came to tell me of it, but, my brother, you will be surprised at what I am going to say. He urgently asked me to get your permission for him to fight the dreadful dragon. He is so wonderfully clever, and wields his arms with so much dexterity, that I should not be surprised if he is right in putting so much confidence in himself. Added to that, he told me he had a secret for sending the most wakeful dragons to sleep; however we need speak no further of it, since it does not seem that much value is to be attached to his action." "However it turned out," said the king, "it would be to his glory, and of great use to us should he be successful. But I fear it would be the result of no half-hearted zeal, and would cost him his life." "No, my brother," added the queen, "do not anticipate that; he told me the most surprising things. You know he is by nature very sincere, and what honour can he hope from dying thoughtlessly? Indeed," she continued, "I promised to obtain for him what he desires so ardently, that if you refuse him, he will die."

"I consent then," said the king, "but I confess it is with regret; let us summon him." He signed to Fortuné to approach, and said, kindly: "The queen has just told me of your desire to fight the dragon that is desolating our land. It is a bold resolve, and I think you can scarcely understand the danger." "I pointed it out to him," said the queen, "but he is so eager to show his zeal in your service, that nothing will deter him; and I augur a fortunate issue."

Fortuné was surprised, but too quick-witted not to comprehend the queen's evil design; but his natural kindliness forbade him to mention it, and without replying, allowed her to go on talking; he contented himself with making low bows, which the king took for fresh entreaties to him to grant his permission. "Go, then," he said, with a sigh, "go where glory summons you. I know your skill in everything, and especially in wielding arms; and the monster will find it difficult to escape your blows." "Sire," replied the knight, "however the combat turns out, I shall be content; either I shall deliver you from a terrible scourge, or die in your service; but grant me one favour I infinitely desire." "Ask what you will," said the king. "I venture," he continued, "to ask for your portrait." It pleased the king hugely that Fortuné should ask for his portrait at a time when his mind must have been filled with so many other things, but the queen felt a new annoyance, that he should not have made her the same request; it would indeed have needed amiability enough and to spare to desire the portrait of so wicked a woman.

The king returned to his palace, and the queen to hers. Fortuné, greatly embarrassed at the promise he had made, sought his horse, and said: "My dear Comrade, here is fine news". "I know it already, sir," he replied. "What shall we do?" asked Fortuné. "We must set out as soon as possible," replied the horse; "procure an order from the king in which he commands you to fight the dragon, and then we shall do our duty". Those words comforted the knight. Early the next day he went to the king, in a travelling suit, as well made as all the others that came out of the leather trunk.

Directly the king saw him, he cried out: "What! are you ready to go?" "I cannot use too much speed in executing your commands, sire," he replied; "I come to bid you farewell." The king could not help feeling sad to see a knight so young, handsome, and perfect about to expose himself to the greatest possible danger.

He embraced him, and gave him his portrait, set in big diamonds. Fortuné took it with extraordinary joy; the king's great merit had touched him to such a degree, that he could imagine no one in the world more delightful than he was, and if he suffered pain at the parting, it was less from fear of being swallowed by the dragon, than from being deprived of so beloved a presence.

In the particular decree, ordering Fortuné to fight the dragon, the king enclosed a general one to all his subjects, commanding them to help him, and give him any assistance he might need. Fortuné took leave of the king, and, in order that nothing in his conduct might seem strange, he went to the queen, whom he found at her toilette, and surrounded by several of her ladies. She changed colour when he entered. With how much she had to reproach herself on his account! He greeted her respectfully, and asked her if she wished to honour him with her orders since he was just starting. Those words finished disconcerting her, and Florida, who knew nothing of what the queen had plotted against the knight, was much dismayed; she would have liked to speak to him privately, but he wisely avoided such embarrassing conversations.

"I pray that the gods," said the queen, "may make you victorious, and bring you back triumphant." "Madam," replied the knight, "your majesty does me too much honour. You know well enough the danger I run. I, too, do not ignore it. However, I am full of confidence, and am, perhaps, on this occasion, the only one who is hopeful." The queen understood what he meant, and had there been fewer people in the room, would doubtless have answered the implied reproach.

The knight returned to his own abode, and ordered his excellent servants to mount their horses and accompany him, since the time had come for them to prove what they could do; they all testified their joy at being able to serve him. In less than an hour they were ready, and set out together, assuring him that they would neglect nothing to give him satisfaction. As soon as they were alone in the country, and no longer fearful of observation, each made trial of his skill. Drinker drank the water of the ponds, and fished out the finest fish for his master's dinner; Fleet-Foot caught stags as they ran, and seized hares, notwithstanding their cunning; Good-Shot gave no quarter to partridges or pheasants, and when the game, venison, and fish were all taken, Strong-Back cheerfully carried them. So far only Quick-Ear had not made himself useful; he listened for truffles, mushrooms, salad, and fine herbs to come forth from the earth. Thus the journey cost Fortuné scarcely anything, and he would have been well enough amused by all these extraordinary things had not his heart been full of what he had just quitted. The king's merit was always present to him, and the queen's malice seemed so great that he could not help hating her.

He went on, wrapped in profound thought, from which he was awakened by the piercing shrieks of many persons; these were the poor peasants the dragon was devouring. Some who had escaped were running at the top of their speed. Fortuné called to them but they would not stop; he followed them, spoke with them, and learnt that the monster was not far off. He asked them how they made sure about it; they told him water was scarce in the country, therefore they only drank rain water, and to preserve it had made a pond. After his fatigues, the dragon came to drink of it, his cries were so loud they could be heard a league off, and that all the people, terribly frightened, hid themselves, and closed the windows and doors of their houses.

The knight entered an inn, not so much to rest as to ask his horse's advice. When every one had retired, he went down to the stable and said: "Comrade, how are we to conquer the dragon?" "Sir," he said, "I will dream of it to-night and tell you in the morning." When Fortuné returned to him, Comrade said: "I think Quick-Ear should listen if the dragon is approaching". Quick-Ear lay down on the ground, and heard the cries of the dragon, although he was still seven leagues off. When the horse was informed of this, he said to Fortuné: "Order Drinker to drink all the water that is in the big pond and Strong-Back to take enough wine there to fill it; you must also put in it raisins, pepper, and other things that cause thirst; order the inhabitants to remain shut up in their houses, and you, sir, do not come out of that, you and your people will choose to stay in; the dragon will not delay to come and drink the pond; the wine will seem good to him, and you will see how successfully it will all turn out".

No sooner had Comrade given these orders than all set to work to carry them out. The knight entered a house whence he could see the pond. He was hardly there before the dreadful dragon came; he drank a little, then ate the breakfast provided for him, and drank so much that he became intoxicated. He could not move but lay on his side, his head bent and his eyes closed. When Fortuné saw him thus, he judged he had not a moment to lose; he came forth, sword in hand, and attacked him with marvellous courage. The dragon, feeling himself pierced on all sides, tried to get up and fall on the knight, but he had not the strength, and was fast losing blood; the knight, delighted at having reduced him to this extremity, called his men to bind the monster with cords and chains, wishing to let the king have the pleasure and glory of giving him his death-stroke; so that there being nothing further to fear, they dragged him to the town.

Fortuné walked at the head of the procession. Approaching the palace he sent Fleet-Foot to inform the king of his success; but it seemed well-nigh incredible until the creature was seen on a machine, made expressly, to which he was bound.

The king came down and embraced Fortuné. "The gods reserved this victory for you," he said, "and I am less glad to see the dragon in that condition than to see you once again, my dear knight". "Sire," he replied, "your majesty must give him the final stroke. I only brought him to receive it at your hands." The king drew his sword and made an end of his most cruel enemy; everybody uttered shouts of joy and acclamation at so unexpected a victory.

Florida, always uneasy, was not long in learning the return of the handsome knight. She hastened to tell the queen, who was so surprised and so overcome with love and hate, that she was unable to reply to what her favourite said. She reproached herself over and over again for the shabby trick she had played him, but she would rather see him dead than indifferent, so that she was uncertain if she was glad or sorry he had returned to a court where his presence would again trouble the repose of her life.

The king, impatient to recount to her the success of so extraordinary an adventure, entered her room leaning on the knight. "Here is the conqueror of the dragon," he said to the queen. "He has just rendered me the most signal service I could hope from a faithful subject. It was to you, madam, he spoke first of his desire to fight the monster; I hope you will take into account the danger to which he has been exposed." The queen, composing her countenance, honoured Fortuné with a gracious welcome and a thousand praises. She found him still more charming than when he set out, and the attention with which she looked at him assured him that her heart was still wounded.

She was not willing to trust to the confession of her eyes alone, so one day when they were hunting with the king, she pretended not to follow the hounds, because she did not feel well. Then turning to the young knight, who was not far off: "You will be good enough," she said, "to remain near me; I wish to dismount and rest a little. Go," she added to her attendants, "do not leave my brother." She then got down from her horse, and with Florida sat beside a brook, where for some time she remained in profound silence.   She was considering the turn she should give to her discourse.

Then raising her eyes, she fixed them on the knight and said : " As good intentions are not always apparent, I fear you have not divined the motives that urged me to persuade the king to send you to fight the dragon.   I was sure from a presentiment that has never deceived me that you would come out of it as a man of courage, and those who were envious of you spoke so ill of your bravery because you had not gone to the army, that some glorious deed like this was wanted to close their mouths.   I should have told you what was said about you," she continued, " and perhaps I ought to have done so ; but I was convinced that your resentment would have its consequences, and that it was, therefore, better to silence those evil-intentioned persons by your intrepid conduct in danger than by an authority which would mark you out rather as a favourite than a soldier.   You see, now, sir knight," she went on, " I have taken a lively interest in all your triumphs, and that it would be very wrong of you to judge otherwise."   " The distance that separates us is so great, madam," he replied, modestly, " that I am neither worthy of the explanation you have offered me, nor of the care you have taken to risk my life in order to save my honour. Heaven has protected me with more kindness than my enemies desired, and I shall ever esteem myself happy in spending in the king's service and in yours a life of less value to me than you think."

Fortuné's respectful reproach disconcerted the queen ; she perceived all he meant it to convey, but he fascinated her too greatly for her to risk estranging him by some sharp reply; on the contrary, she pretended to enter into his feelings and made him relate to her the way in which he had overcome the dragon. Fortuné was careful not to tell any one that it was by the aid of his men ; he declared he had gone straight up to the formidable enemy, and that his skill alone and even his temerity had pulled him through.   But the queen, paying scarcely any attention to what he was saying, interrupted him to ask if he was now convinced of her share in all that concerned him.   The conversation might have been carried further, when he said : " Madam, I hear the sound of the horn ; the king is coming ; will not your majesty mount and go and meet him ? " " No," she said, with an air of disdain, " it will be enough if you go."   " The king would blame me, madam," he added, " if I left you in a place where you might run some danger."   " I will absolve you from your anxiety," she added, in a decided manner.   " Go, your presence importunes me."

At that command the knight made her a low bow, mounted his horse, and rode out of sight, feeling very anxious as to what would be the result of this fresh anger.   He consulted his excellent horse : " Tell me, Comrade," he said,

" if this too loving, passionate queen will find some other monster by whose means to rid herself of me?" "She herself is enough," replied the gentle horse; "she is more of a dragon than the one you killed, and she will exercise your patience and virtue in as great a degree." "Will she cause me to lose the king's favour?" he exclaimed; "that is the only thing I fear." "I have no intention of revealing the future," said Comrade; "be satisfied that I shall watch over everything." He said no more, because he saw the king at the end of a grove. Fortuné told him of the queen's indisposition, and how she had ordered him to remain with her. "She seems to favour you very much," said the king, smiling, "and you seem to open your heart to her rather than to me; I've not forgotten that you asked her to obtain for you permission to fight the dragon." "Sire," replied the knight, "I dare not defend myself from what you say; but I can assure your majesty that I regard your favour very differently from that of the queen, and were it permitted to a subject to make a confidant of his sovereign, I should deem it a very particular joy to confess all the feelings of my heart to you." The king interrupted him by asking where he had left the queen.

While he was proceeding to join her, she was complaining of Fortuné's indifference to Florida. "The sight of him is becoming odious to me," she exclaimed; "either he or I must leave the court. I cannot endure the presence of an ungrateful fellow who dares to treat me so contemptuously. Where is the man who would not consider himself fortunate in finding favour with the all-powerful queen of this kingdom? He is surely the only one in the whole universe. Ah! the gods have reserved him on purpose to torment me."

Florida was glad that her mistress should be angry with Fortuné, and instead of appeasing her wrath she increased it, reminding the queen of many circumstances she had perhaps not cared to observe. Her vexation augmented, and she conceived a fresh plan for the knight's destruction.

As soon as the king reached her, and had shown all proper anxiety about her health, she said: "I confess I do not feel very well, but Fortuné should be enough to cure any one; he is so diverting, and his ideas are so absurd. You must know," she continued, "he has begged me to ask a second favour of your majesty. Confident of success, he desires to take on the rashest undertaking imaginable." "Does he want to fight another dragon?" exclaimed the king. "He now undertakes to overcome several at once," she said; "for let me tell you, he boasts of forcing the emperor to restore our treasure, and to do this he does not require an army." "What a pity it is," replied the king, "that this poor boy should be so mad." "His combat with the dragon," added the queen, "makes him think he can do greater things, and what do you risk in permitting him to act in your service?" "I risk his life, which is dear to me," replied the king; "it would grieve me much to be the cause of his death." "However things go, it follows he must die," she said, "for I assure you he is so eager to recover your treasure, that if you refuse your permission, he will languish away."

The king became very gloomy. "I cannot imagine," he said, "who it is that fills his head with these ideas; it grieves me he should be in such a condition." "But," replied the queen, "he fought the dragon and conquered it, and will perhaps succeed again. My presentiments are generally right, and my heart tells me the issue of his undertaking will be fortunate; I beg you, brother, not to oppose his zeal." "I must summon him," added the king, "and at least point out to him the risk he is running." "That is the very way to annoy him," replied the queen; "he will think you do not wish him to go, and to attempt to prevent it by any consideration applying to himself will not be of the least use, for I have already said everything suitable to the occasion." "Very well," said the king, "let him go; I consent." The delighted queen called Fortuné. "Knight," she said, "thank the king, he grants you the permission you so much desire to seek out the Emperor Matapa, and compel him to restore, willingly or by force, the treasure he carried off from us; make your preparations with the same speed as you did for fighting the dragon."

Fortuné, much surprised, understood by this the queen's anger against him; he felt glad, however, to lay down his life for a king he so much loved, and without making any objections to so extraordinary a mission, he knelt down and kissed the king's hand. On his side the king was much distressed. The queen felt a sort of shame to see with what submission he received his condemnation to death. "Can it be," she said to herself, "that he does love me, and rather than deny what I have said on his behalf, he endures the evil trick I play him without complaining? Ah! if I dared to think so, how I should blame myself for the danger to which I am exposing him!" The king spoke to the knight, and mounted his horse; the queen got into her coach, pretending she still felt indisposed.

Fortuné accompanied the king to the end of the forest. Entering it for the purpose of taking counsel with his horse, he said: "My faithful Comrade, it's all up with me; I must die. The queen has just arranged a plan with which I should never have credited her." "My dear master," replied the horse, "do not be alarmed; although I was not present at the interview, I have known all about it for a long time, and the mission is less terrible than you think." "But you do not know," continued the knight, "that the emperor is the most violent of men, and if I suggest to him the restoration of what he took from the king, his only reply will be to tie a rope round my neck, and have me thrown into the river." " I am quite aware of his violent temper," said Comrade, " but that need not prevent you taking your men with you and starting ; if you perish, we shall all perish, but I anticipate a happier issue."

Somewhat comforted, the knight returned home, gave the necessary orders, and then went to the king for his commands and his own credentials. " You will tell the emperor on my behalf," said the king, " that I demand the restoration of my subjects he keeps in slavery, of my soldiers who are his prisoners, of my horses of which he makes use, and of my furniture and treasure." " What am I to offer him in return ? " asked Fortuné. " Nothing," replied the king, " except my affection." It required no great effort of memory to remember these instructions. He left without seeing the queen ; she seemed offended, but it was scarcely necessary to humour her, for what could she do more in her greatest anger than in her transports of love ? Affection of such a character seemed to him the most terrible thing imaginable. The queen's confidant, who was in the secret, was exasperated with her mistress for thus desiring to sacrifice the flower of all chivalry.

The leather trunk provided Fortuné with all that was necessary for the journey ; he was not content with dressing only himself magnificently, he wished his seven companions to be also well attired. As they all had excellent horses, and Comrade seemed rather to fly through the air than to gallop over the ground, in a very short time they reached the capital city where the Emperor Matapa lived. It was bigger than Paris, Rome and Constantinople put together, and so populous that the cellars, garrets and roofs all swarmed with people.

The prodigious size of the town surprised Fortuné. He asked and easily obtained audience of the emperor, but although he declared the purpose of his embassy with a grace that materially aided his arguments, the emperor could not help smiling. " If you were at the head of five hundred thousand men," he said, " I might listen to you, but I am told you have only seven." " I have not undertaken, sir," said Fortuné, " to use force to make you restore my master's property, but merely my humble remonstrances." " Whatever the means," added the emperor, " you will not obtain what you want, unless you carry out an idea that has just occurred to me ; that is, if you could find a man with a sufficiently big appetite to eat for his breakfast all the bread baked for the inhabitants of this town." The knight was overcome with joy at this proposal, and as he did not reply at once, the emperor burst out laughing. " You see," he said, " it is only natural to reply to your unheard-of proposal by one equally extravagant." " Sire," said Fortuné, " I accept your offer; to-morrow I will bring a man who will eat all the fresh bread, and even all the stale bread in the town ; order it to be brought into the great square, and you shall have the pleasure of seeing him devour it, even to the last crumb." The emperor replied that it should be done. For the remainder of the day nothing was talked of but the madness of the new ambassador, and Matapa swore if he did not keep his word he should die.

Fortuné returned to the ambassador's house, where he was lodging, summoned Glutton, and said : " You must now prepare to eat bread ; everything depends on it ". He then informed him of what he had promised the emperor. " Do not disturb yourself, master," said Glutton, " I will eat so much that they will be tired first." Fortuné felt no doubt of his success, and although the precaution was unnecessary, forbade him to have any supper in order that he might make the better breakfast.

The emperor, empress, and princess took their places on a balcony to have a better view of the proceedings. Fortuné arrived with his little cortège, and when he saw six mountains of bread, higher than the Pyrenees, in the great square, he could not help turning pale. But not so Glutton ; the hope of eating so much bread gave him infinite delight. He begged them not to withhold the least little bit, saying he would even like what the mice had left. The emperor jested with his court over the extravagance of Fortuné and his men, but Glutton, all impatient, asked for the signal to commence ; it was given by the sound of trumpets and drums, and he directly attacked one of the mountains of bread, and ate it in less than a quarter of an hour, and then gobbled up all the rest in the same fashion.

The astonishment of the people cannot be described ; they thought their eyes must be deceiving them, and actually touched the place where the bread had been heaped up to make sure ; that day every one, from the emperor to the cat, had to dine without bread.

Fortuné, vastly pleased with his success, approached the emperor, and asked him very respectfully if it pleased him to keep his word. The emperor, somewhat irritated at having been duped, said : " Sir, it is too much to eat without drinking ; you, or one of your men, must drink all the water in the fountains, reservoirs, and aqueducts of the town, and all the wine that is in the cellars. " Sire," said Fortuné, " you set me most impossible tasks, but if I thought you would restore to my king all his property, I would attempt them." " If you succeed in this undertaking," said the emperor, " I will do so." The knight asked the emperor if he would be present. He replied, the thing was strange enough to rouse his curiosity, and getting into a magnificent chariot, went to the fountain of lions ; there were seven of them in marble, and out of their mouths poured torrents of water, which formed a river, on which you could traverse the town in gondolas.

Drinker approached the great basin, and without stopping to take breath once, drank the fountain as dry as if there had never been any water in it. The fish cried vengeance on him, for they knew not what to do. He acted in the same way with all the rest of the fountains, aqueducts, and reservoirs, and would then have drunk the sea, so thirsty was he still. After such proof, the emperor did not doubt he could drink the wine as well as the water, but every one objected in their annoyance to deliver it up to him. Drinker complained loudly of the injustice done him; he said he should be ill after drinking so much water, and that he meant to have not only the wine but the spirits too. Then Matapa, fearing to seem stingy, consented to Drinker's demands, and Fortuné, seizing the opportunity, entreated the emperor to remember his promise. At those words his countenance assumed a severe expression, and he said he would think of it.

He summoned his council and told them his distress at having promised the young ambassador to restore all he had gained from his master; he had attached to it conditions he thought impossible of fulfilment, and how could he now avoid so prejudicial an act? His daughter, one of the most beautiful girls imaginable, hearing her father speak thus, said: " Sire, you know that so far I have beaten all who ventured to compete with me for the prize in running ; tell the ambassador that if he can reach the goal before me, you undertake to evade your promise no longer".

The emperor embraced her, and thought her advice excellent. The next day he received Fortuné's visit most amiably, and said: " I have still another thing to exact ; you or one of your men must run a race with my daughter. I swear by all the elements that if she loses, I will give your master all he wants." Fortuné accepted the challenge, and Matapa added that the race would take place in two hours. He told his daughter to make her preparations; she had been accustomed to the exercise from her earliest youth. She came to a grove of orange trees three leagues in length, and so well sanded that you could not see a pebble as big as a pin's head. She wore a light gown of .pink silk scattered over with little stars embroidered in gold and silver; her beautiful hair was tied back with a ribbon and fell carelessly over her shoulders ; here shoes were small, without heels, and very pretty; her belt was jewelled and showed off her fine figure. Atalanta would not have dared to compare herself with the princess.

Fortuné arrived accompanied by faithful Fleet-Foot and his other servants : the emperor and all the court took their places. The ambassador said that Fleet-Foot would have the honour of racing with the princess. The leather trunk had provided him with a costume of fine Holland linen trimmed with English lace, flame-coloured silk stockings and feathers of the same hue. He looked very handsome and the princess agreed to race with him; but before they started a cordial which helped to make her swifter and stronger was brought her. Fleet-Foot exclaimed that to make the advantages even for both he ought to have some too. "Certainly," she said, "it would be very unfair of me to object." She ordered some to be poured out for him, but as he was not accustomed to it, and it was very strong, it got into his head at once. He took two or three turns, and then fell down at the foot of an orange tree in a sound sleep.

The signal for the start was given : three times they had commenced, and the princess good-naturedly waited for Fleet-Foot to wake up ; but remembering how important it was that she should pull her father out of his dilemma, she at length commenced running with marvellous grace and swiftness. Fortuné and his men had stationed themselves at the end of the grove, and knew nothing of what had been going on. Suddenly he saw the princess running alone, and only half a league from the winning post. "Ye gods!" he exclaimed, speaking to his horse, "we are lost; I do not see Fleet-Foot." "Sir," said Comrade, "Quick-Ear must listen ; perhaps he can tell us what he is doing." Quick-Ear threw himself on the ground, and although he was two leagues off, he heard Fleet-Foot snoring. "Truly," he said, "there's good reason for his absence ; he is sleeping as if he was in his bed." "What shall we do then?" exclaimed Fortuné. "Master," said Comrade, "Good-Shot must aim an arrow at the tip of his ear in order to awake him." Good-Shot took his bow and aimed so exactly that the arrow pierced Fleet-Foot's ear. The pain awoke him from his slumbers ; he opened his eyes, saw the princess almost at the winning post, and heard the shouts of joy and applause. At first he could not make it out, but he soon remembered what the sleep had made him forget. It seemed he was borne on the wind, eyes could not follow him, and he arrived at the goal the first, with the arrow still in his ear, for he had not had time to take it out.

The emperor was so astonished at the three events that had happened since the ambassador's arrival, that he thought the gods were helping him, and that he could no longer delay fulfilling his promise. "Approach," he said, "and learn that I consent to your taking as much of your master's treasure as you or one of your men can carry away ; but you must not imagine I shall ever give you more, or permit his soldiers, subjects, and horses to go." The ambassador made him a low bow, thanked him for his kindness, and begged him to give the necessary orders.

Matapa, greatly annoyed, spoke to the guards of his treasury, and retired to a villa he had near the town. Fortuné and his men demanded admittance into all the places where the king's furniture, curiosities, money, and jewels were kept. On condition that only one man should carry them, nothing was concealed. With Strong-Back's help, the ambassador carried off all the furniture that was in the emperor's palace, five hundred gold statues bigger than giants, coaches, chariots, all sorts of things without exception, and Strong-Back walked so quickly that he scarcely seemed to be carrying a pound's weight.

When the emperor's ministers saw the palaces dismantled to such a degree that there remained neither chairs, coffers, pots, nor beds, they speedily went to tell him, and his astonishment may be imagined when he learned that one man carried it all. He exclaimed that he would not allow it, and ordered his guards and musketeers to mount their horses and pursue the robbers. Although Fortuné was more than ten leagues in advance, Quick-Ear informed him that he heard a troop of cavalry riding at full speed, and Good-Shot with his excellent sight saw them. They were on the bank of a river. Fortuné said to Drinker: "We have no boat, if you could drink some of this water we might cross it". Drinker did what was required. The ambassador wished to make off as quickly as possible, but his horse said to him: "Don't alarm yourself; let your enemies approach". They reached the river bank, and knowing where the fishermen kept their boats, quickly embarked, and rowed with all their might. Impetuous inflated his cheeks and began to breathe; the river grew rough, the boats were overturned, the little army perished, and no one was left to carry the news to the emperor.

Fortuné's men, delighted at so complete a success, demanded the reward they considered their due; they desired to make themselves masters of all the treasures they had carried off, and a hot dispute arose as to the division.

"If I had not gained the prize," said the runner, "you would have nothing."
"And if I had not heard you snore," said Quick-Ear, "where should we be
now?" "How could you have been awakened without me?" put in Good-
Shot. "Truly," remarked Strong-Back, "I like your disputes; surely I have
the best right to choose, since I have had the trouble of carrying it all; without
my help there would have been nothing to divide." "Things would have been
very different if I had not upset the boat," said Impetuous. "I kept silence
till now," interrupted Glutton, "but I cannot help pointing out that I opened
the ball, and had I left even so much as a crust of bread, everything
would have been lost." "My friends," said Fortuné, with an air of
decision, "you have all done wonders, but let us leave the care of rewarding our services to the king. I should be very sorry to be recompensed
by any other hand than his; trust me, let us leave everything to his good-will.
He sent us to bring back his treasure, not to steal it. The thought alone is
shameful; I wish never to hear it mentioned, and on my part, I assure you, I
shall so well reward you that even if the king neglected you, you would have
nothing to regret."

The seven fairy-gifted men took their master's remonstrance to heart, threw
themselves at his feet, and promised for the future to have no will but his; thus
they finished their journey. But Fortuné in drawing near the town was agitated
by many different emotions. The joy of rendering so important a service to the
king, to the man for whom he had such deep affection; the hope of seeing him
and of being favourably received greatly delighted him; but on the other hand,
the fear of again vexing the queen, and of experiencing fresh persecutions at her
hands and those of Florida, threw him into great despair. On his arrival the
people, charmed with the treasure he brought, welcomed him with loud shouts
that were heard at the palace.

The king could not believe so extraordinary a thing, and hastened to inform
the queen of it; at first she was altogether dismayed, but recovering a little,
said: "You see the gods protect him; he has again succeeded, and I am no longer
surprised that he should undertake what seems impossible to others". As she
finished speaking, Fortuné entered. He informed their majesties of the successful result of his journey, adding that the treasure was in the park, for the quantity
of gold, furniture, and jewellery was so great that there was no place big enough
to put it. The king's affection for so zealous and faithful a subject may easily be
believed.

The knight's presence and the renown of his great deeds re-opened the
wound in the queen's heart that had never been quite cured; she thought him
more lovable than ever, and as soon as she found an opportunity of speaking to

Florida, she began her usual complainings. " You see what I have done to destroy him," she said ; " it seemed to me the only way to forget him, but a strange fatality always brings him back, and in spite of the reasons I have for despising a man so greatly my inferior, and who repays my passion with rank ingratitude, I cannot cease loving him, and I am resolved to marry him privately." " To marry him, madam ! " exclaimed Florida. " Have I heard aright ? " " Yes," replied the queen, " you now know my determination and you must help me. Bring Fortuné this evening to my closet, and I will myself explain to him my intentions towards him." Florida, in despair at being chosen to help on her mistress's marriage with the man she herself loved, did all in her power to persuade the queen not to see Fortuné. She pointed out to her the king's anger should he discover the intrigue, how he would condemn the knight to death, or at the very least to life-long imprisonment, so that she would never see him again. But she only wasted her eloquence ; she saw the queen was beginning to get angry, and there was nothing for it but to obey.

She found Fortuné in the gallery of the palace superintending the arrangement of the gold statues he had brought from Matapa : she told him to come to the queen in the evening. The command made him tremble, and Florida understood his agitation. " Oh ! ye gods," she said, " how I pity you ; how is it that this princess's heart has fixed itself on you ? Alas ! I know a heart less dangerous than hers that dares not declare itself." The knight had no desire to enter into further explanations, he had already trouble enough. As he did not wish to find favour with the queen, he dressed himself very negligently, so that she could not think he had any designs ; but if he could thus easily lay aside embroidery and diamonds, he could not get rid of his personal attractions. He was always amiable, always admirable, and, whatever his mood, there was no one to compare with him.

The queen had taken every care to enhance her beauty by all the arts of the toilette, and observed Fortuné's surprise with pleasure. " Appearances," she said, " are often so deluding that I am glad to make you certain of what you have doubtless believed my feelings towards you to be. When I made the king promise to send you to the emperor, it seemed I wished to sacrifice your life, but, handsome knight, learn that I knew what the result would be, and only desired to procure you immortal glory." " Madam," he said, " you are too far above me to lower yourself by explanations ; I care nothing for the motives that induced your actions, it is sufficient for me that I obeyed the king." " You are far too indifferent," she said, " to the explanation I wish to give you, but it is at length time for me to convince you of my love for you. Approach, Fortuné, approach, and receive my hand as a pledge of my faith."

The poor knight had never been so astounded in his life; twenty times he was on the point of declaring his sex. He dared not do so however, and replied to her expressions of love with the utmost coldness. He put forward many arguments as to the king's anger when he should learn that a subject had dared to contract so important a marriage without his consent. After the queen had tried in vain to remove the fears that seemed to fill him, she suddenly assumed the voice and appearance of a fury. She was beside herself with rage; she threatened and insulted him, beat him, scratched him, and then turning her madness against herself, tore her hair, made her face and breast bleed, rent her veil and lace; then shouting: " Help! Help!" her guards entered the room. She ordered them to thrust the wretched man into a deep dungeon, and then hastened to the king to demand justice for the young monster's violence.

She told her brother how for a long time he had been audacious enough to declare a passion for her, and in the hope that absence and hardship might cure him, she had, as he might have observed, neglected no opportunity of sending him away ; but he was a wretch whom nothing could change; the king could see for himself how violent he had been. She desired he should be brought to trial, and if he refused to permit it, she would seek some other means of satisfaction.

The manner in which she spoke astonished the king; he knew she was a very violent woman, and powerful enough to overturn the kingdom. Fortuné's bold-ness demanded exemplary punishment. The people already knew what had happened, and it was his duty to avenge his sister. But, alas! on whom was this vengeance to fall? on a knight who had exposed himself to the greatest danger in his service, on a man to whom he owed peace and treasure, and for whom he had a special liking. He would have given half his life to save his favourite. He pointed out to the queen his great usefulness, the services he had rendered to the state, his youth, and everything that might induce her to pardon him. She would not listen, and only demanded his death. The king could no longer avoid appointing the judges, and chose those who were most gentle and humane in order that they might be the more disposed to take a lenient view of his fault.

But he was wrong in his conjectures. The judges were anxious to restore their reputation at the expense of the unhappy victim, and as the matter had made a great stir, they clothed themselves in all their severity, and condemned Fortuné without deigning to hear him. He was sentenced to be stabbed three times in the heart, for his heart it was that had been guilty.

The king felt the verdict as much as if it had been pronounced against himself; he banished the judges, but could not save Fortuné, and the queen gloried in the punishment he was to suffer; she thirsted for the poor wretch's

blood. The king made fresh attempts to intercede with her, but by so doing
only increased her rage. At length, the day appointed for the execution arrived ;
the knight was brought out of his prison, where no one had been permitted to
speak with him. He did not know of what crime the queen accused him ; he
imagined it to be some new persecution, on account of his indifference, and the
thing that troubled him most was his belief that the king was a party to the
princess's anger.

Florida, inconsolable at her lover's condition, resolved on a violent remedy—
to poison the queen, and if Fortuné suffered a cruel death, to poison herself.
When she learned his sentence, despair seized her heart, and she thought of
nothing but carrying out her plan. The poison she procured was slower in its
effect than she had imagined, for although it had already been administered to
the queen, she did not yet feel its malignity, and ordered the knight to be
brought into the great courtyard of the palace, and receive his death-wound in
her presence. The executioners led him forth from the dungeon in the usual
way, and he seemed a young lamb led to the sacrifice. The first thing he saw
was the queen in her chariot ; of her own desire she could not be too close to
him, wishing that if possible his blood might spurt over her. The king, on the
other hand, shut himself up in his closet, to grieve unobserved over his favourite's
fate.

When Fortuné had been fastened to the stake, in order that his heart might
be stabbed, his coat and vest were removed ; but picture the consternation of the
large assembly when they saw the alabaster bosom of the real Belle-Belle !
Every one knew she was an innocent girl unjustly accused. The queen's
agitation and distress were so great, that the poison began to take surprising
effect ; she fell into convulsions whence she only revived to utter poignant
regrets. The people who loved Fortuné had already set him free ; the king, who
had abandoned himself to the most profound grief, was informed of the surprising
circumstance ; joy took the place of sorrow ; he hastened to the courtyard of the
palace, and was delighted at Fortuné's metamorphosis. The queen's dying
pangs somewhat moderated his transports ; but when he reflected on her malice
he could not regret her, and he resolved to marry Belle-Belle, and repay with a
crown the infinite obligations he owed her, and straightway declared to her his
intentions. It will easily be understood that they more than satisfied her
desires ; she cared less for the high position than for the love of a king of great
merit for whom she had always had strong affection.

A day was appointed for the celebration of the marriage, and Belle-Belle
resumed her girl's dress and looked much more beautiful in it than in man's
attire. She consulted her horse about her future, and he promised her all that

was pleasant. In gratitude for his valuable services she had a stable built for him, panelled with ebony and ivory; he took his rest on satin mattresses. The princess rewarded her followers in proportion to their services.

Comrade, however, disappeared; Belle-Belle was informed of it, and because she loved him dearly she was distressed to lose him; she had search made everywhere for three days, but in vain. On the fourth day her anxiety caused her to rise with the dawn; she went into the garden, then through the wood, and walked in a big meadow, calling out from time to time: "Comrade, my dear Comrade, where are you? Do you mean to forsake me? I have still need of your wise counsel; return, return, and give it me." As she spoke she saw on a sudden a sun rise in the West; she stopped to wonder at the miracle, and her delight was beyond description when it gradually approached her, and she recognised after a moment her horse, in trappings set thick with precious stones, prancing along in front of a pearl and topaz chariot; it was drawn by six sheep, with shining gold fleeces, the harness was of crimson satin, set with emeralds, bosses were not forgotten, and were placed at the horns and ears. In the chariot Belle-Belle recognised her guardian fairy, her father, and her two sisters, who shouted, clapped their hands, and showed her with many marks of affection that they had come to the wedding. She thought she should die for joy, she knew not what to do or say to testify her love for them. She got into the chariot, and the magnificent equipage entered the palace where everything was ready for the celebration of the grandest fête that had ever been given in the kingdom. The fond king joined his destiny to that of his mistress, and the pretty tale has been handed down through the ages until our own day.

THE PIGEON AND THE DOVE.

ONCE upon a time there was a king and queen who loved each other so dearly that they were an example to all the families in their kingdom. Their country was called the Kingdom of the Deserts.

The queen had had several children, who had all died save one daughter, and if anything consoled the mother for the loss of the others it was the beauty and grace of this daughter. She was the sole joy of the king and queen, but the happiness of the royal family was soon to end; for as the king was out hunting one day, the spirited horse he rode took fright at the sound of shooting. Terrified by the firing, he took the bit between his teeth, and was off like a flash. Just at the edge of a precipice he reared, the king was thrown, and the fall was so terrible that he was killed.

The fatal news plunged the queen into the lowest depths of despair; she was unable to moderate her grief, feeling it too violent to be overcome. She thought only of setting her daughter's affairs in order, so that she herself might die in peace. She had a friend called Queen Fairy because she was very clever, and had great authority in all the empires of the world. The queen wrote to her from her deathbed, saying she wished to breathe her last in her arms, and imploring her to come quickly if she wished to find her alive, for she had most important things to tell her.

Although the fairy had much business on hand, she put it all aside, and mounting her fiery camel that travelled faster than light, soon arrived at the palace. The queen was impatiently awaiting her. She begged her to accept the regency of the kingdom, and to take care of the little Princess Constancia. " If anything," she added, "can relieve my anxiety at leaving her an orphan at so tender an age, it is the hope I have that you will continue to her the friendship you have always had for me, that she may find in you a mother who will make her happier and more perfect than I could have done, and that you will choose her a husband so charming that she will love none but him." " You desire all that can be desired, great queen," said the fairy. " I will neglect nothing for your daughter's welfare; but I have cast her horoscope, and it seems that Fate is angry with Nature for having exhausted all her treasures in creating her ; it is decreed that she shall suffer, and your majesty knows how impossible it is to avoid Fate." "At least," said the queen, "alleviate her misfortunes, and neglect no means of trying to prevent them. By extreme care and foresight this can sometimes be done." Queen Fairy promised to do her best, and the queen, after embracing her beloved Constancia over and over again, passed peacefully away.

The fairy read the stars with the same ease with which we now read the new tales published every day. She learnt that the princess was threatened with the fatal love of a giant whose kingdom was not very far from the land of the Deserts. She knew well that it must be prevented, and found no better way than to hide the princess in one of the ends of the earth, so far from the giant's abode that there would be little likelihood of his troubling her.

As soon as Queen Fairy had chosen ministers capable of ruling the state, and had made such excellent laws that not all the wise men of Greece could have made better, she one night entered Constancia's room, and without waking her placed her on the fiery camel, and set off for a fertile land, where it was possible to live free from ambition and care. It was a veritable Arcadia, inhabited only by shepherds and shepherdesses, who dwelt in huts built by their own hands.

She knew that if the princess reached the age of sixteen without seeing the giant she would be able to return in triumph to her kingdom, but if she saw him before, she would be exposed to great misfortunes. The fairy was therefore most careful to hide her from everybody, and that her beauty might be less apparent dressed her like a shepherdess with a big cap pressed down over her face. But, just as the sun when hidden behind the clouds pierces them with long rays of light, the princess's beauty could not be entirely concealed, and in spite of all the fairy's care, Constancia was spoken of as a masterpiece of the gods that enchanted all beholders.

Her beauty was not the only thing for which she was admired. Queen Fairy had endowed her with a wonderful voice and great skill in playing on all sorts of musical instruments, so that without ever having learned music, she could have given instruction to the Muses and even to divine Apollo.

Thus she had plenty to occupy her; the fairy had told her the reason for keeping her hidden away during her childhood. As she was very intelligent, she agreed to everything with great good sense, and Queen Fairy was astonished that at so tender an age she should display so much docility and wit. The fairy had not visited the Kingdom of the Deserts for several months because she never liked leaving Constancia, but it happened she was greatly needed there, because the ministers only acted under her orders, and they did not all do their duty equally well. She set out, enjoining the princess to shut herself up till her return.

The beautiful princess had a sheep whom she dearly loved; she delighted in making him garlands of flowers, and at other times decking him with knots of ribbon. She had named him Ruson. He was cleverer than all his companions; he knew his mistress's voice, and understood and obeyed her commands without fail. "Ruson," she would say, "go and fetch my distaff." He trotted into her room and brought it, leaping merrily round her. He ate the grass she gathered for him, and would have preferred dying of thirst to drinking in any other way than from the hollow of her hand. He could shut the door, beat time when she sang, and bleat in harmony with the music. Ruson was amiable, and Constancia loved and petted him.

But Ruson's attentions to a pretty ewe of the district were at least as marked as those he paid the princess. Sheep, after all, are only sheep, and the loveliest ewe was more beautiful in Ruson's eyes than Venus herself. Constancia often reproached him for his coquetry. "You little flirt," she said, "can't you remain with me? I love you so much, that for you I neglect the whole flock, and yet to please me you will not leave this wretched ewe." She tied him up with a chain of flowers, but this seemed to annoy him, and he pulled so hard that he broke it. "Ah!" said Constancia, in a rage, "the fairy has often told me that men are as self-willed as you, that they dislike the least constraint, and are the most obstinate animals in the world. Since you resemble them, naughty Ruson, go and seek your fine ewe; if the wolf eats you, you'll be in a nice way, for I shall be unable to help you."

The fond sheep did not profit by Constancia's advice. He spent all his time with his beloved ewe near the princess's cottage. One day when she sat all alone at needlework, she heard such loud and piteous bleating that she feared some fatal accident had happened to Ruson. Greatly distressed, she went out and saw a wolf carrying him off. She forgot the fairy's parting injunctions, and ran after them, shouting: "The wolf! The wolf!" She followed him, casting stones at him with her sheep-hook, but he did not drop his prey. Alas! as she was passing near a wood there came out another sort of wolf—a horrible giant. At the sight of the enormous creature, the princess, paralysed with fear, raised her eyes to heaven to ask its protection, and implored the earth to swallow up the monster. Neither heaven nor earth heeded her; she deserved to be punished for neglecting the fairy's orders.

The giant spread out his arms to prevent her passing. But, however terrible and furious he was, he felt the effects of her beauty. "What rank do you hold among the goddesses?" he said, in a voice louder than thunder. "For don't think I can be deceived, you are no mortal; tell me your name and if you are a maiden or the wife of Jupiter. Who are your brothers and your sisters? I have long sought a goddess for my wife, and I am indeed fortunate in finding you." Fear tied the princess's tongue, and the words died away on her lips.

When he found she did not reply to his gallant questions, he said: "For a goddess, you haven't much wit," and without more ado opened a big sack and put her in. The first thing she saw at the bottom was the wicked wolf and the poor sheep. The giant had amused himself catching them as they ran. "We shall die together, my dear Ruson," she said, kissing him, "but it is a small consolation; it would be far better to escape together."

The sad thought made her cry bitterly; she sighed and sobbed aloud. Ruson bleated, the wolf howled, and the noise awoke a dog, a cat, a cock, and a parrot. They then began making a most horrible noise, a strange uproar for a giant's wallet. At length tired of it, the monster thought of killing them, but contented himself with tying up the sack and throwing it to the top of a tree, marking the spot so that he could fetch it again; he was going to fight a duel with another giant, and all this clamour annoyed him. The princess suspected that however slowly he walked, he would soon be far off, for when he went at only a moderate pace a horse galloping at the top of its speed could not catch him. She drew out her scissors, cut the canvas, pulled out her dear Ruson, the dog, the cat, the cock and the parrot, and afterwards escaped herself, leaving the wolf inside as a reward for trying to eat Ruson. The night was very dark; she was alone in the midst of a forest, not knowing in what direction to turn, seeing neither sky nor earth, and always dreading to meet the giant.

She walked as quickly as she could, and would have fallen hundreds and hundreds of times if the animals whose lives she had saved, grateful for her kindness, had not determined to stand by her. They were of the greatest use on the journey; the cat had such sparkling eyes that they shone like a torch, the dog barked and acted as sentinel, the cock crowed to frighten the lions, the parrot chattered so loudly that people thought a great company of persons must be talking, and thus robbers left a free passage to our travellers, and the sheep walking a few paces in advance, prevented her falling into the big holes he himself had some trouble in avoiding.

Constancia walked on at hazard, commending herself to her good friend the fairy, from whom she hoped for help, although she greatly blamed herself for disobeying her injunctions. But at times she feared even the fairy had forsaken her; she would have liked by some good fortune to have reached the house in which she had secretly been brought up, but as she had no idea of the way, she could not come there without particular good luck.

At daybreak she found herself on the bank of a river that watered the pleasantest meadow imaginable; looking round her, she saw neither dog, cat, cock, nor parrot; Ruson alone kept her company. " Alas! where am I ? " she said; " I do not know this beautiful place. What will become of me ? Who will take care of me ? Ah! little Ruson, you have cost me dear! If I had not run after you I should still be in Queen Fairy's house, and should have to fear neither the giant nor any disastrous accident." It really seemed as if Ruson trembled while he listened and acknowledged his fault. At last the princess, worn out and tired, left off scolding him, and sat down by the water's edge. Trees shaded her from the sun's heat. Her eyes closed, she let herself sink on the grass, and was soon sleeping soundly. Faithful Ruson was her only protector; he touched her, pulled her dress, and to her surprise on waking she saw a young man standing behind the bushes! He had hidden himself on purpose to look at her without being seen; the beauty of his face and form, the dignity of his appearance, and the magnificence of his clothes so greatly astonished the princess, that she quickly got up, resolving to go away. I do not know what secret charm stopped her; she looked timidly at the unknown man. The giant had scarcely alarmed her more, but in that case fear sprang from a different cause. How their looks and actions sufficiently proved the feelings with which they already regarded one another !

They might have remained a long while, conversing only with their eyes, if the prince had not heard the blowing of horns and the baying of hounds. He observed her confusion. " Fear nothing, beautiful shepherdess," he said; " you are in safety here; may it please heaven that those who behold you may be equally safe ! " " Sir," she said, " I implore your protection; I am a poor orphan who can do nothing but tend sheep; procure a flock for me, and I will give it all my care." " Happy the sheep," he said, smiling, " whom you lead to pasture; but, indeed, if you wish it, charming shepherdess, I will speak to my mother, the queen, and it will give me the keenest pleasure from now to be of service to you." " Ah ! sir," said Constancia, "pardon the liberty I have taken ; had I known your rank I should not have dared to address you."

The prince listened in the greatest astonishment; he recognised in her intelligence and good breeding that perfectly corresponded with her great beauty, but scarcely with the simplicity of her gown and the calling of a shepherdess. He tried to reason with her. " Think," he said, " you will be exposed all alone in some wood or meadow, having for sole company your innocent sheep. Can the gentle manners I observe in you accommodate themselves to solitude ? And, besides, who knows if your charms, whose fame will spread through the country side, will not bring on you many annoyances ? I myself, charming shepherdess, shall leave the court to follow you, and what I do, others will do." " Cease to flatter me, sir," she said, " with praise I do not deserve ; I was born in a village, and know only a country life, and I hope you will leave me in peace to tend the queen's flocks should she deign to entrust them to my care. I shall ask her to put me under some shepherdess of greater experience than myself, and as I shall not leave her, I shall certainly not be lonely."

The prince was unable to reply; his hunting companions appeared on a hill. " I must leave you, charming girl," he said, eagerly, " I cannot share with so many people the pleasure of beholding you ; go to the end of the meadow and you will find a house, where, if you say I sent you, you will be quite safe." Constancia, who would have been embarrassed in such grand company, hastened to the place pointed out by the prince whose name was Constancio.

He followed her with his eyes, sighed gently, and mounting his horse again rejoined his companions, but did not continue the hunt. Entering the queen's apartments, he found her extremely angry with an old shepherdess who had rendered a very bad account of her lambs. After scolding her well, the queen told her never to let her see her face again.

This circumstance furthered Constancio's plan ; he told his mother how he had met a young girl who ardently desired to become her servant; that she looked as though she would be careful, and seemed disinterested. The queen, well satisfied with her son's recommendation, took the shepherdess into her service without seeing her, and told the prince to order her to go with the others into the royal pastures. He was very glad that there was no need for her to come to the palace : certain jealous feelings made him fear rivals, although there were none who equalled him in rank or merit. It is true he feared the great nobles less than men of a lower rank, for he thought she would be more likely to care for a simple shepherd than for a prince of the blood.

It would be no easy task to relate all the reflections that followed : how he reproached himself ! he who, until now, had never loved anybody, who had found no one worthy of him! To give himself to a girl of low birth, so that he could not declare his passion without blushing! Wishing to conquer it, and convinced that absence was an unfailing remedy, particularly for a dawning passion, he avoided seeing the shepherdess again. He followed his taste for hunting and sport: he turned away from sheep as if they had been serpents, so that in a short time he became less sensible of his wound. But, on one of the hottest of the dog-days, Constancio, tired with a long chase, found himself on the bank of the river; he followed its course under the shade of the hornbeams that joined their branches overhead to those of the willows, and made the place cool and pleasant. He fell into a deep reverie; he was alone, and thought no more of his companions, when, suddenly, he heard the sweet notes of a voice that seemed to him divine; he stopped to listen, and was not a little surprised to hear these words :—

> " Once did I vow all passion I would scorn,
> But love prevails; my promise I forego.
> By deepest wound, alas! now I am torn,
> For my heart's lord is proud Constancio.
> Late have I seen my love within this glade
> Aweary of his labour in the wood,
> Singing his sorrow, sitting in the shade;
> Ne'er saw I aught so beautiful and good.
> Long I remained o'ercome and motionless,
> From Cupid's hand I saw the arrows dart;
> But with the pain comes highest happiness,
> And from this passion that inflames my heart,
> And penetrates into its depths below,
> Relief nor cure, I never wish to know."

His curiosity outweighed the pleasure he felt at hearing such beautiful sing-ing, and he quickly walked on; the name of Constancio had struck him because it was his own. Yet a shepherd might own it as well as a prince, and so he did not know if the words might be intended for him or another. He had scarcely ascended a small hill, covered with trees, when he perceived at its foot the beautiful Constancia. She was seated beside a brook, whose pleasant murmur seemed to harmonise with her voice. Her faithful sheep, her favourite Ruson, lying on the grass, kept much nearer her than the others; now and then Con-stancia patted him with her sheep-hook, caressed him in a child-like fashion, and each time she touched him, he kissed her hand and gave her a look full of intelligence. " Ah!" whispered the prince, " how happy you would be if you knew the value of those caresses! Why, the shepherdess is even more beautiful than when I met her. Love! love! what do you want of me? ought I to love, or rather can I prevent myself falling in love? Understanding my danger, I took care to avoid her. Great gods! what an impression the first meeting left on me! Aided by my reason, I shunned the sweet maiden. Alas! I find her, but he of whom she sings is the happy shepherd of her choice."

While he was thus arguing with himself, the shepherdess rose to gather her flock together and lead it into another part of the meadow, where she had left her companions. The prince, fearing to lose the opportunity of speaking to her, advanced eagerly: "Charming shepherdess," he said, "may I venture to ask you, if the slight service I rendered you, pleased you?" At sight of him Constancia blushed rosy red. "Sir," she said, "I should have offered you my humblest thanks if it had been fitting for a poor girl like me to speak to a prince like you; but, although I failed to do so, heaven is my witness that I am not ungrateful, and that I pray the gods to grant you every happiness." "Constancia," he replied, "if it is true that my kind offices have touched you, as you declare, you can easily prove it." "What can I do for you, sir?" she replied, eagerly. "You can tell me," he continued, "for whom the words you have just sung are intended." "As I did not compose them," she replied, "I should find it difficult to tell you anything about them." He looked at her attentively while she was speaking, and saw that she blushed; she seemed confused, and kept her eyes cast down. "Why do you hide your feelings from me, Constancia?" he said. "Your countenance betrays the secret of your heart; you are in love." He stopped and looked at her with still more attention. "Sir," she said, "the things that interest me little deserve that a prince should trouble about them, and I am so used to keeping silence in the society of my lambs that I beg you to forgive me if I do not reply to your questions"; and before he had time to stop her away she went.

Sometimes jealousy acts as a torch to rekindle love, and from that moment the prince's passion assumed such force that it was never again extinguished; he discovered in the young girl a thousand charms he had not noticed the first time he saw her. Her abrupt manner of leaving him, added to her words, made him think she must be in love with some shepherd. A profound melancholy took possession of his soul, and, although he had the greatest desire to talk to her, he dared not follow her. He lay down in the place she had just quitted; and trying to recall the words she had sung, wrote them on his tablets and examined them attentively. "She can only have seen this Constancio, who fills her mind, a few days ago," he mused. "He bears my name, and yet how far am I from his good fortune! How coldly she looked at me! She seemed more indifferent to-day than when I met her the first time; all her anxiety was to find a pretext for leaving me." These thoughts sensibly distressed him, for he could not understand how a mere shepherdess could be so indifferent to a great prince.

As soon as he returned he summoned a young man who shared all his pleasures ; he was of good birth and amiable. The prince ordered him to disguise himself as a shepherd, to procure a flock and go every day into the queen's pasture grounds to see what Constancia did, of course unsuspected by her. Mirtain, for that was his name, was too anxious to please his master to refuse to help him. He promised to obey his orders, and the very next day was ready to go to the pasture ground ; those in charge of it would not have admitted him, had he not shown an order from the prince declaring him to be his shepherd, and that he was entrusted with the care of his sheep.

He was immediately allowed to join the rustic company; he was gallant, and easily made himself liked by the shepherdesses, but he noticed a certain dignity in Constancia so far above what she appeared to be, that he could not reconcile so much beauty, wit, and merit with her rustic simple life ; in vain he followed her, she was always alone in the depths of the wood, singing in a pre-occupied manner.

No shepherd dared try to win her favour. It seemed too difficult. Mirtain, however, attempted it, became most attentive to her, and learned by his own experience that she did not desire to enter into any engagement.

Every evening he gave the prince an account of the situation, and all Constancio learned only served to distress him further. " Do not mistake, sir," said Mirtain one day ; " this beautiful girl is in love, and it must be with some one in her own country." " If that was so," replied the prince, " would she not want to return there ? " " How do we know," added Mirtain, " that there are not reasons which prevent her going back to her native land ? Perhaps she is angry with her lover." " Ah ! " exclaimed the prince, " she sings her songs too tenderly for that." " It is true," continued Mirtain, " all the trees are carved with their initials ; and since no one here finds favour with her, it must be some one elsewhere." " Find out her feelings towards me," said the prince. " Be they favourable or not, you can discover what she thinks."

Mirtain did not fail to seek an opportunity of speaking to Constancia. "What is the matter with you, beautiful shepherdess?" he said. "In spite of all the cause you have to be merrier than the rest, you seem melancholy." "And what cause for joy have I?" she said. "I am forced to tend sheep far from my native land; I have no news from my relatives: is that so pleasant?" "No," he replied, "but you are the most charming girl imaginable; you are clever, and sing in most enchanting fashion, and nothing can equal your beauty." "Even if I possessed such advantages," she said, with a deep sigh, "they would make little impression on me." "What?" added Mirtain, "you think it necessary to be born a prince or of the race of immortals to be happy? Ah! let me undeceive you. I am a friend of Prince Constancio, and in spite of the difference of position, I approach him sometimes, study him, fathom his thoughts, and I know that he is not happy." "What troubles his peace?" said the princess. "An unhappy passion," continued Mirtain. "He loves," she replied, anxiously; "how I pity him! But what am I saying?" she continued, blushing; "he is too charming not to be loved in return." "He dares not hope, beautiful shepherdess," he said, "but if you cared to set his mind at rest on that point, he would have more faith in your words than in those of any other person." "It is not for me," she said, "to interfere in the affairs of so great a prince; those you mention are of too confidential a nature for me to enter into. Farewell, Mirtain," she added, abruptly leaving him; "if you wish to please me, never mention the prince or his love affairs again."

She went away much moved, for she was far from indifferent to the prince's merit. The first occasion on which she had seen him had never been erased from her mind, and without that secret charm which held her in spite of herself, she would have left no means untried of finding Queen Fairy. She was, moreover, astonished that the clever creature who knew everything did not come and fetch her, but, in fact, it no longer depended upon her. Directly the giant met the princess, she was compelled for a certain time to submit to fortune and to accomplish her destiny; the fairy had to content herself with coming to see her in a sunbeam; Constancia could not look at it fixedly enough to perceive her.

Constancia noticed the prince's neglect of her with vexation; if chance had not led him to the place where she was singing, he would not have seen her again. She was mortally angry with herself for caring anything about it, and if it is possible to love and hate at the same time, I may say she hated him because she loved him too much. How many tears she shed in secret! Ruson was the only witness; she often confided her troubles to him as if he had been capable of understanding them, and when he frisked in the meadows with the ewes, she said: "Take heed, Ruson, that love does not gain possession of you; that is the greatest of all evils, and if your love is not returned, what will you do, poor little sheep ? ''

These reflections were followed by the reproaches she heaped on herself for caring about a prince who regarded her with indifference. She was most anxious to forget him, but one day she perceived him resting in a pleasant place to dream more at his ease about the shepherdess he shunned. At length feeling very drowsy, he lay down on the grass; she saw him, her liking for him grew, and she could not help composing the words that had caused the prince so much anxiety. But how distressed she was in her turn when Mirtain told her that Constancio was in love. Notwithstanding the strong guard she put on herself, she could not help changing colour several times. Mirtain, who had his reasons for studying her, observed it, and was delighted ; he hastened to tell his master what had taken place.

The prince was much less ready to hope than his confidant; he thought only indifference was to be deduced from her conduct, and blamed therefore the fortunate Constancio whom he imagined she loved, but the very next day he went in search of her. No sooner did she see him than she fled as from a lion or tiger; flight seemed to her the only remedy for her troubles. Since her conversation with Mirtain, she knew she ought to do her utmost to tear Constancio's image from her heart, and the only possibility of success lay in avoiding him.

What could Constancio think when his shepherdess made off so hastily ? Mirtain was with him. "You see," said the prince, "the happy result of all your care ; Constancia hates me, and I dare not follow her and avow my passion." "You have too much consideration for so lowly a person," replied Mirtain ; "and if you like, sir, I will tell her you command her to come to you." "Ah, Mirtain !" exclaimed the prince, "what a difference there is between the lover and the confidant ! I think only of finding favour with this lovely girl, and recognise in her the good breeding that would ill assort with the violent measures you advise; rather than importune her, I would suffer anything." He turned in another direction, with so profound an air of melancholy, that a person even less moved than Constancia would have pitied him.

Directly he had passed out of sight she returned, in order to give herself the pleasure of being in the spot he had just quitted. "It was here," she said, "that he stopped, here that he looked at me ; but alas ! he is quite indifferent to me, and comes to dream of her he loves. But why should I complain ? How could he love a girl he believes so far beneath him ?" At times she felt inclined to tell him her story, but Queen Fairy had so emphatically forbidden her to speak of it, that although obedience in this respect was against her interests, she determined to keep silence.

A few days later, the prince returned again; she as carefully avoided him. He was much distressed thereby, and told Mirtain to reproach her for it; she pretended she had not thought about it, but since he deigned to notice it, she would take care not to do so again. Mirtain, delighted to have gained such a promise, informed his master, and the next day the prince went in search of her. She appeared embarrassed, and when he spoke of his feelings, she became still more so. However great her desire to believe him, she feared to deceive herself, and judging her by what he saw, he did not perhaps wish to dazzle her by a declaration scarcely suited to a poor shepherdess. The thought irritated her; she seemed proud, and received the assurances of his passion so coldly, that his worst suspicions were confirmed. "You are in love with another," he said, "but if I knew him, I call the gods to witness that he should feel my greatest wrath." "I ask no favours of you for any one, sir," she said; "if ever you come to know my feelings, you will find them very different from what you believe." At those words the prince took heart again, but the conversation that followed soon destroyed his hopes. For she protested her unconquerable resistance, and was sure she should never love all her life. The last words plunged him into the deepest grief, but he restrained himself from giving it utterance.

Whether on that account, or because of the excess of his passion that assumed new strength through the very difficulties surrounding it, he fell so dangerously ill that the physicians, ignorant of the cause, despaired of his life. Mirtain, who by the prince's orders had stayed near Constancia, brought her the sad news; she listened with grief, and an emotion difficult to describe. "Do you know any remedy," he said, "for fever, headache, and heartache?" "I know one," she replied, "of herbs and flowers, but everything depends on the manner of applying it." "Will you not come to the palace for that purpose?" he added. "No," she said, blushing, "I am too much afraid of failing." "What!" he continued, "you would neglect a means of restoring him to us? I always thought you hard, but you are ten times more so than I imagined." Mirtain's reproaches gave Constancia pleasure; she was delighted to be urged to visit the prince; it was only for the purpose of receiving such a satisfaction that she had boasted of knowing a remedy to relieve him, for as a matter of fact she knew none.

Mirtain went to the prince's bedside, and told him what the shepherdess had said, and how eager she was for his recovery. "You try to flatter me," said Constancio, "but I forgive you, and even at the expense of deceiving myself, should like to think the beautiful girl had some affection for me. Go to the queen, tell her one of her shepherdesses is in possession of a wonderful secret that will effect my cure ; get leave to bring her : run, Mirtain ; in my condition moments seem centuries."

The queen had not yet seen the shepherdess of whom Mirtain spoke ; she said she had little faith in what those ignorant girls pretended to know ; the idea was exceedingly stupid. " But, madam," he said, " more relief sometimes lies in the use of simples than in all the works of Æsculapius. The prince's sufferings are so great that he is anxious to try what the girl proposes." " Very well," said the queen ; " and if she does not cure him, I shall treat her so harshly that she will have no cause to boast of her skill." Mirtain returned to his master, and told him of the queen's ill-temper, and that he feared its effect on Constancia. " I would rather die ! " exclaimed the prince ; " return and tell my mother to leave the beautiful girl to mind her sheep. What a reward for her trouble ! The very idea adds to my suffering."

Mirtain hastened to the queen to tell her from the prince not to ask Constancia to come ; but as she was naturally very prompt to act, his indecision angered her. " I have already sent for her," she said ; " if she cures my son, I will reward her, and if she fails, I know what I shall do. Return to him and try to amuse him ; his melancholy makes me despair." Mirtain obeyed the queen, and took care not to tell his master of her bad temper, for he would have died of anxiety for his shepherdess.

The royal pasture ground was so close to the town that Constancia was not long in reaching it, and even had the distance been greater, her passion would have made her hasten. When she arrived at the palace, the queen was informed ; but she did not deign to see her, and contented herself with sending a message, advising her to take great care about what she was going to attempt ; if she failed to cure the prince, she would have her sewn up in a sack and thrown into the river. At that threat the princess turned pale, and the blood froze in her veins. " Alas ! " she said to herself, " I deserve the punishment ; when I boasted of possessing medical skill, I told a falsehood. My desire to see Constancio is so unreasonable that I dare not hope for the gods' protection." She gently bent her head, and replying never a word, let her tears flow.

All who saw her, admired her ; she seemed to them more divine than human. " Why do you distrust yourself, charming shepherdess ? " they said. " You carry life and death in your eyes ; one of your glances would be enough to cure our young prince ; come into his room, dry your eyes, and use your remedies without fear."

This way of encouraging her, and the extreme desire she had of seeing him, gave her confidence. She asked permission to go into the garden and gather what was needed ; she took myrtle, clover, herbs, and flowers, some dedicated to Cupid, others to Venus ; a dove's feathers and a few drops of pigeons' blood ; she summoned all the gods and fairies to her aid. Then trembling more than a dove before a kite, she said she was ready to attend the prince. He was lying down, his face pale, and his eyes weary ; but directly he saw her, his colour became healthier, a fact she observed with much joy.

"Sir," she said, "for many days I have desired the restoration of your health ; my zeal led me to tell one of your shepherds that I was acquainted with certain little remedies, and would gladly try to give you some relief ; but the queen has told me that if heaven deserts me in the enterprise, if I do not cure you, she will have me drowned. Imagine my fear, and understand that I interest myself in your recovery for your sake and not for mine." "Fear nothing, lovely shepherdess," he said ; "your kind wishes for the preservation of my life make it so dear to me that I shall do all in my power to take it up again. I had ceased to care for it, alas ! for how could I be happy when I remembered what I heard you sing for Constancio ! Those fatal words and your coldness brought me to the sad state in which you see me ; but, lovely shepherdess, since you command me to live, I will live and for you alone."

Constancia concealed with difficulty 'the pleasure such loving words caused her, but dreading some one might overhear the prince's words, she asked him to let her put bandages on his head and arms of the herbs she had gathered. He stretched out his arms so tenderly that she hastily fastened one of the bandages on them, for fear any one should discover what was going on, and after many little ceremonies intended to impose on his attendants, the prince exclaimed that his sufferings were already much less. And what he said was quite true ; the physicians were summoned, and were much surprised at the remedy, so quick and powerful. But when they saw the shepherdess who had applied it, they ceased to be astonished at anything, and said in their own manner of talking that one of her glances had more power than all the drugs in the world.

The shepherdess was so little affected by the praise showered on her that those who did not know her thought she was stupid. She placed herself in a corner of the room, hiding herself from everybody except her invalid, whom she approached at intervals to soothe his aching head with her gentle touch, or to feel his pulse, and in those short moments he said a thousand pretty things, inspired by the heart rather than the mind. "I hope, sir," she said, "that the sack the queen had made for drowning me in will not be put to such a dreadful use ; your health, which is so precious to me, is nearly re-established." "It only depends on you, sweet Constancia," he replied ; "a small share in your heart is all that is required for the peace and preservation of my life."

The prince rose and went to the queen's apartments. When told he was coming, she refused to believe it; she went quickly forward and was vastly surprised to meet him at the door of her room. "What! is it you, my son, my dear son?" she exclaimed. "To whom am I indebted for this marvellous recovery?" "To your own kindness, madam," said the prince; "you found me the cleverest woman in the whole universe. I entreat you, reward her in proportion to the service she has rendered me." "There is no hurry," replied the queen, harshly; "she is a poor shepherdess who may think herself happy if she always has the privilege of tending my sheep."

At that moment the king arrived; he had been told of the prince's recovery, and on entering the queen's apartments, the first thing he saw was Constancia. Her beauty, like a sun shining with a thousand fires, so dazzled him that for a few moments he was unable to ask those near him who was the marvel he beheld, and how long goddesses had dwelt in his palace. When he recovered himself, he approached her, and learning she was the enchantress who had just cured his son, embraced her, and said gallantly he felt very ill, and implored her to cure him also.

She accompanied him to the queen's room. Now the queen had never seen her; her astonishment cannot be described, she uttered a loud cry and swooned, throwing furious glances at the shepherdess. Constancio and Constancia were terrified. The king did not know what to think of the sudden attack; the whole court was alarmed. At length the queen came to herself, and the king asked her several times what had made her faint. She concealed her alarm and said it was her nerves. But the prince, who knew her well, was very anxious. She spoke to the shepherdess with some show of kindness, saying she wished to keep her with her to look after the flowers in her garden. The princess was overjoyed at the idea of being in a place where she could see Constancio every day.

The king made the queen enter his closet and asked her kindly what was vexing her. "Ah, sire," she exclaimed, "I have had a frightful dream. I have never seen that young shepherdess, and yet my imagination painted her so vividly that I recognised her at once, and in the dream my son married her. I am much mistaken or this beautiful girl will cause me much grief." "You put too much faith in a thing so doubtful," said the king. "I advise you not to act on such principles. Send the shepherdess back to mind your sheep, and do not causelessly distress yourself." The king's advice annoyed the queen, and instead of following it she set to work to find out her son's feelings towards Constancia.

The prince seized every opportunity of seeing her. As she had care of the flowers, she was often in the garden watering them, and when she touched them they seemed to grow more brilliant and beautiful. Ruson kept her company, and although he could not reply, she sometimes spoke to him of the prince. When she met him she was so confused that her eyes discovered to him her heart's secret. He was enchanted, and said to her all that the most tender passion could inspire.

Because of her dream, and even more on account of Constancia's matchless beauty, the queen could not sleep peacefully. She rose before the dawn, hid herself behind fences or in the depths of grottoes to listen to her son's conversation with the beautiful girl; but they were careful to speak very softly, and thus she had only suspicions to go on. This made her still more uneasy, and she treated the prince with scorn, thinking night and day that the shepherdess would ascend the throne.

Constancio kept a most vigilant watch over himself, but every one could see that he loved Constancia, and whether he praised or blamed her, he did both like a man who was fond of her. Constancia on her part could not help talking about the prince to her companions. She often sang the verses she had composed for him, and the queen, hearing her, was as surprised at her wonderful voice as at the subject of her song. "How have I offended you, ye just gods," said the queen, "that you should punish me in the way that hurts me most? Alas! I intended my son for my niece, and with bitter sorrow I see him in love with a wretched shepherdess, who will perhaps make him rebel against my wishes."

While she was distressing herself and thinking of a thousand ways in which to punish Constancia for her beauty and charm, love was making great progress with the young people. Constancia, certain of the prince's sincerity, could no longer conceal from him her noble origin, nor her feelings towards him. The tender avowal and the interesting confidence delighted him to such a degree that in any other place than the queen's garden, he would have thrown himself at her feet in sign of gratitude, and it was with the greatest difficulty that he refrained. There was no longer any need to struggle against his passion; he had loved Constancia as a shepherdess, and it is easy to believe that he simply adored her when he learned her rank. If he found no difficulty in believing the extraordinary tale that a great princess should wander through the world, now a shepherdess, and now a gardener, the reason is that such adventures were common enough in those days, and her appearance and manners sufficiently testified to the truth of her words.

Constancio, full of love and respect, swore to be ever faithful to his princess, and she on her side swore the same. They decided to be married directly the persons on whom they depended should consent to their union. The queen perceived all the strength of this dawning passion; her confidant, who eagerly sought some means of pleasing her, told her one day that Constancia sent Ruson every morning into the prince's apartment, carrying two baskets she had filled with flowers, and that Mirtain led him. At this news the queen lost patience: poor Ruson passed by, she waited for him herself, and in spite of Mirtain's entreaties, took the sheep to her room. She tore the basket of flowers to pieces, and searched so diligently that in a big pink, not yet fully out, she found a scrap of paper that Constancia had cleverly slipped into it, gently blaming the prince for the danger to which he exposed himself every day in the chase. The note contained these verses :—

> " Amidst all my gladness,
> I feel a strange fear.
> I am smitten with sadness
> The while you hunt here.
> The lion and the bear,
> Oh! my prince, mayst thou shun !
> There are those that are fair
> May be readily won.
> Such wild prey to pursue,
> Oh ! no longer delight,
> But those hearts subdue
> That will yield to thy might."

When the queen was giving way to anger against the shepherdess, Mirtain informed his master of the sheep's unlucky adventure. The prince, uneasy, rushed into his mother's room, but she had already gone to the king. " See, sire," she said, " see the noble desires of your son ; he is in love with that miserable shepherdess, who persuaded us she knew a way of curing him. Alas ! her knowledge was only too great ; love taught her, and she restored his health merely to bring him into still greater evils, and if we do not take measures to prevent the misfortunes that are threatening us, my dream will come only too true." " You are hard by nature," said the king, " and you want your son to think only of the princess you destine for him ; the matter is not easy ; you must have some indulgence for youth." " I cannot endure the way in which you spoil him," exclaimed the queen ; " you never find fault with him. All I ask of you is to let me send him away for a while ; absence will do more that all my arguments." The king, liking to keep the peace, consented to the queen's demand, and she immediately returned to her own apartments. There the prince was waiting for her in the greatest anxiety. Without giving him time to speak, she said : " My son, the king has just shown me letters from his brother entreating him to send you to his court to make the acquaintance of the princess destined from child-hood to be your wife. It is only right that you should have an opportunity of judging her merits and of loving her before you join your lives for ever." " I do not desire special rules for myself," said the prince; " it is not customary for sovereigns to visit each other and consult their hearts rather than reasons of state in making an alliance; whether the lady you have chosen for me is ugly or beautiful, stupid or intelligent, I shall obey you all the same." " I understand you, you rogue," exclaimed the queen, suddenly flying into a passion, " I understand; you adore a shepherdess all unworthy of you and fear to leave her: you shall either leave her or I will have her killed before your eyes. But if you will go away without hesitation, and will strive to forget her, I will keep her near my person and love her then as much as I hate her now."

The prince, pale as if on the point of death, considered the line of action he ought to take: on all sides he saw terrible trouble, he knew his mother to be the most cruel and vindictive princess in the world, he feared resistance would irritate her, and that his beloved mistress would thereby suffer. Urged to decide about going away, he consented, but as a man consents to drink a cup of poison he knows will be fatal in its effect.

Having given his promise, he left his mother's room, and entered his own, his heart so oppressed that he thought he must die. He confided his troubles to faithful Mirtain, and in his impatience to tell Constancia, went in search of her. He found her in the depths of a grotto, to which she repaired when the sun made the garden too hot; a small bed of turf was beside the stream that flowed down from the rock. In that peaceful spot, she unfastened the braids of her silky, wavy, bright, blonde hair; she put her naked feet into the water, and its pleasant murmur, joined to the fatigue engendered by her work, made her yield insensibly to the pleasures of sleep. Although her eyes were closed, they still had charms; long black lashes showed up the fairness of her complexion, Graces and Cupids seemed to have assembled round her, modesty and gentleness added to her beauty.

Here the amorous prince found her: he remembered that the first time he saw her she had been asleep; but since then she had inspired in him such tender feeling that he would willingly have yielded up one half his life to have spent the other half beside her. The pleasure of looking at her made him forget his troubles; and when he saw the foot whiter than snow, he could not leave off admiring it, and going nearer, he knelt down and took her hand. She imme-diately awoke, seemed vexed that he should have seen the foot, and, blushing like a red rose that blossoms forth at the coming of the dawn, hid it under her gown.

Alas! the bright colour lasted but a short space, for she noticed the new sadness in the prince's countenance. "What is the matter, sir?" she said, terrified. "I see by your eyes that you are in trouble." "Ah! who would not be distressed, my beloved princess?" he said, letting fall the tears he could not restrain. "They are about to part us; I must go away or expose you to the queen's violence. She knows my affection for you; she has even seen the note you wrote me, so one of her women told me, and without sympathising with my sorrow, inhumanly sends me to her brother." "What are you saying, prince?" she exclaimed; "you think that in order to preserve my life, you must abandon me? How can you conceive such a thing? Let me die before your eyes; it would be a better fate than to live separated from you."

Such tender talk was naturally often interrupted by sobs and tears; the young lovers had not yet experienced the sorrows of absence, and had not even thought about them, and thus new troubles were added to those they had already suffered. They made a thousand vows never to change: the prince promised Constancia to return with the utmost possible speed. "I only go," he said, "to shock my uncle and his daughter, so that he may cease to wish to make me his son-in-law. I shall only strive to displease the princess, and shall succeed." "Then," said Constancia, "you must not let her see you, for when she does she will like you whatever pains you take to the contrary." They both wept bitterly, and looked sorrowfully at one another; they made passionate promises, and it was some consolation to repeat that nothing could change their feelings.

Time passed so swiftly in this sweet converse, that night had fallen before they thought of separating; but the queen, desiring to consult the prince about his equipage, sent Mirtain in search of him. He found him at his mistress's feet, holding her hands in his. When the lovers saw Mirtain they were so overcome, they could scarcely speak: he told his master the queen was asking for him. The prince was obliged to obey her commands, and the princess went away.

The queen found her son so melancholy and changed, that she easily guessed the cause; she did not wish to speak of it to him, it was enough that he should go away. Indeed, everything was prepared with such speed that it seemed as if the fairies had a hand in it. As for the prince, his passion filled his whole mind. He desired Mirtain to remain at court, to give him news of the princess every day; he left her his finest jewels in case she should be in want, and his foresight left nothing undone that so important an occasion demanded.

At last he was obliged to set out. It is impossible to describe the grief of the lovers: if anything could lessen its violence, it was the hope of seeing each other soon again. Constancia now understood the magnitude of her misfortune:

to be a king's daughter, to own large realms, and to be in the power of a cruel queen who sent her son away for fear he should love her—her who was his inferior in nothing, and whom the greatest potentates in the world would passionately desire ; but so the stars had decreed.

The queen, delighted at her son's absence, was only desirous of intercepting the letters written to him ; she succeeded, and discovered that Mirtain was his confidant. She had him arrested on a false charge, and cruelly imprisoned in a distant castle. At this news the prince was very angry, and wrote to the king and queen, demanding that his favourite should be set free. His entreaties were of no avail ; but that was not the only trouble that came upon him.

One day, when the princess rose with the dawn, she went into the garden to pluck the flowers with which the queen's toilette was generally decorated. She saw her faithful Ruson, who was walking on in front, retrace his steps in fear. She was going forward to see the cause, when he pulled her by the gown in order to prevent it, for he was very intelligent. She heard the sharp hissing of serpents, and was immediately surrounded by toads, vipers, scorpions, asps, and snakes. They did not sting her, but rose in the air for the purpose of flinging themselves on her, and always fell back into the same place, unable to advance.

In the midst of her fear, she did not fail to observe the miracle, and she attributed it to a jewelled ring her lover had given her. Wherever she turned she saw the venomous creatures : the groves were full of them ; they lay on the flowers and under the trees. Constancia did not know what to do ; she saw the queen at the window mocking at her fear, and knew she could reckon on no assistance from that quarter. " I must die," she said, courageously ; " these horrible monsters have not come here of their own accord, they have been brought by the queen's orders, and she wishes to behold the end of my wretched life ; and, indeed, so unhappy has it been in the past, that I have no reason to love it, and if I regret it, the just gods are witnesses of the cause."

So saying, she advanced ; and, as she walked towards them, the serpents and their comrades retired before her. She was not more astonished at this than the queen, for the dangerous reptiles had been prepared for a long time to sting the shepherdess to death. The queen thought her son would not be surprised, and would attribute the girl's death to natural causes ; thus she would be absolved from blame : but, since the project had failed, she was forced to have recourse to another plan.

At the end of the forest lived a fairy whom it was impossible to visit on account of the elephants she kept. They ran about the forest, devouring poor travellers, their horses, and even the shoes with which they were shod, so great was their appetite. The queen had made a compact with her that, if by some unheard-of chance, any one should succeed in reaching her palace, she should give them something to carry back that would certainly cause their death.

The queen summoned Constancia, gave her her orders, and told her to set out. Now the princess had heard her companions speak of the dangers of the forest ; and an old shepherdess had once told her that she had happily escaped by the help of a little sheep she took with her: for, however furious the elephants were, the sight of a lamb rendered them perfectly gentle. The same shepherdess told her, further, that being ordered to bring back to the queen a burning girdle, she had been afraid to put it on and had placed it round trees which it burned up, and thus the girdle did not do her the harm the queen had hoped.

At the time the princess had listened to this tale, she never thought it would one day be of use to her ; but when the queen issued her orders in so decided a manner that she was obliged to obey, she prayed the gods to favour her. She took Ruson with her, and set out for the dangerous forest. The queen was delighted. She said to the king : "We shall never see the hateful object of our son's love again; I have sent her to a place where a thousand such as she is, would not serve for the fourth part of the elephants' breakfast". The king told her she was too vindictive, and that he could not help feeling sorry for the most beautiful girl he had ever seen. "Really!" she replied; "well, then, love her, and weep for her death as Constancio did when he parted with her."

Constancia had scarcely entered the forest before she was surrounded by the elephants ; the terrible creatures, delighted with the beautiful sheep who walked along more boldly than his mistress, caressed him with their formidable trunks, as gently as a lady could have done it with her hand, and the princess, fearing the elephants might regard her with a different eye, heavy as he was, took him in her arms. No matter in what direction she went, she always showed him to them, and thus speedily advanced towards the old woman's palace so impossible for others to reach.

She arrived after much fear and trouble; the place was quite unguarded, and so was the fairy, who concealed her astonishment at seeing the princess in her dwelling, for no one had succeeded in getting to it for a very long time. "What is your pleasure, beautiful girl?" she said. The princess humbly told her the queen's demand, and begged her to send her the girdle of affection. "I will not refuse her," she said ; "doubtless it is for you." "I do not know, madam," she replied. "Oh! but I do!" said the fairy, and took from her casket a blue velvet girdle, whence hung long strings for holding purse, knife, and scissors, and made her a present of it. " If you put on this girdle," she said, " as soon as you are in the forest, it will make you beloved by every one."

When Constancia had thanked her, she lifted Ruson, now more necessary than ever, in her arms; the elephants treated him with kindness and respect, and in spite of their desire to eat her, let her pass. She did not forget to put the girdle of affection round a tree, which immediately began to burn as if it was in the biggest fire imaginable. She took it off and carried it from tree to tree, until they burned no more, and then, very tired, arrived at the palace.

When the queen saw her, she was so astonished that she could not keep silent. " What a little rogue you are," she said ; " you have never been to my friend the fairy." " Pardon me, madam," replied Constancia, " I bring you the girdle of affection I demanded on your behalf." " Did you not put it on ? " asked the queen. " It is too magnificent for a poor shepherdess like me," she replied. " Not at all," said the queen ; " I make you a present of it for your trouble ; do not fail to adorn yourself with it. But tell me, whom did you meet on your way ? " " I saw," she said, "intelligent and clever elephants, it would be a pleasure to meet anywhere ; the forest seems to be their kingdom, and there are some among them more tyrannical than the others." The queen was terribly put out, but did not say all she thought, feeling sure that nothing in the world could prevent the girdle burning her. " If the elephants favoured you," she said, softly, " the girdle will avenge me ; you will learn, wretched creature, my affection for you, and the advantage you have gained in finding favour with my son ! "

Constancia returned to her little room, and wept for the absence of her beloved prince; she dared not write to him because the queen had spies in the country who stopped the couriers and seized her son's letters. " Alas ! Constancio," she said, " you will soon receive sad news of me ; you ought never to have gone away and left me to your mother's wrath. You should have defended me, or have received my last sighs ; instead, I am delivered over to her tyranny and am without any consolation."

At dawn she went into the garden to work as usual; the venomous creatures were still there, but her ring protected her from them. She wore the blue velvet girdle. When the queen saw her gathering flowers, as quietly as if she had a mere thread round her waist, her annoyance knew no bounds. " What power interests itself for this shepherdess ? " she exclaimed. " She enchants my son, and with innocent simples restores him to health ; serpents and asps fawn round her feet without hurting her ; elephants grow gentle and kind at the sight of her ; the girdle that through fairy power should burn her, only serves to adorn her. I must try some better plan."

She sent the captain of her guards, in whom she put the greatest confidence, to the harbour to see if there were any ships ready to set out for distant lands ; he found one which was to hoist sail early in the night. The queen was delighted, sent a message to the captain, and proposed to sell him the most beautiful slave imaginable. The merchant was very glad and willing to buy. He came to the palace, and unknown to Constancia, saw her in the garden ; the matchless girl's charms surprised him, and the queen, who understood how to derive profit from everything, and who was, moreover, very avaricious, sold Constancia for a high price.

Constancia, unaware of the fresh trouble in store for her, retired early to her little room, for the pleasure of thinking undisturbed of Constancio, and of replying to one of his letters she had at last received. When the queen entered, Constancia, unable to desist from so pleasant an occupation, was still reading it. The queen had a key with which she could open all the locks in the palace. She was accompanied by two mutes and her captain of the guards. A handkerchief was placed over Constancia's mouth, her hands were bound, and she was carried off. Ruson attempted to follow his mistress : the queen threw herself on him and prevented it, for she feared his bleating would be heard, and wished everything to be done with the greatest secrecy and silence. Thus no help being forthcoming, Constancia was taken to the ship, and as they were only waiting for her to embark, the vessel was soon sailing on the high seas.

She was obliged to make the voyage. Even the Fairy Sovereign had been unable to turn destiny in her favour : all that she could do was to follow her everywhere in a dark cloud, in which she was visible to no one. Prince Constancio, entirely occupied with his passion for the shepherdess, took no pains to please the princess destined to become his wife. Although naturally the most polished of men, he treated her very rudely, and she often complained to her father, who could not help quarrelling with his nephew ; thus the match did not progress. When the queen judged it expedient to write to the prince that Constancia was dying, his sorrow cannot be described. He could no longer submit to restraints in which his life ran at least as much risk as that of his mistress, and like a flash of lightning he departed.

But notwithstanding his speed, he arrived too late. The queen, who foresaw his return, had given out for some days that Constancia was ill ; she kept about her women who talked or kept silent as they were ordered. The rumour of Constancia's death was then spread abroad, and an image said to be her body was buried. The queen, seeking all possible means of convincing the prince of the death, brought Mirtain out of prison to assist at the funeral; the day of the burial was duly announced, and everybody came to mourn the charming girl. The queen, who could assume what expression of countenance she pleased, pretended to feel the loss on the prince's account.

He arrived in the greatest possible anxiety. When he entered the town he asked the first persons he met for news of his beloved Constancia; not recognising him, they told him she was dead. At those fatal words he could no longer restrain his grief; he fell from his horse, lifeless, speechless. People ran up, recognised the prince, hastened to help him, and carried him half dead to the palace.

The king felt his son's pitiable condition deeply. The queen was prepared for it, and thought that time and the crushing of his hopes would cure him, but his grief was too keen for consolation, and his distress, instead of becoming less, increased every moment. For two days he refused to see or speak to any one; then he went to the queen, his eyes full of tears, his appearance wild, his face pale. He told her she was the cause of his beloved Constancia's death, but that her punishment was at hand, since he was about to die, and therefore wished to visit the place where she was buried.

Unable to dissuade him, the queen determined to take him herself to the cypress wood where she had had a tomb erected. When the prince found himself in the place where his mistress was taking her everlasting rest, the words he uttered were so tender and passionate that never had anything like them been spoken before. The queen, in spite of her hard-heartedness, melted into tears. Mirtain was as much distressed as his master, and all who heard him shared his grief. Suddenly impelled by his rage, the prince drew his sword, and approaching the marble that covered the beautiful body, would have killed himself then and there if Mirtain and the queen had not arrested his arm. " No," he said, " nothing in the world shall prevent my dying and rejoining my beloved princess." The queen was surprised to hear him call the shepherdess princess; she did not know if her son was wandering, and would have thought him out of his mind, had it not been for his calm and collected manner.

She asked him why he spoke of Constancia as princess; he replied that she was of royal birth, that her kingdom was called the Kingdom of the Deserts, she was sole heir, and that had not concealment become unnecessary, he should never have mentioned it. " Alas! my son," said the queen, " since Constancia is of a rank equal to your own, be comforted for she is not dead. To lessen your grief, hear my confession : I sold her for a slave to some merchants." " Ah ! " exclaimed the prince, " you tell me this in order to prevent me killing myself; but my

28

resolution is fixed, nothing can turn me from my purpose." " I must then," added the queen, " take measures to convince you," and she ordered the wax figure to be disinterred. On first sight of it he thought it was his dear princess, and fell into a swoon from which he was with difficulty recovered. In vain the queen assured him that Constancia was not dead; after the evil trick she had served him he could not believe her. But Mirtain was able to convince him of the truth; the prince knew his affection for him, and that he was incapable of telling him a falsehood.

He felt a little comforted, for of all misfortunes death is the most terrible, and now he might hope to see his mistress again. But where could he look for her? No one knew the merchants who had bought her; they had not mentioned their destination, and these things formed no slight difficulties. But there is scarcely anything true love cannot overcome. He preferred to perish in pursuit of those who had robbed him of his mistress, than to live without her.

He blamed the queen most severely for her pitiless cruelty; he added she would have ample time to repent of the wicked trick she had played him, for he was about to depart, resolved never to return; thus in destroying one, she had destroyed two. The wretched mother threw herself on her son's neck, wept bitter tears and implored him by his father's old age and her affection not to leave them, that lacking his pleasant society they should die, that he was their one hope, and that if he was absent their neighbours and enemies would take possession of the kingdom. The prince listened coldly and respectfully, but her cruelty to Constancia was always before him; without Constancia all the kingdoms in the world were as nothing to him, and therefore he persisted in his resolve to set out the next day.

In vain the king tried to persuade him to stop. Constancio spent the night in giving orders to Mirtain, and entrusted to his care the faithful sheep. He took with him a large quantity of precious stones, and told Mirtain to keep the rest; he further said that he should send news of his doings to him alone, on condition that he kept it secret, for he wished his mother to suffer all the misery of anxiety.

Day had not yet dawned when impatient Constancio mounted his horse: he gave himself into the hands of fortune, begging her to be kind and aid him to recover his mistress. He did not know which way to go, but as she had embarked in a ship, he thought sailing the seas would be the best way to find her. He went to the most important port, unaccompanied and unknown, and asked about the farthest place to which the ships sailed, about all the coasts, shores and ports at which they touched. Then he embarked, hoping that a passion so pure and strong would not be ever unsatisfied.

As soon as they approached land he got into the long boat and rowed to shore shouting : " Constancia, beautiful Constancia, where are you ?   I seek you and call you in vain.   How much longer are we to be separated ? "   His regrets and laments were lost in the air, and he returned to the ship, his heart sore with grief and his eyes full of tears.

One evening they cast anchor behind a big rock.   He landed as usual, and since the country was unknown and the night dark, his companions did not wish to go on, fearing for their lives.   But the prince attached slight value to life, and began to walk on, falling and picking himself up again a countless number of times.   At length he saw a bright light which seemed to come from a fire ; going nearer he heard a great noise and loud strokes of hammers.   Far from feeling alarmed, he hastened to reach an immense forge, open on all sides ; the furnace was so bright that it seemed as if the sun must be shining.   Thirty giants, each with only one eye in the middle of the forehead, were at work there, forging weapons.

Constancio approached them and said : " If amidst the iron and fire that surround you, you are capable of pity, if by chance you have seen in this neighbourhood the lovely Constancia whom merchants have carried off as a slave, and will tell me where to find her, you may ask and have anything I possess ".   Scarcely had he finished speaking when the noise which on his arrival had ceased, recommenced with even greater force than before.   " Alas ! " he said, " my grief does not touch you, barbarous creatures ; I can expect no help from you."

He was about turning in a different direction when he heard sweet and enchanting music, and looking towards the furnace saw the most beautiful child imagination can conceive.   He shone brighter than the fire out of which he came.   When the prince saw his beauty, the bandage over his eyes, his bow and arrows, he knew it must be Cupid.   It was he indeed, and he exclaimed : " Stop, Constancio ; the passion that consumes you is so pure that I cannot refuse my help.   I am called Virtuous Love ; it is I who wounded you on Constancia's account, and it is I who protect her from the giant that persecutes her.   Queen Fairy is my intimate friend ; we are in alliance to guard her for you, but before revealing where she is at present, I must prove your love."   " Command, Cupid ! what you please," exclaimed the prince ; " whatever it may be, I shall obey you."   " Cast yourself into this fire," replied the child, " and remember that if you do not love faithfully, and one alone, you are lost."   " I need have no fear," said Constancio.   He cast himself into the fire and at once lost consciousness, knowing neither where nor what he was.

He slept for thirty hours, and on waking found himself the handsomest pigeon imaginable. He was no longer in the dreadful furnace, but in a nest of roses, jasmine and honeysuckle. His astonishment was unbounded ; his feathered legs, his many-coloured plumage and his red eyes surprised him vastly ; he wondered at his image in a brook, and wishing to complain, found that although he still had his human power of thought, he could no longer speak.

He regarded his change in form as the crowning stroke of his misfortunes. "Ah! treacherous Cupid," he thought to himself, "is this how you reward the most perfect of all loves ? Must a man be fickle, a traitor, and a perjurer to find favour with you ? I have known you recompense many of that character and afflict those who are really faithful. What can I hope," he continued, "from this extraordinary shape ? I'm a pigeon, and, if like Blue Bird, whose story has always been one of my favourites, I could speak, I would fly high and far, and seek my dear mistress in different countries, and inquire about her from so many people that I could not fail to find her ; but I cannot pronounce her name, and the only remedy left me, is to throw myself down some precipice and so perish."

Full of that dreadful purpose, he flew to the top of a high mountain, intending to throw himself to the bottom, but his wings kept him up in spite of himself. This greatly astonished him, for having never yet been a pigeon, he did not know the use of wings. He then determined to pull out all his feathers, and began to pluck himself most unmercifully.

Thus despoiled, he was about to make another attempt to throw himself from the top of a rock when two girls came up. Directly they saw the unfortunate bird, the one said to the other : "Whence comes this poor pigeon ? From the sharp talons of some bird of prey, or from the jaws of a weasel?" "I do not know whence he comes," replied the younger, "but I know very well where he is going"; and laying hold of the quiet little creature, continued : "He is going to keep company with five of his brothers, of whom I intend to make a pie for Queen Fairy".

Prince Pigeon, hearing her words, far from escaping, approached her so that she might do him the kindness of killing him quickly, but what might have caused his destruction saved him, for the girls found him so polite and friendly that they determined to keep him and make a pet of him. The more beautiful of the two shut him up in a covered basket in which she usually put her needle-work, and they proceeded on their way.

"For some days," said one of them, "our mistress has seemed terribly busy; every moment she is mounting her fiery camel, and night and day travelling from one end of the earth to the other without stopping." "If you were discreet," replied her companion, " I could tell you the reason, for she has imparted it to me." " Of course I can hold my tongue," exclaimed the one who had already spoken ; "you may be quite certain of my silence." " Know then," she replied, " that the Princess Constancia, whom she dearly loves, is persecuted by a giant who wants to marry her; he has shut her up in a tower, and to prevent the marriage Queen Fairy must work great marvels."

The prince heard their conversation from the bottom of the basket ; so far he had thought nothing could add to his misfortunes, but to his great sorrow he learned that he had been mistaken. From what I have told you of his passion, and of the circumstances in which he was placed, his despair at being turned into a pigeon just at the very moment the princess had most need of his help, may be easily imagined. To torment him the more, his vivid imagination pic- tured Constancia in the fatal tower, besieged by the importunity, violence, and ardour of a terrible giant; he dreaded that in her fear she would consent to the marriage. The next minute he thought she would not be afraid, and would ex- pose herself to the fury of such a lover. It would be difficult to describe his state of mind.

When the young girl who was carrying him in her basket returned with her companion to the palace of their fairy mistress, they found her walking in a shady alley of her garden. They prostrated themselves before her, and said : " Great queen, look at this pigeon we have found ; he is gentle, friendly, and if he had feathers he would be very handsome. We have decided to keep him in our room, but if it would amuse you, he can sometimes come into yours." The fairy took the basket in which he was shut, drew him out, and made serious reflections on the strangeness of the world, for it was an extraordinary circumstance that a prince like Constancio should be turned into a pigeon trussed ready for roasting or boiling; and although the change had been brought about solely by her will and agency, she liked to moralise on all sorts of events, and this one struck her as very remarkable. She caressed the pigeon, and he on his side did all in his power to attract her attention, so that she might relieve him from his misery; he bowed pigeon-fashion, drawing back his foot a little; he pecked at her with a caressing air, and although as yet he was new to the ways of pigeons, he was more expert than the oldest and wisest of the race.

Fairy Sovereign carried him into her closet, shut the door, and said : " In spite of your sad plight, I recognise and love you for the sake of my daughter Constancia, who is as little indifferent to you, as you are to her. I am alone to blame for your change of form. I made you enter the fiery furnace in order to test the sincerity of your love, and I find it pure and ardent; you have come well through the trial." The pigeon nodded his head three times in token of gratitude, and listened to what the fairy told him. " As soon as your mother," she continued, " received the money and jewels in exchange for the princess, she most cruelly sent her to the merchants who had bought her. Directly she was on board, they set sail for the East Indies, where they were sure of getting rid of the precious jewel in their possession at the greatest profit. Her tears and entreaties availed nothing to change their resolution ; in vain she told them that Constancio would buy her back with all he possessed in the world. The more they recognised the high price they might expect for her, the more they hastened to get away, fearing lest the prince should be informed of her abduction, and come and snatch their prey from them.

" After travelling half over the world they were overtaken by a furious storm. The princess had succumbed to grief and the fatigues of the voyage, and was dying. Fearful of losing her, they put in at the nearest port ; but while they were disembarking a giant of enormous size, accompanied by several others, came up, and they all shouted together that they wanted to look at the curiosities that were in the ship.

" The first thing the giant saw when he got on board was the young princess. They recognised each other at once. ' Ah, you little rogue ! ' he exclaimed, ' the just and pitiful gods put you once again into my power : do you remember the day I found you, and you cut my sack ? I am very much mistaken if you play me such a trick again.' He seized her as an eagle lays hold of a chicken ; and, in spite of her resistance and the merchants' entreaties, carried her off in his arms, running with all speed to his great tower.

" The tower is on a high mountain ; the sorceress who built it neglected nothing to make it beautiful and strange. There is no door ; you enter by the windows that are very high up ; the diamond walls shine like the sun, and are of a hardness to resist everything. In fact all the richest productions of art and nature are of less worth than its contents. On the way there the furious giant told the lovely Constancia that he wished to marry her and make her the happiest woman in the world ; that she should be mistress of all his treasure ; that he would love her tenderly, and give her cause to bless the good fortune that had brought her to him. By her tears and lamentations he learned her deep despair, and as, in spite of the destiny that had decreed Constancia's destruction, I was secretly looking after everything, I inspired in the giant a feeling of tenderness he had never before experienced, so that instead of flying into a rage, he told the princess he would grant her a year's respite, and during that time would treat her kindly ; but if in that period she did not make up her mind to do what he wished, he would marry her against her will, and afterwards kill her, so that she could choose which she preferred.

" After that terrible declaration he shut her up, giving her the most beautiful girls imaginable for companions in the hope they might be able to rouse her from the deep melancholy into which she was plunged. He placed giants round the tower to prevent any one approaching it, and, indeed, if anybody was fearless enough to do so, he would soon receive his punishment, for they make cruel and formidable guards.

" At length the poor princess seeing no probability of assistance, and only one day wanting to complete the year, is preparing to throw herself off the top of the tower into the sea. This, Sir Pigeon, is her condition. The only remedy I can think of is that you should fly to her, holding in your beak this little ring ; when she puts it on her finger she will change into a dove, and you will easily escape."

The pigeon was most eager to set out, but knew not how to make himself understood. He pulled at the fairy's ruff and at her fringed apron ; he went to the window and tapped the glass with his beak. All this meant in pigeon language: " I entreat you, madam, to send me with your enchanted ring to the princess's assistance ". She understood him perfectly, and responding to his wishes, said: " Go, fly, charming pigeon ; the ring will guide you. Here it is ; take care not to lose it, for you are the only person in the world who can set Constancia free."

As I have already observed, Prince Pigeon had no wings; he had plucked them out in the extremity of his despair. The fairy rubbed him with a marvellous essence that made them grow again so beautiful and wonderful that Venus's doves themselves were not worthy to be compared with him. He was delighted to recover his wings, and taking flight reached the top of the tower at dawn. Its diamond walls were so dazzling that the sun in its greatest brilliance is scarcely so bright. On the keep was an extensive garden, in the centre of which grew an orange tree loaded with flowers and fruit ; the rest of the garden was very curious, and if Prince Pigeon had not been occupied with such important business, he would have found great pleasure in examining it.

He perched on the orange tree, holding the ring in his beak ; he was feeling terribly anxious, when the princess entered the garden. She wore a long white gown, her head was covered with a black veil embroidered in gold ; it fell over her face and reached to the ground on every side. The amorous pigeon might have doubted if it was she, if it had been possible that any other woman could have possessed that noble bearing and dignified appearance. She sat down under the orange tree, and suddenly raising her veil, he remained for some time entranced.

" How vain seem now all sad regrets, all melancholy thoughts," she said ; " my afflicted heart has spent a whole year between hope and fear ; but the fatal moment has arrived. This very day, in a few hours, I must die, or wed the giant. Alas! is it possible that Queen Fairy and Prince Constancio have thus forsaken me? What have I done to them? But what is the use of these reflections? Would it not be wiser to carry out my design?" She rose and courageously made ready to throw herself from the tower; but as the slightest sound terrified her, and she heard the pigeon moving in the tree, she raised her eyes to see what it was; at the same moment he flew to her, and placed in her lap the all-important little ring. The princess, surprised at the caresses of the handsome bird, and at his beautiful plumage, was equally astonished at the present he gave her. She looked at the ring and noticed some mysterious marks on it; she still held it, when unobserved by her, the giant entered the garden.

Some of her waiting-women had informed her terrible lover of the princess's despair, and that rather than marry him she preferred to kill herself. When he heard that she had gone up to the top of the tower, so early in the morning, he feared some fatal catastrophe; his heart was incapable of any cruel action, and her beauty so greatly enchanted him, that he loved her tenderly. O ye gods! what were her feelings when she saw him! She feared he would deprive her of the means she was seeking of putting an end to her existence. Poor pigeon was not a little afraid of the terrible giant. In her confusion, Constancia put the ring on her finger and was immediately changed into a dove, and flew away with all possible speed in the company of the faithful pigeon.

Never was there surprise like that of the giant. After looking at his mistress, now a dove flying through the air, he remained for some time motionless, then uttered cries and groans that shook the mountains and ended only with his life; he flung himself into the sea, and it was far better that he should be drowned than the princess. She and her guide went speeding on their way, and as soon as they were far enough off to have no cause to fear, they halted in a wood almost dark from the number of the trees, and very pleasant on account of the green grass and the beautiful flowers that carpeted the ground. Constancia did not know that the pigeon was her true lover. He was feeling greatly troubled at his inability to tell her so, when he felt an invisible hand loosen his tongue. He was overjoyed, and said to the princess: "Has not your heart told you, charming dove, that your companion is consumed by a passion you yourself have kindled?" "My heart hopes for happiness," she replied, "but dares not flatter itself such will be the case. Alas! who could have imagined it? I was about to succumb to my wretched fate, when you appeared and snatched me from the jaws of death, or from the arms of a monster I feared even more than death."

The prince, delighted to hear his dove speak, and to find her as loving as ever, said to her everything the most ardent and tender passion could inspire.

He related all that had happened since her absence, especially his amazing encounter with Cupid at the forge, and the fairy in her palace, and Constancia was overjoyed to learn that her best friend was still taking charge of her. " Let us go and find her, my dear prince," she said to Constancio, "and thank her for all she has done for us: she will restore us to our natural shapes, and we will return to your kingdom or to mine."

"If you love me as much as I love you," he replied, " I should make you a proposal, in which love alone bears a part. But, charming princess, you will call me strange." " Do not demean your intelligence at the expense of your heart," she rejoined ; " speak without fear. I shall always listen to you with pleasure." " I am of opinion, then, that we should not change our forms. You, a dove, and I, a pigeon, are consumed by the same passion as were Constancio and Constancia. I feel sure that without the cares of our kingdoms, without councils to hold, wars to wage, audiences to give, exempt from continually playing an important part on the world's stage, we shall find it far pleasanter to live only for each other in delightful solitude." "Ah!" exclaimed the dove, "how great and full of charm is your plan ! Young as I am, alas ! I have known so many misfortunes; fate, jealous of my innocent beauty has obstinately persecuted me, and I should be very glad to renounce all the good things it has given me, and to live only for you. Yes, my dear prince, I consent : let us choose some pleasant land and spend our days happily in our changed shapes ; let us lead an innocent life, without ambition, without desires other than those that spring from virtuous love."

" It is I who must guide you," cried Cupid, descending from the heights of Olympus ; " so loving a plan deserves my protection." " And mine, too," said Queen Fairy, suddenly appearing. " I have come to you, to anticipate by a few moments the delight of seeing you." The pigeon and the dove were as much pleased as surprised at this new event. " We will place ourselves under your guidance," said Constancia to the fairy. " Do not forsake us," said Constancio to Cupid. " Come," he said, " to Paphos ; my mother is still worshipped there, and the birds sacred to her are always held in veneration." " No," replied the princess, " we do not seek the community of men ; happy those who can renounce it ! We desire some beautiful solitude."

The fairy struck the ground with her wand and Cupid did the same with a golden arrow. They immediately beheld a most beautiful spot, deserted by all save nature, the loveliest of woods, flowers, meadows, and springs. " Stay here for millions of years," said Cupid, " and swear eternal faith in the presence of this marvellous fairy." " I swear it to my dove," said Pigeon. " I swear it to my pigeon," said Dove. " Your marriage," said the fairy, " could not be celebrated by a god better able to render it happy. Besides, I promise you that if you grow weary of your present forms, you may depend on me, and I will restore you to your original shapes." Pigeon and Dove thanked the fairy, and assured her they should have no need of her good offices, they had had too wide an experience of the misfortunes of life. They asked her if Ruson was still alive to bring him to them. " He has changed his condition," said Cupid. " I had condemned him to be a sheep. I took pity on him, and restored him to the throne from which I had taken him." Constancia felt no longer surprised at the pretty ways she had so liked in him, and implored Cupid to tell her the story of a sheep she had loved so well. " I will come some day and tell it you," he replied, kindly, " but just now am wanted in so many places, that I do not know where to go first. Farewell," he continued, " happy, loving pair ; you can boast of being the wisest folk in my empire."

Queen Fairy remained some time with the newly-married couple. She could not sufficiently praise their disdain for the vanities of the world ; and it is certain they chose the best way to lead a tranquil life. At length she left them ; and it has been ascertained from her and from Cupid that Prince Pigeon and Princess Dove loved each other faithfully to the end of their days.

PRINCESS BELLE-ETOILE.

ONCE upon a time there lived a princess who possessed nothing of her former greatness but the canopy of her throne and the case that had contained her knife, fork, and spoon; the former was of velvet embroidered with pearls, and the latter of gold set with diamonds. She took as much care of them as possible, but the extreme poverty to which she was reduced compelled her from time to time to remove a pearl, a diamond, or an emerald, and have it secretly sold in order that she might have the wherewithal to feed her suite. She was a widow with three young and lovely daughters. She saw that if she brought them up in a manner suitable to their rank they would afterwards feel their misfortunes the more. She, therefore, determined to sell her few remaining possessions and settle with her three daughters in some distant country house, where they could live in a style suited to their small fortune. In crossing a forest she was robbed and scarcely anything was left. The poor princess, more grieved by this last misfortune than by all that had gone before, recognised that she must either earn her living or die of hunger. She had formerly been fond of good eating, and knew how to make excellent sauces. She had never gone anywhere without her little gold kitchen that people came from afar to visit. What had been a mere amusement, now afforded her a means of subsistence. She settled near a large town in a very pretty house. She cooked marvellously good dishes, and, as the people of that land were rather greedy, everybody patronised her. They talked of nothing but the excellent cook, and scarcely gave her time to breathe. Meanwhile her three daughters grew up, and their beauty would have made as great a stir as the princess's sauces, had she not shut them up in a room they rarely left.

On one of the finest days in the year, a little old woman who seemed very tired entered their house; she supported herself on a stick, her body was bent, and her face wrinkled. " I come," she said, " for you to serve me a nice dinner, for I wish before going into the next world to enjoy myself in this." Taking a cane-bottomed chair she sat down near the fire, asking the princess to be quick. As she could not do it all without assistance, she summoned her three daughters;

the eldest was called Roussette, the second Brunette, and the youngest Blondine. She had given them these names on account of the colour of their hair. They were dressed like peasants, with bodices and petticoats of different colours. The youngest was the prettiest and sweetest. Their mother told one to fetch pigeons from the pigeon-house, another to kill chickens, and the last to make pastry. In less than a moment they had laid the table for the old lady very nicely ; the linen was beautifully white, the china well polished, and the courses many and various. The wine was excellent, ice was not forgotten, and the glasses were rinsed every time by the prettiest hands imaginable. All this gave the good old woman a fine appetite. If she ate well, she drank still better. She became a little flustered and said many things which the princess, who pretended not to pay any attention, found very witty.

The dinner ended as cheerfully as it had begun; the old lady rose from the table and said to the princess : " My dear friend, if I had any money I would pay you, but I was ruined a long time ago ; I wanted to come to you in order to get such good cheer. All I can promise you is to send you better customers than my. self." The princess began to smile, and said kindly : " Do not distress yourself, my good mother ; I am always well paid when I give pleasure ". " We were delighted to wait on you," said Blondine, " and if you will take supper here, we shall be even better pleased." " Oh ! what a happy thing it is," exclaimed the old woman, " to be born with a kindly heart. But do you not hope to receive its due reward ? Be sure," she continued, " that the first thing you wish for, without thinking of me, will be granted." ' At the same moment she disappeared, and they never doubted she was a fairy.

The adventure astonished them mightily; they had never seen a fairy before and felt afraid. For five or six months they talked of nothing else, and as soon as they wished for anything, thought of her. Thus nothing turned out as they desired, and they were extremely angry with the fairy. But one day when the king was hunting he came to the good cook's abode to see if she was as clever as people said. He made so much noise in approaching the garden that the three sisters who were picking strawberries heard him. "Ah!" said Roussette, "if I was lucky enough to marry the admiral, I promise to spin with my shuttle and distaff a great quantity of thread, and to weave out of it so much cloth that he would not need to buy any for the sails of his ships." "And I," said Brunette, "if fortune was kind enough to make me the wife of the king's brother, I promise to make him so much lace with my needle that his palace would be filled with it." "And I," added Blondine, "I promise that if the king would wed me, I should have after a short space of time two handsome boys and a beautiful girl; their hair shall fall in ringlets and shall scatter precious stones; they shall have a shining star on the forehead and a rich gold chain round the neck."

One of the king's favourites who had come in advance to inform the hostess of the king's arrival, hearing the sounds of talking in the garden, stopped without making any noise, and was amazed at the beautiful girls' conversation. He promptly repeated it to the king to amuse him; he laughed and commanded them to appear before him.

They came at once in the most graceful manner possible, and greeted the king modestly and respectfully. When he asked them if it was true that they had been talking about the husbands they wished for, they blushed and looked down. He urged them to confess, and at length they gave in. Then he exclaimed: "I do not know what power is acting on me, but I shall not leave this place until I have married the beautiful Blondine." "Sire," said the king's brother, "I ask your permission to wed the pretty Brunette." "Grant me a like favour," added the admiral, "for Roussette charms me infinitely."

The king, glad to find his example followed by the greatest persons in his kingdom, said he approved their choice, and asked the mother for her consent. She replied that it was the greatest joy she could possibly have. The king embraced her, and the prince and the admiral followed suit.

When the king was ready to dine, a table laid for seven with a gold service and loaded with everything of the rarest and best for a good dinner came down the chimney. But the king hesitated to eat; he feared the viands might be only suited to witches' nocturnal revels, and the manner of serving your dinner from the chimney seemed somewhat doubtful.

On the sideboard only gold bowls and vases were to be seen, on which the chasing surpassed the material. At the same moment a swarm of honey-bees appeared in crystal hives, and began the most charming music you can imagine. The whole room was filled with hornets, flies, wasps, and other little insects of that sort who waited on the king with supernatural skill. Three or four thousand flies poured out the wine, and not one ventured to drown himself in it, a surprising example of moderation and discipline. The princess and her daughters understood that all that was happening was to be attributed to the little old woman, and blessed the hour in which they had made her acquaintance.

After the banquet, which lasted so long that night surprised them while they were still at table—a circumstance of which the king felt a little ashamed, for it would seem that at his wedding Bacchus took the place of Cupid—the king rose and said : " Let us end the fête as it should have begun ". He drew a ring from his finger and put it on that of Blondine; the prince and the admiral followed his example. The bees redoubled their songs. They danced and were merry, and all who had accompanied the king congratulated the queen and the princess. As for the admiral's wife, she was not treated with quite so much ceremony, a fact that greatly annoyed her, for she was older than Brunette or Blondine, and yet had not made so good a match as they had.

The king sent his equerry-in-chief to inform his mother of the great events, and to bring his most magnificent chariots in order to take Queen Blondine and her two sisters to the court. The queen-mother was the most cruel and passionate of women. When she learned that her son had married without her knowledge, and above all a girl of low birth, and that the prince had done the same, she had a paroxysm of anger that terrified the whole court. She asked the equerry-in-chief what had made the king enter into so ill-judged a union. He told her that it was in the hope of becoming the father of two boys and a girl with long curly hair, stars on their heads, and gold chains round their necks; these curious things had charmed him. The queen-mother smiled contemptuously at her son's credulity, and her insulting remarks sufficiently proved her wrath.

The chariots had already arrived at the little house. The king invited his mother-in-law to accompany him, and promised she should be treated with the utmost consideration and respect. But she already knew the agitations of a court. " Sire," she said, " I know too much of the world to forsake the peaceful life I have with so much difficulty attained." " What ? " replied the king ; " do you wish to continue keeping an inn ? " " No," she said, " you will allow me something to live on." " Permit me," he added, " to give you a suite and officers." " I thank you," she said, " but when I am alone, I have no enemies to worry me ; if I had servants, I should dread finding foes among them." The king admired the wisdom and moderation of a woman who thought and spoke like a philosopher.

While he was persuading his mother-in-law to come with him, the admiral's wife hid all the fine gold bowls and vases from the sideboard in the bottom of her chariot, wishing to gain every possible advantage, but the fairy who saw every-thing, though herself unseen, changed them into earthen pitchers, so that when Roussette arrived and was going to carry them into her closet, she found nothing that would have repaid her for the trouble.

The king and queen affectionately embraced the wise princess, and assured her that all they possessed was at her disposal. They left the rustic abode and came to the town, preceded by trumpets, hautboys, and drums, whose sounds could be heard afar off. The queen-mother's confidants advised her to conceal her ill-temper, because it would offend the king, and might have unfortunate consequences. She, therefore, controlled herself, and showed only affection for her two daughters-in-law, giving them jewels and praises for all their actions, good or bad.

Queen Blondine and Princess Brunette were great friends, but Roussette hated them both with a mortal hatred. " See," she said, " my sisters' good fortune—one is queen, the other princess of the blood, their husbands adore them ; and I, the eldest, and a hundred times more beautiful than they are, am only married to an admiral, who does not love me as he ought." Her jealousy of her sisters made her take the side of the queen-mother ; for it was well known that her affection for her daughters-in-law was a mere pretence, and that she would welcome any opportunity of doing them an injury.

Shortly before the birth of children to the queen and the princess, a great war broke out, and the king was obliged to lead his army. Thus the young queen and the princess, forced to remain in the power of the queen-mother, begged the king to let them return to their mother, so that she might console them for the absence of their husbands. The king would not give his consent, but implored his wife to remain at the palace, assuring her his mother would treat her kindly. He begged the queen-mother most earnestly to love her daughter-in-law, and take care of her, adding that she could not oblige him more, that he hoped to have beautiful children, and that he awaited the news of their birth with the greatest anxiety. The wicked queen, delighted that her son should confide his wife to her care, promised to think of nothing but her well-being ; and assured him he might set out with a mind perfectly at ease. He departed with so strong a desire to return soon, that he risked his troops in every encounter ; and his good luck made his hardihood not only always successful, but also advanta-geous to the affairs of his realm. The queen was confined before his return. The same day, her sister, the princess, gave birth to a beautiful boy, and died immediately.

Roussette was busy thinking of ways in which to hurt the young queen. When she saw her pretty children, and remembered that she had none, her rage increased ; she resolved to speak to the queen-mother at once, for there was no time to lose. " Madam," she said, " I am so deeply sensible of the honour your majesty does me, in admitting me to your favour, that I willingly put aside my own interests for the sake of yours. I quite understand your annoyance at the ill-judged marriages of your sons. Here are now four children who will perpetuate the fault. Our mother is a poor villager who was starving when she decided to become a cook ; believe me, madam, let us make a fricassee of all those little ones, and so send them out of the world before they can make you blush." "Ah! my dear Roussette," said the queen, embracing her, " how I love you for being so just, and for sympathising as you do with my real annoyances ! I had already resolved on what you suggest ; it is only the means that puzzles me." " That need give you no trouble," said Roussette. " My dog has just had three puppies ; they have each a star on the forehead and a mark round the neck which makes a sort of chain. The queen must be made to think she gave birth to the little animals, and her two sons, her daughter, and the princess's son must be killed."

" Your plan pleases me vastly," she exclaimed ; " I have already given such orders to Feintise, her lady-in-waiting, so that there will no difficulty about the little dogs." " Here they are," said Roussette ; " I brought them with me." She then opened a large bag she always wore at her side, and drew from it three little pups. The queen-mother and she at once dressed them like the queen's children, in lace and fine linen embroidered with gold. They put them in a covered basket, and the wicked queen, accompanied by Roussette, went to Queen Blondine. " I come to thank you," she said, " for the fine heirs you have presented to my son ; they certainly possess heads fitted to wear a crown. I am not surprised that you promised your husband two sons and a daughter with stars on their foreheads, long hair, and gold chains round their necks. Here, take and nurse them yourself, for no woman will care to suckle dogs."

The poor queen thought she should die of grief when she saw the three puppies, and heard the distracting noise they made. She began to cry bitterly, then clasping her hands: " Alas ! madam," she said, " do not add your reproaches to my trouble ; it could not surely be greater. If the gods had allowed me to die before becoming the mother of these little monsters, I should have reckoned myself happy. Alack ! what am I to do ? The king will hate me as much as he used to love me." Sighs and sobs stifled her voice, she could speak no more ; and the queen-mother spent three hours at her bedside pleasantly occupied in insulting her.

She then went away, and Roussette, pretending to sympathise with Blondine's grief, said she was not the first to whom a like misfortune had occurred.

It was of course a trick on the part of the old fairy, who had promised them so many wonderful things, but as it would be very dangerous for her to see the king, she advised her to go with her three puppy children to their poor mother. The queen's tears formed her only reply. It was a very hard heart that would not have been touched by her condition ! Believing herself to be their mother, she actually suckled the horrid animals.

The queen ordered Feintise to take Blondine's children, and the princess's son, and to strangle and bury them, so that no one should know anything about it. When she was on the point of carrying out the command, and even held the fatal cord in her hand, she looked at them, found them so wondrously beautiful, and observed that they promised such extraordinary things, from the stars that shone on their foreheads, that she dared not use her hands to take so august a life.

She had a boat brought to the sea-shore, and put the four children in one cradle into it, and some jewelled necklaces, so that if fate led them to the hands of any one kind-hearted enough to bring them up, he might be rewarded.

Driven before a high wind, Feintise soon lost sight of the boat, and in the same instant the waves grew bigger, the sun was hidden, the clouds and water seemed to meet, and thunderclaps resounded on every side. She never doubted but the frail craft was upset, and felt glad that the poor innocents were no more, because she had dreaded something extraordinary happening in their favour.

The king, his mind always full of the queen, having made a truce for a short period, returned, travelling post ; he arrived twelve hours after the birth of the children. When the queen-mother heard of his arrival, she went to meet him, her appearance betokening great grief ; she held him for some time closely in her arms, moistening his face with her tears, and it seemed as if her grief had deprived her of the power of speech. The king, all trembling, dared not ask what had happened, for he felt sure it must be some terrible misfortune. At last his mother told him, with an effort, that this wife had given birth to three dogs. Feintise then showed them to him, and the admiral's wife, throwing herself at the king's feet, implored him not to kill the queen, but to send her back to her mother ; that so had the queen herself determined, and would consider such treatment a great favour.

The king's despair was so great that he could scarcely breathe ; he looked at the puppies, and was surprised at the star in the middle of their foreheads, and the different colour round their necks. He sank into a chair, turning over many thoughts in his mind, unable to make any final decision. But the queen-mother importuned him to such a degree, that he pronounced sentence of banish-

ment on the innocent queen.   She was immediately put into a litter with
the three dogs, and taken to her mother's house, where she arrived almost
dead.

The gods took pity on the princes and the princess in the boat.   The fairy
who protected them, instead of rain, caused milk to fall into their little mouths,
and the terrible storm that had so suddenly arisen did not do them the least injury.   After drifting along for seven days and seven nights in open sea as gently
as if they had been on a lake, they fell in with a pirate ship.   The captain,
struck even at a distance by the brilliant light of the stars on their foreheads, felt
sure the boat must be full of precious stones.   He verily found some in it, but
was even more delighted with the beauty of the four marvellous children.   The
desire of saving them made him return home in order to give them to his wife,
who was childless, but ardently wished for sons and daughters.

She was troubled to see him return so soon, because he had intended making a long voyage; but she was overjoyed when he delivered to her keeping such
an important treasure.   Together they wondered at the marvel of the stars, the
gold chains that could not be removed from their necks, and their long hair.   Their
astonishment increased when the woman combed their hair, and every second
there fell from it pearls, rubies, diamonds, and emeralds, of various sizes and
all perfect; she told her husband about it, and he was equally surprised.

" I am," he said, " very tired of being a pirate; if these little children's
locks continue to give us such treasures, I will no longer scour the ocean, and
my property will be as great as that of our chief captain's."   The pirate's wife,
whose name was Corsine, was delighted at her husband's determination, and
loved the children all the more in consequence.   She named the princess,
Belle-Etoile; her elder brother, Petit-Soleil; the younger, Heureux; and the
princess's son, Chéri.   So superior in beauty to the other two was Chéri that,
although he had neither star nor necklace, Corsine loved him best.

As she could not rear them without the aid of a nurse, she asked her husband, who was fond of hunting, to catch her some very young fawns.   He easily
succeeded, because the forest in which they dwelt was very large.   Corsine exposed
them on the weather side, and the hinds scenting them, hastened up to suckle
them.   Corsine then hid them, and put the children in their stead, who eagerly
drank the hind's milk.   Twice every day four of them came to Corsine's house
in search of the princes and the princess whom they took for fawns.

Thus passed the princes' early childhood: the pirate and his wife loved
them so passionately that they gave them every care.   The man had been well
educated, and it was less from inclination than from the frowardness of fortune
that he had become a pirate.   He had met Corsine in the house of a princess,

where her mind had been properly cultivated ; she was well-bred, and, although she inhabited a kind of desert, where they subsisted on the booty he brought home from his voyages, she had not forgotten the usages of society. Thus their joy that they were no longer forced to expose themselves to all the dangers inseparable from a pirate's life, was very great, and they were getting rich all the same. About every three days, there fell, as I have already mentioned, a quantity of precious stones from the hair of the princess and her brothers ; those Corsine sold at the nearest town, and brought back all manner of pretty things for her little ones.

When they had passed their earliest infancy, the pirate began seriously to cultivate the charming dispositions heaven had endowed them with. As he never doubted that a great mystery attached to their origin, and his finding them, he wished to show his gratitude to the gods by giving the children a good education, so that, after rendering his house more comfortable, he brought there clever men who taught them the various branches of knowledge with an ease that vastly surprised those learned persons.

The pirate and his wife had never told any one the story of the finding of the four children. They passed for theirs, although their actions proved they sprung from a more illustrious stock. They were extremely fond of one another, which was only natural and polite, but Prince Chéri's affection for Princess Belle-Etoile was more eager and ardent than that of the other two ; no sooner did she express a wish for anything than he attempted even the impossible to procure her what she wanted. He scarcely ever left her ; when she went hunting, he accompanied her ; when she stayed at home, he always found an excuse for remaining with her. Petit-Soleil and Heureux treated her with less affection and respect. She noticed the difference, but Chéri quite made up for it, and she loved him more than the others.

As they grew older their mutual affection increased, and at first they derived only pleasure from the fact. " My dear brother," said Belle-Etoile, " if my wishes could make you happy, you should be one of the greatest kings on the earth." " Alas ! my sister," he replied, " do not grudge me the happiness I find in being near you. I would rather spend an hour with you than possess the high honour you wish for me. When she made a like speech to her brothers, they very naturally replied that they would like nothing better, and to prove them further she added : " I should like you to sit on the greatest throne in the world, even if I were never to see you ". They immediately said : " You are right, my sister ; the one is worth much more than the other ". " You would then be willing," she said, " never to see me again ? " " Certainly," they replied, " we should be quite content to hear from you occasionally."

When she was alone she examined these different ways of loving, and felt her own heart was just like theirs, for although she was fond of Petit-Soleil and Heureux, she did not desire to remain with them all her life, but she burst into tears whenever she thought their father might possibly send Chéri to sea, or put him into the army. Thus love, under the guise of a beautiful disposition, grew up in these young hearts. But at the age of fourteen, Belle-Etoile began to reproach herself for the injustice she thought she was doing her brothers in not loving them equally. She imagined Chéri's attentions and caresses were the cause, and forbade him to seek further means of making himself beloved. "You have found only too many," she said, pleasantly, "and you have succeeded in causing me to make a great difference between you and them." When she spoke thus his joy was intense; far from lessening his love, she increased it, and every day he showed her some fresh gallantry.

They had no idea what their affection tended to, nor did they know its meaning, when one day Belle-Etoile received some new books. She took the first that came to her hand; it contained the story of two young lovers, whose passion began when they thought themselves brother and sister, but afterwards their relatives recognised them and discovered to them that such was not the case, and after many troubles they were married. As Chéri read extremely well, intelligently, and with expression, she asked him to read the tale to her while she finished a piece of needlework she was anxious to complete.

He read the story, and it was not without some emotion that he recognised in it a perfect description of his own feelings. Belle-Etoile was equally surprised; it seemed as if the author had divined all that was passing in her mind. The longer Chéri read, the more he was touched; the longer the princess listened, the more distressed she became; in spite of her efforts her eyes filled, and the tears coursed down her cheeks. Chéri, on his part, made the same effort, but equally in vain; he grew pale, changed colour, and the sound of his voice became strange; they both suffered as much as it is possible to endure. "Ah! my sister," he exclaimed, looking at her sadly, "how happy was Hippolyte in not being Julie's brother!" "We shall not have a similar cause for gladness," she replied, "but alas! we need it as much." So saying, she knew she had said too much, and looked confused; if anything could comfort the prince, it was her state of mind. From that time they both fell into a deep melancholy, without any further explanation. They understood a part of what was passing in their minds, and endeavoured to hide from everybody a secret they would have preferred to ignore themselves, and which they never discussed with each other. However it is only natural to hope, and the princess considered it a favourable sign that Chéri alone had no star on his forehead nor chain round his neck, though he possessed long hair and the gift of scattering precious stones when it was combed like his cousins.

One day the three princes had gone hunting. Belle-Etoile shut herself up in a little room that she liked because it was dark, and she could indulge her dreams there with less interruption than elsewhere ; she made no noise at all. This room was only divided from that of Corsine by a partition wall. Corsine thought the girl was out walking, and Belle-Etoile heard her say to the pirate : " Belle-Etoile is now old enough to be married : if we knew who she was, we should try to find her a husband suited to her rank, or if we could think those who pass for her brothers, were not so, we could give her one of them, for where can she hope to find any one more perfect ? "

" When I found them," said the pirate, " there was nothing to give me any clue to their rank. The precious stones placed in their cradle pointed to the fact that they must belong to wealthy people, but the strange thing was that they all seemed to be of exactly the same age, and it is not usual to have four children at one birth." " I doubt," said Corsine, " if Chéri is their brother ; he has neither star nor necklace." " That is true," replied her husband, " but the diamonds fall from his hair as from that of the others, and considering all the wealth we have amassed by means of these dear children, I have nothing further to wish for than to discover their origin." " We must leave everything to the gods," said Corsine, " who gave them to us, and will, doubtless, at the right time reveal to us the secret."

Belle-Etoile listened attentively to this conversation. Her joy at the hope she might be of illustrious birth cannot be expressed ; for although she had never been wanting in respect to those she believed to be her parents, she had all the same been sorry to know herself the daughter of a pirate. But what delighted her even more was the hope that Chéri was not her brother. She burned with impatience to talk to him, and tell him so strange a circumstance.

She mounted a light bay horse, whose black mane was tied up with diamond buckles, for she had only to comb her hair once to provide the whole hunt with jewels. Her green velvet saddle-cloth was studded with diamonds and embroidered with rubies. She rode swiftly towards the forest in search of her brothers. The sound of horns and the baying of hounds signified to her where they were, and in a moment she had joined them. At sight of her, Chéri left the others and went to meet her. " What a delightful surprise," he exclaimed. " Belle-Etoile ! at length you come to the hunt, you who can never for a moment be persuaded to leave the joys of music and the sciences."

" I have so many things to say to you," she replied, " that wishing to be alone with you, I came in search of you." " Alas ! my sister," he said, sighing,

" what do you want of me ?   It seems to me that for some while past you have been avoiding me." She blushed, cast down her eyes, and remained on her horse, sad and pondering, without replying a word. When her brothers came up she started as from deep slumber, and jumped to the ground, walking on in front. They all followed her, and in the midst of a grass-plot, shaded by trees, she said : " Let us stay here, and I will tell you what I have just heard ".

She related to them the conversation between the pirate and his wife, and how they were not their children. The surprise of the three princes was enormous, and they discussed what they ought to do. One wished to depart without saying anything about it ; another preferred remaining where he was, and the last wanted to go, but at the same time to tell the pirate of their intention. The first argued that his way was best, because the profit gained by combing their hair would certainly make the pirate desirous of keeping them with him ; the second replied that it would be all very well to go away if they had any fixed place to go to and knew something of their rank in life, otherwise it was not exactly pleasant to wander about the world. The last added that it would be most ungrateful to go away without telling their benefactors, and that it would be stupid to remain longer in the depths of a forest where they had no means of learning who they were, and that, therefore, the best method was to speak to the pirate and his wife and ask their consent to their setting out. All agreed to this, and they mounted their horses in order to go and find the pirate and Corsine.

Chéri's heart was full of all the most delightful hopes that can console an afflicted lover. His love helped him partly to divine the future ; he no longer thought himself Belle-Etoile's brother, and giving a little rein to his passion indulged himself in many beautiful dreams. They joined the pirate and Corsine with a mingled expression of joy and anxiety on their countenances. " We do not come," said Petit-Soleil, who was spokesman, " to deny the affection, gratitude, and respect we owe you ; although we have learnt that you are not our father and mother, the pity that induced you to rescue us, the noble education you have given us, all the care and kindness with which you have surrounded us, have formed such close ties that nothing in the world could free us from them. We come, therefore, to renew our sincerest thanks, to beg you to tell us the strange story, and give us your advice, so that guided by you we may have no cause to reproach ourselves."

The pirate and Corsine were much surprised that a thing they had so carefully concealed should have been discovered. " You have been only too well informed," they said, "and we cannot hide the fact that you are not our children, and came into our possession by the merest chance. We know nothing of your rank, but the precious stones that were in your cradle prove that your parents are either great nobles or very rich. Now how can we advise you? If you consult our affections for you, you would then remain with us and console our old age with your pleasant society. If you do not like the castle we have built here, or if living in this solitude wearies you, we would go wherever you pleased, provided it was not to the court. A long experience has made it hateful to us, and would make it equally hateful to you if you knew the continual agitation, hypocrisy, envy, the disparity of rank, the real evil and the pretended good to be found there. We would say more but you would think our advice interested; and so it is, my children, for we want to keep you in this peaceful retreat, although you are at liberty to quit it when you like. Do not, however, fail to remember that here you are in the harbour, and that you go to the stormy sea, and that there trouble is nearly always in excess of joy; that the period of our lives is but short, and we often have to leave the world in the midst of our career; that the great things of the earth are counterfeit stones by which through a strange fatality we allow ourselves to be dazzled, and that the most enduring of all goods is to be able to limit our desires, to enjoy tranquillity, and become wise. ·

The pirate would have spoken longer had not Prince Heureux interrupted him. "'My dear father," he said, " we are too anxious to clear up the mystery of our birth to bury ourselves in a desert. Your teaching is excellent and I wish we were capable of following it, but some indescribable fatality calls us elsewhere. Permit us to fulfil our destiny; we shall return and tell you our adventures." The pirate and his wife began to weep. The princes felt very sorry, especially Belle-Etoile, who had a charming disposition and would never have thought of leaving the desert if she had been sure that Chéri would always stay with her.

The decision made, they thought only of preparing for their embarkation, for as they had been found on the sea they hoped to receive there some revelation of what they desired to know. They took on board their ship a horse for each, and after combing their hair violently in order to leave Corsine as many precious stones as possible, they asked her to give them in exchange the diamond chains found in their cradle. She fetched them from her closet, where she had carefully put them, and fastened them to Belle-Etoile's gown. She could not leave off embracing her, moistening her face with her tears.

Never was there a sadder parting; the pirate and his wife thought they could not survive it. Their sorrow did not arise from interested motives, for they had amassed such a quantity of treasure that they did not want any more. Petit-Soleil, Heureux, Chéri, and Belle-Etoile got into the ship. The pirate had had built for them a very stout and magnificent vessel; the mast was of ebony and cedar, the rigging of green silk mixed with gold, the sails of green and gold cloth, and the decorations beautiful. When it began to move, Cleopatra with her Antony and even the whole of Venus's crew would have lowered their flag before it. The princess was seated under a rich canopy on the poop, her two brothers and her cousin near her, and brighter than the constellations of heaven, their stars gave forth long dazzling rays of light. They determined to go to the place where the pirate had found them. They prepared for a great sacrifice to the gods and fairies to obtain their protection and their guidance to the place of their birth. They caught a dove to sacrifice, but the princess finding it beautiful, took pity on it and saved its life, and to protect it from such a fate let it fly away. "Go," she said, "bird of Venus, and if some day I have need of you, do not forget the benefit you owe me."

The dove flew away. When the sacrifice was ended, they began so charming a concert, that it seemed as if all nature kept silence to listen ; the waves of the sea were at rest, not a wind blew, zephyr alone gently stirred the princess's hair and veil. Then there came forth from the water a mermaid, who sang so well that the princess and her brothers were enchanted. After singing a few songs, she turned towards them and exclaimed : "*Cease to disturb your-selves ; let your ship go as it listeth ; disembark where it stops, and let all who love continue to love*".

Belle-Etoile and Chéri were charmed with the mermaid's words. They had no doubt they were meant for them, and expressing this belief in their glances, their hearts conversed, and neither Petit-Soleil nor Heureux perceived any-thing of it. The ship sailed on at the will of the winds and waves ; the voyage was uneventful, the weather was always fine, and the sea always calm. They were three months at sea, and during the time Prince Chéri often talked with the princess. "What delightful hopes I have, charming star," he said to her one day. "I am not your brother ; this heart that owns your power and will never recognise that of another is not born for crime, and it would be one to love you as I do, if you were my sister. But the kindly mermaid, who gave us counsel, confirmed what I already thought." "Ah ! my brother," she replied, "do not put too much trust in a thing still so obscure that we cannot see it clearly. What would our fate be if we vexed the gods by feelings they disap-proved ? The mermaid's words were so vague, that if we apply them to our-selves, it only proves that we wish to give them that meaning." "Cruel girl !" said the distressed prince ; "you say that less out of fear of the gods than out of hatred for me." Belle-Etoile did not reply, but raising her eyes to the heavens, she heaved so deep a sigh that he could not help regarding it as a favourable sign.

It was the season of the year when the days are long and hot. Towards evening the princess and her brothers came on deck to watch the sun sink into the sea. She sat down, the princes placed themselves near her; they took their instruments, and began a delightful concert. But the ship, driven by a fresh breeze, seemed to sail more swiftly, and quickly doubled a small cape that hid a part of the most beautiful town imaginable; and when it stood fully revealed, the sight surprised our young people. All the palaces were of marble, with gilded roofs, and the rest of the houses were of very fine porcelain. Some evergreen trees mingled their enamelled leaves with the various colours of the marble, gold, and porcelain. They hoped their ship would enter the harbour, but feared it would scarcely find room there, for the number of masts made it look like a floating forest.

Their wish was granted; the ship ran into the harbour, and the quay was immediately crowded with people, who had noticed the magnificent ship. The vessel built by the Argonauts for the quest of the Golden Fleece was not so splendid. The stars, and the beauty of the wondrous children, enchanted all beholders, and the king was informed of the new arrivals. As he could not believe it, and the principal terrace of the palace bordered the sea-shore, he quickly came out upon it, and saw the Princes Petit-Soleil and Chéri lifting the princess in their arms, and carrying her to land; then the horses were disembarked, and their rich trappings corresponded with all the rest. Petit-Soleil mounted one blacker than jet, Heureux's was grey, Chéri's snow-white, and the princess's light-bay. The king admired them all four on their horses, which stepped so majestically that they kept off all who tried to approach them.

The princes, hearing people say " There is the king," raised their eyes, and seeing his dignified bearing, they made a low bow, and passed slowly on, still looking at him. He on his part looked at them, and was not less charmed with the princess's matchless beauty than with the good looks of the young princes. He ordered his equerry to offer them his protection, and everything they might have need of in a land where they were apparently strangers. They received the honour the king did them with much respect and gratitude, and said they only wanted a house in which they could be in seclusion, and would prefer it one or two leagues from the town, because they were very fond of walking. The equerry-in-chief at once ordered them to be given a very beautiful dwelling where they and their attendants could comfortably lodge.

The king's mind was so full of the four children he had just seen, that he went immediately to the queen-mother's apartments to tell her the miracle of the stars shining on their foreheads, and everything he had found to admire in them. She was quite overcome, and asked him, without affectation, how old they were. He replied fifteen or sixteen. She did not show her anxiety, but greatly feared that Feintise had deceived her. The king walked quickly up and down, and said : " How happy must a father be with such handsome sons and so beautiful a daughter ! As for me, wretched monarch, I am the father of three dogs—illustrious successors, indeed ; my crown is well established ! "

The queen-mother listened to these words with a mortal agony. The shining stars, the age of the strangers, were so like those of the princes and their sister, that she had great suspicions Feintise had deceived her, and had saved the king's children instead of killing them. But she had great control over herself, and betrayed nothing of what was passing in her mind ; she would not even send that day to procure information about many things she wanted to know. But the next day she sent her secretary, who, under pretext of giving orders in the house for their greater comfort, was to examine into everything, and report if they had stars on the forehead.

The secretary set out quite early, and arrived just when the princess was beginning her toilet. At that time people did not purchase their complexion of a perfumer—a fair skin remained fair and a dark one did not become fair ; so he saw her before her hair was dressed. It was being combed ; her fair locks, finer than gold thread, fell to the ground in curls. Several baskets were placed round so that the precious stones that fell from her hair might not be lost ; the star on her forehead shone with a dazzling light, and the gold chain round her neck was not less extraordinary than the precious stones which rolled down from the crown of her head. The secretary could scarcely believe his eyes, but the princess chose the biggest pearl, and begged him to keep it in remembrance of her ; it is the same stone that the kings of Spain esteem so highly under the name of Peregrine, which means pilgrim, because it came from a traveller.

The secretary, embarrassed by such generosity, took leave of her, and visited the three princes, with whom he remained a long time in order to obtain the required information. What he told the queen on his return confirmed her suspicions. He told her that Chéri had no star, but that precious jewels fell from his hair as from that of his brothers, and that, in his opinion, he was the handsomest ; that they came from a long distance ; their parents had only allowed them a certain time for visiting foreign lands. This puzzled the queen a little, and she sometimes thought they could not be the king's children after all.

She was hovering thus between hope and fear, when the king, who was very fond of hunting, went to the neighbourhood of their house. The equerry-in-chief, who accompanied him, told him it was the place where, following his commands, he had lodged Belle-Etoile and her brothers. " The queen counselled me," replied the king, " not to visit them ; she thinks they may come from some land infested with the plague, and may bring with them the germs of disease." " The young stranger lady," said the equerry, " is, indeed, very dangerous ; but, sir, I should fear her eyes more than infection of disease." " In truth," said the king, " I agree with you " ; and urging his horse forward heard the sound of musical instruments and voices. He stopped near a large saloon, of which the windows stood open ; and after admiring the sweet symphony he advanced.

The noise of the horses made the princes look out : when they recognised the king, they saluted him respectfully ; they hastened to meet him with a pleased expression of countenance and many marks of submission ; they knelt down and kissed his hands as if they knew he was their father. He embraced them, and felt greatly moved, and could not imagine the reason. He told them they must not fail to come to the palace, for he wanted to talk with them and introduce them to his mother. They thanked him for the honour he showed them, and promised that, as soon as their clothes and equipages were ready, they would certainly come to court.

The king left them to finish the hunt, and kindly sent them half the booty, taking the rest to the queen. " What ! " she said, " is it possible that you have had such poor sport ? You generally kill three times as much game." " Yes," replied the king, " but I gave some to the handsome strangers. I feel drawn towards them in a most surprising manner, and if you had less fear of infection I should lodge them in the palace." The queen-mother was very angry, accused him of failing in respect towards her, and reproached him for so carelessly exposing her to danger.

Directly he left her, she sent for Feintise ; she shut herself up with her in her closet, seized her hair with one hand, and with the other held a dagger at her throat. " Wretch," she said, " I do not know what prevents me from sacrificing you to my just resentment. You have deceived me. You did not kill the four children I delivered over to you to get rid of ; confess your crime, and then, may be, I shall pardon you." Feintise, half dead with fear, threw herself at her feet and told her all ; but she deemed it impossible the children could be alive, because such a frightful storm had arisen that she thought the hail would knock her down. But she asked for time, and promised to get rid of them, one after the other, so that nobody would suspect anything wrong.

The queen, who only desired their death, was somewhat appeased. She told her not to lose a moment, and old Feintise, well knowing her danger, neglected nothing to attain her end. She spied the time when the three princes were hunting, and, taking a guitar, sat beneath the princess's windows and sang these words :—

" Beauty conquers all with her great power,
Happy ye who profit by her hour !
Beauty fades away,
Winter's frost
Will blight the blossoms gay.
Thus dim grows beauty's ray,
Charms are lost,
We count them with dismay.
Upon us then doth seize
Dull despair.
Unhappy, ill at ease,
We seek the aid of these,
Art and care,
With futile hope to please.
Blithe young hearts ! seek every charm to prove
Youth's the age when ev'ry one should love.
Beauty fades away,
Winter's frost
Will blight the blossoms gay.
Thus dim grows beauty's ray,
Charms are lost,
We count them with dismay.
Upon us then doth seize
Dull despair.
Unhappy, ill at ease,
We seek the aid of these,
Art and care,
With futile hope to please."

Belle-Etoile found the song pleasing, and came out on to the balcony to
see who was singing. When she appeared, Feintise, who was well dressed,
made her a low curtesy; the princess returned her greeting and good-humouredly
asked if the words she had just heard applied to the singer of them. " Yes,
charming girl," replied Feintise, " they are for me; but in order that they may
never be applicable to you, I come to give you some advise you must not fail to
take." " And what is it ? " said Belle-Etoile. " If you will allow me to join
you in your room I will tell you," she added. " You can come in," rejoined the
princess, and the old lady entered with a certain courtly air that once acquired
is seldom lost.

" My beautiful girl," said Feintise, without losing a moment, for she feared
some interruption, " heaven has made you entirely charming: you have a shining
star on your forehead and many other marvels are told of you, but you lack one
essentially necessary thing; if you do not possess it I pity you." " And what

may that be?" she replied. "The dancing water," continued our malicious old dame; "if I had had it, you would not see a white hair on my head nor a wrinkle on my face, and I should have the most beautiful teeth imaginable and a charming, youthful appearance. But alas! I learnt the secret too late, my charms were already faded. Take warning by my misfortunes, dear child; it will help to console me, for I feel a most extraordinary affection for you." "But where can I get this dancing water?" asked Belle-Etoile. "From the luminous forest," said Feintise. "You have three brothers, surely one of them loves you enough to fetch it for you. Indeed it would be scarcely kind not to do so, and nothing less will assure your being beautiful a hundred years after your death." "My brothers are very fond of me," said the princess, "and one of them will refuse me nothing. Certainly if this water can do all you say, I will reward you in proportion." The perfidious old dame speedily withdrew, charmed at her good success. She told Belle-Etoile she would visit her frequently.

The princes returned from the chase, one bringing a wild boar, another a hare, and the last a stag. It was all laid at their sister's feet; she received the homage a little contemptuously, for her mind was full of Feintise's advice. She seemed troubled, and Chéri, who was always studying her, was not a quarter of an hour in her company before he noticed it. "What is the matter, my dearest star?" he said. "Do you not like the country we are in? If that is the case let us go away at once. Perhaps our train is not large enough, the furniture beautiful enough, or our food delicate enough. Tell me, I beg, so that I may have the pleasure of being the first to obey you, and of compelling the others to obey you."

"The confidence you inspire in me to tell you what is passing in my mind," she replied, "urges me to confess that unless I have the dancing water I can no longer live; it is to be obtained from the luminous forest, and possessing it, I need fear nothing from the ravages of time." "Do not trouble, my sweet star," he replied, "I will go and fetch it for you, or my death will show you that it is impossible to obtain." "No," she said, "I would rather renounce all the advantages of beauty, and sooner than risk so dear a life I will be hideous; I implore you to think no more of the dancing water, and indeed if I have any influence over you I forbid it."

The prince feigned obedience, but directly she was occupied he mounted his white horse which curvetted and pranced along, taking money and a rich costume with him. There was no need to burden himself with diamonds, for three turns of the comb caused sometimes a million to fall. The number was not always the same; the condition of their mind and health regulated the supply of the precious stones. He took no one with him in order to be more at liberty,.

and that if the quest proved dangerous he might run risks without having to overcome the remonstrances of a zealous and timid attendant.

When supper-time arrived and no Chéri, the princess's anxiety was so great that she could neither eat nor drink. She gave orders that they should search everywhere. The two princes, knowing nothing about the dancing water, told her she worried unnecessarily, that he could not be far off, that she knew how he liked to dream, and that he had doubtless stopped in the forest. She remained quiet till midnight, then lost patience and in tears told her brothers that she was the cause of Chéri's absence, that she had confessed to him a violent desire for the dancing water from the luminous forest, and that doubtless that was where he had gone. They determined to send people in search of him, and she bade them tell him she implored him to return.

Wicked Feintise was dying to know the result of her advice; when she learnt that Chéri had already started, she was much delighted, never doubting that his progress would be quicker than those who had been sent in search of him, and that some accident would happen to him. She hastened to the palace, joyful at the hope, and told the queen all that had taken place. "I confess, madam," she said, "that there is no possible doubt that they are the three princes and their sister; they have stars on the brow, gold chains round the neck, their hair is most lovely, and jewels fall from it at every moment; the princess is wearing the jewels I put in the cradle, though they are not so beautiful as those that fall from her hair. Thus I cannot doubt their return, in spite of the care I thought I took to prevent it. But, madam, I will rid you of them, and as it is the only way in which I can repair my fault, I entreat you to give me time. One of the princes has already gone in search of the dancing water, and he must perish in the attempt, and so I shall prepare many ways for their destruction." "We shall see," said the queen, "if success attends your efforts; count on that alone to turn aside my just anger." Feintise withdrew more alarmed than ever, searching in her mind for every possible means by which she might compass their destruction.

The means employed for that of Prince Chéri was very sure, for the dancing water is not easily obtained, and the misfortunes of those who had attempted to find it were so well known that everybody was acquainted with the road to it. His white horse galloped at a surprising rate; he spurred it on continually, because he wanted to return quickly to Belle-Etoile, and give her all the satisfaction she hoped from his journey. He went on for eight nights following, resting only in the woods under the first tree, and eating nothing but the fruit he found on his road, scarcely giving his horse time to browse the grass. At the end of that period he found himself in a country where the air was so hot that he began to suffer greatly. The heat was not caused by the sun, and he could not understand the reason, when from the top of a mountain he saw the luminous forest. All the trees were burning, but were not consumed, and threw their flames such a distance that the country was arid and barren. He heard serpents hissing and lions roaring in the forest, a fact that vastly astonished him, since it seemed that no animal, the salamander excepted, could live in such a furnace.

After looking at this terrible place he descended the height, pondering how he should act, and more than once saying to himself that he was lost. As he approached the terrible fire, he was seized with a great thirst; he found a spring bubbling up out of the hill, and falling into a big marble basin. He dismounted, and stooped to fill with the water a little gold cup he had brought with him to hold that the princess desired, when he saw a dove drowning in the spring; her wings were wet through; she had no more strength, and had slipped down to the bottom of the basin. Chéri took pity on her and rescued her; he held her up by the feet, for she had drunk so much that she was inflated. Then he warmed her, dried her wings with his handkerchief, and aided her so successfully that in a very short time the poor dove was more cheerful than she had been sad before.

" Prince Chéri," she said, in a sweet and tender voice, " you could not have done a kindness to a more grateful animal than myself; it is not the first time I have received important favours from your family, and I am delighted to be of use to you in my turn. Do not imagine I am ignorant of the purpose of your journey; you undertook it somewhat rashly, for the number of those who have perished here cannot be counted. The dancing water is for women the eighth wonder of the world; it beautifies, regenerates and enriches, but if I do not guide you, you could never obtain it, for the spring boils up out of the earth in the centre of the forest, and falls into a gulf. The road is covered with fallen, burning branches, and I see no other means of getting there except underground; remain quietly here while I make the necessary preparations."

The dove then rose up in the air, flew now high, now low; now here, now there; and exerted herself to such a degree, that by the end of the day she told the prince everything was ready. He held the helpful bird in his arms, kissed it, caressed and thanked it, and followed it on his beautiful white horse. Scarcely had he gone a hundred yards, when he saw two long lines of foxes, snails, moles, ants, and all sorts of animals that burrow in the earth; there was such a vast number of them that he could not imagine by what power they had been gathered together. "It is by my order," said the dove, " that you see all these subterranean folk; they are going to work on your behalf, and very speedily. I should be very glad if you would thank them. "The prince saluted them, and promised to take them to a less barren spot, and gladly entertain them there ; and each animal seemed satisfied.

Chéri having reached the entrance of the passage, left his horse outside; and, half stooping, he went on with the good dove, who led him without accident to the spring. It made so great a noise that he would have become deaf if she had not given him two of her white feathers to stop up his ears. He was vastly surprised to see that the water danced as well as if it had been taught by Favier and Pecourt.* It is true, it danced only old-fashioned dances like the Bocane, the Mariée, and the Saraband.† Several birds, flying in the air, sang tunes, to which the water danced. The prince filled his gold cup, drank himself a couple of draughts, that made him a hundred times handsomer than he was before, and so greatly refreshed him, that he scarcely perceived that of all places in the world the luminous forest was the hottest.

He returned by the same road he had come ; his horse had gone away, but, obedient to his voice, it came at full gallop as soon as he called it. The prince sprang lightly into the saddle, proud of having obtained the dancing water. " Dear dove," he said, " I know not by what miracle your power in this place is so great; the benefits I have gained from it call forth all my gratitude ; and, as freedom is the greatest of goods, I restore yours to you in return for the favours you have shown me." So saying, he let her go. She flew away with rather a sullen air, as if she would have stayed with him against his will. " What inequality ! " he said. " You are more like a man than a dove—one is fickle, the other is not." The dove replied to him from the air : " Eh ! do you know who I am ? " Chéri was astonished that the dove should thus reply to his thought ; he judged her to be very clever, and felt sorry he had let her go. " She might have been useful to me," he said " and I might have learned from her many things that would contribute to the peace of my life." But he came to the conclusion that a good deed is never to be regretted ; and he felt repaid when he thought how she had smoothed the difficulties of procuring the dancing water. The gold cup was closed up, so that the water could neither escape nor evaporate. He was thinking with pleasure of Belle-Etoile's delight at receiving it, and his own joy in seeing her again, when he observed several cavaliers riding at full speed, who no sooner perceived him than, with loud shouts, they pointed him out to one another. He had no fear, he was intrepid

* Favier and Pecourt were famous French dancers in the time of Madame D'Aulnoy.

† Bocane : an old, slow dance ; Mariée : a quick, lively dance; Saraband : a slow Spanish dance in triple time.

enough to be little alarmed at dangers, but he was much annoyed that anything should delay him. He rode quickly up to them and was greatly surprised to recognise some of his servants, who delivered to him little notes, or, more properly, the commands entrusted to them by the princess that he should not expose himself to the perils of the luminous forest. He kissèd Belle-Etoile's handwriting, heaved more than one sigh, and hastened to return to her and put an end to her anxiety.

He found her seated under some trees and in the greatest distress of mind. When she saw him at her feet she knew not how to welcome him. She wanted to scold him for setting out against her orders and to thank him for the charming present he brought her. In the end affection won the day; she kissed her beloved brother and her reproaches were not of a very serious character.

Old Feintise, who was ever watchful, learnt from spies that Chéri had returned handsomer than before his departure, and that the princess, after bathing her face with the dancing water, had become so excessively beautiful, that it was impossible to receive the least of her glances without dying more than half-a-dozen deaths.

Feintise was both astonished and annoyed, for she had reckoned on the prince perishing in the undertaking. But it would not do to be disheartened, and she waited for the hour at which the princess with but few attendants went to a little temple of Diana. She approached her and said in a friendly way: " I am delighted, madam, at the happy result of my advice. One glance at you is enough to know that you possess the dancing water, but if I dared counsel you further, you should endeavour to obtain the singing apple. It is quite a different thing; it adorns the mind to such a degree that there is nothing you would not be able to accomplish. If you wish to convince some one of something, you have only to smell the singing apple : if you wish to speak in public, to write verses or prose to amuse, to cause tears or laughter, the apple can do it all, and it sings so well and so loud that although it can be heard eight leagues off, you are not stunned by the sound."

" I don't want it!" exclaimed the princess; " you nearly caused my brother's death with your dancing water; your advice contains too much danger." " What, madam," replied Feintise, " you would be sorry to be the most learned and witty person in the universe? you can't really think so." " Ah, but what should I have done ? " said Belle-Etoile, " if my dear brother had been brought back dead or dying ? " " He," said the old woman, " will not go again ; the others must take their turn in serving you, and the enterprise is not so dangerous." " Never mind," added the princess, " I am not inclined to expose them." " Truly, how I pity you," said Feintise, " to lose such a splendid opportunity ; but you must reflect on it. Farewell, madam." She went away annoyed at her ill success, and Belle-Etoile remained at the foot of the statue of Diana, irresolute how to proceed. She loved her brothers, but she also loved herself, and felt that nothing would please her better than to possess the singing apple.

She sighed for some time and then began to weep. Petit-Soleil returning from the hunt heard a noise in the temple, entered, and saw the princess, who covered her face with her veil in shame of her wet eyes. He had already noticed her tears, and approaching her implored her to tell him instantly the reason of her sorrow. She refused, replying that she was ashamed of herself ; but the more she concealed her secret the greater became his desire to know it.

At length she told him that the same old woman who had advised her to send for the dancing water had just told her that the singing apple was much more wonderful, because it gave you so much wit as to make you a sort of pro- digy. In truth, she would give the half of her life for such an apple, but she feared the danger of seeking it was too great. " You need have no fear on my account," said her brother, smiling. " I have no desire to render you such a service ; have you not intelligence enough ? Come, come, sister," he continued, " dry your eyes."

Belle-Etoile followed him as annoyed at the way in which he received her confidence as at the impossibility of obtaining the singing apple. Supper was served, and they all four sat down to table ; she could not eat, and Chéri, charming Chéri, who thought only of her, served her the nicest things and pressed her to taste them. At the first mouthful her heart swelled, tears came into her eyes, and, weeping, she left the table. Belle-Etoile in tears ! O ye gods ! what was Chéri's anxiety ! He asked what was the matter and Petit Soleil told him, scoffing so unkindly at his sister that she was offended, withdrew into her own room, and would not speak to any one all the evening.

As soon as Petit-Soleil and Heureux had gone to bed, Chéri mounted his ex- cellent white horse without telling any one where he was going. He left a note for Belle-Etoile with the order that it was to be given her when she awoke. And all that night he rode on, not knowing where he could obtain the singing apple.

The prince's letter was given to the princess on her rising, and her feelings of anxiety and affection on such an occasion may easily be imagined. She hastened to her brothers' room to read it them ; they shared her fears, for they were all most united. They immediately sent nearly all their people after him to force him to return, and abandon so terrible an adventure.

Meanwhile the king did not forget the beautiful children in the forest; he often turned his steps that way, and when he passed near their house and saw them he reproached them for never coming to the palace. They excused themselves at first because they were having a suitable equipage prepared, and now on account of their brother's absence, and promised that on his return they would take advantage of the king's permission, and come and pay their duty to him.

Prince Chéri's passion was too ardent for him not to make all possible speed. At dawn he came upon a handsome young man lying under the trees reading a book; Chéri approached him and said politely: " Allow me to interrupt you to ask you if you know where the singing apple is to be found ? " The young man raised his eyes and smiling pleasantly said: " Do you wish to obtain it ? " " Yes, if it is possible," replied the prince. " Ah, sir ! " added the stranger, " you have no idea of the dangers attending such a quest; this book relates them, and the mere reading terrifies me." " Never mind," said Chéri, " no danger can prevent me making the attempt; only tell me where I can find it." " The book observes," continued the man, " that it is in a vast desert in Libya, that its singing can be heard eight leagues off, and that the dragon who guards it has already devoured five hundred thousand persons who were rash enough to go there." " I shall make five hundred thousand and one," replied the prince, smiling, and with a bow he took his way towards the Libyan desert; his fine horse was of zephyr breed, for Zephyr was his grandfather, and went like the wind, so that his speed was incredible.

He listened in vain, but could nowhere hear the apple singing. He was distressed by the length of the road and the uselessness of his journey, when he saw a poor dove fall at his feet; it was still alive, but surely dying. As he saw no one who could have wounded it, he thought it very probably belonged to Venus, and having escaped from her] dove-cote, naughty Cupid, to try his arrows, had shot it. He took pity on it, dismounted, and lifting it, wiped its white wings, already stained with red blood. Taking from his pocket a gold phial that contained an admirable balm for wounds, he had scarcely put some on the sick dove before it opened its eyes, raised its head, spread its wings, and preened its feathers. Then looking at the prince: " Good-day, Chéri," it said ; " you are destined to save my life, and I to render you great service. You come to gain possession of the singing apple; the enterprise is difficult and worthy of you, because it is guarded by a terrible dragon, with twelve feet, three heads, six wings, and a bronze body." " Ah, my dear dove," said the prince, " how glad I am to see you again, and at a time when I so greatly need your help. Do not refuse it me, my beautiful little bird, for if I had the shame of returning home without the singing apple, I should die of grief; and since you assisted me to get the dancing water I hope you will find a way to make me succeed in this undertaking." ."You touch me truly," replied the dove, tenderly. "Follow me; I am going to fly in front of you, and I hope all will go well."

The prince let her go; after travelling all day they arrived near a mountain of sand. "You must dig here," said the dove. Immediately the prince, letting nothing discourage him, began to dig, sometimes with his hands, sometimes with his sword. At the end of a few hours he found a helmet, cuirass, and the rest of the armour for himself and his horse, made entirely of mirrors. "Arm yourself," said the dove, "and do not fear the dragon; when he sees his reflection in these mirrors, he will be so terrified, thinking they are monsters like himself, that he will run away."

Chéri greatly approved the expedient, armed himself with the mirrors, and taking up the dove again, went on during the whole of the night. At dawn they heard an enchanting melody. The prince begged the dove to tell him what it was. "I feel sure," she said, "only the apple could be so beautiful, because it alone simulates all the various parts of music, and without touching an instrument, seems to play them all in the most perfect fashion." Every step brought them nearer; the prince thought to himself that he would like the apple to sing something suitable to his situation, and at the same moment heard these words:—

> "The most rebellious heart is gained
>   At last by Love:
> Then cease not thy wooing,
> But persevere! Thy cruel
>   Fair one shalt thou move
> By constantly pursuing!"

"Ah!" he exclaimed, replying to the verses, "what a delightful prophecy! I may hope one day to be happy; it has just been foretold me." The dove said nothing; she was no great talker, and only spoke when it was absolutely necessary. As he advanced the beauty of the music increased, and notwithstanding his eagerness he was sometimes so enchanted that he stopped still only to listen. But the sight of the terrible dragon who suddenly appeared with his twelve feet and more than a hundred claws, the three heads and the bronze body, woke him from that sort of lethargy. The monster had scented the prince from afar, and waited to devour him like the others of whom he had made such excellent meals. Their bones were piled round the apple tree on which was the marvellous apple, and they were so high that the trees could not be seen.

The terrible animal advanced leaping; he covered the ground with a very dangerous and poisonous foam. Out of his horrible mouth came fire and little dragons that he threw like darts into the eyes and ears of the knights-errant who wanted to carry off the apple. But when he saw his horrible shape multiplied hundreds and hundreds of times in the prince's mirrors it was his turn to be afraid; he stopped, looked haughtily at the prince loaded with dragons, and only thought of flight. Chéri, observing the happy effect of his armour, pursued him to the entrance of a deep cave, into which he hurried to get out of Chéri's way. He quickly closed up the entrance, and hastened to return to the singing apple.

Climbing over the bones that surrounded it, he looked admiringly at the beautiful tree; it was of amber, the apples of topaz, and the best of all, the one he sought amid all this trouble and danger was to be seen at the top, made of a single ruby with a diamond crown above. The prince, overcome with joy at being able to give Belle-Etoile so rare and perfect a treasure, hastened to break off the amber branch, and, proud of his good fortune, mounted his white horse but could not see the dove. Directly she saw she was no longer needed, she had flown away. Without wasting time in superfluous regrets, and fearing that the dragon whose hisses he could hear might find a way of getting at the apple, he returned with it to the princess.

She had been unable to sleep during his absence; she never ceased reproaching herself for her desire of being more intelligent than the rest, and feared Chéri's death more than her own. "Ah! unfortunate that I am!" she exclaimed, heaving deep sighs, "why was I so vain-glorious? Was it not enough to think and speak well enough to do and say nothing foolish? I shall be properly punished for my vanity if I lose him I love. Alas!" she continued, "perhaps the gods, angry at the feelings I cannot help having towards Chéri, will take him from me by some tragic end."

There was no evil her distressed heart did not imagine when, in the middle of the night, she heard such wonderful music that she could not help getting up and going to the window to hear it better; she knew not what to think of it. Sometimes she thought it was Apollo and the Muses, sometimes Venus, the Graces and Cupids; the melodious sound came ever nearer, and Belle-Etoile listened.

At length the prince arrived. The moon was shining brightly; he stopped under the balcony whence the princess had withdrawn on perceiving a horseman in the distance. The apple immediately sang:—

" Awake, beauteous slumberer ".

The princess, curious to see who sang so well, looked out, and recognising her beloved brother, thought of throwing herself out of the window in order to be sooner with him; she spoke so loud that everybody awoke, and the door was soon opened to admit Chéri. The eagerness with which he entered may be imagined. He held the amber branch with the miraculous fruit at its end in his hand, and as he had smelt it often his intelligence was so great that nothing in the world could be compared to him.

Belle-Etoile ran to meet him in the greatest haste. " Do you think I'm going to thank you, dearest brother?" she said, weeping for joy. " No, it is too dearly bought at the risk you ran to obtain it." " There is no danger," he said, " I would not undergo for the sake of giving you the least pleasure. Receive, Belle-Etoile," he continued, " this unique fruit; no one in the world deserves it so much as you, but what can it give you that you do not already possess?" Petit-Soleil and his brother interrupted the conversation; they were delighted to see the prince again. He told them all about his journey, and the narration lasted till daylight.

Wicked Feintise had returned to her little house after speaking with the queen of her projects; she was too anxious to sleep quietly. She heard the sweet singing of the apple that nothing in nature could equal. She suspected Chéri had actually obtained it! She wept, groaned, wounded her face, tore her hair; her grief was extreme, for instead of injuring the beautiful children as she intended, she actually benefited them through her perfidy.

As soon as it was light, she learnt that the prince's return was only too true. She went to the queen-mother. " Well, Feintise," said that princess, " do you bring me good news? Are the children dead?" " No, madam," she replied, throwing herself at her feet, " but let not your majesty grow impatient, there remains infinite ways of delivering you from them." " Ah! wretched woman!" said the queen, " you are only here to deceive me; you protect them." The old woman protested the contrary, and when she had somewhat appeased her returned to ponder over what she should do next.

For some days she did not appear, but at the end of them she spied about to such purpose that she found the princess walking alone in a glade of the forest awaiting the return of her brothers. " Heaven showers its gifts on you," said the old miscreant, approaching her; " charming star, I hear you have the singing apple, and if such a piece of luck had fallen to my share, I could not be more glad, for it must be confessed my liking for you makes me interested in your good fortune; but," she added, " I cannot refrain from giving you another piece of advice." " Oh! keep your advice to yourself," said the princess, moving away; " the good it brings me cannot make up for the anxiety it has caused me." "Anxiety is not so great an evil," she rejoined, smiling; "it is sometimes sweet and tender." "Be silent," said Belle-Etoile, "I tremble when I think of it." "You are certainly vastly to be pitied," said the old lady, "to be the loveliest and cleverest girl in the world; I beg to sympathise with you." "Yet another blow!" replied the princess; "I know the condition to which my brother's absence reduced me." "Notwithstanding, I must tell you," continued Feintise, "that you lack the little green bird that tells all things; he could tell you your rank, the good and evil chances of life; nothing is so hidden that he cannot reveal it, and when people say Belle-Etoile has the dancing water and the singing apple, they will say at the same time, but since she lacks the little green bird that tells all things she might as well have nothing."

After thus speaking out what was in her mind, she withdrew. The princess, sad and dreamy, began to sigh bitterly. "The woman is right," she said; "of what avail are the benefits I receive from the water and the apple since I do not know whence I come, who are my parents, and by what accident my brothers and I were exposed to the fury of the waves? There must have been something very extraordinary about our birth to cause us to be thus forsaken, and yet to gain the certain protection of the gods to save us from so many dangers; how I should like to know my father and mother, to love them if they are still alive, and to honour their memory if they are dead!" A flood of tears poured down her cheeks like morning dew-drops on the lilies and roses.

Chéri, who was always more anxious to see her than the others were, hastened to return after the hunt. He was on foot, his bow hung carelessly at his side, he carried a few arrows in his hand, his hair was tied together, and so equipped his martial appearance was very pleasing. As soon as the princess saw him, she entered a shady alley that he might not perceive the signs of grief on her countenance, but a mistress cannot move so quickly that an eager lover cannot reach her. The prince came up with her and had scarcely looked at her before he perceived she was in trouble. He was distressed and begged and implored her to tell him the reason; she obstinately refused. At last he pointed one of the arrows at his heart and said: "You do not love me, Belle-Etoile; there is nothing left but to die". This kind of talk greatly alarmed her; she had no longer the strength to keep her secret, but she only revealed it on condition that he would never in his life seek the means of gratifying her desire. He promised and said nothing to prove that he intended to make this third journey.

As soon as she had gone to her room and the princes to theirs, Chéri came downstairs, took his horse from the stable, mounted it and set off without saying a word to anybody. This news threw the family into great consternation. The king, who could not forget them, sent to invite them to dine with him; they replied that their brother had just gone away, that they had no pleasure nor peace without him, and that on his return they would not fail to come to the palace. The princess was inconsolable; the dancing water and the singing apple had no more charms for her, for, Chéri absent, nothing had power to delight her.

The prince wandered over the world, asking the people he met where the little green bird that tells all things was to be found. Most of them did not know, but he fell in with an old man who, bringing him into his house, took the trouble to look on a globe which formed part of his study and amusement. He then told him it was in an arctic region, on the summit of a terrible rock, and showed him the road he must take. To mark his gratitude the prince gave him a little bag of big pearls that had fallen from his hair, and taking leave of him continued his journey.

At dawn he saw the high and steep rock, and on the top the bird speaking like an oracle, saying the wisest things. He thought that with a little skill it would be easy to catch it, for it did not seem at all wild. It came and went, jumping lightly from point to point. The prince dismounted, and going up noiselessly in spite of the roughness of the ascent, he delighted in the thought of giving Belle-Etoile pleasure. He was so near the green bird that he believed he could touch it, when the rock suddenly opened, and he fell, motionless as a statue, into a spacious hall; he could neither move nor bewail the distressing accident. Three hundred knights who had made the same attempt as himself were in like case; they looked at each other, the only thing possible for them to do.

Chéri's prolonged absence caused the princess to fall dangerously ill. The physicians knew that a deep melancholy preyed on her mind. Her brothers loved her dearly and asked her the reason of her trouble. She confessed that night and day she reproached herself for Chéri's absence, and felt that if she did not soon hear something of him she should die. They were touched by her tears, and to cure her Petit-Soleil resolved to go and find his brother.

The prince set out, knowing where the famous bird was. He reached the place, saw the creature and approached it hopefully. At the same moment the rock engulfed him, he fell into the large hall, and the first thing he saw was Chéri, but he could not speak to him.

Belle-Etoile was recovering, and every moment hoped to see her two brothers return, but her hopes were unfulfilled, her distress became greater, and night and day she never ceased lamenting and accusing herself of the princes' ˙ˊ rtunes. Prince Heureux, whose pity for her was not less than his anxiety for his brothers, determined in his turn to go and find them. He told Belle-Etoile, who at first opposed the plan, but he replied that it was his duty to expose himself to danger in order to find those whom he loved best in the world. After tenderly bidding the princess farewell he set out, and she remained alone, a prey to the deepest sorrow.

When Feintise learnt that the third prince had departed she rejoiced exceedingly. She told the queen-mother, and promised her more certainly than ever to destroy the whole of the miserable family. Heureux underwent the same fate as Chéri and Petit-Soleil; he found the rock, saw the beautiful bird, fell like a statue into the hall, recognised the princes but could not speak to them. They were all arranged in crystal niches; they neither slept nor ate, and their enchantment was of the saddest sort, because the only privilege they had was the power to think about and deplore their adventures.

Belle-Etoile, inconsolable at the continued absence of her brothers, reproached herself for delaying so long to follow them. Without further hesitation she ordered her people to wait for her six months, but if in that time neither she nor her brothers returned they were to inform the pirate and his wife of their death. She dressed herself like a man, thinking she would run less risk thus disguised than if she travelled over the world as an adventuress. Feintise, overcome with joy, saw her ride away on her beautiful horse, and hastened to the palace to regale the queen-mother with the good news.

The princess was only armed with a helmet, whose visor she scarcely ever lifted, for her beauty was so delicate and perfect that no one would have believed, as she wished, that she was a knight. The severity of winter made itself felt, and the land in which the little bird who tells all things lived never enjoyed in any season the pleasant warmth of the sun.

Belle-Etoile was feeling terribly cold, but nothing could discourage her, when she saw a dove scarcely less white and cold than the snow on which she was lying. In spite of her impatience to reach the rock she could not let it die, and dismounting, she took it in her hands, warmed it with her breath, and put it in her bosom; the poor little creature did not stir. Belle-Etoile thought it was dead, and felt sorry. She drew it forth, and looking at it said, as if it had been able to understand: "What shall I do, sweet little dove, to save your life?" "Belle-Etoile," replied the creature, "one gentle kiss of your lips will finish what you have so charitably begun." "Not one," said the princess, "but a hundred if they are necessary." She kissed it, and the dove, taking courage, said merrily: "I know you in spite of your disguise; learn that you are undertaking a thing impossible without my help; do then as I advise you.

When you reach the rock, instead of looking for a way to ascend it, stop at the bottom and commence the most beautiful and melodious song you know. The green bird who tells all things will listen and will observe whence the voice comes; then you must feign sleep. I shall stay by you, and when he sees me he will come down from the top of the rock to peck me : at that moment you can take him."

The princess, charmed with the hope, soon reached the rock. She recognised her brothers' horses grazing, and the sight renewed her grief ; she sat down and wept bitterly. But the little green bird said such beautiful and comforting things that any distressed heart would have been made glad. She dried her tears and began to sing so loud and well that the princes in the depths of the enchanted hall had the pleasure of hearing her.

It was the first time they had felt any hope. The little green bird who tells all things listened, and looked whence the voice came ; he saw the princess, who had taken off her helmet to sleep more comfortably, and the dove hovering round her. He quietly flew down and pecked at her, but he had not torn out three feathers before he was caught.

" Ah ! what do you want with me ? " he said. " What have I done to you that you should come so far to make me miserable ? Give me my liberty, I entreat you ; I will do for you whatever you wish in exchange." " I desire," said Belle-Etoile, " that you will restore to me my three brothers ; I do not know where they are, but their horses that are feeding near this rock prove to me that you are keeping them in some place." " Under my left wing is a crimson feather, pull it out," he said, " and touch the rock with it." The princess, lost no time in doing as he said, and immediately saw lightning and heard a noise of wind and thunder that frightened her terribly. In spite of her fear she never released the green bird, dreading that he might escape. She touched the rock again with the crimson feather, and the third time it split from top to bottom. With an air of triumph she entered the hall in which the princes were and so many others. She hastened up to Chéri, who did not recognise her in her doublet and helmet ; and then the enchantment still worked, for he could neither move nor speak. The princess again questioned the green bird, who told her to rub the mouth and eyes of all she wished to disenchant with the crimson feather; she rendered that great service to several kings and monarchs, and especially to our three princes.

Moved by so great a benefaction, they all threw themselves at her feet, calling her the saviour of kings. She then saw that her brothers, deceived by her clothes, did not recognise her; she quickly took off her helmet, stretched out her arms to them, embraced them over, and over again, and very politely asked the other princes who they were. They each told her their tale, and offered to accompany her wherever she wished to go. She replied that although the laws of chivalry gave her some rights over the liberty she had just restored to them, she would not avail herself of them. Thereupon she withdrew with the princes to relate all that had happened since their separation.

The little green bird who tells all things interrupted them to entreat Belle-Etoile to grant him his liberty; she looked for the dove in order to ask her advice, but could not find her. She told the bird that he had cost her so much trouble and anxiety that she could not consent to enjoy her conquest for so short a space. They all four mounted their horses, and left the emperors and kings to go their ways on foot, for during the two or three hundred years they had been there their equipages had perished.

The queen-mother, relieved of the anxiety the return of the beautiful children had caused her, renewed her entreaties to the king to marry again, and succeeded so well that she induced him to choose a princess from among her relations. And as it was necessary to annul the marriage of poor Queen Blondine, who all this time had remained with her mother in the little country house with the three dogs she had named Grief, Distress, and Sorrow on account of all the trouble they had caused, the queen-mother sent to fetch her. She got into a coach, taking the dogs with her; she was dressed in black with a long veil that fell to her feet. So attired she looked more beautiful than the day-star, although through sleeplessness and loss of appetite she had become pale and thin. Everybody pitied her mother, and the king was so distressed that he dared not look at her. But when he thought of the risk he ran of having no heirs but puppies, he consented to everything.

The day for the wedding being fixed, the queen-mother, entreated by the admiral's wife, Roussette, who still hated her unfortunate sister, said that she wished Queen Blondine to come to the fête. Everything was done to render it fine and sumptuous, and as the king was glad of the opportunity to show the strangers his magnificence, he ordered his equerry-in-chief to invite them, and in case they had not returned to leave orders that they might be told of the invitation directly they came back.

The equerry-in-chief found they were still absent, and knowing the pleasure it would give the king to see them, left one of his attendants to wait for them and bring them without delay. Belle-Etoile and the three princes arrived on the very day of the great banquet. The gentleman who had been waiting for them told them the king's story: how he had formerly married a poor, but beautiful and virtuous girl, who had unfortunately given birth to three dogs, that he had sent her away, never wishing to see her more, yet he loved her so dearly that for fifteen years he had refused to entertain any proposal for a second marriage ; that the queen-mother and his subjects had urged him so continually that he had determined to marry a princess of the court, and that they must hasten to come to the wedding.

Belle-Etoile at once put on a pink velvet gown, trimmed with shining diamonds, she let her hair tied with ribbons fall in thick curls on her shoulders ; the star on her forehead threw out a bright light, and the chain round her neck that could not be taken off seemed of a metal more precious even than gold. Indeed never had anything so beautiful been seen by mortal eyes. Her brothers looked equally well, and especially Prince Chéri ; there was something most distinguished in his appearance. They all four got into an ebony and ivory chariot, lined with gold cloth ; the cushions were of the same material, embroidered with precious stones, and it was drawn by twelve white horses. The rest of their equipage was of unequalled magnificence. When Belle-Etoile and her brothers appeared the king and all his court, enchanted, received them at the top.of the staircase. The singing apple made itself heard in a marvellous fashion, the dancing water danced, and the little bird who tells all things spoke more wisely than the oracles. They all bowed low before the king, and taking his hand kissed it with as much affection as respect. He embraced them and said : " Gentle strangers, I thank you for coming hither to-day ; your presence gives me the greatest pleasure ". So saying, he led them into a spacious hall where musicians were playing all manner of instruments, and several tables splendidly served with good cheer left nothing to be desired.

The queen-mother entered, accompanied by her future daughter-in-law, the admiral's wife, Roussette, and all her ladies, leading the poor queen by a leash of leather fastened round her neck, and serving at the same time for the three dogs. They brought her to the middle of the room, where was placed a trough full of bones and broken meats, that the queen-mother had ordered for their dinner.

Although they did not know her, Belle-Etoile and the princes felt so sorry for her misfortunes that the tears came into their eyes ; they were moved either by the contemplation of the changes of fortune, or by reason of the blood that flowed in their veins. But what did the wicked queen think of a return so little desired, and so contrary to her plans ? She looked furiously at Feintise, who ardently desired the earth to open and swallow her up.

The king introduced the beautiful children to his mother, praising them very highly, and in spite of the uneasiness she was feeling, she spoke to them pleasantly, and looked at them as kindly as if she loved them, for at that time dissimulation was largely practised. The banquet went off merrily, although it troubled the king greatly to see his wife eat with the puppies like the lowest of animals, but having decided to please his mother, who wished him to marry again, he made no remonstrance.

At the end of the feast, the king speaking to Belle-Etoile, said: " I know that you possess three matchless treasures; I congratulate you, and beg you to tell us how you obtained them ". "Sire," she replied "I obey you with pleasure. I had been told that the dancing water would make me beautiful, and that the singing apple would give me wit, and for those two reasons I wanted to have them. With regard to the little green bird that tells all things, I had another: we know nothing of our rank, we are children abandoned by our relatives, of whom we know none, and I hoped the wondrous bird might explain to us a thing that fills our minds night and day." "Judging by your appear-ance," said the king, "your rank must be most illustrious.; but, come, tell me truly, who are you?" "Sire," she said, "my brothers and I put off asking him till our return; on reaching home, we received your commands to come to the wedding, and all that I could do was to bring these three curiosities with me to amuse you."

"I am very glad," said the king; "do not delay to let me see them." "You allow yourself to be amused with every trifle proposed to you," said the queen-mother, angrily; "these are nice brats with their curiosities; really that name of itself proves the absurdity of the thing. Fie! fie! I cannot allow these strangers, evidently sprung from the dregs of the people, to abuse your credulity. It is all mere jugglers' tricks, and had it not been for you, they would never have had the honour of sitting at my table."

Belle-Etoile and her brothers knew not what to make of her disagreeable speeches; their countenances expressed confusion and despair at receiving so great an affront before the whole court. But the king, telling his mother that such conduct was most uncalled for, begged the beautiful children not to be annoyed, and held out his hand in token of friendship. Belle-Etoile took a bowl of rock crystal, into which she poured all the dancing water; immediately the water was seen to move, to leap in time, to come and go, to rise like a little stormy sea, to change into a thousand different colours, and to make the crystal bowl move the whole length of the king's table; then suddenly a few drops were thrown in the face of the equerry to whom the children owed so much. He was a man of rare merit, but his ugliness was as great, and he had lost one eye. Directly the water touched him he became so handsome that he was scarcely recognisable, and his eye was restored. The king, who loved him dearly, felt as much joy at the event as the queen-mother felt anger, for she could not endure the applause given to the princes. After the noise had subsided, Belle-Etoile placed on the dancing water the singing apple, made of a single ruby crowned with diamonds, with its amber branch; it began a concert so melodious that a hundred musicians could not have made such sweet sounds. The king and all the court were enchanted, and were still lost in admiration when Belle-Etoile took from her muff a little gold cage of marvellous workmanship, in which was the green bird that tells all things; he fed on powdered diamonds and drank the water distilled from pearls. She took it carefully and put it on the apple, which was silent out of respect and in order to give it the opportunity of speaking. His feathers were so sensitive that they moved if any one opened or closed their eyes near him; they were of every shade of green imaginable. He addressed the king, and asked him what he wanted to know. " We all desire to learn," he said, " who are this beautiful girl and these three knights." " O king! " replied the green bird, in a loud, clear voice, " she is your daughter and two of these princes are your sons; the other, named Chéri, is your nephew." Then with matchless eloquence he told the whole story without omitting the smallest detail.

The king burst into tears, and the poor queen left the trough, the bones, and the dogs, and softly drew near; she wept for joy and for the love of her husband and children, for could she doubt the truth of the tale when she saw in them all the marks by which they might be recognised? The three princes and Belle-Etoile rose, threw themselves at the king's feet, embraced his knees, kissed his hands; he held out his arms to them and pressed them to his heart; nothing was heard but sighs and cries of joy. The king, perceiving that his wife remained timidly by the wall, went to her, caressed her over and over again, himself gave her a chair next his, and made her sit down in it.

Her children kissed her hands and feet; so pathetic and touching a sight had never been seen; everybody wept and lifted their hands and eyes to heaven in token of their gratitude that things so important and yet so hidden should have been made known. The king thanked the princess whom he had intended to marry, and presented her with a large quantity of precious stones. But if he had obeyed his feelings of resentment how would he not have acted with regard to the queen-mother, the admiral's wife, and Feintise? He began to give vent to his anger when the generous queen, her children and Chéri entreated him to be calm, and let their punishment rather than be severe, serve as a warning and an example: the queen-mother was shut up in a tower, the admiral's wife and Feintise were cast into a damp and gloomy dungeon, where they fed with the three puppies, Grief, Distress, and Sorrow, who missing their kind mistress continually bit these women. So they died, after living long enough to repent of their crimes.

The queen-mother, Roussette and Feintise having been removed according to the king's orders, the musicians resumed singing and playing. The joy was without parallel; Belle-Etoile and Chéri were more glad than all the rest put together, seeing they were on the eve of happiness. In fact, the king, finding his nephew the handsomest and cleverest of all the court, told him he would not allow such an auspicious day to pass without celebrating his wedding, and that he therefore gave him his daughter. The prince, overcome with joy, threw himself at his feet, and Belle-Etoile showed equal satisfaction.

It was only fair that the old princess who had lived so long in retirement should leave it to share in the general rejoicing. The same little fairy who had dined at her house and been so kindly welcomed, suddenly appeared to tell her what was happening at court. "Let us take our way there," she said; "on the road I will tell you all the care I have taken of your family." The grateful princess got into her chariot, which shone with gold and azure, was preceded by drums and trumpets, and accompanied by six hundred body-guards who looked like great nobles. The fairy told the princess her grandchildren's adventures and how she had watched over them, that in the form of a mermaid, a dove, in a thousand ways she had protected them. "You see," she added, "a good deed is never thrown away."

Every moment the good princess kissed the fairy's hands to show her gratitude, for she could find no words in which to express her joy. At length they arrived. The king welcomed them with every mark of affection. It will easily be believed that Queen Blondine and her beautiful children were eager to do honour to the illustrious lady, and when they learned all that the fairy had done on their behalf, how she was the gentle dove who had been their guide, nothing could have been added to their words. To put the finishing stroke to the king's joy, she told him that his mother-in-law, whom he had always taken to be a poor peasant, was by birth the Princess Sovereign. That was the only thing wanting to the monarch's happiness. The fête ended with the marriage of Belle-Etoile and Chéri. The pirate and his wife were sent for in order that they might be rewarded for the excellent education they had given the children. And so, after many troubles, every one was made happy.

PRINCE MARCASSIN.

THERE was once upon a time a king and a queen who lived in great sorrow because they had no children. The queen, though still beautiful, was no longer young, so that she did not dare look forward to having any. This made her very sad. She slept little, and was always sighing and praying to the gods and all the fairies to give her what she wished. One day when she was walking in a little wood, after gathering violets and roses she picked some strawberries too, but no sooner had she eaten them than she became very drowsy, and lying down at the foot of a tree, she fell asleep.

She dreamt while she slept that she saw passing through the air three fairies, who stopped just over her head. The first one looking pityingly at her, said: "Here is a lovely queen to whom we should be doing a real service if we were to give her a child". "Very well," said the second, "do so, since you are the eldest of us." "My gift to her," she went on, "is a son, the handsomest, the most amiable, and the best loved in the world." "And mine," said the other, "is that she may see this son happy in whatever he undertakes, always powerful, full of understanding and of justice." The third fairy, when her turn came to name her gift, burst out laughing, and mumbled some words between her teeth that the queen did not hear.

That was her dream. Waking up after a few minutes, she saw nothing in the air nor in the garden. "Alas!" she said, "I am not fortunate enough to justify the hope that my dream may come to pass. What thanks would I not give to the gods and to the good fairies if I had a son!" Gathering some more flowers she returned to the palace more cheerful than usual. The king noticed

this, and begged her to tell him the reason.   She denied him, but he pressed her.
" It is not," she said to him, "a thing deserving of your curiosity ; it is nothing
but a dream, and you will think me very silly to attach any kind of belief to it."
Then she told him that while she was asleep she had seen three fairies in the
air, and what two of them had said, and that the third had burst out laughing
without her being able to hear what she muttered.

" This dream," said the king, " is gratifying to me as it is to you, but that
merry-humoured fairy makes me uneasy, for the most of them are mischievous,
and it is not always a good sign when they laugh."   "As for me," replied the
queen, " I believe that signifies neither good nor ill ; my mind is filled with my
desire to have a son, and a hundred fancies rise out of that.   Besides, what
could happen to him, supposing there were anything true in what I have
dreamt ?   Is he not endowed with all that can be most advantageous to him ?
Heaven grant that I may have this consolation ! "   Thereupon she fell a-weeping.
The king assured her that she was so dear to him that she made up for everything.

When some months had passed the queen knew that she was to have a
child.   Word went round the whole kingdom to send up prayers for her ; the
altars smoked only with the sacrifices offered to the gods for the preservation of
so dear a treasure.   The assembled states sent deputies to compliment their
majesties ; all the princes of the blood, the princesses, and the ambassadors were
at the court when the queen was brought to bed.   The layette for the precious
child was of wonderful beauty, and the nurse excellent.   But how was the public
joy changed to sadness when instead of a fine prince there was born—a little wild
boar !   Everybody shrieked, which frightened the queen very much.   She asked
what was the matter, but they did not wish to tell her for fear she should die of
grief.   So, on the contrary, they assured her she was the mother of a fine boy,
and that she had cause for rejoicing.

But the king was terribly cast down.   He ordered them to put the Marcassin
in a sack and to throw him to the bottom of the sea, so that the memory of an
event so grievous might be lost entirely.   But afterwards he had pity, and
thinking it right to consult the queen on the matter, he gave orders for him to
be fed, and said not a word to his wife till the danger was past of a great disappointment causing her death.   Every day she asked to see her son.   They
told her he was too delicate to be brought from his room to her own, and with
that explanation she was satisfied.

As for Prince Marcassin, he fed like a wild boar in whom the
desire of life is strong.   They had to provide six nurses for him, three of them
dry nurses, in the English fashion.   These would always be giving him Spanish

wines and cordials to drink, which taught him early to be a judge of the best wines. The queen, impatient to caress her baby, told the king that she was well enough to go as far as the child's room, and that she could no longer live without seeing her son. The king heaved a deep sigh, and ordered them to bring hither the heir to the crown. He was swaddled like a child in robes of gold brocade. The queen took him in her arms, and lifting a frill of lace that covered his head . . . Alas! what was her dismay at the fatal sight? That moment seemed as if it must be the last of her life. She looked with sad eyes at the king, not daring to utter a word.

"Do not grieve, my dear queen," he said to her. "I impute no blame to you on account of our misfortune. It is, no doubt, a trick played by some wicked fairy, and if you will give your consent, I shall carry out my first plan, which was to have the little monster drowned." "Ah, sire!" she said, "do not make me your confidant in respect to so cruel a deed. I am the mother of this unfortunate Marcassin. I feel the tenderness within me making appeal for him. Do him no harm, I beg of you. He has already suffered too much in being born a wild boar when he should have been a man."

So deeply did she move the king by her tears and her reasoning that he promised what she desired. The ladies, therefore, who had charge of Marcassin, began to take much more care of him; for till now they had looked on him as an unholy beast soon to serve as food for fishes. It is true that in spite of his ugliness his eyes were seen to be full of intelligence. They had taught him to give his little foot to those who came to salute him as others give their hand. They decked him with diamond bracelets. And in all his ways there was a certain grace.

The queen could not help loving him. She had him often in her arms, at the bottom of her heart thinking him pretty, though she dared not utter this for fear they should think her crazy. But she did say to her friends that her son seemed to be of an amiable disposition. She covered him with endless knots of rose-coloured ribbons, and his ears were pierced. He had a string with which they held him up to teach him to walk on his hind legs. They put shoes on him, and silken stockings fastened over the knee to make his legs look longer. He was beaten when he grunted. In short, in so far as it was possible, they weaned him from his wild-boar habits.

One evening, when the queen was out walking and carrying him in her arms, she passed under the same tree where she had fallen asleep and where she had dreamt all I have already told. The remembrance of that adventure came back to her mind with great vividness. "Here, then," she said, "is the prince so handsome, so perfect, and so happy, that I was going to have! O vain dream! fatal vision! O fairies, what had I done that you should mock me?" She was murmuring those words under her breath, when all of a sudden she saw an oak spring up; and from it there appeared a lady richly dressed, who looking at her in a kindly manner, said: "Do not grieve, great queen, at having given birth to Marcassin. I assure you there will come a time when he will seem beautiful to you." The queen recognised her as one of the three fairies who passing through the air while she slept, had stopped and had willed she might have a son. "It is difficult for me to believe you, madam," she answered. "No matter what intelligence my son may possess, who can love him with such a face?" Once again the fairy answered: "Do not grieve, great queen, at having given birth to Marcassin. I assure you there will come a time when he will seem beautiful to you." She disappeared immediately into the tree, and the tree into the earth, without its even appearing that there ever had been one in that place.

Much astonished at this new adventure, the queen could not help hoping that the fairies would take some care of the royal beast. Quickly did she return to the palace to let the king know what had occurred; but he thought she had invented this means of making his son seem less hateful to him. "I see quite well," she said, "from the way you are listening to me that you do not believe what I am saying. Yet nothing is truer than what I have just told you." "It is very hard," said the king, "to endure the fairies' mockeries. By what means could they ever make anything else of our child than a wild boar? Never do I think of him without being overwhelmed by grief." The queen went out from him more sorrowful than ever. She had hoped that the fairy's promises would soften the king's sadness; yet he would hardly listen to them. So she withdrew, having made up her mind to speak no more to him about her son, and to leave to the gods the task of consoling her husband.

Marcassin began to speak. Like other children he lisped a little; but that did not diminish the queen's pleasure in hearing him, for she had doubted whether he would ever speak at all. He grew very tall, and used often to walk on his hind feet. He wore long garments covering his limbs, and an English cap of black velvet to conceal his head, his ears, and a part of his snout. His tusks, it must be confessed, were terrible; and his bristles stood up in a fearsome way. His look was proud, and his presence betokened a power of absolute command. He ate out of a golden trough, in which truffles, and acorns, and morels, and grass were prepared for him, and no pains were spared to teach him dainty ways and good manners. His mind was naturally superior, and he was of dauntless courage. The king recognising his qualities, began to care more for him than he had done before, and sought out good masters to teach him all they could.

Marcassin was not successful with figure dances, but in round dances and the minuet, where speed and lightness are wanted, he did wonderfully. As to musical instruments, he knew well enough that the lute and the theorbo were not suitable to him; he liked the guitar, and played beautifully on the flute. He rode on horseback with astonishing talent and grace. Hardly a day passed that he did not go to the hunt, attacking furiously with his teeth the fiercest and the most dangerous beasts. His masters perceived in him a quick wit and every possible facility for gaining an accurate knowledge of the sciences. But very bitterly did he feel the ridicule which his wild-boar's face brought upon him, so that he avoided appearing in large assemblies.

His life was passing in happy unconcern, when one day while he was with the queen, he saw a lady enter. She was good-looking, and was followed by three very lovely young girls. Throwing herself at the feet of the queen, she told her she had come to beg her to give them shelter at her court. The death of her husband and great misfortunes had reduced her to extreme poverty, and her birth and her unhappy condition were well enough known to her majesty to justify the hope that she would willingly receive her. The queen was deeply touched at seeing them thus kneeling before her. She embraced them, and said she would gladly receive the three girls; the eldest of whom was called Ismene, the second Zelonide, and the youngest Marthesie. She promised to take care of them, assured the mother she need not be discouraged, that she might remain in the palace where she would be treated with much regard, and might count on the queen's friendship. The mother, charmed with the goodness of the queen, kissed her hand a thousand times, and felt a sudden calm such as she had not known for long.

The fame of Ismene's beauty spread through the court, and very deeply affected a young knight named Coridon, who was no less famous in his own way than she was in hers. Almost at the same time they felt a secret sympathy linking them to each other. The knight was of an amiability untold. He charmed every one, and every one loved him. And as this was an engagement with many advantages for Ismene, the queen saw with pleasure the attentions he paid her, and the favour with which she regarded him. At last their marriage was spoken of; everything seemed pointing that way. They were born for one another, and Coridon neglected nothing in the way of those gay entertainments and all those tender attentions which firmly bind a heart already affected.

But the prince had felt the power of Ismene as soon as he had seen her, without daring to declare his passion. "Ah! Marcassin, Marcassin," he cried, looking at himself in a glass, "could you possibly, with a face so hideous, dare to hope that the fair Ismene would think well of you? I must conquer my passion, for of all misfortunes the greatest is to love without return." He avoided her presence with great care; but as he thought of her none the less he became the prey of a terrible melancholy, and he grew so thin that his bones were sticking through his skin. But his trouble greatly increased when he learnt that Coridon was openly wooing Ismene, that she held him in much esteem, and that ere long the king and the queen would be preparing the wedding-feast.

Hearing this, he felt his love growing stronger and his hope fading away, for it seemed easier to please Ismene while she was merely indifferent than now when her heart was given to Coridon. He understood that silence on his part would be fatal to him, so having watched for a favourable opportunity to speak with her, he found one. One day as she was sitting under some pleasant trees singing the words of a song that her lover had made for her, Marcassin approached her, very much overcome, and sitting down beside her, he asked if it were true, as he had been told, that she was going to marry Coridon. She answered that the queen had commanded her to receive his attentions, and naturally that must end as he had suggested. "Ismene," said he, more gently, "you are so young that I did not think they were planning your marriage. Had I known it I should have proposed to you as a husband the only son of a great king who loves you and who would be delighted to make you happy." At these words Ismene grew pale. Already she had remarked that Marcassin, who naturally was rather shy, used to talk to her with evident pleasure, to give her all the truffles which his wild-boar instinct enabled him to find in the forest, and to present her with the flowers with which his cap was generally decked. She was much afraid lest he himself was the prince of whom he spoke, and she answered: "I am very glad, my lord, to have been in ignorance of the sentiments of the son of this great king. It may be that my family, more ambitious than I myself, would have wished to force me to marry him, and in confidence I tell you that my heart is so entirely Coridon's that it can never belong to any one else." "What!" he replied, "you would refuse the crowned head of him who would put his fortune at your disposal?" "There is nothing I would not refuse," she said. "I have more tenderness than ambition; and I beg of you, my lord, seeing that you have dealings with this prince, to make him promise to leave me alone." "Ah, cruel one!" cried the impatient Marcassin, "you know only too well the prince I mean! His face does not please you. You would not like to bear the name of Queen Marcassin. You have sworn eternal faithfulness to your knight, but think, think of the difference between us. I am not an Adonis, I admit, but I am a formidable wild boar; supreme force is surely worth as much as some trivial graces of manner. Ismene, think of this. Do not drive me to despair ! " While he was speaking, his eyes seemed to be on fire, and his long tusks clacked one against the other with a noise which set the poor girl all of a tremble.

Marcassin went away. Ismene, in great trouble, was shedding a torrent of tears when Coridon approached her. Till now they had only known the delights of a mutual tenderness. Nothing had come in the way of these, and they had ground for hoping that very soon their love would be happily crowned. What then was this young lover's despair when he saw the grief of his fair mistress ? He begged her to tell him the reason of it. She did so ; and it is not possible to describe the sorrow which the news caused him. " I cannot," he said, " secure my happiness at the cost of yours. A crown is offered to you—you must accept it." " Accept it, great gods ! " she cried ; " forget you, and wed a monster ! What have I done, alas ! that you should give me advice so opposed to our love and our happiness ? " Coridon was overcome to such a degree that he could answer nothing, but the tears flowing from his eyes were enough to show the condition of his soul. Ismene, deeply sensible of their common sorrow, said to him hundreds and hundreds of times that she would never change if all the kings of the earth were in question ; and touched by this generosity, he told her hundreds and hundreds of times that it would be best to leave him to die of sorrow and ascend the throne that was offered to her.

While they were disputing this, Marcassin was with the queen, to whom he said that the hope of curing his passion for Ismene had forced him to silence, but that he had struggled in vain ; that she was on the eve of her marriage ; that he felt he had not the strength to bear up under such a misfortune ; and that, in short, he wished to marry her or to die. The queen was much astonished to hear that the wild boar was in love. " Who would have you, my son ; and what kind of children could you hope for ? " " Ismene is so beautiful," said he, " that she could not have ugly children, and even should they take after me, I would face all rather than see her in another's arms." " Have you so little sense of your position," the queen went on, " as to desire a girl whose birth is inferior to your own ? " " And what royal lady is there," he replied, " with so little daintiness as to be willing to marry a wretched pig like me ? " " My son, you are mistaken," answered the queen ; " princesses less than anybody else are free to choose. We shall have you described as fairer than love itself. When the marriage is accomplished, and we have the lady in our keeping, she will be forced to remain with us." " I am not capable," he said, " of such a piece of trickery. I should be in despair at making my wife unhappy." " Can you believe," cried the queen, " that she whom you desire would not be so with you ? Her lover is worthy of her love, and if there is a difference of rank between a sovereign and a subject, there is no less between a wild boar and a most charming man of the world." " So much the worse for me, madam," replied Marcassin, vexed at the reasons she was urging. " It seems to me that you less than any other should insist upon my misfortune. Why did you make me a pig? Is it not unjust to reproach me with a thing which I did not bring about?" "I am not reproach- ing you," answered the queen, deeply moved. " I only want to show you that if you marry a wife who does not love you, you will be unhappy, and you will bring her sorrow. If you could but understand what suffering those forced marriages are the cause of you would not wish to run the risk of one. Is it not better to live alone in peace?" " To do that would want more indifference than I have, madam," he said. " Ismene has touched my heart. She is gentle, and I flatter myself that a delicate handling of her, together with the crown she must hope for, will make her yield. But, however it turns out, if it is my fate to be loveless I shall have the happiness of possessing a wife whom I love."

The queen found his mind was so firmly fixed that she gave up the thought of turning him away from it. She promised to work for the end he de- sired, and without any delay she sent for Ismene's mother. She knew her dis- position—that of an ambitious woman, who would have sacrificed her daughters for an advantage even below that of a crown. As soon as the queen told her that it was her will that Marcassin should marry Ismene, she threw herself at her feet, and assured her that the wedding-day was for her to choose. " But," said the queen, " her affections are engaged : we have commanded her to look on Coridon as her destined husband." "Well, madam," answered the old mother, " we shall command her to look on him henceforth as the man she shall not marry." " The heart does not always consult the reason," replied the queen. " When once it is really attached, it is difficult to subdue it." " If her heart had other desires than mine," said she, " I should tear them from her without mercy." The queen seeing her so determined, felt that she might safely impose on her the task of rendering her daughter submissive.

And, in truth, she hastened to Ismene's chamber, where the poor girl, knowing that the queen had sent for her mother, was anxiously awaiting the return of the latter. And one may easily imagine how her anxiety increased when she was told in a hard and resolute manner that the queen had chosen her for her daughter-in-law, that she must never speak to Coridon any more, and that if she were lacking in obedience she would be strangled. Ismene did not dare answer this threat, but she wept bitterly, and the report was spread abroad very soon that she was going to wed the royal wild boar; for the queen, who had made the king consent, sent her precious stones with which to deck herself when she should come to the palace.

Coridon, in desperation, in spite of all that had been done to prevent his entrance, sought her and spoke to her. When he reached her own private apartment he found her reclining on a couch, the tears streaming down her face. Falling on his knees by her side, and taking her hand: "Alas," said he, "charming Ismene, you are weeping for my sorrows". "They are my sorrows too," she replied. "You are aware, dear Coridon, to what I am condemned. Death is the only possible escape from the outrage they mean to subject me to. Yes, I assure you, I could die more easily than I could give myself to any one else." "No," said he, "live: you will be a queen. It may be that you will grow used to this hideous prince." "That I could not do," she said. "I can imagine nothing in the world more terrible than such a husband. His crown does not lessen my sorrows." "The gods preserve you," he continued, "from so fatal a resolution, beloved Ismene—one which only befits my lot. I am about to lose you; you cannot forbid the step my anguish drives me to." "If you die," she answered, "I shall not survive you; and I feel a certain consolation in the thought that death at least will bring us together."

While they were talking thus, Marcassin took them by surprise. The queen having told him what she had done in his favour, he hastened to express his joy to Ismene, but the presence of Coridon annoyed him to the last degree. He was in a jealous and impatient humour. In a fashion that strongly suggested the wild boar, he ordered him to be gone and never again appear at the court. "What do you mean, cruel prince?" cried Ismene, stopping her lover as he went away. "Do you think you can banish him from my heart as you do now from my presence? No, he is too well planted there. In bringing sorrow on me do not overlook what you are bringing on yourself. Here is the man whom I can love. For you I feel only horror." "And as for me, cruel one," said Marcassin, "I am all love for you. It is useless to confess all your hate for me. None the less will you be my wife, and you will only suffer the more."

Coridon, in despair at having brought this fresh unhappiness on his mistress, went away just at the moment when Ismene's mother came to scold her. She assured the prince that her daughter would forget Coridon altogether, and that there was no reason to delay so charming a wedding. Marcassin, no less eager, said he was going to arrange the day with the queen, the king having left the care of this great festivity in her hands, the truth being that he did not want to have anything to do with it, for this marriage seemed displeasing and ridiculous to him, persuaded as he was that the Marcassin race would be perpetuated in the royal house. The blind indulgence with which the queen regarded her son was a grief to him.

Marcassin feared lest the king should repent of the consent he had given to his desires, so all the preparations for the ceremony were hastened. He had knee breeches made for him, with bunches of ribbon at the knee, and a perfumed doublet, for there was always a slight odour about him which it was difficult to endure. His mantle was embroidered with jewels, his wig was fair as a child's curls, and his hat covered with feathers. Perhaps a more extraordinary figure than he presented was never seen, and no one except her who was condemned to the misfortune of marrying him could look at him without laughing. But, alas! young Ismene had little heart to laugh. In vain they promised her magnificence. She despised it, and was only conscious of the unlucky star she had been born under.

Coridon saw her passing on her way to the temple, looking like a beautiful victim about to be slaughtered. Marcassin, transported with delight, prayed her to banish the deep sadness with which she was overcast; for he wished to make her so happy that all the queens of the earth would envy her. "I confess," he said, "that I am not handsome, but it is said that every man is like some animal. Well, I am most like a wild boar. That is my beast. There is no reason to consider me less amiable on that account, for my heart is full of tenderness and possessed by a strong passion for you." Ismene, without answering, looked at him with a disdainful air, shrugged her shoulders, and let him guess all the horror she felt for him. Her mother was behind her, threatening her in a thousand different ways. "Wretched girl," she said, "do you wish to ruin us along with yourself? Have you no fear lest the prince's love may turn to fury?" But Ismene, occupied with her own trouble, paid not the least attention to these words. Marcassin, who had her hand in his, could not keep from leaping and dancing, whispering in her ears a thousand tender words.

At last the ceremony was over. After the guests had cried three times, "Long live Prince Marcassin! Long live Princess Marcassin," the bridegroom brought his bride to the palace, where all the preparations had been made for a magnificent repast. The king and queen having taken their places, the bride sat down opposite the wild boar, who devoured her with his eyes, so beautiful did he find her; but she was buried in such deep sadness that she saw nothing of what was going on and heard nothing of the loud sounds of the music.

The queen plucked her dress and whispered in her ear: "My child, cast off that cloud of melancholy from you if you wish to please us. You look as if this were your burial rather than your wedding-day." "May the gods but grant that this be the last day of my life!" she answered. "You commanded me to give my heart to Coridon. It was rather from your hand than my choice he received it; but, alas! if you have changed towards him, I have not done so." "Do not speak thus," replied the queen; "it makes me blush for shame and vexation.

Think of the honour my son is doing you, and the gratitude you owe him."
Ismene answered not a word, but let her head fall gently on her breast as she
plunged again into her former reverie.

Marcassin was much distressed at seeing the aversion in which his wife held
him. There were, indeed, moments when he wished his marriage had not taken
place, when he even wished to dissolve it on the spot, but his heart refused consent to any such renunciation. The ball opened. Ismene's sisters shone in
splendour. Little did they care for her sorrows in their delight at the brilliant
position which the alliance gave them. The bride danced with Marcassin; and
really it was frightful to see his face, and still more so to be his wife. The
whole court was so sad that it was impossible to counterfeit joy. The ball did
not last long. The princess was conducted to her apartment; and after the ceremony of disrobing, the queen withdrew. Marcassin, the impatient lover, retired
to bed with much speed. Ismene said she wished to write a letter, and entering
her inner chamber she shut the door, though Marcassin cried out to her to write
quickly, and that this was hardly an hour at which to begin correspondence.

Alas! on entering this inner chamber, what was the sight that fell suddenly
on Ismene's eyes? There was the unhappy Coridon, who had bribed one of her
women to open the door of the secret stair by which he entered. In his hand was
a dagger. "Think not, my charming princess," he said, "that I am come to
reproach you for forsaking me. When we first plighted troth you swore that your
heart would never change; nevertheless you have consented to leave me, and I
blame the gods more than I do you. But neither you nor the gods can make me
bear so great a sorrow. Losing you, princess, there is nothing left me but to
die." Hardly had he uttered these words before he plunged the dagger in his
heart.

Ismene had no time to answer him. "You die, dear Coridon!" she cried
in sore grief. "Then have I nothing left to care for in the world! Its
splendours would be hateful to me; the light of day would be insupportable."
She said no more, but plunging the same dagger into her bosom which smoked
still with the blood of Coridon, she fell lifeless to the ground.

Marcassin was waiting too impatiently for the fair Ismene not to be aware
that she delayed her return. He called her as loud as he could, but there came
no answer. He became very angry. Rising and putting on his dressing-gown,
he ran to the cabinet door and had it forced. He was the first to enter. Alas!
what was his astonishment to find Ismene and Coridon in such a terrible condition! He was like to die of grief and rage. Mingled feelings, now of love, now
of hate, maddened him. He adored Ismene, but he knew that she had only
killed herself in order to put a sudden end to the union they had just contracted.

They ran to the king and queen with the news of what had happened in the prince's apartment. The whole palace rang with laments, for Ismene was beloved and Coridon held in high esteem. The king did not rise; he could not enter with such tenderness as the queen into Marcassin's adventures, and left to her the care of consoling him.

She made Marcassin go to bed. She mingled her tears with his, and when he let her have an opportunity of speaking, and ceased his laments for a moment, she tried to make him see that he was fortunate in being free of one who would never have loved him, and whose heart was already filled with a strong affection; that to kill a great passion was well-nigh impossible, and that she was persuaded he ought to think himself fortunate in her loss. " What matter!" he cried. " I wished to have her for my own, even had she been unfaithful to me. I cannot say she sought to deceive me by feigned caresses; she always showed her horror for me. It is I that have caused her death, and what have I not to reproach myself with on this head?" The queen saw that he was in such deep trouble that she left him with those persons who pleased him most, and withdrew to her own room.

In bed she called to mind all that had happened since the dream in which she had seen the three fairies. " What harm did I do to them," she said, " to make them send such bitter griefs to afflict me? I was hoping for an amiable and charming son; they made him like a wild boar. He is a monstrosity. Poor Ismene preferred to kill herself rather than live with him. The king has never had a happy moment since this unfortunate prince was born; and as for me, I am overpowered with sadness every time I see him."

While she was speaking thus to herself she saw a great light in her room, and near her bed she recognised the fairy who had come out of the trunk of a tree in the wood. The fairy said to her: " O queen! why will you not believe me? Did I not assure you that your Marcassin would bring you much satisfaction? Have you not faith in my sincerity?" " Ah! who could believe?" said the queen. " Nothing have I seen as yet answering in the least degree to your words. Why did you not leave me for the rest of my life without an heir rather than give me one like him?" " We are three sisters," answered the fairy. " Two of us are good; the other one nearly always spoils the good we do. It was she you saw laughing while you slept. Without us your troubles would last even longer, but they will have an end." " Alas! it will be by my death or Marcassin's," said the queen. " I may not tell you," replied the fairy. " I am only allowed to bring you the comfort of some hope." Then she vanished. In the room a pleasant fragrance lingered, and the queen flattered herself that a change for the better was to come.

Marcassin went into deep mourning; he passed many days shut up in his chamber, and covered many a page with the record of his keen regrets for the loss he had sustained. He even desired that these verses should be carved on the tombstone of his wife :—

> " O fate unyielding, harsh decree,
> That banished Ismene everlastingly!
> Veiled are her eyes in the eternal night,
> Her eyes that were our light.
> O fate unyielding, harsh decree,
> That banished Ismene everlastingly! "

Everybody was astonished at his remembering so tenderly one who had shown so much aversion for him. But gradually he began to frequent the society of ladies, and was struck with the charms of Zelonide, Ismene's sister, who was no less charming than she had been, and who bore a great resemblance to her. This resemblance pleased him. When he talked to her he found her full of wit and vivacity. It seemed to him that if anything could console him for the loss of Ismene it would be young Zelonide. She did him many kindnesses, for it never entered her mind that he wished to marry her. Nevertheless he was determined to do so. And one day when the queen was alone in her own apartment, he betook himself there with a livelier air than usual. " Madam," said he, " I have come to ask a favour of you, and at the same time to beg of you not to dissuade me from what is in my mind; for nothing in the world could quench the desire I feel to marry again. Give me your hand upon it, I pray you. It is Zelonide I wish to marry; speak to the king, so that the matter may be arranged without delay." " Ah! my son," said the queen, " what have you then determined on? Have you already forgotten Ismene's despair and her tragic death? How can you hope that her sister will love you better? Are you more lovable than you were, less of a wild boar, less hideous? Be reasonable, my son; do not expose yourself anew every day. Fashioned as you are, it would become you to be retiring." " I agree with you, madam," replied Marcassin; " that is why I wish for a companion. The owls and the toads and the serpents find mates. Am I then inferior to vile beasts? But you are bent on vexing me. Surely a wild boar is worth more than any of those I have named."

" Alas, dear child," said the queen, " the gods will testify to the love I bear you, and to the sorrow with which I am overwhelmed when I look on you. When I set forth all these reasons it is not because I am bent on vexing you. When you have a wife I hope she may love you as much as I do; but there is a difference between the feelings of a wife and those of a mother."

"My mind is made up," said Marcassin. "I beg you, madam, to speak to-day to the king and to Zelonide's mother, so that my marriage may take place as soon as possible." The queen promised, but when she talked to the king of the matter he told her that in respect of her son she was contemptibly weak, and that most certainly still further catastrophes would happen from so unsuitable a marriage. Although the queen was as much persuaded of the truth of this as he was, she did not therefore yield, being desirous of keeping the promise she had given to her son. She accordingly pressed the king so sorely that, wearied of the matter, he told her she might do what she wished, but that if trouble came of it she could only blame her own weakness.

On going back to her own room the queen found Marcassin there awaiting her with the greatest impatience. She told him he might declare his affection to Zelonide, the king having given his consent provided she gave hers, for he did not want the authority with which he was clothed to bring misfortune. "I assure you, madam," said Marcassin, with a swaggering air, "you are the only person that thinks so meanly of me. Every one else praises me, and points to a thousand good qualities which I possess." "Courtiers always do so," said the queen, "and princes are always treated in that fashion. The former do nothing but sing praises, the latter hear nothing but praises sung. How is it possible ever to know one's faults in such a labyrinth? Ah! how happy might the great be if they had friends more attached to their persons than their fortunes." "I am not sure, madam," rejoined Marcassin, "that they would be pleased to hear unpleasant truths. Nobody likes these, no matter to what condition of life they belong. Why, for instance, do you always insist that there is no difference between a wild boar and me, that I inspire terror, and that I should go and hide myself? Have I no obligation towards those who bring me solace, who tell me flattering untruths, and who hide the faults you are so anxious to point out?"

"Oh, well-spring of vanity!" cried the queen, "we find you wherever we turn our eyes! Yes, my son, you are fair and handsome; I advise you to continue your gifts to those who tell you so." "Madam," said Marcassin, "I am well enough aware of my misfortunes. I am perhaps more keenly aware of them than any one else is, but it does not rest in my hands to add an inch to my stature, nor to straighten my figure, nor to exchange my boar's head for a man's with flowing locks. I am willing to be taken to task for ill-temper, impatience, or avarice—in fact, for any defect that can be remedied. But as for my person, you must own, surely, that I am to be pitied and not blamed." Seeing that he was growing angry, the queen told him that since he was so resolved to marry, he might see Zelonide, and come to terms with her.

He was too eager to bring this conversation to an end to stop longer with his mother. Hastening to Zelonide, he entered her room unceremoniously, and finding her in the inner room, he kissed her, saying : " Little sister, I bring news which I cannot think will be displeasing to you. I am desirous that you should marry." " My lord," she said, " if I marry by your direction I am content." " The bridegroom in question," he replied, " is one of the greatest princes in the kingdom, but he is not handsome." " What matter ? " said she. " My mother is so cruel that I shall only be too glad to change my condition." " He whom I speak of," added the prince, " is very much like me." Zelonide looked at him fixedly, and with astonishment in her eyes. " You do not answer, little sister," he said ; " is it joy or grief that makes you silent ? " " I do not call to mind, my lord," she replied, " having seen any one at the court like you." " What ! " he said, " you cannot guess that I mean myself ? Yes, dear child, I love you, and I am come to offer to share my heart and my crown with you." " Ye gods ! what do I hear ? " cried Zelonide, in grief. " What do you hear, ungrateful one ? " said Marcassin. " You hear what should give you more satisfaction than anything else in the world. Can you ever otherwise hope to be a queen ? I am gracious enough to cast my eyes on you. Strive to merit my love, and do not imitate the follies of Ismene." " No," she said, " do not fear that I shall take my life as she did. But, my lord, there are so many persons more amiable and more ambitious than I am. Why do you not choose some one who would appreciate better the honour you destine for me ? I confess to you that my only desire is for a quiet and retired life. Let me arrange my own lot." " You hardly deserve that I should raise you to the throne by violence," he cried, " but a fatal impulse which is beyond my understanding urges me to marry you." Zelonide's only answer was her tears.

He left her full of sadness, and went to seek his mother-in-law to tell her of his intentions, in order that she might persuade Zelonide to do what he desired with a good grace. He told her of the interview that he had just had with her, and the repugnance she had shown for this marriage which was to make her fortune and that of all her house. The ambitious mother knew well enough the advantages she might derive from it ; and when Ismene had killed herself she was much more distressed on account of her own interest than because of any tenderness she had for her. She was beyond measure delighted that this loathsome Marcassin wished to form a new alliance with her family. She threw herself at his feet ; she embraced him, and thanked him a thousand times for an honour which affected her so deeply. She assured him that Zelonide would be obedient, or if not she would plunge a dagger in her eyes. " I must confess," said Marcassin, " that it grieves me to do violence to her; but if I wait till hearts are thrust on me I may wait for the rest of my life. All the beauties think me hideous—yet, nevertheless, I have made up my mind to wed a lovely maiden." "You are right, my lord," replied the wicked old woman. "You must have your own way. If they are not pleased, it is only because they do not know what is to their real advantage."

So strongly did she uphold Marcassin that he told her that the matter was now therefore fully arranged, and that he would turn a deaf ear to the weeping and beseeching of Zelonide. Going home he selected his most magnificent possessions and sent them to his mistress. As her mother was by when they brought her the golden baskets full of jewels, she did not dare refuse them, but she showed the utmost indifference to all they brought her except to a dagger with a handle set in diamonds. She took it in her hand several times, and put it in her girdle, for the ladies of that country were in the habit of carrying them.

Then she said : "I am mistaken if this is not the same dagger that pierced the bosom of my poor sister". "We do not know if that be so, madam," said they to whom she spoke, "but if you think it is, you should never look at it." "On the contrary," she answered, "I admire her courage. Happy is she who is brave enough to do likewise !" "Ah! my sister," cried Marthesie, "what fatal thoughts are passing through your mind? Do you wish to die?" "No," replied Zelonide, firmly. "The altar is not worthy of such a victim, but I take the gods to witness that . . ." She could say no more, for her tears choked her laments and her words.

The amorous Marcassin, on being told how Zelonide had received his gift, was so very angry that he was on the point of breaking off the marriage, never to see her in his life again. But whether from love or from pride, he could not bring his mind to do so, and determined to follow out his first intention with the greatest possible speed. The king and the queen gave him the charge of arranging for the great feast. He ordered it on a magnificent scale; yet there was always in whatever he did a certain smack of the wild boar, which was very extraordinary. The ceremony took place in a vast forest, where tables were placed loaded with venison for all the fierce and savage beasts that might want to come and eat, so that they might share in the feast.

It was here that Zelonide, being conducted hither by her mother and sister, found the king, the queen, their wild-boar son, and all the court, under the thick dark foliage, and here the newly-wedded pair swore to each other eternal love. Marcassin would not have found it difficult to keep his word. As to Zelonide, it was easy to see she obeyed with the greatest unwillingness, though she was able to control herself and partly hide her displeasure. The prince, who liked to look at the hopeful side, thought she was yielding to the force of necessity, and that she would only think henceforth how to please him. This idea made him quite good-tempered again. And when the ball was about to begin he hastened to disguise himself as an astrologer with a long robe. Two court ladies only were of the masquerade besides. He wished all of them to be so much alike that it would be impossible to distinguish them, and it was no easy task to make such well-favoured ladies resemble a hideous pig like him.

One of these ladies was the confidant of Zelonide, and Marcassin was not ignorant of this. It was only out of curiosity that he planned the disguise. After they had danced a very short " entree de ballet," for nothing was more fatiguing to the prince, he went up to his new bride, and, making certain signs, pointed to one of the masked astrologers, which made Zelonide think it was her friend who was by her side, and that she was pointing to Marcassin. "Alas!" she said, "I know it only too well. There is that monster whom the gods in their anger have given me for a husband; but if you love me, we shall rid the earth of him this night." Marcassin understood from her words that she referred to some plot which very nearly concerned him. He whispered low to Zelonide: " I will dare all to serve you ". " Hold then," she answered. " Here is a dagger he sent me. You must hide it in my room and help me to kill him." Marcassin said little in reply, for fear she should recognise the jargon he talked, which was somewhat extraordinary. He took the dagger quietly and left her for a moment.

Afterwards he returned without a mask, presenting his compliments to her, which she received with rather an embarrassed air, for she was turning over in her mind the plan for his ruin; and at that moment he was hardly less anxious than herself. "Is it possible," said he to himself, "that any one so young and beautiful should be so wicked? What have I done to her that she should kill me? True, I am not handsome. I eat in a barbarous fashion. I have some faults, but who has not? With the face of a beast, I am yet a man! How many beasts are there with human faces! Is not this Zelonide, whom I thought so charming, a tigress, a lioness? Ah! how little trust is to be put in appearances!" All this he was muttering between his teeth when she asked him what was the matter. "You are sad, Marcassin. Are you not regretting the honour you have done me?" "No," said he; "I do not change easily. I was thinking of a means of closing the ball before long. I am sleepy."

The princess was delighted to see him drowsy, thinking that she would have less trouble in carrying out her project. The festival ended, Marcassin and his wife were borne away in a stately chariot. The whole palace was lit with lamps in the shape of little pigs, and there was much ceremony in conducting the wild boar and his bride to their apartment. She had no doubt but that her confidant was behind the tapestry, so she went to bed with a silken cord below her pillow.

32

With this she meant to revenge the death of Ismene and the wrong they had done herself in forcing her to a marriage so distasteful to her. Marcassin, profiting by the deep silence that reigned, made pretence of sleeping, and snored till all the furniture in the room shook. "You are asleep at last, you ugly pig!" said Zelonide. "The time has come to take revenge on you for your fatal affection. You will die in the dark night." Softly she rose, and ran to all the corners calling her friend ; but, of course, she was not there, since Zelonide's plan was quite unknown to her.

"Ungrateful friend!" she cried, in a low voice. "You abandon me. After giving me so absolute a promise you do not keep it ; but my courage will stand me instead." Having uttered these words, she passed the silken cord softly round Marcassin's neck, who had only waited for that to spring on her. Two blows of his great tusks on her throat, and she died almost immediately.

Such a catastrophe could not take place without a great stir. Everybody ran and beheld with the utmost astonishment the dying Zelonide. They would have come to her assistance, but he placed himself between with a furious air. And when the queen whom they had gone to fetch arrived, he told her what had happened and what had forced him to extreme violence against the unhappy princess.

The queen could not help lamenting her. "I foresaw only too well the trouble inseparable from your alliance. Let it, at least, serve to cure you of this marriage frenzy by which you are possessed. We could not always be having a wedding-day end with a funeral ceremony." Marcassin did not answer. He had fallen into a deep reverie. He went to bed but could not sleep, reflecting continually on his misfortunes. Secretly he reproached himself with the death of two of the loveliest beings in the world, and the passion he had for them would awake again ceaselessly to torment him.

"Unhappy wretch that I am!" he said to a young lord whom he loved. "I have never tasted happiness in the whole course of my life. If the throne I am to occupy is spoken of, every one says what a pity it will be to see so fair a realm in the possession of a monster. If I share my crown with a poor girl, instead of considering herself happy, she seeks the means of killing herself or me. If I seek solace from my father and mother they abhor me, and cast none but angry looks at me. What must I do in this despair that overwhelms me? I want to leave the court. I shall go to the deepest paths of the forest and lead the life which befits a wild boar of might and spirit. I shall never play the gallant any more. The animals will not reproach me for being uglier than they. It will be easy to be king over them, for I have reason to my share, which will serve me as a means of mastering them. I shall live more peacefully with them than I do now in a court over which I am destined to rule, and I shall not suffer the indignity of marrying a mate who stabs herself, or one that wants to strangle me. Ha! let us flee, let us flee to the woods; let us despise the crown they think I am not fit to wear."

His friend at first wished to dissuade him from so extraordinary a resolution; but he saw that he was so overpowered by his continual strokes of ill-luck that finally he pressed him no longer to remain; and one night when they had forgotten to keep guard round his palace, he made his escape without being seen, to the depths of the forest, where he began to lead the life of his wild-boar kindred.

The king and the queen could not help being touched by a flight which despair alone had driven him to. They sent out hunters to look for him; but how were they to recognise him? Two or three fierce boars were caught and brought home after much danger, but they made such ravage at the court that it was decided not to run any further risks. A general order was given that no more boars should be killed, for fear of meeting the prince.

Marcassin, when he went away, had promised his friend to write to him sometimes. He had taken writing materials with him; and from time to time they found a very illegible letter at the gate of the town, addressed to the young lord. This was a consolation to the queen, informing her as it did that her son still lived.

The mother of Ismene and Zelonide felt deeply the loss of her two daughters. All her magnificent dreams had vanished when they died. She had to bear the reproach of sacrificing them to her ambition, and the thought that only her threat had forced them to give their consent to marry Marcassin. The queen no longer looked on her so favourably as she had done. So she resolved to live in the country with Marthesie, her only daughter, who was much more beautiful than her sisters had been, and in whose gentle manners there was so much charm that no one could look on her with indifference. One day when this maiden was walking in the forest followed by two waiting women, not far from her mother's house, she saw all at once, about twenty paces off, a boar of an enormous size. Her attendants left her and fled. As for Marthesie, she was so terrified that she remained motionless as a statue unable to escape.

Marcassin, for it was he, knew her at once, and by the way she was trembling he saw that she was nearly dead of fright. He did not wish to terrify her more, so, stopping, he said: " Have no fear, Marthesie. I love you too well to do you any hurt. It rests only with you whether I do not serve you. You know what injuries I suffered at the hands of your sisters; a miserable return for my affection, though I must confess that I had deserved their hatred by my obstinacy in determining to have them against their will. Since I have lived in these forests

I have learnt that nothing in the world demands more freedom than the heart. I see that all the animals are happy because they live without constraint. I did not know their maxims before. I know them now, and I feel that I should far rather die than enter on an enforced marriage. If the gods who are angry with me would at last be appeased, if they would make you think favourably of me, I confess, Marthesie, that I should be delighted to unite my fortunes to yours. But, alas! what am I saying? Would you come with a monster like me inside my cavern?"

While Marcassin was speaking Marthesie summoned up strength enough to answer him. "What, my lord!" she cried; "is it possible that I see you in a condition so ill-becoming your birth? The queen, your mother, never lets a day pass without weeping for your griefs." "My griefs!" said Marcassin, interrupting her. "Do not speak thus of my present condition. My lot is cast. It has not been easy to make up my mind to it, but it is done. Do not think, young Marthesie, that a brilliant court will always ensure our most lasting happiness. There are joys more entrancing, and I say again, you could make me know them if you were inclined to join me in this wild life." "And why," she asked, "will you not come back again to a place where you are still beloved?" "Still beloved?" cried he. "No, no, princes covered with disgrace are not beloved. Just as people look for no end of benefits which the great are not in a position to render, so princes are made responsible when evil fortune happens, and are hated more than other people. •

"But why am I trifling in this way?" he cried. "If any of the bears or lions of my neighbourhood were to pass by and to hear me speak, I should be ruined. Make up your mind, therefore, to come without any other thought than that of passing your best days in the narrow retreat of an unfortunate monster, unfortunate no longer if he has you." "Marcassin," she said, "I have had till now no reason to love you. Without you I should still have two sisters who were dear to me. Let me have time before making up my mind to a course so extraordinary." "You may be asking me for time," he said, "only to betray me." "I am not capable of that," she answered; "and I assure you that from this moment no one will know I have seen you." "Will you come back?" he asked. "Certainly," she replied. "Ah! but your mother will forbid it. They will tell her you met a terrible boar. She will not be willing to let you run any further risk. Come then, Marthesie; come with me." "Where will you take me?" she asked. "Into a deep grotto," he answered. "A stream clearer than crystal runs slowly through it, its banks covered with moss and green grasses. A hundred echoes send back the plaints of love-stricken and forsaken shepherds. There shall we live together." "Say rather," she answered, "there shall I be devoured by one of your best friends. They will come to see you and find me, and my last moment will have come. Besides that, my mother, in despair at having lost me, will have me sought for everywhere. These woods are too near her house. I should be discovered."

"Let us go wherever you like," he said. "The preparations of a poor wild boar are soon made ready." "No doubt," she answered, "but mine are more troublesome. I want garments for every season, and ribbons and jewels." "You want loads of trifles and useless things for your toilet! When one has intelligence and reason can one not raise oneself above those petty arrangements? Believe me, Marthesie, they will add nothing to your beauty, and I feel sure they will tarnish its brilliancy. Seek nothing for your complexion but the fresh clear water of the streams. Let your hair, with its curls and its exquisite colour, its texture finer than the spider's web where the silly fly is caught, be your adornment. Your teeth are as white as pearls, and more regular. Be content with their brightness, and leave trinkets to those who are not so fair as you."

"I am well pleased with all you say to me," she answered, "but you will never be able to persuade me to bury myself in the depths of a cavern with only lizards and snails to bear me company. Would it not be better for you to come home with me to your father, the king? I promise you that they will give their consent to our marriage. I shall be delighted. And if you loved me would you not desire to make me happy and to place me in a lofty station?" "I love you, fair mistress," he replied, "but you do not love me. It is ambition that would induce you to take me for a husband, and I have too much delicacy of feeling to reconcile myself to that sort of regard."

"You are naturally inclined to think ill of our sex," replied Marthesie; "but, my lord Marcassin, surely it is yet something that I promise to cherish a sincere friendship for you. Think of this. You will see me again in a few days in this place."

The prince took leave of her and withdrew into his dark grotto, much occupied with what she had said to him. His evil star had made him so hateful to those he loved that till to-day he had never been flattered by a gracious word. This made him much more sensible of Marthesie's kindness. Striving for some means to express his love, the idea occurred to him of preparing a repast for her, and several lambs and roe-bucks felt the force of his carniverous tooth. Then he ranged them in his cavern, waiting for the moment when Marthesie would come to keep her appointment.

She, on her side, did not know how to decide. Had Marcassin been as handsome as he was hideous, had they loved each other as much as Astrea and Celadon did, it would have been all she could do to spend her best days thus in a terrible solitude, and then Marcassin would have had to be Celadon. However, she was not engaged. No one up till now had had the honour of pleasing her; and she was inclined to live with perfect willingness with the prince if he would but leave the forest. She stole out to come and see him, and found him at the appointed meeting-place. He had never failed to go there several times a-day for fear of missing the moment when she would come. As soon as he saw her he ran to her, crouching at her feet, to let her know that wild boars when they wish have most courteous forms of salutation.

Then they withdrew to a place apart, and Marcassin looking at her with his little eyes full of fire and passion, said: "What may I hope from your tenderness?" "You may have great hopes," she replied, "if you are of a mind to return to court, but I own to you that I do not feel capable of passing the rest of my life far away from all society." "Ah," said he, "it is because you do not love me. True, I am not lovable, but I am unhappy, and from pity and generosity you might do for me what for another you would do from inclination." "And how do you know," she answered, "that those feelings have no part in the friendship I have for you? Believe me, Marcassin, I am giving good proof of this in consenting to follow you to your father, the king." "Come to my grotto," said he, "and judge for yourself what you want me to leave for your sake."

At this proposal she hesitated a little, fearing he might keep her against her will. Divining what was in her mind, he said: "Do not be afraid; I shall not seek my happiness by violent means". Marthesie trusted his word. He led her to the farther end of the cavern, where she found all the animals he had slaughtered to regale her. This kind of butchery made her sick. At first she turned away her eyes, and after a moment she would have gone out, but Marcassin, putting on a masterful air and tone, said: "Lovely Marthesie, I am not so indifferent to you as to let you leave me. I take the gods to witness that you will ever reign in my heart. Insuperable difficulties prevent me from going back to my father, the king. Accept here my love and trust. Let this flowing stream, these evergreen vines, this rock, these woods and all that dwell therein, bear witness to our mutual oaths!"

She was not so desirous as he was of plighting troth; but she was shut into the grotto without any means of getting out. Why had she come in? Should she not have foreseen what would happen? She began to weep and to reproach Marcassin. "How can I trust your promises," she asked, "since you break your first one?" "There must be," he said to her, with a wild-boar smile, "something human mingled with the animal in me. This breaking of my promise for which you blame me, this little trick by which I gained my end, these show the man in me, for, to speak frankly, there is more honour amongst animals than amongst men." "Alas!" she answered, "you have the worst part of both—the heart of a man, and the face of a beast. Be then either the one or the other, and after that I shall make up my mind to what you desire." "But, fair Marthesie," he said, "would you wish to stay with me without being my wife? for you may take for granted that I shall not allow you to go out of here. Her tears and prayers were redoubled, but he was not affected by them; and after a long struggle she consented to take him as a bridegroom, and assured him she would love him as fondly as if he were the most comely prince in the world.

He was delighted by her pleasant ways. He kissed her hand a thousand times, and assured her in his turn that she would not be so unhappy as she had reason to think. Then he asked her if she would eat of the animals he had killed. "No," said she, "that is not according to my taste. If you could bring me some fruit I should like it." When he went out he closed the entrance to the cavern so securely that it was impossible for Marthesie to run away. But she had made up her mind as to her lot, and she would not have escaped even had she been able to.

Marcassin loaded three hedgehogs with oranges, sweet limes, citrons, and other fruits. He goaded them by the prickles with which they are covered, and the load reached the grotto quite safely. He entered and begged Marthesie to partake. "Here is your wedding-feast: not like the feasts made for your two sisters, but I hope that the less magnificence there is the more enjoyment there will be." "The gods grant it may be so," she answered. Then taking some water in her hand she drank to the health of the wild boar, which filled him with delight.

The repast was as short as it was frugal. Being over, Marthesie gathered all the moss and grass and flowers that Marcassin brought her and made a bed of it, hard enough to be sure, on which she and the prince lay down. She was most careful to ask him if he liked his pillow high or low, if he had room enough, and on what side he slept best. The good Marcassin thanked her tenderly, and exclaimed from time to time: "I would not change my lot with that of the greatest men. At last I have found what I sought. I am beloved by her whom I love." A hundred pretty things did he say to her, at which she was not astonished, for he was witty, but she rejoiced all the same that he was none the less so because of the solitude in which he lived.

Both fell asleep; but Marthesie, waking up, had the feeling that her bed was softer than when she lay down. Then touching Marcassin gently she found that his head was fashioned like a man's, that his hair was long, that he had arms and hands. She could not help wondering, but she fell asleep again, and when it was day she found that her husband was as much of a wild boar as ever.

They passed the next day like the one before. Marthesie said nothing to her husband of what she had suspected during the night. The hour for retiring came. She touched his head while he was asleep, and again found the same change she had found before. Now she was really in trouble. She could hardly sleep at all; she was filled with continual anxiety, and was always sighing. Marcassin saw this with real despair. "You do not love me," he said, "my dear Marthesie. I am an unfortunate wretch whose face disgusts you. I shall die, and yours will be the fault." "Say rather, cruel wretch, that you will be the death of me," she replied. "The wrong you are doing me affects me so deeply that I cannot endure it." "I do you a wrong?" he cried. "I a cruel wretch? What do you mean? You certainly have no reason to complain." "Do you think I am ignorant that every night you give up your place to a man?" "Wild boars," he said, "and especially those like me, are not of such an easy disposition. Do not harbour a thought so offensive to both of us, dear Marthesie, for, be assured, I should be jealous of the gods themselves. But perhaps you imagine this absurdity in your sleep." Marthesie, ashamed at having spoken of a thing so improbable, replied that she had such faith in his words that, though she had reason to think she was awake when she was touching arms and hands and hair, she would refuse to believe her judgment, and would never again speak of the matter to him.

And in truth she cast aside all the suspicious thoughts that came to her. Six months passed away with little enjoyment on Marthesie's side, for she never left the cavern in case she should meet her mother or the servants of her household. Since the poor mother had lost her daughter she never ceased lamenting. She made the woods resound with her griefs and with the name of Marthesie. At the sound of her voice, which fell well-nigh every day on her ears, she sighed in secret to cause so much pain to her mother and to be helpless to console her; but Marcassin had given her due warning, and she feared him as much as she loved him.

As she was all gentleness, she continued to show great tenderness to the wild boar, who loved her too, in the most passionate way. Yet when she knew that the Marcassin race was to be perpetuated, her sorrow knew no bounds.

One night as she lay awake, weeping softly, she heard talking so near her that though the voices were low, not a word that was said escaped her. It was the good Marcassin, who was praying some one to be less cruel, and to give him the permission he had long been asking. And the answer always came: "No, no; I will not". Marthesie was more troubled than ever. "Who can enter this cavern ? " she said. " My husband has not revealed this secret to me." She had no desire to fall asleep again : she was too full of curiosity. The conversation ended, she heard the person who had been speaking to the prince go out of the cavern, and shortly afterwards Marcassin was snoring like a pig. Very soon she got up to see if it were easy to take away the stone that closed up the entrance to the grotto, but she could not move it. Coming back softly, and without a light, she felt something under her feet, and discovered that it was a wild boar's skin. She took it up and hid it, and waited in silence for the outcome of the affair.

The dawn had hardly appeared when Marcassin got up, and she heard him fumbling about on all sides. While he was searching anxiously the day broke. She saw him so extraordinarily handsome and well made that never was any surprise more delightful than hers. " Ah ! " she cried, " do not keep me in ignorance of my happiness any longer. I know it. I feel it deep down in my heart. Dear prince, by what good fortune have you become the handsomest of all men ? " At first he was surprised at the discovery she had made, but composing himself, he said : " I am about to explain everything to you, dear Marthesie, and, at the same time, to confess that it is to you I owe this delightful metamorphosis.

" You must know that the queen, my mother, was asleep one day in the shade of some trees, when three fairies passed over her head. They recognised her and they stopped. The eldest one gave her a son who was to be witty and handsome. The second improved on this gift, adding in my favour no end of fine qualities. The youngest, with a burst of laughter, said : 'We must vary this affair somewhat. Spring would not be so pleasant if winter did not come before. In order, therefore, that the prince, whom you desire should be charming, may appear more so, my gift to him is that he be a wild boar until he marry three wives, and till the third one find his wild boar's skin.' At these words the three fairies vanished. The queen had heard what the two first had said very distinctly, but as for the one who was injuring me, she was laughing so much that it was impossible to distinguish her words. It is only since our wedding-day that I have been aware of what I have just now told you. When I was going in search of you, thinking only of my passion, I stopped to drink at a stream that flows near my grotto. Whether it was clearer than usual, or whether I was looking at my reflection more attentively, because of my desire to please you, I felt myself to be so hideous that my eyes filled with tears. Without exaggeration, I shed enough to swell the current of the stream, and I said to myself it was impossible that I should please you.

" Desponding at this thought, I made up my mind to go no further. ' I cannot be happy,' I said, 'if I am not beloved, and I can never be loved by any reasonable creature.' I was muttering these words when I saw a lady approach with a boldness that surprised me, for to those who do not know me I have a fearsome look. 'Marcassin,' she said, 'the hour of your happiness draws near, provided that you marry Marthesie, and that she loves you as you are. Be assured that before long you will put off the guise of a wild boar. From your wedding-night even, you will doff that skin that is so hateful to you. But put it on again before daybreak, and say nothing to your wife. Be careful to prevent her knowing anything of it till the time of the great discovery shall arrive.'

"She told me," he continued; "all I have already related to you about my mother, the queen. I thanked her very humbly for the good news she brought me, and went to seek you with feelings of mingled joy and hope such as I had never before experienced. And when I was so happy as to receive proofs of friendship from you my satisfaction increased in every way, and my impatience to share my secret with you was difficult to restrain. The fairy, who knew this, used to come at night and threaten me with the greatest misfortunes if I could not keep silent. 'Ah, madam,' I said to her, 'you surely have never loved, else you would not oblige me to hide anything so delightful from her I love best in the whole world.' She laughed at my distress, and told me not to grieve, for all would turn out well. Yet," he added, "give me back my boar's skin. I must put it on again, in case the fairies are angry." "Whatever happens, dear prince," said Marthesie, "I shall never change towards you. The charming picture of your metamorphosis will always rest with me." "I feel assured," he said, "that the fairies will not make us suffer long. They have charge of us. This bed which seems to you to be of moss is of excellent down and fine wool. It was they who placed all the fine fruits you have eaten at the entrance to the grotto." Marthesie did not neglect to thank the fairies for so many favours.

While she was expressing her gratitude to them Marcassin was making the utmost efforts to get into the skin, but it had grown so small that it would not even cover one of his legs. He pulled it this way and that way with his teeth and his hands, but in vain. He was very sad and was lamenting his misfortune, for he feared with reason lest the fairy who had so effectually turned him into a wild boar should come and clothe him with the skin again for yet a long while. "Alas! my dear Marthesie," said he, "why did you hide this fatal skin? Perhaps it is to punish us for that I cannot use it as I did. If the fairies are angry, how can we pacify them?" Marthesie wept also. It was a very strange thing to weep for, that he could no longer be a wild boar.

At that moment the grotto shook; then the roof opened. They saw six distaffs fall, filled with silk, three of them white, and three black, and they all danced together. A voice came from them which said : " If Marcassin and Marthesie can guess what these white and black distaffs mean they will be happy ". The prince pondered for a while, and then he said : " I guess that the three white distaffs mean the three fairies who gave me gifts at my birth ". " And I," said Marthesie, " guess that the three black ones signify my two sisters and Coridon." At that moment the three fairies took the place of the white distaffs. Ismene, Zelonide, and Coridon appeared also. Never was anything so terrifying as this return from the other world. " We do not come from so far away as you think," they said to Marthesie. " The watchful fairies have had the goodness to take care of us ; and while you were weeping for our death, we were being led into a castle where no delight was wanting save your company."

" What ! " said Marcassin. " Did I not see Ismene and her lover lifeless, and did not Zelonide perish by my hand ? " " No," said the fairies. " A charm was on your eyes that we might deceive you as we wished. Every day that kind of thing occurs. Here a husband thinks his wife is at the ball with him, while she is lying asleep in bed ; there a lover dotes on his fair mistress, while in truth she is as hideous as an ape ; and again, another believes he has killed his enemy, who is living safely in another country." " My mind is in a whirl of doubt," said Prince Marcassin. " It would seem, from what you say, that one must not even believe what one sees." " The rule is not a general one," answered the fairies, " but it cannot be denied that one should suspend one's judgment about many things, and believe that some portion of Faërie may enter into what seems to us most certain."

The prince and his wife thanked the fairies for the lesson they had just received, and for preserving the lives of those who were so dear to them. " But," added Marthesie, throwing herself at their feet, " may I not hope that you will no more make my faithful Marcassin wear that hideous skin ? " " We come to assure you of it," they said, " for it is time to return to the court." Immediately the grotto took the form of a magnificent tent, where the prince found several valets to dress him in gorgeous attire. There were attendants for Marthesie too, and a costume of exquisite work. Nothing was lacking for the adornment of her hair, and of her whole person. Then the dinner was served as a repast ordered by the fairies. What need to say more ?

Never was there such perfect joy. All the grief Marcassin had suffered did not equal the pleasure of seeing himself not only a man, but a wondrous handsome one. After they had risen from table several magnificent carriages, to which the finest horses in the world were harnessed, came up at full speed.

The ladies got into them with the rest of the little company, horse guards marching before and behind. And so did Marcassin return to the palace.

At the court they did not know where this splendid equipage came from. Still less did they know who was in it, till a herald published it in a loud voice, to the sound of trumpets and of kettle-drums. The whole people ran in great delight to meet their prince. Every one was charmed with him, and no one wished to doubt the reality of an event which seemed nevertheless almost incredible. The news was carried to the king and the queen, who came down at once to the courtyard. Prince Marcassin was so much like his father that it would have been difficult to mistake him. And no one did so. And never was there more widespread delight. After some months this was still further increased by the birth of a son, in whose face and character there was not a trace of the wild boar.

THE DOLPHIN.

THERE was once upon a time a king and a queen to whom heaven had given several children; but they loved them only so far as they were good and beautiful. Among the others was a young son called Alidor, whose figure, indeed, was passable, but who, nevertheless, was unbearably ugly. The king and the queen regarded him with much repugnance, and were always telling him to go out of their sight. And as he began to find that all the caresses were for others, and there was nothing but severity for him, he saw that the only thing left for him to do was to go away secretly. He carefully arranged his plans for leaving the kingdom without any one knowing where he was bound for, in hopes that fortune would treat him better in another country than in his own.

When the king and the queen found he had gone they did not know what to do. They considered that he would not appear in that splendour which befits a prince, and that unpleasant things might happen to him, which concerned them more on account of their own reputation than for his sake. They sent couriers after him with orders to bring him back at once, but he was so careful to choose the most out-of-the-way roads that they followed him in vain; and those who had been ordered to seek for him had not returned to the court before he was forgotten there. Every one knew too well how little the king and the queen cared for him to love him as they would have done a happy prince. Alidor was no longer spoken of. Besides, who was there to speak of him? Luck was against him; his kinsfolk hated him; and little thought was given to any merit he might have.

Alidor was just setting out to seek his fortune without knowing very well whither he wished to go, when he met a young man, handsome and well mounted, and who looked as if he were on a journey. They greeted each other and exchanged some courteous words, for a while speaking only of general matters. After some time the traveller learned from Alidor where he was going. "But you yourself," he said, "will you tell me your destination?" "My lord," he answered, "I am a squire in the service of the King of the Woods. I am sent to fetch some horses from a place not far from here." "Is he a savage king?" said the prince. "You call him King of the Woods, and I picture him to myself as living there." "His forefathers," said the squire, "probably lived as you say, but, as for him, he has a great court. The queen, his wife, is one of the loveliest ladies in the world, and their only daughter, Princess Livorette, is endowed with a thousand charms, which delight all who look on her. True, she is still so young that she is not aware of all the attentions paid her, but, nevertheless, no one can help paying homage to her." "You make me very curious to see her," said the prince, "and to spend some time in so delightful a court. But do they look on strangers with favour? I do not flatter myself. I know that nature has not blest me with a handsome face, but in compensation she has given one a good heart." "A very rare possession," said the traveller, "and I rate it much higher than the other. Everything is given its true value in our court, so you may go there perfectly certain of being favourably received." Thereupon he gave him directions as to the road he should take to reach the Kingdom of the Woods, and as he was of an obliging disposition, and marked in his companion an air of nobility which not all his ugliness could mar, he gave him the address of some of his friends who would present him to the king and queen. The prince was much pleased with the courtesy shown him. It promised well for a country if such politeness were native to it, and, as he was only seeking for a spot where he might dwell unknown, he preferred to choose the one now suggested to him to any other. He even felt a particular leading of fortune urging him to choose it. After having taken leave of the traveller he went on his way, thinking at times of the Princess Livorette, in regard to whom he already felt the liveliest curiosity.

When he arrived at the court of the King of the Woods, the friends of his companion by the way received him hospitably, and the king gave him a hearty welcome. He was delighted at having left his own country, for though he was unknown, he could not but be gratified at all the marks of regard shown towards him. It is true things were far otherwise in the queen's apartment, where he had hardly entered before there burst out from all sides long peals of laughter. One lady hid her face so as not to look at him; another ran away. But most clearly of all did the young Livorette, to whom such an example of ill-manners was being given, let the prince see what she thought of his ugliness.

It seemed to him that a princess who laughed in this fashion at a stranger's defects was not very well-bred. Secretly he pitied her. "Alas!" he said, "this is how I was spoiled in my father's house. Princes, it must be confessed, are unfortunate, seeing how their faults are tolerated. Yes, now I understand the poison we drink deep draughts of every day. Should not this fair princess think shame to laugh at me? I come from a distance to pay my respects to her, and to attach myself to her court. It is open to me to journey farther and declare her good qualities or her bad ones. I was not born her subject, and nothing need bind my tongue save her civility. Yet hardly has she cast her eyes on me before she insults me with her mocking airs. But alas!" he went on, looking at her with admiration, "how safe she is from evil words of mine! Never was anything so beautiful revealed to my sight. I admire her, I admire her only too much, and I know only too well that I shall do so all my life."

While he was making these sad reflections, the queen, who was of a kindly disposition, ordered him to come to her, and wishing to appease him she spoke pleasantly to him, asking about his country, his name, and his adventures, and to all her inquiries he replied like a man of intelligence, ready with his answers. His character pleased her, and she told him that whenever he wished to pay his respects to her she would see him with pleasure. She even asked whether he played at any game, and told him to come and play basset with her. As his desire was to please, he made a point of being present when the queen played. He had plenty of money and jewels. In all his actions there was an air of nobility, which counted for not a little in the distinction he gained for himself. And though no one knew who he was, for he took great pains to conceal his birth, they judged of him none the less favourably. The princess was the only one who could not endure him. She burst out laughing in his face; she made faces at him, and was guilty of every trick which her age suggested to her, and which would not have mattered from any one else. But from her it was very different. He took it very seriously, and when he knew her a little better he uttered his complaints. " Don't you think, madam," he said, " that it is somewhat unjust to laugh at me? The same gods that made you the most beautiful princess in the world made me the ugliest of men, and I am their work as well as you." " I know it, Alidor," she said, " but you are the worst bit of work that ever came out of their hands." Thereupon she looked at him fixedly, without taking her eyes off him for a long time, and then she laughed enough to make herself ill.

The prince, who all this time was looking at her, drank long draughts of the poison love was preparing. " I must die," he said to himself, " since I cannot hope to please, and I cannot live without enjoying the favour of Livorette." At last he grew so melancholy that everybody was sorry for him. The queen saw it, for he did not play as he used to. She asked him what was the matter, but could draw nothing more out of him than that he felt a strange langour, which he thought the change of climate had something to do with, and that he meant to go into the country often to take the air. The fact was, he could no longer bear to see the princess every day without hope. He believed he might be cured if he avoided her, but wherever he went his passion followed him. He sought out solitary places, and there he gave himself up to a profound reverie. The sea being near he used often to go fishing, but in vain did he cast his hook and his nets, for he caught nothing. On his return Livorette was nearly always at the window, and when she saw him coming she used to call out with

a sly little air: "Well, Alidor, and have you brought me some nice fish for my supper?" "No, madam," he answered, bowing low, and then passing sadly on. The beautiful princess laughed at him. "Oh, how stupid he is!" she said; "he can't even catch a single sole."

He was miserable at his want of luck and at being constantly laughed at by the princess, and he wanted very much to catch something worth offering to her. He used often to go out in a little sloop, taking with him various kinds of nets, and because of Livorette he took endless pains to do his best. "Am I not indeed unfortunate," he said, "to find in this amusement a new disappointment? I was only seeking to forget the princess; and now she takes a fancy to eat the fish I catch, and fortune is so unkind as to refuse to let me gratify this desire."

Full of sadness he sailed out into the sea further than he had ever done before, and, throwing out his nets in a determined fashion, he was suddenly aware they were so laden that he made haste to draw them back for fear of breaking them. When he had hauled the net on board he looked eagerly to see what was struggling inside it, and he found a fine dolphin, which he took up in his arms, delighted at his success. The dolphin tried hard to get away, struggled violently, and then feigned to be dead, so that Alidor might be put off his guard; but it was no use. "My poor dolphin," said he, "do not torment yourself further. For a certainty I shall take you home to the princess, and you will have the honour of being served up this evening on her table."

"You will be playing me a very bad turn," said the dolphin. "What!" cried the prince, in astonishment, "you can speak! Just gods, what marvel is this!" "If you will be so good and generous as to let me free," the dolphin went on, "I shall render you such real services in the course of my life that you will never need to repent of your kindness." "And what will the princess have for her supper?" said Alidor. "Don't you know the mocking tone she puts on with me? She calls me awkward, stupid, and a hundred other things, and for the sake of my reputation I am forced to sacrifice you." "And so, because the princess sets up as a judge of the gentle art," said the dolphin, "when you are not successful in your haul you think you have no honour and nobility left! Let me live, I pray you. Put back your most humble servant, the dolphin, in the water. There are good deeds whose reward follow hard on their steps."

"Well, be off with you," said the prince, throwing the creature into the sea. "I expect neither good nor ill from you, but you seem to have a strong desire to live. Livorette may add, if she will, still further insults to those she has already heaped on me. What does it matter? You are a remarkable animal, and I shall do as you wish."

The dolphin disappeared from his sight, and at that moment the prince felt that all hope of success had vanished too. Sitting down in the boat, and drawing in the oars, which he placed under his feet, he folded his arms and gave himself up to a deep reverie, out of which he was awakened by a pleasant voice, which seemed to crisp the waves as it rose from the sea. "Alidor, Prince Alidor," said the voice, "here is a friend." Looking down he saw the dolphin turning somersaults on the surface of the water. "Every one must have their turn, that is but just," said the dolphin. "Only a quarter of an hour ago you did me a great kindness. Now ask me to do you a service, and you will see what will happen." "I ask but a small reward for a great service," said the prince. "Send me the best fish in the sea." No sooner said than done. Without casting a net there came bounding into the boat such a quantity of salmon, soles, turbots, oysters, and other shell fish, that Alidor had reason to fear on account of the overloading of the boat. "Stop, stop, my dear dolphin," he cried; "I am overwhelmed by all you are doing for me, but I fear lest your generosity may prove dangerous. Save me, for you see that the situation is serious."

The dolphin pushed the boat to shore, where the prince arrived with all his fish. Four mules could not have carried the amount, so he sat down, and was choosing out the best when he heard the dolphin's voice: "Alidor," it said, thrusting up its big head, "are you at all satisfied with what I have done for you?" "I could not be more so," he answered. "Oh, but you must know that I am also most grateful for your treatment of me, and for your having saved my life. I have, therefore, come to tell you that every time you wish to command my services I shall be ready to obey you. I have more than one kind of power, and if you believe me you may have a proof of it." "Alas!" said the prince, "what should I wish for? I love a princess, and she hates me." "Do you want to love her no longer?" said the dolphin. "No," replied Alidor, "I could not make up my mind to that. Make it possible for me to please her, or let me die." "Will you promise me," continued the dolphin, "never to have any other wife but only Livorette?" "Yes, I promise you," cried the prince. "I have sworn to be faithful to the love I bear to her, and nothing within my power shall ever be wanting on my part to give her pleasure." "We must practise a deception on her," said the dolphin, "for she does not wish to marry you, thinking you ugly, and not really knowing you." "I give my consent to such a deception," replied the prince, "though I have made up my mind that she can never give herself to any one like me." "Time might bring her to reason," said the dolphin, "but let me change you into a canary bird; you may put off the guise whenever you like." "You are master, dear dolphin," answered Alidor. "Well, then," continued the fish, "I desire that you be a canary!" And in that moment the prince saw himself with feathers, and birds' claws, and a tiny beak; and he could whistle and sing admirably. Then, wishing himself Alidor again, he found he was the same as before.

Never was any one more joyful. Burning with impatience to be with the young princess, he called to his attendants, loaded them with the fish, and took the road to the town. Of course Livorette was on her balcony, calling out to him: "Well, Alidor, have you had better luck this time?" "Yes, madam," he said, showing her the great baskets filled with the finest fish in the world. "Oh!" she cried, pouting like a child, "I am quite sorry you have caught so many fish, for I shall never be able to laugh at you again." "You will never want for a pretext, when you wish for one, madam," he answered, and he went on his way, giving orders for all the fish to be sent to her. Then after a moment he took the form of a little canary, and flew on her window sill. As soon as she noticed the bird she came softly forward, holding out her hand to take hold of it, but it flew away from her into the air.

"I came from one of the ends of the earth," it said, "where the fame of your beauty has reached. But, dear princess, it would not be fair that I should come on purpose such a distance and be treated like an ordinary canary. You must promise never to put me in a cage, to let me come and go, and to have no other prison than your sweet eyes." "Ah, dear little bird!" cried Livorette, "ask me whatever you like; I promise never to break one of the conditions you put on me, for there was never seen anything so pretty as you. You speak better than a parrot, and you whistle exquisitely. I love you so much—so much that I am dying to have you for my own." The canary flew down, and lighted on Livorette's head, then on her finger, not only whistling airs, but singing words with the accuracy and in the style of the most skilful musician.

> "Fickle my nature is and light,
>   Yet is my chief desire to bide by thee;
> No gates or bars prepare to stay my flight,
>   If love my gaoler be.
> It is a service sweet, thy yoke to bear,
>   Since it is thine;
> Happier my lot thy livery to wear,
>   Than were an empire mine!"

"I am enchanted," she said to all the ladies, "by the gift that fortune has just sent me." She ran to her mother's room to show her beautiful canary. The queen would have given anything to hear it speak, but not a word would it say except for the princess, and it seemed to have no thought of pleasing any one else.

When night was come Livorette went to her room with the pretty bird, whom she called Bébé. When she began her toilette the canary perched on her mirror, taking the liberty to peck at her ear or her hands every now and again. This delighted her, and Alidor, who up till now had never known any pleasure in his life, felt supremely happy, and had no other desire to be ever anything else than Bébé, the canary. True, he was sad to think that they left him in a room where Livorette's dogs, monkeys, and parrots generally slept. "And so," he said, sorrowfully, "you think so little of me that you cast me off like this!" "It is not casting you off, dear Bébé," she answered, "to put you with what I like best." Then she went out, but the prince remained perched on the mirror. As soon as it was day he flew away to the sea-shore. "Dolphin, dear dolphin," he cried, "let me have a word or two with you. Do not refuse to listen to me." The friendly fish appeared, gravely riding on the water. When Bébé saw him he flew towards him and perched on his head.

"I know all you have done, and all you wish me to do," said the dolphin, "but I declare that you shall not enter Livorette's room till she is betrothed to you, and till the king and the queen have given their consent. After that I shall look upon you as her husband." The prince had so much regard for the fish that he did not insist, but thanked the dolphin a thousand times for the charming disguise he had procured for him, and begged that he would still remain his friend.

Coming back to the palace in his feathered shape, he found the princess in her dressing-gown. She had been searching for him everywhere, and, not having found him, she was now weeping bitterly. "Ah, you little traitor!" she said, "already you have left me! Did I not treat you well enough? Have I not petted you—given you biscuits and sugar and sweets?" "Yes, yes, my princess," said the canary, who was listening through a little hole, "you have shown me some kindness, but you have neglected me too. Do you think I am satisfied to sleep near your ugly cat? He would have eaten me fifty times if I had not taken the precaution to keep awake all night to save myself from his claws." Livorette, moved by his words, looked at him tenderly. Holding out her finger, she said: "Come, Bébé, come and be friends". "Oh! I don't make up so easily," he answered. "I wish the king and the queen to know of this." "Very well," said she, "I shall take you to their room."

She went at once to find them. They were still in bed, talking of an advantageous marriage which had been proposed for their daughter. "Well, dear child," said the queen, "what do you want this morning?" "I bring my little bird," she answered. "It wants to speak to you." "That is most important," said the queen, laughing. "But are we in a condition to give a serious audience?" "Yes, your majesty," replied the canary. "Neither do I appear in your court with all the pomp that befits me, for, the fame of the beauty and the charms of the young princess having reached me, I set off speedily to beg you to give me her hand in marriage. Such as you see me, I am king of a little grove, where oranges and myrtles and honeysuckles grow, the most charming spot in all the Canary Isles. I have a great number of subjects of my own kind, who are forced to pay me a large tribute of flies and worms. The princess might eat her fill, and she would never want for music, for I have even amongst my kinsmen some nightingales that would sing their best for her. We should live here in your court as long as you liked. I only need, your majesty, a little millet, some rape-seed, and fresh water. When you give the word for us to retire to our own states, distance will be no bar to our receiving news of you, and sending you ours in return. We shall have flying couriers to serve us, and I think I may say without vanity that you will get a great deal of satisfaction from a son-in-law like me." He ended up by whistling two or three airs, and chirping pleasantly. The king and the queen laughed till they could laugh no longer. "We have no wish," said they, "to refuse Livorette to you. Yes, pretty canary bird, we give her to you, provided she consents." "With all my heart," she said. " I have never been so happy in my life as I am now to marry Prince Bébé." Thereupon he plucked one of the finest feathers from his tail and offered it to her as a wedding present. Livorette accepted it graciously, and stuck it in her hair, which was wonderfully beautiful.

When she went back to her own apartment she told her ladies-in-waiting that she had a great piece of news for them—that the king and the queen had just betrothed her to a reigning prince. On hearing this, one flew towards her and embraced her knees, another kissed her hands. They asked her with the utmost eagerness who the prince was to whom the most beautiful princess in all the world was to be given. " Here he is," said she, drawing out the little canary from the inside of her sleeve, and showing them her betrothed. At the sight of him they laughed heartily, and many a jest was made about the perfect innocence of their fair mistress.

Livorette made haste to dress and return to her mother's room, for the queen loved her so dearly that she always liked to have her near her. But the canary flew away, and assumed his ordinary shape as Alidor, that he might pay his court to the queen. "Come," cried the queen when she saw him, "come and congratulate my daughter on her marriage with Bébé. Do you not think that we have found a fine lord for her?" Alidor entered into the spirit of the jest, and as he was gayer than he had ever been in his life he said a hundred pretty things, and the queen was much entertained. But Livorette continued to laugh at him, and contradicted every word he said to her. It would have made him very melancholy to see her in this mood if he had not remembered that his friend, the fish, was going to help him to overcome this aversion.

When the princess went to bed, she would have left her canary in the room with the animals, but he began to grumble, and, flying round her, followed her into her own, and perched himself neatly on a piece of porcelain, from which they dared not chase him for fear of breaking it. " If you begin to sing too early in the morning, Bébé," said Livorette, " and waken me, I shall not forgive you." He promised her to be quiet till she should order him to sing his little song, and with that assurance they retired for the night. Hardly was the princess in bed before she fell into so deep a sleep that there can be no doubt the dolphin had a hand in it. She snored even like a little pig, which is not natural in a child. But Bébé did not snore. To do so he would first have had to shut his eyes. Leaving the porcelain vase, he came and placed himself near his charming bride, so quietly that she did not wake. As soon as day had come he again took his canary shape, and flew away to the edge of the sea, where, as Alidor, he sat down on a little rock, the surface of which was smooth and covered with samphire. Then he looked all round to see if his dear friend, the dolphin, were near. He called him several times, and while he waited he was reflecting with pleasure on his happiness. "Oh, fairies," he said, "whose praises we sing, and whose power is indeed so extraordinary, could your art make any other mortal as happy as I am?" This thought suggested to him the following words :—

> "Good friend, to whose staunch aid I owe
> That the full bliss of love I know,
> My perfect happiness in other's ear
>   I may not say.
> For at my heart there gnaws the horrid fear
> The jealous gods should wrest my love away."

When he was murmuring these words he felt the rock shaking violently. Then through an opening there came out a little old dwarf woman, leaning her tottering frame on a crutch. It was Grognette the fairy, who was no better than Grognon. "Really, my lord Alidor," she said, "I think you are taking a great liberty in seating yourself on my rock. I do not know what should hinder me from throwing you to the bottom of the sea just to teach you that, if the fairies cannot make a happier mortal than you, they can at least make an unhappy one whenever they like." "Madam," replied the prince, astonished at this adventure, "I did not know you lived here. I should certainly have been very careful not to fail in the respect due to your palace." "Excuses will avail you nothing," she continued. "You are ugly and presumptuous, and I want the pleasure of seeing you suffer." "Alas!" said he, "what have I done to you?" "I don't know," she answered, "but I shall treat you as if I did." "The dislike you bear to me is very extraordinary," said he, "and if I did not hope that the gods would protect me against you, I would anticipate the ills with which you threaten me by taking my own life." Grognette went on muttering threats, and then retired into her rock again, which closed up.

The prince, in deep distress, did not wish to sit down, having no desire for a fresh quarrel with an ill-omened dwarf. "I was too satisfied with my lot," said he, "and now comes a little fury to trouble it. What harm will she do me? Ah, doubtless, it will not be on me that she will vent her anger. It will rather be on the fair lady whom I love. O dolphin, dolphin, I beg you to come and console me!" At that moment the fish appeared near the shore. "Well, what do you wish?" it said. "I was coming to thank you for all the kindnesses you have done me. I am now married to Livorette, and, in the ardour of my joy, I was hastening so that you might share it with me when a fairy . . ." "I know," said the dolphin, interrupting him. "It was Grognette, the most malicious and strangest creature on earth. For any one to be happy is quite enough to displease her. But what annoys me most of all is that she has power, and that she means to oppose my plans for your good." "What a strange creature!" replied Alidor; "how have I offended her?" "What, you a man, and wonder at human injustice! In truth, you men never think of justice. It would be all you could do were you fish, and even we in our kingdom of the seas are not too just. Every day we see the big ones swallowing up the little. It should not be endured, for the smallest herring has its right as a citizen of the water as much as a terrible whale."

"If I interrupt you," said the prince, "it is only to ask if I may never let Livorette know that I am her husband." "Enjoy the time that is," answered the dolphin, "without taking thought for the future." And, having said these words, he disappeared below the water. The prince became a canary again, and flew to his dear princess, who was searching everywhere for him. "Will you always make me anxious in this way, you little runaway?" she said as soon as she saw him. "I fear lest you should be lost, and then I should die of sorrow." "No, my Livorette," he replied, "I shall never get lost, for your sake." "Can you answer for it?" she continued. "Might they not lay snares and spread nets for you? Or, if you fell into the trap laid for you by some fair lady, how do I know you would return?" "Oh, what an unjust suspicion!" said he; "you do not know me." "Forgive me, Bébé," said she, smiling. "I have heard it said that little importance is attached to being loyal to a wife, and since I am yours I fear lest you should change."

Conversations like these delighted the canary, for they showed him that he was loved. And yet he was so only as a little bird. At times a keen pang would shoot through his heart. "Is it justifiable, the trick I have played on her?" he said to the dolphin. "I know that the princess does not love me, that she thinks me ugly, and that none of my faults have escaped her. I have every reason to think that she would not wish me for a husband, and, nevertheless, I have become so. If she comes to know it one day, what reproaches will she not heap on me? What shall I say to her? I should die of sorrow if I were to displease her." But the fish said to him: "Your reflections do not pull together with your love. If every lover were to make such, there would never any more be ladies carried off or disappointed. Enjoy the present time, for less happy days are in store for you."

Alidor was very much troubled by this warning. He knew quite well that Grognette the fairy still had a grudge against him for having sat down on her rock when she was underneath. He prayed the dolphin still to help him as before.

There was a great deal of talk about the marriage of the princess with a handsome young prince whose states were not far away. Ambassadors came from him to ask for her hand, and received a cordial welcome from the king. This news was most alarming to Alidor, who, without delay, betook himself to the sea-shore, and, calling his good friend the fish, he told him what he feared. " Think," said he, " how desperate is my situation ! Either I must lose my wife and see her married to another, or declare my marriage and be separated from her for the remainder of my life." " I have no power to prevent Grognette doing you an injury," said the dolphin. " I am no less grieved than you are, and you yourself cannot be more occupied with your affairs than I am. Yet pluck up courage. I can tell you nothing more at present, but you may count on my goodwill as on something which will never fail you." The prince thanked him with all his heart, and went back to the princess.

He found her in the midst of her women, one holding her head, and another her arm, while she was complaining of illness. As at that moment he was not in his canary guise he dared not go near her, though her illness made him very anxious. As soon as she saw him she smiled in spite of all she was suffering. " Alidor," she said, " I think I am going to die. It is a great grief to me now that the ambassadors have come, for I hear all kinds of good reports of the prince who asks me to marry him." " But, madam," he replied, with a forced smile, " have you forgotten that you have chosen a husband ? " " What, my canary ? " said she. " Ha, ha ! I know he will not be angry, though I love him tenderly all the same." " To share your heart with another would perhaps not content him," said Alidor. " Well, no matter," added Livorette. " I shall be very pleased to be queen over a great kingdom." " But, madam," he went on, " he offered you one." " Oh, what a fine kingdom ! " she answered, " a little jasmine wood ! That might do for a bee or a linnet—but not for me."

Her waiting-women, thinking that she was talking too much for her health, begged Alidor to withdraw. Then they made her lie down, and Bébé came and chided her gently for her want of faithfulness. As she was not very ill, she went to see the queen. But from that day there scarcely passed one in which she did not suffer. Her languor changed her appearance ; and she grew thin and discontented. Months passed away in this fashion. They did not know what to do ; and what more especially troubled the court was that the ambassadors who had come with the demand for her hand were urging her parents to give her into their charge. The queen heard of a very skilful physician who might be able to cure her. She sent an equipage for him, and forbade them to tell him the rank of the sick princess, so that he might speak out more freely. When he arrived the queen hid herself in order to listen. But he, seeing her, looked at her for a little and said with a smile : " Is it possible that your court doctors did not know what ailed this little lady ? The fact is, before long she will bestow a fine boy on her family." They did not give him time to finish what he was going to say. All the court ladies loaded him with reproaches, and taking him by the shoulders they pushed him out, hooting him loudly the while.

Bébé, who was in Livorette's room, did not, like the others, think that this country doctor was a fool. Several times it had occurred to him that the princess was to bear a child, and so he went to the sea-shore to consult his friend the fish, who seemed to be of the same opinion. " I advise you," said he, " to go away ; for I fear lest they should find you by her when she is asleep, and you would both be lost." " Ah!" said the prince, mournfully, " do you think I can live apart from her who is dearer than all in the world ? Why should I be careful of my life ? The time is coming when it will be hateful to me. I must see Livorette, or die !" The dolphin felt pity for him, and shed some tears, though dolphins have not the habit of weeping, and he did what he could to console his dear friend. It was all Grognette's doing without a doubt.

The queen related to the king the leech's fancy. Livorette was called. To the questions they asked she answered with as much sincerity as innocence. They spoke even to her waiting-women, whose evidence was satisfactory in every way. So their majesties' minds were set at rest till the day when the princess gave birth to the prettiest baby that ever was. How can we possibly describe the astonishment, the anger of the king, the grief of the queen, the anxiety of Alidor, the surprise of the ambassadors and of all the court ? Where did the child come from ? Who was its father ? No one could tell, and young Livorette knew as little as the child itself. But the king treated the matter with the utmost seriousness. His daughter's tears and vows were of no avail. He made up his mind to have her thrown along with her son from the top of a mountain into a precipice with jagged sides, where she would die a cruel death. He told the queen of his intention, but she was so terribly distressed at the thought that she fell as if dead at his feet. He was touched by her sad condition, and when she had come to herself somewhat he tried to console her, but she told him she would never know a moment of joy or of health till he had revoked so terrible an order. Throwing herself on her knees, the tears stream-ing down her cheeks, she begged him to kill her, and spare the lives of Livorette and her son. She had had the infant fetched on purpose that the king might be touched by his innocence. The lamentations of the queen, and the cries of the little child, moved him with compassion. Throwing himself into an armchair, he covered his face with his hands, and pondered and sighed for long before he could utter a word. At last he said to the queen that for her sake he was willing to put off the death of the princess and her son, but that she must understand it was only deferred ; that nothing but blood could wash away a stain so shameful to their house.   The queen thought that much had already been gained in getting the death of her dear daughter and her grandson deferred : so she made no further stipulations, and gave her consent to the princess being shut up in a tower, where the light of the sun did not even come to gladden her eyes.   In that sad place she was left to mourn her cruel fate.   If anything could have comforted her in her sorrows it would have been her perfect innocence.   She never saw her child, and was given no news of it.   "Just heaven!" she cried, "what have I done to be overwhelmed with such bitter griefs?"

Alidor, in deepest sorrow, was at the end of his powers of endurance. Gradually his mind gave way, and at last he went mad altogether.   His moans and cries were heard ceaselessly in the woods.   He would throw away money and jewels on the road.   His clothes were in rags, his hair in tangles, his beard unshaven ; and all this, added to his natural ugliness, made him almost horrible to look on.   Every one pitied him greatly, and would have done so even more had not the princess's misfortune filled the minds of everybody in the land. The ambassadors who had come to ask her in marriage heartily wished themselves at home again, for they were, in a manner, ashamed at having come for her.   The king, for his part, saw them go willingly enough, for their presence was a grief to him.   And as for the dolphin, hidden in the depths of the sea, he appeared no more, leaving the field free to Grognette the fairy to do all the harm she could to the prince and the princess.

Although the little prince grew lovelier than a sunny day, the king had only preserved his life that he might be the means of proving who was his father. He said nothing to the queen ; but one day he announced that all the courtiers should bring a gift to rejoice the heart of his grandson.   They all obeyed ; and, when the king was told that a large number were assembled, he led the queen into the great audience-chamber.   They were followed by the nurse carrying in her arms the lovely child clad in brocade of gold and silver.   They each came forward to kiss his little hand, and to give him, one a jewelled rose, one artificial fruits, another a golden lion, an agate wolf, an ivory horse, a spaniel, a parrot, a butterfly.   He accepted everything with indifference. The king, apparently quite careless, was nevertheless watching what the child was doing.   He noticed that he did not show any affection to one more than to the other.   He gave orders for a further announcement : that if any one failed to come he would be judged guilty and punished as such.   At these threats there was greater haste than ever ; and the king's squire, who had met Alidor on his travels and who was the cause of his having come to the court, finding him in the depths of a cave, in which he generally hid himself since his reason had gone, called to him: "Come, Alidor, do you wish to be the only one to give nothing to the little prince? Have you not heard the proclamation? Do you wish the king to sentence you to death?" "Yes, then, I do," replied the poor prince, with a wandering look. "Why should you come and disturb my peace?" "Do not be angry," said the squire; "I only speak for the purpose of urging you to make an appearance." "Yes; I am most becomingly dressed," said Alidor, laughing, "for paying a visit to the royal monkey!" "If it is only a question of providing you with clothes," said the squire, "I can furnish you with very fine ones." "Very well," said the other; "it is long since I have seen myself in stately apparel."

He came out of the cave and betook himself quietly enough to the squire's house; who, being one of the grandest courtiers, gave him a choice of several magnificent dresses. But he would only wear a black one, and in spite of all remonstrances went without cravat, or hat, or shoes. Till he had reached the door he forgot about the gift to be presented to the prince; but he did not trouble himself long about the matter. Seeing a pin lying on the ground he picked it up to serve as his gift, and went hopping into the hall, rolling his eyes, and hanging out his tongue in such a way that, added to his natural ugliness, one could hardly bear to look at him. The nurse, fearing lest the little prince should be terrified, would have turned his face the other way, and signed to Alidor to go away; but as soon as the child saw him he held out his arms, laughing, and showing such extraordinary delight that Alidor had to be brought to him. Then the child threw his arms round his neck, kissed him again and again, and refused to be taken away from him. And Alidor, in spite of his madness, was no less tender towards the child.

The king stood transfixed with astonishment at this most strange event. He hid his anger from the assembly, but as soon as the audience was ended, without saying a word to the queen, he gave commands to two lords, whom he honoured with especial confidence, to go and fetch the Princess Livorette from the tower in which she had been languishing for four years, and to put her into a barrel along with Alidor and the little prince, to provide them with a pot of milk, a bottle of wine and a loaf, and to fling them to the bottom of the sea.

The lords, horrified at receiving so cruel an order, fell at his feet and humbly begged him to spare his daughter and his grandson. "Alas, sire!" said they, "if your majesty had but allowed yourself to know what she has suffered for four years past, you would think she had been sufficiently punished, without now adding so cruel a death. Consider, she is your only daughter, intended by the gods to wear your crown one day. You are accountable for her life to your subjects. There is great promise in her son. Will you cut him off in his infancy?" "Yes, I will," said the king, wrathful at the resistance shown to his command, "and if you do not carry out my orders you will die along with her."

The courtiers knew with sorrow that their struggles against the king's determination were in vain, so they withdrew with downcast heads and tears in their eyes. They gave orders that a barrel large enough to contain the princess, her son, and Alidor, and the little supply of provisions, should be procured. Then, repairing to the tower, they found her lying on some straw, with irons on her feet and hands. For four years she had not seen the light of day. With profound respect did they greet her, telling her the command they had received from her father. So loud was her sobbing that she could hardly hear what they said. And yet she well understood their message, and mingled her tears with theirs. "Alas!" she said, "the gods are witnesses of my innocence. I am only sixteen years old. I was destined to wear more crowns than one, and now you are going to cast me to the bottom of the sea like the guiltiest of creatures. But do not think I am seeking to corrupt your fidelity or begging you to find some pretext by which my life may be saved. For many a day the king has accustomed me to long for death. I would willingly die could my poor child be saved. What crime is he guilty of? Is not his innocence enough to save him from the fury of the king? Is it possible he is doomed to perish with me? Is it not enough for my father to take my life? Does one victim not satisfy him?"

The lords who were listening to her could not say a word in reply. They could only obey, they said to the princess. "Well," she answered, "break the chains that bind me; I am ready to follow you." The guards came. They filed off the irons with which her hands and feet were loaded, causing her a great deal of pain the while, but she bore all with wonderful patience. She went out of the prison lovely as the sunbeam from the bosom of the wave, and all who saw her wondered no less at her courage than at her bewitching beauty, which, in spite of all her sorrows, was greater than ever, her languid air becoming her no less than her former vivacity.

Alidor and the little prince were waiting at the sea-shore, where they had been brought by the guards, the one knowing just as little as the other what was to be done to them. When the princess saw her son she took him in her arms, kissing him a thousand times with the utmost tenderness. When she was told that it was on account of Alidor she was to be drowned, she said she was very glad they had named the man whom she cared for least in the whole world, and that while preparing her destruction they were none the less justifying her. Alidor began laughing as soon as he saw her. "Ha, little princess, where do you come from ? " he said. "We have had fine doings since you left. Livorette is no longer at the palace, and I have been raving mad. They say," he went on, "we are to voyage together to the bottom of the sea. Listen, princess: you must wake me every morning, for I shall sleep till mid-day if you don't take care."

And he would have said more had not Livorette, as with a last effort, entered the first into the barrel, clasping her son in her arms. Alidor threw himself headlong in, leaping for joy at being on his way to the kingdom of the soles, where the turbot is king, and uttering a stream of nonsense. Then they closed up the barrel, and from the top of a rock that jutted into the sea they threw it down. All the spectators were sobbing and uttering long cries of despair, and as they withdrew their hearts were full of deepest sadness. As for Alidor, he was wonderfully calm. The first thing he did was to seize the loaf and eat the whole of it. Then he found the bottle of wine, and began to drink it in a cheerful way, singing songs just as if he had been present at some merry feast. "Alidor," said the princess, "leave me at least to die in peace, and do not daze me with your mistimed joy." "What harm have I done you, princess," he asked, "that you should wish me to be sad? Do you know I have a secret to tell you. Somewhere here about, where exactly I do not know, there is a certain fish called a dolphin. He is my best friend, and has promised to obey me whenever I command. That is why, my beautiful Livorette, I am not uneasy, for I shall call to him to help us as soon as we are either hungry or thirsty, or whenever we feel we should like to sleep in some superb palace. He will build one expressly for us." "Call him then, you silly," said the princess. "Why do you put off what cannot brook delay? If you wait till I am hungry you will

wait a long time. Alas! my heart is too sad for me to think of food. But my son here is dying. He will be suffocated in this vile barrel. Make haste then, I beg of you, so that I may see if you are telling the truth, for a madman like you may well be deceived."

Alidor immediately called the dolphin. " Dolphin, my fishy friend, come here at once, I command you, and do all that I tell you." " Here I am," said the dolphin ; " speak." " Are you there ? " asked the prince. " This barrel is so well closed that I cannot see." " Only say what you desire," said the dolphin. " I should like to listen to beautiful music," Alidor replied, and at that moment the music began. " What ! " said the princess with impatience, " are you laughing at me with your music ? Isn't it rather a useless thing to hear fine music when you are drowning ? " " But, princess, you were neither hungry nor thirsty. What do you wish for ? " " Give me your power of commanding the dolphin," she answered. " Dolphin, dolphin," cried Alidor, " I command you to do all that Princess Livorette desires, without failing in one particular." " Very well," said the dolphin, " I shall do so." And without a moment's delay she told him to bear them away to the loveliest island in the world, and to build on it the finest palace that ever was seen, with exquisite gardens, surrounded by streams, one full of wine and another of water, with a garden full of flowers and a tree in the middle, whose stem should be silver and its branches gold, with three oranges growing on it, one of diamond, another of ruby, and a third of emerald. The palace was to be painted and gilded, and all her story represented on its walls. " Is that all ? " said the dolphin. " It is a good deal," she answered. " Not very much," he replied, " seeing that it is done already." " Well, then, I wish you," she said, " to tell me one thing I do not know and which perhaps you do." " I understand," said the dolphin. " You want to know who is the father of your little prince. It is Bébé the canary, and Bébé is none other than Prince Alidor who is with you." " Ah, my lord Dolphin ! " cried Livorette, " you are laughing at me." " I swear," said he, " by Neptune's trident, by Scylla and Charybdis, by all the caverns of the sea, by its shells, by its treasures, by its tritons, by its naiads, by the happy omens that the pilot draws at sight of me. Lastly, I swear by yourself, dear Livorette, that I am true and honourable, and that I do not lie." " After so many oaths," she said, " I cannot but believe you, though, to tell the truth, what I have just heard is one of the most astonishing things in the world. I order you then to restore Alidor to reason, to give him all the intelligence possible, and to endow his conversation with charm. Let him be a hundred times handsomer than he was ugly, and tell me why you called him prince, for that title sounds pleasantly in my ears." The dolphin obeyed in these particulars as he had done before. He told Livorette the prince's adventures, who was his father, who was his mother, and all about his ancestors and kinsfolk; for he had absolute knowledge of the past, the present, and the future, and was as good as a professional genealogist. Such fish are not to be found every day. Dame Fortune has her say in the making of them.

While they were talking, the barrel struck on an island. The dolphin, having raised it gradually, threw it on the shore; and as soon as it was there it opened. The princess, the prince, and the child were at liberty to come out of their prison. The first thing that Alidor did was to cast himself at Livorette's feet. He had quite recovered his reason, and his wit was ever so much brighter than it had been before. He had grown so handsome: all his features were so much changed for the better that she hardly recognised him. With the utmost gentleness he begged to be forgiven for his metamorphosis into the canary, excusing himself in a way which was both respectful and affectionate. At last she gave her pardon for a marriage, to which, perhaps, she would not have consented if he had taken other means of bringing it about. It is true the dolphin had given him such a comely shape that she had never seen his equal at her father's court. He confirmed all the dolphin had told her about his rank, a matter most essential to the satisfaction of this princess; for, in fact, what would it avail to be the friend of the fairies when one cannot change one's birth? When heaven does not place us in that position in which we would have desired to be born, only virtue and merit can repair the loss: but often it is repaired with such generosity as to bring abundant consolation.

The princess was in the best of humours. From the midst of terrible danger she had been saved, and she was deeply sensible of it, and gave thanks to the gods. Then she looked out towards the sea for their good friend, the dolphin. There he was, and she thanked him, as was her duty, for having preserved her life. The prince was no less grateful. Their son, who spoke very prettily, and was much more intelligent than children of his age generally are, complimented him too in a way that delighted the good dolphin, who turned somersaults over and over and over again to please the little boy.

But suddenly they heard a loud sound of trumpets, fifes, and hautboys, and the neighing of horses. It was the prince and princess's equipage and their guards, all in gorgeous attire. There were ladies in the carriages who alighted as soon as they came in sight, to kiss the hem of the princess's robe. She would have prevented it, seeing in them evident marks of rank which deserved her consideration. But they told her that the orders from the dolphin were to acknowledge the prince and princess king and queen of the island, where were many obedient subjects and much happiness in store for them. Alidor and Livorette were delighted to see the honour paid them by such courteous and agreeable persons, and responded to the homage with as much graciousness as dignity. Then they got into an open carriage, drawn by eight winged horses, who bore them away, now mounting to the clouds, now coming down so gradually that they were hardly aware of the descent. This way of driving is pleasant: you are not jolted, and need fear no fatigue.

They were still near the middle region of the air when they saw on the slope of a hill lying along the sea-coast, a palace of so marvellous a structure that, though all the walls were made of silver, they could yet see right through the rooms, which were furnished, they saw, in the most superb style and with the most exquisite taste imaginable. The gardens were still more beautiful. There were countless fountains, and nature had scattered delicious springs all about in profusion. The prince and his wife were at a loss where to bestow their greatest praise, so perfect did each thing seem to them. When they had entered the palace, from all sides cries rose of " Long live Prince Alidor! Long live the Princess Livorette! May pleasures surround them while they dwell here!" The music of instruments and of sweet voices made a pleasant symphony the while.

Before long they were served with an excellent repast, of which they stood in much need, the sea air and the way they had been cast adrift having fatigued them terribly. So, sitting down, they partook of the repast with appetite. When. they had finished the warden of the royal treasure entered and asked them if they would be pleased to spend some little time after their meal in the neighbouring gallery. They went, and saw along the walls large wells and buckets made of perfumed Spanish leather, ornamented with gold. They asked what they were for, and the warden told them that streams of metal flowed into these wells, and when money was wanted one had nothing to do but to let down a bucket and to say: " I wish to draw up louis, pistoles, quadruples, crowns, or other coins ". At the word the water took the wished-for form, and the bucket came up full of gold or silver or coins, and yet the spring never dried up for those who made good use of it. But, as had happened several times, when misers let down the bucket with the sole intention of amassing gold and keeping it locked up, they drew it up full of frogs and adders, to their great terror, and sometimes to their great hurt, according to the degree of their avarice. The prince and princess admired these wells, looking on them as one of the finest and rarest things in the whole world. To test the result they let down the bucket, and back it came filled with little grains of gold. When they asked why the gold was not already coined, the warden told them they were waiting to know the arms of the prince and princess so as to stamp them. " Ah ! " said

Alidor, " we are too much indebted to the generous dolphin to have any other image on them than his." In an instant all the grains were changed into gold pieces, with a dolphin on each.

The hour for retiring having come, Alidor, timid and respectful, went to his own room, and the princess and her son to theirs. At past eleven o'clock next morning the princess was still asleep. The prince had risen early to go to the hunt, and to be back again before she should be awake. When he learnt he might see her without disturbing her he went to her room, followed by a train of gentlemen carrying great golden vessels filled with the game he had killed. He presented them to his dear princess, who accepted them graciously, thanking him again and again for his goodness to her, which gave him the opportunity of telling her that never had he loved her with more ardour than now, and that he prayed her to name the time when their marriage would be celebrated with pomp.

" Ah! my lord," she said, " my mind is made up on that point. I shall never consent except with the permission of my royal father and mother." Never did lover receive a crueller blow. " Fair princess, to what fate do you condemn me?" he said. " Do you not know that what you desire is impossible? Hardly have we escaped from the horrible barrel into which they had put us for our destruction, and you are already imagining that they will consent to my desires. Ah, perhaps you wish to punish me for the strong passion I feel for you. I am aware that you mean to give your heart and your hand to the prince who sent ambassadors to you at the time when I changed myself into a canary." " You are quite wrong in your judgment of my feeling," she said. " I respect you, I love you, and I have forgiven all the ills you drew down on me by a disguise which you should not have assumed; for, being the son of a king, might you not have felt assured that my father would have been pleased to make an alliance with you?"

" A great affection does not reason so coolly," he answered. " I have taken the first step which has led me to happiness, but you are so hard, and if you do not take back the cruel word you have just uttered it is all up with me." " I cannot take it back," she said. " You must know that this night while I was sleeping quietly I felt myself being roughly pulled. Opening my eyes, I saw by a torch, which cast a sombre light, the most hideous little creature in the world looking at me steadily with angry eyes. ' Do you know me?' she said. ' No, madam,' I answered, ' nor do I wish to.' ' Ah! you are laughing,' said she. ' No,' I replied, ' I swear I am telling the truth.' ' My name is Grognette, the fairy,' said she. ' I have good reason to be angry with Alidor, who sat down on my rock. In fact, he has a particular faculty for displeasing me. I forbid you, therefore, to consider him as your husband till you have your father and mother's consent, and if you disobey me I shall take my revenge on your son. He shall die, and his death will be followed by a thousand other misfortunes which you will not be able to escape.' At these words she blew flames of fire on me. They covered me, and I thought I was going to be burnt, when she said : ' I spare you on condition that you obey my orders '."

The prince knew well from the name and the description of Grognette that the princess's story was true. "Alas !" he said, "why did you ask our friend, the fish, to cure my madness ? I was less to be pitied then than now. Mind and reason, what purpose do they serve except to make me suffer ? Let me go and beg him to take away my reason again. It is an irksome good." The princess was deeply moved. She truly loved the prince, finding in him all kinds of fine qualities, and thinking all he did and said perfect in grace. She wept, and he could not help feeling joy at the sight of her tears flowing for his sake. It gave him much more pleasure to know her feelings for him than his own for her had given him when he was the canary, and this so comforted him in his sadness that he threw himself at her feet and kissed her hands. "My dear Livorette," he said, "be assured I have no will where you are concerned. I own you as the absolute mistress of my fate."

Livorette was deeply conscious of what this submission had cost him, and ceaselessly did she turn over in her mind the means whereby she might obtain the permission so necessary to their happiness. It was, in fact, the one thing lacking, for there were no pleasures imaginable that the inhabitants of the island did not try to give them. Their rivers were full of fish, their forests of game, their orchards of fruit, their fields of wheat, their meadows of grass, their wells of gold and silver. There were no wars and no law-suits. It was a land where youth, health, beauty, wit, books, pure water, good wine abounded, and where snuff-boxes never gave out ! And Livorette was as much in love with Alidor as Alidor with Livorette.

Every now and again they would go to pay their respects to the dolphin, who was always glad to see them. When they spoke of Grognette, the fairy, and of the commands she had put upon the princess, and when they begged him to be their friend in this matter, he always had some comforting words with which to console them. Yet he would give no absolute promise. So two years passed away. Alidor wished to send ambassadors to the King of the Woods, and asked the dolphin's advice on the subject, but the dolphin said that Grognette would kill them without any doubt, and that perhaps the gods themselves would in the end interfere in favour of the prince and princess.

But meanwhile the queen had learnt the sad fate prepared for her daughter, her grandson, and Alidor. Never was sorrow greater than hers. Joy and good health were hers no more. Every spot where she had once seen the princess recalled her sorrow, and she could not keep from heaping endless reproaches on the king. "Cruel father!" she said, "how could you make up your mind to drown the poor child? She was our only one, and the gods had given her to us. We should have waited till the gods had taken her from us." For some time the king took these words coolly, but at last he himself began to feel the full extent of his loss. He missed his daughter no less than his wife did, and secretly he was bitten by remorse for sacrificing his tenderness to his reputation. Unwilling that the queen should know how he suffered, he endeavoured to hide his sorrow under an air of hardness. But as soon as he found himself alone he would cry out: "My daughter, my dear daughter, where are you? Have I then lost you, the only consolation of my old age? And I have lost you by my own doing!"

At last, overcome one day by the queen's grief and his own, he confessed to her that since that fatal day when he had given orders for Livorette and her son to be cast into the sea he had not had a moment's peace. Her plaintive shadow followed him wheresoever he went; the innocent cries of her son rung in his ears, and he feared he would die for the sorrow of it all. This news made the queen much more unhappy than before. "Now I shall suffer your grief as well as my own. What shall bring us comfort, sire?" The king said he had heard tell of a fairy who for some little time back had been living in the forest of the bears, and that he would go and consult her. "I will gladly go with you," said the queen, "though I am not quite clear what I want to ask her; for the death of our dear Livorette and of the little prince is only too certain." "All the same," said the king, "we must see her." So he ordered them to make ready his state carriage at once, and all that might be necessary for a journey of thirty leagues. They set off early next day and soon arrived at the dwelling of the fairy; who, having read by the stars that the king and queen were coming to visit her, came hastily forward to greet them.

As soon as their majesties saw her they got down out of their carriage, and, having embraced her with every sign of friendship, they could not keep from weeping bitterly. "Sire," said the fairy, "I know why you have come. You are in deep distress at having brought about the death of the princess, your daughter. I know no other remedy for your sorrow than to advise both of you to set out in a fair ship for the dolphin's isle. It is a long way from here, but you will find there a fruit which will make you forget your grief. I counsel you to lose no time. It is your only means of consolation. As for you, madam," she said to the queen, "your condition moves me so deeply that your troubles seem as if they were my own." The king and queen thanked the fairy for her good counsel, bestowed valuable gifts on her, and begged her to have the goodness, during their absence, to take an especial charge of their kingdom, so that no neighbours might bethink themselves of making war. She promised all they asked, and they went back to their capital comforted in some degree, in that they could look forward to a mitigation of their sorrow.

A ship was fitted out. They went on board, and set sail for the high sea guided by a pilot who had been in the dolphin's isle. For some days the wind was favourable; but afterwards it became so contrary, and the storm rose to such a pitch, that after being tossed about by it the vessel split on a rock without there being a chance of saving it. All those who were on board were suddenly separated from each other, with no hope of escaping from the terrible danger.

All this time the king was only thinking of his daughter. "I am fully deserving of the punishment which the gods send me," he said, "since it was I that exposed Livorette and her son to the fury of the waves." These thoughts so tortured him that he had given up all thoughts of seeking to prolong his life, when he saw the queen on a dolphin's back, where she had found a refuge on falling from the ship. She was holding out her arms to him in her eagerness to join him, and praying that the good dolphin might reach him and save him along with her. And that is just what happened; for at the moment when the king was on the point of sinking, the good fish approached him, and with the queen's aid he got on its back. She was full of joy at finding him again, and begged him to pluck up heart, since there was every evidence that heaven had their safety in its keeping. And, in fact, towards the close of day, the ever-serviceable dolphin carried them to a pleasant shore on which they landed, no more fatigued than if they had but just come from their berths in the stern.

It was the very island over which Livorette and Alidor were reigning. They were walking along the shore, Livorette holding her son by the hand, and a numerous retinue following them, when they saw to their great surprise two persons on the dolphin's back. They went forward, naturally, to offer hospitality to them. But what was the surprise of the prince and princess to recognise the king and queen! They saw, however, that they were not recognised in their turn; which was not extraordinary seeing that the king and queen had not set eyes on their daughter for six years. A girl changes greatly in such a time. And Alidor, from being ugly and mad, had now become handsome, and his reason was restored to him. The child too had grown. So their majesties were far from being aware that they saw before them their dear daughter and their grandson.

Livorette could hardly restrain her tears. At every word she said to her father and mother, or that she heard them say, her bosom swelled, and her voice, changing its tone every minute, was trembling with agitation. " Madam," said the king to her, " see at your feet a monarch in deep distress, a queen in despair. We were shipwrecked near by. All those who were with us have perished. We are alone, stripped of all our treasures and with none to help us. Sad examples are we of the fickleness of fortune." " Sire," said the princess, " you could have landed in no country where help would have been given to you with more pleasure. Forget your misfortunes, I beg of you. And you, madam," she said to the queen, " let me embrace you." And at the word she threw herself on her neck, while the queen pressed her in her arms with such extraordinary tenderness, because of her likeness to her dear Livorette, that she all but fainted.

Alidor invited them to ride in his chariot, which they agreed to, and they were driven to the castle, where all the beauty and the magnificence filled the king with surprise. Never a moment passed but some pleasure was prepared for them ; but what gave them most joy was that the prince's vessels, which had been not far away from the spot where the shipwreck of the king had taken place, had saved the ship and all on board, and brought the crew to the dolphin's isle, even while the king was lamenting their death.

At last, one day after they had spent some time with the prince and princess, the king begged them to give them the means of returning to their own kingdom. " Alas ! " said the queen, " I shall not conceal from you our misfortune, the saddest that could ever happen to a father and mother." Thereupon she told the story of Livorette ; the griefs that overwhelmed them ever since the cruel torture to which the king had doomed her ; the advice of the fairy who dwelt in the forest of the bears, and their intention of going to the dolphin's isle. " And here we have reached it by the strangest navigation possible. But beyond the pleasure of seeing you we have found nothing here to comfort us, and the fairy who induced us to come has not foretold correctly what would happen."

The princess had listened to her dear mother with such pity and filial feeling that she could not keep her tears back. The queen was indeed grateful to seen how keenly she felt her sorrows. She begged the gods to reward her, and, embracing her again and again, she called her her daughter and her child without knowing why.

At last, the ship being ready, the departure of the king and the queen was fixed for the next day. The princess had been keeping one of the most beautiful things about the palace for them to see as they were going away. It was the rare tree in the flower-bed, whose stem was of silver and the branches of gold, and from which hung three oranges of diamonds, rubies and emeralds. There were three guardians whose duty it was to watch it night and day, lest an attempt should be made to take it, and the fruit should really be carried off. When Alidor and Livorette had taken the king and queen to this place, they let them for some time remain admiring at their leisure the beauty of this wonderful tree, which had not its like in the world. After they had spent more than four hours inspecting it, they returned to the place where the prince and the princess were waiting for them to partake of a magnificent repast. In the room there was a table with only two covers, and when the king asked why, they told him that they wished to have the honour of serving them. So they begged their majesties to be seated. Livorette and Alidor and their child brought wine to the king and queen, serving them on their knees, carving the meat for them, placing it neatly on their majesties' plates, choosing the best and the most delicate portions. Soft and pleasant harmonies were heard the while. Suddenly the three guardians of the rare tree entered with a terrified air, with sad news to tell : the fine diamond and ruby oranges had been stolen, and it could only have been by those persons who had just been to see them—which meant the king and the queen. They were of course offended, and, both rising from the table, they said they are willing to be searched before the whole court. At the same time the king undid his scarf and opened his vest, while the queen undid her bodice. But what was the astonishment of one and the other to see the diamond and the ruby oranges fall down. "Ah! sire," cried the princess, "what a reward is this for the kind and respectful treatment you have received in our island! It is an evil return for a good welcome from hosts who paid you all respect." The king and the queen, in confusion at these reproaches, tried all sorts of means in order to justify themselves, protesting that they were incapable of committing the theft, that those who accused them did not know them, and that they themselves could not understand how it had all happened.

At these words the princess, throwing herself at the feet of her father and mother, said : " Sire, I am the unhappy Livorette you placed in the barrel along with Alidor and my son. You accused me of a crime to which I had never consented. Misfortune came upon me without more knowledge on my part than your majesties had when the oranges were hidden in your bosoms. I dare beseech you to believe and to pardon me!" The hearts of the king and queen were pierced by these words. They lifted their daughter up, and all but strangled her, so closely did they clasp her in their arms. She presented Prince Alidor and the little prince to them. It is easier to imagine than to describe the joy of these illustrious personages.

The wedding of the prince and princess was celebrated with great pomp. The dolphin was present in the shape of a young monarch of marvellous beauty and wit. Ambassadors were sent to the father and mother of Alidor with precious gifts, and charged to relate all that had happened. The life of the prince and princess was as long and happy after this as it had been full of sorrow and complications in the beginning. Livorette returned with her husband to her father's kingdom, but her son stayed behind in the dolphin's isle.

ABERDEEN UNIVERSITY PRESS.

CPSIA information can be obtained at www.ICGtesting.com
Printed in the USA
LVOW09*0551270816

502070LV00019B/141/P